Torture and Truth

America, Abu Ghraib, and the War on Terror

Because War is
complete Insanity
and unpredictable.
Friction in WAR

ALSO BY MARK DANNER

The Massacre at El Mozote:
A Parable of the Cold War

The Road to Illegitimacy:
One Reporter's Travels Through the 2000 Florida Vote Recount

Torture and Truth

America, Abu Ghraib, and the War on Terror

Mark Danner

NEW YORK REVIEW BOOKS

New York

THIS IS A NEW YORK REVIEW BOOK

PUBLISHED BY THE NEW YORK REVIEW OF BOOKS

TORTURE AND TRUTH:
AMERICA, ABU GHRAIB, AND THE WAR ON TERROR
by Mark Danner

This edition published in 2004
in the United States of America by
The New York Review of Books
1755 Broadway
New York, NY 10019
www.nybooks.com

Cover design by Milton Glaser, Inc.

Distributed to the trade by Publishers Group West

A catalog record for this book is available from the Library of Congress

ISBN 1-59017-152-7
Printed in the United States of America on acid-free paper.
November 2004
3 5 7 8 10 8 6 4 2

War pulls from all Directions unexpectably

For Robert B. Silvers

Table of Contents

Acknowledgments

This book began life as a series of articles for *The New York Review of Books*. I would like to thank the editors and staff of the *Review* for their skill, their patience, and their forbearance. In particular, I thank Rea Hederman, the publisher of the *Review*, who had the idea for the book, and Michael Shae, who brought it to press; Barbara Epstein, the co-editor and co-founder of the *Review*, and Jenie Hederman, Ann Kjellberg, Scott Staton, Elaine Blair, Hugh Eakin, Jonathan Shainin, and Pearl Kan.

Finally, I would like to thank Robert B. Silvers, co-editor of *The New York Review of Books* since its founding, who over many years has given me unfailing help, counsel, and friendship. Bob Silvers's dedication, energy, loyalty, and faith are legendary. Indeed, those who have had the great good luck to work with him share a simple secret: a writer could have no better editor. This book, like so much else, would not exist without him and I dedicate it to him in friendship and appreciation.

Introduction

THIS BOOK IS about torture, and about how a democracy, when faced with incontrovertible evidence that members of its military and security services are engaging in torture, moves, or fails to move, to confront that fact. The democracy in question is the United States and the evidence that it faced was the photographs of abuses in Abu Ghraib prison in Iraq that were first broadcast on the CBS television network on April 28, 2004, and published in *The New Yorker* a few days later. Though the photographs, by virtue of their nearly instantaneous broadcast throughout the world, are the best-known, they are by no means the only evidence, or even the most important. Indeed, as I argue in these pages, though the photographs first announced Abu Ghraib to the world and gave impetus to the investigation of what happened there, as the months passed and more evidence accumulated the images have increasingly had the opposite effect, helping to block a full public understanding of how the scandal arose and how what Americans did at Abu Ghraib was ultimately tied to what they had been doing in Afghanistan, Guantánamo, and elsewhere in the "war on terror"—and, finally, to what officials had been deciding in Washington. Among other things, this book is an attempt to put more of that evidence before the public, in an easily accessible and comprehensible form.

The book is divided into three parts. The first part, the main text, collects my reporting on the Abu Ghraib scandal, which was originally published in three articles in *The New York Review of Books* in 2004. The second part, called "Addenda" and intended to place the Abu Ghraib story in the broader context of the Iraq war, collects articles I wrote about the war itself, including my reporting from Iraq during the fall of 2003. The third part, the

Appendices, collects the primary documents of the Abu Ghraib story and is in turn divided into three: the first appendix, entitled "Disputation," includes letters, memoranda, and reports drafted by officials of the Bush administration struggling to define the status of prisoners taken in the "war on terror" and to decide what techniques of interrogation could lawfully be applied to them; the second, "Revelation," includes the photographs of the abuses, the detailed depositions of some of those abused, and the Red Cross investigators' eyewitness account of what happened in Abu Ghraib; and finally "Investigation" collects the various reports initiated by officials of the US government into the scandal, including those by Major General Antonio M. Taguba, by Lieutenant General Anthony R. Jones and Major General George R. Fay, and by former secretary of defense James R. Schlesinger and the commission he headed.

My hope is that readers will go beyond my account of Abu Ghraib and the general issue of torture to look at the primary documents themselves. As I write, less than five months after the photographs were first broadcast, few of the major facts about what went on in Abu Ghraib remain hidden. Thanks to investigations, but even more to the leaks that occasioned them, we know, certainly in broad outline, what happened at the prison and how what happened there derived from decisions made in Afghanistan, Guantánamo, and, ultimately, Washington, D.C. This makes Abu Ghraib a peculiarly contemporary kind of scandal: like other scandals that have erupted during the Iraq war and the war on terror, it is not about revelation or disclosure but about the failure, once wrongdoing is disclosed, of politicians, officials, the press, and, ultimately, citizens to act. The scandal is not about uncovering what is hidden, it is about seeing what is already there—and acting on it. It is not about information; it is about politics.

MARK DANNER

September 17, 2004

A NOTE ON THE TEXT

The reader will find all notes at the end of each chapter.

The texts of most of the documents quoted here—including the Taguba, Red Cross, Fay, and Schlesinger reports—will be found reprinted in full in the Appendices beginning on page 73.

I

TORTURE AND TRUTH

IN NOVEMBER of 2003 in Iraq, I traveled to Falluja during the early days of what would become known as the "Ramadan Offensive"—when suicide bombers in the space of less than an hour destroyed the Red Cross headquarters and four police stations, and daily attacks by insurgents against US troops doubled, and the American adventure in Iraq entered a bleak tunnel from which it has yet to emerge. I inquired of a young man there why the people of that city were attacking Americans more frequently each day. How many of the attacks, I wanted to know, were carried out by foreign fighters? How many by local Islamists? And how many by what US officers called "FRLS"—former regime loyalists?[1]

The young man—I'll call him Salih—listened, answered patiently in his limited but eloquent English, but soon became impatient with what he plainly saw as my American obsession with categories and particulars. Finally he interrupted my litany of questions, pushed his face close to mine, and spoke to me slowly and emphatically:

> For Fallujans it is a *shame* to have foreigners break down their doors. It is a *shame* for them to have foreigners stop and search their women. It is a *shame* for the foreigners to put a bag over their heads, to make a man lie on the ground with your shoe on his neck. This is a great *shame*, you understand? This is a great *shame* for the whole tribe.
>
> It is the *duty* of that man, and of that tribe, to get revenge on this soldier—to kill that man. Their duty is to attack them, to *wash the shame*. The shame is a *stain*, a dirty thing; they have to *wash* it. No sleep—we cannot sleep until we have revenge. They have to kill soldiers.

He leaned back and looked at me, then tried one more time. "The Americans," he said, "*provoke* the people. They don't *respect* the people."

I thought of Salih and his impatience as I paged through the reports of General Taguba and the Red Cross,* for they treat not just of "abuses" or "atrocities" but the entire American "liberation" of Iraq and how it has gone wrong; they are dispatches from the scene of a political disaster. Salih came strongly to mind as I read one of the less lurid sections of the Red Cross report, entitled "Treatment During Arrest," in which the anonymous authors tell how Iraqis they'd interviewed described "a fairly consistent pattern... of brutality by members of the [Coalition Forces] arresting them":

> Arresting authorities entered houses usually after dark, breaking down doors, waking up residents roughly, yelling orders, forcing family members into one room under military guard while searching the rest of the house and further breaking doors, cabinets and other property. They arrested suspects, tying their hands in the back with flexi-cuffs, hooding them, and taking them away. Sometimes they arrested all adult males present in a house, including elderly, handicapped or sick people... pushing people around, insulting, taking aim with rifles, punching and kicking and striking with rifles.

Of course, this is war; those soldiers had intelligence to gather, insurgents to find, a rebellion to put down. However frightening such nighttime arrests might be, Iraqis could at least expect that these soldiers were accountable, that they had commanding officers and a clear chain of command, that there were bases to which one could go and complain. These were, after all, Americans. And yet:

> In almost all instances..., arresting authorities provided no information about who they were, where their base was located, nor did they explain the cause of arrest. Similarly, they rarely informed the arrestee or his family where he was being taken and for how long, resulting in the de facto "disappearance" of the arrestee.... Many [families] were left without news for months, often fearing that their relatives were dead.

We might pass over with a shiver the word "disappearance," with its unfortunate

---

* The texts of these reports, and other documents quoted here, can be found in the Appendices, beginning on page 73.

associations, and say to ourselves, once again, that this was war: insurgents were busy killing American soldiers and had to be rooted out, even if it meant one or two innocent civilians were sucked up into the system. And then one comes upon this quiet little sentence:

> Certain [Coalition Forces] military intelligence officers told the ICRC that in their estimate between *70 percent and 90 percent of the persons deprived of their liberty in Iraq had been arrested by mistake.* [emphasis added]

In the fall of 2003 Abu Ghraib contained within its walls—as the war heated up and American soldiers, desperate for "actionable intelligence," spent many an autumn evening swooping down on Iraqi homes, kicking in doors, and carrying away hooded prisoners into the night—well over eight thousand Iraqis. Could it be that "between 70 percent and 90 percent" of them were "arrested by mistake"? And if so, which of the naked, twisted bodies that television viewers and newspaper readers around the world have been gazing at these last weeks were among them? Perhaps the seven bodies piled up in that great coil, buttocks and genitals exposed to the camera? Or the bodies bound one against another on the cellblock floor? Or the body up against the bars, clenched before the teeth of barking police dogs?

Consider the naked body wearing only the black hood, hands clasped above its head: Pfc. Lynndie England, she of the famous leash, frames the body like a car salesman displaying next year's model, grinning back at the camera, pointing to its genitals with her right hand, flashing a thumbs-up with her left. This body belongs to Hayder Sabbar Abd, a thirty-four-year-old Shiite from Nasiriya, also known as Abu Ghraib Prisoner Number 13077. Last June, at a military checkpoint in the south, according to *The New York Times*, Mr. Abd "tried to leave the taxi he was riding in." Suspicious behavior, rendered more suspicious by the fact that Mr. Abd had served eighteen years in the Iraqi army, part of that time in the Republican Guard. The Americans took him to a detention center at Baghdad airport, and from there to the big military prison at Um Qasr, and finally, after three months, to Abu Ghraib. A strange odyssey through Occupied Iraq, made stranger by the fact that during that time, Mr. Abd says, "he was never interrogated, and never charged with a crime." "The truth is," he told Ian Fisher of *The New York Times*, "we were not terrorists. We were not insurgents. We were just ordinary people. And American intelligence knew this."

3

As I write, we know nothing of what "American intelligence knew"—apart from a hint here or there, this critical fact is wholly absent from both reports, as it has been from the public hearings of Secretary of Defense Donald Rumsfeld and other officials. General Taguba, following his orders, concentrates instead on the activities of the military police, hapless amateurs who were "tasked" to "set physical and mental conditions for favorable interrogation of witnesses" and whose work, thanks to digital photography, has now been displayed so vividly to the citizens of the world. It is this photography that has let us visualize something of what happened to Mr. Abd one night in early November 2003, following a fight among prisoners, when he and six other men were brought to what was known as "the hard site" at Abu Ghraib, the wing for the most dangerous prisoners:

> The seven men were all placed in hoods, he said, and the beating began. "They beat our heads on the walls and the doors," he said. "I don't really know: I couldn't see." He said his jaw had been broken, badly enough that he still has trouble eating. In all, he said, he believes that he received about 50 blows over about two hours.
>
> "Then the interpreter told us to strip," he said. "We told him: 'You are Egyptian, and you are a Muslim. You know that as Muslims we can't do that.' When we refused to take off our clothes, they beat us and tore our clothes off with a blade."
>
> It was at this moment in the interview…that several pages of the photographs made public last week were produced.… He quickly and unemotionally pointed out all his friends—Hussein, Ahmed, Hashim—naked, hooded, twisted around each other.
>
> He also saw himself, as degraded as possible: naked, his hand on his genitals, a female soldier, identified in another report as Pvt. Lynndie England, pointing and smiling with a cigarette in her mouth. Mr. Abd said one of the soldiers had removed his hood, and the translator ordered him to masturbate while looking at Private England.…
>
> "She was laughing, and she put her hands on her breasts," Mr. Abd said. "Of course, I couldn't do it. I told them that I couldn't, so they beat me in the stomach, and I fell to the ground. The translator said, 'Do it! Do it! It's better than being beaten.' I said, 'How can I do it?' So I put my hand on my penis, just pretending."

All the while, he said, the flash of the camera kept illuminating the dim room that once held prisoners of Mr. Hussein. . . .[2]

Such scenes, President Bush tells us, "do not represent America." But for Iraqis, what does? To Salih and other Iraqis they represent the logical extension of treatment they have seen every day under a military occupation that began harshly and has grown, under the stress of the insurgency, more brutal. As another young Iraqi man told me in November,

> The attacks on the soldiers have made the army close down. You go outside and there's a guy on a Humvee pointing a machine gun at you. You learn to raise your hands, to turn around. You come to hate the Americans.

This of course is a prime goal of the insurgents; they cannot defeat the Americans militarily but they can defeat them politically. For the insurgents, the path to such victory lies in provoking the American occupiers to do their political work for them; the insurgents ambush American convoys with "improvised explosive devices" placed in city neighborhoods so the Americans will respond by wounding and killing civilians, or by imprisoning them in places like Abu Ghraib.[3] The insurgents want to place the outnumbered, overworked American troops under constant fear and stress so they will mistreat Iraqis on a broad scale and succeed in making themselves hated.

In this project, as these reports make clear, the methods used at Abu Ghraib played a critical part. For if Americans are learning about these "abuses" for the first time, news about what has been happening at Abu Ghraib and other prisons has been spreading throughout Iraq for many months. And if the Iraqis, with their extensive experience of Abu Ghraib and the purposes it served in the national imagination, do not regard such methods as "abuses," neither do the investigators of the Red Cross:

> These methods of physical and psychological coercion *were used by the military intelligence in a systematic way to gain confessions and extract information* or other forms of co-operation from persons who had been arrested in connection with suspected security offences or deemed to have an "intelligence value." [emphasis added]

What, according to the Red Cross, were these "methods of physical and psychological coercion"?

- Hooding, used to prevent people from seeing and to disorient them, and also to prevent them from breathing freely. One or sometimes two bags, sometimes with an elastic blindfold over the eyes which, when slipped down, further impeded proper breathing. Hooding was sometimes used in conjunction with beatings thus increasing anxiety as to when blows would come. The practice of hooding also allowed the interrogators to remain anonymous and thus to act with impunity. Hooding could last for periods from a few hours to up to two to four consecutive days ...;
- Handcuffing with flexi-cuffs, which were sometimes made so tight and used for such extended periods that they caused skin lesions and long-term after-effects on the hands (nerve damage), as observed by the ICRC;
- Beatings with hard objects (including pistols and rifles), slapping, punching, kicking with knees or feet on various parts of the body (legs, sides, lower back, groin). ...;
- Being paraded naked outside cells in front of other persons deprived of their liberty, and guards, sometimes hooded or with women's underwear over the head ...;
- Being attached repeatedly over several days ... with handcuffs to the bars of their cell door in humiliating (i.e. naked or in underwear) and/or uncomfortable position causing physical pain;
- Exposure while hooded to loud noise or music, prolonged exposure while hooded to the sun over several hours, including during the hottest time of the day when temperatures could reach ... 122 degrees Fahrenheit ... or higher;
- Being forced to remain for prolonged periods in stress positions such as squatting or standing with or without the arms lifted.

The authors of the Red Cross report note that when they visited the "isolation section" of Abu Ghraib in mid-October 2003, they "directly witnessed and documented a variety of methods used to secure the cooperation" of prisoners, among them "the practice of keeping [prisoners] completely naked in totally empty concrete cells and in total darkness. ..." When the Red Cross delegates "requested an explanation from the authorities ... the military intelligence officer in charge of the interrogation explained that this practice was 'part of the process.'"

> The ICRC medical delegate examined persons . . . presenting signs of con-
> centration difficulties, memory problems, verbal expression difficulties,
> incoherent speech, acute anxiety reactions, abnormal behavior and sui-
> cidal tendencies. These symptoms appeared to have been caused by the
> methods and duration of interrogation.

This "process" is not new; indeed, like so many of the news stories presented as "revelation" during these last few months, it has appeared before in the American press. After the arrest in Pakistan more than a year ago of Khalid Sheik Mohammed, the al-Qaeda operations chief, "senior American officials" told *The New York Times* that "physical torture would not be used against Mr. Mohammed":

> They said his interrogation would rely on what they consider acceptable
> techniques like sleep and light deprivation and the temporary withhold-
> ing of food, water, access to sunlight and medical attention.
>   American officials acknowledged that such techniques were recently
> applied as part of the interrogation of Abu Zubaydah, the highest-
> ranking Qaeda operative in custody until the capture of Mr. Mohammed.
> Painkillers were withheld from Mr. Zubaydah, who was shot several
> times during his capture in Pakistan.[4]

In the same article, published more than a year before the Abu Ghraib photographs were made public, a number of American officials discussed the "methods and techniques" applied in interrogations at Afghanistan's Bagram Air Base, at Guantánamo, and at other secret prisons now holding the thousands who have been arrested and confined by American and allied forces since the attacks of September 11:

> Routine techniques include covering suspects' heads with black hoods
> for hours at a time and forcing them to stand or kneel in uncomfortable
> positions in extreme cold or heat. . . . In some cases, American officials
> said, women are used as interrogators to try to humiliate men. . . .
>   Disorientation is a tool of interrogation and therefore a way of life.

To that end, the building—an unremarkable hangar—is lighted twenty-four hours a day, making sleep almost impossible, said Muhammad Shah, an Afghan farmer who was held there for eighteen days.

Colonel King said it was legitimate to use lights, noise and vision restriction, and to alter, without warning, the time between meals, to blur a detainee's sense of time. He said sleep deprivation was "probably within the lexicon...."

Two former prisoners said they had been forced to stand with their hands chained to the ceiling and their feet shackled in the isolation cells.

The "methods of physical and psychological coercion" that the Red Cross delegates witnessed at Abu Ghraib were indeed, as the "military intelligence officer in charge of the interrogation" told them frankly, "part of" a "process" that has been deployed by American interrogators in the various American-run secret prisons throughout the world since September 11. What separates Abu Ghraib from the rest is not the "methods of physical and psychological coercion used" but the fact that, under the increasing stress of the war, the pressing need for intelligence, and the shortage of available troops and other resources in Iraq, military policemen like Pfc. England, who had little or no training, were pressed into service to "soften up" the prisoners and, as the Taguba report puts it, set "the conditions for successful exploitation of the internees." And so when Specialist Sabrina Harman was asked about the prisoner who was placed on a box with electric wires attached to his fingers, toes, and penis, in an image now famous throughout the world, she replied that "her job was to keep detainees awake," that "MI [military intelligence] wanted to get them to talk," and that it was the job of her and her colleagues "to do things for MI and OGA [Other Government Agencies, a euphemism for the CIA] to get these people to talk." The military police, who, General Taguba notes, had "no training in interrogation," were told, in the words of Sergeant Javal S. Davis, to "loosen this guy up for us." "Make sure he has a bad night." "Make sure he gets the treatment."

As for the unusual methods used—"breaking of chemical lights and pouring the phosphoric liquid on detainees," "using military working dogs to frighten and intimidate detainees," "beating detainees with a broom handle and a chair," "threatening male detainees with rape," "sodomizing a detainee with a chemical light and perhaps a broom stick," and the rest of the sad litany General Taguba patiently sets out—Sergeant Davis told investigators that he "assumed that if they were doing things out of the ordinary or outside the guidelines, someone would have said something. Also the wing belongs to MI and it appeared MI personnel approved of the abuse."

Many of the young Americans smiling back at us in the photographs will soon be on trial. It is unlikely that those who ran "the process" and issued the orders will face the same tribunals. Iraqis will be well aware of this, even if Americans are not. The question is whether Americans have traveled far enough from the events of September 11 to go beyond the photographs, which show nothing more than the amateur stooges of "the process," and look squarely at the process itself, the process that goes on daily at Abu Ghraib, Guantánamo, Bagram, and other secret prisons in Iraq and around the world.

To date the true actors in those lurid scenes, who are professionals and no doubt embarrassed by the garish brutality of their apprentices in the military police, have remained offstage. None has testified. The question we must ask in coming days, as Specialist Jeremy Sivits and other young Americans face public courts-martial in Baghdad, is whether or not we as Americans can face a true revelation. We must look squarely at the photographs and ask: Is what has changed only what we know, or what we are willing to accept?

—*The New York Review of Books*, May 12, 2004

NOTES

1. See "Delusions in Baghdad," pp. 60–71.

2. See "Iraqi Recounts Hours of Abuse by US Troops," *The New York Times*, May 5, 2004, p. A1.

3. See "Iraq: The New War," pp. 53–59.

4. See Don Van Natta Jr., "Questioning Terror Suspects in a Dark and Surreal World," *The New York Times*, March 9, 2003.

II

THE LOGIC OF TORTURE

We've now had fifteen of the highest-level officials involved in this entire operation, from the secretary of defense to the generals in command, and nobody knew that anything was amiss, no one approved anything amiss, nobody did anything amiss. We have a general acceptance of responsibility, but there's no one to blame, except for the people at the very bottom of one prison.

—Senator Mark Dayton (D-Minn.)
Armed Services Committee
May 18, 2004

WHAT IS DIFFICULT is separating what we now know from what we have long known but have mostly refused to admit. Though the events and disclosures of the last weeks have taken on the familiar clothing of a Washington scandal—complete with full-dress congressional hearings, daily leaks to reporters from victim and accused alike, and of course the garish, spectacular photographs and videos from Abu Ghraib—beyond that bright glare of revelation lies a dark area of unacknowledged clarity. Behind the exotic brutality so painstakingly recorded in Abu Ghraib, and the multiple tangled plotlines that will be teased out in the coming weeks and months about responsibility, knowledge, and culpability, lies a simple truth, well known but not yet publicly admitted in Washington: that since the attacks of September 11, 2001, officials of the United States, at various locations around the world, from Bagram in Afghanistan to Guantánamo in Cuba to Abu Ghraib in Iraq, have been torturing prisoners.

They did this, in the felicitous phrasing of General Taguba's report, in order to "exploit [them] for actionable intelligence" and they did it, insofar as this is possible, with the institutional approval of the United States government, complete with memoranda from the President's counsel and officially promulgated decisions, in the case of Afghanistan and Guantánamo, about the nonapplicability of the Geneva Conventions and, in the case of Iraq, about at least three different sets of interrogation policies, two of them modeled on earlier practice in Afghanistan and Cuba.[1] They did it under the gaze of Red Cross investigators, whose confidential reports—which, after noting that "methods of physical and psychological coercion were used by the military intelligence in a systematic way to gain confessions and extract information," then set out these "methods" in stark and sickening detail—were handed over to American military and government authorities and then mysteriously "became lost in the Army's bureaucracy and weren't adequately addressed."[2] Or so three of the highest-ranking military officers in the land blandly explained to senators on the Armed Services Committee on May 18, 2004. On that same day, as it happened, an unnamed "senior Army officer who served in Iraq" told reporters for *The New York Times* that in fact the Army *had* addressed the Red Cross report—"by trying to curtail the international organization's spot inspections of the prison":

> After the International Committee of the Red Cross observed abuses in one cellblock on two unannounced inspections in October and complained in writing on Nov. 6, the military responded that inspectors should make appointments before visiting the cellblock. That area was the site of the worst abuses.... Brig. Gen. Janis Karpinski, commander of the 800th Military Police Brigade, whose soldiers guarded the prisoners, said that despite the serious allegations in the Red Cross report, senior officers in Baghdad had treated it in "a light-hearted manner."[3]

Why had these "senior officers" treated the grave allegations of the Red Cross, now the subject of so much high-level attention, in "a light-hearted manner"? The most plausible answer is that they did so not because they were irresponsible or incompetent or evil but because they were well aware that this report—like the others that had been issued by the Red Cross, and by Amnesty International and Human Rights Watch and other well-known organizations—would have no bearing whatever on what the American military did or did not do in Iraq.

The officers almost certainly knew that, whatever the investigators of the Red Cross observed and wrote, American policies in Abu Ghraib prison were governed by entirely different concerns, and were sanctioned, even as the insurgency in Iraq gained strength and the demand for "actionable intelligence" became more urgent, by their most senior commanders—among others, by Lieutenant General Ricardo Sanchez, the overall commander in Iraq, who on October 12, 2003 (about the time Red Cross investigators were making their two unannounced inspections), signed a classified memorandum calling for interrogators at Abu Ghraib to work with military police guards to "manipulate an internee's emotions and weaknesses" and to assume control over the "lighting, heating... food, clothing, and shelter" of those they were questioning.[4]

Six weeks later, Brigadier General Karpinski herself wrote to Red Cross officials to say that "military necessity" required the isolation of prisoners of "significant intelligence value" who were not, she asserted, entitled to "obtain full [Geneva Convention] protection," despite the Bush administration's stated position that the conventions would be "fully applicable" in Iraq.[5] We now have a good deal of evidence about how military policemen at Abu Ghraib, who had been ordered (according to Sergeant Samuel Provance, one of the first soldiers in military intelligence to speak to reporters) to "strip down prisoners and embarrass them as a way to help 'break' them,"[6] attempted, whether enthusiastically or reluctantly, to fulfill these orders.

ᶻᵃ ᶻᵃ ᶻᵃ

We can begin with the story of the as-yet-anonymous prisoner who on January 21, 2004, gave a sworn statement—obtained by *The Washington Post* —to the military's Criminal Investigation Division about his time in Abu Ghraib:

> The first day they put me in a dark room and started hitting me in the head and stomach and legs.
>
> They made me raise my hands and sit on my knees. I was like that for four hours. Then the Interrogator came and he was looking at me while they were beating me. Then I stayed in this room for 5 days, naked with no clothes.... They put handcuffs on my hand and they cuffed me high for 7 or 8 hours. And that caused a rupture to my right hand and I had a

cut that was bleeding and had pus coming from it. They kept me this way on 24, 25, and 26 October. And in the following days, they also put a bag over my head, and of course, this whole time I was without clothes and without anything to sleep on. And one day in November, they started different type of punishment, where an American Police came in my room and put the bag over my head and cuffed my hands and he took me out of the room into the hallway. He started beating me, him, and 5 other American Police. I could see their feet, only, from under the bag.

A couple of those police they were female because I heard their voices and I saw two of the police that were hitting me before they put the bag over my head. One of them was wearing glasses. I couldn't read his name because he put tape over his name. Some of the things they did was make me sit down like a dog, and they would hold the string from the bag and they made me bark like a dog and they were laughing at me. . . . One of the police was telling me to crawl in Arabic, so I crawled on my stomach and the police were spitting on me when I was crawling and hitting me. . . .

Then the police started beating me on my kidneys and then they hit me on my right ear and it started bleeding and I lost consciousness. . . .

A few days before they hit me on my ear, the American police, the guy who wears glasses, he put red woman's underwear over my head. And then he tied me to the window that is in the cell with my hands behind my back until I lost consciousness. And also when I was in Room #1 they told me to lay down on my stomach and they were jumping from the bed onto my back and my legs. And the other two were spitting on me and calling me names, and they held my hands and legs. After the guy with the glasses got tired, two of the American soldiers brought me to the ground and tied my hands to the door while laying down on my stomach. One of the police was pissing on me and laughing on me. . . . And the soldier and his friend told me in a loud voice to lie down, so I did that. And then the policeman was opening my legs, with a bag over my head, and he sat down between my legs on his knees and I was looking at him from under the bag and they wanted to do me because I saw him and he was opening his pants, so I started screaming loudly and the other police starting hitting me with his feet on my neck and he put his feet on my head so I couldn't scream. . . . And then they put the loudspeaker inside the room and they closed the door and he was yelling in the microphone.

...They took me to the room and they signaled me to get on to the floor. And one of the police he put a part of his stick that he always carries inside my ass and I felt it going inside me about 2 centimeters, approximately. And I started screaming, and he pulled it out and he washed it with water inside the room. And then two American girls that were there when they were beating me, they were hitting me with a ball made of sponge on my dick. And when I was tied up in my room, one of the girls, with blonde hair, she is white, she was playing with my dick.... And they were taking pictures of me during all these instances.[7]

What is one to make of this Dantesque nightmare journey? The very outlandishness of the brutality might lead one to think such acts, if not themselves fantasies, must be the product of a singularly sadistic mind—and that indeed, as the Army has maintained, we are dealing here with the abuses of a half-dozen or so unstable personalities, left unsupervised, their natures darkened and corrupted by the stresses of war and homesickness and by the virtually unlimited power that had been granted them. That the abuse reported by many other Abu Ghraib detainees in their affidavits, and depicted in the photographs, is very similar does not of course disprove the Army's "few bad apples" defense; on the contrary, perhaps these half-dozen or so miscreants simply terrorized their cellblock, inflicting similar abhorrent acts on anyone they pleased. But then we come upon the following report, written by the Reuters bureau chief in Baghdad and published in the magazine *Editor and Publisher*, about the treatment of three Iraqi employees of Reuters—two cameramen and a driver—who were filming near the site of the downing of a US helicopter near Falluja in early January when troops of the 82nd Airborne Division arrived:

When the soldiers approached them they were standing by their car, a blue Opel. Salem Uraiby [who had worked for Reuters as a cameraman for twelve years] shouted "Reuters, Reuters, journalist, journalist." At least one shot was fired into the ground close to them.

They were thrown to the ground and soldiers placed guns to their heads. Their car was searched. Soldiers found their camera equipment and press badges and discovered no weapons of any kind. Their hands were cuffed behind their backs and they were thrown roughly into a Humvee where they lay on the floor. . . .

Once they arrived at the US base (this was [forward operating base] Volturno near Fallujah) they were kept in a holding area with around 40 other prisoners in a large room with several open windows. It was bitterly cold. . . .

Bags were alternately placed on their heads and taken off again. Deafening music was played on loudspeakers directly into their ears and they were told to dance around the room. Sometimes when they were doing this, soldiers would shine very bright [flashlights] directly into their eyes and hit them with the [flashlights]. They were told to lie on the floor and wiggle their backsides in the air to the music. They were told to do repeated press ups and to repeatedly stand up from a crouching position and then return to the crouching position.

Soldiers would move between them, whispering things in their ear. . . . Salem says they whispered that they wanted to have sex with him and were saying "come on, just for two minutes." They also said he should bring his wife so they could have sex with her. . . .

Soldiers would whisper in their ears "One, two, three . . ." and then shout something loudly right beside their ear. All of this went on all night. . . . Ahmad said he collapsed by morning. Sattar said he collapsed after Ahmad and began vomiting. . . .

When they were taken individually for interrogation, they were interrogated by two American soldiers and an Arab interpreter. All three shouted abuse at them. They were accused of shooting down the helicopter. Salem, Ahmad, and Sattar all reported that for their first interrogation they were told to kneel on the floor with their feet raised off the floor and with their hands raised in the air.

If they let their feet or hands drop they were slapped and shouted at. Ahmad said he was forced to insert a finger into his anus and lick it. He was also forced to lick and chew a shoe. For some of the interrogation tissue paper was placed in his mouth and he had difficulty breathing and speaking. Sattar too said he was forced to insert a finger into his anus and lick it. He was then told to insert this finger in his nose during questioning, still kneeling with his feet off the ground and his other arm in the air. The Arab interpreter told him he looked like an elephant. . . .

Ahmad and Sattar both said that they were given badges with the letter "C" on it. They did not know what the badges meant but whenever
they were being taken from one place to another in the base, if any soldier saw their badge they would stop to slap them or hurl abuse.[8]

Different soldiers, different unit, different base; and yet it is obvious that
much of what might be called the "thematic content" of the abuse is very similar: the hooding, the loud noises, the "stress positions," the sexual humiliations, the threatened assaults, and the forced violations—all seem to emerge
from the same script, a script so widely known that apparently even random
soldiers the Reuters staffers encountered in moving about the Volturno base
knew their parts and were able to play them. All of this, including the commonly recognized "badge," suggests a clear program that had been purposely
devised and methodically distributed with the intention, in the words of General Sanchez's October 12 memorandum, of helping American troops
"manipulate an internee's emotions and weaknesses."

❧ ❧ ❧

I think what happened is that you took a sophisticated concept at
Gitmo, where the Geneva Convention did not apply... and you put it in
the hands of people [in Iraq] who should have been driving trucks, or
doing something else instead of guarding prisoners. It was a disaster
waiting to happen.

—Senator Lindsey Graham (R-S.C.)
Armed Services Committee

What "sophisticated concept" does Senator Graham have in mind? How can
what seems to be random and bizarre brutality possibly be described as
"sophisticated"?

Though we are limited here to what is publicly known, as Senator Graham
with his security clearances is not, it is still possible to chart, in the history of
"extreme interrogation" since the late Fifties, a general move toward more
"scientific" and "touch-less" techniques, the lineaments of which are all too
evident in the morbid accounts now coming out of Iraq. The most famous
compilation of these techniques can be found in the CIA's manual *KUBARK
Counterintelligence Interrogation*, produced in 1963, and in particular its

chapter "The Coercive Counterintelligence Interrogation of Resistant Sources," which includes the observation that

> all coercive techniques are designed to induce regression.... The result of external pressures of sufficient intensity is the loss of those defenses most recently acquired by civilized man.... "Relatively small degrees of homeostatic derangement, fatigue, pain, sleep, loss, or anxiety may impair these functions."[9]

The intent of such "homeostatic derangement," according to the CIA manual, is to induce "the debility-dependence-dread state," causing the prisoner to experience the "emotional and motivational reactions of intense fear and anxiety."

> ...The circumstances of detention are arranged to *enhance within the subject his feelings of being cut off from the known and the reassuring, and of being plunged into the strange....* Control of the source's environment permits the interrogator to determine his diet, sleep pattern and other fundamentals. Manipulating these into irregularities, so that the subject becomes disorientated, is very likely to create feelings of fear and helplessness. [emphasis added]

Thus the hooding, the sleep deprivation, the irregular and insufficient meals, and the exposure to intense heat and cold. As a later version of the manual puts it, the "questioner"

> is able to manipulate the subject's environment, to create unpleasant or intolerable situations, to disrupt patterns of time, space, and sensory perception.... Once this disruption is achieved, the subject's resistance is seriously impaired. He experiences a kind of psychological shock, which may only last briefly, but during which he is far...likelier to comply.... Frequently the subject will experience a feeling of guilt. *If the "questioner" can intensify these guilt feelings, it will increase the subject's anxiety and his urge to cooperate as a means of escape.*[10] [emphasis added]

Viewed in this light, the garish scenes of humiliation pouring out in the photographs and depositions from Abu Ghraib—the men paraded naked down the cellblock with hoods on their heads, the forced masturbation, the forced homosexual activity, and all the rest—begin to be comprehensible; they are in fact staged operas of fabricated shame, intended to "intensify" the prisoner's "guilt feelings, increase his anxiety and his urge to cooperate." While many of the elements of abuse seen in the reports from Iraq, particularly the sensory deprivation and "stress positions," resemble methods used by modern intelligence services, including the British in Northern Ireland, some of the techniques seem clearly designed to exploit the particular sensitivities of Arab culture to public embarrassment, particularly in sexual matters.

The American military, of course, is well aware of these cultural sensitivities; in fall 2003, for example, the Marine Corps offered to its troops, along with a weeklong course on Iraq's customs and history, a pamphlet which included these admonitions:

> Do not shame or humiliate a man in public. Shaming a man will cause him and his family to be anti-Coalition.
>
> The most important qualifier for all shame is for a third party to witness the act. If you must do something likely to cause shame, remove the person from view of others.
>
> Shame is given by placing hoods over a detainee's head. Avoid this practice.
>
> Placing a detainee on the ground or putting a foot on him implies you are God. This is one of the worst things we can do.
>
> Arabs consider the following things unclean:
>
> Feet or soles of feet.
>
> Using the bathroom around others. Unlike Marines, who are used to open-air toilets, Arab men will not shower/use the bathroom together.
>
> Bodily fluids. . . .[11]

These precepts, intended to help Marines get along with the Iraqis they were occupying by avoiding doing anything, however unwittingly, that might offend them, are turned precisely on their heads by interrogators at Abu Ghraib and other American bases. Detainees are kept hooded and bound; made to crawl and grovel on the floor, often under the feet of the American soldiers; forced to put shoes in their mouths. And in all of this, as the Red Cross report noted, the *public* nature of the humiliation is absolutely critical; thus the parading of naked bodies, the forced masturbation in front of female soldiers, the confrontation of one naked prisoner with one or more others, the forcing together of naked prisoners in "human pyramids." And all of this was made to take place in full view not only of foreigners, men and women, but also of that ultimate third party: the ubiquitous digital camera with its inescapable flash, there to let the detainee know that the humiliation would not stop when the act itself did but would be preserved into the future in a way that the detainee would not be able to control. Whatever those taking them intended to do with the photographs, for the prisoners the camera had the potential of exposing his humiliation to family and friends, and thus served as a "shame multiplier," putting enormous power in the hands of the interrogator. The prisoner must please his interrogator, else his shame would be unending.

If, as the manuals suggest, the road to effective interrogation lay in "intensifying guilt feelings," and with them "the subject's anxiety and his urge to cooperate as a means of escape," then the bizarre epics of abuse coming out of Abu Ghraib begin to come into focus, slowly resolving from what seems a senseless litany of sadism and brutality to a series of actions that, however abhorrent, conceal within them a certain recognizable logic. Apart from the Reuters report, we don't know much about what went on in the interrogation rooms themselves; up to now, the professionals working within those rooms have mostly refused to talk.[12] We do know, from the statements of several of the military policemen, that the interrogators gave them specific instructions: "Loosen this guy up for us. Make sure he has a bad night. Make sure he gets the treatment." When one of these soldiers, Sergeant Javal S. Davis, was asked why he didn't protest the abusive behavior, he answered that he "assumed that if they were doing anything out of the ordinary or outside the guidelines, someone would have said something. Also, the wing belongs to [Military Intelligence] and it appeared that MI personnel approved the abuse." He went on, speaking about one of the other accused policemen:

> The MI staffs, to my understanding, have been giving Graner compliments on the way he has been handling the MI holds [i.e., prisoners held by military intelligence]. Example being statements like "Good job, they're breaking down real fast"; "They answer every question"; "They're giving out good information, finally"; and "Keep up the good work"—stuff like that.[13]

As a lawyer for another of the accused, Staff Sergeant Ivan Fredericks, told reporters:

> The story is not necessarily that there was a direct order. Everybody is far too subtle and smart for that.... Realistically, there is a description of an activity, a suggestion that it may be helpful and encouragement that this is exactly what we needed.

These statements were made by accused soldiers who have an obvious motive to shift the blame. Though few in military intelligence have spoken, and three have reportedly claimed the equivalent of Fifth Amendment protection,[14] one who has talked to journalists, Sergeant Samuel Provance, confirmed Sergeant Davis's assertion that the policemen were following orders:

> Military intelligence was in control. Setting the conditions for interrogations was strictly dictated by military intelligence. They weren't the ones carrying it out, but they were the ones telling the MPs to wake the detainees up every hour on the hour....

Provance told the reporters that "the highest ranking officers at the prison were involved and that the Army appears to be trying to deflect attention away from the military intelligence's role."[15]

One needn't depend on the assertions of those accused to accept that what happened in Abu Ghraib and elsewhere in Iraq was not the random brutality of "a few bad apples" (which, not surprisingly, happens to be the classic defense governments use in torture cases). One needn't depend on the wealth of external evidence, including the fall 2003 visit to Abu Ghraib by Major General Geoffrey Miller, then the commander of Guantánamo (and now commander of Abu Ghraib), in which, according to the Taguba report, he reviewed "current Iraqi Theater ability to rapidly exploit internees for actionable intelligence"[16]; or Lieutenant General Sanchez's October 12 memorandum, issued after General Miller's visit, instructing intelligence officers to work more closely with military policemen to "manipulate an internee's emotions and weaknesses"; or statements from Thomas M. Pappas, the colonel in charge of intelligence, that he felt "enormous pressure," as the insurgency increased in intensity, to "extract more information from prisoners."[17] The internal evidence—the awful details of the abuse itself and the clear logical narrative they take on when set against what we know of the interrogation methods of the American military and intelligence agencies—is quite enough to show that what happened at Abu Ghraib, whatever it was, did not depend on the sadistic ingenuity of a few bad apples.

This is what we know. The real question now, as so often, is not what we know but what we are prepared to do.

ва ва ва

> Should we remain in Algeria? If you answer "yes," then you must accept all the necessary consequences.
>
> —Colonel Philippe Mathieu
> *The Battle of Algiers* (1965)

When, as a young intelligence officer, the late General Paul Aussaresses arrived in war-torn Algeria a half-century ago and encountered his first captured insurgent, he discovered that methods of interrogation were widely known and fairly simple:

> When I questioned them I started by asking what they knew and they clearly indicated that they were not about to talk....
>
> Then without any hesitation, the policemen showed me the technique used for "extreme" interrogations: first, a beating, which in most cases was enough; then other means, such as electric shocks...; and finally water. Torture by electric shock was made possible by generators used to power field radio transmitters, which were extremely common in Algeria. Electrodes were attached to the prisoner's ears or testicles, then electric charges of varying intensity were turned on. This was apparently a well-known procedure....[18]

Aussaresses remarks that "almost all the French soldiers who served in Algeria knew more or less that torture was being used but didn't question the methods because they didn't have to face the problem directly." When as a responsible officer he gives a full report to his commander on his methods —which are yielding, as he notes, "very detailed explanations and other names, allowing me to make further arrests"—he encounters an interesting response:

"Are you sure there aren't other ways of getting people to talk?" he asked me nervously. "I mean methods that are . . ."

"Faster?" I asked.

"No, that's not what I mean."

"I know what you mean, Colonel. You're thinking of cleaner ways. You feel that none of this fits in with our humanistic tradition."

"Yes, that's what I mean," answered the Colonel.

"Even if I did agree with you, sir, to carry out the mission you've given me, I must avoid thinking in moral terms and only do what is most useful."

Aussaresses's logic is that of a practical soldier: a traditional army can defeat a determined guerrilla foe only through superior intelligence; superior intelligence can be wrested from hardened insurgents in time to make it "actionable" only through the use of "extreme interrogation"—torture; therefore, to have a chance of prevailing in Algeria the French army must torture. He has nothing but contempt for superior officers, like his colonel, who quail at the notion of "getting their hands dirty"—to say nothing of the politicians who, at the least sign of controversy over the methods he is obliged to employ, would think nothing of abandoning him as "a rotten apple."

It has long since become clear that President Bush and his highest officials, as they confronted the world on September 11, 2001, and in the days after, made a series of decisions about methods of warfare and interrogation that General Aussaresses, the practical soldier, would have well understood. The effect of those decisions—among them, the decision to imprison indefinitely those seized in Afghanistan and elsewhere in the war on terror, the decision to designate those prisoners as "unlawful combatants" and to withhold from them the protections of the Geneva Convention, and finally the decision to employ "high pressure methods" to extract "actionable intelligence" from them —was officially to transform the United States from a nation that did not torture to one that did. And the decisions were not, at least in their broad outlines, kept secret. They were known to officials of the other branches of the government and, eventually, to the public.

The direct consequences of those decisions, including details of the methods of interrogation applied in Guantánamo and at Bagram Air Base, began to emerge more than a year ago. It took the Abu Ghraib photographs, however, set against the violence and chaos of an increasingly unpopular war in

Iraq, to bring Americans' torture of prisoners up for public discussion. And just as General Aussaresses would recognize some of the methods Americans are employing in their secret interrogation rooms—notably, the practice of "water-boarding," strapping prisoners down and submerging them until they are on the point of drowning, long a favorite not only of the French in Algeria but of the Argentines, Uruguayans, and others in Latin America[19]—the general would smile disdainfully at the contradictions and hypocrisies of America's current scandal over Abu Ghraib: the "disgust" expressed by high officials over what the Abu Ghraib photographs reveal, the senior American officers in their ribbons prevaricating before the senators, and the continuing insistence that what went on in Abu Ghraib was only, as President Bush told the nation, "disgraceful conduct by a few American troops, who dishonored our country and disregarded our values."

General Aussaresses argued frankly for the necessity of torture but did not reckon on its political cost to what was, in the end, a political war. The general justified torture, as so many do, on the "ticking bomb" theory, as a means to protect lives immediately at risk; but in Algeria, as now in Iraq, torture, once sanctioned, is inevitably used much more broadly; and finally it becomes impossible to weigh what the practice gains militarily in "actionable intelligence" against what it loses politically, in an increasingly estranged population and an outraged world. Then as now, this was a political judgment, not a military one; and those who made it helped lose the generals' war.

A half-century later, the United States is engaged in another political war: not only the struggle against the insurgency in Iraq but the broader effort, if you credit the administration's words, to "transform the Middle East" so that "it will no longer produce ideologies of hatred that lead men to fly airplanes into buildings in New York and Washington." We can't know the value of the intelligence the torturers managed to extract, though top commanders admitted to *The New York Times* on May 27, 2004, that they learned "little about the insurgency" from the interrogations. What is clear is that the Abu Ghraib photographs and the terrible story they tell have done great damage to what was left of America's moral power in the world, and thus its power to inspire hope rather than hatred among Muslims. The photographs "do not represent America," or so the President asserts, and we nod our heads and agree. But what exactly does this mean? As so often, it took a comic, Rob Corddry on *The Daily Show with Jon Stewart*, to point out the grim contradiction in this:

There's no question what took place in that prison was horrible. But the Arab world has to realize that the US shouldn't be judged on the actions of a...well, we shouldn't be judged on actions. It's our principles that matter, our inspiring, abstract notions. Remember: Just because torturing prisoners is something we did, doesn't mean it's something we *would* do.[20]

Over the next weeks and months, Americans will decide how to confront what their fellow citizens did at Abu Ghraib, and what they go on doing at Bagram and Guantánamo and other secret prisons. By their actions they will decide whether they will begin to close the growing difference between what Americans say they are and what they actually do. Iraqis and others around the world will be watching to see whether all the torture will be stopped and whether those truly responsible for it, military and civilian, will be punished. This is, after all, as our President never tires of saying, a war of ideas. Now, as the photographs of Abu Ghraib make clear, it has also become a struggle over what, if anything, really does represent America.

—The New York Review of Books, May 27, 2004

NOTES

1. "In Abu Ghraib prison alone, senior officials have testified that no less than three sets of interrogation policies were put in play at different times—those cited in Army field manuals, those used by interrogators who previously worked in Afghanistan and a third set created by Iraq's commanding general after policies used at Guantánamo Bay." From Craig Gordon, "High-Pressure Tactics: Critics Say Bush Policies—Post 9/11—Gave Interrogators Leeway to Push Beyond Normal Limits," *Newsday*, May 23, 2004.

2. See Edward Epstein, "Red Cross Reports Lost, Generals Say: 'The System Is Broken,' Army Commander Tells Senate Panel about Abu Ghraib Warnings," *San Francisco Chronicle*, May 20, 2004.

3. See Douglas Jehl and Eric Schmitt, "Officer Says Army Tried to Curb Red Cross Visits to Prison in Iraq," *The New York Times*, May 19, 2004.

4. See R. Jeffrey Smith, "Memo Gave Intelligence Bigger Role: Increased Pressure Sought on Prisoners," *The Washington Post*, May 21, 2004.

5. See Douglas Jehl and Neil A. Lewis, "US Disputed Protected Status of Iraq Inmates," *The New York Times*, May 23, 2004.

6. See Josh White and Scott Higham, "Sergeant Says Intelligence Directed Abuse," *The Washington Post*, May 20, 2004.

7. See "Translation of Sworn Statement Provided by _____, Detainee #_____, 1430/21 Jan 04," available along with thirteen other affidavits from Iraqis, at "Sworn Statements by Abu Ghraib Detainees," www.washingtonpost.com, and reproduced on pp. 247–248. The name was withheld by *The Washington Post* because the witness "was an alleged victim of sexual assault."

8. See Greg Mitchell, "Exclusive: Shocking Details on Abuse of Reuters Staffers in Iraq," *Editor and Publisher*, May 19, 2004, which includes excerpts from the Baghdad bureau chief's report.

9. *See* KUBARK *Counterintelligence Interrogation—July 1963*, archived at "Prisoner Abuse: Patterns from the Past," National Security Archive Electronic Briefing Book No. 122, p. 83; www.gwu.edu/~nsarchiv/NSAEBB/NSA-EBB122. "KUBARK" is a CIA codename.

10. *See Human Resource Exploitation Training Manual—1983*, National Security Archive Electronic Briefing Book No. 122, "Non-coercive Techniques"; www.gwu.edu /~nsarchiv/NSAEBB /NSAEBB122.

11. See "Semper Sensitive: From a Handout That Accompanies a Weeklong Course on Iraq's Customs and History," Marine Division School, *Harper's*, June 2004, p. 26.

12. Though we do know something of what has gone on at other American interrogation centers, for example, the American air base at Bagram, Afghanistan. See Don Van Natta Jr., "Questioning Terror Suspects in a Dark and Surreal World," *The New York Times*, March 9, 2003.

13. See Scott Higham and Joe Stephens, "Punishment and Amusement," *The Washington Post*, May 22, 2004.

14. See Richard A. Serrano, "Three Witnesses in Abuse Case Aren't Talking: Higher-ups and a Contractor Out to Avoid Self-incrimination," *San Francisco Chronicle*, May 19, 2004.

15. See White and Higham, "Intelligence Officers Tied to Abuses in Iraq."

16. See General Antonio M. Taguba, "Article 15-6 Investigation of the 800th Military Police Brigade" (The Taguba Report), reproduced on page 283.

17. See Douglas Jehl, "Officers Say US Colonel at Abu Ghraib Prison Felt Intense Pressure to Get Inmates to Talk," *The New York Times*, May 18, 2004.

18. See Paul Aussaresses, *The Battle of the Casbah: Terrorism and Counter-Terrorism in Algeria, 1955–1957*, translated by Robert L. Miller (Enigma, 2002).

19. See James Risen, David Johnston, and Neil A. Lewis, "Harsh CIA Methods Cited in Top Qaeda Interrogations," *The New York Times*, May 13, 2004.

20. Rob Corddry, *The Daily Show with Jon Stewart*, Comedy Central, May 6, 2004.

III

THE SECRET ROAD
TO ABU GHRAIB

"Free societies in the Middle East will be hopeful societies, which no longer feed resentments and breed violence for export.... The terrorists are fighting freedom with all their cunning and cruelty because freedom is their greatest fear—and they should be afraid, because freedom is on the march."

—President George W. Bush,
Republican National Convention, New York, September 2, 2004

"It was discovered that freedom in this land is not ours. It is the freedom of the occupying soldiers in doing what they like...abusing women, children, men, and the old men and women whom they arrested randomly and without any guilt. No one can ask them what they are doing, because they are protected by their freedom.... No one can punish them, whether in our country or their country. They expressed the freedom of rape, the freedom of nudity and the freedom of humiliation."

—Sheik Mohammed Bashir,
Friday prayers, Um al-Oura, Baghdad, June 11, 2004[1]

THEY HAVE LONG since taken their place in the gallery of branded images, as readily recognizable in much of the world as Marilyn struggling with her billowing dress or Michael dunking his basketball: Hooded Man, a dark-caped figure tottering on a box, supplicant arms outstretched, wires trailing from his fingers; and Leashed Man, face convulsed in humiliation above his leather collar, naked body twisted at the feet of the American female in camouflage pants who gazes down at him without expression, holding the leash casually in hand. The ubiquity of these images in much of the world suggests not only their potency but their usefulness and their adaptability. For the first of the many realities illuminated by the Global War on Terror—or the GWOT, as General George R. Fay and the panel chaired by James R. Schlesinger designate it in their reports[2]—is the indisputable fact that much of the world sees America rather differently from the way Americans see themselves.

Out of the interlocking scandals and controversies symbolized by Hooded Man and Leashed Man, the pyramids of naked bodies, the snarling dogs, and all the rest, and known to the world by the collective name of Abu Ghraib, one can extract two "master narratives," both dependent on the power and mutability of the images themselves. The first is that of President Bush, who presented the photographs as depicting "disgraceful conduct by a few American troops, who dishonored our country and disregarded our values"— behavior that, the President insisted, "does not represent America." And the aberrant, outlandish character of what the photographs show—the nudity, the sadism, the pornographic imagery—seemed to support this "few bad apples" argument, long the classic defense of states accused of torture.

The facts, however, almost from day one, did not: the Red Cross report, the Army's own Taguba report, even the photographs themselves, some of which depicted military intelligence soldiers assisting in abuses they supposedly knew nothing about—all strongly suggested that the images were the brutal public face of behavior that involved many more people than the seven military police who were quickly charged. The new reports not only decisively prove what was long known, widening the circle of direct blame for what happened at Abu Ghraib to nearly fifty people, including military intelligence soldiers and officers (although subsequent disclosures suggest the number is at least twice that). More important, the reports suggest how procedures that "violated established interrogation procedures and applicable laws" had their genesis not in Iraq but in interrogation rooms in Afghanistan and Guantánamo Bay, Cuba—and ultimately in decisions made by high officials in Washington.

As General George R. Fay writes, in a section of his report that was classified and kept from the public,

> Policies and practices developed and approved for use on Al Qaeda and
> Taliban detainees [in Afghanistan and Guantánamo] who were not

afforded the protection of the Geneva Conventions, now applied to detainees who did fall under the Geneva Conventions' protections.

According to General Fay, these "policies and practices" included, among others, "removing clothing, isolating people for long periods of time, using stress positions, exploiting fear of dogs and implementing sleep and light deprivation."

What we know as "the Abu Ghraib scandal" has in fact become an increasingly complex story about how Americans in Afghanistan and Cuba and Iraq came to commit acts, with the apparent approval of the highest officials, that clearly constitute torture. The images themselves, however, having helped force open the door to broader questions of how the Bush administration has treated prisoners in the War on Terror, are now helping to block that door; for the images, by virtue of their inherent grotesque power, strongly encourage the view that "acts of brutality and purposeless sadism," which clearly did occur, lay at the heart of Abu Ghraib. Even public officials charged with investigating the scandal—these are the fourth and fifth full reports on the matter, with at least four more to come—at the same time seek to contain it by promoting the view that Abu Ghraib in its essence was about individual misbehavior and sadism: "Animal House on the night shift," as former secretary of defense Schlesinger characterized it, even as his own report showed in detail that it was a great deal more.

The second "master narrative" of Abu Ghraib is that of the Muslim preacher Sheik Mohammed Bashir, quoted above, and many other Arabs and Muslims who point to the scandal's images as perfect symbols of the subjugation and degradation that the American occupiers have inflicted on Iraq and the rest of the Arab world. In this sense the Hooded Man and the Leashed Man fill a need, serving as powerful brand images advertising a preexisting product. Imagine, for a moment, an Islamic fundamentalist trying to build a transnational movement by arguing that today "nations are attacking Muslims like people attacking a plate of food," and by exhorting young Muslims to rise up and follow the Prophet's words:

> And why should ye not fight in the cause of Allah and of those who, being weak, are ill-treated (and oppressed)?—women and children— whose cry is: "Oh Lord, rescue us from this town, whose people are oppressors; and raise for us from thee one who will help!"

For such an Islamic fundamentalist, quoting these words to give legitimacy to his call for jihad against the United States—as Osama bin Laden did in his famous 1998 fatwa "Jihad Against Jews and Crusaders"[3]—what better image of Arab ill-treatment and oppression could be devised than that of a naked Arab man lying at the feet of a short-haired American woman in camouflage garb, who stares immodestly at her Arab pet while holding him by the throat with a leash? Had bin Laden sought to create a powerful trademark image for his international product of global jihad, he could scarcely have done better hiring the cleverest advertising firm on Madison Avenue.

And not only are these photographs perfect masterpieces of propaganda; they have, to paraphrase Henry Kissinger, the considerable advantage of being true. Or, to put it another way: if the Hooded Man and the Leashed Man and the naked human pyramids and the rest shocked Americans because of their perverse undermining of the normal, they shocked Iraqis and other Arabs because the images seemed to confirm so vividly and precisely a reality that many had suspected and feared but had tried not to believe.

⁂ ⁂ ⁂

"I always knew the Americans would bring electricity back to Baghdad. I just never thought they'd be shooting it up my ass."

—Young Iraqi translator, Baghdad, November 2003

On first setting eyes on the Hooded Man in April 2004, I thought instantly of this joke, which I'd heard in a Baghdad street six months before. At that moment, the insurgency, wholly unanticipated by American officers on the ground and stubbornly denied by their political masters in Washington, had been gaining strength for months.[4] Enormous suicide bombings had killed hundreds, had driven the United Nations, the Red Cross, and many other international organizations from the country, and had turned Baghdad into a city of stone, its public buildings and hotels and many of its roads encircled by massive concrete blast barriers and its American occupation government wholly inaccessible behind the barbed-wire and machine-gun nests of the grim fortress called the Green Zone.

The only Americans most Iraqis saw were the sunglasses-wearing machine-gunners atop the up-armored Humvees and Bradley fighting vehicles that barreled through traffic several times a day. These patrols were coming under increasingly frequent attack, usually from the ubiquitous "improvised explosive devices," or IEDs, which insurgents concealed in garbage cans or behind telephone poles. By November the number of attacks against Americans had doubled, to nearly forty a day. In May 2003, the month President Bush declared that "major combat" was over, forty-one Americans died in Iraq; in November, six months later, 110 died. And by and large, as was clear in Iraq at the time, and as these reports amply confirm, the American officers had very little idea who was killing their troops and had become increasingly desperate to find out. General Fay writes in his report that

> as the pace of operations picked up in late November–early December 2003, it became a common practice for maneuver elements to round up large quantities of Iraqi personnel [i.e., civilians] in the general vicinity of a specified target as a cordon and capture technique. Some operations were conducted at night....

Representatives of the Red Cross, who visited Abu Graib nearly thirty times in this period, offered a more vivid account of "cordon and capture":

> Arresting authorities entered houses usually after dark, breaking down doors, waking up residents roughly, yelling orders, forcing family members into one room under military guard while searching the rest of the house and further breaking doors, cabinets and other property. They arrested suspects, tying their hands in the back with flexi-cuffs, hooding them, and taking them away. Sometimes they arrested all adult males present in a house, including elderly, handicapped or sick people. Treatment often included pushing people around, insulting, taking aim with rifles, punching and kicking and striking with rifles. Individuals were often led away in whatever they happened to be wearing at the time of arrest—sometimes in pyjamas or underwear....

In this way the Americans arrested thousands of Iraqis—or, as Schlesinger puts it, "they reverted to rounding up any and all suspicious-looking persons —all too often including women and children. The flood of incoming detainees contrasted sharply with the trickle of released individuals." Soon the population of the US military's detention system approached ten thousand and very few Iraqis did not have some family member or friend who had gained intimate familiarity with American "cordon and capture." When Sheik Bashir complained to the Sunni faithful at the Um al-Oura mosque that Friday in June of the occupying soldiers "abusing women, children, men, and the old men and women whom they arrested randomly and without any guilt," he had no need to point to photographs. In Baghdad and Falluja eight months before, I had heard the same bitter complaints, not only about the brutality of the tactics but about the obvious randomness of the arrests, which General Fay now confirms:

> SCT Jose Garcia, assigned to the Abu Ghraib Detainee Assessment Board, estimated that 85–90 percent of the detainees were of no intelligence value.... Large quantities of detainees with little or no intelligence value swelled Abu Ghraib's population and led to a variety of overcrowding difficulties.... Complicated and unresponsive release procedures ensured that these detainees stayed at Abu Ghraib—even though most had no value.

Among the many disadvantages of these nighttime sweeps as a tactic for fighting an insurgency was that prisoners scooped up in this way soon flooded the system, inundating the very prisons where detainees were meant to be "exploited for actionable intelligence." And having filled Abu Ghraib largely with Iraqis of "no intelligence value"—whose families in most cases had no way to confirm where they were—the overwhelmed American command could not devise a way to get them out again, especially when faced with the strong opposition of those who had arrested them in the first place:

> Combat Commanders desired that no security detainee be released for fear that any and all detainees could be threats to coalition forces.... The [chief of intelligence, Fourth Infantry Division] informed [Major General] Fast that the Division Commander did not concur with the release of any detainees for fear that a bad one may be released along with the good ones.

Major General Fast, the senior intelligence officer in Iraq, described the attitude of the combat commanders as, "We wouldn't have detained them if we wanted them released." A sensible attitude, one might think, but as General Fay points out, the combat soldiers, in their zeal to apprehend Iraqis who might conceivably be supporting those shadowy figures attacking American troops, neglected to filter out those who clearly didn't belong in prison. The capturing soldiers

> failed to perform the proper procedures at the point-of-capture and beyond with respect to handling captured enemy prisoners of war and detainees (screening, tactical interrogation, capture cards, sworn statements, transportation, etc.). Failure of capturing units to follow these procedures contributed to facility overcrowding, an increased drain on scarce interrogator and linguist resources to sort out the valuable detainees from innocents who should have been released soon after capture, and ultimately, to *less actionable intelligence.* [My emphasis.]

The system was self-defeating and, not surprisingly, "interrogation operations in Abu Ghraib suffered from the effects of a broken detention operations system." Indeed, these reports are full of "broken systems" and "under-resourced" commands, from Abu Ghraib itself, a besieged, sweltering, stinking hell-hole under daily mortar attack that lacked interpreters, interrogators, guards, detainee uniforms, and just about everything else, including edible food, and that, at its height, was staggering under an impossible prisoner-to-guard ratio of seventy-five to one, all the way up to the command staff of Lieutenant General Ricardo Sanchez, which lacked, among other vital resources, two thirds of its assigned officers. In Iraq, as the Schlesinger report puts it bluntly, "there was not only a failure to plan for a major insurgency, but also to quickly and adequately adapt to the insurgency that followed after major combat operations." And though they don't say so explicitly, it is clear that the writers of these reports put much of the blame for this not on the commanders on the ground but on the political leadership in Washington, who, rather than pay the political cost of admitting the need for more troops—admitting, that is, that they had made mistakes in planning for the war and in selling it to the public—decided to "tough it out," at the expense of the men and women in the field and, ultimately, the Iraqis they had been sent to "liberate." All told, the reports offer a vivid and damning picture of a war that is understaffed, undersupplied, underresourced, and, above all, undermanned.

In this sense Abu Ghraib is at once a microcosm of the Iraq war in all its failures and the proverbial canary in the mineshaft, warning of what is to come. In fighting a guerrilla war, the essential weapon is not tanks or helicopters but intelligence, and the single essential tool to obtain it is reliable political support among the population. In such a war, arresting and imprisoning thousands of civilians in murkily defined "cordon and capture" raids is a blatantly self-defeating tactic, and an occupying army's resort to it means not only that the occupier lacks the political support necessary to find and destroy the insurgents but that it has been forced by the insurgents to adopt tactics that will further lessen that support and create still more insurgents. It is, in short, a strategy of desperation and, in the end, a strategy of weakness.

By late summer 2003—a time when Bush administration officials had expected to start "drawing down" American forces "in theater" until a stabilization force of no more than 30,000 Americans remained in Iraq—the US military, even with 130,000 troops, was losing the initiative to an insurgency that seemed to have come out of nowhere and, after carrying out its increasingly bloody IED attacks and suicide bombings, regularly managed to disappear back into the same place. Officials in Washington were growing worried and impatient, and intelligence officers in Iraq were feeling the pressure.

In mid-August, a captain in military intelligence (MI) sent his colleagues an e-mail—recently shown to me—in which, clearly responding to an earlier request from interrogators, he sought to define "unlawful combatants," distinguishing them from "lawful combatants [who] receive protections of the Geneva Convention and gain combat immunity for their warlike acts." After promising to provide "an ROE"—rules of engagement—"that addresses the treatment of enemy combatants, specifically, unprivileged belligerents," the captain asks the interrogators for "input...concerning what their special interrogation knowledge base is and more importantly, what techniques would they feel would be effective techniques." Then, reminding the intelligence people to "provide Interrogation techniques 'wish list' by 17 AUG 03," the captain signs off this way:

> The gloves are coming off gentlemen regarding these detainees, Col Boltz has made it clear that we want these individuals broken. Casualties are mounting and we need to start gathering info to help protect our fellow soldiers from any further attacks. I thank you for your hard work and your dedication.
>
> MI ALWAYS OUT FRONT!

On August 31 Major General Geoffrey Miller, the commander of the US detention camp in Guantánamo, would arrive, ordered to Iraq "to review current Iraqi Theater ability to rapidly exploit internees for actionable intelligence." He and his team would bring with them news and advice drawn from the American government's and the US military's latest thinking on interrogation. For those at Abu Ghraib charged with "breaking" prisoners, help was on the way.

ঌ ঌ ঌ

"In the case of Khalid Shaikh Mohammed, a high-level detainee who is believed to have helped plan the attacks of Sept. 11, 2001, CIA interrogators used graduated levels of force, including a technique known as "water-boarding," in which a prisoner is strapped down, forcibly pushed under water and made to believe he might drown."[5]

—*The New York Times*, May 13, 2004

In the matter of Americans' use of torture there are, to paraphrase Donald Rumsfeld, the things we know, the things we know we don't know, and the things we don't know we don't know. We know, for example, that much of the 9/11 Commission report's meticulous account of the unfolding of the World Trade Center plot comes from secret interrogations of Khalid Shaikh Mohammed and other "high value detainees." We know we don't know where he and his score or so fellows are being held—and neither, reportedly, does President Bush, who "informed the CIA that he did not want to know where they are"[6]—though it is likely that the CIA is holding them at a secret military base somewhere in Asia, perhaps in Afghanistan, Thailand, or even Jordan. We know we don't know specifically what "graduated levels of force" means, though we have a general idea:

After apprehending suspects, US take-down teams—a mix of military special forces, FBI agents, CIA case officers and local allies—aim to disorient and intimidate them on the way to detention facilities.

According to Americans with direct knowledge and others who have witnessed the treatment, captives are "softened up" by MPs and US Army Special Forces troops who beat them up and confine them in tiny rooms. The alleged terrorists are commonly blindfolded and thrown into walls, bound in painful positions, subjected to loud noises and deprived of sleep.[7]

We do know, finally, what "water-boarding" is, though it is not clear what version of this torture the Americans are applying. There is, for example, the version French policemen and soldiers used on prisoners during the Algerian War, as in this account from Bechir Boumaza, a thirty-one-year-old Algerian interrogated in Paris in 1958:

> I was taken off the bar [on which he had been hung and subjected to electric torture] and my guards started their football again [beating and kicking him], perhaps for a quarter hour. Then they led me, still naked and blindfolded, into a neighboring room on the same floor. I heard: "We'll have to kill him, the bastard."
>
> Then they laid me on a bench, flat on my stomach, head extending into the air, and tied my arms against my body with cords. Again the same question, which I refused to answer. By tilting the bench very slowly, they dipped my head into a basin filled with stinking liquid—dirty water and urine, probably. I was aware of the gurgling liquid reaching my mouth, then of a dull rumbling in my ears and a tingling sensation in my nose.
>
> "You asked for a drink—take all you want."
>
> The first time I did drink, trying to appease an insupportable thirst. I wanted to vomit immediately.
>
> "He's puking, the bastard."
>
> And my head was pushed back into the basin. . . .
>
> From time to time one of them would sit on my back and bear down on my thighs. I could hear the water I threw up fall back into the basin. Then the torture would continue.[8]

The Latin American version, called *el submarino*, uses a wooden table, an oil drum filled with water, and a set of hooks linking the two, so that when the interrogators lift the table, the prisoner's head is submerged. Here is the account of Irina Martinez, an Argentine student activist, who was arrested at her parents' house in Buenos Aires in 1977, during the Dirty War:

> She was immediately blindfolded. Her first torture session was in a basement full of soldiers, where she was stripped naked, tied, and

beaten. "They slapped my face, pinched my breasts. 'You have to talk, this is your last opportunity, and this is your salvation.' And then they put me on a table. And I thought, 'Well, if they are going to kill me, I hope they kill me pretty soon.' They pushed my head underwater, so I could not breathe. They take you out, ask you things, they put you in, they take you out—so you cannot breathe all the time. 'Who did you receive this from? Who do you know?' Who can control anything when you cannot breathe? They pull you out, you try to grab for air, so they put you back in so you swallow water, and it is winter and you are very cold and very scared and they do that for a long time. Even if you are a good swimmer you cannot stand it anymore. . . ."[9]

Water-boarding, as those Americans who used the method on Khalid Shaikh Mohammed and other "high value detainees" surely know, is very effective in inducing fear; as a Uruguayan army interrogator put it, "There is something more terrifying than pain, and that is the inability to breathe." It is most effective, as these examples suggest, when combined with other techniques, including stress positions, sensory and sleep deprivation, and direct "physical coercion," or beatings.

We don't know precisely when officers of the CIA began applying such "enhanced interrogation techniques," as the agency calls them, to their "high value detainees," but we can see signs of the trend toward using these techniques very soon after the attacks of September 11, and also signs of strong interest in learning immediately the results of interrogation coming from high up in the security bureaucracies, including from the office of Secretary of Defense Rumsfeld. As early as October 2001, after the capture of John Walker Lindh in Afghanistan, a Navy admiral told the intelligence officer interrogating Lindh that "the secretary of defense's counsel has authorized him to 'take the gloves off' and ask whatever he wanted."[10]

Lindh's interrogators stripped the young American, who had been shot in the foot, taped him to a stretcher, propped it up against a shipping container in the cold open air of Afghanistan, and proceeded to interrogate him in marathon sessions that went on for days. According to documents that were leaked to a *Los Angeles Times* reporter, Lindh's responses during these interrogation sessions were cabled back to the Defense Department as often as every hour. During the coming months and years, as the United States gradually built a network of secret and semisecret prisons in Bagram and

Kandahar, Afghanistan; Guantánamo, Cuba; Qatar and Diego Garcia, as well as Abu Ghraib and Camp Cropper, Iraq, this direct attention from senior officials in Washington has remained constant. As Lieutenant Colonel Steven Jordan, the head of the Joint Intelligence and Debriefing Center at Abu Ghraib, told General Taguba in December 2003, "Sir, I was told a couple times...that some of the reporting was getting read by Rumsfeld, folks out of Langley [CIA headquarters], some very senior folks." For Jordan, that meant a lot of pressure to produce. It also meant that what went on at Abu Ghraib and other interrogation centers was very much the focus of the most senior officials in Washington.

ða ða ða

In the last chapter, I wrote about the case of an Iraqi man who had spent time in Abu Ghraib and had given a sworn statement, after his release, to investigators of the US Army's Criminal Investigation Command (CID). This statement had been leaked, along with those of twelve other detainees, to *The Washington Post*, which posted them on its Web site. Here now is General Fay's full account of what happened to the anonymous prisoner, and his analysis of who was responsible:

In October 2003, DETAINEE-07, reported alleged multiple incidents of physical abuse while in Abu Ghraib. DETAINEE-07 was a [military intelligence] hold and considered of potentially high value. He was interrogated on 8, 21 and 29 October; 4 and 23 November and 5 December. DETAINEE-07's claims of physical abuse (hitting) started on his first day of arrival. He was left naked in his cell for extended periods, cuffed in his cell in stressful positions ("High cuffed"), left with a bag over his head for extended periods, and denied bedding or blankets. DETAINEE-07 described being made to "bark like a dog, being forced to crawl on his stomach while MPs spit and urinated on him, and being struck causing unconsciousness."

On another occasion DETAINEE-07 was forced to lie down while MPs jumped onto his back and legs. He was beaten with a broom and a chemical light was broken and poured over his body. DETAINEE-04 witnessed the abuse with the chem.-light. During this abuse a police stick was used to sodomize DETAINEE-07 and two female MPs were hitting him, throwing a ball at his penis, and taking photographs. This investigation surfaced no photographic evidence of the chemical light abuse or sodomy. DETAINEE-07 also alleged that CIVILIAN-17, MP Interpreter, Titan Corp., hit DETAINEE-07 once, cutting his ear to an extent that required stitches. He told SOLDIER-25, analyst, B/321 [Military Intelligence Brigade], about this hitting incident during an interrogation. SOLDIER-25 asked the MPs what had happened to the detainee's ear and was told he had fallen in his cell. SOLDIER-25 did not report the detainee's abuse. SOLDIER-25 claimed the detainee's allegation was made in the presence of CIVILIAN-21, Analyst/Interrogator, CACI [Corporation], which CIVILIAN-21 denied hearing this report. Two photos taken at 2200 hours, 1 November 2003, depict a detainee with stitches in his ear; however, we could not confirm the photo was DETAINEE-07.

Based on the details provided by the detainee and the close correlation to other known MP abuses, it is highly probable DETAINEE-07's allegations are true. SOLDIER-25 failed to report the detainee's allegation of abuse. His statements and available photographs do not point to direct [military intelligence] involvement. However, MI interest in this detainee, his placement in Tier 1A of the Hard Site, and initiation of the abuse once he arrived there, combine to create a circumstantial connection to MI (knowledge or implicit tasking of the MPs to "set conditions") which are difficult to ignore. MI should have been aware of what was being done to this detainee based on the frequency of interrogations and high interest in his intelligence value.

What is interesting here is not simply that General Fay confirms the account of Detainee-07 but the strange Kabuki dance the general performs when he comes to the point of assigning responsibility. During a period of about two months, military police beat the detainee savagely into unconsciousness, ripped his ear, urinated on him, "high-cuffed" him to the bars of his cell for hours so that the skin of his hand split and oozed pus, and sodomized him with a police baton—to give only a brief summary of what, in the detainee's statement, is an exhaustive and exhausting catalog of imaginative and extremely disgusting tortures carried out over many days. Now during this time, as General Fay meticulously confirms, military intelligence soldiers interrogated Detainee-07 on at least six occasions, as befits a prisoner judged of "potentially high value." General Fay, however, finds here only a "circumstantial connection to MI," concluding that the intelligence officers "should have been aware of what was being done to this detainee."

The problem here is that it is quite obvious from the report that military intelligence officers were "aware of what was being done to the detainee"—indeed, that they ordered it. During Detainee-07's first beating, according to his statement, "the Interrogator came and he was looking at me while they were beating me." The general doesn't mention this; indeed, throughout his patient recounting of his forty-four "serious incidents"—his careful sifting of them into categories ("Nudity/ Humiliation," "Assault," "Sexual Assault," "Use of Dogs," "The 'Hole,'" and "Other"), his determination to classify them according to responsibility ("MI," "MP," "MI/MP," or "UNK," for unknown), and his dogged effort to separate what he calls "violent/sexual abuse incidents" (which is to say those, generally speaking, committed by military police, which were not a matter of policy) from "misinterpretation/confusion incidents" (those committed by military intelligence soldiers, who, however, were "confused" about what was permitted at Abu Ghraib as a matter of policy)—throughout all this runs a tone of faintly hysterical absurdity. Throughout we see distinctions that are not distinctions at all, and that recall nothing so much as the darkest passages of *Catch-22*; for example, this passage, on "sleep adjustment":

> Sleep adjustment was brought with 519 [Military Intelligence Battalion] from Afghanistan. It is also a method used at GTMO [Guantánamo]....
> At Abu Ghraib, however, the MPs were not trained, nor informed as to how they actually should do the sleep adjustment. The MPs were just told to keep a detainee awake for a time specified by the interrogator. The MPs used their own judgment as to how to keep them awake. Those techniques included taking the detainees out of their cells, stripping them and giving them cold showers. CPT Wood stated she did not know this was going on and thought the detainees were being kept awake by the MPs banging on the cell doors, yelling, and playing loud music.

Abu Ghraib was a mess; training was deficient; the chain of command was dysfunctional. But that military intelligence soldiers would have had no idea what was being done to prisoners whom they spent hours and hours each day interrogating is simply not credible.

What is credible, or at least comprehensible, is the subtle bureaucratic strategy that has been adopted in these reports, and which has been visible, indeed obvious, from the moment the story of Abu Ghraib broke. For at that moment, in late April, a bureaucratic and political war erupted over torture and its implications, and over Abu Ghraib and how broad-reaching and damaging the scandal that bore its name was going to be. On one side were those within the administration, many of whom had opposed the use of "enhanced interrogation tactics" from the beginning, including many in the judge advocate generals' offices of the various military services and career lawyers in the Justice Department, who for the last four months have been leaking a veritable flood of documents detailing legally questionable and politically damaging administration decisions about torture and interrogation. On the other side are those at the highest political levels of the Department of Defense, the Department of Justice, and the White House who have struggled, so far successfully, to keep Abu Ghraib from becoming what it early on threatened to be: a scandal that could bring down many senior officials in the Department of Defense, and perhaps the administration itself.

With no fear of a full, top-to-bottom investigation from a Congress that is firmly in Republican hands, administration officials, and particularly those at the Department of Defense, have managed to orchestrate a slowly unfolding series of inquiries, almost all of them carried out within the military by officers who by definition can only direct their gaze down the chain of command, not up it, and who are each empowered to examine only a limited and precisely defined number of links in the chain that connects the highest levels of the government to what happened on the ground in Abu Ghraib and elsewhere in the war on terror. Thus General Taguba investigated the military police, General Paul Mikolashek, as the Army's inspector general, reported on detention procedures, General Fay on military intelligence, and so on.

Beyond the reports themselves, the key strategy of the defense is both to focus on the photographs and to isolate the acts they depict—which, if not the most serious, are those with the most political effect—from any inference that they might have resulted, either directly or indirectly, from policy. Thus the dogged effort to isolate these acts as "violence/sexual abuse incidents" that originated wholly in the minds of sadistic military police during the wee hours, and that, above all, had nothing whatever to do with what was done "to set the conditions" for interrogation—even though this division is quite artificial and many of the latter activities, as vividly demonstrated by the sufferings of Detainee-07, were conducted by precisely the same people and were equally, or more, disgusting, sadistic, and abusive.

Only against this background can one properly appreciate the opening paragraph of former secretary Schlesinger's report, five powerfully peculiar sentences, in which the bureaucratic priorities of this political containment effort have thoroughly corrupted the language:

> The events of October through December 2003 on the night shift of Tier 1 at Abu Ghraib prison were acts of brutality and purposeless sadism. We now know these abuses occurred at the hands of both military police and military intelligence personnel. The pictured abuses, unacceptable even in wartime, were not part of authorized interrogations nor were they even directed at intelligence targets. They represent deviant behavior and a failure of military leadership and discipline. However, we do know that some of the egregious abuses at Abu Ghraib which were not photographed did occur during interrogation sessions and that abuses during interrogation sessions occurred elsewhere.

Mr. Schlesinger and his fellow commissioners begin by defining all the events at Abu Ghraib as "acts of brutality and purposeless sadism," though they admit, in the next sentence, that they in fact occurred "at the hands of both military police and military intelligence." The next sentence abruptly and arbitrarily narrows the subject from "the events . . . on the night shift" to "the pictured abuses"—that is, those in the photographs—which the writers say were not "even directed at intelligence targets." These "represent deviant behavior"—except for the fact, as they go on to concede in the fifth sentence (where perhaps counsel intervened), that "some of the egregious abuses . . . which were not photographed did occur during interrogation sessions." It is a strange tangle of self-contradictory and oddly qualified sentences which seems designed to allow Mr. Schlesinger and others in the administration to contend that their report proved decisively that the abuses at Abu Ghraib were nothing more than the photographs—an argument that in fact the report that follows decisively disproves.

The "celebrity abuses"—those known through the photographs—are segregated firmly within the realm of "acts of brutality and purposeless sadism," as Mr. Schlesinger calls them—"Animal House on the night shift"—and thereby sealed off entirely from the responsibility of policymakers. Even now seven hapless MPs are being prosecuted—two have already pleaded guilty—but only, in effect, for taking pictures; that is, only for those acts which can be said to have taken place outside the realm of interrogation or of acts "setting the conditions for interrogation." On the other hand, acts of brutality that can't be attributed entirely to sadistic military police, and which clearly involved military intelligence and the process of interrogation—those, that is, that risk implicating policymakers, who in the end are responsible for deciding what the interrogators can and cannot do—are ascribed in the reports to "misinterpretation/confusion" on the part of the intelligence people about what interrogation techniques could and could not be used at Abu Ghraib. These actions, after all, are where the political danger lies; for knowledge about "interrogation techniques" leads to knowledge about the official doctrine that allowed those techniques, doctrine leads to policy, and policy leads to power.

⋐ ⋐ ⋐

Nixon: Do you think we want to go this route now? Let it hang out?
Dean: Well, it isn't really that.
Haldeman: It's a limited hang-out.
Ehrlichman: It's a modified, limited hang-out.

—The White House, March 22, 1973

The delicate bureaucratic construction now holding the Abu Ghraib scandal firmly in check rests ultimately on President Bush's controversial decision, on February 7, 2002, to withhold protection of the Geneva Convention both from al-Qaeda and from Taliban fighters in Afghanistan. The decision rested on the argument, in the words of White House Counsel Alberto Gonzalez, that "the war against terrorism is a new kind of war," in fact, a "new paradigm [that] renders obsolete Geneva's strict limitations on questioning of enemy prisoners and renders quaint some of its provisions. . . ." In a prefiguring of later bureaucratic wars, lawyers in the State Department and many in the military services fought against this decision, arguing, prophetically, that it "would undermine the United States military culture, which is based on a strict adherence to the law of war."

For torture, this decision was Original Sin: it made legally possible the adoption of the various "enhanced interrogation techniques" that have been used at CIA secret prisons and at the US military's prison at Guantánamo Bay. As it turns out, however, for the administration, Bush's decision was also Amazing Grace, because, by implying that the US military must adhere to wholly different rules when interrogating, say, Taliban prisoners in Guantá-namo, who do not enjoy Geneva Convention protection, and Iraqi insurgents at Abu Ghraib, who do, it makes it possible to argue that American interroga-tors, when applying the same techniques at Abu Ghraib that they had earlier used in Afghanistan or at Guantánamo, were in fact taking part not in "violent/sexual abuse incidents," like their sadistic military police colleagues, but instead in "misinterpretation/confusion incidents."

A central figure in all this is Major General Geoffrey Miller, who when last we saw him, in late August 2003, was on his way from Guantánamo, where he commanded the detention facility, to Abu Ghraib, where he had been ordered "to review current Iraqi Theater ability to rapidly exploit internees for action-able intelligence." General Miller's report, which remains secret but was made available to me, recommends, among other things, that those in charge of Abu Ghraib should "dedicate and train a detention guard force subordinate to [the Joint Interrogation and Debriefing Center] that sets conditions for the suc-cessful interrogation and exploitation of internees/detainees. This action," he adds, "is now in progress." The MPs, in other words, should be working for the interrogators and spending significant time "softening up" prisoners, by keeping them awake, "making sure this one has a bad night," etc.—doing, that is, precisely what the accused military police, no doubt self-servingly, claimed they were doing in at least some of those dreadful photographs.

Before he left Iraq, General Miller also "left behind a whole series of [Stan-dard Operating Procedures] that could be used as a start point for [Abu Ghraib] interrogation operations." After returning to Guantánamo, the general dispatched to Iraq a follow-up team who, according to General Fay, brought with it the secretary of defense's letter of April 16, 2003, "outlining the tech-niques authorized for use with the GTMO detainees." Various parts of the bureaucracy, both inside and outside the Department of Defense, had been fighting over these interrogation techniques since the previous December. On December 2, Secretary Rumsfeld had approved, among other techniques, yelling at detainees, use of stress positions, use of isolation, deprivation of light and auditory stimuli, use of hoods, use of twenty-hour interrogation, removal of clothing, use of mild physical contact, and "use of detainees' indi-vidual phobias (such as fear of dogs) to induce stress."

Six weeks later, reportedly after vigorous opposition from lawyers in the Department of the Navy, among others, Rumsfeld rescinded these instruc-tions and convened a working group to recommend suitable methods for

Guantánamo. Though the derivation of interrogation techniques eventually adopted for Iraq is almost Talmudic in its intricacy, and though the list of methods permitted changed at least three times during the critical fall of 2003, Fay makes it clear in his report that Lieutenant General Sanchez's command in Iraq "relied heavily on the series of SOPs [standard operating procedures] which MG G. Miller provided to develop not only the structure, but also the interrogation policies for detainee operations." Other sources include, according to a classified section of Fay's report made available to me, the interrogation policy of the shadowy, elite unit Joint Task Force-121, which spent its time searching for "high value targets" in Iraq. "At some point," Fay says, the leading military intelligence battalion at Abu Ghraib "came to possess the JTF-121 interrogation policy" and the first set of interrogation rules used by this unit "were derived almost verbatim from JTF-121 policy," which

> included the use of stress positions during fear-up harsh interrogation approaches, as well as presence of military working dogs, yelling, loud music, and light control. The memo also included sleep management and isolation approaches.

On September 14, Lieutenant General Sanchez signed a policy that included elements of the JTF-121 procedures and elements drawn from General Miller's GTMO policy, including the use of dogs, stress positions, yelling, loud music, light control, and isolation, among other techniques.

The policy at Abu Ghraib would change at least twice more but what is critical here is Fay's point, included in a still-secret section of the report, that "policies and practices developed and approved for use on Al Qaeda and Taliban detainees who were not afforded the protection of the Geneva Conventions, now applied to detainees who did fall under the Geneva Conventions' protections." Sanchez later tried to define, unilaterally, some of his detainees as "unlawful combatants"—and the e-mail I quoted earlier, sent in August 2003 by a captain in military intelligence, suggests that interrogators feeling the pressure to produce results were eager that this be done. But in fact, as Schlesinger points out, Sanchez had no authority to make such a determination.

This confusion over doctrine supposedly allowed some of the more gruesome practices that are so patiently set out in General Fay's report, including sensory deprivation, routine nudity and humiliation, "exploiting the Arab fear of dogs," and prolonged isolation of a particularly revolting kind:

> DETAINEE-14 was detained in a totally darkened cell measuring about 2 meters long and less than a meter across, devoid of any window, latrine or water tap, or bedding. On the door the [Red Cross] delegates noticed the inscription "the Gollum," and a picture of the said character from the film trilogy "Lord of the Rings."

The Red Cross delegates got no farther than the door. Detainee-14 was one of eight detainees to whom General Sanchez denied them access.

The fact is that countless details in these reports give the lie to any supposed rigid division between the "violent/sexual acts incidents" and the "misinterpretation/confusion incidents," not only because in many cases military police really were setting "the conditions for the successful interrogation and exploitation of internees/detainees," as Major General Miller recommended they should, but because general practices, like the extensive use of nudity, "likely contributed," as General Fay wrote in his report, to "an escalating 'de-humanization' of the detainees and set the stage for additional and more severe abuses to occur."

There simply was no clear dividing line, no point where sadistic abuses became instances of "misinterpretation/confusion"—where, that is, an interrogator simply erred in applying a technique that while permitted in Afghanistan or Guantánamo, constituted a violation in Iraq of the Geneva Conventions. How isolated could the so-called "Animal House on the night shift" abuses of the military police have been from military intelligence when, as we learn in the Fay report, one of the most notorious images, that of "several naked detainees stacked in a 'pyramid,'" served as a "screen saver" on one of the computers in the military intelligence office?

ﺋﺎ ﺋﺎ ﺋﺎ

James Harding (Financial Times): Mr. President, I want to return to the question of torture. What we've learned from these memos this week is that the Department of Justice lawyers and the Pentagon lawyers have essentially worked out a way that US officials can torture detainees without running afoul of the law. So when you say you want the US to adhere to international and US laws, that's not very comforting. This is a moral question: Is torture ever justified?

President Bush: Look, I'm going to say it one more time.... Maybe I can be more clear. The instructions went out to our people to adhere to law. That ought to comfort you. We're a nation of law. We adhere to laws. We have laws on the books. You might look at these laws, and that might provide comfort for you. And those were the instructions . . . from me to the government.

—News conference,
Sea Island, Georgia, June 10, 2004

As I write, four months have passed since a series of bizarre photographs were broadcast on American television and entered the consciousness of the world. Seven military police, those "few bad apples," have been indicted and two have pled guilty. According to the military's latest account, reported in *The New York Times*, thirteen service members have been discharged, and fifty-four have suffered some form of "lesser disciplinary action," while fifty-seven others have been "referred to court-martial proceedings"—although it is impossible to know how many such "proceedings" will result in actual charges and trials, and it seems unlikely that any would before the election in November. What has been on trial thus far, however, is the acts depicted in the photographs and these acts, while no doubt constituting abuse, have been carefully insulated from any charge that they represent, or derived from, US policy—a policy that permits torture. Thus far, in the United States at least, there has been relatively little discussion about torture and whether the agents of the US government should be practicing it.

The twenty-seven military intelligence officers and soldiers implicated in General Fay's report, meanwhile, have so far escaped indictment. A number of them have claimed the equivalent of Fifth Amendment protection and military prosecutors have so far declined to bring cases against them. Until they do, or offer grants of immunity for their testimony, it will be difficult to prosecute successfully the remaining military policemen, who include those men and women accused of the most serious photographed crimes. On the other hand, at least some of the military intelligence officers may be in a position to implicate officials above them. Such a threat, however implicit, might be a powerful lever to dissuade the administration from prosecution, at least before the election.

As for Major General Geoffrey Miller, the former commander of GTMO, he is now in command of Abu Ghraib. It is unclear precisely who ordered Major General Miller to make his "assessment visit" to Abu Ghraib late last summer, and if it is true, as seems likely and as many believe, that these orders originated at the top levels of the Pentagon—perhaps even from the office of the county's leading "intelligence junkie," Secretary of Defense Donald Rumsfeld—then no proof of this has emerged. Nor, at this point, would such proof, or anything short of evidence linking Rumsfeld directly to what was shown in the photographs, make a decisive difference. The fact that the legal trail at Abu Ghraib has been directed toward the abuses that appear in the photographs means that the question of policy—of whether the United States should be torturing prisoners, of what the political and moral costs of this will finally be, and of what responsibility those who ultimately direct that policy really bear—has hardly been seriously debated, whether in Congress or anywhere else. Only now, more than four months after the photographs were broadcast to the world, and after eight prominent retired generals and admirals wrote to President Bush publicly demanding a truly independent and far-reaching investigation, has there been some small sign that the administration, perhaps finally pressed by a reluctant Republican Senate, might eventually be forced to go beyond the piecemeal and dilatory efforts it has so far grudgingly made.

If that does happen, it will have been long in coming—and again, almost certainly, and critically for the administration, no results could be known until after the election. So far, officials of the Bush administration, who counted on the fact that the public, and much of the press, could be persuaded to focus on the photographs—the garish signboards of the scandal and not the scandal itself—have been proved right. This makes Abu Ghraib a peculiarly contemporary kind of scandal, with most of its plotlines exposed to view—but with few willing to follow them and fewer still to do much about them. As with other controversies over the Iraq war, the revelations have been made, the behavior exposed, but the moral will to act, or even to debate what action might be warranted, seems mostly lacking.

Meantime the Hooded Man has taken his place among the symbols calling forth, in some parts of the world, a certain image of the United States and what it stands for. Sheik Bashir, who said of the occupying soldiers that "no one can punish them, whether in our country or their country," has thus far been proved right. Only those at the lowest rung of the ladder have so far been punished and the matter of what was actually happening within the interrogation rooms of Abu Ghraib, not to mention in the secret detention centers of the CIA, has hardly been debated. The Iraqis know this, even if many Americans do not. Meanwhile the political damage to US interests in the world has been very great. As the military strategist Anthony Cordesman put it,

> We need to understand that this image is going to be used for years to come. We are dealing with an ideological climate in which the extremists are the threat, not the moderates. And they are going to use these images for years to come, and they are going to couple them to images like Israeli treatment of the Palestinians and find ways of tying this to all their conspiracy theories and hostile images of the West. And the end result is that they will be tools for insurgents and extremists and terrorists.[11]

There is no weighing such ongoing damage against the intelligence that these techniques may have gained. How can such things as these be quantified? According to the Schlesinger report,

> There were five cases of detainee deaths as a result of abuse by U.S. personnel during interrogations.... There are 23 cases of detainee deaths still under investigation....

The words are blunt, though a writer less fond of euphemism might have put the matter even more plainly: "American interrogators have tortured at least five prisoners to death." And from what we know, Mr. Schlesinger's figures, if anything, substantially understate the case.

It has become a cliché of the Global War on Terror—the GWOT, as these reports style it—that at a certain point, if the United States betrays its fundamental principles in the cause of fighting terror, then "the terrorists will have won." The image of the Hooded Man, now known the world over, raises a stark question: Is it possible that that moment of defeat could come and go, and we will never know it?

—*The New York Review of Books*, October 7, 2004

NOTES

1. 'See Edward Cody, "Iraqis Put Contempt for Troops on Display," *The Washington Post*, June 12, 2004.

2. Major General George R. Fay, *AR 15-6 Investigation of the Abu Ghraib Detention Facility and the 205th Military Intelligence Brigade*; and James R. Schlesinger, Harold Brown, Tillie K. Fowler, and General Charles A. Horner (USAF-Ret.), *Final Report of the Independent Panel to Review DoD Detention Operations*. Both reports are reproduced at the back of this book, beginning on pages 329 and 403, respectively.

3. See Osama bin Laden, "Jihad Against Jews and Crusaders," February 28, 1998, in *Voices of Terror*, edited by Walter Laqueur (Reed, 2004), pp. 410–412.

4. See my "Delusions in Baghdad," pp. 60–71.

5. See James Risen, David Johnston, and Neil A. Lewis, "Harsh CIA Methods Cited in Top Qaeda Interrogations," *The New York Times*, May 13, 2004.

6. See Risen, Johnston, and Lewis, "Harsh CIA Methods Cited in Top Qaeda Interrogations."

7. See Dana Priest and Barton Gellman, "US Decries Abuse but Defends Interrogations," *The Washington Post*, December 26, 2002.

8. See *The Gangrene*, translated by Robert Silvers (Lyle Stuart, 1960), pp. 81–82.

9. See John Conroy, *Unspeakable Acts, Ordinary People: The Dynamics of Torture* (University of California Press, 2000), pp. 170–171.

10. See Richard A. Serrano, "Prison Interrogators' Gloves Came Off Before Abu Ghraib," *Los Angeles Times*, June 9, 2004.

11. Anthony Cordesman, "Goal in Iraq Is to 'Get the Best Compromise You Can,'" interview with Bernard Gwertzman, Council on Foreign Relations, May 11, 2004.

Addenda:

THE CONTEXT

IV

IRAQ: THE NEW WAR

—August 28, 2003

WE SEE THE WORLD through the stories we tell, and until recently the story most Americans told themselves about the war in Iraq was a simple and dramatic narrative of imminent threat, daring triumph, and heroic liberation—a story neatly embodied in images of a dictator's toppling statue and a president in full flight gear swaggering across a carrier deck. Those pictures, once so bright and clear, have now faded, giving place to a second, darker story beneath: the story of an unfinished war, undertaken for murky reasons, that has left young Americans ruling indefinitely over people who do not welcome them and who are killing more and more of them each day. As long as Saddam Hussein remains at large, as long as the weapons our leaders said were threatening us are not found, and as long as Iraqis go on killing Americans, this second, darker story may come to blot out and finally to mock the memory of the first.

As the war's ending and, increasingly, its beginning grow more cloudy, Americans are confronted on their television screens with a violent present that day by day becomes more difficult to comprehend. That the attacks on American soldiers in Iraq "do not pose a strategic threat to the mission," in the words of the American proconsul L. Paul Bremer, is true but meaningless. The war in Iraq—in the streets of Baghdad no less than in the halls of Congress or in the stump speeches of the campaign trail—is in its essence political, not military. Like the terrorists who hijacked American airliners and flew them into American buildings, the fighters daily ambushing American troops are attacking not American military power but American will. And thanks to the way President Bush and his colleagues chose to build the case for war, and the errors they have made in prosecuting it, American will is an increasingly vulnerable target. In the end defeat or victory in Iraq will be judged not by who controls Baghdad but by whether the war has left Americans more secure than they were before it was undertaken. All the ringing presidential pronouncements of "Mission Accomplished!" will not change the reality: America could still lose this war.

Like the strikes on the World Trade Center and the Pentagon, the attacks in Iraq —ambushes and assassinations of American troops; sabotage of Iraqi oil pipelines, water mains, electrical lines, and other critical infrastructure; suicide bombings of UN headquarters and other "soft" targets—are aimed not at defeating American forces directly but at creating a political spectacle that will impress, frighten, and persuade a number of audiences, among them the Iraqi people, the Arab world, and finally the American public. During a briefing on July 16, General John Abizaid, who succeeded General Tommy Franks as head of Central Command, described the authors of these attacks as

> ... mid-level Ba'athist, Iraqi intelligence people, Special Security Organization people, Special Republican Guard people that have organized at the regional level in cellular structure and are conducting what I would describe as a classical guerrilla-type campaign against us. ... We're seeing a cellular organization of six to eight people, armed with RPGs, machine guns, etc., attacking us at ... times and places of their choosing. ... There are some foreign fighters. ... Remember in the early stages of capturing Baghdad, there were an awful lot of foreign fighters, and it's possible that ... they've reformed and reorganized.[1]

The enemy in Iraq, in other words, is dynamic and changeable, a shadowy and loose group of forces made up of former officers and soldiers of the vast security and intelligence organs of the *ancien régime*; foreign-born jihadis, or ideological commandos, who have slipped into Iraq from Saudi Arabia, Syria, and other Islamic countries and are determined to confront and defeat the United States; and, perhaps increasingly, young, unemployed Iraqis, angry at the American occupation and the difficulties it has brought, eager to avenge a relative's death or a personal affront, or simply desperate to earn some easy money by hiring themselves out to attack Americans. We know little of this shadowy world, and depend for what we do know on military sources, named and unnamed, and inferences drawn from the pattern, character, and frequency of the attacks; but it is likely that the relative weight and influence of its various actors, and the alliances and rivalries among them, are in a constant state of flux, as are the opposition's political interests and the tactics it adopts to achieve them. On this, General Abizaid, in the same briefing, set out the salient point:

> War is a struggle of wills. You look at the Arab press; they say, "We drove the Americans out of Beirut, we drove them out of Somalia; ... we'll drive them out of Baghdad."

To these names of the familiar symbols of a great power's defeat and withdrawal in the face of a determined irregular force—whether using suicide bombings (Beirut, 1983) or guerrilla warfare (Mogadishu, 1993)—General Abizaid might have added the name of Afghanistan. For the jihadis, in particular, Iraq presents the chance to do to the American empire in the Middle East what they believe they did a decade ago to the Soviet empire in Central Asia—to force on the occupier a long, bloody stalemate leading to retreat and, finally, to collapse.

By now it is clear that this campaign began long before the fall of Baghdad last

April. As early as January 2003, according to *Newsweek*, the Iraqi secret police issued an order instructing its forces to "do what's necessary after the fall of the Iraqi leadership to the American-British-Zionist Coalition forces," and setting out eleven steps, among them, "looting and burning all the government institutions that belong to our Directorates and other ones," and sowing chaos in the country by sabotaging power plants and assassinating imams and other public figures.[2]

It now seems likely that much of the looting and plundering that Secretary of Defense Rumsfeld dismissed as mere "untidiness," the inevitable concomitant of the coming of democracy, constituted the first stage of a carefully planned "war beyond the war." Secretary Rumsfeld's strategy of "going in light"—of conquering Iraq with a quick, highly focused attack employing a minimum of troops—left the Americans uniquely vulnerable to this kind of planned chaos and the widespread feeling of insecurity it fostered. As the military commentator Anthony Cordesman put it,

> The same strategy designed to deliver a carefully focused attack on the regime did not provide enough manpower to simultaneously occupy and secure the areas that the Coalition liberated...and deal with the wide range of local, regional, ethnic and religious divisions [the Coalition] encountered.[3]

The weeks of looting and disorder that followed not only continued the destruction of Iraq's infrastructure, preventing the Americans from supplying the country with electricity and other basic services. More important, the looting and mayhem destroyed American political authority even before it could be established; such political authority is rooted in the monopoly of legitimate violence, which the Americans, after standing by during weeks of chaos and insecurity, were never able to attain.

During the last four months, the tactics of those opposing or defying the occupation have steadily evolved, as General Abizaid acknowledged, "getting more organized... learning...adapting to our tactics, techniques and procedures.... They're better coordinated...less amateurish...more sophisticated." As the tactics of the Iraqis have changed—from the intensive looting and mayhem of the first weeks, to the hit-and-run small-arms attacks of late spring and early summer, to the more sophisticated use of radio-controlled and timed explosives of July and August, and finally to the suicide truck bombings of late summer—the American forces, adapting in their turn, have responded by launching a series of large-scale raids against opposition strongholds in the so-called "Sunni Triangle" of central Iraq. These raids netted a large haul of weapons and explosives and hundreds of prisoners; they also further alienated from the occupation many Iraqis who might have been disposed to welcome it, or at least to tolerate it.

This is the dynamic that various opponents of the occupation must try to sustain. By whatever means, they aim to produce in Iraq growing political anger and discontent and to focus that anger and discontent on the occupiers, thus alienating more and more Iraqis, who might join the anti-occupation forces, actively support them, or at least count themselves sympathetic to the cause. Since the numbers of the armed opposition, as Paul Bremer noted, are far too small to defeat the Americans militarily, their strategy relies on provoking the Americans to take actions that will create among Iraqis the broader support needed to sustain a guerrilla war.

By launching paramilitary attacks almost daily, the opponents hope to force the Americans to adopt increasingly aggressive and intrusive tactics that will further alienate a citizenry already frustrated by their failure to bring order to the country. By blowing up electrical pylons, sabotaging water mains, destroying oil pipelines, and staging attacks on the United Nations and other nongovernmental organizations, they hope to further degrade the quality of life of ordinary Iraqis, who are increasingly shocked and angered by the Americans' failure to provide basic services. By threatening and assassinating Iraqis who collaborate with the Americans, they hope to show Iraqis that the occupiers cannot protect them, further slowing the rate of reconstruction, deepening the country's bitter political divisions, and making the daunting task of building a stable politics friendly to America all the more difficult.

That Iraqis loyal to a security-obsessed totalitarian regime of three decades would seek to fight the Americans who have overthrown it is not surprising. Nor should it be surprising that jihadis from outside and inside Iraq should seize the opportunity to attack infidels occupying an Islamic country. What is surprising is the degree to which the Americans, through their own lack of attention to the critical political tasks of the war's aftermath, have in effect assisted their efforts. The civilian leadership of the Pentagon remains in thrall to fashionable concepts of war-fighting such as "Shock and Awe" and "Network-Centric Warfare," which emphasize information, speed, and the use of light forces, but which leave out, in the words of the military historian Kenneth W. Kagan, "the most important component of war," which is to provide "a reliable recipe for translating the destruction of the enemy's ability to continue to fight into the accomplishment of the political objectives of the conflict."[4]

The obligation to provide such a "reliable recipe" in Iraq falls in the end to US political leaders, but they have largely abdicated this responsibility. Shortly before the war, the President, discarding many months of effort by the State Department, handed over control of occupation planning to Pentagon officials, who hastily constructed a plan based largely on optimistic assumptions about the warmth of the Iraqis' attitude toward the Americans, and about the ease with which new leaders could be imposed on the existing governing institutions. Many of these expectations, which were encouraged by favored Iraqi expatriates, dovetailed perfectly with the Pentagon's own reluctance to provide sufficient military police and dirty its hands with other distasteful "nation-building" tasks. When their assumptions proved unfounded, administration officials were excruciatingly slow to admit reality and make adjustments. These first weeks of the occupation, in which security in Baghdad collapsed, chaos ruled the streets, and the fledgling occupation authority daily issued conflicting statements and made promises it did not keep, were a fiasco. They proved an enormous boon to violent opponents, providing them, in the lawless streets of postwar Iraq, the political equivalent of a warm petri dish in which to grow.[5]

As near as one can tell, the Bush administration launched its war against Iraq for three broad reasons:

1. *Weapons of Mass Destruction*: To disarm Iraq of its alleged chemical and biological weapons and eliminate its nuclear program.

2. *National Security*: To remove Iraq as a threat to American dominance of the Persian Gulf and to Israel, and make it America's central ally and base in the region, replacing an increasingly unstable and Islamicist Saudi Arabia, from which American troops could be withdrawn.[6]

3. *Regional Transformation*: To make Iraq an example of Arab democracy as the first step in "the transformation of the Middle East" which, in the words of National Security Adviser Condoleezza Rice, "is the only guarantee that it will no longer produce ideologies of hatred that lead men to fly airplanes into buildings in New York and Washington."[7]

Nearly six months after the war was launched, these three rationales for America's first preemptive war have been stood on their heads.

Different officials clearly lent different weight to these arguments, but we know, thanks to Deputy Secretary of Defense Paul Wolfowitz, that "bureaucratic reasons"—"because it was the one reason everyone could agree on"—at least in part led the administration to focus on the first. More important, in the wake of September 11, the argument that Saddam might give weapons of mass destruction to terrorists who would attack the US, or might use them to attack Persian Gulf nations and Israel, was clearly the most politically potent—the principal argument likely to convince the broad mass of Americans to support a preemptive war. It was also the only argument that, as embodied in a number of United Nations resolutions, had some degree of international legitimacy.

By now, however, the argument that Iraq threatened vital US interests with weapons of mass destruction seems to have been disproved: no weapons have been found, and even if some are eventually uncovered it seems highly implausible that they could have posed an imminent threat.[8] The collapse of the case for weapons of mass destruction and the revelations about how the administration relentlessly and recklessly exaggerated the evidence of the threat have left the occupation of Iraq with a singularly fragile foundation of public support.

That support is likely to be further eroded by the continuing violence and combat deaths in Iraq, for which the President did nothing to prepare the country. President Bush's approval ratings have declined steadily since his triumphant landing on the USS *Lincoln* last May and in some polls have now dipped below his pre–September 11 lows. With a lackluster economic record—he looks to be the first president since Herbert Hoover to see the total number of jobs decline during his term—President Bush has relied on his aggressive foreign policy and his claimed competence in national security to sustain his political strength. He has used the war on terror politically with great skill and ruthlessness and apparently plans to make it the heart of his reelection effort, scheduling the 2004 Republican convention in New York so as to recall the 9/11 anniversary.

All of this ensures that the Democratic candidates will make the war in Iraq—the exaggerations about weapons of mass destruction that led to it, the Americans who continue to die in a war advertised to the public as "a cakewalk," the billion dollars a week the country is paying for a war that has no visible conclusion—a central issue in the campaign. The controversy in July 2003 over "the sixteen words" in the President's State of the Union speech, which claimed falsely that Saddam Hussein had sought uranium oxide from Africa, and the damage this controversy did to the President's popularity, suggest that Bush, far from launching his reelection campaign energized by a triumphant war, may find Iraq to be a political albatross around his neck.

However good this news may be for Democrats and their supporters, it is unlikely to be good for the Iraqis. The Bush administration has proved unwilling so far to provide the protection and resources necessary to rebuild the country. At the same time, the administration, holding to a policy that poisoned international relations before the war, is doggedly refusing to grant the modicum of authority to the United Nations that would be necessary to bring in anything more than a token number of troops from other countries, particularly from India, Pakistan, and Turkey. Whether in one month or three, this attitude may well change. Indeed, faced with the prospect of running for reelection on the record of an increasingly unpopular and inconclusive war, the administration, shielded by as many international forces as it can muster, may be tempted to take the equivalent of Senator George Aitken's long-ago advice about Vietnam: Declare victory and go home.

As one who argued strenuously against invading Iraq, I find this prospect particularly troubling to contemplate. Having invaded and occupied Iraq, and unleashed a horde of political demons there, the United States faces a number of extremely difficult choices, one of the worst of which is precipitous withdrawal. Already Secretary Wolfowitz's notion that the invasion would "demonstrate especially to the Arab and Muslim world that there is a better way than the way of the terrorist" has acquired a grimly ironic cast.[9] For all its grandiose talk about establishing in Iraq "a shining example for the Arab world," the administration has so far not been willing to devote the necessary troops or resources to the task. The recent influx of jihadis hoping to take advantage of the chaos in Iraq in order to make of it "the new Afghanistan" suggests another possibility: that Iraq, far from becoming a symbol of the promise of democracy in the Middle East, may become afflicted with a low-level and prolonged nationalist war which the Islamists would use to attract recruits and build their movement politically, while they use terror and other guerrilla tactics to bleed and diminish the United States and weaken its position in the Middle East.

That, of course—like "the war after the war" itself—is a political project, not a military one. Not for the first time, the United States has shown itself to be a strange, hybrid creature, military giant and political dwarf. But Iraq is not Lebanon, from which the US could sail away and invade Grenada; the stakes are much higher. "You can't just get up and walk away from Iraq like you did Lebanon," said Ghassan Salame, the former Lebanese government minister and scholar, who was working for the UN headquarters in Baghdad when it was bombed. "No matter how bad it gets. If Iraq turns into anarchy, it's likely to spill into the rest of the Gulf. It would be a catastrophe."[10]

This is the national security argument, stood on its head: Saddam Hussein, it was said, with his weapons of mass destruction and his reckless ambitions, would inevitably acquire nuclear weapons and threaten both the established order in the Middle East and US access to its oil supplies in the Persian Gulf. Since he posed a lingering threat to the US, why not eliminate that threat now, when the American people, in the wake of the September 11 attacks, could be persuaded to support a preemptive war?

The irony, nearly six months after the US launched this war, is that while Saddam Hussein has been unseated, the threat that Iraq posed to the Gulf has not been removed. Indeed, it may be that the United States, with its overwhelming military power, has succeeded only in transforming an eventual and speculative threat into a concrete and immediate one. Now the Bush administration finds itself trying to perform the tightrope walk of building a stable and friendly government beneath the shadow of escalating violence and a growing and inevitable nationalism—and it does so in the face of an impatient and bewildered public and an approaching election campaign. The administration began its Iraq venture with an air of absolute determination, taking a kind of grim pride in defying the United Nations and "doing what is right." America, and Iraq, will need a different kind of determination now—and a new-found honesty to go with it.

—*The New York Review of Books*, August 28, 2003

NOTES

1. Department of Defense news briefing, July 16, 2003.

2. See Scott Johnson and Evan Thomas, "Still Fighting Saddam," *Newsweek*, July 21, 2003, p. 22.

3. Anthony Cordesman, "Iraq and Conflict Termination: The Road to Guerrilla War?," Center for Strategic and International Studies, July 28, 2003.

4. See "War and Aftermath," *Policy Review*, August and September 2003, p. 9.

5. See Mark Fineman, Robin Wright, and Doyle McManus, "Preparing for War, Stumbling to Peace," *Los Angeles Times*, July 18, 2003.

6. See Jeffrey Sachs, "The Real Target of the War in Iraq Was Saudi Arabia," *Financial Times*, August 23, 2003, and Robert Badinter, "La vraie raison de la guerre qui s'annonce," *Le Nouvel Observateur*, February 20, 2003. As both authors make clear, the administration was reluctant to discuss publicly the displacement of the Saudis as a motive for the war.

7. See Dana Milbank, "Patience on Iraq Policies Urged," *The Washington Post*, August 26, 2003, p. 1.

8. See Rolf Ekeus, "Iraq's Real Weapons Threat," *The Washington Post*, June 29, 2003, p. B7, who argues convincingly that Iraq destroyed its remaining weapons and focused "on design and engineering, with the purpose of activating production" in the event of war with Iran.

9. See "Deputy Secretary Wolfowitz Interview on PBS with Charlie Rose," August 4, 2003, Department of Defense transcript.

10. Quoted in Robert Baer, "Will Lebanon's Horror Become Iraq's?," *The Washington Post*, August 24, 2003.

V

DELUSIONS IN BAGHDAD

—November 19, 2003

AUTUMN IN BAGHDAD IS cloudy and gray. Trapped in rush-hour traffic one October morning, without warning my car bucked up and back, like a horse whose reins had been brutally pulled. For a jolting instant the explosion registered only as the absence of sound, a silent blow to the stomach; and then a beat later, as hearing returned, a faint tinkling chorus: the store windows, all along busy Karrada Street, trembling together in their sashes. They were tinkling still when over the rooftops to the right came the immense eruption of oily black smoke.

Such dark plumes have become the beacons, the lighthouses, of contemporary Baghdad, and we rushed to follow, bumping over the center divider, vaulting the curb, screeching through the honking chaos of Seventies-vintage American cars, trailing the blasting horns and screaming tires for two, three, four heart-pounding moments until, barely three blocks away, at one end of a pleasant residential square, behind a gaggle of blue-shirted Iraqi security men running in panic about the grass, shouting, waving their AK-47s, we came upon two towering conflagrations, rising perhaps a dozen feet in the air, and, perfectly outlined in the bright orange flames, like skeletons preserved in amber, the blackened frames of what moments before had been a van and a four-wheel drive.

Between the two great fires rose a smaller one, eight or nine feet high, enclosing a tangled mass of metal. Pushing past the Iraqis, who shouted angrily, gesturing with their guns, I ran forward, toward the flames: the heat was intense. I saw slabs of smashed wall, hunks of rubble, glass, and sand scattered about, and behind it all an immense curtain of black smoke obscuring everything: the building, part of the International Red Cross compound, that stood there, the wall that had guarded it, the remains of the people who, four minutes before, had lived and worked there.

"Terrorism," the US Army lieutenant colonel had told me ruefully the week before, "is Grand Theater," and, as a mustached security man yanked me roughly by the arm, spinning me away from the flames, I saw that behind me the front rows had quickly filled: photographers with their long lenses, khaki vests, and shoulder bags struggled to push their way through the Iraqi security men, who, growing angrier, shouted and cursed, pushing them back. Swinging their AK-47s, they managed to form a ragged perimeter against what was now a jostling, roiling crowd, while camera crews in the vanguard surged forward. Now a US Army Humvee appeared; four American soldiers leaped out and plunged into the crowd, assault rifles raised, and began to scream, in what I had come to recognize as a characteristic form of address, "GET. THE FUCK. BACK! GET. THE FUCK. BACK!" Very young men in tan camouflage fatigues, armed, red-faced, flustered; facing them, the men and women of the world press, Baghdad division, assembled in their hundreds in less than a quarter of an hour: in the front row, those who, like me, had had the dumb luck to be in the neighborhood; behind them network crews who had received a quick tip from an embassy contact or an Iraqi stringer, or had simply heard or felt the explosion and pounded their way up to the hotel roof, scanning the horizon anxiously, locating the black beacon, and racing off to cover the story—or, as Lieutenant Colonel George Krivo put it bitterly, to "*make* the story. Here, media is the total message: I now have an understanding of McLuhan you wouldn't believe. Kill twenty people here? In front of that lens it's killing twenty thousand."

Behind the flames and the dark smoke, amid the shattered walls and twisted metal, a dozen people lay dead, many of whom had been unlucky enough to find themselves passing the front of the International Red Cross compound when, at half past eight in the morning, a man later claimed to be of Saudi nationality drove an ambulance with Red Cross markings up to the security checkpoint and detonated what must have been several thousand pounds of explosives, collapsing forty feet of the protective wall and sending a huge sandbag barrier cascading forward.[1] The Red Cross compound, with its security wall and sandbags and manned checkpoints, was a "hardened target"—as were, indeed, the three Baghdad police stations that, within the next forty-five minutes, suicide bombers struck, in the neighborhoods of al-Baya'a, al-Shaab, and al-Khadra.

In the rhetoric of security, all of these attacks failed dismally. "From what our indications are," Brigadier General Mark Hertling told Fox News that afternoon, "none of those bombers got close to the target." In the rhetoric of politics, however, the attacks were a brilliant *coup de théâtre*. In less than an hour, four men, by killing forty people, including one American soldier and twenty Iraqi police, had succeeded in dominating news coverage around the world, sending television crews rushing about Baghdad in pursuit of the latest plume of smoke and broadcasting the message, via television screens in a hundred countries, first and foremost the United States, that Baghdad, US official pronouncements notwithstanding, remained a war zone.

Within a week, as members of the Red Cross left Iraq and many of the few remaining international organizations followed close behind, the attackers had set in motion, at the "highest levels" of the Bush administration, a "reevaluation" of American policy. Within two weeks, even as President Bush went on vowing publicly that the United States "would not be intimidated," he abruptly recalled L. Paul Bremer, the American administrator in Iraq, who rushed back to Washington so hurriedly he left the prime minister of Poland, one of America's few major allies in Iraq, waiting forlornly for an appointment that never came.

After two days of intensive consultations, administration officials unveiled a new policy. They decided to discard what had been a carefully planned, multiyear process that would gradually transform the authoritarian Iraqi state into a democracy—seven clearly defined steps intended to allow democratic parties, practices, and institutions to take root, develop, and grow, eventually leading to a new constitution written and ratified by the Iraqi people and, finally, a nationwide election and handover of power from American administrators to the elected Iraqi politicians it produced. The administration put in its place a hastily improvised rush to "return power to the Iraqis." In practice, this meant that in seven months the United States would hand over sovereignty to unelected Iraqis (presumably those on the American-appointed Governing Council, many of them former exiles, who had been pressing for such a rapid granting of power since before the war). Elections and a constitution would come later.[2] Despite President Bush's fervent protestations to the contrary, this was clearly a dramatic change in his policy of "bringing democracy to Iraq"—and, by extension, of making Iraq the first step in what he recently described as his "forward strategy of democracy in the Middle East."

If victory in war is defined as accomplishing the political goals for which military means were originally brought to bear, then eight months after it invaded Iraq, the United States remains far from victory. If the political goal of the war in Iraq was to remove Saddam Hussein and his Baathist regime and establish in their place a stable, democratic government, then that goal, during the weeks I spent in Iraq in late October and early November of 2003, seemed to be growing ever more distant.

When I arrived in Baghdad, Iraqi insurgents were staging about fifteen attacks a day on American troops; by the time I left the number of daily attacks had more than doubled, to thirty-five a day. Though military leaders like Lieutenant General Ricardo Sanchez, the overall commander, have repeatedly denigrated the attacks on his troops as "strategically and operationally insignificant," those attacks led the CIA to conclude, in a report leaked in mid-November, that the "US-led drive to rebuild the country as a democracy could collapse unless corrective actions are taken immediately."[3] The United States fields by far the most powerful military in the world, spending more on defense than the rest of the world combined, and as I write a relative handful of lightly armed insurgents, numbering in the tens of thousands or perhaps less, using the classic techniques of guerrilla warfare and suicide terrorism, are well on the way toward defeating it.

"What we have here," Lieutenant Colonel William Darley told me, "is basically a constabulary action. I mean, this is pretty much the Old West here. Peacekeeping. Where are the regiment on regiment, division on division engagements? We've seen almost nothing above the squad level. Basically this is not a real war." I heard this view, in various versions, expressed by American military men all over Iraq, from staff officers to combat commanders to lieutenants on the ground. Most of these men I found deeply impressive: well trained, well schooled, extremely competent. What joined them together, as the war grew steadily worse for American forces, was an inability, or perhaps a reluctance, to recognize what was happening in Iraq *as a war*.

"There's a deep cultural bias in the United States that if a military doesn't resemble ours, it's no good," the military strategist George Freidman of the private intelligence company Stratfor told me. "We have the strongest conventional forces in the world. So no one fights us conventionally. They fight us asymmetrically."

In Iraq, asymmetric warfare has meant a combination of guerrilla attacks on US and other coalition forces and terrorist attacks on a variety of prominent nonmilitary targets, including hotels, embassies, and international organizations. Beginning late this spring, the guerrilla attacks were centered in Baghdad and the so-called "Sunni Triangle" north and west of the capital but, since mid-autumn, they have increasingly spread to the north and, more slowly, the south of the country. Since late summer, highly effective terrorist attacks, including suicide bombings, have grown steadily more audacious and sophisticated, particularly in their use of the international press to multiply their political effect. In responding to both lines of attack, US intelligence—the "center of gravity" in any guerrilla war—has seemed poor or nonexistent.

The guerrilla attacks have built on, and worsened, the American occupation's unpopularity among many Iraqis, capitalizing on, among other things, the US military's failure to provide security during the early weeks of the occupation and the daily humiliations and occasional brutalities that come with the presence of an occupying army. The terrorist attacks have served to consolidate and then worsen the international isolation the Americans have labored under since the catastrophic diplomatic decisions that led up to the war and have succeeded in depriving the coalition of additional military forces and international help in rebuilding the country.

Terrorism is certainly—as the lieutenant colonel put it—Grand Theater. Or to put it a slightly different way, terrorism is a form of talk. To hear what is being said, one must look at the sequence of major bombings in Iraq over the last several months:

August 7, Jordanian Embassy: A suicide car bomber kills nineteen people.
August 19, United Nations Headquarters: A suicide truck bomber kills twenty-three, including the UN's chief envoy in Iraq.
September 22, UN Headquarters: A suicide car bomber kills two and wounds nineteen.
October 9, police station: A suicide car bomber kills ten.
October 12, Baghdad Hotel: A suicide car bomber kills eight and wounds thirty-two.
October 14, Turkish Embassy: A suicide car bomber kills two and wounds thirteen.
October 27, Red Cross Headquarters and four police stations: Car bombers kill about forty and wound two hundred.
November 12, Italian Carabinieri Headquarters, Nasiriya: A truck bomber kills thirty-one.

Behind these attacks—I list only the major ones—one can see a rather methodical intention to sever, one by one, with patience, care, and precision, the fragile lines that still tie the occupation authority to the rest of the world. Suicide bombers struck at the countries that supported the Americans in the war (Jordan), that support the occupation with troops (Italy) or professed a willingness to do so (Turkey). They struck at the heart of an "international community" that could, with increased involvement, help give the occupation both legitimacy (the United Nations) and material help in rebuilding the country (the Red Cross). Finally they repeatedly struck at Iraqis collaborating with occupation authorities, whether as members of the American-selected Governing Council (several of whom lived in the Baghdad Hotel) or as policemen trained and paid by Americans.

By striking at the Jordanians, the bombers helped to ensure that no Arab country will contribute troops to support the occupation. By striking at the Turks, they helped force them to withdraw their controversial offer to send soldiers. By striking at the United Nations and the Red Cross, they not only forced the members of those two critical institutions to flee the country but led most other nongovernmental organizations, who would have been central to supplying expertise and resources to rebuilding Iraq, to leave as well. And by striking at the homes of several members of the Governing Council (wounding one member and, in a separate incident, assassinating another), they forced those officials to join the Americans behind their isolating wall of security, further separating them from Iraqis and underlining their utter political reliance on the Americans.

"Signs and symbols," the Italian security officer said. "Terrorism is nothing but signs and symbols." He looked at the sandbags and barbed wire, the rows of concrete Jersey barriers and armed guards that surrounded his embassy. "None of this will matter," he told me. "If they want to hit us, they will, and though they won't get to the building, it will still be a victory because it will kill people and make news. Terror," he said, "is quite predictable." What, I asked, did the signs and symbols mean? He spoke matter-of-factly: that anyone who helps the Americans will be a target; that the Americans cannot protect their allies and provide security to Iraqis; that the disorder is growing and that deciding to work with the Americans, who in their isolation are looking like a less-than-dominant and in any event ephemeral presence, is not the most prudent of bets; that the war, whatever fine words President Bush may pronounce from his aircraft carrier, is not over. Terror, he said, has a logic of its own. Two weeks after we spoke a suicide bomber killed nineteen Italians at Nasiriya.

Autumn in Baghdad is sunny and bright. Drive about the bustling city of tan, sun-dried brick and you will hear the noise of honking horns and see crowded markets, the streets overwhelmed by an enormous postwar expansion of traffic, the sidewalks cluttered with satellite disks and other new products flooding into the newly opened Iraqi market. During the last several months, however, a new city has taken root amid these busy streets and avenues, spreading rapidly as it superimposes itself over the old tan brick metropolis: a new grim city of concrete. It is constructed of twelve-foot-high gray concrete barriers, endless roadblocks manned by squads of men with Kalashnikovs, walls of enormous steel-reinforced bags of earth and rubble and mile upon mile of coiled razor wire, and studded here and there with tanks rooted behind sandbags and watchful soldiers in combat fatigues. This city has a vaguely postmodern, apocalyptic feel, "a bit of Belfast here, a bit of Cyprus there, here and there a sprinkling of West Bank," as one network cameraman put it to me.

Many streets, including several of the grand ceremonial avenues of Saddam's capital, are now entirely lined with raw concrete a dozen feet high, giving the driver the impression of advancing down a stone tube. Behind these walls entire chunks of Baghdad have effectively vanished, notably the great park and building complex that had housed Saddam's Republican Palace and now comprises the so-called Green Zone—a four-and-a-half-square-mile concrete bunker that has at its heart the head-quarters of the Coalition Provisional Authority.

To enter the palace you must secure, first, an appointment—hard to get, and made immeasurably harder by the fact that most members of the CPA are difficult or impossible to reach by telephone—and then make your way down several hundred yards of sidewalk lined with razor wire. Your journey will be broken by three checkpoints, two military (concrete cordons, sandbags, machine guns) and one civilian. At two of these you present two identifications and submit to full body searches, standing with your legs parted and arms extended and staring straight ahead, in a ritual I found myself repeating, on a busy day in Baghdad, a dozen or more times. Finally, after securing an identification badge, you must wait for a military escort to drive you to the palace, where yet another series of checks and searches will be performed.

Inside Saddam's Republican Palace—his huge likeness in the central atrium is discreetly masked by a large blue cloth—you will find, amid the dark marble floors and sconces and chandeliers, a great many Americans striding purposefully about, some in uniform but many in casual civilian clothing: chinos, jeans, sport shirts. They look bright, crisp, self-assured, and extremely young; they look, in other words, like what they are: junior staffers from Washington, from the Capitol, the departments and various agencies and think tanks. After all the combat fatigues on the city streets ("During my two weeks here," an oil industry contractor told me, "I've not seen one American who wasn't in uniform"), it is a bit of a shock to find this great horde of young American civilians secreted in Saddam's marble-lined hideaway, now become Baghdad's own Emerald City.

I spoke to one young expert from the Governance Department at some length about the Americans' "seven-point plan" to install democracy in Iraq, which was then stalled at point three: writing the constitution. (To summarize very crudely, the Shia, the majority on the Governing Council and in the country, were insisting that the writers of the constitution be chosen in a nationwide election; the others, fearing the Shia's numerical dominance, were pushing for the writers to be "selected" under various methods. This deadlock over the constitution is a precise reflection of the larger "governance problem" in Iraq—beginning with Shia numerical dominance—that would need to be resolved if Iraq is ever to become a working democracy.) I found myself impressed with the young woman's knowledge and commitment. In general, the CPA members seem dedicated and well-meaning—they'd have to be, to come to Baghdad;

they are also entirely isolated, traveling twice daily by military-driven bus within the bunkered compound from their places of work in the bunkered palace to their places of rest in the bunkered Rasheed Hotel.

Or rather they made that trip until October 26, 2003, when, just before six in the morning, a person or persons unknown towed a small blue two-wheeled trailer—to any observer (including, presumably, the soldier manning the checkpoint a couple hundred yards away), it looked like a generator, a common sight in electricity-starved Iraq—up to the park across from which the Rasheed stood resplendent behind its impressive concrete barriers, quickly opened the trailer's doors, turned it around, and directed it toward the hotel, and ran off, no doubt looking back to gaze in satisfaction a few moments later when a dozen or so converted French-made air-to-surface missiles whooshed out of their tubes and began peppering the rooms in which the Americans running the occupation slept, wounding seventeen people, killing one (a lieutenant colonel), and coming within a few yards of killing the visiting Paul L. Wolfowitz, United States deputy secretary of defense and mastermind of the Iraq war.

My friend in Governance was thrown from her bed and, finding her door jammed shut by the blast damage, and taking "one look at the smoke coming from under that jammed door and realizing if I didn't get out of there I was going to die," she climbed out on the ledge and crept along it, ten floors up, to the room next door and the smoke-filled, chaotic hallway beyond. The Rasheed was evacuated and many of its former occupants found themselves sleeping on quickly assembled cots in Saddam's palace. As for my friend's "seven-point plan," two weeks later President Bush decided to abandon it. Instead of confronting the problem that had blocked the writing of a new Iraqi constitution—the question of how the fact of Shia numerical dominance, and other unresolved conflicts in the Iraqi state, would be integrated into a functioning Iraqi democracy—the President, faced with mounting attacks from Iraqis opposed to the new political dispensation he had declared himself committed to create, decided to abandon the effort.

Security underlies everything in Iraq; it is the fault line running squarely beneath the occupation and the political world that will emerge from it. As I look back, perhaps my most frightening moment in the country came not at the Red Cross bombing, or at an ambush on the highway between Falluja and Ramadi where five civilians were killed, or at various other scenes of violence of one kind or another, but at a press conference the afternoon of the Rasheed attack, when General Martin E. Dempsey, the impressive commander of the First Infantry Division, characterized the rocket launcher—the cleverly disguised weapon that some unknown persons had used to pierce successfully the huge security perimeter around the Rasheed and thereby kill and wound, under the noses of tens of thousands of US soldiers, the Americans who were supposedly running Iraq, and nearly kill the deputy secretary of defense—as "not very sophisticated ... a science project, made in a garage with a welder, a battery, and a handful of wire." What frightened me was the possibility that General Dempsey—a sophisticated man who no doubt had read the literature on counterinsurgency and knew well "the lessons" of the British in Malaya and the French in Algeria and the

Americans in Vietnam, but who, like almost every other impressive American commander in Iraq, had been trained to fight with, and against, large armored formations—was aware of the condescension evident in his tone.

"The idea behind these stay-behind insurgent groups is that they're *clandestine*, they use what's *available*—an old drainpipe, whatever," said a private security officer working for an American television network who, like many of the security professionals in Iraq, was a veteran of Britain's elite Special Air Service. "They don't need to be sophisticated, they need to be *effective*—and that device that hit the Rasheed was very effective." Raymond Bonner, a *New York Times* reporter, made a somewhat broader point: "The good news is it was a science project put together in a garage. The bad news is it was a science project put together in a garage."

Ten days later, when a colleague, a strong advocate of the United States' invasion, declared to me with some impatience, "The United States will not *lose*. The United States has *absolute military superiority in Iraq!*,"[4] I remembered Bonner's comment. In view of the progress of the war against the US coalition—the spreading activities of the opposition, the growing sophistication of their methods, the increasing numbers of Americans being killed—is the fact that the United States has "absolute military superiority" in Iraq good or bad news? All differences aside (and there are a great many differences), people commonly made the same point about Vietnam; but if it is true that "the United States had absolute military superiority in Vietnam," then what exactly do those words mean—and what do they tell us about those who utter them?

Fall in Falluja is dusty and bright. Here, on an average day in late October, insurgents attacked American soldiers eight times, twice the rate of a month before, according to General Chuck Swannack, commander of the 82nd Airborne Division. The method of choice was IEDs—"improvised explosive devices," in military parlance—planted, presumably, by FRLs, or "former regime loyalists." On the road leading into town, just emerging from the cloverleaf off the main highway, I saw the aftermath of one such attack. Late that afternoon, as an American armored convoy rumbled up the highway into the city, someone set off what the general described as

> a very sophisticated device, three barrels of flammable material rigged to a triggering mechanism, using a remote-controlled trigger. As our squad was clearing the cloverleaf, the individuals set off the device, killed a paratrooper, and then some individuals directed fire at us with AK-47s from the houses.

General Swannack's men dismounted, returned fire, stormed the houses, and arrested several civilians, leading them roughly away in flexi-cuffs. It was a typical day in Falluja, with a typical score: one dead American soldier, two dead civilians, several civilians wounded, several arrested, with an indeterminate number of family members, neighbors, and friends of those killed, wounded, and arrested left furious at the Americans and nursing strong grievances, which tribal honor, an especially strong force in Falluja, now demanded they personally avenge—by killing more Americans. As for the handful of "individuals" who had set off the device and opened fire on the Americans, they managed—as they do in all but a few such ambushes—to get away clean.

As I write, 423 Americans have died in Iraq since the United States invaded in March and more than 2,300 have been wounded there, many grievously; and the rate at which Americans are being killed and wounded is increasing. But while these tolls are having a discernible effect on President Bush's popularity among Americans, the major goal of this kind of warfare is not only to kill and wound Americans but to increase Iraqi recruits, both active and passive, who will oppose the occupation; its major product, that is, is *political*. "The point," said General Swannack, "is to get the Americans to fire back and hopefully they'll get some Iraqi casualties out of that and they can publicize that."

After first estimating the guerrilla strength in and around Falluja at 20,000, the general revised his figure: "Probably about a thousand people out there really want to attack us and kill us and another nineteen thousand or so really really don't like us." Such estimates vary wildly around Iraq, depending on whom you ask. General Sanchez recently put the total number of the opposition nationwide at five thousand. Whatever the numbers, the guerrillas' main business is to make them grow, particularly the number of strong sympathizers; and all evidence suggests that thus far they are succeeding.

Saddam's Iraq was a national security state dominated by the interlocking intelligence services of the government and the elite security units of the army, all of it rooted in the enormous Baath Party, a highly elaborated structure that over a half-century spread and proliferated into every institution in the country and that originally grew from a complex network of conspiratorial cells of three to seven members. Saddam's elite Republican Guard numbered 80,000; his even more select Special Republican Guard numbered 16,000; his Fedayeen Saddam, a paramilitary force—in effect, Saddam's brownshirts—numbered 40,000. The Mukhabarat and the various intelligence services, of which there were perhaps a dozen, numbered thousands more. All of these men were highly trained, well armed, and tested for their political loyalty. Few of them died in the war.

In May, in an astonishing decision that still has not been adequately explained, American administrator L. Paul Bremer vastly increased the number of willing Iraqi foot soldiers by abruptly dissolving the regular Iraqi army, which had been established by King Faisal I in 1921, and thereby sent out into bitter shame and unemployment 350,000 of those young Iraqis who were well trained, well armed, and deeply angry at the Americans. Add to these a million or so tons of weapons and munitions of all sorts, including rockets and missiles, readily available in more than a hundred mostly unguarded arms depots around the country, as well as vast amounts of money stockpiled during thirty-five years in power (notably on March 18, 2003, when Saddam sent three tractor trailers to the Central Bank and relieved it of more than a billion dollars in cash), and you have the makings of a well-manned, well-funded insurgency.

During the months since the fall of Baghdad in April, that insurgency has grown and evolved. Its methods have moved from assassinations of isolated US soldiers, to attacks on convoys with small arms, to increasingly sophisticated and frequent ambushes of convoys with remote-controlled explosives and attacks on helicopters with rocket-propelled grenades and missiles. While there seems to be some regional coordination among groups, it is clear that the opposition is made up of many different organizations, some regionally based, some local; some are explicitly Saddamist, some more broadly Baathist, some Islamist, and some frankly anti-Saddam and nationalist. "I don't see a vision by these disparate groups of insurgents or partisans," said Ahmed S. Hashim, a professor at the Naval War College who has closely studied the opposition. "But at this stage they do not need one. They are making our stay uncomfortable, they have affected our calculus and are driving a wedge between us. What I know is the coalition is losing ground among Iraqis." Within and among these groupings a competitive politics now exists, an armed politics that will evolve and develop, depending on how successful they are in attacking the Americans and forcing them to adjust their policies and, eventually, to leave the country.

By now much evidence exists, including documents apparently prepared by Iraqi intelligence services, to suggest that this insurgency, at least in its broad outlines, was planned before the war and that the plan included looting, sabotage, and assassination of clerics.[5] Particularly damaging was the looting, in which government ministries and other public buildings, including museums, libraries, and universities, were thoroughly ransacked, down to the copper pipes and electrical wiring in the walls, and then burned, and the capital was given over to weeks of utter lawlessness while American soldiers stood by and watched. This was an enormously important political blow against the occupation, undermining any trust or faith Iraqis might have had in their new rulers and destroying any chance the occupiers had to establish their authority. Most of all, the looting created an overwhelming sense of insecurity and trepidation, a sense that the insurgents, with their bombings and attacks, have built on to convince many Iraqis that the Americans have not achieved full control and may well not stay long enough to attain it.

All of this is another way of saying that if security is the fault line running beneath political development in Iraq, then politics is the fault line running beneath security. By now the failures in planning and execution that have dogged the occupation—the lack of military police, the refusal to provide security in the capital, the dissolution of the Iraqi army—are well known.[6] All have originated in Washington, many born of struggles between the leading departments of government, principally the State Department, the CIA, and the Pentagon, which the White House has never managed to resolve. (The most obvious product of these struggles was the President's decision, barely two months before the invasion, to discard the year of occupation planning by the State Department and shift control to the Pentagon, which proved itself wholly unprepared to take on the task.)

In Iraq, after the Big Bang of the American invasion, a new political universe is slowly being born. Part of this Iraqi political universe is called the Governing Council, and it does its work behind the concrete barriers of the Green Zone. Another part works at the level of nascent local government throughout the country. Still another works in the mosques of the south and among the Shiite religious establishment known as the Hawza. And yet another part—now a rather large and powerful part—is armed and clandestine and is making increasingly sophisticated and effective use of guerrilla warfare and terrorism, hoping to force the Americans from the country and claim its share of power. The Americans seek to define the armed claimants as illegitimate—essentially, as not part of the recognized universe at all. But in order to enforce that definition—to confine the game to the actors they regard as legitimate—the Americans must prove themselves able to make use of their power, both military and political, more effectively.

As I write, on November 19, 2003, US military forces in Iraq are conducting Operation Iron Hammer, striking with warplanes and artillery bases thought to be occupied by Iraqi insurgents. American television broadcasts are filled with dramatic footage of huge explosions illuminating the night sky. In Tikrit, Saddam's political base and a stronghold of the opposition, the Americans staged a military show of force, sending tanks and other armored vehicles rumbling through the main street. "They need to understand," Lieutenant Colonel Steve Russell told ABC News, "it's more than just Humvees we'll be using in these attacks."

The armed opposition in Iraq seems unlikely to be impressed. However many insurgents the Americans manage to kill in bombing runs and artillery barrages, the toll on civilians, in death and disruption, is also likely to be high, as will damage to the fragile sense of normalcy that Americans are struggling to achieve and the opposition forces are determined to destroy. Large-scale armored warfare looks and sounds impressive, inspiring overwhelming fear; but it is not discriminate, which makes it a blunt and ultimately self-defeating instrument to deploy against determined guerrillas. In general, the American military, the finest and most powerful in the world, is not organized and equipped to fight this war, and the part of it that is—the Special Forces—are almost entirely occupied in what seems a never-ending hunt for Saddam. For American leaders, and particularly President Bush, this has become the quest for the Holy Grail: finding Saddam will be an enormous political boon. For the American military, this quest has the feel of a more traditional and familiar kind of war. "We are a hierarchy and we like to fight hierarchies," says military strategist John Arquilla. "We think if we cut off the head we can end this."

Whatever the political rewards of finding Saddam, they will not likely include putting a definitive end to the insurgency in Iraq.[7] "The Americans need to get out of their tanks, get out from behind their sunglasses," a British military officer, a veteran of Northern Ireland told me. "They need to get on the ground where they can get to know people and encourage them to tell them where the bad guys are." As I write, operations on the ground seem to be moving in the opposite direction. In any event it is difficult to impress an opponent with a military advance plainly meant to cover a political retreat.

President Bush's audacious project in Iraq was always going to be difficult, perhaps impossible, but without political steadfastness and resilience, it had no chance to succeed. This autumn in Baghdad, a ruthless insurgency, growing but still in its infancy, has managed to make the President retreat from his project, and has worked, with growing success, to divide Iraqis from the Americans who claim to govern them. These insurgents cannot win, but by seizing on Washington's mistakes and working relentlessly to widen the fault lines in occupied Iraq, they threaten to prevent what President Bush told Americans he sent the US military to achieve: a stable, democratic, and peaceful Iraq, at the heart of a stable and democratic Middle East.

—*The New York Review of Books*, November 19, 2003

NOTES

1. For the Saudi claim, see Mohammad Bazzi, "Saudis Suspected in 2 Iraq Attacks," *Newsday*, November 11, 2003.

2. See Susan Sachs, "US Is Set to Return Power to Iraqis as Early as June," *The New York Times*, November 15, 2003.

3. See Jonathan S. Landay, "CIA Has a Bleak Analysis of Iraq," *Philadelphia Inquirer*, November 12, 2003.

4. Christopher Hitchens made the comment, in a debate with me at the University of California at Berkeley on November 4, 2003. See "Has Bush Made Us Safer? Iraq, Terror and American Power," at webcast.berkeley.edu/events/archive.html.

5. See Michael Hirsh, Rod Nordland, and Mark Hosenball, "About-Face in Iraq," *Newsweek*, November 24, 2003; and Douglas Jehl, "Plan for Guerrilla Action May Have Predated War," *The New York Times*, November 15, 2003.

6. See Mark Fineman, Robin Wright, and Doyle McManus, "Preparing for War, Stumbling to Peace," *Los Angeles Times*, July 18, 2003; and David Rieff, "Blueprint for a Mess," *The New York Times Magazine*, November 2, 2003.

7. See Ahmed S. Hashim, "The Sunni Insurgency in Iraq," *Middle East Institute Policy Brief*, August 15, 2003, who notes that the "elimination of Saddam and his dynasty may demoralize pro-regime insurgents but may actually embolden anti-regime and anti-US insurgents who may have held back in the past . . . because of the barely submerged fears that the regime could come back."

Appendices:

TORTURE AND TRUTH
IN WORDS AND PICTURES

FROM THE MOMENT the Abu Ghraib photographs were released on the CBS News program *60 Minutes II* on April 28, 2004, and then published a few days later in *The New Yorker*, along with an article by Seymour M. Hersh, the torture scandal has been driven by documents: first the photographs themselves, then the Taguba report, the Red Cross report, the depositions from prisoners taken by the Criminal Investigation Command of the US Army, and finally the series of investigations undertaken by officers and former officials in the wake of the release of the photographs themselves.

In the way of Washington, the scandal, which had been set off by a leak of photographs, brought in its wake more leaks, until, six weeks after the emergence of the photographs, during June 2004, a series of documents was released to the press that showed in detail the struggles among senior officials within the executive branch—notably, in the Department of Justice, the Department of Defense, and the White House itself—over how to treat those prisoners captured in Afghanistan and later in Iraq, and what methods to use in interrogating them. Not only the documents themselves but the manner of their release offer the careful reader the vision of a bureaucratic war, in which officials of various departments and agencies struggle over how far the US government may legally extend its power in prosecuting the war on terror. As I write that bureaucratic war is still being fought.

The documents that follow are arranged under three headings. The first section, "Disputation," includes a series of memoranda, letters, and reports that take up two questions: First, should the Geneva Convention apply to the conflict in Afghanistan and Geneva Convention protection be extended to members of al-Qaeda and members of the Taliban? And second: What methods of interrogation can legally and properly be applied to these prisoners?

The second section, "Revelation," includes reproductions of the digital photographs taken at Abu Ghraib prison in fall 2003 that have been released to the press; the depositions of thirteen Abu Ghraib prisoners that were taken by the US Army's Criminal Investigation Command that were released to the press; and the full text of the Red Cross report that was based on a series of twenty-nine visits by Red Cross investigators during the summer and fall of 2003.

The third section, "Investigation," includes the full texts of the reports by Major General Antonio M. Taguba, who investigated the activities of the military police; by Lieutenant General Anthony R. Jones and Major General George R. Fay, who investigated the actitivies of military intelligence; and by former secretary of defense James R. Schlesinger and the commission he headed, which essentially investigated the investigations themselves.

—MARK DANNER
September 17, 2004

APPENDIX I

Disputation:

ARGUING TORTURE

SHORTLY AFTER THE attacks on September 11, 2001, marked the official start of the global war on terror—or the GWOT, as some writers of these documents refer to it—another, quieter struggle broke out among officials of the United States government concerning how that war was to be fought: its extent, its limits, and its rules. Thanks to the photographs from Abu Ghraib and the leaks of documents that followed their broadcast in April 2004, we now know a good deal about that internal bureaucratic war and how it took shape within the United States government during the months after 9/11.

The documents that follow describe two substantial arguments over what US policy should be in this "new kind of war," as the President's counsel, Alberto Gonzalez, calls it. The first argument concerns who should be protected—specifically, whether prisoners who might be members of al-Qaeda or the Taliban should be entitled to the protections of the Geneva Convention. On one side are those in the White House and the Department of Justice who argue against extending such protection, contending, in Mr. Gonzalez's words, that "this new paradigm renders obsolete Geneva's strict limitations on questioning of enemy prisoners and renders quaint some of its provisions" (see page 84). On the other side are those in the Department of State and in some parts of the Department of Defense who fear that such a decision "will reverse over a century of US policy and practice in supporting the Geneva conventions and undermine the protections of the law of war for our troops" (see page 91).

The second argument is over how far American military and intelligence personnel are permitted to go in interrogating prisoners—and specifically, what techniques constitute torture, which the United States has bound itself, by international treaty and by domestic statute, to prohibit. Again, the discussion is driven by aggressive arguments put forward by lawyers in the Office of Legal Counsel of the Department of Justice, who contend that "physical pain amounting to torture must be equivalent in intensity to the pain accompanying serious physical injury, such as organ failure, impairment of bodily function, or even death" (see page 115)—a standard which, if adopted, would allow extremely brutal interrogation methods. These documents show how discussion within the government about what constitutes torture evolved, under the press of events and government pressure for "actionable intelligence"—first from prisoners in Afghanistan and Guantánamo, then from prisoners in Iraq—into a discussion among policymakers and military officers about what specific methods of interrogation should be permitted in Guantánamo—and, ultimately, in the prison at Abu Ghraib.

The final document, published here for the first time, is the report by Major General Geoffrey D. Miller (see page 205), then commander of Guantánamo, who traveled to Abu Ghraib in August 2003 to "review current Iraqi theater ability to rapidly exploit internees for actionable intelligence." Major General Miller recommended, among other things, that those in charge of Abu Ghraib "dedicate and train a detention guard force...that sets conditions for the successful interrogation and exploitation of internees/detainees." In General Miller's visit, two paths meant to be kept separate in effect converge, and interrogation methods officially intended for use only on prisoners not protected by the Geneva Convention, like those in Guantánamo, "migrate" to Iraq (in the words of James R. Schlesinger in his report) and are employed on prisoners there who are entitled to such protection. At this writing Major General Miller is commander of Abu Ghraib prison.

—MD

WHO IS PROTECTED?: THE DEBATE OVER POWS

I

Federal Register: November 16, 2001 (Volume 66, Number 222)
Presidential Documents
Page 57831-57836

Military Order of November 13, 2001
Detention, Treatment, and Trial of Certain Non-Citizens in the
War Against Terrorism

By the authority vested in me as President and as Commander in Chief of the
Armed Forces of the United States by the Constitution and the laws of the United
States of America, including the Authorization for Use of Military Force Joint Reso-
lution (Public Law 107-40, 115 Stat. 224) and sections 821 and 836 of title 10,
United States Code, it is hereby ordered as follows:

Section 1. Findings.

(a) International terrorists, including members of al Qaida, have carried out
attacks on United States diplomatic and military personnel and facilities abroad and
on citizens and property within the United States on a scale that has created a state of
armed conflict that requires the use of the United States Armed Forces.

(b) In light of grave acts of terrorism and threats of terrorism, including the terrorist attacks on September 11, 2001, on the headquarters of the United States Department of Defense in the national capital region, on the World Trade Center in New
York, and on civilian aircraft such as in Pennsylvania, I proclaimed a national emergency on September 14, 2001 (Proc. 7463, Declaration of National Emergency by
Reason of Certain Terrorist Attacks).

c) Individuals acting alone and in concert involved in international terrorism possess both the capability and the intention to undertake further terrorist attacks
against the United States that, if not detected and prevented, will cause mass deaths,
mass injuries, and massive destruction of property, and may place at risk the continu-
ity of the operations of the United States Government.

(d) The ability of the United States to protect the United States and its citizens, and
to help its allies and other cooperating nations protect their nations and their citizens,
from such further terrorist attacks depends in significant part upon using the United
States Armed Forces to identify terrorists and those who support them, to disrupt
their activities, and to eliminate their ability to conduct or support such attacks.

(e) To protect the United States and its citizens, and for the effective conduct of military operations and prevention of terrorist attacks, it is necessary for individuals subject to this order pursuant to section 2 hereof to be detained, and, when tried, to be
tried for violations of the laws of war and other applicable laws by military tribunals.

(f) Given the danger to the safety of the United States and the nature of international terrorism, and to the extent provided by and under this order, I find consistent with section 836 of title 10, United States Code, that it is not practicable to apply in military commissions under this order the principles of law and the rules of evidence generally recognized in the trial of criminal cases in the United States district courts.

(g) Having fully considered the magnitude of the potential deaths, injuries, and property destruction that would result from potential acts of terrorism against the United States, and the probability that such acts will occur, I have determined that an extraordinary emergency exists for national defense purposes, that this emergency constitutes an urgent and compelling government interest, and that issuance of this order is necessary to meet the emergency.

Sec. 2. Definition and Policy.

(a) The term "individual subject to this order" shall mean any individual who is not a United States citizen with respect to whom I determine from time to time in writing that:

(1) there is reason to believe that such individual, at the relevant times,

(i) is or was a member of the organization known as al Qaida;

(ii) has engaged in, aided or abetted, or conspired to commit, acts of international terrorism, or acts in preparation therefor, that have caused, threaten to cause, or have as their aim to cause, injury to or adverse effects on the United States, its citizens, national security, foreign policy, or economy; or

(iii) has knowingly harbored one or more individuals described in subparagraphs (i) or (ii) of subsection 2(a)(1) of this order; and

(2) it is in the interest of the United States that such individual be subject to this order.

(b) It is the policy of the United States that the Secretary of Defense shall take all necessary measures to ensure that any individual subject to this order is detained in accordance with section 3, and, if the individual is to be tried, that such individual is tried only in accordance with section 4.

(c) It is further the policy of the United States that any individual subject to this order who is not already under the control of the Secretary of Defense but who is under the control of any other officer or agent of the United States or any State shall, upon delivery of a copy of such written determination to such officer or agent, forthwith be placed under the control of the Secretary of Defense.

Sec. 3. Detention Authority of the Secretary of Defense.

Any individual subject to this order shall be—

(a) detained at an appropriate location designated by the Secretary of Defense outside or within the United States;

(b) treated humanely, without any adverse distinction based on race, color, religion, gender, birth, wealth, or any similar criteria;

(c) afforded adequate food, drinking water, shelter, clothing, and medical treatment;

(d) allowed the free exercise of religion consistent with the requirements of such detention; and

(e) detained in accordance with such other conditions as the Secretary of Defense may prescribe.

Sec. 4. Authority of the Secretary of Defense Regarding Trials of Individuals Subject to this Order.

(a) Any individual subject to this order shall, when tried, be tried by military commission for any and all offenses triable by military commission that such individual is alleged to have committed, and may be punished in accordance with the penalties provided under applicable law, including life imprisonment or death.

(b) As a military function and in light of the findings in section 1, including subsection (f) thereof, the Secretary of Defense shall issue such orders and regulations, including orders for the appointment of one or more military commissions, as may be necessary to carry out subsection (a) of this section.

(c) Orders and regulations issued under subsection (b) of this section shall include, but not be limited to, rules for the conduct of the proceedings of military commissions, including pretrial, trial, and post-trial procedures, modes of proof, issuance of process, and qualifications of attorneys, which shall at a minimum provide for—

(1) military commissions to sit at any time and any place, consistent with such guidance regarding time and place as the Secretary of Defense may provide;

(2) a full and fair trial, with the military commission sitting as the triers of both fact and law;

(3) admission of such evidence as would, in the opinion of the presiding officer of the military commission (or instead, if any other member of the commission so requests at the time the presiding officer renders that opinion, the opinion of the commission rendered at that time by a majority of the commission), have probative value to a reasonable person;

(4) in a manner consistent with the protection of information classified or classifiable under Executive Order 12958 of April 17, 1995, as amended, or any successor Executive Order, protected by statute or rule from unauthorized disclosure, or otherwise protected by law, (A) the handling of, admission into evidence of, and access to materials and information, and (B) the conduct, closure of, and access to proceedings;

(5) conduct of the prosecution by one or more attorneys designated by the Secretary of Defense and conduct of the defense by attorneys for the individual subject to this order;

(6) conviction only upon the concurrence of two-thirds of the members of the commission present at the time of the vote, a majority being present;

(7) sentencing only upon the concurrence of two-thirds of the members of the commission present at the time of the vote, a majority being present; and

(8) submission of the record of the trial, including any conviction or sentence, for review and final decision by me or by the Secretary of Defense if so designated by me for that purpose.

Sec. 5. Obligation of Other Agencies to Assist the Secretary of Defense.

Departments, agencies, entities, and officers of the United States shall, to the maximum extent permitted by law, provide to the Secretary of Defense such assistance as he may request to implement this order.

Sec. 6. Additional Authorities of the Secretary of Defense.

(a) As a military function and in light of the findings in section 1, the Secretary of Defense shall issue such orders and regulations as may be necessary to carry out any of the provisions of this order.

(b) The Secretary of Defense may perform any of his functions or duties, and may exercise any of the powers provided to him under this order (other than under section 4(c)(8) hereof) in accordance with section 113(d) of title 10, United States Code.

Sec. 7. Relationship to Other Law and Forums.

(a) Nothing in this order shall be construed to—

(1) authorize the disclosure of state secrets to any person not otherwise authorized to have access to them;

(2) limit the authority of the President as Commander in Chief of the Armed Forces or the power of the President to grant reprieves and pardons; or

(3) limit the lawful authority of the Secretary of Defense, any military commander, or any other officer or agent of the United States or of any State to detain or try any person who is not an individual subject to this order.

(b) With respect to any individual subject to this order—

(1) military tribunals shall have exclusive jurisdiction with respect to offenses by the individual; and

(2) the individual shall not be privileged to seek any remedy or maintain any proceeding, directly or indirectly, or to have any such remedy or proceeding sought on the individual's behalf, in (i) any court of the United States, or any State thereof, (ii) any court of any foreign nation, or (iii) any international tribunal.

(c) This order is not intended to and does not create any right, benefit, or privilege, substantive or procedural, enforceable at law or equity by any party, against the United States, its departments, agencies, or other entities, its officers or employees, or any other person.

(d) For purposes of this order, the term "State" includes any State, district, territory, or possession of the United States.

(e) I reserve the authority to direct the Secretary of Defense, at any time hereafter, to transfer to a governmental authority control of any individual subject to this order. Nothing in this order shall be construed to limit the authority of any such governmental authority to prosecute any individual for whom control is transferred.

Sec. 8. Publication.

This order shall be published in the Federal Register.

[signed]

GEORGE W. BUSH

THE WHITE HOUSE
November 13, 2001.

2

DRAFT
1/25/2002—3:30 pm

January 25, 2002

MEMORANDUM FOR THE PRESIDENT

FROM: ALBERTO R. GONZALES

SUBJECT: DECISION RE APPLICATION OF THE GENEVA
CONVENTION ON PRISONERS OF WAR TO THE
CONFLICT WITH AL QAEDA AND THE TALIBAN

Purpose

On January 18, I advised you that the Department of Justice had issued a formal legal opinion concluding that the Geneva Convention III on the Treatment of Prisoners of War (GPW) does not apply to the conflict with al Qaeda. I also advised you that DOJ's opinion concludes that there are reasonable grounds for you to conclude that GPW does not apply with respect to the conflict with the Taliban. I understand that you decided that GPW does not apply and, accordingly, that al Qaeda and Taliban detainees are not prisoners of war under the GPW.

The Secretary of State has requested that you reconsider that decision. Specifically, he has asked that you conclude that GPW does apply to both al Qaeda and the Taliban. I understand, however, that he would agree that al Qaeda and Taliban fighters could be determined not to be prisoners of war (POWs) but only on a case-by-case basis following individual hearings before a military board.

This memorandum outlines the ramifications of your decision and the Secretary's request for reconsideration.

Legal Background

As an initial matter, I note that you have the constitutional authority to make the determination you made on January 18 that the GPW does not apply to al Qaeda and the Taliban. (Of course, you could nevertheless, as a matter of policy, decide to apply the principles of GPW to the conflict with al Qaeda and the Taliban.) The Office of Legal Counsel of the Department of Justice has opined that, as a matter of international and domestic law, GPW does not apply to the conflict with al Qaeda. OLC has further opined that you have the authority to determine that GPW does not apply to the Taliban. As I discussed with you, the grounds for such a determination may include:

- A determination that Afghanistan was a failed state because the Taliban did not exercise full control over the territory and people, was not recognized by the international community, and was not capable of fulfilling its international obligations (e.g., was in widespread material breach of its international obligations).
- A determination that the Taliban and its forces were, in fact, not a government, but a militant, terrorist-like group.

OLC's interpretation of this legal issue is definitive. The Attorney General is charged by statute with interpreting the law for the Executive Branch. This interpretive authority extends to both domestic and international law. He has, in turn, delegated this role to OLC. Nevertheless, you should be aware that the Legal Adviser to the Secretary of State has expressed a different view.

Ramifications of Determination that GPW Does Not Apply

The consequences of a decision to adhere to what I understood to be your earlier determination that the GPW does not apply to the Taliban include the following:

Positive:

- Preserves flexibility:
  - As you have said, the war against terrorism is a new kind of war. It is not the traditional clash between nations adhering to the laws of war that formed the backdrop for GPW. The nature of the new war places a high premium on other factors, such as the ability to quickly obtain information from captured terrorists and their sponsors in order to avoid further atrocities against American civilians, and the need to try terrorists for war crimes such as wantonly killing civilians. In my judgment, this new paradigm renders obsolete Geneva's strict limitations on questioning of enemy prisoners and renders quaint some of its provisions requiring that captured enemy be afforded such things as commissary privileges, scrip (i.e., advances of monthly pay), athletic uniforms, and scientific instruments.
  - Although some of these provisions do not apply to detainees who are not POWs, a determination that GPW does not apply to al Qaeda and the Taliban eliminates any argument regarding the need for case-by-case determinations of POW status. It also holds open options for the future conflicts in which it may be more difficult to determine whether an enemy force as a whole meets the standard for POW status.
  - By concluding that GPW does not apply to al Qaeda and the Taliban, we avoid foreclosing options for the future, particularly against nonstate actors.

- Substantially reduces the threat of domestic criminal prosecution under the War Crimes Act (18 U.S.C. 2441).
  - That statute, enacted in 1996, prohibits the commission of a "war crime" by or against a U.S. person, including U.S. officials. "War crime" for these purposes is defined to include any grave breach of GPW or any violation of common Article 3 thereof (such as "outrages against personal dignity"). Some of these provisions apply (if the GPW applies) regardless of whether the individual being detained qualifies as a POW. Punishments for violations of Section 2441 include the death penalty. A determination that the GPW is not applicable to the Taliban would mean that Section 2441 would not apply to actions taken with respect to the Taliban.
  - Adhering to your determination that GPW does not apply would guard effectively against misconstruction or misapplication of Section 2441 for several reasons.
    - First, some of the language of the GPW is undefined (it prohibits, for example, "outrages upon personal dignity" and "inhuman treatment"), and it is difficult to predict with confidence what actions might be deemed to constitute violations of the relevant provisions of GPW.
    - Second, it is difficult to predict the needs and circumstances that could arise in the course of the war on terrorism.
    - Third, it is difficult to predict the motives of prosecutors and independent counsels who may in the future decide to pursue unwarranted charges based on Section 2441. Your determination would create a reasonable basis in law that Section 2441 does not apply, which would provide a solid defense to any future prosecution.

Negative:

On the other hand, the following arguments would support reconsideration and reversal of your decision that the GPW does not apply to either al Qaeda or the Taliban:

- Since the Geneva Conventions were concluded in 1949, the United States has never denied their applicability to either U.S. or opposing forces engaged in armed conflict, despite several opportunities to do so. During the last Bush Administration, the United States stated that it "has a policy of applying the Geneva Conventions of 1949 whenever armed hostilities occur with regular foreign armed forces, even if arguments could be made that the threshold standards for the applicability of the Conventions . . . are not met."
- The United States could not invoke the GPW if enemy forces threatened to mistreat or mistreated U.S. or coalition forces captured during operations in Afghanistan, or if they denied Red Cross access or other POW privileges.
- The War Crimes Act could not be used against the enemy, although other criminal statutes and the customary law of war would still be available.

- Our position would likely provoke widespread condemnation among our allies and in some domestic quarters, even if we make clear that we will comply with the core humanitarian principles of the treaty as a matter of policy.
- Concluding that the Geneva Convention does not apply may encourage other countries to look for technical "loopholes" in future conflicts to conclude that they are not bound by GPW either.
- Other countries may be less inclined to turn over terrorists or provide legal assistance to us if we do not recognize a legal obligation to comply with the GPW.
- A determination that GPW does not apply to al Qaeda and the Taliban could undermine U.S. military culture which emphasizes maintaining the highest standards of conduct in combat, and could introduce an element of uncertainty in the status of adversaries.

Response to Arguments for Applying GPW to the al Qaeda and the Taliban

On balance, I believe that the arguments for reconsideration and reversal are unpersuasive.

- The argument that the U.S. has never determined that GPW did not apply is incorrect. In at least one case (Panama in 1989) the U.S. determined that GPW did not apply even though it determined for policy reasons to adhere to the convention. More importantly, as noted above, this is a new type of warfare—one not contemplated in 1949 when the GPW was framed—and requires a new approach in our actions towards captured terrorists. Indeed, as the statement quoted from the administration of President George Bush makes clear, the U.S. will apply GPW "whenever hostilities occur with regular foreign armed forces." By its terms, therefore, the policy does not apply to a conflict with terrorists, or with irregular forces, like the Taliban, who are armed militants that oppressed and terrorized the people of Afghanistan.
- In response to the argument that we should decide to apply GPW to the Taliban in order to encourage other countries to treat captured U.S. military personnel in accordance with the GPW, it should be noted that your policy of providing humane treatment to enemy detainees gives us the credibility to insist on like treatment for our soldiers. Moreover, even if GPW is not applicable, we can still bring war crimes charges against anyone who mistreats U.S. personnel. Finally, I note that our adversaries in several recent conflicts have not been deterred by GPW in their mistreatment of captured U.S. personnel, and terrorists will not follow GPW rules in any event.
- The statement that other nations would criticize the U.S. because we have determined that GPW does not apply is undoubtedly true. It is even possible that some nations would point to that determination as a basis for failing to cooperate with us on specific matters in the war against terrorism. On the

other hand, some international and domestic criticism is already likely to flow from your previous decision not to treat the detainees as POWs. And we can facilitate cooperation with other nations by reassuring them that we fully support GPW where it is applicable and by acknowledging that in this conflict the U.S. continues to respect other recognized standards.

- In the treatment of detainees, the U.S. will continue to be constrained by (i) its commitment to treat the detainees humanely and, to the extent appropriate and consistent with military necessity, in a manner consistent with the principles of GPW, (ii) its applicable treaty obligations, (iii) minimum standards of treatment universally recognized by the nations of the world, and (iv) applicable military regulations regarding the treatment of detainees.
- Similarly, the argument based on military culture fails to recognize that our military remain bound to apply the principles of GPW because that is what you have directed them to do.

3

United States Department of State
Washington, D.C. 20520

MEMORANDUM

TO: Counsel to the President
           Assistant to the President for National Security Affairs

FROM: Colin L. Powell [initialed 26/1]

SUBJECT: Draft Decision Memorandum for the President on the Applicability of
           the Geneva Convention to the Conflict in Afghanistan

I appreciate the opportunity to comment on the draft memorandum. I am concerned that the draft does not squarely present to the President the options that are available to him. Nor does it identify the significant pros and cons of each option. I hope that the final memorandum will make clear that the President's choice is between

> Option 1: Determine that the Geneva Convention on the treatment of Prisoners of War (GPW) does not apply to the conflict on "failed State" or some other grounds. Announce this position publicly. Treat all detainees consistent with the principles of the GPW;

and

> Option 2: Determine that the Geneva Convention does apply to the conflict in Afghanistan, but that members of al Qaeda as a group and the Taliban individually or as a group are not entitled to Prisoner of War status under the Convention. Announce this position publicly. Treat all detainees consistent with the principles of the GPW.

The final memorandum should first tell the President that both options have the following advantages—that is there is no difference between them in these respects:

- Both provide the same practical flexibility in how we treat detainees, including with respect to interrogation and length of the detention.
- Both provide flexibility to provide conditions of detention and trial that take into account constraints such as feasibility under the circumstances and necessary security requirements.
- Both allow us not to give the privileges and benefits of POW status to al Qaeda and Taliban.

- Neither option entails any significant risk of domestic prosecution against U.S. officials.

The memorandum should go on to identify the separate pros and cons of the two options as follows:

Option 1—Geneva Convention does not apply to the conflict

Pros:

- This is an across-the-board approach that on its face provides maximum flexibility, removing any question of case-by-case determination for individuals.

Cons:

- It will reverse over a century of U.S. policy and practice in supporting the Geneva conventions and undermine the protections of the law of war for our troops, both in this specific conflict and in general.
- It has a high cost in terms of negative international reaction, with immediate adverse consequences for our conduct of foreign policy.
- It will undermine public support among critical allies, making military cooperation more difficult to sustain.
- Europeans and others will likely have legal problems with extradition or other forms of cooperation in law enforcement, including in bringing terrorists to justice.
- It may provoke some individual foreign prosecutors to investigate and prosecute our officials and troops.
- It will make us more vulnerable to domestic and international legal challenge and deprive us of important legal options:

  — It undermines the President's Military Order by removing an important legal basis for trying the detainees before Military Commissions.
  — We will be challenged in international fora (UN Commission on Human Rights; World Court; etc.).
  — The Geneva Conventions are a more flexible and suitable legal framework than other laws that would arguably apply (customary international human rights, human rights conventions). The GPW permits long-term detention without criminal charges. Even after the President determines hostilities have ended, detention continues if criminal investigations or proceedings are in process. The GPW also provides clear authority for transfer of detainees to third countries.

— Determining GPW does not apply deprives us of a winning argument to oppose habeas corpus actions in U.S. courts.

Option 2—Geneva Convention applies to the conflict

Pros:

- By providing a more defensible legal framework, it preserves our flexibility under both domestic and international law.
- It provides the strongest legal foundation for what we actually intend to do.
- It presents a positive international posture, preserves U.S. credibility and moral authority by taking the high ground, and puts us in a better position to demand and receive international support.
- It maintains POW status for U.S. forces, reinforces the importance of the Geneva Conventions, and generally supports the U.S. objective of ensuring its forces are accorded protection under the Convention.
- It reduces the incentives for international criminal investigations directed against U.S. officials and troops.

Cons:

- If, for some reason, a case-by-case review is used for Taliban, some may be determined to be entitled to POW status. This would not, however, affect their treatment as a practical matter.

I hope that you can restructure the memorandum along these lines, which it seems to me will give the President a much clearer understanding of the options available to him and their consequences. Quite aside from the need to identify options and their consequences more clearly, in its present form, the draft memorandum is inaccurate or incomplete in several respects. The most important factual errors are identified on the attachment.

ᨀ ᨀ ᨀ

Comments on the [Gonzales] Memorandum of January 25, 2002

Purpose

(Second paragraph) The Secretary of State believes that al Qaeda terrorists as a group are not entitled to POW status and that Taliban fighters could be determined not to be POWs either as a group or on a case-by-case basis.

Legal Background

(First bullet) The Memorandum should note that any determination that Afghanistan is a failed state would be contrary to the official U.S. government position. The United States and the international community have consistently held Afghanistan to its treaty obligations and identified it as a party to the Geneva Conventions.

(Second paragraph) The Memorandum should note that the OLC interpretation does not preclude the President from reaching a different conclusion. It should also note that the OLC opinion is likely to be rejected by foreign governments and will not be respected in foreign courts or international tribunals which may assert jurisdiction over the subject matter. It should also note that OLC views are not definitive on the factual questions which are central to its legal conclusions.

Ramifications of Determination that GPW Does Not Apply

(Positive) The Memorandum identifies several positive consequences if the President determines the GPW does not apply. The Memorandum should note that these consequences would result equally if the President determines that the GPW does apply but that the detainees are not entitled to POW status.

(Negative. First bullet) The first sentence is correct as it stands. The second sentence is taken out of context and should be omitted. The U.S. position in Panama was that Common Article 3 of the Geneva Conventions did apply.

Response to Arguments for Applying GPW to the al Qaeda and the Taliban

(First bullet) The assertion in the first sentence is incorrect. The United States has never determined that the GPW did not apply to an armed conflict in which its forces have been engaged. With respect to the third sentence, while no-one anticipated the precise situation that we face, the GPW was intended to cover all types of armed conflict and did not by its terms limit its application.

(Fourth bullet) The point is not clear. If we intend to conform our treatment of the detainees to universally recognized standards, we will be complying with the GPW.

4

Office of the Attorney General
Washington, D.C. 20530

February 1, 2002

The President
The White House
Washington, DC

Dear Mr. President:

With your permission, I would like to comment on the National Security Council's discussion concerning the status of Taliban detainees. It is my understanding that the determination that al Qaeda and Taliban detainees are not prisoners of war remains firm. However, reconsideration is being given to whether the Geneva Convention III on prisoners of war applies to the conflict in Afghanistan.

There are two basic theories supporting the conclusion that Taliban combatants are not legally entitled to Geneva Convention protections as prisoners of war:

1. During relevant times of the combat, Afghanistan was a failed state. As such it was not a party to the treaty, and the treaty's protections do not apply;
2. During relevant times, Afghanistan *was* a party to the treaty, but Taliban combatants are not entitled to Geneva Convention III prisoner of war status because they acted as unlawful combatants.

If a <u>determination</u> is made that Afghanistan was a failed state (Option 1 above) and not a party to the treaty, various legal risks of liability, litigation, and criminal prosecution are minimized. This is a result of the Supreme Court's opinion in *Clark v. Allen* providing that when a President <u>determines</u> that a treaty does not apply, his determination is fully discretionary and will not be reviewed by the federal courts.

Thus, a Presidential determination against treaty applicability would provide the highest assurance that no court would subsequently entertain charges that American military officers, intelligence officials, or law enforcement officials violated Geneva Convention rules relating to field conduct, detention conduct or interrogation of detainees. The War Crimes Act of 1996 makes violation of parts of the Geneva Convention a crime in the United States.

In contrast, if a determination is made under Option 2 that the Geneva Convention applies but the Taliban are <u>interpreted</u> to be unlawful combatants not subject to the treaty's protections, *Clark v. Allen* does not accord American officials the same protection from legal consequences. In cases of Presidential <u>interpretation</u> of treaties which are confessed to apply, courts occasionally refuse to defer to Presidential interpretation. *Perkins v. Elg* is an example of such a case. If a court chose to review for itself the facts underlying a Presidential interpretation that detainees were unlawful combatants, it could involve substantial criminal liability for involved U.S. officials.

We expect substantial and ongoing legal challenges to follow the Presidential resolution of these issues. These challenges will be resolved more quickly and easily if they are foreclosed from judicial review under the *Clark* case by a Presidential determination that the Geneva Convention III on prisoners of war does not apply based on the failed state theory outlined as Option 1 above.

In sum, Option 1, a determination that the Geneva Convention does not apply, will provide the United States with the highest level of legal certainty available under American law.

It may be argued that adopting Option 1 would encourage other states to allege that U.S. forces are ineligible for Geneva Convention III protections in future conflicts. From my perspective, it would be far more difficult for a nation to argue falsely that America was a "failed state" than to argue falsely that American forces had, in some way, forfeited their right to protections by becoming unlawful combatants. In fact, the North Vietnamese did exactly that to justify mistreatment of our troops in Vietnam. Therefore, it is my view that Option 2, a determination that the Geneva Convention III applies to the conflict in Afghanistan and that Taliban combatants are not protected because they were unlawful, could well expose our personnel to a greater risk of being treated improperly in the event of detention by a foreign power.

Option 1 is a legal option. It does not foreclose policy and operational considerations regarding actual treatment of Taliban detainees. Option 2, as described above, is also a legal option, but its legal implications carry higher risk of liability, criminal prosecution, and judicially-imposed conditions of detainment—including mandated release of a detainee.

Clearly, considerations beyond the legal ones mentioned in this letter will shape and perhaps control ultimate decision making in the best interests of the United States of America.

Sincerely,

[signed]

John Ashcroft
Attorney General

5

THE LEGAL ADVISER
DEPARTMENT OF STATE
WASHINGTON

February 2, 2002

MEMORANDUM

TO: Counsel to the President

FROM: William H. Taft, IV [initialed]

SUBJECT: Comments on Your Paper on the Geneva Convention

The paper should make clear that the issue for decision by the President is whether the Geneva Conventions apply to the conflict in Afghanistan in which U.S. armed forces are engaged. The President should know that a decision that the Conventions do apply is consistent with the plain language of the Conventions and the unvaried practice of the United States in introducing its forces into conflict over fifty years. It is consistent with the advice of DOS lawyers and, as far as is known, the position of every other party to the Conventions. It is consistent with UN Security Council Resolution 1193 affirming that "All parties to the conflict (in Afghanistan) are bound to comply with their obligations under international humanitarian law and in particular the Geneva Conventions. . . ." It is not inconsistent with the DOJ opinion that the Conventions generally do not apply to our world-wide effort to combat terrorism and to bring al Qaeda members to justice.

From a policy standpoint, a decision that the Conventions apply provides the best legal basis for treating the al Qaeda and Taliban detainees in the way we intend to treat them. It demonstrates that the United States bases its conduct not just on its policy preferences but on its international legal obligations. Agreement by all lawyers that the War Crimes Act does not apply to our conduct means that the risk of prosecution under that statute is negligible. Any small benefit from reducing it further will be purchased at the expense of the men and women in our armed forces that we send into combat. A decision that the Conventions do not apply to the conflict in Afghanistan in which our armed forces are engaged deprives our troops there of any claim to the protection of the Convention in the event they are captured and weakens the protections afforded by the Conventions to our troops in future conflicts.

The structure of the paper suggesting a distinction between our conflict with al Qaeda and our conflict with the Taliban does not conform to the structure of the Conventions. The Conventions call for a decision whether they apply to the conflict in Afghanistan. If they do, their provisions are applicable to all persons involved in that conflict—al Qaeda, Taliban, Northern Alliance, U.S. troops, civilians, etc. If the Conventions do not apply to the conflict, no one involved in it will enjoy the benefit of their protections as a matter of law.

6

U.S. Department of Justice
Office of Legal Counsel

Office of the Assistant Attorney General   Washington, D.C. 20530

February 7, 2002

Memorandum for Alberto R. Gonzales
Counsel to the President

*Re: Status of Taliban Forces Under
Article 4 of the Third Geneva Convention of 1949*

You have asked for our Office's views concerning the status of members of the Taliban militia under Article 4 of the 1949 Geneva Convention (III) Relative to the Treatment of Prisoners of War ("GPW"). Assuming the accuracy of various facts provided to us by the Department of Defense ("DoD"), we conclude that the President has reasonable factual grounds to determine that no members of the Taliban militia are entitled to prisoner of war ("POW") status under GPW. First, we explain that the Taliban militia cannot meet the requirements of Article 4(A)(2), because it fails to satisfy at least three of the four conditions of lawful combat articulated in Article 1 of the Annex to the 1907 Hague Convention (IV) Respecting the Laws and Customs of War on Land ("Hague Convention"), which are expressly incorporated into Article 4(A)(2). Second, we note that neither Article 4(A)(1) nor Article 4(A)(3) apply to militia, and that the four conditions of lawful combat contained in the Hague Convention also govern Article 4(A)(1) and (3) determinations in any case. Finally, we explain why there is no need to convene a tribunal under Article 5 to determine the status of the Taliban detainees.

I.

Article 4(A) of GPW defines the types of persons who, once they have fallen under the control of the enemy, are entitled to the legal status of POWs. The first three categories are the only ones relevant to the Taliban. Under Article 4(A)(1), individuals who are "members of the armed forces of a Party to the conflict," are entitled to POW status upon capture. Article 4(A)(3) includes as POWs members of "regular armed forces who profess allegiance to a government or an authority not recognized by the Detaining Power."

Article 4(A)(2) includes as POWs members of "other militias" and "volunteer corps," including "organized resistance movements" that belong to a Party to the conflict. In addition, members of militias and volunteer corps must "fulfill" four conditions: (a) "being commanded by a person responsible for his subordinates"; (b) "having a fixed distinctive sign recognizable at a distance"; (c) "carrying arms openly"; and (d) "conducting their operations in accordance with the laws and customs of war." Those four conditions reflect those required in the 1907 Hague Convention IV. *See Commentary to the Geneva Convention Relative to the Treatment of Prisoners of War* 49 (Red Cross 1952) ("Red Cross Commentary") ("during the 1949 Diplomatic Conference...there was unanimous agreement that the categories of persons to whom the Convention is applicable must be defined, in harmony with the Hague Regulations").

Should "any doubt arise as to whether persons, having committed a belligerent act and having fallen into the hands of the enemy," GPW Article 5 requires that these individuals "enjoy the protections of" the Convention until a tribunal has determined their status.

Thus, in deciding whether members of the Taliban militia qualify for POW status, the President must determine whether they fall within any of these three categories. Under Article II of the Constitution, the President possesses the power to interpret treaties on behalf of the Nation. Memorandum for John Bellinger, III, Senior Associate Counsel and Legal Adviser to the National Security Council, from John C. Yoo, Deputy Assistant Attorney General and Robert J. Delahunty, Special Counsel, Office of Legal Counsel, *Re: Authority of the President to Suspend Certain Provisions of the ABM Treaty* (Nov. 15, 2001). This includes, of course, the power to apply treaties to the facts of a given situation. Thus, the President may interpret GPW, in light of the known facts concerning the operation of Taliban forces during the Afghanistan conflict, to find that all of the Taliban forces do not fall within the legal definition of POW. A presidential determination of this nature would eliminate any legal "doubt" as to the prisoners' status, as a matter of domestic law, and would therefore obviate the need for article 5 tribunals.

We believe that, based on the facts provided by the Department of Defense, see Rear Admiral L.E. Jacoby, U.S. Navy, J-2, *Information Paper, Subject: Background Information on Taliban Forces* (Feb. 6, 2002), the President has reasonable grounds to conclude that the Taliban, as a whole, is not legally entitled to POW status under Articles 4(A)(1) through (3).

II.

As the Taliban have described themselves as a militia, rather than the armed forces of Afghanistan, we begin with GPW's requirements for militia and volunteer corps under Article 4(A)(2). Based on the facts presented to us by DoD, we believe that the President has the factual basis on which to conclude that the Taliban militia, as a group, fails to meet three of the four GPW requirements, and hence are not legally entitled to POW status.

First, there is no organized command structure whereby members of the Taliban militia report to a military commander who takes responsibility for the actions of his subordinates. The Taliban lacks a permanent, centralized communications infrastructure. Periodically, individuals declared themselves to be "commanders" and organized groups of armed men, but these "commanders" were more akin to feudal lords than military officers. According to DoD, the Taliban militia functioned more as many different armed groups that fought for their own tribal, local, or personal interests.

Moreover, when the armed groups organized, the core of the organization was often al Qaeda, a multinational terrorist organization, whose existence was not in any way accountable to or dependent upon the sovereign state of Afghanistan. We have previously concluded, as a matter of law, that al Qaeda members are not covered by GPW. See Memorandum for Alberto R. Gonzales, Counsel to the President and William J. Haynes II, General Counsel of the Department of Defense, from Jay S. Bybee, Assistant Attorney General, Re: Applications of Treaties and Laws to al Qaeda and Taliban Detainees (Jan. 22, 2002). After October 7, when the United States armed forces began aerial bombing of al Qaeda and Taliban targets in Afghanistan, the distinction between Taliban and al Qaeda became even more blurred as al Qaeda assumed the lead in organizing the defense.

DoD's facts suggest that to the extent the Taliban militia was organized at all, it consisted of a loose array of individuals who had shifting loyalties among various Taliban and al Qaeda figures. According to DoD, the Taliban lacked the kind of organization characteristic of the military. The fact that at any given time during the conflict the Taliban were organized into some structured organization does not answer whether the Taliban leaders were responsible for their subordinates within the meaning of GPW. Armed men who can be recruited from other units, as DoD states, through defections and bribery are not subject to a commander who can discipline his troops and enforce the laws of war.

Second, there is no indication that the Taliban militia wore any distinctive uniform or other insignia that served as a "fixed distinctive sign recognizable at a distance." DoD has advised us that the Taliban wore the same clothes they wore to perform other daily functions, and hence they would have been indistinguishable from civilians. Some have alleged that members of the Taliban would wear black turbans, but apparently this was done by coincidence rather than design. Indeed, there is no indication that black turbans were systematically worn to serve as an identifying feature of the armed group.

Some of the Taliban militia carried a tribal flag. DoD has stated that there is no indication that any individual members of the Taliban wore a distinctive sign or insignia that would identify them if they were not carrying or otherwise immediately identified with a tribal flag. Moreover, DoD has not indicated that tribal flags marked only military, as opposed to civilian, groups.

Third, the Taliban militia carried arms openly. This fact, however, is of little significance because many people in Afghanistan carry arms openly. Although Taliban forces did not generally conceal their weapons, they also never attempted to distinguish themselves from other individuals through the arms they carried or the manner in which they carried them. Thus, the Taliban carried their arms openly, as GPW requires military groups to do, but this did not serve to distinguish the Taliban from the rest of the population. This fact reinforces the idea that the Taliban could neither be distinguished by their uniforms and insignia nor by the arms they carried from Afghani civilians.

Finally, there is no indication that the Taliban militia understood, considered themselves bound by, or indeed were even aware of, the Geneva Conventions or any other body of law. Indeed, it is fundamental that the Taliban followed their own version of Islamic law and regularly engaged in practices that flouted fundamental international legal principles. Taliban militia groups have made little attempt to distinguish between combatants and non-combatants when engaging in hostilities. They have killed for racial or religious purposes. Furthermore, DoD informs us of widespread reports of Taliban massacres of civilians, raping of women, pillaging of villages, and various other atrocities that plainly violate the laws of war.

Based on the above facts, apparently well known to all persons living in Afghanistan and joining the Taliban, we conclude that the President can find that the Taliban militia is categorically incapable of meeting the Hague conditions expressly spelled out in Article 4(A)(2) of GPW.

III.

One might argue that the Taliban is not a "militia" under Article 4(A)(2), but instead constitutes the "armed forces" of Afghanistan. Neither Article 4(A)(1), which grants POW status to members of the armed forces of a state party, nor Article 4(A)(3), which grants POW status to the armed forces of an unrecognized power, defines the term "armed forces." Unlike the definition of militia in Article 4(A)(2), these two other categories contain no conditions that these groups must fulfill to achieve POW status. Moreover, because GPW does not expressly incorporate Article 4(A)(2)'s four conditions into either Article 4(A)(1) or (3), some might question whether members of regular armed forces need to meet the Hague conditions in order to qualify for POW status under GPW.

We conclude, however, that the four basic conditions that apply to militias must also apply, at a minimum, to members of armed forces who would be legally entitled to POW status. In other words, an individual cannot be a POW, even if a member of an armed force, unless forces also are: (a) "commanded by a person responsible for his subordinates"; (b) "hav[e] a fixed distinctive sign recognizable at a distance"; (c) "carry[] arms openly"; and (d) "conduct[] their operations in accordance with the laws and customs of war." Thus, if the President has the factual basis to determine that Taliban prisoners are not entitled to POW status under Article 4(A)(2) as members of a militia, he therefore has the grounds to also find that they are not entitled to POW status as members of an armed force under either Article 4(A)(1) or Article 4(A)(3).

Article 4(A)'s use of the phrase "armed force," we believe, incorporated by reference the four conditions for militia, which originally derived from the Hague

Convention IV. There was no need to list the four Hague conditions in Article 4(A)(1) because it was well understood under preexisting international law that all armed forces were already required to meet those conditions. As would have been understood by the GPW's drafters, use of the term "armed forces" incorporated the four criteria, repeated in the definition of militia, that were first used in the Hague Convention IV.

The view that the definition of an armed force includes the four criteria outlined in Hague Convention IV and repeated in GPW is amply supported by commentators. As explained in a recently-issued Department of the Army pamphlet, the four Hague conditions are "arguably part and parcel of the definition of a regular armed force. It is unreasonable to believe that a member of a regular armed force could conduct military operations in civilian clothing, while a member of the militia or resistance groups cannot. Should a member of the regular armed forces do so, it is likely that he would lose his claim to immunity and be charged as a spy or as an illegal combatant." Major Geoffrey S. Corn & Major Michael L. Smidt, *"To Be Or Not To Be, That Is The Question": Contemporary Military Operations and the Status of Captured Personnel*, Department of the Army Pamphlet 27-50-319, 1999-Jun. Army Law. 1, 14 n.127 (1999). One scholar has similarly concluded that "[u]nder the Hague Convention, a person is a member of the armed forces of a state only if he satisfies the [four enumerated] criteria." Gregory M. Travalio, *Terrorism, International Law, and the Use of Military Force*, 18 Wis. Int'l L.J. 145, 184 n.140 (2000). *See also* Michael N. Schmitt, *Bellum Americanum: The U.S. View of Twenty-First Century War and Its Possible Implications For the Law of Armed Conflict*, 19 Mich. J. Int'l L. 1051, 1078 (1998) ("[U]nder the Regulations annexed to Hague Convention IV, combatants were those who were members of the regular armed forces (or formal militia), were commanded by a person responsible for their conduct, wore a fixed distinctive emblem (or uniform), carried their weapons openly, and conducted operations in accordance with the law of war. The 1949 Geneva Convention on Prisoners of War extended this status to members of an organized resistance movement which otherwise complied with the Hague IV requirements.").

Further, it would be utterly illogical to read "armed forces" in Article 4(A)(1) and (3) as somehow relieving members of armed forces from the same POW requirements imposed on members of a militia. There is no evidence that any of the GPW's drafters or ratifiers believed that members of the regular armed forces ought to be governed by *lower standards* in their conduct of warfare than those applicable to militia and volunteer forces. Otherwise, a sovereign could evade the Hague requirements altogether simply by designating all combatants as members of the sovereign's regular armed forces. A sovereign, for example, could evade the status of spies as unlawful combatants simply by declaring all spies to be members of the regular armed forces, regardless of whether they wore uniforms or not. Further, it would make little sense to construe GPW to deny some members of militias or volunteer corps POW protection for failure to satisfy the Hague conditions (under Article 4(A)(2)), while conferring such status upon other members simply because they have become part of the regular armed forces of a party (under Article 4(A)(1)).

This interpretation of "armed force" in GPW finds direct support in the International Committee of the Red Cross, the non-governmental organization primarily responsible for, and most closely associated with, the drafting and successful completion of GPW. After the Conventions were established, the Committee started work on a Commentary on all of the Geneva Conventions. In its discussion of Article 4(A)(3) of GPW, the ICRC construed both Article 4(A)(1) and (3) to require all regular armed forces to satisfy the four Hague IV (and Article 4(A)(2)) conditions:

> [t]he expression "members of regular armed forces" denotes armed forces which differ from those referred to in sub-paragraph (1) of this paragraph in one respect only: the authority to which they profess allegiance is not recognized by the adversary as a Party to the conflict. These "regular armed forces" have all the material characteristics and all the attributes of armed forces in the sense of sub-paragraph (1): they wear uniform, they have an organized hierarchy and they know and respect the laws and customs of war. The delegates to the 1949 Diplomatic Conference were therefore fully justified in considering that there was no need to specify for such armed forces the requirements stated in sub-paragraph (2) (a), (b), (c) and (d).

Red Cross Commentary at 62-63 (emphasis added).

Numerous scholars have similarly interpreted GPW as applying the four conditions to Article 4(A)(1) and (3) as well as to Article 4(A)(2). As Professor Howard S. Levie, a leading expert on the laws of war and the Geneva Conventions in particular, has explained in his authoritative treatise:

> This enumeration [of the four conditions] does not appear in subparagraph 1, dealing with the regular armed forces. This does not mean that mere membership in the regular armed forces will automatically entitle an individual who is captured to prisoner-of-war status if his activities prior to and at the time of capture have not met these requirements. The member of the regular armed forces wearing civilian clothes who is captured while in enemy territory engaged in an espionage or sabotage mission is entitled to no different treatment than that which would be received by a civilian captured under the same circumstances. Any other interpretation would be unrealistic as it would mean that the dangers inherent in serving as a spy or saboteur could be immunized merely by making the individual a member of the armed forces; and that members of the armed forces could act in a manner prohibited by other areas of the law of armed conflict and escape the penalties therefore, still being entitled to prisoner-of-war status.

Howard S. Levie, 59 International Law Studies: Prisoners of War in International Armed Conflict 36-37 (Naval War College 1977). Oxford Professor Ingrid Detter has similarly concluded that, under the 1949 Geneva Conventions, to be a combatant, a person would have to be:

(a) commanded by a person responsible for his subordinates;
(b) having a fixed distinctive sign recognizable at a distance;
(c) carrying arms openly;
(d) conducting their operations in accordance with the laws and customs of war.

The same requirements as apply to irregular forces are presumably also valid for members of regular units. However, this is not clearly spelt out: there is no textual support for the idea that members of regular armed forces should wear uniform. On the other hand, there is ample evidence that this is a rule of law which has been applied to a number of situations to ascertain the status of a person. Any regular soldier who commits acts pertaining to belligerence in civilian clothes loses his privileges and is no longer a lawful combatant. "Unlawful" combatants may thus be either members of the regular forces or members of resistance or guerilla movements who do not fulfil the conditions of lawful combatants.

Ingrid Detter, The Law of War 136-37 *(Cambridge 2d ed. 2000)*. See also Christopher C. Burris, *The Prisoner of War Status of PLO Fedayeen*, 22 N.C. J. Int'l L. & Com. Reg. 943, 987 n.308 (1997) ("I am using Article 4A(2)'s four criteria because the armed forces of the Palestinian Authority, over 30,000 men under arms organized into roughly ten or more separate para-military units, are more characteristic of militia units than the regular armed forces of a state. This is because these units are organized as police/security units, not exclusive combat units. See Graham Usher, Palestinian Authority, Israeli Rule, The Nation, Feb. 5, 1996, at 15, 16. Whether the Palestinian Authority's forces are considered militia or members of the armed forces, they still must fulfill Article 4A(2)'s four criteria.").[1]

Therefore, it is clear that the term "armed force" includes the four conditions first identified by Hague Convention IV and expressly applied by GPW to militia groups. In other words, in order to be entitled to POW status, a member of an armed force must (a) be "commanded by a person responsible for his subordinates"; (b) "hav[e] a fixed distinctive sign recognizable at a distance"; (c) "carry[] arms openly"; and (d) "conduct[] their operations in accordance with the laws and customs of war." We believe that the President, based on the facts supplied by DoD, has ample grounds upon which to find that members of the Taliban have failed to meet three of these four criteria, regardless of whether they are characterized as members of a "militia" or of an "armed force." The President, therefore, may determine that the Taliban, as a group, are not entitled to POW status under GPW.

IV.

Under Article 5 of GPW, "[s]hould any doubt arise as to whether persons . . . belong to any of the categories enumerated in Article 4, such persons shall enjoy the protection of the present Convention until such time as their status has been determined by a competent tribunal." As we understand it, DoD in the past has presumed prisoners to be entitled to POW status until a tribunal determines otherwise. The presumption and tribunal requirement are triggered, however, only if there is "any doubt" as to a prisoner's Article 4 status.

Under Article II of the Constitution, the President possesses the power to interpret treaties on behalf of the Nation.[2] We conclude, in light of the facts submitted to us by the Department of Defense and as discussed in Parts II and III of this memorandum, that the President could reasonably interpret GPW in such a manner that none of the Taliban forces fall within the legal definition of POWs as defined by Article 4. A presidential determination of this nature would eliminate any legal "doubt" as to the prisoners' status, as a matter of domestic law, and would therefore obviate the need for Article 5 tribunals.

This approach is also consistent with the terms of Article 5. As the International Committee of the Red Cross has explained, the "competent tribunal" requirement of Article 5 applies "to cases of doubt as to whether persons having committed a belligerent act and having fallen into the hands of the enemy belong to any of the categories enumerated in Article 4." *Red Cross Commentary* at 77. Tribunals are thus designed to determine whether a particular set of facts falls within one of the Article 4 categories; they are not intended to be used to resolve the proper interpretation of those categories. The President, in other words, may use his constitutional power to interpret treaties and apply them to the facts, to make the determination that the Taliban are unlawful combatants. This would remove any "doubt" concerning whether members of the Taliban are entitled to POW status.

We therefore conclude that there is no need to establish tribunals to determine POW status under Article 5.

Please let us know if we can provide further assistance.

[signed]

Jay S. Bybee
Assistant Attorney General

NOTES

1. The only federal court we are aware of that has addressed this issue denied Article 4(A)(3) status to defendants because they could not satisfy the Hague conditions. In *United States v. Buck*, 690 F. Supp. 1291 (S.D.N.Y. 1988), the defendants claimed that they were entitled to POW status as military officers of the Republic of New Afrika, "a sovereign nation engaged in a war of liberation against the colonial forces of the United States government." *Id.* at 1293. That nation, it was contended, included "all people of African ancestry living in the United States." *Id.* at

1296. The court refused to extend POW status to the defendants. After determining that GPW did not apply at all due to the absence of an armed conflict as understood under Article 2, the court alternatively reasoned that the defendants could not satisfy any of the requirements of Article 4. *See id.* at 1298 (stating that, even if GPW applied, "it is entirely clear that these defendants would not fall within Article 4, upon which they initially relied"). The court first concluded that the defendants failed to meet the four Hague conditions expressly spelled out in Article 4(A)(2). The court then rejected POW status under Article 4(A)(3) "[f]or comparable reasons":

> Article 4(A)(2) requires that to qualify as prisoners of war, members of "organized resistance movements" must fulfill the conditions of command by a person responsible for his subordinates; having a fixed distinctive sign recognizable at a distance; carrying arms openly; and conducting their operations in accordance with the laws and customs of war. The defendants at bar and their associates cannot pretend to have fulfilled those conditions. *For comparable reasons*, Article 4(3)'s reference to members of "regular armed forces who profess allegiance to a government or an authority not recognized by the Detaining Power," also relied upon by defendants, does not apply to the circumstances of this case.

Id. (emphasis added). The court reached this conclusion even though the Hague conditions are not explicitly spelled out in Article 4(A)(3). Nothing in the court's discussion suggests that it would have construed Article 4(A)(1) any differently.

2. *See* Memorandum for John Bellinger, III, Senior Associate Counsel and Legal Adviser to the National Security Council, from John C. Yoo, Deputy Assistant Attorney General and Robert J. Delahunty, Special Counsel, Office of Legal Counsel, *Re: Authority of the President to Suspend Certain Provisions of the ABM Treaty* (Nov. 15, 2001).

7

THE WHITE HOUSE
WASHINGTON

February 7, 2002

MEMORANDUM FOR THE VICE PRESIDENT
THE SECRETARY OF STATE
THE SECRETARY OF DEFENSE
THE ATTORNEY GENERAL
CHIEF OF STAFF TO THE PRESIDENT
DIRECTOR OF CENTRAL INTELLIGENCE
ASSISTANT TO THE PRESIDENT FOR
NATIONAL SECURITY AFFAIRS
CHAIRMAN OF THE JOINT CHIEFS OF STAFF

SUBJECT: Humane Treatment of al Qaeda and Taliban Detainees

1. Our recent extensive discussions regarding the status of al Qaeda and Taliban detainees confirm that the application of the Geneva Convention Relative to the Treatment of Prisoners of War of August 12, 1949 (Geneva) to the conflict with al Qaeda and the Taliban involves complex legal questions. By its terms, Geneva applies to conflicts involving "High Contracting Parties," which can only be states. Moreover, it assumes the existence of "regular" armed forces fighting on behalf of states. However, the war against terrorism ushers in a new paradigm, one in which groups with broad, international reach commit horrific acts against innocent civilians, sometimes with the direct support of states. Our Nation recognizes that this new paradigm— ushered in not by us, but by terrorists—requires new thinking in the law of war, but thinking that should nevertheless be consistent with the principles of Geneva.

2. Pursuant to my authority as Commander in Chief and Chief Executive of the United States, and relying on the opinion of the Department of Justice dated January 22, 2002, and on the legal opinion rendered by the Attorney General in his letter of February 1, 2002, I hereby determine as follows:

   a. I accept the legal conclusion of the Department of Justice and determine that none of the provisions of Geneva apply to our conflict with al Qaeda in Afghanistan or elsewhere throughout the world because, among other reasons, al Qaeda is not a High Contracting Party to Geneva.

   b. I accept the legal conclusion of the Attorney General and the Department of Justice that I have the authority under the Constitution to suspend Geneva as between the United States and Afghanistan, but I decline to exercise that authority at this time. Accordingly, I determine that the provisions of Geneva will apply to our present conflict with the Taliban. I reserve the right to exercise this authority in this or future conflicts.

   c. I also accept the legal conclusion of the Department of Justice and determine that common Article 3 of Geneva does not apply to either al Qaeda or Taliban detainees, because, among other reasons, the relevant conflicts are international in scope and common Article 3 applies only to "armed conflict not of an international character."

   d. Based on the facts supplied by the Department of Defense and the recommendation of the Department of Justice, I determine that the Taliban detainees are unlawful combatants and, therefore, do not qualify as prisoners of war under Article 4 of Geneva. I note that, because Geneva does not apply to our conflict with al Qaeda, al Qaeda detainees also do not qualify as prisoners of war.

3. Of course, our values as a Nation, values that we share with many nations in the world, call for us to treat detainees humanely, including those who are not legally entitled to such treatment. Our Nation has been and will continue to be a strong supporter of Geneva and its principles. As a matter of policy, the United States Armed Forces shall continue to treat detainees humanely and, to the extent appropriate and consistent with military necessity, in a manner consistent with the principles of Geneva.

4. The United States will hold states, organizations, and individuals who gain control of United States personnel responsible for treating such personnel humanely and consistent with applicable law.

5. I hereby reaffirm the order previously issued by the Secretary of Defense to the United States Armed Forces requiring that the detainees be treated humanely and, to the extent appropriate and consistent with military necessity, in a manner consistent with the principles of Geneva.

6. I hereby direct the Secretary of State to communicate my determinations in an appropriate manner to our allies, and other countries and international organizations cooperating in the war against terrorism of global reach.

NSC DECLASSIFICATION REVIEW [E.O. 12958 as amended]
DECLASSIFIED IN FULL ON 6/17/2004
by R. Soubers
Reason: 1.5 (d)
Declassify on: 02/07/12

[signed]

George Bush

WHAT IS TORTURE?:
THE DEBATE OVER INTERROGATION

I

U.S. Department of Justice
Office of Legal Counsel

Office of the
Deputy Assistant Attorney General   Washington, D.C. 20530

August 1, 2002

The Honorable Alberto R. Gonzales
Counsel to the President
The White House
Washington, D.C.

Dear Judge Gonzales:

You have requested the views of our Office concerning the legality, under international law, of interrogation methods to be used during the current war on terrorism. More specifically, you have asked whether interrogation methods used on captured al Qaeda operatives, which do not violate the prohibition on torture found in 18 U.S.C. § 2340–2340A, would either: a) violate our obligations under the Torture Convention,[1] or b) create the basis for a prosecution under the Rome Statute establishing the International Criminal Court (ICC).[2] We believe that interrogation methods that comply with § 2340 would not violate our international obligations under the Torture Convention, because of a specific understanding attached by the United States to its instrument of ratification. We also conclude that actions taken as part of the interrogation of al Qaeda operatives cannot fall within the jurisdiction of the ICC, although it would be impossible to control the actions of a rogue prosecutor or judge. This letter summarizes our views; a memorandum opinion will follow that will more fully explain our reasoning.

I.

Section 2340A makes it a criminal offense for any person "outside the United States [to] commit[] or attempt[] to commit torture."[3] The act of torture is defined as an:

> act committed by a person acting under the color of law specifically intended to inflict severe physical or mental pain or suffering (other than pain or suffering incidental to lawful sanctions) upon another person within his custody or physical control.

18 U.S.C.A. § 2340(1); *see id.* § 2340A. Thus, to convict a defendant of torture, the prosecution must establish that: (1) the torture occurred outside the United States; (2) the defendant acted under the color of law; (3) the victim was within the defendant's custody or physical control; (4) the defendant specifically intended to cause severe physical or mental pain or suffering; and (5) that the act inflicted severe physical or mental pain or suffering. *See also* S. Exec. Rep. No. 101–30, at 6 (1990) ("For an act to be 'torture,' it must...cause severe pain and suffering, and be intended to cause severe pain and suffering."). As we have explained elsewhere, in order to violate the statute a defendant must have specific intention to inflict severe pain or suffering—in other words, "the infliction of such pain must be the defendant's precise objective." See Memorandum for Alberto R. Gonzales, Counsel to the President, from: Jay S. Bybee, Assistant Attorney General, Office of Legal Counsel, *Re: Standards of Conduct for Interrogation under 18 U.S.C. §§ 2340–2340A* at 3 (August 1, 2002).

Section 2340 further defines "severe mental pain or suffering" as:

the prolonged mental harm caused by or resulting from—

(A) the intentional infliction or threatened infliction of severe physical pain or suffering;

(B) the administration or application, or threatened administration or application, of mind-altering substances or other procedures calculated to disrupt profoundly the senses or the personality;

(C) the threat of imminent death; or

(D) the threat that another person will imminently be subjected to death, severe physical pain or suffering, or the administration or application of mind-altering substances or other procedures calculated to disrupt profoundly the senses or personality.

18 U.S.C. § 2340(2). As we have explained, in order to inflict severe mental or suffering, a defendant both must commit one of the four predicate acts, such as threatening imminent death, and intend to cause "prolonged mental harm."

II.

You have asked whether interrogation methods used on al Qaeda operatives that comply with 18 U.S.C. §§ 2340–2340A nevertheless could violate the United States' obligations under the Torture Convention. The Torture Convention defines torture as:

any act by which *severe* pain or suffering, whether physical or mental, is intentionally inflicted on a person for such purposes as obtaining from him or a third person information or a confession, punishing him for an act he or a third person has committed or is suspected of having committed, or intimidating or coercing him or a third person, or for any reason based on discrimination of any kind, when such pain or suffering is inflicted by or at the instigation of or with the consent or acquiescence of a public official or other person acting in an official capacity.

Article 1(1) (emphasis added).

Despite the apparent differences in language between the Convention and § 2340, international law clearly could not hold the United States to an obligation different than that expressed in § 2340. When it acceded to the Convention, the United States attached to its instrument of ratification a clear understanding that defined torture in the exact terms used by § 2340. The first Bush administration submitted the following understanding of the treaty:

> The United States understands that, in order to constitute torture, an act must be *specifically intended* to inflict severe physical or mental pain or suffering and that mental pain or suffering refers to prolonged mental pain caused by or resulting from (1) the intentional infliction or threatened infliction of severe physical pain or suffering; (2) administration or application, or threatened administration or application, of mind altering substances or other procedures calculated to disrupt profoundly the senses or the personality; (3) the threat of imminent death; or (4) the threat that another person will imminently be subjected to death, severe physical pain or suffering, or the administration or application of mind-altering substances or other procedures calculated to disrupt profoundly the senses or personality.

S. Exec. Rep. No. 101–30, at 36. The Senate approved the Convention based on this understanding, and the United States included the understanding in its instrument of ratification.[4]

This understanding accomplished two things. First, it made crystal clear that the intent requirement for torture was specific intent. By its terms, the Torture Convention might be read to require only general intent although we believe the better argument is that that the Convention's use of the phrase "intentionally inflicted" also created a specific intent-type standard. Second, it added form and substance to the otherwise amorphous concept of *mental* pain or suffering. In so doing, this understanding ensured that mental torture would rise to a severity comparable to that required in the context of physical torture.

It is one of the core principles of international law that in treaty relations a nation is not bound without its consent. Under international law, a reservation made when ratifying a treaty validly alters or modifies the treaty obligation, subject to certain conditions that will be discussed below. Vienna Convention on the Law of Treaties, May 23, 1969, 1155 U.N.T.S. 331 (entered into force Jan. 27, 1980); 1 Restatement of the

Law (Third) of the Foreign Relations Law of the United States § 313 (1987).[5] The right to enter reservations applies to multilateral international agreements just as in the more familiar context of bilateral agreements. *Id.* Under international law, therefore, the United States thus is bound only by the text of the Torture Convention as modified by the first Bush administration's understanding.[6] As is obvious from its text, Congress codified the understanding almost verbatim when it enacted § 2340. The United States' obligation under the Torture Convention is thus identical to the standard set by § 2340. Conduct that does not violate the latter does not violate the former. Put another way, so long as the interrogation methods do not violate § 2340, they also do not violate our international obligations under the Torture Convention.

Although the Vienna Convention on Treaties recognizes several exceptions to the right to make reservations, none of them apply here.[7] First, a reservation is valid and effective unless it purports to defeat the object and purpose of the treaty. Vienna Convention, art. 19. Our initial research indicates that international law has provided little guidance regarding the meaning of the "object and purpose" test. Nonetheless, it is clear that here the United States had not defeated the object and purpose of the Torture Convention. The United States nowhere reserved the right to conduct torture; in fact, it enacted Section 2340 to expand the prohibition on torture in its domestic criminal law. Rather than defeat the object of the Torture Convention, the United States simply accepted its prohibition and attempted, through the Bush administration's understanding, to make clear the scope and meaning of the treaty's obligations.

Second, a treaty reservation will not be valid if the treaty itself prohibits states from taking reservations. The Torture Convention nowhere prohibits state parties from entering reservations. To be sure, two provisions of the Torture Convention—the competence of the Committee Against Torture, art. 28, and the mandatory jurisdction of the International Court of Justice, art. 30—specifically note that nations may take reservations from their terms. Nonetheless, the Convention contains no provision that explicitly attempts to preclude states from exercising their basic right under international law to enter reservations to other provisions. Without such a provision, we do not believe that the Torture Convention precludes reservations.

Third, in regard to multilateral agreements, a treaty reservation may not be valid if it is objected to in a timely manner by other states. Vienna Convention art. 20. If another state does not object within a certain period of time, it is deemed to have acquiesced in the reservation. Even if, however, another nation objects, that only means that the provision of the treaty to which the reservation applies is not in force between the two nations—unless the objecting nation opposes entry into force of the treaty as a whole between the two nations. *Id.* art 21(3). Here, no nation appears to have objected to the United States' further definition of torture. Only one nation, Germany, appears to have commented on the United States' reservations, and even Germany did not oppose any U.S. reservation outright.

Thus, we conclude that the Bush administration's understanding created a valid and effective reservation to the Torture Convention. Even if it were otherwise, there is no international court to review the conduct of the United States under the Convention. In an additional reservation, the United States refused to accept the jurisdiction of the ICJ (which, in any event, could hear only a case brought by another state, not by an individual) to adjudicate cases under the Convention. Although the Convention creates a Committee to monitor compliance, it can only conduct studies and has no enforcement powers.

III.

You have also asked whether interrogations of al Qaeda operatives could be subject to criminal investigation and prosecution by the ICC. We believe that the ICC cannot take action based on such interrogations.

First, as noted earlier, one of the most established principles of international law is that a state cannot be bound by treaties to which it has not consented. Although President Clinton signed the Rome Statute, the United States has withdrawn its signature from the agreement before submitting it to the Senate for advice and consent—effectively terminating it. The United States, therefore, cannot be bound by the provisions of the ICC Treaty nor can U.S. nationals be subject to ICC prosecution. We acknowledge, however, that the binding nature of the ICC treaty on non-parties is a complicated issue and do not attempt to definitively answer it here.

Second, even if the ICC could in some way act upon the United States and its citizens, interrogation of an al Qaeda operative could not constitute a crime under the Rome Statute. Even if certain interrogation methods being contemplated amounted to torture (and we have no facts that indicate that they would), the Rome Statute makes torture a crime subject to the ICC's jurisdiction in only two contexts. Under article 7 of the Rome Statute, torture may fall under the ICC's jurisdiction as a crime against humanity if it is committed as "part of a widespread and systematic attack directed against any civilian population." Here, however, the interrogation of al Qaeda operatives is not occurring as part of such an attack. The United States' campaign against al Qaeda is an attack on a non-state terrorist organization, not a civilian population. If anything, the interrogations are taking place to elicit information that could prevent attacks on civilian populations.

Under article 8 of the Rome statute, torture can fall within the ICC's jurisdiction as a war crime. In order to constitute a war crime, torture must be committed against "persons or property protected under the provisions of the relevant Geneva Conventions." Rome Statute, art. 8. On February 27, 2002, the President determined that neither members of the al Qaeda terrorist network nor Taliban soldiers were entitled to the legal status of prisoners of war under the Convention Relative to the Treatment of Prisoners of War, 6 U.S.T. 3517 ("GPW"). As we have explained elsewhere, members of al Qaeda cannot receive the protections accorded to POWs under GPW because al Qaeda is a non-state terrorist organization that has not signed the Conventions. Memorandum for Alberto R. Gonzales, Counsel to the President and William J. Haynes, II, General Counsel, Department of Defense, from Jay S. Bybee, Assistant Attorney General, Office of Legal Counsel, *Re: Application of Treaties and Laws to al Qaeda and Taliban Detainees* at 8 (Jan. 22, 2002). The President has appropriately determined that al Qaeda members are not POWs under the GPW, but rather are illegal combatants, who are not entitled to the protections of any of the Geneva Conventions. Interrogation of al Qaeda members, therefore, cannot constitute a war crime because article 8 of the Rome Statute applies only to those protected by the Geneva Conventions.

We cannot guarantee, however, that the ICC would decline to investigate and prosecute interrogations of al Qaeda members. By the terms of the Rome Statute, the ICC is not checked by any other international body, not to mention any democratically-elected or accountable one. Indeed, recent events indicate that some nations even believe that the ICC is not subject to the authority of the United Nations Security Council. It is possible that an ICC official would ignore the clear limitations imposed by the Rome Statute, or at least disagree with the President's interpretation of GPW. Of course, the problem of the "rogue prosecutor" is not limited to questions about the interrogation of al Qaeda operatives, but is a potential risk for any number of actions that have been undertaken during the Afghanistan campaign, such as the collateral loss of civilian life in the bombing of legitimate military targets. Our Office can only provide the best reading of international law on the merits. We cannot predict the political actions of international institutions.

Please let us know if we can be of further assistance.

Sincerely,

[signed]

John C. Yoo
Deputy Assistant Attorney General

NOTES

1. Convention Against Torture and Other Cruel, Inhuman or Degrading Treatment or Punishment, adopted Dec. 10, 1984, S. Treaty Doc. No. 100-20 (1988), 1465 U.N.T.S. 85 (entered into force June 26, 1987)

2 U.N. Doc. A/CONF. 183/9 (1998), reprinted in 37 I.L.M. 999 (1998) [hereinafter ICC Statute].

3. If convicted of torture, a defendant faces a fine or up to twenty years' imprisonment or

both. If, however, the act resulted in the victim's death, a defendant may be sentenced to life imprisonment or to death. *See* 18 U.S.C.A. § 2340A(a). Whether death results from the act also affects the applicable statute of limitations. Where death does not result, the statute of limitations is eight years; if death results, there is no statute of limitations. *See* 18 U.S.C.A. § 3286(b) (West Supp. 2002); *id.* § 2332b(g)(5)(B) (West Supp. 2002). Section 2340A as originally enacted did not provide for the death penalty as a punishment. *See* Omnibus Crime Bill, Pub. L. No. 103-322, Title VI, Section 60020, 108 Stat. 1979 (1994) (amending section 2340A to provide for the death penalty); H. R. Conf. Rep. No. 103-711, at 388 (1994) (noting that the act added the death penalty as a penalty for torture).

Most recently, the USA Patriot Act, Pub. L. No. 107-56, 115 Stat. 272 (2001), amended section 2340A to expressly codify the offense of conspiracy to commit torture. Congress enacted this amendment as part of a broader effort to ensure that individuals engaged in the planning of terrorist activities could be prosecuted irrespective of where the activities took place. See H. R. Rep. No. 107-236, at 70 (2001) (discussing the addition of "conspiracy" as a separate offense for a variety of "Federal terrorism offense[s]").

4. See http://www.un.org/Depts/Treaty/final/ts2/newfiles/part_boo/iv_boo/iv_9.html.

5. Although, under domestic law, the Bush administration's definition of torture was categorized as an "understanding," it was deposited with the instrument of ratification as a condition of the United States' ratification, and so under international law we consider it to be a reservation if it indeed modifies the Torture Convention standard. See Restatement (Third) at § 313 cmt. g.

6. Further, if we are correct in our suggestion that the Torture Convention itself creates a heightened intent standard, then the understanding attached by the Bush Administration is less a modification of the Convention's obligations and more of an explanation of how the United States would implement its somewhat ambiguous terms.

7. It should be noted that the United States is not a signatory to the Vienna Convention, although it has said that it considers some of its provisions to be customary international law.

2

U.S. Department of Justice
Office of Legal Counsel

Office of the Assistant Attorney General   Washington, D.C. 20530

August 1, 2002

Memorandum for Alberto R. Gonzales
Counsel to the President

*Re: Standards of Conduct for Interrogation under
18 U.S.C. §§ 2340–2340A*

You have asked for our Office's views regarding the standards of conduct under the Convention Against Torture and Other Cruel, Inhuman and Degrading Treatment or Punishment as implemented by Sections 2340– 2340A of title 18 of the United States Code. As we understand it, this question has arisen in the context of the conduct of interrogations outside of the United States. We conclude below that Section 2340A proscribes acts inflicting, and that are specifically intended to inflict, severe pain or suffering, whether mental or physical. Those acts must be of an extreme nature to rise to the level of torture within the meaning of Section 2340A and the Convention. We further conclude that certain acts may be cruel, inhuman, or degrading, but still not produce pain and suffering of the requisite intensity to fall within Section 2340A's proscription against torture. We conclude by examining possible defenses that would negate any claim that certain interrogation methods violate the statute.

In Part I, we examine the criminal statute's text and history. We conclude that for an act to constitute torture as defined in Section 2340, it must inflict pain that is difficult to endure. Physical pain amounting to torture must be equivalent in intensity to the pain accompanying serious physical injury, such as organ failure, impairment of bodily function, or even death. For purely mental pain or suffering to amount to torture under Section 2340, it must result in significant psychological harm of significant duration, e.g., lasting for months or even years. We conclude that the mental harm also must result from one of the predicate acts listed in the statute, namely: threats of imminent death; threats of infliction of the kind of pain that would amount to physical torture; infliction of such physical pain as a means of psychological torture; use of drugs or other procedures designed to deeply disrupt the senses, or fundamentally alter an individual's personality; or threatening to do any of these things to a third party. The legislative history simply reveals that Congress intended for the statute's definition to track the Convention's definition of torture and the reservations, understandings, and declarations that the United States submitted with its ratification. We conclude that the statute, taken as a whole, makes plain that it prohibits only extreme acts.

In Part II, we examine the text, ratification history, and negotiating history of the Torture Convention. We conclude that the treaty's text prohibits only the most extreme acts by reserving criminal penalties solely for torture and declining to require such penalties for "cruel, inhuman, or degrading treatment or punishment." This confirms our view that the criminal statute penalizes only the most egregious conduct. Executive branch interpretations and representations to the Senate at the time of ratification further confirm that the treaty was intended to reach only the most extreme conduct.

In Part III, we analyze the jurisprudence of the Torture Victims Protection Act, 28 U.S.C. § 1350 note (2000), which provides civil remedies for torture victims, to predict the standards that courts might follow in determining what actions reach the threshold of torture in the criminal context. We conclude from these cases that courts are likely to take a totality-of-the-circumstances approach, and will look to an entire course of conduct, to determine whether certain acts will violate Section 2340A. Moreover, these cases demonstrate that most often torture involves cruel and extreme physical pain. In Part IV, we examine international decisions regarding the use of sensory deprivation techniques. These cases make clear that while many of these techniques may amount to cruel, inhuman or degrading treatment, they do not produce pain or suffering of the necessary intensity to meet the definition of torture. From these decisions, we conclude that there is a wide range of such techniques that will not rise to the level of torture.

In Part V, we discuss whether Section 2340A may be unconstitutional if applied to interrogations undertaken of enemy combatants pursuant to the President's Commander-in-Chief powers. We find that in the circumstances of the current war against al Qaeda and its allies, prosecution under Section 2340A may be barred because enforcement of the statute would represent an unconstitutional infringement of the President's authority to conduct war. In Part VI, we discuss defenses to an allegation that an interrogation method might violate the statute. We conclude that, under the current circumstances, necessity or self-defense may justify interrogation methods that might violate Section 2340A.

I. 18 U.S.C. §§ 2340–2340A

Section 2340A makes it a criminal offense for any person "outside the United States [to] commit[] or attempt[] to commit torture."[1] Section 2340 defines the act of torture as an:

> act committed by a person acting under the color of law specifically intended to inflict severe physical or mental pain or suffering (other than pain or suffering incidental to lawful sanctions) upon another person within his custody or physical control.

18 U.S.C.A. § 2340(1); *see id.* § 2340A. Thus, to convict a defendant of torture, the prosecution must establish that: (1) the torture occurred outside the United States; (2) the defendant acted under the color of law; (3) the victim was within the defendant's custody or physical control; (4) the defendant specifically intended to cause severe physical or mental pain or suffering; and (5) that the act inflicted severe physical or mental pain or suffering. *See also* S. Exec. Rep. No. 101–30, at 6 (1990) ("For an act to be 'torture,' it must . . . cause severe pain and suffering, and be intended to cause severe pain and suffering."). You have asked us to address only the elements of specific intent and the infliction of severe pain or suffering. As such, we have not addressed the elements of "outside the United States," "color of law," and "custody or control."[2] At your request, we would be happy to address these elements in a separate memorandum.

A. "Specifically Intended"

To violate Section 2340A, the statute requires that severe pain and suffering must be inflicted with specific intent. *See* 18 U.S.C. § 2340(1). In order for a defendant to have acted with specific intent, he must expressly intend to achieve the forbidden act. *See United States v. Carter*, 530 U.S. 255, 269 (2000); Black's Law Dictionary at 814 (7th ed. 1999) (defining specific intent as "[t]he intent to accomplish the precise criminal act that one is later charged with"). For example, in *Ratzlaf v. United States*, 510 U.S. 135, 141 (1994), the statute at issue was construed to require that the defendant act with the "specific intent to commit the crime." (Internal quotation marks and citation omitted.) As a result, the defendant had to act with the express "purpose to disobey the law" in order for the *mens rea* element to be satisfied. *Ibid.* (internal quotation marks and citation omitted).

Here, because Section 2340 requires that a defendant act with the specific intent to inflict severe pain, the infliction of such pain must be the defendant's precise objective. If the statute had required only general intent, it would be sufficient to establish guilt by showing that the defendant "possessed knowledge with respect to the *actus reus* of the crime." *Carter*, 530 U.S. at 268. If the defendant acted knowing that severe pain or suffering was reasonably likely to result from his actions, but no more, he would have acted only with general intent. *See id.* at 269; Black's Law Dictionary 813 (7th ed. 1999) (explaining that general intent "usu[ally] takes the form of recklessness (involving actual awareness of a risk and the culpable taking of that risk) or negligence (involving blameworthy inadvertence)"). The Supreme Court has used the following example to illustrate the difference between these two mental states:

> [A] person entered a bank and took money from a teller at gunpoint, but deliberately failed to make a quick getaway from the bank in the hope of being arrested so that he would be returned to prison and treated for alcoholism. Though this defendant knowingly engaged in the acts of using force and taking money (satisfying "general intent"), he did not intend permanently to deprive the bank of its possession of the money (failing to satisfy "specific intent").

Carter, 530 U.S. at 268 (citing 1 W. LaFave & A. Scott, Substantive Criminal Law §
3.5, at 315 (1986)).

As a theoretical matter, therefore, knowledge alone that a particular result is certain
to occur does not constitute specific intent. As the Supreme Court explained in the
context of murder, "the . . . common law of homicide distinguishes…between a person
who knows that another person will be killed as a result of his conduct and a person
who acts with the specific purpose of taking another's life[.]" *United States v. Bailey*,
444 U.S. 394, 405 (1980). "Put differently, the law distinguishes actions taken
'because of' a given end from actions taken 'in spite of their unintended but foreseen
consequences." *Vacco v. Quill*, 521 U.S. 793, 802–03 (1997). Thus, even if the defendant knows that severe pain will result from his actions, if causing such harm is not his
objective, he lacks the requisite specific intent even though the defendant did not act in
good faith. Instead, a defendant is guilty of torture only if he acts with the express purpose of inflicting severe pain or suffering on a person within his custody or physical
control. While as a theoretical matter such knowledge does not constitute specific intent,
juries are permitted to infer from the factual circumstances that such intent is present.
See, e.g., United States v. Godwin, 272 F.3d 659, 666 (4th Cir. 2001); *United States v.
Karro*, 257 F.3d 112, 118 (2d Cir. 2001); *United States v. Wood*, 207 F.3d 1222, 1232
(10th Cir. 2000); *Henderson v. United States*, 202 F.2d 400, 403 (6th Cir. 1953).
Therefore, when a defendant knows that his actions will produce the prohibited result,
a jury will in all likelihood conclude that the defendant acted with specific intent.

Further, a showing that an individual acted with a good faith belief that his conduct
would not produce the result that the law prohibits negates specific intent. *See, e.g.,
South Atl. Lmtd. Ptrshp. of Tenn. v. Reise*, 218 F.3d 518, 531 (4th Cir. 2002). Where a
defendant acts in good faith, he acts with an honest belief that he has not engaged in
the proscribed conduct. *See Cheek v. United States*, 498 U.S. 192, 202 (1991); *United
States v. Mancuso*, 42 F.3d 836, 837 (4th Cir. 1994). For example, in the context of
mail fraud, if an individual honestly believes that the material transmitted is truthful,
he has not acted with the required intent to deceive or mislead. *See, e.g., United States
v. Sayakhom*, 186 F.3d 928, 939–40 (9th Cir. 1999). A good faith belief need not be a
reasonable one. *See Cheek*, 498 U.S. at 202.

Although a defendant theoretically could hold an unreasonable belief that his acts
would not constitute the actions prohibited by the statute, even though they would as
a certainty produce the prohibited effects, as a matter of practice in the federal criminal justice system it is highly unlikely that a jury would acquit in such a situation.
Where a defendant holds an unreasonable belief, he will confront the problem of proving to the jury that he actually held that belief. As the Supreme Court noted in *Cheek*,
"the more unreasonable the asserted beliefs or misunderstandings are, the more likely
the jury… will find that the Government has carried its burden of proving" intent. *Id.*
at 203–04. As we explained above, a jury will be permitted to infer that the defendant
held the requisite specific intent. As a matter of proof, therefore, a good faith defense
will prove more compelling when a reasonable basis exists for the defendant's belief.

B. "Severe Pain or Suffering"

The key statutory phrase in the definition of torture is the statement that acts amount to torture if they cause "severe physical or mental pain or suffering." In examining the meaning of a statute, its text must be the starting point. *See INS v. Phinpathya*, 464 U.S. 183, 189 (1984) ("This Court has noted on numerous occasions that in all cases involving statutory construction, our starting point must be the language employed by Congress,... and we assume that the legislative purpose is expressed by the ordinary meaning of the words used.") (internal quotations and citations omitted). Section 2340 makes plain that the infliction of pain or suffering per se, whether it is physical or mental, is insufficient to amount to torture. Instead, the text provides that pain or suffering must be "severe." The statute does not, however, define the term "severe." "In the absence of such a definition, we construe a statutory term in accordance with its ordinary or natural meaning." *FDIC v. Meyer*, 510 U.S. 471, 476 (1994). The dictionary defines "severe" as "[u]nsparing in exaction, punishment, or censure" or "[I]nflicting discomfort or pain hard to endure; sharp; afflictive; distressing; violent; extreme; as *severe* pain, anguish, torture." Webster's New International Dictionary 2295 (2d ed. 1935); *see* American Heritage Dictionary of the English Language 1653 (3d ed. 1992) ("extremely violent or grievous: *severe* pain") (emphasis in original); IX The Oxford English Dictionary 572 (1978) ("Of pain, suffering, loss, or the like: Grievous, extreme" and "of circumstances...: hard to sustain or endure"). Thus, the adjective "severe" conveys that the pain or suffering must be of such a high level of intensity that the pain is difficult for the subject to endure.

Congress's use of the phrase "severe pain" elsewhere in the United States Code can shed more light on its meaning. *See, e.g., West Va. Univ. Hosps., Inc. v. Casey*, 499 U.S. 83, 100 (1991) ("[W]e construe [a statutory term] to contain that permissible meaning which fits most logically and comfortably into the body of both previously and subsequently enacted law."). Significantly, the phrase "severe pain" appears in statutes defining an emergency medical condition for the purpose of providing health benefits. *See, e.g.,* 8 U.S.C. § 1369 (2000); 42 U.S.C. § 1395w-22 (2000); *id.* § 1395x (2000); *id.* § 1395dd (2000); *id.* § 1396b (2000); *id.* § 1396u-2 (2000). These statutes define an emergency condition as one "manifesting itself by acute symptoms of sufficient severity (including *severe pain*) such that a prudent lay person, who possesses an average knowledge of health and medicine, could reasonably expect the absence of immediate medical attention to result in—placing the health of the individual... (i) in serious jeopardy, (ii) serious impairment to bodily functions, or (iii) serious dysfunction of any bodily organ or part." *Id.* § 1395w-22(d)(3)(B) (emphasis added). Although these statutes address a substantially different subject from Section 2340, they are nonetheless helpful for understanding what constitutes severe physical pain. They treat severe pain as an indicator of ailments that are likely to result in permanent and serious physical damage in the absence of immediate medical treatment. Such damage must rise to the level of death, organ failure, or the permanent impairment of a significant body function. These statutes suggest that "severe pain," as used in

Section 2340, must rise to a similarly high level—the level that would ordinarily be associated with a sufficiently serious physical condition or injury such as death, organ failure, or serious impairment of body functions—in order to constitute torture.[3]

C. "Severe mental pain or suffering"

Section 2340 gives further guidance as to the meaning of "severe mental pain or suffering," as distinguished from severe physical pain and suffering. The statute defines "severe mental pain or suffering" as:

> the prolonged mental harm caused by or resulting from—
> (A) the intentional infliction or threatened infliction of severe physical pain or suffering;
> (B) the administration or application, or threatened administration or application, of mind-altering substances or other procedures calculated to disrupt profoundly the senses or the personality;
> (C) the threat of imminent death; or
>
> (D) the threat that another person will imminently be subjected to death, severe physical pain or suffering, or the administration or application of mind-altering substances or other procedures calculated to disrupt profoundly the senses or personality.

18 U.S.C. § 2340(2). In order to prove "severe mental pain or suffering," the statute requires proof of "prolonged mental harm" that was caused by or resulted from one of four enumerated acts. We consider each of these elements.

1. "Prolonged Mental Harm"

As an initial matter, Section 2340(2) requires that the severe mental pain must be evidenced by "prolonged mental harm." To prolong is to "lengthen in time" or to "extend the duration of, to draw out." Webster's Third New International Dictionary 1815 (1988); Webster's New International Dictionary 1980 (2d ed. 1935). Accordingly, "prolong" adds a temporal dimension to the harm to the individual, namely, that the harm must be one that is endured over some period of time. Put another way, the acts giving rise to the harm must cause some lasting, though not necessarily permanent, damage. For example, the mental strain experienced by an individual during a lengthy and intense interrogation—such as one that state or local police might conduct upon a criminal suspect—would not violate Section 2340(2). On the other hand, the development of a mental disorder such as posttraumatic stress disorder, which can last months or even years, or even chronic depression, which also can last for a considerable period of time if untreated, might satisfy the prolonged harm requirement. See American Psychiatric Association, *Diagnostic and Statistical Manual of Mental*

Disorders 426, 439–45 (4th ed. 1994) ("DSM-IV"). *See also* Craig Haney & Mona Lynch, *Regulating Prisons of the Future: A Psychological Analysis of Supermax and Solitary Confinement*, 23 N.Y.U. Rev. L. & Soc. Change 477, 509 (1997) (noting that posttraumatic stress disorder is frequently found in torture victims); *cf.* Sana Loue, *Immigration Law and Health* § 10:46 (2001) (recommending evaluating for post-traumatic stress disorder immigrant-client who has experienced torture).[4] By contrast to "severe pain," the phrase "prolonged mental harm" appears nowhere else in the U.S. Code nor does it appear in relevant medical literature or international human rights reports.

Not only must the mental harm be prolonged to amount to severe mental pain and suffering, but also it must be caused by or result from one of the acts listed in the statute. In the absence of a catchall provision, the most natural reading of the predicate acts listed in Section 2340(2)(A)–(D) is that Congress intended it to be exhaustive. In other words, other acts not included within Section 2340(2)'s enumeration are not within the statutory prohibition. *See Leatherman v. Tarrant County Narcotics Intelligence & Coordination Unit*, 507 U.S. 163, 168 (1993) ("*Expressio unius est exclusio alterius.*"); Norman Singer, 2A Sutherland on Statutory Construction § 47.23 (6th ed. 2000) ("[W]here a form of conduct, the manner of its performance and operation, and the persons and things to which it refers are designated, there is an inference that all omissions should be understood as exclusions.") (footnotes omitted). We conclude that torture within the meaning of the statute requires the specific intent to cause prolonged mental harm by one of the acts listed in Section 2340(2).

A defendant must specifically intend to cause prolonged mental harm for the defendant to have committed torture. It could be argued that a defendant needs to have specific intent only to commit the predicate acts that give rise to prolonged mental harm. Under that view, so long as the defendant specifically intended to, for example, threaten a victim with imminent death, he would have had sufficient *mens rea* for a conviction. According to this view, it would be further necessary for a conviction to show only that the victim factually suffered prolonged mental harm, rather than that the defendant intended to cause it. We believe that this approach is contrary to the text of the statute. The statute requires that the defendant specifically intend to inflict severe mental pain or suffering. Because the statute requires this mental state with respect to the infliction of severe mental pain, and because it expressly defines severe mental pain in terms of prolonged mental harm, that mental state must be present with respect to prolonged mental harm. To read the statute otherwise would read the phrase "the prolonged mental harm caused by or resulting from" out of the definition of "severe mental pain or suffering."

A defendant could negate a showing of specific intent to cause severe mental pain or suffering by showing that he had acted in good faith that his conduct would not amount to the acts prohibited by the statute. Thus, if a defendant has a good faith belief that his actions will not result in prolonged mental harm, he lacks the mental state necessary for his actions to constitute torture. A defendant could show that he acted in good faith by taking such steps as surveying professional literature, consulting with experts, or reviewing evidence gained from past experience. *See, e.g., Ratlzlaf,* 510 U.S. at 142 n.10 (noting that where the statute required that the defendant act with the specific intent to violate the law, the specific intent element "might be negated by, e.g., proof that defendant relied in good faith on advice of counsel.") (citations omitted). All of these steps would show that he has drawn on the relevant body of knowledge concerning the result proscribed that the statute, namely prolonged mental harm. Because the presence of good faith would negate the specific intent element of torture, it is a complete defense to such a charge. *See, e.g., United States v. Wall,* 130 F.3d 739, 746 (6th Cir. 1997); *United States v. Casperson,* 773 F.2d 216, 222–23 (8th Cir. 1985).

2. Harm Caused By Or Resulting From Predicate Acts

Section 2340(2) sets forth four basic categories of predicate acts. First in the list is the "intentional infliction or threatened infliction of severe physical pain or suffering." This might at first appear superfluous because the statute already provides that the infliction of severe physical pain or suffering can amount to torture. This provision, however, actually captures the infliction of physical pain or suffering when the defendant inflicts physical pain or suffering with general intent rather than the specific intent that is required where severe physical pain or suffering alone is the basis for the charge. Hence, this subsection reaches the infliction of severe physical pain or suffering when it is but the means of causing prolonged mental harm. Or put another way, a defendant has committed torture when he intentionally inflicts severe physical pain or suffering with the specific intent of causing prolonged mental harm. As for the acts themselves, acts that cause "severe physical pain or suffering" can satisfy this provision.

Additionally, the threat of inflicting such pain is a predicate act under the statute. A threat may be implicit or explicit. *See, e.g., United States v. Sachdev,* 279 F.3d 25, 29 (1st Cir. 2002). In criminal law, courts generally determine whether an individual's words or actions constitute a threat by examining whether a reasonable person in the same circumstances would conclude that a threat had been made. *See, e.g., Watts v. United States,* 394 U.S. 705, 708 (1969) (holding that whether a statement constituted a threat against the president's life had to be determined in light of all the surrounding circumstances); *Sachdev,* 279 F.3d at 29 ("a reasonable person in defendant's position would perceive there to be a threat, explicit, or implicit, of physical injury"); *United States v. Khorrami,* 895 F.2d 1186, 1190 (7th Cir. 1990) (to establish that a threat was made, the statement must be made "in a context or under such circumstances wherein a reasonable person would foresee that the statement would be interpreted by those to whom the maker communicates a statement as a serious expression of an intention to inflict bodily harm upon [another individual]") (citation and internal quotation marks omitted); *United States v. Peterson,* 483 F.2d 1222, 1230 (D.C. Cir. 1973) (perception of threat of imminent harm necessary to establish self-defense had to be "objectively reasonable in light of the surrounding circumstances"). Based on this common approach, we believe that the existence of a threat of severe pain or suffering should be assessed from the standpoint of a reasonable person in the same circumstances.

Second, Section 2340(2)(B) provides that prolonged mental harm, constituting torture, can be caused by "the administration or application or threatened administration or application, of mind-altering substances or other procedures calculated to disrupt profoundly the senses or the personality." The statute provides no further definition of what constitutes a mind-altering substance. The phrase "mind-altering substances" is found nowhere else in the U.S. Code nor is it found in dictionaries. It is, however, a commonly used synonym for drugs. *See, e.g., United States v. Kingsley*, 241 F.3d 828, 834 (6th Cir.) (referring to controlled substances as "mind-altering substance[s]") *cert. denied*, 122 S. Ct. 137 (2001); *Hogue v. Johnson*, 131 F.3d 466, 501 (5th Cir. 1997) (referring to drugs and alcohol as "mind-altering substance[s]"), *cert. denied*, 523 U.S. 1014 (1998). In addition, the phrase appears in a number of state statutes, and the context in which it appears confirms this understanding of the phrase. *See, e.g.*, Cal. Penal Code § 3500(c) (West Supp. 2000) ("Psychotropic drugs also include mind-altering...drugs...."); Minn. Stat. Ann. § 260B.201(b) (West Supp. 2002) ("'chemical dependency treatment'" define as programs designed to "reduc[e] the risk of the use of alcohol, drugs, or other mind-altering substances").

This subparagraph, however, does not preclude any and all use of drugs. Instead, it prohibits the use of drugs that "disrupt profoundly the senses or the personality." To be sure, one could argue that this phrase applies only to "other procedures," not the application of mind-altering substances. We reject this interpretation because the terms of Section 2340(2) expressly indicate that the qualifying phrase applies to both "other procedures" *and* the "application of mind-altering substances." The word "other" modifies "procedures calculated to disrupt profoundly the senses." As an adjective, "other" indicates that the term or phrase it modifies is the remainder of several things. *See* Webster's Third New International Dictionary 1598 (1986) (defining "other" as "the one that remains of two or more"); Webster's Ninth New Collegiate Dictionary 835 (1985) (defining "other" as "being the one (as of two or more) remaining or not included"). Or put another way, "other" signals that the words to which it attaches are of the same kind, type, or class as the more specific item previously listed. Moreover, where statutes couple words or phrases together, it "denotes an intention that they should be understood in the same general sense." Norman Singer, 2A Sutherland on Statutory Construction § 47:16 (6th ed. 2000); *see also Beecham v. United States*, 511 U.S. 368, 371 (1994) ("That several items in a list share an attribute counsels in favor of interpreting the other items as possessing that attribute as well."). Thus, the pairing of mind-altering substances with procedures calculated to disrupt profoundly the senses or personality and the use of "other" to modify "procedures" shows that the use of such substances must also cause a profound disruption of the senses or personality.

For drugs or procedures to rise to the level of "disrupt[ing] profoundly the senses or personality," they must produce an extreme effect. And by requiring that they be "calculated" to produce such an effect, the statute requires for liability the defendant has consciously designed the acts to produce such an effect. 28 U.S.C. § 2340(2)(B). The word "disrupt" is defined as "to break asunder; to part forcibly; rend," imbuing the verb with a connotation of violence. Webster's New International Dictionary 753 (2d ed. 1935); *see* Webster's Third New International Dictionary 656 (1986) (defining disrupt as "to break apart: Rupture" or "destroy the unity or wholeness of"); IV The Oxford English Dictionary 832 (1989) (defining disrupt as "[t]o break or burst asunder; to break in pieces; to separate forcibly"). Moreover, disruption of the senses or personality alone is insufficient to fall within the scope of this subsection; instead, that disruption must be profound. The word "profound" has a number of meanings, all of which convey a significant depth. Webster's New International Dictionary 1977 (2d ed. 1935) defines profound as: "Of very great depth; extending far below the surface or top; unfathomable[;] . . . [c]oming from, reaching to, or situated at a depth or more than ordinary depth; not superficial; deep-seated; chiefly with reference to the body; as a *profound* sigh, wound, or pain[;] . . . [c]haracterized by intensity, as of feeling or quality; deeply felt or realized; as, *profound* respect, fear, or melancholy; hence, encompassing; thoroughgoing; complete; as, *profound* sleep, silence, or ignorance." *See* Webster's Third New International Dictionary 1812 (1986) ("having very great depth: extending far below the surface . . . not superficial"). Random House Webster's Unabridged Dictionary 1545 (2d ed. 1999) also defines profound as "originating in or penetrating to the depths of one's being" or "pervasive or intense; thorough; complete" or "extending, situated, or originating far down, or far beneath the surface." By requiring that the procedures and the drugs create a *profound* disruption, the statute requires more than that the acts "forcibly separate" or "rend" the senses or personality. Those acts must penetrate to the core of an individual's ability to perceive the world around him, substantially interfering with his cognitive abilities, or fundamentally alter his personality.

The phrase "disrupt profoundly the senses or personality" is not used in mental health literature nor is it derived from elsewhere in U.S. law. Nonetheless, we think the following examples would constitute a profound disruption of the senses or personality. Such an effect might be seen in a drug-induced dementia. In such a state, the individual suffers from significant memory impairment, such as the inability to retain any new information or recall information about things previously of interest to the individual. *See* DSM-IV at 134.[5] This impairment is accompanied by one or more of the following: deterioration of language function, e.g., repeating sounds or words over and over again; impaired ability to execute simple motor activities, e.g., inability to dress or wave goodbye; "[in]ability to recognize [and identify] objects such as chairs or pencils" despite normal visual functioning; or "[d]isturbances in executive level functioning," i.e., serious impairment of abstract thinking. *Id.* at 134–35. Similarly, we think that the onset of "brief psychotic disorder" would satisfy this standard. *See id.* at 302–03. In this disorder, the individual suffers psychotic symptoms, including among other things, delusions, hallucinations, or even a catatonic state. This can last for one day or even one month. *See id.* We likewise think that the onset of obsessive-compulsive disorder behaviors would rise to this level. Obsessions are intrusive thoughts unrelated to reality. They are not simple worries, but are repeated doubts or even "aggressive or horrific impulses." *See id.* at 418. The DSM-IV further explains that compulsions include "repetitive behaviors (e.g., hand washing, ordering, checking)" and that "[b]y definition, [they] are either clearly excessive or are not connected in a realistic way with what they are designed to neutralize or prevent." *See id.* Such compulsions or obsessions must be "time-consuming." *See id.* at 419. Moreover, we think that pushing someone to the brink of suicide, particularly where the person comes from a culture with strong taboos against suicide, and it is evidenced by acts of self-mutilation, would be a sufficient disruption of the personality to constitute a "profound disruption." These examples, of course, are in no way intended to be exhaustive list. Instead, they are merely intended to illustrate the sort of mental health effects that we believe would accompany an action severe enough to amount to one that "disrupt[s] profoundly the senses or the personality."

The third predicate act listed in Section 2340(2) is threatening a prisoner with "imminent death." 18 U.S.C. § 2340(2)(C). The plain text makes clear that a threat of death alone is insufficient; the threat must indicate that death is "imminent." The "threat of imminent death" is found in the common law as an element of the defense of duress. *See Bailey*, 444 U.S. at 409. "[W]here Congress borrows terms of art in which are accumulated the legal tradition and meaning of centuries of practice, it presumably knows and adopts the cluster of ideas that were attached to each borrowed word in the body of learning from which it was taken and the meaning its use will convey to the judicial mind unless otherwise instructed. In such case, absence of contrary direction may be taken as satisfaction with widely accepted definitions, not as a departure from them." *Morissette v. United States*, 342 U.S. 246, 263 (1952). Common law cases and legislation generally define imminence as requiring that the threat be almost immediately forthcoming. 1 Wayne R. LaFave & Austin W. Scott, Jr., Substantive Criminal Law § 5.7, at 655 (1986). By contrast, threats referring vaguely to things that might happen in the future do not satisfy this immediacy requirement. *See United States v. Fiore*, 178 F.3d 917, 923 (7th Cir. 1999). Such a threat fails to satisfy this requirement not because it is too remote in time but because there is a lack of certainty that it will occur. Indeed, timing is an indicator of certainty that the harm *will* befall the defendant. Thus, a vague threat that someday the prisoner *might* be killed would not suffice. Instead, subjecting a prisoner to mock executions or playing Russian roulette with him would have sufficient immediacy to constitute a threat of imminent death. Additionally, as discussed earlier, we believe that the existence of a threat must be assessed from the perspective of a reasonable person in the same circumstances.

Fourth, if the official threatens to do anything previously described to a third party, or commits such an act against a third party, that threat or action can serve as the necessary predicate for prolonged mental harm. *See* 18 U.S.C. § 2340(2)(D). The statute does not require any relationship between the prisoner and the third party.

3. Legislative History

The legislative history of Sections 2340–2340A is scant. Neither the definition of torture nor these sections as a whole sparked any debate. Congress criminalized this conduct to fulfill U.S. obligations under the U.N. Convention Against Torture and Other Cruel, Inhuman or Degrading Treatment or Punishment ("CAT"), adopted Dec. 10, 1984, S. Treaty Doc. No. 100–20 (1988), 1465 U.N.T.S. 85 (entered into force June 26, 1987), which requires signatories to "ensure that all acts of torture are offenses under its criminal law." CAT art. 4. These sections appeared only in the Senate version of the Foreign Affairs Authorization Act, and the conference bill adopted them without amendment. See H. R. Conf. Rep. No. 103–482, at 229 (1994). The only light that the legislative history sheds reinforces what is already obvious from the texts of Section 2340 and CAT: Congress intended Section 2340's definition of torture to track the definition set forth in CAT, as elucidated by the United States' reservations, understandings, and declarations submitted as part of its ratification. See S. Rep. No. 103–107, at 58 (1993) ("The definition of torture emanates directly from article 1 of the Convention."); id. at 58–59 ("The definition for 'severe mental pain and suffering' incorporates the understanding made by the Senate concerning this term.").

4. Summary

Section 2340's definition of torture must be read as a sum of these component parts. See *Argentine Rep. v. Amerada Hess Shipping Corp.*, 488 U.S. 428, 434–35 (1989) (reading two provisions together to determine statute's meaning); *Bethesda Hosp. Ass'n v. Bowen*, 485 U.S. 399, 405 (1988) (looking to "the language and design of the statute as a whole" to ascertain a statute's meaning). Each component of the definition emphasizes that torture is not the mere infliction of pain or suffering on another, but is instead a step well removed. The victim must experience intense pain or suffering of the kind that is equivalent to the pain that would be associated with serious physical injury so severe that death, organ failure, or permanent damage resulting in a loss of significant body function will likely result. If that pain or suffering is psychological, that suffering must result from one of the acts set forth in the statute. In addition, these acts must cause long-term mental harm. Indeed, this view of the criminal act of torture is consistent with the term's common meaning. Torture is generally understood to involve "intense pain" or "excruciating pain," or put another way, "extreme anguish of body or mind." Black's Law Dictionary at 1498 (7th Ed. 1999); Random House Webster's Unabridged Dictionary 1999 (1999); Webster's New International Dictionary 2674 (2d ed. 1935). In short, reading the definition of torture as a whole, it is plain that the term encompasses only extreme acts.[6]

II. U.N. Convention Against Torture and Other Cruel Inhuman or Degrading Treatment or Punishment.

Because Congress enacted the criminal prohibition against torture to implement CAT, we also examine the treaty's text and history to develop a fuller understanding of the context of Sections 2340–2340A. As with the statute, we begin our analysis with the treaty's text. See *Eastern Airlines Inc. v. Floyd*, 499 U.S. 530, 534–35 (1991)

("When interpreting a treaty, we begin with the text of the treaty and the context in which the written words are used.) (quotation marks and citations omitted). CAT defines torture as:

> any act by which *severe* pain or suffering, whether physical or mental, is intentionally inflicted on a person for such purposes as obtaining from him or a third person information or a confession, punishing him for an act he or a third person has committed or is suspected of having committed, or intimidating or coercing him or a third person, or for any reason based on discrimination of any kind, when such pain or suffering is inflicted by or at the instigation of or with the consent or acquiescence of a public official or other person acting in an official capacity.

Article 1(1) (emphasis added). Unlike Section 2340, this definition includes a list of purposes for which such pain and suffering is inflicted. The prefatory phrase "such purposes as" makes clear that this list is, however, illustrative rather than exhaustive. Accordingly, severe pain or suffering need not be inflicted for those specific purposes to constitute torture; instead, the perpetrator must simply have a purpose of the same kind. More importantly, like Section 2340, the pain and suffering must be severe to reach the threshold of torture. Thus, the text of CAT reinforces our reading of Section 2340 that torture must be an extreme act.[7]

CAT also distinguishes between torture and other acts of cruel, inhuman, or degrading treatment or punishment.[8] Article 16 of CAT requires state parties to "undertake to prevent . . . other acts of cruel, inhuman or degrading treatment or punishment *which do not amount to torture* as defined in article 1." (Emphasis added). CAT thus establishes a category of acts that are not to be committed and that states must endeavor to prevent, but that states need not criminalize, leaving those acts without the stigma of criminal penalties. CAT reserves criminal penalties and the stigma attached to those penalties for torture alone. In so doing, CAT makes clear that torture is at the farthest end of impermissible actions, and that it is distinct and separate from the lower level of "cruel, inhuman, or degrading treatment or punishment." This approach is in keeping with CAT's predecessor, the U.N. Declaration on the Protection from Torture. That declaration defines torture as "an aggravated and deliberate form of cruel, inhuman or degrading treatment or punishment." Declaration on Protection from Torture, UN Res. 3452, Art. 1(2) (Dec. 9, 1975).

A. Ratification History

Executive branch interpretation of CAT further supports our conclusion that the treaty, and thus Section 2340A, prohibits only the most extreme forms of physical or mental harm. As we have previously noted, the "division of treaty-making responsibility between the Senate and the President is essentially the reverse of the division of law-making authority, with the President being the draftsman of the treaty and the Senate holding the authority to grant or deny approval." *Relevance of Senate Ratification History to Treaty Interpretation*, 11 Op. O.L.C. 28, 31 (Apr. 9, 1987) ("Sofaer Memorandum"). Treaties are negotiated by the President in his capacity as the "sole organ of the federal government in the field of international relations." *United States v. Curtiss-Wright Export Corp.*, 299 U.S. 304, 320 (1936). Moreover, the President is responsible for the day-to-day interpretation of a treaty and retains the power to unilaterally terminate a treaty. *See Goldwater v. Carter*, 617 F.2d 697, 707–08 (D.C. Cir.) (en banc) *vacated and remanded with instructions to dismiss on other grounds*, 444 U.S. 996 (1979). The Executive's interpretation is to be accorded the greatest weight in ascertaining a treaty's intent and meaning. *See, e.g., United States v. Stuart*, 489 U.S. 353, 369 (1989) ("'the meaning attributed to treaty provisions by the Government agencies charged with their negotiation and enforcement is entitled to great weight'") (quoting *Sumitomo Shoji America, Inc. v. Avagliano*, 457 U.S. 176, 184–85 (1982)); *Kolovrat v. Oregon*, 366 U.S. 187, 194 (1961) ("While courts interpret treaties for themselves, the meaning given them by the department of government particularly charged with their negotiation and enforcement is given great weight."); *Charlton v. Kelly*, 229 U.S. 447, 468 (1913) ("A construction of a treaty by the political departments of the government, while not conclusive upon a court..., is nevertheless of much weight.").

A review of the Executive branch's interpretation and understanding of CAT reveals that Congress codified the view that torture included only the most extreme forms of physical or mental harm. When it submitted the Convention to the Senate, the Reagan administration took the position that CAT reached only the most heinous acts. The Reagan administration included the following understanding:

> The United States understands that, in order to constitute torture, an act must be a deliberate and calculated act of an extremely cruel and inhuman nature, specifically intended to inflict excruciating and agonizing physical or mental pain or suffering.

S. Treaty Doc. No. 100-20, at 4–5. Focusing on the treaty's requirement of "severity," the Reagan administration concluded, "The extreme nature of torture is further emphasized in [this] requirement." S. Treaty Doc. No. 100-20, at 3 (1988); S. Exec. Rep. 101-30, at 13 (1990). The Reagan administration also determined that CAT's definition of torture fell in line with "United States and international usage, [where it] is usually reserved for extreme deliberate and unusually cruel practices, for example, sustained systematic beatings, application of electric currents to sensitive parts of the body and tying up or hanging in positions that cause extreme pain." S. Exec. Rep. No. 101-30, at 14 (1990). In interpreting CAT's definition of torture as reaching only such extreme acts, the Reagan administration underscored the distinction between torture and other cruel, inhuman, or degrading treatment or punishment. In particular, the administration declared that article 1's definition of torture ought to be construed in light of article 16. *See* S. Treaty Doc. No. 100-20, at 3. Based on this distinction, the administration concluded that: "'Torture' is thus to be distinguished from lesser forms of cruel, inhuman, or degrading treatment or punishment, which are to be deplored and prevented, but are not so universally and categorically condemned as to warrant the severe legal consequences that the Convention provides in case of torture." S. Treaty Doc. 100-20, at 3. Moreover, this distinction was "adopted in order to emphasize that torture is at the extreme end of cruel, inhuman and degrading treatment or punishment." S. Treaty Doc. No. 100-20, at 3. Given the extreme nature of torture, the administration concluded that "rough treatment as generally falls into the category of 'police brutality,' while deplorable, does not amount to 'torture.'" S. Treaty Doc. No. 100-20, at 4.

Although the Reagan administration relied on CAT's distinction between torture and "cruel, inhuman, or degrading treatment or punishment," it viewed the phrase "cruel, inhuman, or degrading treatment or punishment" as vague and lacking in a universally accepted meaning. Of even greater concern to the Reagan administration was that because of its vagueness this phrase could be construed to bar acts not prohibited by the U.S. Constitution. The administration pointed to *Case of X v. Federal Republic of Germany* as the basis for this concern. In that case, the European Court of Human Rights determined that the prison officials' refusal to recognize a prisoner's sex change might constitute degrading treatment. *See* S. Treaty Doc. No. 100-20, at 15 (citing European Commission on Human Rights, *Dec. on Adm.*, Dec. 15, 1977, *Case of X v. Federal Republic of Germany* (No. 6694/74), 11 Dec. & Rep. 16)). As a result of this concern, the Administration added the following understanding:

> The United States understands the term, "cruel, inhuman or degrading treatment or punishment," as used in Article 16 of the Convention, to mean the cruel, unusual, and inhumane treatment or punishment prohibited by the Fifth, Eighth and/or Fourteenth Amendments to the Constitution of the United States.

S. Treaty Doc. No. 100-20, at 15–16. Treatment or punishment must therefore rise to the level of action that U.S. courts have found to be in violation of the U.S. Constitution in order to constitute cruel, inhuman, or degrading treatment or punishment. That which fails to rise to this level must fail, *a fortiori*, to constitute torture under Section 2340.[9]

The Senate did not give its advice and consent to the Convention until the first Bush administration. Although using less vigorous rhetoric, the Bush administration joined the Reagan administration in interpreting torture as only reaching extreme acts. To ensure that the Convention's reach remained limited, the Bush administration submitted the following understanding:

> The United States understands that, in order to constitute torture, an act must be specifically intended to inflict severe physical or mental pain or suffering and that mental pain or suffering refers to prolonged mental pain caused by or resulting from (1) the intentional infliction or threatened infliction of severe

physical pain or suffering; (2) administration or application, or threatened administration or application, of mind altering substances or other procedures calculated to disrupt profoundly the senses or the personality; (3) the threat of imminent death; or (4) the threat that another person will imminently be subjected to death, severe physical pain or suffering, or the administration or application of mind-altering substances or other procedures calculated to disrupt profoundly the senses or personality.

S. Exec. Rep. No. 101-30, at 36. This understanding accomplished two things. First, it ensured that the term "intentionally" would be understood as requiring specific intent. Second, it added form and substance to the otherwise amorphous concept of *mental* pain or suffering. In so doing, this understanding ensured that mental torture would rise to a severity seen in the context of physical torture. The Senate ratified CAT with this understanding, and as is obvious from the text, Congress codified this understanding almost verbatim in the criminal statute.

To be sure, it might be thought significant that the Bush administration's language differs from the Reagan administration understanding. The Bush administration said that it had altered the CAT understanding in response to criticism that the Reagan administration's original formulation had raised the bar for the level of pain necessary for the act or acts to constitute torture. *See* Convention Against Torture: Hearing Before the Senate Comm. On Foreign Relations, 101st Cong. 9–10 (1990) ("1990 Hearing") (prepared statement of Hon. Abraham D. Sofaer, Legal Adviser, Department of State). While it is true that there are rhetorical differences between the understandings, both administrations consistently emphasize the extraordinary or extreme acts required to constitute torture. As we have seen, the Bush understanding as codified in Section 2340 reaches only extreme acts. The Reagan understanding, like the Bush understanding, ensured that "intentionally" would be understood as a specific intent requirement. Though the Reagan administration required that the "act be deliberate and calculated" *and* that it be inflicted with specific intent, in operation there is little difference between requiring specific intent alone and requiring that the act be deliberate and calculated. The Reagan understandings also made express what is obvious from the plain text of CAT: torture is an extreme form of cruel and inhuman treatment. The Reagan administration's understanding that the pain be "excruciating and agonizing" is in substance not different from the Bush administration's proposal that the pain must be severe.

The Bush understanding simply took a rather abstract concept—excruciating and agonizing mental pain—and gave it a more concrete form. Executive branch representations made to the Senate support our view that there was little difference between these two understandings and that the further definition of mental pain or suffering merely sought remove the vagueness created by concept of "agonizing and excruciating" mental pain. *See* 1990 Hearing, at 10 (prepared statement of Hon. Abraham D. Sofaer, Legal Adviser, Department of State) ("no higher standard was intended" by the Reagan administration understanding than was present in the Convention or the Bush understanding); *id.* at 13–14 (statement of Mark Richard, Deputy Assistant Attorney General, Criminal Division, Department of Justice) ("In an effort to overcome this unacceptable element of vagueness [in the term "mental pain"], we have proposed an understanding which defines severe mental pain constituting torture with sufficient specificity... to protect innocent persons and meet constitutional due process requirements.") Accordingly, we believe that the two definitions submitted by the Reagan and Bush administrations had the same purpose in terms of articulating a legal standard, namely, ensuring that the prohibition against torture reaches only the most extreme acts. Ultimately, whether the Reagan standard would have been even higher is a purely academic question because the Bush understanding clearly established a very high standard.

Executive branch representations made to the Senate confirm that the Bush administration maintained the view that torture encompassed only the most extreme acts. Although the ratification record, i.e., testimony, hearings, and the like, is generally not accorded great weight in interpreting treaties, authoritative statements made by representatives of the Executive Branch are accorded the most interpretive value. See Sofaer Memorandum, at 35–36. Hence, the testimony of the Executive branch witnesses defining torture, in addition to the reservations, understandings and declarations that were submitted to the Senate by the Executive branch, should carry the highest interpretive value of any of the statements in the ratification record. At the Senate hearing on CAT, Mark Richard, Deputy Assistant Attorney General, Criminal Division, Department of Justice, offered extensive testimony as to the meaning of torture. Echoing the analysis submitted by the Reagan administration, he testified that "[t]orture is understood to be that barbaric cruelty which lies at the top of the pyramid of human rights misconduct." 1990 Hearing, at 16 (prepared statement of Mark Richard). He further explained, "As applied to physical torture, there appears to be some degree of consensus that the concept involves conduct, the mere mention of which sends chills down one's spine[.]" *Id.* Richard gave the following examples of conduct satisfying this standard: "the needle under the fingernail, the application of electrical shock to the genital area, the piercing of eyeballs, etc." *Id.* In short, repeating virtually verbatim the terms used in the Reagan understanding, Richard explained that under the Bush administration's submissions with the treaty "the essence of torture" is treatment that inflicts "excruciating and agonizing physical pain." *Id.* (emphasis added).

As to mental torture, Richard testified that "no international consensus had emerged [as to] what degree of mental suffering is required to constitute torture[,]" but that it was nonetheless clear that severe mental pain or suffering "does not encompass the normal legal compulsions which are properly a part of the criminal justice system[:] interrogation, incarceration, prosecution, compelled testimony against a friend, etc.—notwithstanding the fact that they may have the incidental effect of producing mental strain." *Id.* at 17. According to Richard, CAT was intended to "condemn as torture intentional acts such as those designed to damage and destroy the human personality." *Id.* at 14. This description of mental suffering emphasizes the requirement that any mental harm be of significant duration and lends further support for our conclusion that mind-altering substances must have a profoundly disruptive effect to serve as a predicate act.

Apart from statements from Executive branch officials, the rest of a ratification record is of little weight in interpreting a treaty. *See generally* Sofaer Memorandum. Nonetheless, the Senate understanding of the definition of torture largely echoes the administrations' views. The Senate Foreign Relations Committee Report on CAT opined: "[f]or an act to be 'torture' it must be an *extreme* form of cruel and inhuman treatment, cause *severe* pain and suffering and be *intended to cause severe* pain and suffering." S. Exec. Rep. No. 101-30, at 6 (emphasis added). Moreover, like both the Reagan and Bush administrations, the Senate drew upon the distinction between torture and cruel, inhuman or degrading treatment or punishment in reaching its view that torture was extreme.[10] Finally, the Senate concurred with the administrations' concern that "cruel, inhuman, or degrading treatment or punishment" could be construed to establish a new standard above and beyond that which the Constitution mandates and supported the inclusion of the reservation establishing the Constitution as the baseline for determining whether conduct amounted to cruel, inhuman, degrading treatment or punishment. *See* 136 Cong. Rec. 36,192 (1990); S. Exec. Rep. 101-30, at 39.

B. Negotiating History

CAT's negotiating history also indicates that its definition of torture supports our reading of Section 2340. The state parties endeavored to craft a definition of torture that reflected the term's gravity. During the negotiations, state parties offered various formulations of the definition of torture to the working group, which then proposed a definition based on those formulations. Almost all of these suggested definitions illustrate the consensus that torture is an extreme act designed to cause agonizing pain. For example, the United States proposed that torture be defined as "includ[ing] any act by which extremely severe pain or suffering . . . is deliberately and maliciously inflicted on a person." J. Herman Burgers & Hans Danelius, *The United Nations Convention Against Torture: A Handbook on the Convention Against Torture and Other Cruel Inhuman and Degrading Treatment or Punishment* 41 (1988) ("CAT Handbook"). The United Kingdom suggested an even more restrictive definition, i.e., that torture be defined as the "*systematic and intentional* infliction of *extreme* pain or suffering rather than *intentional* infliction of *severe* pain or suffering." *Id.* at 45 (emphasis in original). Ultimately, in choosing the phrase "severe pain," the parties concluded that this phrase "sufficient[ly] . . . convey[ed] the idea that only acts of a certain gravity shall . . . constitute torture." *Id.* at 117.

In crafting such a definition, the state parties also were acutely aware of the distinction they drew between torture and cruel, inhuman, or degrading treatment or punishment. The state parties considered and rejected a proposal that would have defined torture merely as cruel, inhuman or degrading treatment or punishment. *See id.* at 42. Mirroring the Declaration on Protection From Torture, which expressly defined torture as an "aggravated and deliberate form of cruel, inhuman or degrading treatment or punishment," some state parties proposed that in addition to the definition of torture set out in paragraph 2 of article 1, a paragraph defining torture as "an aggravated and deliberate form of cruel, inhuman or degrading treatment or punishment" should be included. *See id.* at 41; *see also* S. Treaty Doc. No. 100-20, at 2 (the U.N. Declaration on Protection from Torture (1975) served as "a point of departure for the drafting of [CAT]"). In the end, the parties concluded that the addition of such a paragraph was superfluous because Article 16 "impl[ies]" that torture is the gravest form of such treatment or punishment." *CAT Handbook* at 80; *see* S. Exec. Rep. No. 101-30, at 13 ("The negotiating history indicates that [the phrase 'which do not amount to torture'] was adopted in order to emphasize that torture is at the extreme end of cruel, inhuman and degrading treatment or punishment and that Article 1 should be construed with this in mind.").

Additionally, the parties could not reach a consensus about the meaning of "cruel, inhuman, or degrading treatment or punishment." *See CAT Handbook* at 47. Without a consensus, the parties viewed the term as simply "'too vague to be included in a convention which was to form the basis for criminal legislation in the Contracting States.'" *Id.* This view evinced by the parties reaffirms the interpretation of CAT as purposely reserving criminal penalties for torture alone.

CAT's negotiating history offers more than just support for the view that pain or suffering must be extreme to amount to torture. First, the negotiating history suggests that the harm sustained from the acts of torture need not be permanent. In fact, "the United States considered that it might be useful to develop the negotiating history which indicates that although conduct resulting in permanent impairment of physical or mental faculties is indicative of torture, it is not an essential element of the offence." *Id.* at 44. Second, the state parties to CAT rejected a proposal to include in CAT's definition of torture the use of truth drugs, where no physical harm or mental suffering was apparent. This rejection at least suggests that such drugs were not viewed as amounting to torture per se. *See id.* at 42.

C. Summary

The text of CAT confirms our conclusion that Section 2340A was intended to proscribe only the most egregious conduct. CAT not only defines torture as involving severe pain and suffering, but also it makes clear that such pain and suffering is at the extreme end of the spectrum of acts by reserving criminal penalties solely for torture. Executive interpretations confirm our view that the treaty (and hence the statute) prohibits only the worst forms of cruel, inhuman, or degrading treatment or punishment. The ratification history further substantiates this interpretation. Even the negotiating history displays a recognition that torture is a step far-removed from other cruel, inhuman or degrading treatment or punishment. In sum, CAT's text, ratification history and negotiating history all confirm that Section 2340A reaches only the most heinous acts.

III. U.S. Judicial Interpretation

There are no reported cases of prosecutions under Section 2340A. *See* Beth Stephens, *Corporate Liability: Enforcing Human Rights Through Domestic Litigation*, 24 Hastings Int'l & Comp. L. Rev. 401, 408 & n.29 (2001); Beth Van Schaack, *In Defense of Civil Redress: The Domestic Enforcement of Human Rights Norms in the Context of the Proposed Hague Judgments Convention*, 42 Harv. Int'l L. J. 141, 148–49 (2001); Curtis A. Bradley, *Universal Jurisdiction and U.S. Law*, 2001 U. Chi. Legal F. 323, 327–28. Nonetheless, we are not without guidance as to how United States courts would approach the question of what conduct constitutes torture. Civil suits filed under the Torture Victims Protection Act ("TVPA"), 28 U.S.C. § 1350 note (2000), which supplies a tort remedy for victims of torture, provide insight into what acts U.S. courts would conclude constitute torture under the criminal statute.

The TVPA contains a definition similar in some key respects to the one set forth in Section 2340. Moreover, as with Section 2340, Congress intended for the TVPA's definition of torture to follow closely the definition found in CAT. *See Xuncax v. Gramajo*, 886 F. Supp. 162, 176 n.12 (D. Mass 1995) (noting that the definition of torture in the TVPA tracks the definitions in Section 2340 and CAT).[11] The TVPA defines torture as:

> (1) . . . any act, directed against an individual in the offender's custody or physical control, by which severe pain or suffering (other than pain or suffering arising only from or inherent in, or incidental to, lawful sanctions), whether physical or mental, is intentionally inflicted on that individual for such purposes as obtaining from that individual or a third person information or a confession, punishing that individual for an act that individual or a third person has committed or is suspected of having committed, intimidating or coercing that individual or a third person, or for any reason based on discrimination of any kind; and
>
> (2) mental pain or suffering refers to prolonged mental harm caused by or resulting from—
>
> (A) the intentional infliction or threatened infliction of severe physical pain or suffering;
>
> (B) the administration or application, or threatened administration or application, of mind altering substances or other procedures calculated to disrupt profoundly the senses or the personality;
>
> (C) the threat of imminent death; or
>
> (D) the threat that another individual will imminently be subjected to death, severe physical pain or suffering, or the administration or application of mind altering substances or other procedures calculated to disrupt profoundly the senses or personality.

28 U.S.C. § 1350 note § 3(b). This definition differs from Section 2340's definition in

two respects. First, the TVPA definition contains an illustrative list of purposes for which such pain may have been inflicted. *See id.* Second, the TVPA includes the phrase "arising only from or inherent in, or incidental to lawful sanctions"; by contrast, Section 2340 refers only to pain or suffering "incidental to lawful sanctions." *Id.* Because the purpose of our analysis here is to ascertain acts that would cross the threshold of producing "severe physical or mental pain or suffering," the list of illustrative purposes for which it is inflicted, generally would not affect this analysis.[12] Similarly, to the extent that the absence of the phrase "arising only from or inherent in" from Section 2340 might affect the question of whether pain or suffering was part of lawful sanctions and thus not torture, the circumstances with which we are concerned here are solely that of interrogations, not the imposition of punishment subsequent to judgment. These differences between the TVPA and Section 2340 are therefore not sufficiently significant to undermine the usefulness of TVPA cases here.[13]

In suits brought under the TVPA, courts have not engaged in any lengthy analysis of what acts constitute torture. In part, this is due to the nature of the acts alleged. Almost all of the cases involve physical torture, some of which is of an especially cruel and even sadistic nature. Nonetheless, courts appear to look at the entire course of conduct rather than any one act, making it somewhat akin to a totality-of-the-circumstances analysis. Because of this approach, it is difficult to take a specific act out of context and conclude that the act in isolation would constitute torture. Certain acts do, however, consistently reappear in these cases or are of such a barbaric nature, that it is likely a court would find that allegations of such treatment would constitute torture: (1) severe beatings using instruments such as iron barks, truncheons, and clubs; (2) threats of imminent death, such as mock executions; (3) threats of removing extremities; (4) burning, especially burning with cigarettes; (5) electric shocks to genitalia or threats to do so; (6) rape or sexual assault, or injury to an individual's sexual organs, or threatening to do any of these sorts of acts; and (7) forcing the prisoner to watch the torture of others. Given the highly contextual nature of whether a set of acts constitutes torture, we have set forth in the attached appendix the circumstances in which courts have determined that the plaintiff has suffered torture, which include the cases from which these seven acts are drawn. While we cannot say with certainty that acts falling short of these seven would not constitute torture under Section 2340, we believe that interrogation techniques would have to be similar to these in their extreme nature and in the type of harm caused to violate the law.

Despite the limited analysis engaged in by courts, a recent district court opinion provides some assistance in predicting how future courts might address this issue. In *Mehinovic v. Vuckovic*, 198 F. Supp. 2d 1322, (N.D. Ga. 2002), the plaintiffs, Bosnian Muslims, sued a Bosnian Serb, Nikola Vuckovic, for, among other things, torture and cruel and inhumane treatment. The court described in vivid detail the treatment the plaintiffs endured. Specifically, the plaintiffs experienced the following:

Vuckovic repeatedly beat Kemal Mehinovic with a variety of blunt objects and boots, intentionally delivering blows to areas he knew to already be badly injured, including Mehinovic's genitals. *Id.* at 1333–34. On some occasions he was tied up and hung against windows during beatings. *Id.* Mehinovic, was subjected to the game of "Russian roulette." *See id.* Vuckovic, along with other guards, also forced Mehinovic to run in a circle while the guards swung wooden planks at him. *Id.*

Like Mehinovic, Muhamed Bicic was beaten repeatedly with blunt objects, to the point of loss of consciousness. *See Id* at 1335. He witnessed the severe beatings of other prisoners, including his own brother. "On one occasion, Vuckovic ordered Bicic to get on all fours while another soldier stood or rode on his back and beat him with a baton—a game the soldiers called 'horse.'" *Id.* Bicic, like Mehinovic, was subjected to the game of Russian roulette. Additionally, Vuckovic and the other guards forcibly extracted a number of Bicic's teeth. *Id.* at 1336.

Safet Hadzialijagic was subjected to daily beatings with "metal pipes, bats, sticks, and weapons." *Id.* at 1337. He was also subjected to Russian roulette. *See id.* at 1336–37. Hadzialijagic also frequently saw other prisoners being beaten or heard their screams as they were beaten. Like Bicic, he was subjected to the teeth extraction incident. On one occasion, Vuckovic rode Hadzialijagic like a horse, simultaneously hitting him in the head and body with a knife handle. During this time, other soldiers kicked and hit him. He fell down during this episode and was forced to get up and continue carrying Vuckovic. *See id.* "Vuckovic and the other soldiers [then] tied Hadzialijagic with a rope, hung him upside down, and beat him. When they noticed that Hadzialijagic was losing consciousness, they dunked his head in a bowl used as a toilet." *Id.* Vuckovic then forced Hadzialijagic to lick the blood off of Vuckovic's boots and kicked Hadzialijagic as he tried to do so. Vuckovic then used his knife to carve a semi-circle in Hadzialijagic's forehead. Hadzialijagic went into cardiac arrest just after this incident and was saved by one of the other plaintiffs. *See id.*

Hasan Subasic was brutally beaten and witnessed the beatings of other prisoners, including the beating and death of one of his fellow prisoners and the beating of Hadzialijagic in which he was tied upside down and beaten. *See id.* at 1338–39. *Id.* at 1338. Subasic also was subjected to the teeth pulling incident. Vuckovic personally beat Subasic two times, punching him and kicking him with his military boots. In one of these beatings, "Subasic had been forced into a kneeling position when Vuckovic kicked him in the stomach." *Id.*

The district court concluded that the plaintiffs suffered both physical and mental torture at the hands of Vuckovic.[14] With respect to physical torture, the court broadly outlined with respect to each plaintiff the acts in which Vuckovic had been at least complicit and that it found rose to the level of torture. Regarding Mehinovic, the court determined that Vuckovic's beatings of Mehinovic in which he kicked and delivered other blows to Mehinovic's face, genitals, and others body parts, constituted torture. The court noted that these beatings left Mehinovic disfigured, may have broken ribs, almost caused Mehinovic to lose consciousness, and rendered him unable to eat for a period of time. As to Bicic, the court found that Bicic had suffered severe physical pain and suffering as a result of Vuckovic's repeated beatings of him in which Vuckovic used various instruments to inflict blows, the "horse" game, and the teeth pulling incident. *See id.* at 1346. In finding that Vuckovic inflicted severe physical pain on

Hadzialijagic, the court unsurprisingly focused on the beating in which Vuckovic tied Hadzialijagic upside down and beat him. *See id.* The court pointed out that in this incident, Vuckovic almost killed Hadzialijagic. *See id.* The court further concluded that Subasic experienced severe physical pain and thus was tortured based on the beating in which Vuckovic kicked Subasic in the stomach. *See id.*

The court also found that the plaintiffs had suffered severe mental pain. In reaching this conclusion, the court relied on the plaintiffs' testimony that they feared they would be killed during beatings by Vuckovic or during the "game" of Russian roulette. Although the court did not specify the predicate acts that caused the prolonged mental harm, it is plain that both the threat of severe physical pain and the threat of imminent death were present and persistent. The court also found that the plaintiffs established the existence of prolonged mental harm as each plaintiff "*continues* to suffer long-term psychological harm as a result of [their] ordeals." *Id.* (emphasis added). In concluding that the plaintiffs had demonstrated the necessary "prolonged mental harm," the court's description of that harm as ongoing and "long-term" confirms that, to satisfy the prolonged mental harm requirement, the harm must be of a substantial duration.

The court did not, however, delve into the nature of psychological harm in reaching its conclusion. Nonetheless, the symptoms that the plaintiffs suffered and continue to suffer are worth noting as illustrative of what might in future cases be held to constitute mental harm. Mehinovic had "anxiety, flashbacks, and nightmares and has difficulty sleeping." *Id.* at 1334. Similarly, Bicic, "suffers from anxiety, sleeps very little, and has frequent nightmares" and experiences frustration at not being able to work due to the physical and mental pain he suffers. *Id.* at 1336. Hadzialijagic experienced nightmares, at times required medication to help him sleep, suffered from depression, and had become reclusive as a result of his ordeal. *See id.* at 1337–38. Subasic, like the others, had nightmares and flashbacks, but also suffered from nervousness, irritability, and experienced difficulty trusting people. The combined effect of these symptoms impaired Subasic's ability to work. *See id.* at 1340. Each of these plaintiffs suffered from mental harm that destroyed his ability to function normally, on a daily basis, and would continue to do so into the future.

In general, several guiding principles can be drawn from this case. First, this case illustrates that a single incident can constitute torture. The above recitation of the case's facts shows that Subasic was clearly subjected to torture in a number of instances, e.g., the teeth pulling incident, which the court finds to constitute torture in discussing Bicic. The court nevertheless found that the beating in which Vuckovic delivered a blow to Subasic's stomach while he was on his knees sufficed to establish that Subasic had been tortured. Indeed, the court stated that this incident "caus[ed] Subasic to suffer severe pain." *Id.* at 1346. The court's focus on this incident, despite the obvious context of a course of torturous conduct, suggests that a course of conduct is unnecessary to establish that an individual engaged in torture. It bears noting, however, that there are no decisions that have found an example of torture on facts that show the action was isolated, rather than part of a systematic course of conduct. Moreover, we believe that had this been an isolated instance, the court's conclusion that this act constituted torture would have been in error, because this single blow does not reach the requisite level of severity.

Second, the case demonstrates that courts may be willing to find that a wide range of physical pain can rise to the necessary level of "severe pain or suffering." At one end of the spectrum is what the court calls the "nightmarish beating" in which Vuckovic hung Hadzialijagic upside down and beat him, culminating in Hadzialijagic going into cardiac arrest and narrowly escaping death. *Id.* It takes little analysis or insight to conclude that this incident constitutes torture. At the other end of the spectrum, is the court's determination that a beating in which "Vuckovic hit plaintiff Subasic and kicked him in the stomach with his military boots while Subasic was forced into a kneeling position[]" constituted torture. *Id.* To be sure, this beating caused Subasic substantial pain. But that pain pales in comparison to the other acts described in this case. Again, to the extent the opinion can be read to endorse the view that this single act and the attendant pain, considered in isolation, rose to the level of "severe pain or suffering," we would disagree with such a view based on our interpretation of the criminal statute.

The district court did not attempt to delineate the meaning of torture. It engaged in no statutory analysis. Instead, the court merely recited the definition and described the acts that it concluded constituted torture. This approach is representative of the approach most often taken in TVPA cases. The adoption of such an approach suggests that torture generally is of such an extreme nature—namely, the nature of acts are so shocking and obviously incredibly painful—that courts will more likely examine the totality of the circumstances, rather than engage in a careful parsing of the statute. A broad view of this case, and of the TVPA cases more generally, shows that only acts of an extreme nature have been redressed under the TVPA's civil remedy for torture. We note, however, that *Mehinovic* presents, with the exception of the single blow to Subasic, facts that are well over the line of what constitutes torture. While there are cases that fall far short of torture, see *infra* app., there are no cases that analyze what the lowest boundary of what constitutes torture. Nonetheless, while this case and the other TVPA cases generally do not approach that boundary, they are in keeping with the general notion that the term "torture" is reserved for acts of the most extreme nature.

IV. International Decisions

International decisions can prove of some value in assessing what conduct might rise to the level of severe mental pain or suffering. Although decisions by foreign or international bodies are in no way binding authority upon the United States, they provide guidance about how other nations will likely react to our interpretation of the CAT and Section 2340. As this Part will discuss, other Western nations have generally used a high standard in determining whether interrogation techniques violate the international prohibition on torture. In fact, these decisions have found various aggressive interrogation methods to, at worst, constitute cruel, inhuman, and degrading treatment, but not torture. These decisions only reinforce our view that there is a clear distinction between the two standards and that only extreme conduct, resulting in pain that is of an intensity often accompanying serious physical injury, will violate the latter.

A. European Court of Human Rights

An analogue to CAT's provisions can be found in the European Convention on Human Rights and Fundamental Freedoms (the "European Convention"). This convention prohibits torture, though it offers no definition of it. It also prohibits cruel, inhuman, or degrading treatment or punishment. By barring both types of acts, the European Convention implicitly distinguishes between them and further suggests that torture is a grave act beyond cruel, inhuman, or degrading treatment or punishment. Thus, while neither the European Convention nor the European Court of Human Rights decisions interpreting that convention would be authority for the interpretation of Sections 2340–2340A, the European Convention decisions concerning torture nonetheless provide a useful barometer of the international view of what actions amount to torture.

The leading European Court of Human Rights case explicating the differences between torture and cruel, inhuman, or degrading treatment or punishment is *Ireland v. the United Kingdom* (1978).[15] In that case, the European Court of Human Rights examined interrogation techniques somewhat more sophisticated than the rather rudimentary and frequently obviously cruel acts described in the TVPA cases. Careful attention to this case is worthwhile not just because it examines methods not used in the TVPA cases, but also because the Reagan administration relied on this case in reaching the conclusion that the term torture is reserved in international usage for "extreme, deliberate, and unusually cruel practices." S. Treaty Doc. 100–20, at 4.

The methods at issue in *Ireland* were:

(1) Wall Standing. The prisoner stands spread eagle against the wall, with fingers high above his head, and feet back so that he is standing on his toes such that all of his weight falls on his fingers.

(2) Hooding. A black or navy hood is placed over the prisoner's head and kept there except during the interrogation.

(3) Subjection to Noise. Pending interrogation, the prisoner is kept in a room with a loud and continuous hissing noise.

(4) Sleep Deprivation. Prisoners are deprived of sleep pending interrogation.

(5) Deprivation of Food and Drink. Prisoners receive a reduced diet during detention and pending interrogation.

The European Court of Human Rights concluded that these techniques used in combination, and applied for hours at a time, were inhuman and degrading but did not amount to torture. In analyzing whether these methods constituted torture, the court treated them as part of a single program. *See Ireland.* ¶ 104. The court found that this program caused "if not actual bodily injury, at least intense physical and mental suffering to the person subjected thereto and also led to acute psychiatric disturbances during the interrogation." *Id.* ¶ 167. Thus, this program "fell into the category of inhuman treatment[.]" *Id.* The court further found that "[t]he techniques were also degrading since they were such as to arouse in their victims feeling of fear, anguish and inferiority capable of humiliating and debasing them and possible [sic] breaking their physical or moral resistance." *Id.* Yet, the court ultimately concluded:

> Although the five techniques, as applied in combination, undoubtedly amounted to inhuman and degrading treatment, although their object was the extraction of confession, the naming of others and/or information and although they were used systematically, they did not occasion suffering of the particular *intensity* and *cruelty* implied by the word torture...

Id. (emphasis added). Thus, even though the court had concluded that the techniques produce "intense physical and mental suffering" and "acute psychiatric disturbances," they were not sufficient intensity or cruelty to amount to torture.

The court reached this conclusion based on the distinction the European Convention drew between torture and cruel, inhuman, or degrading treatment or punishment. The court reasoned that by expressly distinguishing between these two categories of treatment, the European Convention sought to "attach a special stigma to deliberate inhuman treatment causing very serious and cruel suffering." *Id.* ¶ 167. According to the court, "this distinction derives principally from a difference in the intensity of the suffering inflicted." *Id.* The court further noted that this distinction paralleled the one drawn in the U.N. Declaration on the Protection from Torture, which specifically defines torture as "'an aggravated and deliberate form of cruel, inhuman or degrading treatment or punishment.'" *Id.* (quoting U.N. Declaration on the Protection From Torture).

The court relied on this same "intensity/cruelty" distinction to conclude that some physical maltreatment fails to amount to torture. For example, four detainees were severely beaten and forced to stand spread eagle up against a wall. *See id.* ¶ 110. Other detainees were forced to stand spread eagle while an interrogator kicked them "continuously on the inside of the legs." *Id.* ¶ 111. Those detainees were beaten, some receiving injuries that were "substantial" and, others received "massive" injuries. *See id.* Another detainee was "subjected to...'comparatively trivial' beatings" that resulted in a perforation of the detainee's eardrum and some "minor bruising." *Id.* ¶ 115. The court concluded that none of these situations "attain[ed] the particular level [of severity] inherent in the notion of torture." *Id.* ¶ 174.

B. Israeli Supreme Court

The European Court of Human Rights is not the only other court to consider whether such a program of interrogation techniques was permissible. In *Public Committee Against Torture in Israel v. Israel*, 38 I.L.M. 1471 (1999), the Supreme Court of Israel reviewed a challenge brought against the General Security Service ("GSS") for its use of five techniques. At issue in *Public Committee Against Torture In Israel* were: (1) shaking, (2) the Shabach, (3) the Frog Crouch, (4) the excessive tightening of hand-cuffs, and (5) sleep deprivation. "Shaking" is "the forceful shaking of the suspect's upper torso, back and forth, repeatedly, in a manner which causes the neck and head to dangle and vacillate rapidly." *Id.* ¶ 9. The "Shabach" is actually a combination of methods wherein the detainee

> is seated on a small and low chair, whose seat is tilted forward, towards the ground. One hand is tied behind the suspect, and placed inside the gap between the chair's seat and back support. His second hand is tied behind the chair, against its back support. The suspect's head is covered by an opaque sack, falling down to his shoulders. Powerfully loud music is played in the room.

Id. ¶ 10.

The "frog crouch" consists of "consecutive, periodical crouches on the tips of one's toes, each lasting for five minute intervals." *Id.* ¶ 11. The excessive tightening of hand-cuffs simply referred to the use handcuffs that were too small for the suspects' wrists. *See id.* ¶ 12. Sleep deprivation occurred when the Shabach was used during "intense non-stop interrogations."[16] *Id.* ¶ 13.

While the Israeli Supreme Court concluded that these acts amounted to cruel, and inhuman treatment, the court did not expressly find that they amounted to torture. To be sure, such a conclusion was unnecessary because even if the acts amounted only to cruel and inhuman treatment the GSS lacked authority to use the five methods. Nonetheless, the decision is still best read as indicating that the acts at issue did not constitute torture. The court's descriptions of and conclusions about each method indicate that the court viewed them as merely cruel, inhuman or degrading but not of the sufficient severity to reach the threshold of torture. While its descriptions discuss necessity, dignity, degradation, and pain, the court carefully avoided describing any of these acts as having the severity of pain or suffering indicative of torture. *See id.* at ¶¶ 24–29. Indeed, in assessing the *Shabach* as a whole, the court even relied upon the European Court of Human Right's *Ireland* decision for support and it did not evince disagreement with that decision's conclusion that the acts considered therein did not constitute torture. *See id.* 30.

Moreover, the Israeli Supreme Court concluded that in certain circumstances GSS officers could assert a necessity defense.[17] CAT, however, expressly provides that "[n]o exceptional circumstance whatsoever, whether a state of war or a threat of war, inter-nal political instability or any other public emergency may be invoked as a justification of torture." Art. 2(2). Had the court been of the view that the GSS methods constituted torture, the Court could not permit this affirmative defense under CAT. Accordingly, the court's decision is best read as concluding that these methods amounted to cruel and inhuman treatment, but not torture.

In sum, both the European Court on Human Rights and the Israeli Supreme Court have recognized a wide array of acts that constitute cruel, inhuman, or degrading treatment or punishment, but do not amount to torture. Thus, they appear to permit, under international law, an aggressive interpretation as to what amounts to torture, leaving that label to be applied only where extreme circumstances exist.

V. The President's Commander-in-Chief Power

Even if an interrogation method arguably were to violate Section 2340A, the statute would be unconstitutional if it impermissibly encroached on the President's constitutional power to conduct a military campaign. As Commander-in-Chief, the President has the constitutional authority to order interrogations of enemy combatants to gain intelligence information concerning the military plans of the enemy. The demands of the Commander-in-Chief power are especially pronounced in the middle of a war in which the nation has already suffered a direct attack. In such a case, the information gained from interrogations may prevent future attacks by foreign enemies. Any effort to apply Section 2340A in a manner that interferes with the President's direction of such core war matters as the detention and interrogation of enemy combatants thus would be unconstitutional.

A. The War with Al Qaeda

At the outset, we should make clear the nature of the threat presently posed to the nation. While your request for legal advice is not specifically limited to the current circumstances, we think it is useful to discuss this question in the context of the current war against the al Qaeda terrorist network. The situation in which these issues arise is unprecedented in recent American history. Four coordinated terrorist attacks, using hijacked commercial airliners as guided missiles, took place in rapid succession on the morning of September 11, 2001. These attacks were aimed at critical government buildings in the Nation's capital and landmark buildings in its financial center. These events reach a different scale of destructiveness than earlier terrorist episodes, such as the destruction of the Murrah Building in Oklahoma City in 1994. They caused thousands of deaths. Air traffic and communications within the United States were disrupted; national stock exchanges were shut for several days; and damage from the attack has been estimated to run into the tens of billions of dollars. Moreover, these attacks are part of a violent campaign against the United States that is believed to include an unsuccessful attempt to destroy an airliner in December 2001; a suicide bombing attack in Yemen on the *U.S.S. Cole* in 2000; the bombings of the United States Embassies in Kenya and in Tanzania in 1998; a truck bomb attack on a U.S. military housing complex in Saudi Arabia in 1996; an unsuccessful attempt to destroy the World Trade Center in 1993; and the ambush of U.S. servicemen in Somalia in 1993. The United States and its overseas personnel and installations have been attacked as a result of Usama Bin Laden's call for a "jihad against the U.S. government, because the U.S. government is unjust, criminal and tyrannical."[18]

In response, the Government has engaged in a broad effort at home and abroad to counter terrorism. Pursuant to his authorities as Commander-in-Chief, the President in October, 2001, ordered the Armed Forces to attack al Qaeda personnel and assets in Afghanistan, and the Taliban militia that harbored them. That military campaign appears to be nearing its close with the retreat of al Qaeda and Taliban forces from their strongholds and the installation of a friendly provisional government in Afghanistan. Congress has provided its support for the use of forces against those linked to the September 11 attacks, and has recognized the President's constitutional power to use force to prevent and deter future attacks both within and outside the United States. S. J. Res. 23, Pub. L. No. 107-40, 115 Stat. 224 (2001). We have reviewed the President's constitutional power to use force abroad in response to the September 11 attacks in a separate memorandum. *See* Memorandum for Timothy E. Flanigan, Deputy Counsel to the President, from John C. Yoo, Deputy Assistant Attorney General, Office of Legal Counsel, *Re: The President's Constitutional Authority to Conduct Military Operations Against Terrorists and Nations Supporting Them* (Sept. 25, 2001) ("September 11 War Powers Memorandum"). We have also discussed the President's constitutional authority to deploy the armed forces domestically to protect against foreign terrorist attack in a separate memorandum. *See* Memorandum for Alberto R. Gonzales, Counsel to the President and William J. Haynes, II, General Counsel, Department of Defense, from John C. Yoo, Deputy Assistant Attorney General and Robert J. Delahunty, Special Counsel, Office of Legal Counsel, *Re: Authority for Use of Military Force to Combat Terrorist Activities Within the United States* at 2–3 (Oct. 17, 2001). The Justice Department and the FBI have launched a sweeping investigation in response to the September 11 attacks, and last fall Congress enacted legislation to expand the Justice Department's powers of surveillance against terrorists. *See* The USA Patriot Act, Pub. L. No. 107-56, 115 Stat. 272 (Oct. 26, 2001). This spring, the President proposed the creation of a new cabinet department for homeland security to implement a coordinated domestic program against terrorism.

Despite these efforts, numerous upper echelon leaders of al Qaeda and the Taliban, with access to active terrorist cells and other resources, remain at large. It has been reported that the al Qaeda fighters are already drawing on a fresh flow of cash to rebuild their forces. *See* Paul Haven, *U.S.: al-Qaida Trying to Regroup*, Associated Press, Mar. 20, 2002. As the Director of the Central Intelligence Agency has recently testified before Congress, "Al-Qa'ida and other terrorist groups will continue to plan to attack this country and its interests abroad. Their modus operandi is to have multiple attack plans in the works simultaneously, and to have al-Qa'ida cells in place to conduct them." Testimony of George J. Tenet, Director of Central Intelligence, Before the Senate Armed Services Committee at 2 (Mar. 19, 2002). Nor is the threat contained to Afghanistan. "Operations against US targets could be launched by al-Qa'ida cells already in place in major cities in Europe and the Middle East. Al-Qa'ida can also exploit its presence or connections to other groups in such countries as Somalia, Yemen, Indonesia, and the Philippines." *Id.* at 3. It appears that al Qaeda continues to enjoy information and resources that allow it to organize and direct active hostile forces against this country, both domestically and abroad.

Al Qaeda continues to plan further attacks, such as destroying American civilian airliners and killing American troops, which have fortunately been prevented. It is clear that bin Laden and his organization have conducted several violent attacks on the United States and its nationals, and that they seek to continue to do so. Thus, the capture and interrogation of such individuals is clearly imperative to our national security and defense. Interrogation of captured al Qaeda operatives may provide information concerning the nature of al Qaeda plans and the identities of its personnel, which may prove invaluable in preventing further direct attacks on the United States and its citizens. Given the massive destruction and loss of life caused by the September 11 attacks, it is reasonable to believe that information gained from al Qaeda personnel could prevent attacks of a similar (if not greater) magnitude from occurring in the United States. The case of Jose Padilla, a.k.a. Abdullah Al Mujahir, illustrates the importance of such information. Padilla allegedly had journeyed to Afghanistan and Pakistan, met with senior al Qaeda leaders, and hatched a plot to construct and detonate a radioactive dispersal device in the United States. After allegedly receiving training in wiring explosives and with a substantial amount of currency in his position, Padilla attempted in May, 2002, to enter the United States to further his scheme. Interrogation of captured al Qaeda operatives allegedly allowed U.S. intelligence and law enforcement agencies to track Padilla and to detain him upon his entry into the United States.

B. Interpretation to Avoid Constitutional Problems

As the Supreme Court has recognized, and as we will explain further below, the President enjoys complete discretion in the exercise of his Commander-in-Chief authority and in conducting operations against hostile forces. Because both "[t]he executive power and the command of the military and naval forces is vested in the President," the Supreme Court has unanimously stated that it is *the President alone []* who is constitutionally invested with the *entire charge of hostile operations.*" *Hamilton v. Dillin*, 88 U.S. (21 Wall.) 73, 87 (1874) (emphasis added). That authority is at its height in the middle of a war.

In light of the President's complete authority over the conduct of war, without a clear statement otherwise, we will not read a criminal statute as infringing on the President's ultimate authority in these areas. We have long recognized, and the Supreme Court has established a canon of statutory construction that statutes are to be construed in a manner that avoids constitutional difficulties so long as a reasonable alternative construction is available. *See, e.g., Edward J. DeBartolo Corp. v. Florida Gulf Coast Bldg. & Constr. Trades Council*, 485 U.S. 568, 575 (1988) (citing *NLRB v. Catholic Bishop of Chicago*, 440 U.S. 490, 499–501, 504 (1979)) ("[W]here an otherwise acceptable construction of a statute would raise serious constitutional problems, [courts] will construe [a] statute to avoid such problems unless such construction is plainly contrary to the intent of Congress."). This canon of construction applies especially where an act of Congress could be read to encroach upon powers constitutionally committed to a coordinate branch of government. *See, e.g., Franklin v.*

Massachusetts, 505 U.S. 788, 800–1 (1992) (citation omitted) ("Out of respect for the separation of powers and the unique constitutional position of the President, we find that textual silence is not enough to subject the President to the provisions of the [Administrative Procedure Act]. We would require an express statement by Congress before assuming it intended the President's performance of his statutory duties to be reviewed for abuse of discretion."); *Public Citizen v. United States Dep't of Justice*, 491 U.S. 440, 465–67 (1989) (construing Federal Advisory Committee Act not to apply to advice given by American Bar Association to the President on judicial nominations, to avoid potential constitutional question regarding encroachment on Presidential power to appoint judges).

In the area of foreign affairs, and war powers in particular, the avoidance canon has special force. *See, e.g., Dep't of Navy v. Egan*, 484 U.S. 518, 530 (1988) ("unless Congress specifically has provided otherwise, courts traditionally have been reluctant to intrude upon the authority of the Executive in military and national security affairs."); *Japan Whaling Ass'n v. American Cetacean Soc'y*, 478 U.S. 221, 232–33 (1986) (construing federal statutes to avoid curtailment of traditional presidential prerogatives in foreign affairs). We do not lightly assume that Congress has acted to interfere with the President's constitutionally superior position as Chief Executive and Commander in Chief in the area of military operations. *See Egan*, 484 U.S. at 529 (quoting *Haig v. Agee*, 453 U.S. 280, 293–94 (1981)). *See also Agee*, 453 U.S. at 291 (deference to Executive Branch is "especially" appropriate "in the area . . . of . . . national security").

In order to respect the President's inherent constitutional authority to manage a military campaign against al Qaeda and its allies, Section 2340A must be construed as not applying to interrogations undertaken pursuant to his Commander-in-Chief authority. As our Office has consistently held during this Administration and previous Administrations, Congress lacks authority under Article I to set the terms and conditions under which the President may exercise his authority as Commander-in-Chief to control the conduct of operations during a war. *See, e.g.,* Memorandum for Daniel J. Bryant, Assistant Attorney General, Office of Legislative Affairs, from Patrick F. Philbin, Deputy Assistant Attorney General, Office of Legal Counsel, *Re: Swift Justice Authorization Act* (Apr. 8, 2002); Memorandum for Timothy E. Flanigan, Deputy Counsel to the President, from John C. Yoo, Deputy Assistant Attorney General, Office of Legal Counsel, *Re: The President's Constitutional Authority to Conduct Military Operations Against Terrorists and Nations Supporting Them* (Sep. 25, 2001) ("Flanigan Memorandum"); Memorandum for Andrew Fois, Assistant Attorney General, Office of Legislative Affairs, from Richard L. Shiffrin, Deputy Assistant Attorney General, Office of Legal Counsel, *Re: Defense Authorization Act* (Sep. 15, 1995). As we discuss below, the President's power to detain and interrogate enemy combatants arises out of his constitutional authority as Commander in Chief. A construction of Section 2340A that applied the provision to regulate the President's authority as Commander-in-Chief to determine the interrogation and treatment of enemy combatants would raise serious constitutional questions. Congress may no more regulate the President's ability to detain and interrogate enemy combatants than it may regulate his ability to direct troop movements on the battlefield. Accordingly, we would construe Section 2340A to avoid this constitutional difficulty, and conclude that it does not apply to the President's detention and interrogation of enemy combatants pursuant to his Commander-in-Chief authority.

This approach is consistent with previous decisions of our Office involving the application of federal criminal law. For example, we have previously construed the congressional contempt statute not to apply to Executive branch officials who refuse to comply with congressional subpoenas because of an assertion of executive privilege. In a published 1984 opinion, we concluded that

> if executive officials were subject to prosecution for criminal contempt whenever they carried out the President's claim of executive privilege, it would significantly burden and immeasurably impair the President's ability to fulfill his constitutional duties. Therefore, the separation of powers principles that underlie the doctrine of executive privilege also would preclude an application of the contempt of Congress statute to punish officials for aiding the President in asserting his constitutional privilege.

Prosecution for Contempt of Congress of an Executive Branch Offical Who Has Asserted A Claim of Executive Privilege, 8 Op. O.L.C. 101, 134 (May 30, 1984). Likewise, we believe that, if executive officials were subject to prosecution for conducting interrogations when they were carrying out the President's Commander-in-Chief powers, "it would significantly burden and immeasurably impair the President's ability to fulfill his constitutional duties." These constitutional principles preclude an application of Section 2340A to punish officials for aiding the President in exercising his exclusive constitutional authorities. *Id.*

C. The Commander-in-Chief Power

It could be argued that Congress enacted 18 U.S.C. § 2340A with full knowledge and consideration of the President's Commander-in-Chief power, and that Congress intended to restrict his discretion in the interrogation of enemy combatants. Even were we to accept this argument, however, we conclude that the Department of Justice could not enforce Section 2340A against federal officials acting pursuant to the President's constitutional authority to wage a military campaign.

Indeed, in a different context, we have concluded that both courts and prosecutors should reject prosecutions that apply federal criminal laws to activity that is authorized pursuant to one of the President's constitutional powers. This Office, for example, has previously concluded that Congress could not constitutionally extend the congressional contempt statute to Executive branch officials who refuse to comply with congressional subpoenas because of an assertion of executive privilege. We opined that "courts ... would surely conclude that a criminal prosecution for the exercise of a presumptively valid, constitutionally based privilege is not consistent with the

Constitution." 8 Op. O.L.C. at 141. Further, we concluded that the Department of Justice could not bring a criminal prosecution against a defendant who had acted pursuant to an exercise of the President's constitutional power. "The President, through a United States Attorney, need not, indeed may not, prosecute criminally a subordinate for asserting on his behalf a claim of executive privilege. Nor could the Legislative Branch or the courts require or implement the prosecution of such an individual." *Id.* Although Congress may define federal crimes that the President, through the Take Care Clause, should prosecute, Congress cannot compel the President to prosecute outcomes taken pursuant to the President's own constitutional authority. If Congress could do so, it could control the President's authority through the manipulation of federal criminal law.

We have even greater concerns with respect to prosecutions arising out of the exercise of the President's express authority as Commander in Chief than we do with prosecutions arising out of the assertion of executive privilege. In a series of opinions examining various legal questions arising after September 11, we have explained the scope of the President's Commander-in-Chief power.[19] We briefly summarize the findings of those opinions here. The President's constitutional power to protect the security of the United States and the lives and safety of its people must be understood in light of the Founders' intention to create a federal government "cloathed with all the powers requisite to the complete execution of its trust." *The Federalist* No. 23, at 147 (Alexander Hamilton) (Jacob E. Cooke ed. 1961). Foremost among the objectives committed to that trust by the Constitution is the security of the nation. As Hamilton explained in arguing for the Constitution's adoption, because "the circumstances which may affect the public safety" are not "reducible within certain determinate limits,"

> it must be admitted, as a necessary consequence, that there can be no limitation of that authority, which is to provide for the defence and protection of the community, in any matter essential to its efficacy.

Id. at 147–48. Within the limits that the Constitution itself imposes, the scope and distribution of the powers to protect national security must be construed to authorize the most efficacious defense of the nation and its interests in accordance "with the realistic purposes of the entire instrument." *Lichter v. United States*, 334 U.S. 742, 782 (1948).

The text, structure and history of the Constitution establish that the Founders entrusted the President with the primary responsibility, and therefore the power, to ensure the security of the United States in situations of grave and unforeseen emergencies. The decision to deploy military force in the defense of United States interests is expressly placed under Presidential authority by the Vesting Clause, U.S. Const. Art. I, § 1, cl. 1, and by the Commander-in-Chief Clause, *id.*, § 2, cl. 1.[20] This Office has long understood the Commander-in-Chief Clause in particular as an affirmative grant of authority to the President. *See, e.g.*, Memorandum for Charles W. Colson, Special Counsel to the President, from William H. Rehnquist, Assistant Attorney General,

Office of Legal Counsel, *Re: The President and the War Power: South Vietnam and the Cambodian Sanctuaries* (May 22, 1970) ("Rehnquist Memorandum"). The Framers understood the Clause as investing the President with the fullest range of power understood at the time of the ratification of the Constitution as belonging to the military commander. In addition, the structure of the Constitution demonstrates that any power traditionally understood as pertaining to the executive—which includes the conduct of warfare and the defense of the nation—unless expressly assigned in the Constitution to Congress, is vested in the President. Article II, Section 1 makes this clear by stating that the "executive Power shall be vested in a President of the United States of America." That sweeping grant vests in the President an unenumerated "executive power" and contrasts with the specific enumeration of the powers—those "herein"—granted to Congress in Article I. The implications of constitutional text and structure are confirmed by the practical consideration that national security decisions require the unity in purpose and energy in action that characterize the Presidency rather than Congress.[21]

As the Supreme Court has recognized, the Commander-in-Chief power and the President's obligation to protect the nation imply the ancillary powers necessary to their successful exercise. "The first of the enumerated powers of the President is that he shall be Commander-in-Chief of the Army and Navy of the United States. And, of course, the grant of war power includes all that is necessary and proper for carrying those powers into execution." *Johnson v. Eisentrager*, 339 U.S. 763, 788 (1950). In wartime, it is for the President alone to decide what methods to use to best prevail against the enemy. *See, e.g.*, Rehnquist Memorandum; Flanigan Memorandum at 3. The President's complete discretion in exercising the Commander-in-Chief power has been recognized by the courts. In the *Prize Cases*, 67 U.S. (2 Black) 635, 670 (1862), for example, the Court explained that whether the President "in fulfilling his duties as Commander in Chief" had appropriately responded to the rebellion of the southern states was a question "to be *decided by him*" and which the Court could not question, but must leave to "the political department of the Government to which this power was entrusted."

One of the core functions of the Commander in Chief is that of capturing, detaining, and interrogating members of the enemy. *See, e.g.*, Memorandum for William J. Haynes, II, General Counsel, Department of Defense, from Jay S. Bybee, Assistant Attorney General, Office of Legal Counsel, *Re: The President's Power as Commander in Chief to Transfer Captured Terrorists to the Control and Custody of Foreign Nations* at 3 (March 13, 2002) ("the Commander-in-Chief Clause constitutes an independent grant of substantive authority to engage in the detention and transfer of prisoners captured in armed conflicts"). It is well settled that the President may seize and detain enemy combatants, at least for the duration of the conflict, and the laws of war make clear that prisoners may be interrogated for information concerning the enemy, its strength, and its plans.[22] Numerous Presidents have ordered the capture, detention, and questioning of enemy combatants during virtually every major conflict in the Nation's history, including recent conflicts such as the Gulf, Vietnam, and Korean wars. Recognizing this authority, Congress has never attempted to restrict or interfere with the President's authority on this score. *Id.*

Any effort by Congress to regulate the interrogation of battlefield combatants would violate the Constitution's sole vesting of the Commander-in-Chief authority in the President. There can be little doubt that intelligence operations, such as the detention and interrogation of enemy combatants and leaders, are both necessary and proper for the effective conduct of a military campaign. Indeed, such operations may be of more importance in a war with an international terrorist organization than one with the conventional armed forces of a nation-state, due to the former's emphasis on secret operations and surprise attacks against civilians. It may be the case that only successful interrogations can provide the information necessary to prevent the success of covert terrorist attacks upon the United States and its citizens. Congress can no more interfere with the President's conduct of the interrogation of enemy combatants than it can dictate strategic or tactical decisions on the battlefield. Just as statutes that order the President to conduct warfare in a certain manner or for specific goals would be unconstitutional, so too are laws that seek to prevent the President from gaining the intelligence he believes necessary to prevent attacks upon the United States.

VI. Defenses

In the foregoing parts of this memorandum, we have demonstrated that the ban on torture in Section 2340A is limited to only the most extreme forms of physical and mental harm. We have also demonstrated that Section 2340A, as applied to interrogations of enemy combatants ordered by the President pursuant to his Commander-in-Chief power would be unconstitutional. Even if an interrogation method, however, might arguably cross the line drawn in Section 2340, and application of the statute was not held to be an unconstitutional infringement of the President's Commander-in-Chief authority, we believe that under the current circumstances certain justification defenses might be available that would potentially eliminate criminal liability. Standard criminal law defenses of necessity and self-defense could justify interrogation methods needed to elicit information to prevent a direct and imminent threat to the United States and its citizens.

A. Necessity

We believe that a defense of necessity could be raised, under the current circumstances, to an allegation of a Section 2340A violation. Often referred to as the "choice of evils" defense, necessity has been defined as follows:

> Conduct that the actor believes to be necessary to avoid a harm or evil to himself or to another is justifiable, provided that:
> (a) the harm or evil sought to be avoided by such conduct is greater than that sought to be prevented by the law defining the offense charged; and

(b) neither the Code nor other law defining the offense provides exceptions or defenses dealing with the specific situation involved; and

(c) a legislative purpose to exclude the justification claimed does not otherwise plainly appear.

Model Penal Code § 3.02. *See* also Wayne R. LaFave & Austin W. Scott, 1 Substantive Criminal Law § 5.4 at 627 (1986 & 2002 supp.) ("LaFave & Scott"). Although there is no federal statute that generally establishes necessity or other justifications as defenses to federal criminal laws, the Supreme Court has recognized the defense. See *United States v. Bailey*, 444 U.S. 394, 410 (1980) (relying on LaFave & Scott and Model Penal Code definitions of necessity defense).

The necessity defense may prove especially relevant in the current circumstances. As it has been described in the case law and literature, the purpose behind necessity is one of public policy. According to LaFave and Scott, "the law ought to promote the achievement of higher values at the expense of lesser values, and sometimes the greater good for society will be accomplished by violating the literal language of the criminal law." LaFave & Scott, at 629. In particular, the necessity defense can justify the intentional killing of one person to save two others because "it is better that two lives be saved and one lost than that two be lost and one saved." *Id.* Or, put in the language of a choice of evils, "the evil involved in violating the terms of the criminal law (. . . even taking another's life) may be less than that which would result from literal compliance with the law (. . . two lives lost)." *Id.*

Additional elements of the necessity defense are worth noting here. First, the defense is not limited to certain types of harms. Therefore, the harm inflicted by necessity may include intentional homicide, so long as the harm avoided is greater (i.e., preventing more deaths). *Id.* at 634. Second, it must actually be the defendant's intention to avoid the greater harm; intending to commit murder and then learning only later that the death had the fortuitous result of saving other lives will not support a necessity defense. *Id.* at 635. Third, if the defendant reasonably believed that the lesser harm was necessary, even if, unknown to him, it was not, he may still avail himself of the defense. As LaFave and Scott explain, "if A kills B reasonably believing it to be necessary to save C and D, he is not guilty of murder even though, unknown to A, C and D could have been rescued without the necessity of killing B." *Id.* Fourth, it is for the court, and not the defendant to judge whether the harm avoided outweighed the harm done. *Id.* at 636. Fifth, the defendant cannot rely upon the necessity defense if a third alternative is open and known to him that will cause less harm.

It appears to us that under the current circumstances the necessity defense could be successfully maintained in response to an allegation of a Section 2340A violation. On September 11, 2001, al Qaeda launched a surprise covert attack on civilian targets in the United States that led to the deaths of thousands and losses in the billions of dollars. According to public and governmental reports, al Qaeda has other sleeper cells within the United States that may be planning similar attacks. Indeed, al Qaeda plans apparently include efforts to develop and deploy chemical, biological and nuclear weapons of mass destruction. Under these circumstances, a detainee may possess information that could enable the United States to prevent attacks that potentially could equal or surpass the September 11 attacks in their magnitude. Clearly, any harm that might occur during an interrogation would pale to insignificance compared to the harm avoided by preventing such an attack, which could take hundreds or thousands of lives.

Under this calculus, two factors will help indicate when the necessity defense could appropriately be invoked. First, the more certain that government officials are that a particular individual has information needed to prevent an attack, the more necessary interrogation will be. Second, the more likely it appears to be that a terrorist attack is likely to occur, and the greater the amount of damage expected from such an attack, the more that an interrogation to get information would become necessary. Of course, the strength of the necessity defense depends on the circumstances that prevail, and the knowledge of the government actors involved, when the interrogation is conducted. While every interrogation that might violate Section 2340A does not trigger a necessity defense, we can say that certain circumstances could support such a defense.

Legal authorities identify an important exception to the necessity defense. The defense is available "only in situations wherein the legislature has not itself, in its criminal statute, made a determination of values." *Id.* at 629. Thus, if Congress explicitly has made clear that violation of a statute cannot be outweighed by the harm avoided, courts cannot recognize the necessity defense. LaFave and Israel provide as an example an abortion statute that made clear that abortions even to save the life of the mother would still be a crime; in such cases the necessity defense would be unavailable. *Id.* at 630. Here, however, Congress has not explicitly made a determination of values vis-à-vis torture. In fact, Congress explicitly removed efforts to remove torture from the weighing of values permitted by the necessity defense.[23]

B. Self-Defense

Even if a court were to find that a violation of Section 2340A was not justified by necessity, a defendant could still appropriately raise a claim of self-defense. The right to self-defense, even when it involves deadly force, is deeply embedded in our law, both as to individuals and as to the nation as a whole. As the Court of Appeals for the D.C. Circuit has explained:

> More than two centuries ago, Blackstone, best known of the expositors of the English common law, taught that "all homicide is malicious, and of course amounts to murder, unless... excused on the account of accident or self-preservation...." Self-defense, as a doctrine legally exonerating the taking of human life, is as viable now as it was in Blackstone's time.

United States v. Peterson, 483 F.2d 1222, 1228–29 (D.C. Cir. 1973). Self-defense is a common-law defense to federal criminal law offenses, and nothing in the text, structure or history of Section 2340A precludes its application to a charge of torture. In the absence of any textual provision to the contrary, we assume self-defense can be an appropriate defense to an allegation of torture.

The doctrine of self-defense permits the use of force to prevent harm to another person. As LaFave and Scott explain, "one is justified in using reasonable force in defense of another person, even a stranger, when he reasonably believes that the other is in immediate danger of unlawful bodily harm from his adversary and that the use of such force is necessary to avoid this danger." *Id.* at 663–64. Ultimately, even deadly force is permissible, but "only when the attack of the adversary upon the other person reasonably appears to the defender to be a deadly attack." *Id.* at 664. As with our discussion of necessity, we will review the significant elements of this defense.[24] According to LaFave and Scott, the elements of the defense of others are the same as those that apply to individual self-defense.

First, self-defense requires that the use of force be *necessary* to avoid the danger of unlawful bodily harm. *Id.* at 649. A defender may justifiably use deadly force if he reasonably believes that the other person is about to inflict unlawful death or serious bodily harm upon another, and that it is necessary to use such force to prevent it. *Id.* at 652. Looked at from the opposite perspective, the defender may not use force when the force would be as equally effective at a later time and the defender suffers no harm or risk by waiting. *See* Paul H. Robinson, 2 Criminal Law Defenses § 131(c) at 77 (1984). If, however, other options permit the defender to retreat safely from a confrontation without having to resort to deadly force, the use of force may not be necessary in the first place. La Fave and Scott at 659–60.

Second, self-defense requires that the defendant's belief in the necessity of using force be reasonable. If a defendant honestly but unreasonably believed force was necessary, he will not be able to make out a successful claim of self-defense. *Id.* at 654. Conversely, if a defendant reasonably believed an attack was to occur, but the facts subsequently showed no attack was threatened, he may still raise self-defense. As LaFave and Scott explain, "one may be justified in shooting to death an adversary who, having threatened to kill him, reaches for his pocket as if for a gun, though it later appears that he had no gun and that he was only reaching for his handkerchief." *Id.* Some authorities, such as the Model Penal Code, even eliminate the reasonability element, and require only that the defender honestly believed—regardless of its unreasonableness—that the use of force was necessary.

Third, many legal authorities include the requirement that a defender must reasonably believe that the unlawful violence is "imminent" before he can use force in his defense. It would be a mistake, however, to equate imminence necessarily with timing—that an attack is immediately about to occur. Rather, as the Model Penal Code explains, what is essential is that, the defensive *response* must be "immediately necessary." Model Penal Code § 3.04(1). Indeed, imminence may be merely another way of expressing the requirement of necessity. Robinson at 78. LaFave and Scott, for example, believe that the imminence requirement makes sense as part of a necessity defense because if an attack is not immediately upon the defender, the defender has other options available to avoid the attack that do not involve the use of force. LaFave and Scott at 656. If, however, the fact of the attack becomes certain and no other options remain, the use of force may be justified. To use a well-known hypothetical, if A were to kidnap and confine B, and then tell B he would kill B one week later, B would be justified in using force in self-defense, even if the opportunity arose before the week had passed. *Id.* at 656; *see also* Robinson at § 131(c)(1) at 78. In this hypothetical, while the attack itself is not imminent, B's use of force becomes immediately necessary whenever he has an opportunity to save himself from A.

Fourth, the amount of force should be proportional to the threat. As LaFave and Scott explain, "the amount of force which [the defender] may justifiably use must be reasonably related to the threatened harm which he seeks to avoid." LaFave and Scott at 651. Thus, one may not use deadly force in response to a threat that does not rise to death or serious bodily harm. If such harm may result, however, deadly force is appropriate. As the Model Penal Code § 3.04(2)(b) states, "[t]he use of deadly force is not justifiable... unless the actor believes that such force is necessary to protect himself against death, serious bodily injury, kidnapping or sexual intercourse compelled by force or threat."

Under the current circumstances, we believe that a defendant accused of violating Section 2340A could have, in certain circumstances, grounds to properly claim the defense of another. The threat of an impending terrorist attack threatens the lives of hundreds if not thousands of American citizens. Whether such a defense will be upheld depends on the specific context within which the interrogation decision is made. If an attack appears increasingly likely, but our intelligence services and armed forces cannot prevent it without the information from the interrogation of a specific individual, then the more likely it will appear that the conduct in question will be seen as necessary. If intelligence and other information support the conclusion that an attack is increasingly certain, then the necessity for the interrogation will be reasonable. The increasing certainty of an attack will also satisfy the imminence requirement. Finally, the fact that previous al Qaeda attacks have had as their aim the deaths of American citizens, and that evidence of other plots have had a similar goal in mind, would justify proportionality of interrogation methods designed to elicit information to prevent such deaths.

To be sure, this situation is different from the usual self-defense justification, and, indeed, it overlaps with elements of the necessity defense. Self-defense as usually discussed involves using force against an individual who is about to conduct the attack. In the current circumstances, however, an enemy combatant in detention does not himself present a threat of harm. He is not actually carrying out the attack; rather, he has participated in the planning and preparation for the attack, or merely has knowledge of the attack through his membership in the terrorist organization. Nonetheless, leading scholarly commentators believe that interrogation of such individuals using methods that might violate Section 2340A would be justified under the doctrine of self-defense, because the combatant by aiding and promoting the terrorist plot "has culpably caused the situation where someone might get hurt. If hurting him is the only means to prevent the death or injury of others put at risk by his actions, such torture should be permissible, and on the same basis that self-defense is permissible." Michael S. Moore, *Torture and the Balance of Evils*, 23 Israel L. Rev. 280, 323 (1989) (symposium on Israel's Landau Commission Report).[25] Thus, some commentators believe that by helping to create the threat of loss of life, terrorists become culpable for the threat even though they do not actually carry out the attack itself. They may be hurt in an interrogation because they are part of the mechanism that has set the attack in motion, *id.* at 323, just as is someone who feeds ammunition or targeting information to an attacker. Under the present circumstances, therefore, even though a detained enemy combatant may not be the exact attacker—he is not planting the bomb, or piloting a hijacked plane to kill civilians—he still may be harmed in self-defense if he has knowledge of future attacks because he has assisted in their planning and execution.

Further, we believe that a claim by an individual of the defense of another would be further supported by the fact that, in this case, the nation itself is under attack and has the right to self-defense. This fact can bolster and support an individual claim of self-defense in a prosecution, according to the teaching of the Supreme Court in *In re Neagle*, 135 U.S. 1 (1890). In that case, the State of California arrested and held deputy U.S. Marshal Neagle for shooting and killing the assailant of Supreme Court Justice Field. In granting the writ of habeas corpus for Neagle's release, the Supreme Court did not rely alone upon the marshal's right to defend another or his right to self-defense. Rather, the Court found that Neagle, as an agent of the United States and of the executive branch, was justified in the killing because, in protecting Justice Field, he was acting pursuant to the executive branch's inherent constitutional authority to protect the United States government. *Id.* at 67 ("We cannot doubt the power of the president to take measures for the protection of a judge of one of the courts of the United States who, while in the discharge of the duties of his office, is threatened with a personal attack which may probably result in his death."). That authority derives, according to the Court, from the President's power under Article II to take care that the laws are faithfully executed. In other words, Neagle as a federal officer not only could raise self-defense or defense of another, but also could defend his actions on the ground that he was implementing the Executive Branch's authority to protect the United States government.

If the right to defend the national government can be raised as a defense in an individual prosecution, as *Neagle* suggests, then a government defendant, acting in his official capacity, should be able to argue that any conduct that arguably violated Section 2340A was undertaken pursuant to more than just individual self-defense or defense of another. In addition, the defendant could claim that he was fulfilling the Executive Branch's authority to protect the federal government, and the nation, from attack. The September 11 attacks have already triggered that authority, as recognized both under domestic and international law. Following the example of *In re Neagle*, we conclude that a government defendant may also argue that his conduct of an interrogation, if properly authorized, is justified on the basis of protecting the nation from attack.

There can be little doubt that the nation's right to self-defense has been triggered under our law. The Constitution announces that one of its purposes is "to provide for the common defense." U.S. Const., Preamble. Article I, § 8 declares that Congress is to exercise its powers to "provide for the common Defence." *See also* 2 Pub. Papers of Ronald Reagan 920, 921 (1988–89) (right of self-defense recognized by Article 51 of the U.N. Charter). The President has a particular responsibility and power to take steps to defend the nation and its people. *In re Neagle*, 135 U.S. at 64. *See also* U.S. Const., art. IV, § 4 ("The United States shall . . . protect [each of the States] against Invasion"). As Commander-in-Chief and Chief Executive, he may use the armed forces to protect the nation and its people. *See, e.g., United States v. Verdugo-Urquidez*, 494 U.S. 259, 273 (1990). And he may employ secret agents to aid in his work as Commander-in-Chief. *Totten v. United States*, 92 U.S. 105, 106 (1876). As the Supreme Court observed in *The Prize Cases*, 67 U.S. (2 Black) 635 (1862), in response to an armed attack on the United States "the President is not only authorized but bound to resist force by force . . . without waiting for any special legislative authority." *Id.* at 668. The September 11 events were a direct attack on the United States, and as we have explained above, the President has authorized the use of military force with the support of Congress.[26]

As we have made clear in other opinions involving the war against al Qaeda, the nation's right to self-defense has been triggered by the events of September 11. If a government defendant were to harm an enemy combatant during an interrogation in a manner that might arguably violate Section 2340A, he would be doing so in order to prevent further attacks on the United States by the al Qaeda terrorist network. In that case, we believe that he could argue that his actions were justified by the Executive branch's constitutional authority to protect the nation from attack. This national and international version of the right to self-defense could supplement and bolster the government defendant's individual right.

Conclusion

For the foregoing reasons, we conclude that torture as defined in and proscribed by Sections 2340–2340A, covers only extreme acts. Severe pain is generally of the kind difficult for the victim to endure. Where the pain is physical, it must be of an intensity akin to that which accompanies serious physical injury such as death or organ failure. Severe mental pain requires suffering not just at the moment of infliction but it also requires lasting psychological harm, such as seen in mental disorders like posttraumatic stress disorder. Additionally, such severe mental pain can arise only from the predicate acts listed in Section 2340. Because the acts inflicting torture are extreme, there is significant range of acts that though they might constitute cruel, inhuman, or degrading treatment or punishment fail to rise to the level of torture.

Further, we conclude that under the circumstances of the current war against al Qaeda and its allies, application of Section 2340A to interrogations undertaken pursuant to the President's Commander-in-Chief powers may be unconstitutional. Finally, even if an interrogation method might violate Section 2340A, necessity or self-defense

could provide justifications that would eliminate any criminal liability.
Please let us know if we can be of further assistance.

[signed]

Jay S. Bybee
Assistant Attorney General

APPENDIX

Cases in which U.S. courts have concluded the defendant tortured the plaintiff:

- Plaintiff was beaten and shot by government troops while protesting the destruction of her property. *See Wiwa v. Royal Dutch Petroleum*, 2002 WL 319887 at *7 (S.D.N.Y. Feb. 28, 2002).

- Plaintiff was removed from ship, interrogated, and held incommunicado for months. Representatives of defendant threatened her with death if she attempted to move from quarters where she was held. She was forcibly separated from her husband and unable to learn of his welfare or whereabouts. *See Simpson v. Socialist People's Libyan Arab Jamahiriya*, 180 F. Supp. 2d 78, 88 (D.D.C. 2001) (Rule 12(b)(6) motion).

- Plaintiff was held captive for five days in a small cell that had no lights, no window, no water, and no toilet. During the remainder of his captivity, he was frequently denied food and water and given only limited access to the toilet. He was held at gunpoint, with his captors threatening to kill him if he did not confess to espionage. His captors threatened to cut off his fingers, pull out his fingernails, and shock his testicles. *See Daliberti v. Republic of Iraq*, 146 F. Supp. 2d 19, 22–23, 25 (D.D.C. 2001) (default judgment).

- Plaintiff was imprisoned for 205 days. He was confined in a car park that had been converted into a prison. His cell had no water or toilet and had only a steel cot for a bed. He was convicted of illegal entry into Iraq and transferred to another facility, where he was placed in a cell infested with vermin. He shared a single toilet with 200 other prisoners. While imprisoned he had a heart attack but was denied adequate medical attention and medication. *See Daliberti v. Republic of Iraq*, 146 F. Supp. 2d 19, 22–23 (D.D.C. 2001) (default judgment).

- Plaintiff was imprisoned for 126 days. At one point, a guard attempted to execute him, but another guard intervened. A truck transporting the plaintiff ran over pedestrian at full speed without stopping. He heard other prisoners being beaten and he feared being beaten. He had serious medical conditions that were not promptly or adequately treated. He was not given sufficient food or water. *See Daliberti v. Republic of Iraq,* 146 F. Supp. 2d 19, 22–23 (D.D.C. 2001) (default judgment).

- Allegations that guards beat, clubbed, and kicked the plaintiff and that the plaintiff was interrogated and subjected to physical and verbal abuse sufficiently stated a claim for torture so as to survive Rule 12(b)(6) motion. *See Price v. Socialist People's Libyan Arab Jamahiriya,* 110 F. Supp. 2d 10 (D.D.C. 2000).

- Plaintiffs alleged that they were blindfolded, interrogated and subjected to physical, mental, and verbal abuse while they were held captive. Furthermore, one plaintiff was held eleven days without food, water, or bed. Another plaintiff was held for four days without food, water, or a bed, and was also stripped naked, blindfolded, and threatened with electrocution of his testicles. The other two remaining plaintiffs alleged that they were not provided adequate or proper medical care for conditions that were life threatening. The court concluded that these allegations sufficiently stated a claim for torture and denied defendants Rule 12(b)(6) motion. *See Daliberti v. Republic v. Iraq,* 97 F. Supp. 2d 38, 45 (D.D.C. 2000) (finding that these allegations were "more than enough to meet the definition of torture in the [TVPA]").

- Plaintiff's kidnappers pistol-whipped him until he lost consciousness. They then stripped him and gave him only a robe to wear and left him bleeding, dizzy, and in severe pain. He was then imprisoned for 1,908 days. During his imprisonment, his captors sought to force a confession from him by playing Russian Roulette with him and threatening him with castration. He was randomly beaten and forced to watch the beatings of others. Additionally, he was confined in a rodent and scorpion infested cell. He was bound in chains almost the entire time of his confinement. One night during the winter, his captors chained him to an upper floor balcony, leaving him exposed to the elements. Consequently, he developed frostbite on his hands and feet. He was also subjected to a surgical procedure for an unidentified abdominal problem. *See Cicippio v. Islamic Republic of Iran,* 18 F. Supp. 2d 62 (D.D.C. 1998).

- Plaintiff was kidnapped at gunpoint. He was beaten for several days after his kidnapping. He was subjected to daily torture and threats of death. He was kept in solitary confinement for two years. During that time, he was blindfolded and chained to the wall in a six-foot by six-foot room infested with rodents. He was shackled in a stooped position for 44 months and he developed eye infections as a result of the blindfolds. Additionally, his captors did the following: forced him to kneel on spikes, administered electric shocks to his hands; battered his feet with iron bars and struck him in the kidneys with a rifle; struck him on the side of his head with a hand grenade, breaking his nose and jaw; placed boiling tea kettles on his shoulders; and they laced his food with arsenic. *See Cicippio v. Islamic Republic of Iran*, 18 F. Supp. 2d 62 (D.D.C. 1998).

- Plaintiff was pistol-whipped, bound and gagged, held captive in darkness or blindfold for 18 months. He was kept chained at either his ankles or wrists, wearing nothing but his undershorts and a t-shirt. As for his meals, his captors gave him pita bread and dry cheese for breakfast, rice with dehydrated soup for lunch, and a piece of bread for dinner. Sometimes the guards would spit into his food. He was regularly beaten and incessantly interrogated; he overheard the deaths and beatings of other prisoners. *See Cicippio v. Islamic Republic of Iran*, 18 F. Supp. 2d 62, (D.D.C. 1998).

- Plaintiff spent eight years in solitary or near solitary confinement. He was threatened with death, blindfolded and beaten while handcuffed and fettered. He was denied sleep and repeatedly threatened with death. At one point, while he was shackled to a cot, the guards placed a towel over his nose and mouth and then poured water down his nostrils. They did this for six hours. During this incident, the guards threatened him with death and electric shock. Afterwards, they left him shackled to his cot for six days. For the next seven months, he was imprisoned in a hot, unlit cell that measured 2.5 square meters. During this seven-month period, he was shackled to his cot—at first by all his limbs and later by one hand or one foot. He remained shackled in this manner except for the briefest moments, such as when his captors permitted him to use the bathroom. The handcuffs cut into his flesh. *See Hilao v. Estate of Marcos*, 103 F.3d 789, 790 (9th Cir. 1996). The court did not, however, appear to consider the solitary confinement per se to constitute torture. *See id.* at 795 (stating that to the extent that [the plaintiff's] years in solitary confinement do not constitute torture, they clearly meet the definition of prolonged arbitrary detention").

- High-ranking military officers interrogated the plaintiff and subjected him to mock executions. He was also threatened with death. *See Hilao v. Estate of Marcos*, 103 F.3d 789, 795 (9th Cir. 1996).

- Plaintiff, a nun, received anonymous threats warning her to leave Guatemala. Later, two men with a gun kidnapped her. They blindfolded her and locked her in an unlit room for hours. The guards interrogated her and regardless of the answers she gave to their questions, they burned her with cigarettes. The guards then showed her surveillance photographs of herself. They blindfolded her again, stripped her, and raped her repeatedly. *See Xuncax v. Gramajo*, 886 F. Supp. 162, 176 (1995).

- Plaintiffs were beaten with truncheons, boots, and guns and threatened with death. Nightsticks were used to beat their backs, kidneys, and the soles of their feet. The soldiers pulled and squeezed their testicles. When they fainted from the pain, the soldiers revived them by singeing their nose hair with a cigarette lighter. They were interrogated as they were beaten with iron barks, rifle butts, helmets, and fists. One plaintiff was placed in the "djak" position, i.e., with hands and feet bound and suspended from a pole. Medical treatment was withheld for one week and then was sporadic and inadequate. See *Paul v. Avril*, 901 F. Supp. 330, 332 (S.D. Fla. 1994).

- Alien subjected to sustained beatings for the month following his first arrest. After his second arrest, suffered severe beatings and was burned with cigarettes over the course of an eight-day period. *Al-Saher v. INS*, 268 F.3d 1143, 1147 (9th Cir. 2001) (deportation case).

- Decedent was attacked with knifes and sticks, and repeatedly hit in the head with the butt of a gun as he remained trapped in his truck by his attackers. The attackers then doused the vehicle with gasoline. Although he managed to get out of the truck, he nonetheless burned to death. *Tachiona v. Mugabe*, No. 00 Civ. 6666VMJCF, 2002 WL 1424598 at *1 (S.D.N.Y. July 1, 2002).

- Decedent was attacked by spear, stick, and stone wielding supporters of defendant. He was carried off by the attackers and "was found dead the next day, naked and lying in the middle of the road[.]" From the physical injuries, it was determined that he had been severely beaten. According to his death certificate, he died from "massive brain injury from trauma; [] assault; and [] laceration of the right lung." *Tachiona v. Mugabe*, No. 00 Civ. 6666VMJCF, 2002 WL 1424598 at *2 (S.D.N.Y. July 1, 2002).

- Decedent was abducted, along with five others. He and the others were severely beaten and he was forced to drink diesel oil. He was then summarily executed. *Tachiona v. Mugabe*, No. 00 Civ. 6666VMJCF, 2002 WL 1424598 at *4 (S.D.N.Y. July 1, 2002).

- Forced sterilization constitutes torture. *Bi Zhu Lin v. Ashcroft*, 183 F. Supp. 2d 551 (D. Conn. 2002) (noting determination by immigration judge that such conduct constitutes torture).

There are two cases in which U.S. courts have rejected torture claims on the ground that the alleged conduct did not rise to the level of torture. In *Faulder v. Johnson*, 99 F. Supp. 2d 774 (S.D. Tex. 1999), the district court rejected a death row inmate's claim that psychological trauma resulting from repeated stays of his execution and his 22-year wait for that execution was torture under CAT. The court rejected this contention because of the United States' express death penalty reservation to CAT. *See id*. In *Eastman Kodak v. Kavlin*, 978 F. Supp. 1078, 1093 (S.D. Fla. 1997), the plaintiff was held for eight days in a filthy cell with drug dealers and an AIDS patient. He received no food, no blanket and no protection from other inmates. Prisoners murdered one another in front of the plaintiff. *Id*. The court flatly rejected the plaintiff's claim that this constituted torture.

NOTES

1. If convicted of torture, a defendant faces a fine or up to twenty years' imprisonment or both. If, however, the act resulted in the victim's death, a defendant may be sentenced to life imprisonment or to death. *See* 18 U.S.C.A. § 2340A(a). Whether death results from the act also affects the applicable statute of limitations. Where death does not result, the statute of limitations is eight years; if death results, there is no statute of limitations. *See* 18 U.S.C.A. § 3286(b) (West Supp. 2002); *id*. § 2332b(g)(5)(B) (West Supp. 2002). Section 2340A as originally enacted did not provide for the death penalty as a punishment. *See* Omnibus Crime Bill, Pub. L. No. 103–322, Title VI, Section 60020, 108 Stat. 1979 (1994) (amending section 2340A to provide for the death penalty); H. R. Conf. Rep. No. 103–711, at 388 (1994) (noting that the act added the death penalty as a penalty for torture).

Most recently, the USA Patriot Act, Pub. L. No. 107–56, 115 Stat. 272 (2001), amended section 2340A to expressly codify the offense of conspiracy to commit torture. Congress enacted this amendment as part of a broader effort to ensure that individuals engaged in the planning of terrorist activities could be prosecuted irrespective of where the activities took place. *See* H. R. Rep. No. 107–236, at 70 (2001) (discussing the addition of "conspiracy" as a separate offense for a variety of "Federal terrorism offense[s]").

2. We note, however, that 18 U.S.C. § 2340(3) supplies a definition of the term "United States." It defines it as "all areas under the jurisdiction of the United States including any of the places described in" 18 U.S.C. §§ 5 and 7, and in 49 U.S.C. § 46501(2). Section 5 provides that United States "includes all places and waters, continental or insular, subject to the jurisdiction of the United States." By including the definition set out in Section 7, the term "United States" as used in Section 2340(3) includes the "special maritime and territorial jurisdiction of the United States." Moreover, the incorporation by reference to Section 46501(2) extends the definition of the "United States" to "special aircraft jurisdiction of the United States."

3. One might argue that because the statute uses "or" rather than "and" in the phrase "pain or suffering" that "severe physical suffering" is a concept distinct from "severe physical pain." We believe the better view of the statutory text is, however, that they are not distinct concepts. The statute does not define "severe mental pain" and "severe mental suffering" separately. Instead, it gives the phrase "severe mental pain or suffering" a single definition. Because "pain or suffering" is single concept for the purposes of "severe mental pain or suffering," it should likewise be read as a single concept for the purposes of severe physical pain or suffering. Moreover, dictionaries define the words "pain" and "suffering" in terms of each other. *Compare, e.g.*, Webster's Third New International Dictionary 2284 (1993) (defining suffering as "the endurance of . . . pain" or "a pain endured"); Webster's Third New International Dictionary 2284 (1986) (same); XVII The Oxford English Dictionary 125 (2d ed. 1989) (defining suffering as "the bearing or undergoing of pain"); *with, e.g.*, Random House Webster's Unabridged Dictionary 1394

(2d ed. 1999) (defining "pain" as "physical suffering"); The American Heritage Dictionary of the English Language 942 (College ed. 1976) (defining pain as "suffering or distress"). Further, even if we were to read the infliction of severe physical suffering as distinct from severe physical pain, it is difficult to conceive of such suffering that would not involve severe physical pain. Accordingly, we conclude that "pain or suffering" is a single concept within the definition of Section 2340.

4. The DSM-IV explains that posttraumatic disorder ("PTSD") is brought on by exposure to traumatic events, such as serious physical injury or witnessing the deaths of others and during those events the individual felt "intense fear" or "horror." *Id.* at 424. Those suffering from this disorder reexperience the trauma through, *inter alia*, "recurrent and intrusive distressing recollections of the event," "recurrent distressing dreams of the event," or "intense psychological distress at exposure to internal or external cues that symbolize or resemble an aspect of the traumatic event." *Id.* at 428. Additionally, a person with PTSD "[p]ersistent[ly]" avoids stimuli associated with the trauma, including avoiding conversations about the trauma, places that stimulate recollections about the trauma; and they experience a numbing of general responsiveness, such as a "restricted range of affect (e.g., unable to have loving feelings)," and "the feeling of detachment or estrangement from others." *Ibid.* Finally, an individual with PTSD has "[p]ersistent symptoms of increased arousal," as evidenced by "irritability or outbursts of anger," "hypervigilance," "exaggerated startle response," and difficulty sleeping or concentrating. *Ibid.*

5. Published by the American Psychiatric Association, and written as a collaboration of over a thousand psychiatrists, the DSM-IV is commonly used in U.S. courts as a source of information regarding mental health issues and is likely to be used in trial should charges be brought that allege this predicate act. *See, e.g., Atkins v. Virginia*, 122 S. Ct. 2242, 2245 n.3 (2002); *Kansas v. Crane*, 122 S. Ct. 867, 871 (2002); *Kansas v. Hendricks*, 521 U.S. 346, 359–60 (1997); *McClean v. Merrifield*, No. 00-CV-0120E(SC), 2002 WL 1477607 at *2 n.7 (W.D.N.Y. June 28, 2002); *Peeples v. Coastal Office Prods.*, 203 F. Supp. 2d. 432, 439 (D. Md. 2002); *Lassiegne v. Taco Bell Corp.*, 202 F. Supp. 2d 512, 519 (E.D. La. 2002).

6. Torture is a term also found in state law. Some states expressly proscribe "murder by torture." *See, e.g.*, Idaho Code § 18-4001 (Michie 1997); N.C. Gen. Stat. Ann. § 14–17 (1999); *see also* Me. Rev. Stat. Ann. tit. 17-A, § 152-A (West Supp. 2001) (aggravated attempted murder is "[t]he attempted murder...accompanied by torture, sexual assault or other extreme cruelty inflicted upon the victim"). Other states have made torture an aggravating factor supporting imposition of the death penalty. *See, e.g.*, Ark. Code Ann. § 5-4-604(8)(B); Del. Code Ann. tit. 11, § 4209(e)(1)(*l*) (1995); Ga. Code Ann. § 17-10-30(b)(7) (1997); 720 Ill. Comp. Stat. Ann. 5/9-1(b)(14) (West Supp. 2002); Mass. Ann. Laws ch. 279, § 69(a) (Law. Co-op. 1992); Mo. Ann. Stat. § 565.032(2)(7) (West 1999); Nev. Rev. Stat. Ann. 200-033(8) (Michie 2001); N.J. Stat. Ann. § 2C:11-3 (West Supp. 2002) (same); Tenn. Code Ann. § 39-13-204(i)(5) (Supp. 2001); *see also* Alaska Stat. § 12.55.125(a)(3) (2000) (term of 99 years' imprisonment mandatory where defendant subjected victim to "substantial physical torture"). *All of these laws support the conclusion that torture is generally an extreme act far beyond the infliction of pain or suffering alone.*

California law is illustrative on this point. The California Penal Code not only makes torture itself an offense, see Cal. Penal Code § 206 (West Supp. 2002), it also prohibits murder by torture, see Cal. Penal Code § 189 (West Supp. 2002), and provides that torture is an aggravating circumstance supporting the imposition of the death penalty, see Cal. Penal Code § 190.2 (West Supp. 2002). California's definitions of torture demonstrate that the term is reserved for especially cruel acts inflicting serious injury. Designed to "fill[] a gap in existing law dealing with extremely violent and callous criminal conduct[,]" *People v. Hale*, 88 Cal. Rptr. 2d 904, 913 (1999) (internal quotation marks and citation omitted), Section 206 defines the offense of torture as:

[e]very person who, with the intent to cause *cruel* or *extreme* pain and suffering for the purpose of revenge, extortion, persuasion, or for any sadistic purpose, inflicts great bodily injury… upon the person of another, is guilty of torture. The crime of torture does not require any proof that the victim suffered pain.

(Emphasis added). With respect to sections 190.2 and 189, neither of which are statutorily defined, California courts have recognized that torture generally means an "[a]ct or process of inflicting severe pain, esp[ecially] as a punishment to extort confession, or in revenge…. Implicit in that definition is the requirement of an intent to cause pain and suffering in addition to death." *People v. Barrera*, 18 Cal. Rptr. 2d 395, 399 (Ct. App. 1993) (quotation marks and citation omitted). Further, "murder by torture was and is considered among the most reprehensible types of murder because of the calculated nature of the acts causing death." *Id.* at 403 (quoting *People v. Wiley*, 133 Cal. Rptr. 135, 138 (1976) (in bank)). The definition of murder by torture special circumstance, proscribed under Cal. Penal Code § 190.2, likewise shows an attempt to reach the most heinous acts imposing pain beyond that which a victim suffers through death alone. To establish murder by torture special circumstance, the "intent to kill, intent to torture, and infliction of an extremely painful act upon a living victim" must be present. *People v. Bemore*, 94 Cal. Rptr. 2d 840, 861 (2000). The intent to torture is characterized by a "sadistic intent to cause the victim to suffer pain in addition to the pain of death.'" *Id.* at 862 (quoting *People v. Davenport*, 221 Cal. Rptr. 794, 875 (1985)). Like the Torture Victims Protection Act and the Convention Against Torture, discussed *infra* at Parts II and III, each of these California prohibitions against torture require an evil intent—such as cruelty, revenge or even sadism. Section 2340 does not require this additional intent, but as discussed *supra* pp. 2–3, requires that the individual specifically intended to cause severe pain or suffering. Furthermore, unlike Section 2340, neither section 189 nor section 206 appear to require proof of actual pain to establish torture.

7. To be sure, the text of the treaty requires that an individual act "intentionally." This language might be read to require only general intent for violations of the Torture Convention. We believe, however, that the better interpretation is that the use of the phrase "intentionally" also created a specific intent-type standard. In that event, the Bush administration's understanding represents only an explanation of how the United States intended to implement the vague language of the Torture Convention. If, however, the Convention established a general intent standard, then the Bush understanding represents a modification of the obligation undertaken by the United States.

8. Common article 3 of Geneva Convention on prisoners of war, Convention Relative to the Treatment of Prisoners of War, 6 U.S.T. 3517 ("Geneva Convention III") contains somewhat similar language. Article 3(1)(a) prohibits "violence to life and person, in particular murder of all kinds, mutilation, *cruel treatment and torture*." (Emphasis added). Article 3(1)(c) additionally prohibits "outrages upon personal dignity, in particular, humiliating and degrading treatment." Subsection (c) must forbid more conduct than that already covered in subsection (a) otherwise subsection (c) would be superfluous. Common article 3 does not, however, define either of the phrases "outrages upon personal dignity" or "humiliating and degrading treatment." International criminal tribunals, such as those respecting Rwanda and former Yugoslavia have used common article 3 to try individuals for committing inhuman acts lacking any military necessity whatsoever. Based on our review of the case law, however, these tribunals have not yet articulated the full scope of conduct prohibited by common article 3. Memorandum for John C. Yoo, Deputy Assistant Attorney General, Office of Legal Counsel, from James C. Ho, Attorney-Advisor, Office of Legal Counsel, *Re: Possible Interpretations of Common Article 3 of the 1949 Geneva Convention Relative to the Treatment of Prisoners of War* (Feb. 1, 2002).

We note that Section 2340A and CAT protect any individual from torture. By contrast, the standards of conduct established by common article 3 of Convention III, do not apply to "an armed conflict between a nation-state and a transnational terrorist organization." Memorandum for Alberto R. Gonzales, Counsel to the President and William J. Haynes, II, General Counsel, Department of Defense, from Jay S. Bybee, Assistant Attorney General, Office of Legal Counsel, *Re: Application of Treaties and Laws to al Qaeda and Taliban Detainees* at 8 (Jan. 22, 2002).

9. The vagueness of "cruel, inhuman and degrading treatment" enables the term to have a far-ranging reach. Article 3 of the European Convention on Human Rights similarly prohibits such treatment. The European Court of Human Rights has construed this phrase broadly, even assessing whether such treatment has occurred from the subjective stand point of the victim. *See* Memorandum from James C. Ho, Attorney-Advisor to John C. Yoo, Deputy Assistant Attorney General, *Re: Possible Interpretations of Common Article 3 of the 1949 Geneva Convention Relative to the Treatment of Prisoners of War* (Feb. 1, 2002) (finding that European Court of Human Right's construction of inhuman or degrading treatment "is broad enough to arguably forbid even standard U.S. law enforcement interrogation techniques, which endeavor to break down a detainee's 'moral resistance' to answering questions.").

Moreover, despite the Reagan and Bush administrations' efforts to limit the reach of the cruel, inhuman and degrading treatment language, it appears to still have a rather limitless reach. *See id.* (describing how the Eighth Amendment ban on "cruel and unusual punishment" has been used by courts to, *inter alia*, "engage in detailed regulation of prison conductions, including the exact size of cells, exercise, and recreational activities, quality of food, access to cable television, internet, and law libraries.")

10. Hearing testimony, though the least weighty evidence of meaning of all of the ratification record, is not to the contrary. Other examples of torture mentioned in testimony similarly reflect acts resulting in intense pain: the "gouging out of childrens' [sic] eyes, the torture death by molten rubber, the use of electric shocks," cigarette burns, hanging by hands or feet. 1990 Hearing at 45 (Statement of Winston Nagan, Chairman, Board of Directors, Amnesty International USA); *id.* at 79 (Statement of David Weissbrodt, Professor of Law, University of Minnesota, on behalf of the Center for Victims of Torture, the Minnesota Lawyers International Human Rights Committee).

' 11. *See also* 137 Cong. Rec. 34,785 (statement of Rep. Mazzoli) ("Torture is defined in accordance with the definition contained in [CAT]"); *see also* Torture Victims Protection Act: Hearing and Markup on H.R. 1417 Before the Subcomm. On Human Rights and International Organizations of the House Comm. on Foreign Affairs, 100th Cong. 38 (1988) (Prepared Statement of the Association of the Bar of the City of New York, Committee on International Human Rights) ("This language essentially tracks the definition of 'torture' adopted in the Torture Convention.").

12. This list of purposes is illustrative only. Nevertheless, demonstrating that a defendant harbored any of these purposes "may prove valuable in assisting in the establishment of intent at trial." Matthew Lippman, *The Development and Drafting of the United Nations Convention Against Torture and Other Cruel Inhuman or Degrading Treatment or Punishment*, 17 B.C. Int'l & Comp. L. Rev. 275, 314 (1994).

13. The TVPA also requires that an individual act "intentionally." As we noted with respect to the text of CAT, see *supra* n. 7, this language might be construed as requiring general intent. It is not clear that this is so. We need not resolve that question, however, because we review the TVPA cases solely to address the acts that would satisfy the threshold of inflicting "severe physical or mental pain or suffering."

14. The court also found that a number of acts perpetrated against the plaintiffs constituted

cruel, inhuman, or degrading treatment but not torture. In its analysis, the court appeared to fold into cruel, inhuman, or degrading treatment two distinct categories. First, cruel, inhuman, or degrading treatment includes acts that "do not rise to the level of 'torture.'" *Id.* at 1348. Second, cruel, inhuman, or degrading treatment includes acts that "do not have the same purposes as 'torture.'" *Id.* By including this latter set of treatment as cruel, inhuman or degrading, the court appeared to take the view that acts that would otherwise constitute torture fall outside that definition because of the absence of the particular purposes listed in the TVPA and the treaty. Regardless of the relevance of this concept to the TVPA or CAT, the purposes listed in the TVPA are not an element of torture for purposes of sections 2340–2340A.

15. According to one commentator, the Inter-American Court of Human Rights has also followed this decision. *See* Julie Lantrip, *Torture and Cruel, Inhuman and Degrading Treatment in the Jurisprudence of the Inter-American Court of Human Rights*, 5 ILSA J. Int'l & Comp. L. 551, 560–61 (1999). The Inter-American Convention to Prevent and Punish Torture, however, defines torture much differently than it is defined in CAT or U.S. law. *See* Inter-American Convention to Prevent and Punish Torture, opened for signature Dec. 9, 1985, art. 2, OAS T.S. No. 67 (entered into force Feb. 28, 1987, but the United States has never signed or ratified it). It defines torture as "any act intentionally performed whereby physical or mental pain or suffering is inflicted on a person for purposes of criminal investigation, as a means of intimidation, as personal punishment, as a preventive measure, as a penalty or for any other purpose. Torture shall also be understood to be the use of methods upon a person intended to obliterate the personality of the victim or to diminish his physical or mental capacities, even if they do not cause physical pain or mental anguish." Art. 2. While the Inter-American Convention to Prevent and Punish Torture does not require signatories to criminalize cruel, inhuman, or degrading treatment or punishment, the textual differences in the definition of torture are so great that it would be difficult to draw from that jurisprudence anything more than the general trend of its agreement with the *Ireland* decision.

16. The court did, however, distinguish between this sleep deprivation and that which occurred as part of routine interrogation, noting that some degree of interference with the suspect's regular sleep habits was to be expected. *Public Committee Against Torture in Israel* ¶ 23.

17. In permitting a necessity defense, the court drew upon the ticking time bomb hypothetical proffered by the GSS as a basis for asserting a necessity defense. In that hypothetical, the GSS has arrested a suspect, who holds information about the location of a bomb and the time at which it is set to explode. The suspect is the only source of this information, and without that information the bomb will surely explode, killing many people. Under those circumstances, the court agreed that the necessity defense's requirement of imminence, which the court construed as the "imminent nature of the act rather than that of danger," would be satisfied. *Id.* ¶ 34. It further agreed "that in appropriate circumstances" this defense would be available to GSS investigators. *Id.* ¶ 35.

18. *See Osama Bin Laden v. The U.S.: Edicts and Statements*, CNN Interview with Osama bin Laden, March 1997, *available at* http://www.pbs.org/wgbh/pages/frontline/shows/binladen /who/edicts.html.

19. *See, e.g.*, September 11 War Powers Memorandum; Memorandum for Alberto R. Gonzales, Counsel to the President, from Patrick F. Philbin, Deputy Assistant Attorney General, Office of Legal Counsel, *Re: Legality of the Use of Military Commissions to Try Terrorists* (Nov. 6, 2001).

20. *See Johnson v. Eisentrager*, 339 U.S. 763, 789 (1950) (President has authority to deploy United States armed forces "abroad or to any particular region"); *Fleming v. Page*, 50 U.S. (9 How.) 603, 614–15 (1850) ("As commander-in-chief, [the President] is authorized to direct the movements of the naval and military forces placed by law at his command, and to employ them in the manner he may deem most effectual") *Loving v. United States*, 517 U.S. 748, 776 (1996)

(Scalia, J., concurring in part and concurring in judgment) (The "inherent powers" of the Commander in Chief "are clearly extensive."); *Maul v. United States*, 274 U.S. 501, 515–16 (1927) (Brandeis & Holmes, JJ., concurring) (President "may direct any revenue cutter to cruise in any waters in order to perform any duty of the service"); *Commonwealth of Massachusetts v. Laird*, 451 F.2d 26, 32 (1st Cir. 1971) (the President has "power as Commander-in-Chief to station forces abroad"); *Ex parte Vallandigham*, 28 F.Cas. 874, 922 (C.C.S.D. Ohio 1863) (No. 16,816) (in acting "under this power where there is no express legislative declaration, the president is guided solely by his own judgment and discretion"); *Authority to Use United States Military Forces in Somalia*, 16 Op. O.L.C. 6, 6 (Dec. 4, 1992) (Barr, Attorney General).

21. Judicial decisions since the beginning of the Republic confirm the President's constitutional power and duty to repel military action against the United States and to take measures to prevent the recurrence of an attack. As Justice Joseph Story said long ago, "[i]t may be fit and proper for the government, in the exercise of the high discretion confided to the executive, for great public purposes, to act on a sudden emergency, or to prevent an irreparable mischief, by summary measures, which are not found in the text of the laws." *The Apollon*, 22 U.S. (9 Wheat.) 362, 366–67 (1824). If the President is confronted with an unforeseen attack on the territory and people of the United States, or other immediate, dangerous threat to American interests and security, it is his constitutional responsibility to respond to that threat with whatever means are necessary. *See, e.g., The Prize Cases*, 67 U.S. (2 Black) 635, 668 (1862) ("If a war be made by invasion of a foreign nation, the President is not only authorized but bound to resist force by force . . . without waiting for any special legislative authority."); *United States v. Smith*, 27 F. Cas. 1192, 1229–30 (C.C.D.N.Y. 1806) (No. 16,342) (Paterson, Circuit Justice) (regardless of statutory authorization, it is "the duty . . . of the executive magistrate . . . to repel an invading foe"); *see also* 3 Story, *Commentaries* § 1485 ("[t]he command and application of the public force . . . to maintain peace, and to resist foreign invasion" are executive powers).

22. The practice of capturing and detaining enemy combatants is as old as war itself. *See* Allan Rosas, The Legal Status of Prisoners of War 44–45 (1976). In modern conflicts, the practice of detaining enemy combatants and hostile civilians generally has been designed to balance the humanitarian purpose of sparing lives with the military necessity of defeating the enemy on the battlefield. *Id.* at 59–80. While Article 17 of the Geneva Convention Relative to the Treatment of Prisoners of War, Aug. 12, 1949, 6 U.S.T. 3517, places restrictions on interrogation of enemy combatants, members of al Qaeda and the Taliban militia are not legally entitled to the status of prisoners of war as defined in the Convention. See Memorandum for Alberto R. Gonzales, Counsel to the President and William J. Haynes, II, General Counsel, Department of Defense, from Jay S. Bybee, Assistant Attorney General, Office of Legal Counsel, *Re: Application of Treaties and Laws to al Qaeda and Taliban Detainees* (Jan. 22, 2002).

23. In the CAT, torture is defined as the intentional infliction of severe pain or suffering "for such purpose[] as obtaining from him or a third person information or a confession." CAT art. 1.1. One could argue that such a definition represented an attempt to to indicate that the good of obtaining information—no matter what the circumstances—could not justify an act of torture. In other words, necessity would not be a defense. In enacting Section 2340, however, Congress removed the purpose element in the definition of torture, evidencing an intention to remove any fixing of values by statute. By leaving Section 2340 silent as to the harm done by torture in comparison to other harms, Congress allowed the necessity defense to apply when appropriate.

Further, the CAT contains an additional provision that "no exceptional circumstances whatsoever, whether a state of war or a threat of war, internal political instability or any other public emergency, may be invoked as a justification of torture." CAT art. 2.2. Aware of this provision of the treaty, and of the definition of the necessity defense that allows the legislature to provide for an exception to the defense, *see* Model Penal Code § 3.02(b), Congress did not incorporate CAT article 2.2 into Section 2340. Given that Congress omitted CAT's effort to bar a necessity or wartime defense, we read Section 2340 as permitting the defense.

24. Early cases had suggested that in order to be eligible for defense of another, one should have some personal relationship with the one in need of protection. That view has been discarded. LaFave & Scott at 664.

25. Moore distinguishes that case from one in which a person has information that could stop a terrorist attack, but who does not take a hand in the terrorist activity itself, such as an innocent person who learns of the attack from her spouse. Moore, 23 Israel L. Rev. at 324. Such individuals, Moore finds, would not be subject to the use of force in self-defense, although they might be under the doctrine of necessity.

26. While the President's constitutional determination alone is sufficient to justify the nation's resort to self-defense, it also bears noting that the right to self-defense is further recognized under international law. Article 51 of the U.N. Charter declares that "[n]othing in the present Charter shall impair the inherent right of individual or collective self-defense if an armed attack occurs against a Member of the United Nations until the Security Council has taken the measures necessary to maintain international peace and security." The attacks of September 11, 2001, clearly constitute an armed attack against the United States, and indeed were the latest in a long history of al Qaeda sponsored attacks against the United States. This conclusion was acknowledged by the United Nations Security Council on September 28, 2001, when it unanimously adopted Resolution 1373 explicitly "reaffirming the inherent right of individual and collective self-defence as recognized by the charter of the United Nations." This right of self-defense is a right to effective self-defense. In other words, the victim state has the right to use force against the aggressor who has initiated an "armed attack" until the threat has abated. The United States, through its military and intelligence personnel, has a right recognized by Article 51 to continue using force until such time as the threat posed by al Qaeda and other terrorist groups connected to the September 11th attacks is completely ended." Other treaties re-affirm the right of the United States to use force in its self-defense. *See,* e.g., Inter-American Treaty of Reciprocal Assistance, art. 3, Sept. 2, 1947, T.I.A.S. No. 1838, 21 U.N.T.S. 77 (Rio Treaty); North Atlantic Treaty, art. 5, Apr. 4, 1949, 63 Stat. 2241, 34 U.N.T.S. 243.

3

DEPARTMENT OF DEFENSE
JOINT TASK FORCE 170
GUANTANAMO BAY, CUBA
APO AE 08860

JTF-J2   11 October 2001

MEMORANDUM FOR Commander, Joint Task Force 170

SUBJECT: Request for Approval of Counter-Resistance Strategies

1. (S/NF)(U) PROBLEM: The current guidelines for interrogation procedures at GTMO limit the ability of interrogators to counter advanced resistance.

2. (S/NF)(U) Request approval for use of the following interrogation plan.

a. Category I techniques. During the initial category of interrogation the detainee should be provided a chair and the environment should be generally comfortable. The format of the interrogation is the direct approach. The use of rewards like cookies or cigarettes may be helpful. If the detainee is determined by the interrogator to be uncooperative, the interrogator may use the following techniques.

(1) Yelling at the detainee (not directly in his ear or to the level that it would cause physical pain or hearing problems)
(2) Techniques of deception:
(a) Multiple interrogator techniques.
(b) Interrogator identity. The interview may identify himself as a citizen of a foreign nation or as an interrogator from a country with a reputation for harsh treatment of detainees.

b. Category II techniques. With the permission of the GIC, Interrogation Section, the interrogator may use the following techniques.

(1) The use of stress positions (like standing), for a maximum of four hours.
(2) The use of falsified documents or reports.
(3) Use of the isolation facility for up to 30 days. Request must be made to through the OIC, Interrogation Section, to the Director, Joint Interrogation Group (JIG). Extensions beyond the initial 30 days must be approved by the Commanding General. For selected detainees, the OIC, Interrogation Section, will approve all contacts with the detainee, to include medical visits of a non-emergent nature.

(4) Interrogating the detainee in an environment other than the standard interrogation booth:

(5) Deprivation of high and auditory stimuli.

(6) The detainee may also have a hood placed over his head during transportation and questioning. The hood should not restrict breathing in any way and the
detainee should be under direct observation when hooded.

(7) The use of 20-hour interrogations.

(8) Removal of all comfort items (including religions items).

(9) Switching the detainee from hot rations to MREs.

(10) Removal of clothing.

(11) Forced grooming (shaving of facial hair etc.)

(12) Using detainees individual phobias (such as fear of dogs) to induce stress.

c. Category III techniques. Techniques in this category may be used only by submitting
a request through the Director, JIG, for approval by the Commanding General with
appropriate legal review and information to Commander, USSOUTHCOM. These techniques are required for a very small percentage of the most uncooperative detainees (less
than 3%). The following techniques and other aversive techniques, such as those used in
U.S. military interrogation resistance training or by other U.S. government agencies, may
be utilized in a carefully coordinated manner to help interrogate exceptionally resistant
detainees. Any of these techniques that require more than light grabbing, poking, or pushing, will be administered only by individuals specifically trained in their safe application.

(1) The use of scenarios designed to convince the detainee that death or
severely painful consequences are imminent for him and/or his family.

(2) Exposure to cold weather or water (with appropriate medical monitoring).

(3) Use of a wet towel and dripping water to induce the misperception of
suffocation.

(4) Use of mild, non-injurious physical contact such as grabbing, poking in the
chest with the finger, and light pushing.

3. (U) The POC for this memorandum is the undersigned at 13476.

[signed]

JERALD PHIFER
LTC, USA
Director, J2

Declassify Under the Authority of Executive Order 12958
By Executive Secretary, Office of the Secretary of Defense
By William P. Marriott, CAPT, USN, June 21, 2004

4a

DEPARTMENT OF DEFENSE
Joint Task Force 170
Guantanamo Bay, Cuba
APO AE 09880

JTF 170-CG   11 October 2002

MEMORANDUM FOR Commander, Joint Task Force 170

SUBJECT: Legal Review of Aggressive Interrogation Techniques

1. I have reviewed the memorandum on Counter-Resistance Strategies, dated 11 Oct 02, and agree that the proposed strategies do not violate applicable federal law. Attached is a more detailed legal analysis that addresses the proposal.

2. I recommend that interrogators be properly trained in the use of the approved methods of interrogation, and that interrogations involving category II and category III methods undergo a legal review prior to their commencement.

3. This matter is forwarded to you for your recommendation and action.

[signed]

DIANE E. BEAVER
LTC, USA
Staff Judge Advocate

2 Encls
1. JTF 170-J2 Memo,
   11 Oct 02
2. JTF 170-SJA Memo,
   11 Oct 02

4b

DEPARTMENT OF DEFENSE
Joint Task Force 170
Guantanamo Bay, Cuba
APO AE 09880

JTF 170-SJA   11 October 2002

SUBJECT: Legal Brief on Proposed Counter-Resistance Strategies

1. (S/NF)(U) ISSUE: To ensure the security of the United States and its Allies, more aggressive interrogation techniques than the ones presently used, such as the methods proposed in the attached recommendation, may be required in order to obtain information from detainees that are resisting interrogation efforts and are suspected of having significant information essential to national security. This legal brief references the recommendations outlined in the JTF-170-J2 memorandum, dated 11 October 2002.

2. (S/NF)(U) FACTS: The detainees currently held at Guantánamo Bay, Cuba (GTMO), are not protected by the Geneva Conventions (GC). Nonetheless, DoD interrogators trained to apply the Geneva Conventions have been using commonly approved methods of interrogation such as rapport-building through the direct approach, rewards, the multiple interrogator approach, and the use of deception. However, because detainees have been able to communicate among themselves and debrief each other about their respective interrogations, their interrogation resistance strategies have become more sophisticated. Compounding this problem is the fact that there is no established clear policy for interrogation limits and operations at GTMO, and many interrogators have felt in the past that that they could not do anything that could be considered "controversial." In accordance with President Bush's 7 February 2002 directive, the detainees are not Enemy Prisoners of War (EPW). They must be treated humanely and subject to military necessity, in accordance with the principles of GC.

3. (S/NF)(U) DISCUSSION: The Office of the Secretary of Defense (OSD) has not adopted specific guidelines regarding interrogation techniques for detainee operations at GTMO. While the procedures outlined in Army FM 34-52 Intelligence Interrogation (28 September 1992) are utilized, they are constrained by, and conform to the GC and applicable international law, and therefore are not binding. Since the detainees are not EPWs, the Geneva Conventions limitations that ordinarily would govern captured enemy personnel interrogations are not binding on US personnel

conducting detainee interrogations at GTMO. Consequently, in the absence of specific binding guidance, and in accordance with the President's directive to treat the detainees humanely, we must look to applicable international and domestic law in order to determine the legality of the more aggressive interrogation techniques recommended in the J2 proposal.

a. (U) INTERNATIONAL LAW: Although no international body of law directly applies, the more notable international treaties and relevant law are listed below.

(1)(U) In November of 1994, the United States ratified The Convention Against Torture and Other Cruel, Inhumane or Degrading Treatment or Punishment. However, the United States took a reservation to Article 16, which defined cruel, inhumane and degrading treatment or punishment, by instead deferring to the current standard articulated in the 8th Amendment to the United States Constitution. Therefore, the United States is only prohibited from committing those acts that would otherwise be prohibited under the United States Constitutional Amendment against cruel and unusual punishment. The United States ratified the treaty with the understanding that the convention would not be self-executing, that is, that it would not create a private cause of action in US Courts. This convention is the principal UN treaty regarding torture and other cruel, inhumane, or degrading treatment.

(2)(U) The International Covenant on Civil and Political Rights (ICCPR), ratified by the United States in 1992, prohibits inhumane treatment in Article 7, and arbitrary arrest and detention in Article 9. The United States ratified it on the condition that it would not be self-executing, and it took a reservation to Article 7 that we would only be bound to the extent that the United States Constitution prohibits cruel and unusual punishment.

(3)(U) The American Convention on Human rights forbids inhumane treatment, arbitrary imprisonment, and requires the state to promptly inform detainees of the charges against them, to review their pretrial confinement, and to conduct a trial within a reasonable time. The United States signed the convention on 1 June 1977, but never ratified it.

(4)(U) The Rome Statute established the International Criminal Court and criminalized inhumane treatment, unlawful deportation, and imprisonment. The United States not only failed to ratify the Rome Statute, but also later withdrew from it.

(5)(U) The United Nations' Universal Declaration of Human Rights prohibits inhumane or degrading punishment, arbitrary arrest, detention, or exile. Although international declarations may provide evidence of customary international law (which is considered binding on all nations even without a treaty), they are not enforceable by themselves.

(6)(U) There is some European case law stemming from the European Court of Human Rights on the issue of torture. The Court ruled on allegations of torture and other forms of inhumane treatment by the British in the Northern Ireland conflict. The British authorities developed practices of interrogation such as forcing detainees to stand for long hours, placing black hoods over their heads, holding the detainees prior to interrogation in a room with continuing loud noise, and depriving them of sleep, food, and water. The European Court concluded that these acts did not rise to the level of torture as defined in the Convention Against Torture, because torture was defined as an aggravated form of cruel, inhuman, or degrading treatment or punishment. However, the Court did find that these techniques constituted cruel, inhuman, and degrading treatment. Nonetheless, and as previously mentioned, not only is the United States not a part of the European Human Rights Court, but as previously stated, it only ratified the definition of cruel, inhuman, and degrading treatment consistent with the US Constitution. See also *Mehinovic v. Vuckovic*, 198 F. Supp. 2d 1322 (N.D. Geor. 2002); *Committee Against Torture v. Israel*, Supreme Court of Israel, 6 Sep 99, 7 BHRC 31; *Ireland v. UK* (1978), 2 EHRR 25.

b. (U) Domestic Law: Although the detainees' interrogations are not occurring in the continental United States, US personnel conducting said interrogations are still bond by applicable Federal Law, specifically, the Eighth Amendment of the United States Constitution, 18 USC §2340, and for military interrogators, the Uniform Code of Military Justice (UCMI).

(1)(U) The Eighth Amendment of the United States Constitution provides that excessive bail shall not be required, nor excessive fines imposed, nor cruel and unusual punishment inflicted. There is a lack of Eighth Amendment case law relating in the context of interrogations, as most of the Eighth Amendment litigation in federal court involves either the death penalty or 42 USC §1983 actions from inmates based on prison conditions. The Eighth Amendment applies as to whether or not torture or inhumane treatment has occurred under the federal torture statute.[1]

(a)(U) A principal case in the confinement context that is instructive regarding Eighth Amendment analysis (which is relevant because the United States adopted the Convention Against Torture, Cruel, Inhumane and Degrading Treatment, it did so deferring to the Eighth Amendment of the United States Constitution) and conditions of confinement if a US court were to examine the issue is *Hudson v. McMillan*, 503 US 1 (1992). The issue in *Hudson* stemmed from a 42 USC §1983 action alleging that a prison inmate suffered minor bruises, facial swelling, loosened teeth, and a cracked dental plate resulting from a beating by prison guards while he was cuffed and shackled. In this case the Court held that there was no governmental interest in beating an inmate in such a manner. The Court further ruled that the use of excessive physical force against a prisoner might constitute cruel and unusual punishment, even though the inmate does not suffer serious injury.

(b)(U) In *Hudson*, the court relied on *Whitley v. Albert*, 475 US 312 (1986), as the seminal case that establishes whether a constitutional violation has occurred. The Court stated that the extent of the injury suffered by an inmate is only one of the factors to be considered, but that there is no significant injury requirement in order to establish an Eighth Amendment violation, and that the absence of serious injury is relevant to, but does not end, the Eighth Amendment inquiry. The Court based its decision on the "...settled rule that the unnecessary and wanton infliction of pain...constitutes cruel and unusual punishment forbidden by the Eighth Amendment." *Whitley* at 319, quoting *Ingraham v. Wright*, 430 US 651, 670 (1977). The *Hudson* Court then held that in the excessive force or conditions of confinement context, the Eighth Amendment violation test delineated by the Supreme Court in *Hudson* is that when prison officials maliciously and sadistically use force to cause harm, contemporary standards of decency are always violated, whether or not significant injury is evident. The extent of injury suffered by an inmate is one factor that may suggest whether the use of force could plausibly have been thought necessary in a particular situation, but the question of whether the measure taken inflicted unnecessary and wanton pain and suffering, ultimately turns on whether force was applied in a good faith effort to maintain or restore discipline, or maliciously and sadistically for the *very* (emphasis added) purpose of causing harm. If so, the Eighth Amendment claim will prevail.

(c)(U) At the District Court level, the typical conditions-of-confinement claims involve a disturbance of the inmate's physical comfort, such as sleep deprivation or loud noise. The Eighth Circuit ruled in *Singh v. Holcomb*, 1992 US App. LEXIS 24790, that an allegation by an inmate that he was constantly deprived of sleep, which resulted in emotional distress, loss of memory, headaches, and poor concentration, did not show either the extreme deprivation level, or the officials' culpable state of mind required to fulfill the objective component of an Eighth Amendment conditions-of-confinement claim.

(d)(U) In another sleep deprivation case alleging an Eighth Amendment violation, the Eighth Circuit established a totality of the circumstances test, and stated that if a particular condition of detention is reasonably related to a legitimate government objective, it does not, without more, amount to punishment. In *Ferguson v. Cape Girardeau County*, 88 F.3d 647 (8th Cir. 1996), the complainant was confined to a 5-1/2 by 5-1/2-foot cell without a toilet or sink, and was forced to sleep on a mat on the floor under bright lights that were on twenty-four hours a day. His Eighth Amendment claim was not successful because he was able to sleep at some point, and because he was kept under those conditions due to a concern for his health, as well as the perceived danger that he presented. This totality of the circumstances test has also been adopted by the Ninth Circuit. In *Green v. CSO Strack*, 1995 US App. LEXIS 14451, the Court held that threats of bodily injury are insufficient to state a claim under the Eighth Amendment, and that sleep deprivation did not rise to a constitutional violation where the prisoner failed to present evidence that he either lost sleep or was otherwise harmed.

(e)(U) Ultimately, an Eighth Amendment analysis is based primarily on whether the government had a good faith legitimate, governmental interest, and did not act maliciously and sadistically for the very purpose of causing harm.

(2)(U) The torture statute (18 USC §2340) is the United States' codification of the signed and ratified provisions of the Convention Against Torture and Other Cruel, Inhuman or Degrading Treatment or Punishment, and pursuant to subsection 2340B, does not create any substantive or procedural rights enforceable by law by any party in any civil proceeding.

(a)(U) The statue provides that "whoever outside the United States commits or attempts to commit torture shall be fined under this title or imprisoned not more than 20 years, or both, and if death results to any person from conduct prohibited by this subsection, shall be punished by death or imprisoned for any term of years or for life."

(b)(U) Torture is defined as "an act committed by a person acting under color of law *specifically intended* (emphasis added) to inflict severe physical or mental pain or suffering (other than pain or suffering incident to lawful sanctions) upon another person within his custody or physical control." The statute defines "severe mental pain or suffering" as "the *prolonged mental harm caused by or resulting* (emphasis added) from the intentional infliction or threatened infliction of severe physical pain or suffering; or the administration or application, or threatened administration or application, of mind-altering substances or other procedures calculated to disrupt profoundly the senses of the personality; or the threat of imminent death; or the threat that another person will imminently be subjected to death, severe physical pain or suffering, or the administration or application of mind-altering substances or other procedures calculated to disrupt profoundly the senses or personality."

(c)(U) Case law in the context of the federal torture statute and interrogations is also lacking, as the majority of the case law involving torture relates to either the illegality of brutal tactics used by the police to obtain confessions (in which the Court simply states that these confessions will be deemed as involuntary for the purposes of admissibility and due process, but does not actually address torture or the Eighth Amendment), or the Alien Torts Claim act, in which federal courts have defined that certain uses of force (such as kidnapping, beating and raping of a body with the consent or acquiescence of a public official, see *Ortiz v. Ggramsle*, 886 F.Supp. 162 (D.Mass. 1995)), constituted torture. However, no case law on point within the context of 18 USC 2340.

(3)(U) Finally, US military personnel are subject to the Uniform Code of Military Justice. The punitive articles of that could potentially be violated depending on the circumstances and results of an interrogation are: Article 93 (cruelty and maltreatment), Article 118 (murder), Article 199 (manslaughter), Article 124 (maiming), Article 128 (assault), Article 134 (communicating a threat, and negligent homicide), and the inchoate offenses of attempt (Article 80), conspiracy (Article 81), accessory after the fact (Article 78), and solicitation (Article 82). Article 128 is the article most likely to be violated because a simple assault can be consummated by an unlawful demonstration of violence which creates in the mind of another a reasonable apprehension of receiving immediate bodily harm, and a specific intent to actually inflict bodily harm is not required.

4. (S/NF)(U) ANALYSIS: the counter-resistance techniques proposed in the JTF-170-J2 memorandum are lawful because they do not violate the Eighth Amendment to the United States Constitution or the federal torture statute as explained below. An international law analysis is not required for the current proposal because the Geneva Conventions do not apply to these detainees since they are not EPWs.

(a)(S/NF)(U) Based on the Supreme Court framework utilized to assess whether a public official has violated the Eighth Amendment, so long as the force used could plausibly have been thought necessary in a particular situation to achieve a legitimate governmental objective, and it was applied in a good faith effort and not maliciously or sadistically for the very purpose of causing harm, the proposed techniques are likely to pass constitutional muster. The federal torture statute will not be violated so long as any of the proposed strategies are not specifically intended to cause severe physical pain or suffering or prolonged mental harm. Assuming that severe physical pain is not inflicted, absent any evidence that any of these strategies will in fact cause prolonged and long-lasting mental harm, the proposed methods will not violate the statute.

(b)(S/NF)(U) Regarding the Uniform Code of Military Justice, the proposal to grab, poke in the chest, push lightly, and place a wet towel or hood over the detainee's head would constitute a per se violation of Article 128 (Assault). Threatening a detainee with death may also constitute a violation of Article 128, or also Article 134 (communicating a threat). It would be advisable to have permission or immunity in advance from the convening authority, for military members utilizing these methods.

(c)(S/NF)(U) Specifically, with regard to Category I techniques, the use of mild and fear-related approaches such as yelling at the detainee is not illegal because in order to communicate a threat, there must also exist an intent to injure. Yelling at the detainee is legal so long as the yelling is not done with the intent to cause severe physical damage or prolonged mental harm. Techniques of deception such as multiple interrogator techniques, and deception regarding interrogator identity are all permissible methods of interrogation, since there is no legal requirement to be truthful while conducting an interrogation.

(d)(S/NF)(U) With regard to Category II methods, the use of stress positions such as the proposed standing for hours, the use of isolation for up to thirty days, and interrogating the detainee in an environment other than the standard interrogation booth are all legally permissible so long as no severe physical pain is inflicted and prolonged mental harm intended, and because there is a legitimate governmental objective in obtaining the information necessary that the high value detainees on which these methods would be utilized possess, for the protection of the national security of the United States, its citizens, and allies. Furthermore, these methods would not be utilized for the "very malicious and sadistic purpose of causing harm," and absent medical evidence to the contrary, there is no evidence that prolonged mental harm would result from the use of these strategies. The use of falsified documents is legally permissible because interrogators may use deception to achieve their purpose.

(e)(S/NF)(U) The deprivation of light and auditory stimuli, the placement of a hood over the detainee's head during transportation and questioning, and the use of 20-hour interrogations are all legally permissible so long as there is an important governmental objective, and it is not done for the purpose of causing harm or with the intent to cause prolonged mental suffering. There is no legal requirement that detainees must receive four hours of sleep per night, but if a US Court ever had to rule on this procedure, in order to pass Eighth Amendment scrutiny, and as a cautionary measure, they should receive some amount of sleep so that no severe physical or mental harm will result. Removal of comfort items is permissible because there is no legal requirement to provide comfort items. The requirement is to provide adequate food, water, shelter, and medical care. The issue of removing published religious items or materials would be relevant if these were United States citizens with a First Amendment right. Such is not the case with the detainees. Forced grooming and removal of clothing are not illegal, so long as it is not done to punish or cause harm, as there is a legitimate governmental objective to obtain information, maintain health standards in the camp and protect both the detainees and the guards. There is no illegality in removing hot meals because there is no specific requirement to provide hot meals, only adequate food. The use of the detainees' phobias is equally permissible.

(f)(S/NF)(U) With respect to the Category III advanced counter-resistance strategies, the use of scenarios designed to convince the detainee that death or severely painful consequences are imminent is not illegal for the same aforementioned reasons that there is a compelling governmental interest and it is not done intentionally to cause prolonged harm. However, caution should be utilized with this technique because the torture statute specifically mentions making death threats as an example of inflicting mental pain and suffering. Exposure to cold weather or water is permissible with appropriate medical monitoring. The use of a wet towel to induce the misperception of suffocation would also be permissible if not done with the specific intent to cause prolonged mental harm, and absent medical evidence that it would. Caution should be exercised with this method, as foreign courts have already advised about the potential mental harm that this method may cause. The use of physical contact with the detainee, such as pushing and poking, will technically constitute and assault under Article 128, UCMJ.

5 (S/NF)(U) RECOMMENDATION: I recommend that the proposed methods of interrogation be approved, and that the interrogators be properly trained in the use of the approved methods of interrogation. Since the law requires examination of all facts under a totality of circumstances test, I further recommend that all proposed interrogations involving Category II and III methods must undergo a legal, medical, behavioral science, and intelligence review prior to their commencement.

6(U) POC; Captain Michael Borders, x3536.

[signed]

DIANE E. BEAVER
LTC, USA
Staff Judge Advocate

Declassify Under the Authority of Executive Order 12958
By Executive Secretary, Office of the Secretary of Defense
By William P. Marriott, CAPT, USN, June 21, 2004

NOTES

1. Notwithstanding the argument that US personnel are bound by the Constitution, the detainees confined at GTMO have no jurisdictional standing to bring a section 1983 action alleging an Eighth Amendment violation in US Federal Court.

5

DEPARTMENT OF DEFENSE
Joint Task Force 170
Guantanamo Bay, Cuba
APO AE 09880

JTF 170-CG   11 October 2002

MEMORANDUM for Commander, United States Southern Command,
3511 NW 91st Avenue, Miami, Florida 33172-1217

SUBJECT: Counter-Resistance Strategies

1. Request that you approve the interrogation techniques delineated in the enclosed
Counter-Resistance Strategies memorandum. I have reviewed this memorandum and
the legal review provided to me by the JTF-170 Staff Judge Advocate and concur with
the legal analysis provided.

2. I am fully aware of the techniques currenctly employed to gain valuable intelligence in support of the Global War on Terrorism. Although these techniques have
resulted in significant exploitable intelligence, the same methods have become less
effective over time. I believe the methods and techniques delineated in the accompanying J-2 memorandum will enhance our efforts to extract additional information.
Based on the analysis provided by the JTF-170 SJA, I have concluded that these techniques do not violate U.S. or international law.

3. My point of contact for this issue is LTC Jerald Phifer at DSN 660-3476.

[signed]

MICHAEL B. DUNLAVEY
Major General, USA
Commanding

2 Encls.
1. JTF 170-J2 Memo,
   11 Oct 02
2. JTF 170-SJA Memo,
   11 Oct 02

6

DEPARTMENT OF DEFENSE
UNITED STATES SOUTHERN COMMAND
OFFICE OF THE COMMANDER
3511 NW 91ST AVENUE
MIAMI, FL 33172-1217

SCCDR   25 October 2002

MEMORANDUM FOR Chairman of the Joint Chiefs of Staff,
Washington, DC 20318-9999

SUBJECT: Counter-Resistance Techniques

1. The activities of Joint Task Force 170 have yielded critical intelligence support for forces in combat, combatant commanders, and other intelligence/law enforcement entities prosecuting the War on Terrorism. However, despite our best efforts, some detainees have tenaciously resisted our current interrogation methods. Our respective staffs, the Office of the Secretary of Defense, and Joint Task Force 170 have been trying to identify counter-resistant techniques that we can lawfully employ.

2. I am forwarding Joint Task Force 170's proposed counter-resistance techniques. I believe the first two categories of techniques are legal and humane. I am uncertain whether all the techniques in the third category are legal under US law, given the absence of judicial interpretation of the US torture statute. I am particularly troubled by the use of implied or expressed threats of death of the detainee or his family. However, I desire to have as many options as possible at my disposal and therefore request that Department of Defense and Department of Justice lawyers review the third category of techniques.

3. As part of any review of Joint Task Force 170's proposed strategy, I welcome any suggested interrogation methods that others may propose. I believe we should provide our interrogators with as many legally permissible tools as possible.

4. Although I am cognizant of the important policy ramifications of some of these proposed techniques, I firmly believe that we must quickly provide Joint Task Force 170 counter-resistance techniques to maximize the value of our intelligence collection mission.

[signed]

James T. Hill
General, US Army
Commander

Encls.
1. JTF 170 CDR Memo
   dtd 11 October, 2002
2. JTF 170 SJA Memo
   dtd 11 October, 2002
3. JTF 170 J-2 Memo
   dtd 11 October, 2002

Declassify Under the Authority of Executive Order 12958
By Executive Secretary, Office of the Secretary of Defense
By William P. Marriott, CAPT, USN
June 21, 2004

7

GENERAL COUNSEL OF THE DEPARTMENT OF DEFENSE
1600 DEFENSE PENTAGON
WASHINGTON, D.C. 20301-1600

ACTION MEMO

November 27, 2002 (1:00 PM)

DEPSEC _____

FOR: SECRETARY OF DEFENSE

FROM: William J. Haynes II, General Counsel [initialed]

SUBJECT: Counter-Resistance Techniques

- The Commander of USSOUTHCOM has forwarded a request by the Commander of Joint Task Force 170 (now JTF GTMO) for approval of counter-resistance techniques to aid in the interrogation of detainees at Guantánamo Bay (Tab A).

- The request contains three categories of counter-resistance techniques, with the first category the least aggressive and the third category the most aggressive (Tab B).

- I have discussed this with the Deputy, Doug Feith and General Myers. I believe that all join in my recommendation that, as a matter of policy, you authorize the Commander of USSOUTHCOM to employ, in his discretion, only Categories I and II and the fourth technique listed in Category III ("Use of mild, non-injurious physical contact such as grabbing, poking in the chest with the finger, and light pushing").

- While all Category III techniques may be legally available, we believe that, as a matter of policy, a blanket approval of Category III techniques is not warranted at this time. Our Armed Forces are trained to a standard of interrogation that reflects a tradition of restraint.

RECOMMENDATION: That SECDEF approve the USSOUTHCOM Commander's use of those counter-resistance techniques listed in Categories I and II and the fourth technique listed in Category III during the interrogation of detainees at Guantánamo Bay.

SECDEF DECISION

Approved [signed D. Rumsfeld]   Disapproved _____ Other _____

However, I stand for 8–10 hours a day. Why is standing limited to 4 hours? D.R.
[added by hand]

DEC 02 2002

Attachments
As stated

cc: CJCS, USD(P)

Declassified Under Authority of Executive Order 12958
By Executive Secretary, Office of the Secretary of Defense
William P. Marriott, CAPT, USN
June 18, 2004

8

SECRETARY OF DEFENSE
1000 DEFENSE PENTAGON
WASHINGTON, DC 20301-1000

JAN 15 2003

MEMORANDUM FOR COMMANDER USSOUTHCOM

SUBJECT: Counter-Resistance Techniques (U)

(S) My December 2, 2002, approval of the use of all Category II techniques and one Category III technique during interrogations at Guantanamo is hereby rescinded. Should you determine that particular techniques in either of these categories are warranted in an individual case, you should forward that request to me. Such a request should include a thorough justification for the employment of those techniques and a detailed plan for the use of such techniques.

(U) In all interrogations, you should continue the humane treatment of detainees, regardless of the type of interrogation technique employed.

(U) Attached is a memo to the General Counsel setting in motion a study to be completed within 15 days. After my review, I will provide further guidance.

[signed Donald Rumsfeld]

Classified by: Secretary Rumsfeld
Reason: 1.5(c)
Declassify on: 10 years

Declassify Under the Authority of Executive Order 12958
By Executive Secretary, Office of the Secretary of Defense
By William P. Marriott, CAPT, USN
June 21, 2004

9

SECRETARY OF DEFENSE
1000 DEFENSE PENTAGON
WASHINGTON, DC 20301-1000

JAN 15 2003

MEMORANDUM FOR THE GENERAL COUNSEL OF
THE DEPARTMENT OF DEFENSE

SUBJECT: Detainee Interrogations (U)

(U) Establish a working group within the Department of Defense to assess the legal, policy, and operational issues relating to the interrogations of detainees held by the U.S. Armed Forces in the war on terrorism.

(U) The working group should consist of experts from your Office, the Office of the Under Secretary of Defense for Policy, the Military Departments, and the Joint Staff. The working group should address and make recommendations as warranted on the following issues:

- (S) Legal conditions raised by interrogation of detainees held by U.S. Armed Forces.
- (S) Policy considerations with respect to the choice of interrogation techniques, including:
  - (S) contribution to intelligence collection
  - (S) effect on treatment of captured US military personnel
  - (S) effect on detainee prosecutions
  - (S) historical role of US armed forces in conducting interrogations
- (S) Recommendations for employment of particular interrogation techniques by DoD interrogators.

(U) You should report your assessment and recommendations to me within 15 days.

[signed Donald Rumsfeld]

Classified by: Secretary Rumsfeld
Reason: 1.5(c)
Declassify on: 10 years

Declassify Under the Authority of Executive Order 12958
By Executive Secretary, Office of the Secretary of Defense
By William P. Marriott, CAPT, USN
June 21, 2004

IO

Unclassifed When Attachment is Removed

GENERAL COUNSEL OF THE DEPARTMENT OF DEFENSE
1600 Defense Pentagon
Washington, D.C. 20301-1600

Jan 17 2003

MEMORANDUM FOR THE GENERAL COUNSEL OF THE DEPARTMENT OF THE AIR FORCE

SUBJECT: Working Group to Assess Legal, Policy, and Operational Issues Relating to Interrogation of Detainees Held by the U.S. Armed Forces in the War on Terrorism (U)

(U) You are hereby designated as the Chair of an interdepartmental working group and my executive agent to prepare an assessment and recommendations for me that are responsive to the attached memorandum of the Secretary of Defense, "Detainee Interrogations," dated January 15, 2003. In carrying out these responsibilities, you should call upon the resources of the offices of those indicated as recipients of copies of this memorandum, including requesting their participation, or that of members of their staffs, in this working group.

(U) Please provide me with periodic updates as available. I expect your effort to address and provide recommendations, as warranted, pertaining to the issues set out in the Secretary's memorandum. Your analysis should take into account the various potential geographic locations where U.S. Armed Forces may hold detainees.

(U) You should provide your assessment and recommendations to me by January 29, 2003. I appreciate your willingness to assume this important responsibility.

[signed]

William J. Haynes II

Attachment:
As stated.

cc:
Under Secretary of Defense (Policy)

Acting Assistant Secretary of Defense (SO/LIC)
General Counsel of the Department of the Army
General Counsel of the Department of the Navy
Director of the Joint Staff
Director, Joint Intelligence Agency
Counsel of the Commander of the Marine Corps
The Judge Advocate General of the Army
The Judge Advocate General of the Navy
The Judge Advocate General of the Air Force
Staff Judge Advocate General for the Commandant of the Marine Corps

I I

WORKING GROUP REPORT ON DETAINEE INTERROGATIONS IN THE GLOBAL WAR ON TERRORISM:
Assessment of Legal, Historical, Policy, and Operational Considerations

April 4, 2003

I. Introduction

(S/NF)(U) On January 15, 2003, the Secretary of Defense (SECDEF), directed the General Counsel of the Department of Defense (DOD GC) to establish a working group within the Department of Defense (DOD) to assess the legal, policy, and operational issues relating to the interrogations of detainees held by the United States Armed Forces in the war on terrorism. [Attachment 1 not included here.]

(S/NF)(U) On January 16, 2003, the DOD GC asked the General Counsel of the Department of the Air Force to convene this working group, comprised of representatives of the following entities: the Office of the Undersecretary of Defense (Policy), the Defense Intelligence Agency, the General Counsels of the Air Force, Army, and Navy and Counsel to the Commandant of the Marine Corps, the Judge Advocates General of the Air Force, Army, Navy, and Marines, and the Joint Staff Legal Counsel and J5. [Attachment 2 not included here.] The following assessment is the result of the collaborative efforts of those organizations, after consideration of diverse views, and was informed by a Department of Justice opinion.

(S/NF)(U) In preparing this assessment, it was understood that military members, civilian employees of the United States, and contractor employees currently participate in interrogations of detainees. Further, those who participate in the decision processes are comprised of military personnel and civilians.

(U) Our review is limited to the legal and policy considerations applicable to interrogation techniques applied to unlawful combatants in the Global War on Terrorism interrogated outside the sovereign territory of the United States by DOD personnel in DOD interrogation facilities. Interrogations can be broadly divided into two categories, strategic and tactical. This document addresses only strategic interrogations that are those conducted: (i) at a fixed location created for that purpose; (ii) by a task force or higher level component; and (iii) other than in direct and immediate support of on-going military operations. All tactical interrogations, including battlefield interrogations, remain governed by existing doctrine and procedures and are not directly affected by this review.

(U) In considering interrogation techniques for possible application to unlawful combatants in the "strategic" category, it became apparent that those techniques could be divided into three types: (i) routine (those that have been ordinarily used by interrogators for routine interrogations), (ii) techniques comparable to the first type but not formally recognized, and (iii) more aggressive counter-resistance techniques than would be used in routine interrogations. The third type would only be appropriate when presented with a resistant detainee who there is good reason to believe possesses critical intelligence. Many of the techniques of the second and third types have been requested for approval by USSOUTHCOM and USCENTCOM. The working group's conclusions regarding these three types of techniques, including recommendations for appropriate safeguards, are presented at the end of this report.

(U) This assessment comes in the context of a major threat to the security of the United States by terrorist forces who have demonstrated a ruthless disregard for even minimal standards of civilized behavior, with a focused intent to inflict maximum casualties on the United States and its people, including its civilian population. In this context, intelligence regarding their capabilities and intentions is of vital interest to the United States and its friends and allies. Effective interrogations of those unlawful combatants who are under the control of the United States have proven to be and will remain a critical source of this information necessary to national security.

(U) (C) Pursuant to the Confidential Presidential Determination, dated February 7, 2002 (Humane Treatment of al-Qaida and Taliban Detainees), the President determined that members of al-Qaida and the Taliban are unlawful combatants and therefore are not entitled to the protections of the Geneva Conventions as prisoners of war or otherwise. However, as a matter of policy, the President has directed U.S. Armed Forces to treat al-Qaida and Taliban detainees "humanely" and "to the extent appropriate and consistent with military necessity, in a manner consistent with the principles" of the Geneva Conventions. Due to the unique nature of the war on terrorism in which the enemy covertly attacks innocent civilian populations without warning, and further due to the critical nature of the information believed to be known by certain of the al-Qaida and Taliban detainees regarding future terrorist attacks, it may be appropriate for the appropriate approval authority to authorize as a military necessity the interrogation of such unlawful combatants in a manner beyond that which may be applied to a prisoner of war who is subject to the protections of the Geneva Conventions.

(U) In considering this issue, it became apparent that any recommendations and decisions must take into account the international and domestic law, past practices and pronouncements of the United States, DOD policy considerations, practical interrogation considerations, the views of other nations, and the potential impacts on the United States, its Armed Forces generally, individual interrogators, and those responsible for authorizing and directing specific interrogation techniques.

(U) We were asked specifically to recommend techniques that comply with all applicable law and are believed consistent with policy considerations not only of the United States but which may be unique to DOD. Accordingly, we undertook that analysis and conducted a technique-specific review that has produced a summary chart [not included here] for use in identifying the recommended techniques.

[...]

V. Techniques

(U) The purpose of all interviews and interrogations is to get the most information from a detainee with the least intrusive method, always applied in a humane and law-ful manner with sufficient oversight by trained investigators or interrogators. Operat-ing instructions must be developed based on command policies to insure uniform, careful, and safe application of any interrogations of detainees.

(S/NF)(U) Interrogations must always be planned, deliberate actions that take into account numerous, often interlocking factors such as a detainee's current and past per-formance in both detention and interrogation, a detainee's emotional and physical strengths and weaknesses, an assessment of possible approaches that may work on a certain detainee in an effort to gain the trust of the detainee, strengths and weaknesses of interrogators, and augmentation by other personnel for a certain detainee based on other factors.

(S/NF)(U) Interrogation approaches are designed to manipulate the detainee's emotions and weaknesses to gain his willing cooperation. Interrogation operations are never conducted in a vacuum; they are conducted in close cooperation with the units detaining the individuals. The policies established by the detaining units that pertain to searching, silencing, and segregating also play a role in the interrogation of a detainee. Detainee interrogation involves developing a plan tailored to an individ-ual and approved by senior interrogators. Strict adherence to policies/standard oper-ating procedures governing the administration of interrogation techniques and oversight is essential.

(S/NF)(U) Listed below are interrogation techniques all believed to be effective but with varying degrees of utility. Techniques 1–19, 22–26 and 30, applied singly, are purely verbal and/or involve no physical contact that could produce pain or harm and no threat of pain or harm. It is important that interrogators be provided reason-able latitude to vary techniques depending on the detainee's culture, strengths, weak-nesses, environment, extent of training in resistance techniques as well as the urgency of obtaining information that the detainee is known to have. Each of the techniques requested or suggested for possible use for detainees by USSOUTHCOM and USCENTCOM is included. Some descriptions include certain limiting parameters;

these have been judged appropriate by senior interrogators as to effectiveness.

(S/NF)(U) *While techniques are considered individually within this analysis, it must be understood that in practice, techniques are usually used in combination; the cumulative effect of all techniques to be employed __must__ be considered before any decisions are made regarding approval for particular situations.* The title of a particular technique is not always fully descriptive of a particular technique. With respect to the employment of any techniques involving physical contact, stress or that could produce physical pain or harm, a detailed explanation of that technique must be provided to the decision authority prior to any decision.

Note: Techniques 1–17 are further explained in Field Manual 34-52.

   1. (S/NF)(U) Direct: Asking straightforward questions.
   2. (S/NF)(U) Incentive/Removal of Incentive: Providing a reward or removing a privilege, above and beyond those that are required by the Geneva Convention, from detainees (Privileges above and beyond POW-required privileges).
   3. (S/NF)(U) Emotional Love: Playing on the love a detainee has for an individual or group.
   4. (S/NF)(U) Emotional Hate: Playing on the hatred a detainee has for an individual or group.
   5. (S/NF)(U) Fear Up Harsh: Significantly increasing the fear level in a detainee.
   6. (S/NF)(U) Fear Up Mild: Moderately increasing the fear level in a detainee.
   7. (S/NF)(U) Reduced Fear: Reducing the fear level in a detainee.
   8. (S/NF)(U) Pride and Ego Up: Boosting the ego of a detainee.
   9. (S/NF)(U) Pride and Ego Down: Attacking or insulting the ego of a detainee, not beyond the limits that would apply to a POW.
   10. (S/NF)(U) Futility: Invoking the feeling of futility of a detainee.
   11. (S/NF)(U) We Know All: Convincing the detainee that the interrogator knows the answer to questions he asks the detainee.
   12. (S/NF)(U) Establish Your Identity: Convincing the detainee that the interrogator has mistaken the detainee for someone else.
   13. (S/NF)(U) Repetition Approach: Continuously repeating the same question to the detainee within interrogation periods of normal duration.
   14. (S/NF)(U) File and Dossier: Convincing detainee that the interrogator has a damning and inaccurate file, which must be fixed.
   15. (S/NF)(U) Mutt and Jeff: A team consisting of a friendly and harsh interrogator. The harsh interrogator might employ the Pride and Ego Down technique.
   16. (S/NF)(U) Rapid Fire: Questioning in rapid succession without allowing detainee to answer.
   17. (S/NF)(U) Silence: Staring at the detainee to encourage discomfort.
   18. (S/NF)(U) Change of Scenery Up: Removing the detainee from the standard interrogation setting (generally to a location more pleasant, but no worse).

19. (S/NF)(U) Change of Scenery Down: Removing the detainee from the standard interrogation setting and placing him in a setting that may be less comfortable; would not constitute a substantial change in environmental quality.

20. (S/NF)(U) Hooding: This technique is questioning the detainee with a blindfold in place. For interrogation purposes, the blindfold is not on other than during interrogation.

21. (S/NF)(U) Mild Physical Contact: Lightly touching a detainee or lightly poking the detainee in a completely non-injurious manner. This also includes softly grabbing of shoulders to get the detainee's attention or to comfort the detainee.

22. (S/NF)(U) Dietary Manipulation: Changing the diet of a detainee; no intended deprivation of food or water; no adverse medical or cultural effect and without intent to deprive subject of food or water, e.g., hot rations to MREs.

23. (S/NF)(U) Environmental Manipulation: Altering the environment to create moderate discomfort (e.g., adjusting temperature or introducing an unpleasant smell). Conditions would not be such that they would injure the detainee. Detainee would be accompanied by interrogator at all times.

24. (S/NF)(U) Sleep Adjustment: Adjusting the sleeping times of the detainee (e.g., reversing sleep cycles from night to day). This technique is NOT sleep deprivation.

25. (S/NF)(U) False Flag: Convincing the detainee that individuals from a country other than the United States are interrogating him.

26. (S/NF)(U) Threat of Transfer: Threatening to transfer the subject to a 3rd country that subject is likely to fear would subject him to torture or death. (The threat would not be acted upon nor would the threat include any information beyond the naming of the receiving country.)

(S/NF)(U) The following list includes additional techniques that are considered effective by interrogators, some of which have been requested by USCENTCOM and USSOUTHCOM. They are more aggressive counter-resistance techniques that may be appropriate for detainees who are extremely resistant to the above techniques, and who the interrogators strongly believe have vital information. All of the following techniques indicate the need for technique-specialized training and written procedures to insure the safety of all persons, along with appropriate, specified levels of approval and notification for each technique.

27. (S/NF)(U) Isolation: Isolating the detainee from other detainees while still complying with basic standards of treatment.

28. (S/NF)(U) Use of Prolonged Interrogations: The continued use of a series of approaches that extend over a long period of time (e.g., 20 hours per day per interrogation).

29. (S/NF)(U) Forced Grooming: Forcing a detainee to shave hair or beard. (Force applied with intention to avoid injury. Would not use force that would cause serious injury.)

30. (S/NF)(U) Prolonged Standing: Lengthy standing in a "normal" position (non-stress). This has been successful, but should never make the detainee exhausted to the point of weakness or collapse. Not enforced by physical restraints. Not to exceed four hours in a 24-hour period.

31. (S/NF)(U) Sleep Deprivation: Keeping the detainee awake for an extended period of time. (Allowing individual to rest briefly and then awakening him, repeatedly.) Not to exceed 4 days in succession.

32. (S/NF)(U) Physical Training: Requiring detainees to exercise (perform ordinary physical exercises actions) (e.g., running, jumping jacks); not to exceed 15 minutes in a two-hour period; not more than two cycles, per 24-hour periods) Assists in generating compliance and fatiguing the detainees. No enforced compliance.

33. (S/NF)(U) Face slap/Stomach slap: A quick glancing slap to the fleshy part of the cheek or stomach. These techniques are used strictly as shock measures and do not cause pain or injury. They are only effective if used once or twice together. After the second time on a detainee, it will lose the shock effect. Limited to two slaps per application; no more than two applications per interrogation.

34. (S/NF)(U) Removal of Clothing: Potential removal of all clothing; removal to be done by military police if not agreed to by the subject. Creating a feeling of helplessness and dependence. This technique must be monitored to ensure the environmental conditions are such that this technique does not injure the detainee.

35. (S/NF)(U) Increasing Anxiety by Use of Aversions: Introducing factors that of themselves create anxiety but do not create terror or mental trauma (e.g., simple presence of dog without directly threatening action). This technique requires the commander to develop specific and detailed safeguards to insure detainee's safety.

VI. Evaluation of Useful Techniques

(S/NF)(U) The working group considered each of the techniques enumerated in Section V, *supra*, in light of the legal, historical, policy and operational considerations discussed in this paper. In the course of that examination it became apparent that any decision whether to authorize a technique is essentially a risk benefit analysis that generally takes into account the expected utility of the technique, the likelihood that any technique will be in violation of domestic or international law, and various policy considerations. Generally, the legal analysis that was applied is that understood to comport with the views of the Department of Justice. Although the United States, as a practical matter, may be the arbiter of international law in deciding its application to our national activities, the views of other nations are relevant in considering their reactions, potential effects on our captured personnel in future conflicts, and possible liability to prosecution in other countries and international forums for interrogators, supervisors and commanders involved in interrogation processes and decisions.

(S/NF)(U) The Conclusions section of this analysis, *infra*, summarizes salient conclusions that were applied to our analysis of individual techniques. As it suggests, the lawfulness and the effectiveness of individual techniques will, in practice, depend on the specific facts. The lawfulness will depend in significant part on procedural protections that demonstrate a legitimate purpose and that there was no *intent* to inflict significant mental or physical pain—and, in fact, avoid that. Because of this, the assessment of each technique presumed that the safeguards and procedures described in the "DOD-Specific Policy Considerations" section of this paper would be in place. The importance of this is underscored by the fact that, in practice, techniques are usually applied in combination, and as the legal analysis of this paper indicates, the significance and effect on an individual detainee of the specific combination of techniques employed, and their manner of application will determine the lawfulness of any particular interrogation.

(S/NF)(U) In addition, the lawfulness of the application of any particular technique, or combination of techniques, may depend on the practical necessity for imposition of the more exceptional techniques. As the analysis explains, legal justification for action that could otherwise be unlawful (e.g., relying upon national necessity and self-defense) depends in large part on whether the specific circumstances would justify the imposition of more aggressive techniques. Interrogation of an individual known to have facts essential to prevent an immediate threat of catastrophic harm to large populations may support use of "exceptional" techniques, particularly when milder techniques have been unavailing. But this is a determination that will always be case-specific. Consequently, use of each technique should be a decision level appropriate to the gravity of the particular case (both for the nation and for the detainee).

(S/NF)(U) The chart at Attachment 3 [not included here] reflects the result of the risk/benefit assessment for each technique considered, "scored" for each technique, relevant considerations and given an overall recommendation. In addition, it notes specific techniques that, based on this evaluation, should be considered "exceptional techniques" (marked with an "E") subject to particular limitations described in the "DOD-Specific Policy Considerations" section (generally, not routinely available to interrogators, use limited to specifically designated locations and specifically trained interrogators, special safeguards, and appropriately senior employment decision levels specified). For each "exceptional" technique, a recommendation for employment decision level is indicated as well.

VII. Conclusions Relevant to Interrogation of Unlawful Combatants Under DOD Control Outside the United States

(S/NF)(U) As a result of the foregoing analysis of legal, policy, historical, and operational considerations, the following general conclusions can be drawn relevant to interrogation of unlawful combatants captured in the war on terrorism under DOD control outside the United States:

(S/NF)(U) Under the Third Geneva Convention, U.S. forces are required to treat captured personnel as POWs until an official determination is made as to their status. Once a determination has been made that captured personnel are unlawful combatants, as is currently the case with captured Taliban and al-Qaida operatives, they do not have a right to the protections of the Third Geneva Convention.

(U) Customary international law does not provide legally-enforceable restrictions on the interrogation of unlawful combatants under DOD control outside the United States.

(U) The United States Constitution does not protect those individuals who are not United States citizens and who are outside the sovereign territory of the United States.

(S/NF)(U) Under the Torture Convention, no person may be subjected to torture. Torture is defined as an act specifically *intended* to inflict severe physical or mental pain or suffering and that mental pain or suffering refers to *prolonged* mental harm caused by or resulting from (1) the *intentional* infliction or *threatened infliction of severe physical pain or suffering*; (2) the administration or application, or threatened application, of mind altering substances or other procedures *calculated* to disrupt profoundly the senses or personality; (3) the threat of imminent death; or (4) the threat that another person will *imminently* be subjected to death, severe physical pain or suffering, or the administration or application, or threatened application, of mind altering substances or other procedures calculated to disrupt profoundly the senses or personality.

(S/NF)(U) Under the Torture Convention, no person may be subjected to cruel, inhuman or degrading treatment. The United States has defined its obligations under the Torture Convention as conduct prohibited by the 5th, 8th, and 14th Amendments to the Constitution of the United States. These terms, as defined by U.S. courts, could be understood to mean: to inflict pain or harm without a legitimate purpose; to inflict pain or injury for malicious or sadistic reasons; to deny the minimal civilized measures of life's necessities and such denial reflects a deliberate indifference to health and safety; and to apply force and cause injury so severe and so disproportionate to the legitimate government interest being served that it amounts to a brutal and inhumane abuse of official power literally shocking the conscience.

(U) For actions outside the United States and the special maritime and territorial jurisdiction of the United States, 18 U.S.C. § 2340 applies. For actions occurring within the United States and the special maritime and territorial jurisdiction of the United States, various Federal statutes would apply.

(S/NF)(U) The President has directed, pursuant to his Military Order dated

November 13, 2001, that the U.S. Armed Forces treat detainees humanely and that the detainees be afforded adequate food, drinking water, shelter, clothing and medical treatment.

(S/NF)(U) Pursuant to the Confidential Presidential Determination, dated February 7, 2002, the U.S. Armed Forces are to treat detainees in a manner consistent with the *principles* of Geneva, to the extent *appropriate* and consistent with *military necessity.*

(U) Under Article 10 of the Torture Convention, the United States is obligated to ensure that law enforcement and military personnel involved in interrogations are educated and informed regarding the prohibition against torture, and under Article 11, systematic reviews of interrogation rules, methods, and practices are also required.

(U) Members of the U.S. Armed Forces are, at all times and all places, subject to prosecution under the UCMJ for, among other offenses, acts which constitute assault, assault consummated by a battery, assault with the intent to inflict grievous bodily harm, manslaughter, unpremeditated murder, and maltreatment of those subject to their orders. Under certain circumstances, civilians accompanying the Armed Forces may be subject to the UCMJ.

(U) Civilian employees and employees of DOD contractors may be subject to prosecution under the Federal Criminal Code for, among other offenses, acts which constitute assault (in various degrees), maiming, manslaughter, and murder.

(S/NF)(U) Defenses relating to Commander-in-Chief authority, necessity and self-defense or defense of others may be available to individuals whose actions would otherwise constitute these crimes, and the extent of availability of those defenses will be fact-specific. Certain relevant offenses require specific intent to inflict particular degrees of harm or pain, which could be refuted by evidence to the contrary (e.g., procedural safeguards). Where the Commander-in-Chief authority is being relied upon, a Presidential written directive would serve to memorialize this authority.

(S/NF)(U) The lawfulness and appropriateness of the use of many of the interrogation techniques we examined can only be determined by reference to specific details of their application, such as appropriateness and safety for the particular detainee, adequacy of supervision, specifics of the application including their duration, intervals between applications, combination with other techniques, and safeguards to avoid harm (including termination criteria and the presence or availability of qualified medical personnel). (We have recommended appropriate guidance and protections.)

(S/NF)(U) Other nations, including major partner nations, may consider use of techniques more aggressive than those appropriate for POWs violative of international law or their own domestic law, potentially making U.S. personnel involved in the use of such techniques subject to prosecution for perceived human rights violations in other nations or to being surrendered to international fora, such as the ICC; this has the potential to impact future operations and overseas travel of such personnel.

(S/NF)(U) Some nations may assert that the U.S. use of techniques more aggressive than those appropriate for POWs justifies similar treatment for captured U.S. personnel.

(S/NF)(U) Should information regarding the use of more aggressive interrogation techniques than have been used traditionally by U.S. forces become public, it is likely to be exaggerated or distorted in the U.S. and international media accounts, and may produce an adverse effect on support for the war on terrorism.

(S/NF)(U) The more aggressive the interrogation technique used, the greater the likelihood that it will affect adversely the admissibility of any acquired statements or confessions in prosecutions against the person interrogated, including in military commissions (to a lesser extent than in other U.S. courts).

(S/NF)(U) Carefully drawn procedures intended to prevent unlawful levels of pain or harm not only serve to avoid unlawful results but should provide evidence helpful to demonstrate that the specific intent required for certain offenses did not exist.

(S/NF)(U) General use of exceptional techniques (generally, having substantially greater risk than those currently, routinely used by U.S. Armed Forces interrogators), even though lawful, may create uncertainty among interrogators regarding the appropriate limits of interrogations. They should therefore be employed with careful procedures and only when fully justified.

(S/NF)(U) Participation by U.S. military personnel in interrogations which use techniques that are more aggressive than those appropriate for POWs would constitute a significant departure from traditional U.S. military norms and could have an adverse impact on the cultural self-image of U.S. military forces.[76]

(S/NF)(U) The use of exceptional interrogation techniques should be limited to specified strategic interrogation facilities; when there is a good basis to believe that the detainee possesses critical intelligence; when the detainee is medically and operationally evaluated as suitable (considering all techniques in combination); when interrogators are specifically trained for the technique(s); a specific interrogation plan (including reasonable safeguards, limits on duration, intervals between applications, termination criteria and the presence or availability of qualified medical personnel); when there is appropriate supervision; and, after obtaining appropriate specified senior approval level for use with any specific detainee (after considering the foregoing and receiving legal advice).

VIII. Recommendations

(U) We recommend:

(S/NF)(U) 1. The working group recommends that techniques 1–26 [...] be approved for use with unlawful combatants outside the United States, subject to the general limitations set forth in this Legal and Policy Analysis; and that techniques 27–35 be approved for use with unlawful combatants outside the United States subject to the general limitations as well as the specific limitations regarding "exceptional" techniques as follows: conducted at strategic interrogation facilities; where there is a good basis to believe that the detainee possesses critical intelligence; the detainee is medically and operationally evaluated as suitable (considering all techniques to be used in combination); interrogators are specifically trained for the technique(s); a specific interrogation plan (including reasonable safeguards, limits on duration, intervals between applications, termination criteria and the presence or availability of qualified medical personnel) is developed; appropriate supervision is provided; and, appropriate specified senior level approval is given for use with any specific detainee (after considering the foregoing and receiving legal advice).

(S/NF)(U) 2. SECDEF approve the strategic interrogation facilities that are authorized to use the "exceptional techniques" (such facilities at this time include Guantánamo, Cuba; additional strategic interrogation facilities will be approved on a case-by-case basis).

(S/NF)(U) 3. As the Commander-in-Chief authority is vested in the President, we recommend that any exercise of that authority by DOD personnel be confirmed in writing through presidential directive or other document.

(S/NF)(U) 4. That DOD policy directives and implementing guidance be amended as necessary to reflect the determinations in paragraph one and subsequent determinations concerning additional possible techniques.

(S/NF)(U) 5. That commanders and supervisors, and their legal advisers, involved with the decisions related to employment of "exceptional techniques" receive specialized training regarding the legal and policy considerations relevant to interrogations that make use of such techniques.

(S/NF)(U) 6. That OASD (PA) prepare a press plan to anticipate and address potential public inquiries and misunderstandings regarding appropriate interrogation techniques.

(S/NF)(U) 7. That a procedure be established for requesting approval of additional interrogation techniques similar to that for requesting "supplementals" for ROEs; the process should require the requestor to describe the technique in detail, justify its utility, describe the potential effects on subjects, known hazards and proposed safeguards, provide a legal analysis, and recommend an appropriate decision level regarding use on specific subjects. This procedure should ensure that SECDEF is the approval authority for the addition of any technique that could be considered equivalent in degree to any of the "exceptional techniques" addressed in this report (in the chart numbers 27–35, labeled with an "E"), and that he establish the specific decision level required for application of such techniques.

(S/NF)(U) 8. DOD establish specific understandings with other agencies using DOD detailed interrogators regarding the permissible scope of the DOD interrogator's activities.

Classified by: Secretary Rumsfeld
Reason: 1.5(C)
Declassify on: 10 years

NOTE

76. Those techniques considered in this review that raise this concern are relatively few in number and generally indicated by yellow or red (or green with a significant footnote) under major partner views in Attachment 3 [not included here].

12

SECRETARY OF DEFENSE
1000 DEFENSE PENTAGON
WASHINGTON, DC 20301-1000

APR 16 2003

MEMORANDUM FOR THE COMMANDER, US SOUTHERN COMMAND

SUBJECT: Counter-Resistance Techniques in the War on Terrorism (S)

(S/NF)(U) I have considered the report of the Working Group that I directed be established on January 15, 2003.

(S/NF)(U) I approve the use of specified counter-resistance techniques, subject to the following:

(U) a. The techniques I authorize are those lettered A–X, set out at Tab A.

(U) b. These techniques must be used with all the safeguards described at Tab B.

(S)(U) c. Use of these techniques is limited to interrogations of unlawful combatants held at Guantánamo Bay, Cuba.

(S)(U) d. Prior to the use of these techniques, the Chairman of the Working Group on Detainee Interrogations in the Global War on Terrorism must brief you and your staff.

(S/NF)(U) I reiterate that US Armed Forces shall continue to treat detainees humanely and, to the extent appropriate and consistent with military necessity, in a manner consistent with the principles of the Geneva Conventions. In addition, if you intend to use techniques B, I, O, or X, you must specifically determine that military necessity requires its use and notify me in advance.

(S/NF)(U) If, in your view, you require additional interrogation techniques for a particular detainee, you should provide me, via the Chairman of the Joint Chiefs of Staff, a written request describing the proposed technique, recommended safeguards, and the rationale for applying it with an identified detainee.

(S)(U) Nothing in this memorandum in any way restricts your existing authority to maintain good order and discipline among detainees.

[signed Donald Rumsfeld]

Attachments:
As stated
Declassified Under Authority of Executive Order 12958
Executive Secretary, Office of the Secretary of Defense
William P. Marriott, CAPT, USN, June 18, 2004

> Classified By: Secretary of Defense
> Reason: 1.5(a)
> Declassify On: 2 April 2013

NOT RELEASABLE TO FOREIGN NATIONALS

TAB A

INTERROGATION TECHNIQUES

(S/NF)(U) The use of techniques A–X is subject to the general safeguards as provided below as well as specific implementation guidelines to be provided by the appropriate authority. Specific implementation guidance with respect to techniques A–Q is provided in Army Field Manual 34-52. Further implementation guidance with respect to techniques R–X will need to be developed by the appropriate authority.

(S/NF)(U) Of the techniques set forth below, the policy aspects of certain techniques should be considered to the extent those policy aspects reflect the views of other major U.S. partner nations. Where applicable, the description of the technique is annotated to include a summary of the policy issues that should be considered before application of the technique.

A. (S/NF)(U) Direct: Asking straightforward questions.

B. (S/NF)(U) Incentive/Removal of Incentive: Providing a reward or removing a privilege, above and beyond those that are required by the Geneva Convention, from detainees. [Caution: Other nations that believe that detainees are entitled to POW protections may consider that provision and retention of religious items (e.g., the Koran) are protected under international law (see, Geneva III, Article 34). Although the provisions of the Geneva Convention are not applicable to the interrogation of unlawful combatants, consideration should be given to these views prior to application of the technique.]

C. (S/NF)(U) Emotional Love: Playing on the love a detainee has for an individual or group.

D. (S/NF)(U) Emotional Hate: Playing on the hatred a detainee has for an individual or group.

E. (S/NF)(U) Fear Up Harsh: Significantly increasing the fear level in a detainee.

F. (S/NF)(U) Fear Up Mild: Moderately increasing the fear level in a detainee.

G. (S/NF)(U) Reduced Fear: Reducing the fear level in a detainee.

H. (S/NF)(U) Pride and Ego Up: Boosting the ego of a detainee.

I. (S/NF)(U) Pride and Ego Down: Attacking or insulting the ego of a detainee, not beyond the limits that would apply to a POW. [Caution: Article 17 of Geneva III provides, "Prisoners of war who refuse to answer may not be, threatened, insulted, or exposed to any unpleasant or disadvantageous treatment of any kind." Other nations that believe that detainees are entitled to POW protections may consider this technique inconsistent with the provisions of Geneva. Although the provisions of Geneva are not applicable to the interrogation of unlawful combatants, consideration should be given to these views prior to application of the technique.]

J. (S/NF)(U) Futility: Invoking the feeling of futility of a detainee.

K. (S/NF)(U) We Know All: Convincing the detainee that the interrogator knows the answer to questions he asks the detainee.

L. (S/NF)(U) Establish Your Identity: Convincing the detainee that the interrogator has mistaken the detainee for someone else.

M. (S/NF)(U) Repetition Approach: Continuously repeating the same question to the detainee within interrogation periods of normal duration.

N. (U) File and Dossier: Convincing detainee that the interrogator has a damning and inaccurate file, which must be fixed.

O. (S/NF)(U) Mutt and Jeff: A team consisting of a friendly and harsh interrogator. The harsh interrogator might employ the Pride and Ego Down technique. [Caution: Other nations that believe that POW protections apply to detainees may view this technique as inconsistent with Geneva III, Article 13 which provides that POWs must be protected against acts of intimidation. Although the provisions of Geneva are not applicable to the interrogation of unlawful combatants, consideration should be given to these views prior to application of the technique.]

P. (S/NF)(U) Rapid Fire: Questioning in rapid succession without allowing detainee to answer.

Q. (S/NF)(U) Silence: Staring at the detainee to encourage discomfort.

R. (S/NF)(U) Change of Scenery Up: Removing the detainee from the standard interrogation setting (generally to a location more pleasant, but no worse).

S. (S/NF)(U) Change of Scenery Down: Removing the detainee from the standard interrogation setting and placing him in a setting that may be less comfortable; would not constitute a substantial change in environmental quality.

T. (S/NF)(U) Dietary Manipulation: Changing the diet of a detainee; no intended deprivation of food or water; no adverse medical or cultural effect and without intent to deprive subject of food or water, e.g., hot rations to MREs.

U. (S/NF)(U) Environmental Manipulation: Altering the environment to create moderate discomfort (e.g., adjusting temperature or introducing an unpleasant smell). Conditions would not be such that they would injure the detainee. Detainee would be accompanied by interrogator at all times. [Caution: Based on court cases in other countries, some nations may view application of this technique in certain circumstances to be inhumane. Consideration of these views should be given prior to use of this technique.]

V. (S/NF)(U) Sleep Adjustment: Adjusting the sleeping times of the detainee (e.g., reversing sleep cycles from night to day.) This technique is NOT sleep deprivation.

W. (S/NF)(U) False Flag: Convincing the detainee that individuals from a country other than the United States are interrogating him.

X. (S/NF)(U) Isolation: Isolating the detainee from other detainees while still complying with basic standards of treatment. [Caution: The use of isolation as an interrogation technique requires detailed implementation instructions, including specific guidelines regarding the length of isolation, medical and psychological review, and approval for extensions of the length of isolation by the appropriate level in the chain of command. This technique is not known to have been generally used for interrogation purposes for longer than 30 days. Those nations that believe detainees are subject to POW protections may view use of this technique as inconsistent with the requirements of Geneva III, Article 13 which provides that POWs must be protected against acts of intimidation; Article 14 which provides that POWs are entitled to respect for their person; Article 34 which prohibits coercion and Article 126 which ensures access and basic standards of treatment. Although the provisions of Geneva are not applicable to the interrogation of unlawful combatants, consideration should be given to these views prior to application of the technique.]

TAB B

GENERAL SAFEGUARDS

(U)(S/NF) Application of these interrogation techniques is subject to the following general safeguards: (i) limited to use only at strategic interrogation facilities; (ii) there is a good basis to believe that the detainee possesses critical intelligence; (iii) the detainee is medically and operationally evaluated as suitable (considering all techniques to be used in combination); (iv) interrogators are specifically trained for the technique(s); (v) a specific interrogation plan (including reasonable safeguards, limits on duration, intervals between applications, termination criteria and the presence or availability of qualified medical personnel) has been developed; (vi) there is appropriate supervision; and, (vii) there is appropriate specified senior approval for use with any specific detainee (after considering the foregoing and receiving legal advice).

(U) The purpose of all interviews and interrogations is to get the most information from a detainee with the least intrusive method, always applied in a humane and lawful manner with sufficient oversight by trained investigators or interrogators. Operating instructions must be developed based on command policies to insure uniform, careful, and safe application of any interrogations of detainees.

(U)(S/NF) Interrogations must always be planned, deliberate actions that take into account numerous, often interlocking factors such as a detainee's current and past performance in both detention and interrogation, a detainee's emotional and physical strengths and weaknesses, an assessment of possible approaches that may work on a certain detainee in an effort to gain the trust of the detainee, strengths and weaknesses of interrogators, and augmentation by other personnel for a certain detainee based on other factors.

(U)(S/NF) Interrogation approaches are designed to manipulate the detainee's emotions and weaknesses to gain his willing cooperation. Interrogation operations are never conducted in a vacuum; they are conducted in close cooperation with the units detaining the individuals. The policies established by the detaining units that pertain to searching, silencing, and segregating also play a role in the interrogation of a detainee. Detainee interrogation involves developing a plan tailored to an individual and approved by senior interrogators. Strict adherence to policies/standard operating procedures governing the administration of interrogation techniques and oversight is essential.

(U)(S/NF) It is important that interrogators be provided reasonable latitude to vary techniques depending on the detainee's culture, strengths, weaknesses, environment, extent of training in resistance techniques as well as the urgency of obtaining information that the detainee is known to have.

(U)(S/NF) While techniques are considered individually within this analysis, it must be understood that in practice, techniques are usually used in combination; the cumulative effect of all techniques to be employed must be considered before any decisions are made regarding approval for particular situations. The title of a particular technique is not always fully descriptive of a particular technique. With respect to the employment of any techniques involving physical contact, stress or that could produce physical pain or harm, a detailed explanation of that technique must be provided to the decision authority prior to any decision.

Classified By: Secretary of Defense
Reason: 1.5(a)
Declassify On: 2 April 2013

NOT RELEASABLE TO FOREIGN NATIONALS

13

ASSESSMENT OF DoD COUNTERTERRORISM INTERROGATION AND DETENTION OPERATIONS IN IRAQ (U)

1. (S/NF) Introduction — From 31 August to 9 September 2003, MG Geoffrey Miller, US Army, Commander, Joint Task Force Guantanamo (JTF-GTMO) led a team of personnel experienced in strategic interrogation (Annex A) to HQ, CJTF-7, Baghdad, to conduct assistance visits to CJTF-7, TF-20, and the Iraqi Survey Group (ISG) to discuss current theater ability to rapidly exploit internees for actionable intelligence. The team focused on three areas: intelligence integration, synchronization, and fusion; interrogation operations and detention operations. The team used JTF-GTMO operational procedures and interrogation authorities as baselines.

2. (S/NF) Executive Summary — The dynamic operational environment in Iraq requires an equally dynamic intelligence apparatus. To improve velocity and operational effectiveness of counterterrorism interrogation, attention in three major mission areas is needed. The team observed that the Task Force did not have authorities and procedures in place to affect a unified strategy to detain, interrogate, and report information from detainees/internees in Iraq. Additionally, the corps commander's information needs required an in-theater analysis capability integrated throughout the interrogation operations structure to allow for better and faster reach-back to other worldwide intelligence databases. Last, the detention operations function must act as an enabler for interrogation.

(S/NF) The command has initiated a system to drive the rapid exploitation of internees to answer CJTF-7, theater, and national level counter terrorism requirements. This is the first stage toward the rapid exploitation of detainees. Receipt of additional resources currently in staffing will produce a dramatic improvement in the speed of delivering actionable intelligence and leveraging the effectiveness of the interrogation efforts. Our assessment is, given the implementation of the attached recommendations, a significant improvement in actionable intelligence will be realized within thirty days.

3. (S/NF) Functions: Integration — Synchronization — Fusion (Point of contact (POC) is MR David Becker [phone number deleted])

    a. (U) Integration — Defined as: to organize HUMINT collection and analytical resources under a coordinating authority that can rapidly task, direct, conduct analysis, and action intelligence gained from interrogations.

(S/NF) Observation—HUMINT collection and analysis is being performed by several autonomous entities in the theater, resulting in duplication of effort and imperfect information flow.

(S/NF) Recommendation — Establish a robust coordinating authority to direct and coordinate all HUMINT collection and analysis in Iraq. Supplement this authority with a collection management operation focused to support the needs of the Global War on Terrorism (GWOT), the Theater Commander and CJTF-7 Commanders' intelligence and targeting objectives. Additional resources are required for the CJTF-7 CJ2X to sustain this effort.

(S/NF) Observation—HUMINT collection priorities were not clearly defined, leading to ambiguous collection efforts. There are a large number of collection priorities that require a clear prioritization as to which requirements support the commander's critical information requirements.

(S/NF) Recommendation/Action In-progress — CJTF-7 CJ2X has established a clear method of prioritization for collection requirements. Requirements are now being combined into areas of focus to drive interrogation tasking and operations.

b. (U) Synchronization — Defined as: to establish a defined process and procedure to integrate the prioritization and tasking of all interrogation assets. (POC Is MR John Antonitis, [phone number deleted])

(S/NF) Observation — No written guidance specifically addressing interrogation policies and authorities was disseminated to units.

(S/NF) Recommendation/Action In-progress — CJTF-7 is drafting approval documents containing the authorities, policies and practices to outline requirements to process, interrogate, and exploit security internees.

(S/NF) Observation—DoD assets and other autonomous entities are active in the theater collecting information and conducting analysis under independent chains of command. Information sharing is not fully integrated. The various organizations are generally unaware of each other's capabilities, interests, and mutual information needs. They also lack protocols for coordinating access to internees, and for sharing the information collected and analysis performed.

(S/NP) Recommendation—CJTF-7 is establishing a HUMINT Collection and Targeting meeting that provides a weekly forum for system information sharing, internee access, and tasking protocols to fully leverage the participation of all entities active in the theater (to include Special Operations Forces (SOP), the Criminal Investigative Task Force, Central Intelligence Agency, and the Iraqi Survey Group) to support the CJTF-7 commander's intelligence and targeting objectives.

c. (U) **Fusion** — Fusion is defined as assuring that all required resources and actions to support internee operations are properly integrated, supervised, executed and assessed to support the commander's intent. (POC is CDR Jorge Gracia [phone number deleted].)

(S/NF) Observation — The resiliency and global reach of GWOT targets requires much closer cooperation between the strategic analytical community and the collectors and analysts in the field. Military intelligence analysts at the CJTF-7 ACE, CJ2X, and in the field are closely focused on the tactical mission and are generally unaware of the assets and capabilities of the broader national intelligence community and the existence of dedicated CT analytical centers, such as DIA's Joint Intelligence Task Force Combating Terrorism (JITF-CT) and the CIA's Counterterrorism Center (CTC).

(S/NF) Recommendation—Expedite the exchange of Counterterrorism information and analysis between collectors in the field and the national intelligence community by integrating the Interrogator Tiger Teams with analysts at the CJTF-7 CJ2X and national intelligence community through JITF-CT. Energize the analysis-collection feedback loop of the intelligence cycle with robust, timely, GWOT oriented, collection management planning and execution.

4. (U) **Interrogation** — Setting the conditions to exploit internees to respond to questions that answer theater commanders' critical questions. (POC is CW3 Edward Traywick [phone number deleted])

(S/NF) Summary—Tactical interrogation operations differ greatly from strategic interrogation operations. The interrogators within CJTF-7 have been accomplishing the tactical mission, at a high rate of professionalism and effectiveness since the beginning of the war. As the CJTF transitions to a new phase of operations, the category of internees to interrogate and analytical backstopping required necessitates transition to strategic interrogation operations. The interrogation mission is hindered by an absence of analytical resources and reach-back data systems. The detention operation does not yet set conditions for successful interrogations. Interrogations are conducted without a clear strategy for implementing a long-term approach strategy and clearly defined interrogation policies and authorities. To achieve rapid exploitation of internees it is necessary to integrate detention operations, interrogation operations and collection management under one command authority.

(S/NF) Observation—There is minimal analytical support to the interrogation mission. Interrogators continue to use tactical interrogation methods in a transitioning strategic environment.

(S/NF) Recommendation—Establish and train Interrogation Tiger Teams comprised of one interrogator and one analyst, both with SCI access. CJTF-7 has established an initial cadre of integrated Interrogation Tiger Teams from current assets and scheduled deploying interrogators and analysts to attend strategic interrogator and analyst training at Tiger Team University, USAICS, and Fort Huachuca in October 03.

(S/NF) Observation—CJFT-7s two interrogation facilities operate with their own independent collection focus without an integrated coordinating element. Coordination between facilities is conducted informally and inconsistently.

(S/NF) Recommendation—Consolidate the interrogation mission at one Joint Interrogation Debriefing Center (JIDC)/strategic interrogations facility under CJTF-7 command. This action has been initiated.

(S/NF) Observation—Detention operations do not enable the interrogation mission.

(S/NF) Recommendation—Dedicate and train a detention guard force subordinate to the JIDC Commander that sets the conditions for the successful interrogation and exploitation of internees/detainees. This action is now in progress.

(S/NF) Observation—The lack of awareness of available analytical databases by interrogators and analysts limits the ability to conduct effective integrated interrogation operations.

(S/NF) Recommendation—Train analysts to incorporate databases including DIMS, CT-link, web-safe, CIA Source, Harmony, and Coliseum in interrogation planning and execution. This training is provided at Tiger Team University and can be leveraged with a sustained theater training program.

(S/NF) Observation—Analysts at JIDC (Joint Interrogation Debriefing Center) interrogation operations section have limited access to automated intelligence systems that would allow the analyst to reach back to national level resources. The primary collection facilities (Abu Gharib) requires at a minimum 2 JWICS terminal to meet full operational capability.

(S/NF) Recommendation—Provide the necessary systems and bandwidth to enable direct analytical support to interrogation operations. See paragraph 6 (Information Technology).

(S/NF) Observation—There is no Behavioral Science Consultation Team (BSCT) to support interrogation operations. These teams comprised of operational behavioral psychologists and psychiatrists are essential in developing integrated interrogation strategies and assessing interrogation intelligence production.

(S/NF) Recommendation—Provide I BSCT to support interrogation operations.

(S/NF) Observation—The system procedures to rapidly transfer/return fully exploited internee intelligence sources back to the internee general population or recommend their release require assessment and streamlining.

(S/NF) Recommendation—Assess and refine transfer criteria to support continued rapid exploitation of high value internees and the release of fully exploited or low value internees in a more timely manner.

(S/NF) Observation — Task Force 20 (TF-20) lacks adequate number of trained interrogator-analyst Tiger Teams for mission requirements.

(S/NF) Recommendation: That CJTF-7 provide TF-20 Tiger Team support.

(S/NF) Observation—The application of emerging strategic interrogation strategies and techniques contain new approaches and operational art. Legal review and recommendations of internee interrogation operations by a dedicated command staff judge advocate is required to maximize interrogation effectiveness.

(S/NF) Recommendation — Dedicate a judge advocate(s) to advise commanders and interrogation leadership on requirements to operate within approved interrogation authorities, responsible for the detention and intelligence missions. This action is in progress.

5. (U) Detention Operations (POC is CSM Vannatta [phone number deleted])

(U) Functions — Provide a safe, secure and humane environment that supports the expeditious collection of intelligence.

(S/NF) Summary—The importance of the rapid collection and dissemination of intelligence is vital for success and must be emphasized in the conduct of detention operations. It is essential that the guard force be actively engaged in setting the conditions for successful exploitation of the internees. Joint strategic interrogation operations are hampered by lack of active control of the internees within the detention environment. The pending establishment of the theater joint interrogation detention center at Abu Gharib will consolidate both detention and strategic interrogation operations and result in synergy between MP and MI resources and an integrated, synchronized and focused strategic interrogation effort.

(S/NF) Observation — Minimal operational procedures and guidance were available for internee in-processing, collection and integration of intelligence, security procedures, internee discipline standards and procedures for reacting to emergencies situations in the detention facilities.

(S/NF) Recommendation — Develop a comprehensive set of detention physical security SOPs. Conduct training for detention center leadership and staff on the implementation of these procedures. JTF-GTMO SOPs for physical security and detention operations were provided to CJTF-7 staff.

(S/NF) Observation — Some of the detention facility guard force interviewed were unable to apply their standing orders and Rules of Engagement procedures to hypothetical Situations — e.g. escaping internees.

(S/NF) Recommendation — Scenario-based training for the current operational and future theater operational environment is recommended to ensure standing procedures (e.g. Rules of Engagement) are known and their application thoroughly understood by the detention leadership and staff.

(S/NF) Observation — Detention operations must be structured to ensure detention environment focuses the internee's confidence and attention on their interrogators. The MP detention staff should be an integrated element supporting the interrogation functions and received orientation training to support interrogation operations.

(S/NF) Recommendation—Assign, train, and sustain interrogator and detention staff team building focused on improving the collection of intelligence. MP detention staff training programs utilized by JTF-GTMO were provided to CJTF-7 for consideration and baseline implementation.

Observation — Disciplinary procedures for internees are arbitrary or not clearly defined.

(S/NF) Recommendation /Action In-progress — The unit is updating its operating procedures for implementing disciplinary measures related to detainee operations.

(S/NF) Observation—Males, females and juveniles are detained in the same camp in close proximity to each other. Full utilization of a classification system that is sensitive to group dynamics is not currently in place.

(S/NF) Recommendation / Action In-progress — Procedures to segregate males, females, and juvenile internees in the detention facility to prevent unauthorized contact are being refined.

(S/NF) Observation—Some detainees who had infectious medical conditions were detained in the general internee population. This mingling of internees could result in possible contamination of other detainees and soldier detention staff. Detainees suffering from apparent mental illness were segregated in a holding pen that was normally used for disciplinary purposes.

(S/NF) Recommendation—Special needs sections of the detention facility should be developed for internees with contagious medical conditions and internees who exhibit mental illness.

6. (U) Information Technology (IT) (POC is CPT Alberto Hernandez [phone number deleted].)

(U) Functions — IT focus is streamlined information gathering resulting in rapid intelligence analysis and exploitation.

(S/NF) Observation—Current information management systems do not support rapid, integrated exploitation of intelligence community databases.

(S/NF) Recommendation—Create a robust automated knowledge center, incorporating information and documents currently located in diverse data stores to allow for sharing of all information on internees. (See Annex B for specific IT comments.)

7. (U) Conclusion—Actions to improve the Task Force's ability to conduct counterterrorist strategic interrogations were being developed at the time of this report's drafting. Provision of resources is crucial to success. Expeditious fill of two leadership billets—one as Chief of the HUMINT Operations Center (HOC) and the other as Chief, HUMINT Analysis Center (HAC), CJTF-7, is essential to enable successful joint, integrated interrogation operations. Concurrently, assignment of expert analysts is required to form Tiger Teams and populate the HAC.

GEOFFREY D. MILLER
Major General, U.S. Army

Annex A: *Assessment Team Members*

Team Leader

| MG Geoffrey Miller, USA | JTF-GTMO) | Commander |

Synchronization Team

MR John Antonitis	DIA	Former JTF-GTMO Joint Interrogation Group Dir.
MR David Becker	DIA/DHS	Former JTF-GTMO Interrogation Control Ele.Chief
MR Dennis Jamison	CIA	Former JTF-GTMO CTC Chief
CDR Jorge Gracia, USNR	JITF-CT	Former JTF-GTMO Analysis Chief
LTC Diane Beaver, USA	JATF SOUTH	Former JTF-GTMO Staff Judge Advocate
CPT Alberto Hernandez, USA	JTF-GTMO	Information Technology Chief
MR Blame Thomas	CITF	Former JTP-GTMO Crim. Invest. Task Force Chief

Interrogation Operation Team

LtCol Ted Moss, USAF	DIA/DHS	Former JTF-GTMO Interrogation Control Ele Chief
CW3 Edward Traywick, USA	470th MI BDE	Former GTMO Saudi Team Chief
CW3 Waldo Sotolongo, USA	JTF-GTMO	Central Asia Team Chief
SSGT David Smith, USA	JTF-GTMO	Central Asia Team Analyst
MSG Andrew Carter, USA	JTF-GTMO	Saudi Team Noncommissioned Officer-in-Charge
SSG Hugh Shisler, USA	JTF-GTMO	Saudi Team Analyst
SSG Lara Scarpazo, USA	JTF-GTMO	Special Projects Interrogator
SSG Greg Wyse, USA	JTF-GTMO	Special Projects Analyst

Detention Operations Team

| CSM John Vannatta, USA | JTF-GTMO | Camp Delta Superintendent |
| CPT Brian Pitts, USA | JTF-GTMO | Camp Delta Company Commander |

Annex B: Information Technology Solutions

The goal of a theater-wide intelligence information technology initiative is *fused intelligence* which will allow for a faster interrogation cycle, faster exchange of information, minimize manual processes, eliminate redundancy, manpower savings, rapid data mining, focused interrogation plan, and an automated collection plan.

ISSUES

— There isn't sufficient bandwidth or connectivity available to support current interrogation operations and consolidated internee database for near-real time information sharing

  • Some locations have SIPR connectivity but it is slow and unreliable. Some locations do not have enough SIPR drops to support the mission and personnel.

— There are diverse data stores to include MS Excel spreadsheets, MS Access databases, MS Word documents that are not shared by the various internee camps

  • There isn't a theater level network that reaches out to all the units for the purpose of sharing folder, files, and documents, with the exception of email. Email is not an effective way of sharing information for the purpose of conducting data mining and intelligence exploitation.

— There are no standardized information gathering and reporting methods that will allow for tracking of information collected from internees from the time of capture and through the intelligence requirements management and interrogation process.

  • There isn't a comprehensive collection management and dissemination system in place.

— There isn't an effective method to link internees to other internees or associates, organizations, locations, and facilities or to associate documents to internees to allow analysts to quickly search all information pertaining to an internee.

OPTIONS

— Implement a theater level network that supports folder, file, and document sharing.

  • Ensure bandwidth is adequate to support the network traffic and all the users.

- Ensure that all units have access to the network with adequate number of workstations to support the mission, especially for those units that capture and/or initially process internees and those units that conduct analysis and interrogations.

— Develop a database that incorporates the various data stores, from the time of capture and through the intelligence analysis and interrogation process.

- The web-based Joint Detainee Information Management System (JDIMS) developed for and currently utilized by JTF Guantanamo, with some tailoring and modifications, will be adequate to meet this need of a consolidated internee database. The database also contains a collection management and dissemination module that manages all requirements and reporting on internees. It also contains an online reports writing feature, which allows the analysts and interrogators to create reports and immediately share information.

- The Detention Information Management System (DIMS) also developed for and utilized by JTF Guantanamo to capture initial detainee information as well as operational data gathered by the military police, will allow for input of internee information from the time of capture and throughout their stay at the detention facilities when not being interrogated

- A Joint Detainee Information Management System-Iraq will share data with JTF Guantanamo detainee database and make it available to the intelligence community. By sharing detainee information, the intelligence community will benefit from a web-based single source of detainee information readily available to them via the SIPR network.

- A similar system should be implemented in Afghanistan for the detainee operations conducted there.

The goal of a worldwide-integrated detainee database is to address the needs of detainee interrogation operations and to share information regardless of location. It is the tool to bridge intelligence and technology in order to achieve information dominance and efficient operational control over the detainee/internee population and allow for near-real time data mining, information visualization, and intelligence exploitation to combat the Global War on Terrorism.

APPENDIX II

Revelation

THE STORY BREAKS

SOMETIME IN NOVEMBER 2003, Specialist Joseph M. Darby returned to his posting at Abu Ghraib prison in Iraq and heard about a shooting incident that had occurred while he was away on leave. Darby asked the military policeman in charge of the night shift, Specialist Charles A. Graner Jr., if he had any pictures of the incident; Graner handed Darby two CDs. As Darby discovered, the CDs contained hundreds of photographs showing US military policemen and intelligence soldiers abusing prisoners, many of them naked. When Darby confronted Graner, who had been a prison guard in civilian life, Graner replied, according to an account published in *The Washington Post*, "The Christian in me says it's wrong, but the corrections officer in me says, 'I love to make a grown man piss himself.'"

In Darby, apparently, the Christian was stronger, for on January 13, 2004, he turned over the CDs to the Army's Criminal Investigation Command (CID), which led CID officers to launch an investigation, and to interview a number of Iraqis who claimed to have been abused at Abu Ghraib. The statements of thirteen of those Iraqis, which describe in detail what happened to them in the prison, were leaked to *The Washington Post* and appear in the following pages, after the reproductions of the photographs themselves. The photographs were leaked, reportedly by a relative of one of the accused military policemen, to the CBS news program *Sixty Minutes II* in mid-April 2003—though CBS delayed broadcasting them for two weeks, until April 28, at the personal request of General Richard B. Myers, the Chairman of the Joint Chiefs of Staff.

According to a reconstruction by the *Post*, the photographs released in

April, and another set released some weeks later, were taken across seven days in October, November, and December 2003. (They are arranged here, insofar as possible, in the order in which they were taken.) During October officials of the International Committee of the Red Cross visited Abu Ghraib—they visited the prison a total of twenty-nine times during the spring and fall of 2003—and offered, in their report, the only contemporaneous eyewitness account by outside observers of what was happening there. The Red Cross report, dated February 2004, was never intended to be made public. Red Cross officials submitted an earlier version of the report to United States Army officers in Iraq as early as November 2003, but, several senior generals testified to the Senate Armed Services Committee, the reports "became lost in the Army's bureaucracy and weren't adequately addressed." As an unnamed senior officer told *The New York Times*, the Army was sufficiently aware of the report's contents to respond to it "by trying to curtail the international organization's spot inspections of the prison," and by contending, in a letter sent on December 24 over the signature of Brigadier General Janis Karpinski, that the isolation of some prisoners from the representatives of the Red Cross was a "military necessity." The text of the Red Cross report was leaked to *The Wall Street Journal* in early May 2004.

—MD

Appendix II: Revelation—The Story Breaks

THE PHOTOGRAPHS

[date unknown]

SPC Charles A. Graner Jr., leaning against the wall and labeled as No. 1, identified four other soldiers in this photograph (Nos. 4, 5, 6, and 8) as military intelligence officers. No. 2 is a civilian translator. [October 25, 2003]

[October 17, 2003]

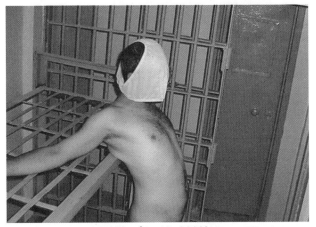

[October 18, 2003]

[October 24, 2003]

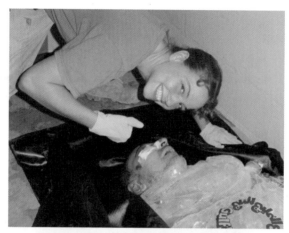

[November 5, 2003]

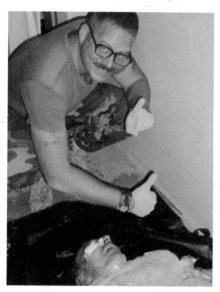

[November 4, 2003 (?)]

[November 5, 2003]

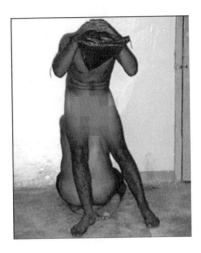

[November 8, 2003]

[November 8, 2003]

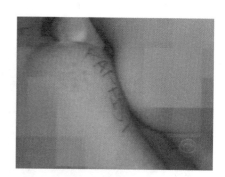

[November 8, 2003]

[November 18, 2003]

[November 29, 2003]

[December 12, 2003]

[circa December 18, 2003]

THE DEPOSITIONS:
THE PRISONERS SPEAK

SWORN STATEMENTS BY
ABU GHRAIB DETAINEES

These documents, obtained by The Washington Post, *are the official English translations of previously secret sworn statements by detainees at the Abu Ghraib prison in Iraq. Some of the names have been withheld from these statements by washingtonpost.com because they are alleged victims of sexual assault.*

SWORN STATEMENT

LOCATION: TIRE 1A, Baghdad Correctional Facility

DATE: 16 Jan 04
TIME: 1722

FILE NUMBER: 0003-04-CID149-83130

LAST NAME, FIRST NAME, MIDDLE NAME:
AL-SHEIKH, Ameen Sa'eed

SOCIAL SECURITY NUMBER: NDRS #151362

GRADE/STATUS: CIV/DETAINEE

ORGANIZATION OR ADDRESS: Baghdad Correctional Facility, Abu Ghraib, Iraq
APO AE 09335

I, Ameen Sa'eed AL-SHEIKH, want to make the following Statement under oath:
I am Ameen Sa'eed AL-SHEIKH. I was arrested on the 7 Oct 2003. They brought
me over to Abu Ghraib Prison they put me in a tent for one night. During this night
the guards every one or two hours and threaten me with torture and punishment.
The second day they transferred me to the hard site. Before I got in, a soldier put a
sand bag over my head. I didn't see anything after that. They took me inside the
building and started to scream at me. The stripped me naked, they asked me, "Do
you pray to Allah?" I said, "Yes." They said, "Fuck you" and "Fuck him." One of
them said, "You are not getting out of here health, you are getting out of here
handicap." And he said to me, "Are you married?" I said, "Yes." They said, "If
your wife saw you like this, she will be disappointed." One of them said, "But if I
saw her now, she would not be disappointed now because I would rape her." Then
one of them took me to the shower, removed the sand bag, and I saw him; a black
man, he told me to take a shower and he said he would come inside and rape me
and I was very scared. Then they put the sand bag over my head and took me to
cell #5. And for the next five days I didn't sleep because they use to come to my
cell, asking me to stand up for hours and hours. And they slammed the outer door,
which made a loud scary noise inside the cell. And this black soldier took me once
more to the showers, stood there staring at my body. And he threaten he was going
to rape me again. After that, they started to interrogate me. I lied to them so they
threaten me with hard punishment. Then other interrogators came over and told
me, "If you tell the truth, we will let you go as soon as possible before Ramadan,"
so I confessed and said the truth. Four days after that, they took me to the camp and
I didn't see those interrogators anymore. New interrogators came and reinterrogated

me. After I told them the truth they accused me of being lying to them. After 18 days in the camp, they sent me to the hard site. I asked the interrogators why? They said they did not know. Two days before Ied (End of Ramadan), an interrogator came to me with a women and an interpreter. He said I'm one step away from being in prison forever. He started the interrogation with this statement and end it with this statement. The first day of Ied, the incident of "Firing" happened, I got shot with several bullets in my body and got transferred to the hospital. And there, the interrogator "Steve" came to me and threaten me with the hardest torture when I go back to the prison. I said to him, "I'm sorry about what happened." He said to me, "Don't be sorry now, because you will be sorry later." After several days he came back and said to me, "If I put you under torture, do you think this would be fair?" I said to him, "Why?" He said he needed more information from me. I told him, "I already told you everything I know." He said, "We'll see when you come back to the prison." After 17 or 18 days, I was released from the hospital, went back to Abu Ghraib, he took me somewhere and the guard put a pistol to my head. He said, "I wish I can kill you right now." I spend the night at this place and next morning they took me to the hard site. They received me there with screaming, shoving, pushing and pulling. They forced me to walk from the main gate to my cell. Otherwise they would beat my broken leg. I was in a very bad shape. When I went to the cell, they took my crutches and I didn't see it since. Inside the cell, they asked me to strip naked; they didn't give me blanket or clothes or anything. Every hour or two, soldiers came, threatening me they were going to kill me and torture me and I'm going to be in prison forever and they might transfer me to Guantanamo Bay. One of them came and told me that he failed to shoot me the first time, but he will make sure he will succeed next time. And he said to me they were going to throw a pistol or a knife in my cell, then shoot me. Sometime they said, "We will make you wish to die and it will not happen." The night guard came over, his name is GRANER, open the cell door, came in with a number of soldiers. They forced me to eat pork and they put liquor in my mouth. They put this substance on my nose and forehead and it was very hot. The guards started to hit me on my broken leg several times with a solid plastic stick. He told me he got shot in his leg and he showed me the scare and he would retaliate from me for this. They stripped me naked. One of them told me he would rape me. He drew a picture of a woman to my back and makes me stand in shameful position holding my buttocks. Someone else asked me, "Do you believe in anything?" I said to him, "I believe in Allah." So he said, "But I believe in torture and I will torture you. When I go home to my country, I will ask whoever comes after me to torture you." Then they handcuffed me and hung me to the bed. They ordered me to curse Islam and because they started to hit my broken leg, I cursed my religion. They ordered me to thank Jesus that I'm alive. And I did what they ordered me. This is against my belief. They left me hang from the bed and after a little while I lost consciousness. When I woke up, I found myself still hang between the bed and the floor. Until now, I lost feeling in three fingers in my right hand. I sat on the bed, one of them stood by the door and pee'd on me. And he said, "GRANER, your prisoner pee'd on himself." And then GRANER came and laughed. After several hours GRANER came and uncuffed me, then I slept. In the morning until now, people I don't know come over and humiliate me and threaten that they will torture me. The second night, GRANER came hand hung me to the cell door. I told him, "I have a broken shoulder, I'm afraid it will break again, cause the doctor told me 'don't put your arms behind your back.'" He said, "I don't care." Then he hung me to the door for more than eight hours. I was screaming from pain the whole night. GRANER and others use to come and ask me, "does it hurt." I said, "Yes." They said, "Good." And they smack me on the back of the head. After that, a soldier came and uncuffed me. My right shoulder and my wrist was in bad shape and great pain. (When I was hung to the door, I lost consciousness several times) Then I slept. In the morning I told the doctor that I think my shoulder is broken because I can't my hand. I feel sever pain. He checked my shoulder and told me, "I will bring another doctor to see you tomorrow." The next day, the other doctor checked my shoulder and said to me, he's taking me to the hospital the next day for X-rays. And the next day he took me to the hospital and X-rayed my shoulder and the doctor told me, "Your shoulder is not broke, but your shoulder is badly hurt." Then they took me back to the hard site. Every time I leave and come back. I have to crawl back to my cell because I can't walk. The next day, other soldiers came at night and took photos of me while I'm naked. They humiliated me and made of me and threaten me. After that, the interrogators came over and identify the person who gave me the pistols between some pictures. And this guy wasn't in the pictures. When I told them that, they said they will torture me and they will come every single night to ask me the same question accompanied with soldiers having weapons and they point a weapon to my head and threaten that they will kill me, sometime with dogs and they hang me to the door allowing the dogs to try to bite me. This happened for a full week or more.

Q: IEM
A: Ameen Sa'eed AL-SHEIKH
Q: Have you ever seen GRANER beating a prisoner?
A: No.
Q: Have you ever seen GRANER/any guards pile naked prisoners over each other?
A: No.
Q: Have you ever seen GRANER/any guards taking photographs of prisoners?
A: No.
Q: Have you ever seen GRANER/any guards taking photographs during punishment time?
A: No.
Q: Have you ever seen GRANER/any soldiers taking photographs while beating prisoners?
A: No.
Q: Have you ever seen any soldier positioning naked prisoners on top of each other?

A: No.
Q: Have you ever seen any guard/American soldier position naked prisoners in sexual positions?
A: No. ////End of Statement///

Translated By:
[signed]
Gawdat HUSSEIN
Interpreter, Category II
Titan Corporation Inc
Camp Doha, Kuwait

Prisoner Interview/Interrogation Team (PIT)(CID)(FWD)
Baghdad Correctional Facility
Abu Ghraib, IZ APO AE 09335

AFFIDAVIT
I, Hiadar Saber Abed Miktub AL-ABOODI, HAVE READ OR HAD READ TO ME THIS STATEMENT, WHICH BEGINS ON PAGE 1, AND ENDS ON PAGE 3. I FULLY UNDERSTAND THE CONTENTS OF THE ENTIRE STATEMENT MADE BY ME. THE STATEMENT IS TRUE. I HAVE INITIALED THE BOTTOM OF EACH PAGE CONTAINING THE STATEMENT. I HAVE MADE THIS STATEMENT FREELY WITHOUT HOPE OR BENEFIT OR REGARD, WITHOUT THREAT OF PUNISHMENT, AND WITHOUT COERCION, UNLAWFUL INFLUENCE, OR UNLAWFUL INDUCEMENT.

WITNESSES:
Gawdat Hussein

TRANSLATION OF STATEMENT PROVIDED BY
Abdou Hussain Saad FALEH, Detainee #18470, 1610/16 JAN 04:

"On the third day, after five o'clock, Mr. Grainer came and took me to Room #37, which is the shower room, and he started punishing me. Then he brought a box of food and he made me stand on it with no clothing, except a blanket. Then a tall black soldier came and put electrical wires on my fingers and toes and on my penis, and I had a bag over my head. Then he was saying "which switch is on for electricity." And he came with a loudspeaker and he was shouting near my ear and then he brought the camera and he took some pictures of me, which I knew because of the flash of the camera. And he took the hood off and he was describing some poses he wanted me to do, and the I was tired and I fell down. And then Mr. Grainer came and made me stand up on the stairs and made me carry a box of food. I was so tired and I dropped it. He started screaming at me in English. He made me lift a white chair high in the air. Then the chair came down and then Mr. Joyner took the hood off my head and took me to my room. And I slept after that for about an hour and then I woke up at the headcount time. I couldn't go to sleep after that because I was very scared."

TRANSLATED BY: VERIFIED BY:

[signed]   [signed]

Mr. Abdelilah ALAZADI   Mr. Johnson ISHO
Translator, Category II   Translator, Category II
Titan Corporation   Titan Corporation

Assigned to:
    Prisoner Interview/Interrogation Team (PIT)(CID)(FWD)
    10th Military Police Battalion (CID)(ABN)(FWD)
    3rd Military Police Group (CID), USACIDC
    Abu Ghraib Prison Complex (ABPC)
    Abu Ghraib, Iraq APO AE 09335

TRANSLATION OF STATEMENT PROVIDED BY
Thaar Salman DAWOD, Detainee #150427, 1440/17 JAN 04:

"I went to the Solitary Confinement on the Sep/10/2003. I was there for 67 days of suffering and little to eat and the torture I saw myself. When I asked the guard Joyner about the time and he cuffed my hand to the door then when his duty ended the second guard came, his name is Grainer, he released my hand from the door and he cuffed my hand in the back. Then I told him I did not do anything to get punished this way so when I said that he hit me hard on my chest and he cuffed me to the window of the room about 5 hours and did not give me any food that day and I stayed without food for 24 hours. I saw lots of people getting naked for a few days getting punished in the first days of Ramadan. They came with two boys naked and they were cuffed together face to face and Grainer was beating them and a group of guards were watching and taking pictures from top and bottom and there was three female soldiers laughing at the prisoners. The prisoners, two of them, were young. I don't know their names."

TRANSLATED BY: VERIFIED BY:

[signed]   [signed]

Mr. Johnson ISHO   Mr. Abdelilah ALAZADI
Translator, Category II   Translator, Category II
Titan Corporation   Titan Corporation

Assigned to:
    Prisoner Interview/Interrogation Team (PIT)(CID)(FWD)
    10th Military Police Battalion (CID)(ABN)(FWD)
    3rd Military Police Group (CID), USACIDC
    Abu Ghraib Prison Complex (ABPC)
    Abu Ghraib, Iraq APO AE 09335

TRANSLATION OF STATEMENT PROVIDED BY
Abd Alwhab YOUSS, Detainee # 150425, 1445/17 JAN 04:

"One day while in the prison the guard came and found a broken toothbrush, and they said that I was going to attack the American Police; I said that the toothbrush wasn't mine. They said we are taking away your clothes and mattress for 6 days and we are not going to beat you. But the next day the guard came and cuffed me to the cell door for 2 hours, after that they took me to a closed room and more than five guards poured cold water on me, and forced me to put my head in someone's urine that was already in that room. After that they beat me with a broom and stepped on my head with their feet while it was still in the urine. They pressed my ass with a broom and spit on it. Also a female soldier, whom I don't know the name was standing on my legs. They used a loudspeaker to shout at me for 3 hours, it was cold. But to tell the truth in daytime Joiner gave me my clothes and at night Grainer took them away. The truth is they gave me my clothes after 3 days, they didn't finish the 6 days and thank you."

TRANSLATED BY: VERIFIED BY:

[signed]   [signed]

Mr. Abdelilah ALAZADI   Mr. Johnson ISHO
Translator, Category II   Translator, Category II
Titan Corporation   Titan Corporation

Assigned to:
    Prisoner Interview/Interrogation Team (PIT)(CID)(FWD)
    10th Military Police Battalion (CID)(ABN)(FWD)
    3rd Military Police Group (CID), USACIDC
    Abu Ghraib Prison Complex (ABPC)
    Abu Ghraib, Iraq APO AE 09335

TRANSLATION OF VERBAL STATEMENT PROVIDED BY
Asad Hamza HANFOSH, Detainee # 152529, 1605/17 JAN 04:

"One the date of November 5, 2003, when the US forces transferred to Isolation, when they took me out of the car, an American soldier hit me with his hand on my face. And then they stripped me naked and they took me under the water and then he made me crawl the hallway until I was bleeding from my chest to my knees and my hands. And after that he put me back into the cell and an hour later he took me out from the cell the second time to the shower room under cold water and them he made me get up on a box, naked, and he hit me on my manhood. I don't know with what, then I fell down on the ground. He made me crawl on the ground. And then he tied my hands in my cell naked until morning time until Joyner showed up and released my hands and took me back to my room and gave me my clothes back. About two days later my interrogation came up, when it was done a white soldier wearing glasses picked me from the room I was in. He grabbed my head and hit it against the wall and then tied my hand to the bed until noon the next day and then two days later the same soldier and he took all my clothes and my mattress and he didn't give me anything so I can sleep on except my jump suit for 3 days. Then Joyner came and gave me a blanket and my clothes a second time."

TRANSLATED BY: VERIFIED BY:

[signed]   [signed]

Mr. Johnson ISHO   Mr. Abdelilah ALAZADI
Translator, Category II   Translator, Category II
Titan Corporation   Titan Corporation

Assigned to:
    Prisoner Interview/Interrogation Team (PIT)(CID)(FWD)
    10th Military Police Battalion (CID)(ABN)(FWD)
    3rd Military Police Group (CID), USACIDC
    Abu Ghraib Prison Complex (ABPC)
    Abu Ghraib, Iraq APO AE 09335

TRANSLATION OF STATEMENT PROVIDED BY
Shalan Said ALSHARONI, Detainee # 150422, 1630/17 JAN 04:

"One of those days the guards tortured the prisoners. Those guards are Grainer, Davis and another man. First they tortured the man whose name is Amjid Iraqi. They stripped him of his clothes and beat him until he passed out and they cursed him and when they took off of his head I saw blood running from his head. They took him to solitary confinement and they were beating him every night.

The evening shift was sad for the prisoners. They brought three prisoners handcuffed to each other and they pushed the first one on top of the others to look like they are gay and when they refused, Grainer beat them up until they put them on top of each other and they took pictures of them. And after that they beat up an Iraqi whose name is Asaad whom they ordered to stand on a food carton and they were pouring water on him and it was the coldest of times. When they torture him they took gloves and they beat his dick and testicles with the gloves and they handcuffed him to the cell door for half a day without food or water. After that they brought young Iraqi prisoners and Grainer tortured them by pouring water on them from the second floor until one of them started crying and screaming and started saying "my heart." They brought the doctors to treat him and they thought he was going to die. After they brought six people and they beat them up until they dropped on the floor and one of them his nose was cut and the blood was running from his nose and he was screaming but no one was responding and all this beating from Grainer and Davis and another man, whom I don't know the name. The Doctor came to stitch the nose and the Grainer asked the doctor to learn how to stitch and it's true, the guard learned how to stitch. He took the string and the needle and he sat down to finish the stitching until the operation succeeded. And then the other man came to take pictures of the injured person who was laying on the ground. And after that they beat up the rest of the group until they fall to the ground. Every time one of them fell on the ground they drag them up to stand on his feet. Grainer beat up a man whose name is Ali the Syrian and he was beating him until he gotten almost crazy. And he was telling him go up to the second floor as he was naked. And they opened the prisoners cells to see him running naked. And after they put him in his cell for four days they were pouring water on him and he couldn't sleep. Before that he was in cell number 4. They hanged him and he was screaming but no one helped him.

There was a translator named Abu Adell the Egyptian. He was helping Grainer and Davis and others whom I don't know, like they were watching a live movie of three young guys being put up by Abu Adell on top of each other. And everyone was taking pictures of this whole thing with cameras. This is what I saw and what I remember to be true."

TRANSLATED BY: VERIFIED BY:

[signed]   [signed]

Mr. Abdelilah ALAZADI   Mr. Johnson ISHO
Translator, Category II   Translator, Category II
Titan Corporation   Titan Corporation

Assigned to:
    Prisoner Interview/Interrogation Team (PIT)(CID)(FWD)
    10th Military Police Battalion (CID)(ABN)(FWD)
    3rd Military Police Group (CID), USACIDC
    Abu Ghraib Prison Complex (ABPC)
    Abu Ghraib, Iraq APO AE 09335

SWORN STATEMENT

LOCATION: Baghdad Correctional Facility

DATE: 17 JAN 04
TIME: 1731

FILE NUMBER: 0003-04-CID 149-83130

LAST NAME, FIRST NAME, MIDDLE NAME:
AL-YASSERI, Nori Samir Gunbar

SOCIAL SECURITY NUMBER: ISN #7787

GRADE/STATUS: CIV/INTERNEE

ORGANIZATION OR ADDRESS: Prison 2A, Baghdad Correction Facility, Abu Ghraib, APO AE 09335

I, Nori Samir Gunbar AL-YASSERI, want to make the following Statement under oath: One day in Ramadan, I don't know the exact date; we were involved in a fight in Compound 2, so they transferred us to the hardsite. As soon as we arrived, they put sandbags over our heads and they kept beating us and called us bad names. After they removed the sandbags they stripped us naked as a newborn baby. Then they ordered us to hold our penises and stroke it and this was only during the night. They started to take photographs as if it was a porn movie. And they treated us like animals not humans. They kept doing this for a long time. No one showed us mercy. Nothing but cursing and beating. Then they started to write words on our buttocks, which we didn't know what it means. After that they left us for the next two days naked with no clothes, with no mattresses, as if we were dogs. And every single night this military guy comes over and beat us and handcuffed us until the end of his shift at 0400. This was for three days and he didn't serve us dinner except for bread and tea. If we had chicken, he would throw it away. The first night when they stripped us naked they made us get on our hands and knees and they started to pile us one on top of the other. They started to take pictures from the front and from the back. And if anyone want to know the details of this, take the negative from the night guard and you will find everything I said was true. The next day the day shift gave us clothes and when the night shift started, the same guard who tortured us the night before came and took the clothes and left us naked and handcuffed to the bed. At the end of his shift he uncuffed us and then he punch us in the stomach and hit us on the head and face. Then he goes home. I kept thinking what is he going to do to us the next night, this white man with the white glasses. When I see him I'm scared to death. Again, watch the pictures in his belongings. He and the two short female soldiers and the black soldier during this dark night. When we were naked he ordered us to stroke, acting like we're masturbating and when we start to do that he would bring another inmate and sit him down on his knees in front of the penis and take photos which looked like this inmate was putting the penis in his mouth.

Before that, I felt that someone was playing with my penis with a pen. After this they make Hashim (NFI) stand in front of me and they forced me to slap him on the face, but I refused cause he is my friend. After this they asked Hashim to hit me, so he punched my stomach. I asked him to do that, so they don't beat him like they had beaten me when I refused to hit Hashim. Nori Samir, Hussein, Mustafa Mahadi Saleh, Hashim, Hiadar, Hathem, Ahmed Sabri; those are the names of the people who were there at this night which we felt like 1000 nights.

Q: IEM
A: Nori Samir Gunbar AL-YASSERI
Q: How many soldiers were there that night?
A: 3 men and 2 women.
Q: Do you know the names of the soldiers?
A: I don't know the soldiers names, but I know what one of them looks like and this was their supervisor. The reason why I know him because I saw him every single night I spent there.
Q: What did the supervisor look like?
A: He's white, muscular, wearing clear medical glasses. He had a blu tattoo on one of his shoulders. I don't know which shoulder and I don't know what tattoo it resembled. And he works every night from 4 pm to 4 am. ///End of Statement///

Translated By:
[signed] Gawdat HUSSEIN
Interpreter, Category II
Titan Corporation Inc.
Camp Doha, Kuwait
Date: 17 Jan 04

AFFIDAVIT
I, Nori Samir Gunbar AL-YASSERI, HAVE READ OR HAD READ TO ME THIS STATE-MENT, WHICH BEGINS ON PAGE 1, AND ENDS ON PAGE 2. I FULLY UNDERSTAND THE CONTENTS OF THE ENTIRE STATEMENT MADE BY ME. THE STATEMENT IS TRUE. I HAVE INITIALED THE BOTTOM OF EACH PAGE CONTAINING THE STATE-MENT. I HAVE MADE THIS STATEMENT FREELY WITHOUT HOPE OF BENEFIT OR REWARD, WITHOUT THREAT OF PUNISHMENT, AND WITHOUT COERCION, UNLAW-FUL INFLUENCE, OR UNLAWFUL INDUCEMENT.

WITNESSES:
Gawdat Hussein

TRANSLATION OF STATEMENT PROVIDED BY
Mustafa Jassim MUSTAFA, Detainee #150542, 1610/17 JAN 04:

"Two days before Ramadan Grainer the guard came with the other guards, they brought two prisoners and they made them take off all their clothes down to naked by the two guards Grainer and Davis and then they were beating them a lot. One of the prisoners was bleeding from a cut he got over his eye. Then they called the doctor who came and fixed him. After that they stated beating him again.

They removed all my clothes down to naked for seven days and they were bringing a group of people to watch me naked.

They brought a prisoner with a civil case, his name is [name blacked out]. He was brought by Grainer the guard and Davis and there was a third guard, I don't know his name. They beat him a lot then they removed all his clothing then they put wire up his ass and they started taking pictures of him.

Grainer used to hang the prisoners by hand to the doors and windows in a way that was very painful for several hours and we heard them screaming.

One day Grainer and Davis brought 6 generals and they stripped them down to naked. They started torturing them and taking pictures and they were enjoying that. When the doctor came to fix the injured person, Grainer took the needle from the doctor and started stitching the cut on the injured person.

A few days before Ramadan, Grainer and Davis, and another person that came with them used beat up a man named "Amjed" who was in room number one. They were beating his very hard with a stick and Grainer was pissing on him and beating him for about a week until they injured his eye and the doctor came.

Grainer and Davis, and a third man, used to beat up a prisoner who was from Syria and strip him all night. We heard him screaming all night.

Every time a new prisoner came Grainer and Davis stripped them, beat them and took pictures. I remember one prisoner named "Wessam."

Important Point:

All the guards excluding Grainer and Davis are very good with the prisoners and the prisoners like them and respect them and are very happy with them. They give a good image of the United States and they prove by their good treatment the big difference between the Baath Party and the United States."

TRANSLATION OF STATEMENT PROVIDED BY
Mustafa Jassim MUSTAFA, Detainee #150542, 1140/18 JAN 04:

"Before Ramadan, Grainer started covering all the rooms with bed sheets. Then I heard screams coming from Room #1, at that time I was in Room #50 and it's right below me so I looked into the room. I saw [name blacked out] in Room #1, who was naked and Grainer was putting the phosphoric light up his ass. [Name blacked out] was screaming for help. There was another tall white man who was with

Grainer, he was helping him. There was also a white female soldier, short, she was taking pictures of [name blacked out]. [Name blacked out] is now in cell #50."

TRANSLATED BY: VERIFIED BY:

[signed]   [signed]

Mr. Johnson ISHO   Mr. Abdelilah ALAZADI
Translator, Category II   Translator, Category II
Titan Corporation   Titan Corporation

Assigned to:
    Prisoner Interview/Interrogation Team (PIT)(CID)(FWD)
    10th Military Police Battalion (CID)(ABN)(FWD)
    3rd Military Police Group (CID), USACIDC
    Abu Ghraib Prison Complex (ABPC)
    Abu Ghraib, Iraq APO AE 09335

TRANSLATION OF STATEMENT PROVIDED BY
Hussein Mohssein Mata AL-ZAYIADI, Detainee #19446, 1242/18 JAN 04:

"I was in the solitary confinement, me and my friends. We were treated badly. They took our clothes off, even the underwear and they beat us very hard, and they put a hood over my head. And when I told them I am sick they laughed at me and beat me. And one of them brought my friend and told him "stand here" and they brought me and had me kneel in front of my friend. They told my friend to masturbate and told me to masturbate also, while they were taking pictures. After that they brought my friends, Haidar, Ahmed, Nouri, Ahzem, Hashiem, Mustafa, and I, and they put us 2 on the bottom, 2 on top of them, and 2 on top of those and one on top. They took pictures of us and we were naked. After the end of the beating, they took us to our separate cells and they opened the water in the cell and told us to lay face down in the water and we stayed like that until the morning, in the water, naked, without clothes. Then one of the other shift gave us clothes, but the second shift took the clothes away at night and handcuffed us to the beds.

The number of the guards was 4. Two of them male, and one of them had a chain tattoo on his arm and wearing eyeglasses. The other one had a tattoo on his back like a dragon. The female wearing eyeglasses was short and had short hair. The second female hair was yellow and she was medium height.

Q: IEM
A: Hussein Mohssein Mata AL-ZAYIADI
Q: How did you feel when the guards were treating you this way?
A: I was trying to kill myself but I didn't have any way of doing it.
Q: Did the guards force you to crawl on your hands and knees on the ground?
A: Yes. They forced us to do this thing.
Q: What were the guards doing while you were crawling on your hands and knees?
A: They were sitting on our backs like riding animals.
Q: When you were on each other, what were the guards doing?
A: They were taking pictures and writing on our asses.
Q: How many times did the guards treat you this way?
A: The first time, when I just go in, and the second day they put us in the water and handcuffed us.
Q: Did you see the guards treat the other inmates this way?
A: I didn't see, but I heard screams and shouts in another area."

TRANSLATED BY: VERIFIED BY:

[signed]   [signed]

Mr. Abdelilah ALAZADI   Mr. Johnson ISHO
Translator, Category II   Translator, Category II
Titan Corporation   Titan Corporation

Assigned to:
    Prisoner Interview/Interrogation Team (PIT)(CID)(FWD)
    10th Military Police Battalion (CID)(ABN)(FWD)
    3rd Military Police Group (CID), USACIDC
    Abu Ghraib Prison Complex (ABPC)
    Abu Ghraib, Iraq APO AE 08335

TRANSLATION OF STATEMENT PROVIDED BY
Kasim Mehaddi HILAS, Detainee #151108, 1300/18 JAN 04:

"In the name of God, I swear to God that everything I witnessed everything I am talking about. I am not saying this to gain any material thing, and I was not pressured to do this by any forces. First, I am going to talk only about what happened to me in Abu Ghraib Jail. I will not talk about what happened when I was in jail before, because they did not ask me about that, but it was very bad.

1. They stripped me of all my clothes, even my underwear. They gave me woman's underwear, that was rose color with flowers in it and they put the bag over my face. One of them whispered in my ear, "today I am going to fuck you," and he said this in Arabic. Whoever was with me experienced the same thing. That's what the American soldiers did, and they had a translator with them, named Abu Hamid and a female soldier, who's skin was olive colored and this was on October 3 or 4, 2003 around 3 or 4 in the afternoon. When they took me to the cell, the translator Abu Hamid came with an American soldier and his rank was sergeant (I believe). And he called told me "faggot" because I was wearing the woman's underwear, and my answer was "no." Then he told me "why are you wearing this underwear," then I told them "because you make me wear it." The transfer from Camp B to the Isolation was full of beatings, but the bags were over our heads, so we couldn't see their faces. And they forced me to wear this underwear all the time, for 51 days. And most of the days I was wearing nothing else.

2. I faced more harsh punishment from Grainer. He cuffed my hands with irons behind my back to the metal of the window, to the point my feet were off the ground and I was hanging there, for about 5 hours just because I asked about the time, because I wanted to pray. And then they took all my clothes and he took the female underwear and he put it over my head. After he released me from the window, he tied me to my bed until before dawn. He took me to the shower room. After he took me to the shower room, he brought me to my room again. He prohibited me from eating food that night, even though I was fasting that day. Grainer and the other two soldiers were taking pictures of every thing they did to me. I don't know if they took a picture of me because they beat me so bad I lost consciousness after an hour or so.

3. They didn't give us food for a whole day and a night, while we were fasting for Ramadan. And the food was only one package of emergency food.

Now I am talking about what I saw:

1. They brought three prisoners completely naked and they tied them together with cuffs and they stuck one to another. I saw the American soldiers hitting them with a football and they were taking pictures. I saw Grainer punching one of the prisoners right in his face very hard when he refused to take off his underwear and I heard them begging for help. And also the American soldiers told to do like homosexuals (fucking). And there was one of the American soldiers they called

Sergeant (black skin) there was 7 to 8 soldiers there also. Also female soldiers were taking pictures and that was in the first day of Ramadan. And they repeated the same thing the second day of Ramadan. And they were ordering them to crawl while they were cuffed together naked.

2. I saw [name blacked out] fucking a kid, his age would be about 15–18 years. The kid was hurting very bad and they covered all the doors with sheets. Then when I heard the screaming I climbed the door because on top it wasn't covered and I saw [name blacked out], who was wearing the military uniform putting his dick in the little kid's ass. I couldn't see the face of the kid because his face wasn't in front of the door. And the female soldier was taking pictures. [Name blacked out], I think he is [name blacked out] because of his accent, and he was not skinny or short, and he acted like a homosexual (gay). And that was in cell #23 as best as I remember.

3. In the cell that is almost under it, on the North side, and I was right across from it on the other side. They put the sheets again on the doors. Grainer and his helper they cuffed one prisoner in Room #1, named [name blacked out], he was Iraqi citizen. They tied him to the bed and they were inserted the phosphoric light in his ass and he was yelling for God's help. [Name blacked out] used to get hit and punished a lot because I heard him screaming and they prohibited us from standing near the door when they do that. That was Ramadan, around 12 midnight approximately when I saw them putting the stick in his ass. The female soldier was taking pictures.

4. I saw more than once men standing on a water bucket that was upside down and they were totally naked. And carrying chairs over their heads standing under the fan of the hallway behind the wooden partition and also in the shower.

Not one night for all the time I was there passed without me seeing, hearing or feeling what was happening to me.

And I am repeating the oath / I swear on Allah almighty on the truth of what I said. Allah is my witness."

TRANSLATED BY: VERIFIED BY:

[signed]   [signed]

Mr. Johnson ISHO   Mr. Abdelilah ALAZADI
Translator, Category II   Translator, Category II
Titan Corporation   Titan Corporation

Assigned to:
    Prisoner Interview/Interrogation Team (PIT)(CID)(FWD)
    10th Military Police Battalion (CID)(ABN)(FWD)
    3rd Military Police Group (CID), USACIDC
    Abu Ghraib Prison Complex (ABPC)
    Abu Ghraib, Iraq APO AE 09335

TRANSLATION OF STATEMENT PROVIDED BY
Mohanded Juma JUMA, Detainee #152307, 1200/18 JAN 04:

"I am going to start from the first day I went into A1. They stripped me from my clothes and all the stuff that they gave me and I spent 6 days in that situation. And then they gave me a blanket only 3 days after that, they gave me a mattress, and after a short period of time, approximately at 2 at night, the door opened and Grainer was there. He cuffed my hands behind my back and he cuffed my feet and he took me to the shower room. When they finished interrogating me, the female interrogator left. And then Grainer and another man, who looked like Grainer but doesn't have glasses, and has a thin mustache, and he was young and tall, came into the room. They threw pepper on my face and the beating started. This went on for a half hour. And then he started beating me with the chair until the chair was broken. After that they started choking me. At that time I thought I was going to die, but it's a miracle I lived. And then they started beating me again. They concentrated on beating me in my heart until they got tired from beating me. They took a little break and then they started kicking me very hard with their feet until I passed out.

In the second scene at the night shift, I saw a new guard that wears glasses and has a red face. He charged his pistol and pointed it at a lot of the prisoners to threaten them with it. I saw things no one would see, they are amazing. They come in the morning shift with two prisoners and they were father and son. They were both naked. They put them in front of each other and they counted 1, 2, 3, and then removed the bags from their heads. When the son saw his father naked he was crying. He was crying because of seeing his father. And then at night, Grainer used to throw the food into the toilet and said "go take it and eat it." And I saw also in Room #5 they brought the dogs. Grainer brought the dogs and they bit him in the right and left leg. He was from Iran and they started beating him up in the main hallway of the prison."

TRANSLATED BY: VERIFIED BY:

[signed]   [signed]

Mr. Johnson ISHO   Mr. Abdelilah ALAZADI
Translator, Category II   Translator, Category II
Titan Corporation   Titan Corporation

Assigned to:
    Prisoner Interview/Interrogation Team (PIT)(CID)(FWD)
    10th Military Police Battalion (CID)(ABN)(FWD)
    3rd Military Police Group (CID), USACIDC
    Abu Ghraib Prison Complex (ABPC)
    Abu Ghraib, Iraq APO AE 09335

SWORN STATEMENT

LOCATION: Rusafa II Prison Compound, Baghdad

DATE: 20 Jan 04
TIME: 1520

FILE NUMBER: 0003-04-CID 148-83130

LAST NAME, FIRST NAME, MIDDLE NAME:
AL-ABOODI, Hiadar Sabar Abed Miktub

SOCIAL SECURITY NUMBER: ISN #13077

GRADE/STATUS: CIV/DETAINEE

ORGANIZATION OR ADDRESS:
Rusafa II Prison Compound, Baghdad, Iraq

I, Hiadar Saber Abed Miktub AL-ABOODI, want to make the following Statement under oath: When first I went to the hard site, the Americans soldiers took me, there were two soldiers, a translator named Abu Hamed. We stood in the hallway before the hard site and they started taking off our clothes one after another. After they took off my clothes the American soldier removed who was wearing glasses, night guard, and I saw an American female soldier which they call her Ms. Maya, in front of me they told me to stroke my penis in front of her. And then they covered my head again, and as I was doing whatever they asked me to do, they removed the bag off my head, and I saw my friend, he was the one in front of me on the floor. And then they told me to sit on the floor facing the wall. They brought another prisoner on my back and he was also naked. Then they ordered me to bend onto my knees and hands on the ground. And then they placed three others on our backs, naked. And after that they order me to sleep on my stomach and they ordered the other guy to sleep on top of me in the same position and the same way to all of us. And there were six of us. They were laughing, taking pictures, and they were stepping on our hands with their feet. And they started taking one after another and they wrote on our bodies in English. I don't know what they wrote, but they were taking pictures after that. Then, after that they forced us to walk like dogs on our hands and knees. And we had to bark like a dog and if we didn't do that, they start hitting us hard on our face and chest with no mercy. After that, they took us to our cells, took the mattresses out and dropped water on the floor and they made us sleep on our stomachs on the floor with the bags on our head and they took pictures of everything. Mr. Joyner shows up in the morning and give us our mattresses, blankets and food, but the second guy who wears the glasses was the opposite; he takes the mattresses, tie our hands, hit us and don't give us food. All that lasted for 10 days and the translator Abu Hamed was there. I only saw him when I arrived, but after that I knew he was there because I heard his voice during all of that. ///End of Statement////

Translated by: Verified by:

[signed]   [signed]

Lauriene H. DICE   Johnson ISHO
Interpreter, Category II   Interpreter, Category II
Titan Corporation Inc.   Titan Corporation Inc.
Camp Doha, Kuwait   Camp Doha, Kuwait

Prisoner Interview/Interrogation Team (PIT)(CID)(FWD)
Baghdad Correctional Facility
Abu Ghraib, Iraq APO AE 09335

AFFIDAVIT
I, Hiadar Saber Abed Miktub AL-ABOODI, HAVE READ OR HAD READ TO ME THIS
STATEMENT, WHICH BEGINS ON PAGE 1, AND ENDS ON PAGE 2.
I FULLY UNDERSTAND THE CONTENTS OF THE ENTIRE STATEMENT MADE BY ME.
THE STATEMENT IS TRUE. I HAVE INITIALED THE BOTTOM OF EACH PAGE CON-
TAINING THE STATEMENT. I HAVE MADE THIS STATEMENT FREELY WITHOUT HOPE
OF BENEFIT OR REGARD, WITHOUT THREAT OF PUNISHMENT, AND WITHOUT
COERCION, UNLAWFUL INFLUENCE, OR UNLAWFUL INDUCEMENT.

WITNESSES:
Johnson ISHO
Laureine H. DICE

TRANSLATION OF SWORN STATEMENT PROVIDED BY
[name blacked out], Detainee #[number blacked out], 1430/21 JAN 04:

"I am the person named above. I entered Abu Ghraib prison on 10 Jul 2003, that was after they brought me from Baghdadi area. They put me in the tent area and then they brought me to Hard Site. The first day they put me in a dark room and started hitting me in the head and stomach and legs.

They made me raise my hands and sit on my knees. I was like that for four hours. Then the Interrogator came and he was looking at me while they were beating me. Then I stayed in this room for 5 days, naked with no clothes. They then took me to another cell on the upper floor. On 15 Oct 2003 they replaced the Army with the Iraqi Police and after that time they started punishing me in all sorts of ways. And the first punishment was bringing me to Room #1, and they put handcuffs on my hand and they cuffed me high for 7 or 8 hours. And that caused a rupture to my right hand and I had a cut that was bleeding and had pus coming from it. They kept me this way on 24, 25 and 26 October. And in the following days, they also put a bag over my head, and of course, this whole time I was without clothes and without anything to sleep on. And one day in November, they started different type of punishment, where an American Police came in my room and put the bag over my head and cuffed my hands and he took me out of the room into the hallway. He started beating me, him, and 5 other American Police. I could see their feet, only, from under the bag. A couple of those police they were female because I heard their voices and I saw two of the police that were hitting me before they put the bag over my head. One of them was wearing glasses. I couldn't read his name because he put tape over his name. Some of the things they did was make me sit down like a dog, and they would hold the string from the bag and they made me bark like a dog and they were laughing at me. And that policeman was a tan color, because he hit my head to the wall. When he did that, the bag came off my head and one of the police was telling me to crawl in Arabic, so I crawled on my stomach and the police were spitting on me when I was crawling and hitting me on my back, my head and my feet. It kept going on until their shift ended at 4 o'clock in the morning. The same thing would happen in the following days.

And I remember also one of the police hit me on my ear, before the usual beating, cuffing, bagging, dog position and crawling until 6 people gathered. And one of them was an Iraqi translator named Shaheen, he is a tan color, he has a mustache. Then the police started beating me on my kidneys and then they hit me on my right ear and it started bleeding and I lost conciousness. Then the Iraqi translator picked me up and told me "You are going to sleep." The when I went into the room, I woke up again. I was unconscious for about two minutes. The policeman dragged me into the room where he washed my ear and they called the doctor. The Iraqi doctor came and told me he couldn't take me to the clinic, so he fixed me in the hallway. When I woke up, I saw 6 of the American Police.

A few days before they hit me on my ear, the American police, the guy who wears glasses, he put red woman's underwear over my head. And then he tied me to the window that is in the cell with my hands behind my back until I lost consciousness. And also when I was in Room #1 they told me to lay down on my stomach and they were jumping from the bed onto my back and my legs. And the other two were spitting on me and calling me names, and they held my hands and legs. After the guy with the glasses got tired, two of the American soldiers brought me to the ground and tied my hands to the door while laying down on my stomach. One of the police was pissing on me and laughing on me. He then released my hands and I want and washed, and then the soldier came back into the room, and the soldier and his friend told me in a loud voice to lie down, so I did that. And then the policeman was opening my legs, with a bag over my head, and he sat down between my legs on his knees and I was looking at him from under the bag and they wanted to do me because I saw him and he was opening his pants, so I started screaming loudly and the other police starting hitting me with his feet on my neck and he put his feet on my head so I couldn't scream. Then they left and the guy with the glasses comes back with another person and he took me out of the room and they put me inside the dark room again and they started beating me with the broom that was there. And then they put the loudspeaker inside the room and they closed the door and he was yelling in the microphone. Then they broke the glowing finger and spread it on me until I was glowing and they were laughing. They took me to the room and they signaled me to get on to the floor. And one of the police he put a part of his stick that he always carries inside my ass and I felt it going inside me about 2 centimeters, approximately. And I started screaming, and he pulled it out and he washed it with water inside the room. And the two American girls that were there when they were beating me, they were hitting me with a ball made of sponge on my dick. And when I was tied up in my room, one of the girls, with blonde hair, she is white, she was playing with my dick. I saw inside this facility a lot of punishment just like what they did to me and more. And they were taking pictures of me during all these instances."

TRANSLATED BY: VERIFIED BY:

[signed]   [signed]

Mr. Johnson ISHO   Mr. Abdelilah ALAZADI
Translator, Category II   Translator, Category II
Titan Corporation   Titan Corporation

Assigned to:
    Prisoner Interview/Interrogation Team (PIT)(CID)(FWD)
    10th Military Police Battalion (CID)(ABN)(FWD)
    3rd Military Police Group (CID), USACIDC
    Abu Ghraib Prison Complex (ABPC)
    Abu Ghraib, Iraq APO AE 09335

THE WITNESSES:
THE RED CROSS REPORT

REPORT OF THE INTERNATIONAL COMMITTEE OF
THE RED CROSS (ICRC) ON THE TREATMENT BY THE
COALITION FORCES OF PRISONERS OF WAR AND
OTHER PROTECTED PERSONS BY THE GENEVA CON-
VENTIONS IN IRAQ DURING ARREST, INTERNMENT
AND INTERROGATION

FEBRUARY 2004

TABLE OF CONTENTS

6. Seizure and confiscation of personal belongings of persons deprived of their liberty
7. Exposure of persons deprived of their liberty to danger tasks
8. Protection of persons deprived of their liberty against shelling

EXECUTIVE SUMMARY

In its "Report on the Treatment by the Coalition Forces of Prisoners of War and other protected persons in Iraq," the International Committee of the Red Cross (ICRC) draws the attention of the Coalition Forces (hereafter called "the CF") to a number of serious violations of International Humanitarian Law. These violations have been documented and sometimes observed while visiting prisoners of war, civilian internees and other protected persons by the Geneva Conventions (hereafter called persons deprived of their liberty when their status is not specifically mentioned) in Iraq between March and November 2003. During its visits to places of internment of the CF, the ICRC collected allegations during private interviews with persons deprived of their liberty relating to the treatment by the CF of protected persons during their capture, arrest, transfer, internment and interrogation.

The main violations, which are described in the ICRC report and presented confidentially to the CF, include:

- Brutality against protected persons upon capture and initial custody, sometimes causing death or serious injury
- Absence of notification of arrest of persons deprived of their liberty to their families causing distress among persons deprived of their liberty and their families
- Physical or psychological coercion during interrogation to secure information
- Prolonged solitary confinement in cells devoid of daylight
- Excessive and disproportionate use of force against persons deprived of their liberty resulting in death or injury during their period of internment

Serious problems of conduct by the CF affecting persons deprived of their liberty are also presented in the report:

- Seizure and confiscation of private belongings of persons deprived of their liberty
- Exposure of persons deprived of their liberty to dangerous tasks
- Holding persons deprived of their liberty in dangerous places where they are not protected from shelling

According to allegations collected by ICRC delegates during private interviews with persons deprived of their liberty, ill-treatment during capture was frequent. While certain circumstances might require defensive precautions and the use of force on the part of battle group units, the ICRC collected allegations of ill-treatment following capture which took place in Baghdad, Basrah, Ramadi and Tikrit, indicating a consistent pattern with respect to times and places of brutal behavior during arrest. The repetition of such behavior by CF appeared to go beyond the reasonable, legitimate and proportional use of force required to apprehend suspects or restrain persons resisting arrest or capture, and seemed to reflect a usual modus operandi by certain CF battle group units.

According to the allegations collected by the ICRC, ill-treatment during interrogation was not systematic, except with regard to persons arrested in connection with suspected security offences or deemed to have an "intelligence" value. In these cases, persons deprived of their liberty under supervision of the Military Intelligence were at high risk of being subjected to a variety of harsh treatments ranging from insults, threats and humiliations to both physical and psychological coercion, which in some cases was tantamount to torture, in order to force cooperation with their interrogators.

The ICRC also started to document what appeared to be widespread abuse of power and ill-treatment by the Iraqi police which is under the responsibility of the Occupying Powers, including threats to hand over persons in their custody to the CF so as to extort money from them, effective hand over of such persons to the custody of the CF on allegedly fake accusations, or invoking CF orders or instructions to mistreat persons deprived of their liberty during interrogation.

In the case of the "High Value Detainees" held in Baghdad International Airport, their continued internment, several months after their arrest, in strict solitary confinement in cells devoid of sunlight for nearly 23 hours a day constituted a serious violation of the Third and Fourth Geneva Conventions.

The ICRC was also concerned about the excessive and disproportionate use of force by some detaining authorities against persons deprived of their liberty involved during their internment during periods of unrest or escape attempts that caused death and serious injuries. The use of firearms against persons deprived of their liberty in circumstances where methods without using firearms could have yielded the same result could amount to a serious violation of International Humanitarian Law. The ICRC reviewed a number of incidents of shootings of persons deprived of their liberty with live bullets, which have resulted in deaths or injuries during periods of unrest related to conditions of internment or escape attempts. Investigations initiated by the CF into these incidents concluded that the use of firearms against persons deprived of their liberty was legitimate. However, non-lethal measures could have been used to obtain the same results and quell the demonstrations or neutralize persons deprived of their liberty trying to escape.

Since the beginning of the conflict, the ICRC has regularly brought its concerns to the attention of the CF. The observations in the present report are consistent with those made earlier on several occasions orally and in writing to the CF throughout

2003. In spite of some improvements in the material conditions of internment, allegations of ill-treatment perpetrated by members of the CF against persons deprived of their liberty continued to be collected by the ICRC and thus suggested that the use of ill-treatment against persons deprived of their liberty went beyond exceptional cases and might be considered as a practice tolerated by the CF.

The ICRC report does not aim to be exhaustive with regard to breaches of International Humanitarian Law by the CF in Iraq. Rather, it illustrates priority areas that warrant attention and corrective action on the part of CF, in compliance with their International Humanitarian Law obligations.

Consequently the ICRC asks the authorities of the CF in Iraq:

- to respect at all times the human dignity, physical integrity and cultural sensitivity of the persons deprived of their liberty held under their control
- to set up a system of notifications of arrest to ensure quick and accurate transmission of information to the families of persons deprived of their liberty
- to prevent all forms of ill-treatment, moral or physical coercion of persons deprived of their liberty in relation to interrogation
- to set up an internment regime which ensures the respect of the psychological integrity and human dignity of the persons deprived of their liberty
- to ensure that all persons deprived of their liberty are allowed sufficient time every day outside in the sunlight, and that they are allowed to move and exercise in the outside yard
- to define and apply regulations and sanctions compatible with International Humanitarian Law and to ensure that persons deprived of their liberty are fully informed upon arrival about such regulations and sanctions to thoroughly investigate violations of International Humanitarian Law in order to determine responsibilities and prosecute those found responsible for violations of International Humanitarian Law
- to ensure that battle group units arresting individuals and staff in charge of internment facilities receive adequate training enabling them to operate in a proper manner and fulfill their responsibilities as arresting authority without resorting to ill-treatment or making excessive use of force

INTRODUCTION

1. The International Committee of the Red Cross (ICRC) is mandated by the High Contracting Parties to the Geneva Conventions to monitor the full application of and respect for the Third and Fourth Geneva Conventions regarding the treatment of persons deprived of their liberty. The ICRC reminds the High Contracting Parties concerned, usually in a confidential way, of their humanitarian obligations under all four Geneva Conventions, in particular the Third and Fourth Geneva Conventions as far as the treatment of persons deprived of their liberty is concerned and under Protocol I of

1977 additional to the Geneva Conventions, confirmed and reaffirmed rules of customary law and universally acknowledged principles of humanity.

The information contained in this report is based on allegations collected by the ICRC in private interviews with persons deprived of their liberty during its visits to places of internment of the Coalition Forces (CF) between March and November 2003. The allegations have been thoroughly revised in order to present this report as factually as possible. The report is also based on other accounts given either by fellow persons deprived of their liberty inside internment facilities or by family members. During this period, the ICRC conducted some 29 visits in 14 internment facilities in the central and southern parts of the country. The testimonies were collected in Camp Cropper (Core Holding Area, Military Intelligence section, "High Value Detainees" section); Al-Salihlyye, Tasferat and Al-Russafa prisons; Abu Ghraib Correctional Facility (including Camp Vigilant and the "Military Intelligence" section); Umm Qasr and Camp Bucca, as well as several temporary internment places such as Tallil Transshipment Place, Camp Condor, Amarah Camp and the Field Hospital in Shaibah.

The ICRC conditions for visits to persons deprived of their liberty in internment facilities are common for all countries where the organization operates. They can be expressed as follows:

- The ICRC must have access to all persons deprived of their liberty who come within its mandate in their place of internment
- The ICRC must be able to talk freely and in private with the persons deprived of their liberty of its choice and to register their identity
- The ICRC must be authorized to repeat its visits to the persons deprived of their liberty
- The ICRC must be notified of arrests, transfers and releases by the detaining authorities

Each visit to persons deprived of their liberty is carried out in accordance with ICRC's working procedures expressed as follows:

- At the beginning of each visit, the ICRC delegates speak with the detaining authorities to present the ICRC's mandate and the purpose of the visit as well as to obtain general information on internment conditions, total of interned population and movements of persons deprived of their liberty (release, arrest, transfer, death, hospitalization).
- The ICRC delegates, accompanied by the detaining authorities tour the internment premises.
- The ICRC delegates hold private interviews with persons of their choice who are deprived of their liberty, with no time limit in a place freely chosen and if necessary register them.
- At the end of each visit, the delegates hold a final talk with the detaining authorities to inform them about the ICRC's findings and recommendations.

2. The aim of the report is to present information collected by the ICRC concerning the treatment of prisoners of war by the CF, civilian internees and other protected persons deprived of their liberty during the process of arrest, transfer, internment and interrogation.

3. The main places of internment where mistreatment allegedly took place included battle group unit stations; the military intelligence sections of Camp Cropper and Abu Ghraib Correctional Facility; Al-Baghdadi, Heat Base and Habbania Camp in Ramadi governorate; Tikrit holding area (former Saddam Hussein Islamic School); a former train station in Al-Khaïm, near the Syrian border, turned into a military base; the Ministry of Defense and Presidential Palace in Baghdad, the former *mukhabarat* office in Basrah, as well as several Iraqi police stations in Baghdad.

4. In most cases, the allegations of ill-treatment referred to acts that occurred prior to the internment of persons deprived of their liberty in regular internment facilities, while they were in the custody of arresting authorities or military and civilian intelligence personnel. When persons deprived of their liberty were transferred to regular internment facilities, such as those administered by the military police, where the behavior of guards was strictly supervised, ill-treatment of the type described in this report usually ceased. In these places, violations of provisions of International Humanitarian Law relating to the treatment of persons deprived of their liberty were a result of the generally poor standard of internment conditions (long term internment in unsuitable temporary facilities) or of the use of what appeared to be excessive force to quell unrest or to prevent attempted escapes.

1. TREATMENT DURING ARREST

5. Protected persons interviewed by ICRC delegates have described a fairly consistent pattern with respect to times and places of brutality by members of the CF arresting them.

6. Arrests as described in these allegations tended to follow a pattern. Arresting authorities entered houses usually after dark, breaking down doors, waking up residents roughly, yelling orders, forcing family members into one room under military guard while searching the rest of the house and further breaking doors, cabinets and other property. They arrested suspects, tying their hands in the back with flexi-cuffs, hooding them, and taking them away. Sometimes they arrested all adult males present in a house, including elderly, handicapped or sick people. Treatment often included pushing people around, insulting, taking aim with rifles, punching and kicking and striking with rifles. Individuals were often led away in whatever they happened to be wearing at the time of arrest—sometimes in pyjamas or underwear—and were denied the opportunity to gather a few essential belongings, such as clothing, hygiene items,

medicine or eyeglasses. Those who surrendered with a suitcase often had their belongings confiscated. In many cases personal belongings were seized during the arrest, with no receipt being issued (*see section 6, below*).

7. Certain CF military intelligence officers told the ICRC that in their estimate between 70% and 90% of the persons deprived of their liberty in Iraq had been arrested by mistake. They also attributed the brutality of some arrests to the lack of proper supervision of battle group units.

8. *In accordance with provisions of International Humanitarian Law which oblige the CF to treat prisoners of war and other protected persons humanely and to protect them against acts of violence, threats thereof, intimidation and insults (Art. 13, 14, 17, 87, Third Geneva Convention; Art. 5, 27, 31, 32, 33 Fourth Geneva Convention), the ICRC asks the authorities of CF to respect at all times the human dignity, physical integrity and cultural sensitivity of the persons deprived of their liberty held under their control. The ICRC also asks the authorities of CF to ensure that battle group units arresting individuals receive adequate training enabling them to operate in a proper manner and fulfill their responsibilities without resorting to brutality or using excessive force.*

1.1. Notification to families and information for arrestees

9. In almost all instances documented by the ICRC, arresting authorities provided no information about who they were, where their base was located, nor did they explain the cause of arrest. Similarly, they rarely informed the arrestee or his family where he was being taken and for how long, resulting in the de facto "disappearance" of the arrestee for weeks or even months until contact was finally made.

10. When arrests were made in the streets, along the roads, or at checkpoints, families were not informed about what had happened to the arrestees until they managed to trace them or received news about them through persons who had been deprived of their liberty but were later released, visiting family members of fellow persons deprived of their liberty, or ICRC Red Cross Messages. In the absence of a system to notify the families of the whereabouts of their arrested relatives, many were left without news for months, often fearing that their relatives unaccounted for were dead.

11. Nine months into the present conflict, there is still no satisfactorily functioning system of notification to the families of captured or arrested persons, even though hundreds of arrests continue to be carried out every week. While the main places of internment (Camp Bucca and Abu Ghraib) are part of a centralized notification system through the National Information Bureau (and their data are forwarded electronically to the ICRC on a regular basis), other places of internment such as Mossul or Tikrit are not. Notifications from those places therefore depend solely on capture or internment cards as stipulated by the Third and Fourth Geneva Conventions.

Since March 2003 capture cards have often been filled out carelessly, resulting in unnecessary delays of several weeks or months before families were notified, and sometimes resulting in no notification at all. It is the responsibility of the detaining authority to see to it that each capture or internment card is carefully filled out so that the ICRC is in a position to effectively deliver them to families. The current system of General Information Centers (GIC), set up under the responsibility of the Humanitarian Assistance Coordination Centers (HACC), while an improvement, remains inadequate, as families outside the main towns do not have access to them, lists made available are not complete and often outdated and do not reflect the frequent transfers from one place of internment to another. In the absence of a better alternative, the ICRC's delivery of accurate capture cards remains the most reliable, prompt and effective system to notify the families, provided cards are properly filled out.

The ICRC has raised this issue repeatedly with the detaining authorities since March 2003, including at the highest level of the CF in August 2003. Despite some improvement, hundreds of families have had to wait anxiously for weeks and sometimes months before learning of the whereabouts of their arrested family members. Many families travel for weeks throughout the country from one place of internment to another in search of their relatives and often come to learn about their whereabouts informally (through released detainees) or when the person deprived of his liberty is released and returns home.

12. Similarly, transfers, cases of sickness at the time of arrest, deaths, escapes or repatriations continue to be notified only insufficiently or are not notified at all by the CF to the families in spite of their obligation to do so under International Humanitarian Law.

13. *In accordance with provisions of both the Third Geneva Convention (Art. 70, 122, 123) and the Fourth Geneva Convention (Art. 106, 136, 137, 138, 140), the ICRC reminds the CF of their treaty-based obligation to notify promptly the families of all prisoners of war and other protected persons captured or arrested by them. Within one week, prisoners of war and civilian internees must be allowed to fill out capture or internment cards mentioning at the very least their capture/arrest, address (current place of detention/ internment) and state of health. These cards must be forwarded as rapidly as possible and may not be delayed in any manner. As long as there is no centralized system of notifications of arrest set up by CF, it is of paramount importance that these capture cards be filled out properly, so as to allow the ICRC to transmit them rapidly to the concerned families.*

14. *The same obligation of notification to families of captured or arrested persons applies to transfers, cases of sickness, deaths, escapes and repatriation and identification of the dead of the adverse party. All these events must be notified to the ICRC with the full details of the persons concerned, so as to allow the ICRC to inform the concerned families (Art. 120, 121, 122, 123 Third Geneva Convention; Art. 129, 130, 136, 137, 140 Fourth Geneva Convention).*

2. TREATMENT DURING TRANSFER AND INITIAL CUSTODY

15. The ICRC collected several allegations indicating that following arrest, persons deprived of their liberty were ill-treated, sometimes during transfer from their place of arrest to their initial internment facility. This ill-treatment would normally stop by the time the persons reached a regular internment facility, such as Camp Cropper, Camp Bucca or Abu Ghraib. The ICRC also collected one allegation of death resulting from harsh conditions of interment and ill-treatment during initial custody.

16. One allegation collected by the ICRC concerned the arrest of nine men by the CF in a hotel in Basrah on 13 September 2003. Following their arrest, the nine men were made to kneel, face and hands against the ground, as if in a prayer position. The soldiers stamped on the back of the neck of those raising their head. They confiscated their money without issuing a receipt. The suspects were taken to Al-Hakimiya, a former office previously used by the *mukhabarat* in Basrah and then beaten severely by CF personnel. One of the arrestees died following the ill-treatment ([name blacked out] aged 28, married, father of two children). Prior to his death, his co-arrestees heard him screaming and asking for assistance.

The issued "International Death Certificate" mentioned "Cardio-respiratory arrest—asphyxia" as the condition directly leading to the death. As to the cause of that condition, it mentioned "Unknown" and "Refer to the coroner. "The certificate did not bear any other mention. An eyewitness' description of the body given to the ICRC mentioned a broken nose, several broken ribs and skin lesions on the face consistent with beatings. The father of the victim was informed of his death on 18 September, and was invited to identify the body of his son. On 3 October, the commander of the CF in Basrah presented to him his condolences and informed him that an investigation had been launched and that those responsible would be punished. Two other persons deprived of their liberty were hospitalised with severe injuries. Similarly, a week later, an ICRC medical doctor examined them in the hospital and observed large haematomas with dried scabs on the abdomen, buttocks, sides, thigh, wrists, nose and forehead consistent with their accounts of beatings received.

17. During a visit of the ICRC in Camp Bucca on 22 September 2003, a 61-year old person deprived of his liberty alleged that he had been tied, hooded and forced to sit on the hot surface of what he surmised to be the engine of a vehicle, which had caused severe burns to his buttocks. The victim had lost consciousness. The ICRC observed large crusted lesions consistent with his allegation.

18. The ICRC examined another person deprived of his liberty in the "High Value Detainees" section in October 2003 who had been subjected to a similar treatment. He had been hooded, handcuffed in the back, and made to lie face down, on a hot surface during transportation. This had caused severe skin burns that required three months' hospitalization. At the time of the interview he had been recently discharged from

hospital. He had to undergo several skin grafts, the amputation of his right index finger, and suffered the permanent loss of the use of his left fifth finger secondary to burn-induced skin retraction. He also suffered extensive burns over the abdomen, anterior aspects of the lower extremities, the palm of his right hand and the sole of his left foot. The ICRC recommended to the CF that the case be investigated to determine the cause and circumstances of the injuries and the authority responsible for the ill-treatment. At the time of writing the results of the report were still pending.

18. During transportation following arrest, persons deprived of their liberty were almost always hooded and tightly restrained with flexi-cuffs. They were occasionally

[missing text]

haematoma and linear marks compatible with repeated whipping or beating. He had wrist marks compatible with tight flexi-cuffs.

The ICRC also collected allegations of deaths as a result of harsh internment conditions, ill-treatment, lack of medical attention, or the combination thereof, notably in Tikrit holding area formerly known as the Saddam Hussein Islamic School.

22. Some CF military intelligence officers told the ICRC that the widespread ill-treatment of persons deprived of their liberty during arrest, initial internment and "tactical questioning" was due to a lack of military police on the ground to supervise and control the behavior and activities of the battle groups units, and the lack of experience of intelligence officers in charge of the "tactical questioning."

23. *In accordance with provisions of International Humanitarian Law which oblige the CF to treat prisoners of war and other protected persons humanely and to protect them against acts of violence, threats thereof, intimidation and insults (Art. 13, 14, 17, 87, Third Geneva Convention; Articles 5, 27, 31, 32, 33, Fourth Geneva Convention), the ICRC asks the authorities of the CF to respect at all times the human dignity, physical integrity and cultural sensitivity of the persons deprived of their liberty held in Iraq under their control.*

The ICRC also asks the authorities of the CF to ensure that battle group units transferring and/or holding individuals receive adequate training enabling them to operate in a proper manner and meet their responsibilities without resorting to brutality or using excessive force.

3. TREATMENT DURING INTERROGATION

24. Arrests were usually followed by temporary internment at battle group level or at initial interrogation facilities managed by military intelligence personnel, but accessible to other intelligence personnel (especially in the case of security detainees). The ill-treatment by the CF personnel during interrogation was not systematic, except with

regard to persons arrested in connection with suspected security offences or deemed to have an "intelligence" value. In these cases, persons deprived of their liberty supervised by the military intelligence were subjected to a variety of ill-treatments ranging from insults and humiliation to both physical and psychological coercion that in some cases might amount to torture in order to force them to cooperate with their interrogators. In certain cases, such as in Abu Ghraib military intelligence section, methods of physical and psychological coercion used by the interrogators appeared to be part of the standard operating procedures by military intelligence personnel to obtain confessions and extract information. Several military intelligence officers confirmed to the ICRC that it was part of the military intelligence process to hold a person deprived of his liberty naked in a completely dark and empty cell for a prolonged period to use inhumane and degrading treatment, including physical and psychological coercion, against persons deprived of their liberty to secure their cooperation.

3.1. Methods of ill-treatment

25. The methods of ill-treatment most frequently alleged during interrogation included

- Hooding, used to prevent people from seeing and to disorient them, and also to prevent them from breathing freely. One or sometimes two bags, sometimes with an elastic blindfold over the eyes which, when slipped down, further impeded proper breathing. Hooding was sometimes used in conjunction with beatings thus increasing anxiety as to when blows would come. The practice of hooding also allowed the interrogators to remain anonymous and thus to act with impunity. Hooding could last for periods from a few hours to up to 2 to 4 consecutive days, during which hoods were lifted only for drinking, eating or going to the toilets;
- Handcuffing with flexi-cuffs, which were sometimes made so tight and used for such extended periods that they caused skin lesions and long-term after-effects on the hands (nerve damage), as observed by the ICRC;
- Beatings with hard objects (including pistols and rifles), slapping, punching, kicking with knees or feet on various parts of the body (legs, sides, lower back, groin);
- Pressing the face into the ground with boots;
- Threats (of ill-treatment, reprisals against family members, imminent execution or transfer to Guantánamo);
- Being stripped naked for several days while held in solitary confinement in an empty and completely dark cell that included a latrine;
- Being held in solitary confinement combined with threats (to intern the individual indefinitely, to arrest other family members, to transfer the individual to Guantánamo), insufficient sleep, food or water deprivation, minimal access to showers (twice a week), denial of access to open air and prohibition of contacts with other persons deprived of their liberty;

- Being paraded naked outside cells in front of other persons deprived of their liberty, and guards, sometimes hooded or with women's underwear over the head;
- Acts of humiliation such as being made to stand naked against the wall of the cell with arms raised or with women's underwear over the head for prolonged periods—while being laughed at by guards, including female guards, and sometimes photographed in this position;
- Being attached repeatedly over several days, for several hours each time, with handcuffs to the bars of their cell door in humiliating (i.e. naked or in underwear) and/or uncomfortable position causing physical pain;
- Exposure while hooded to loud noise or music, prolonged exposure while hooded to the sun over several hours, including during the hottest time of the day when temperatures could reach 50 degrees Celsius (122 degrees Fahrenheit) or higher;
- Being forced to remain for prolonged periods in stress positions such as squatting or standing with or without the arms lifted.

26. These methods of physical and psychological coercion were used by the military intelligence in a systematic way to gain confessions and extract information or other forms of cooperation from persons who had been arrested in connection with suspected security offences or deemed to have an "intelligence value."

3.2. Military Intelligence section, "Abu Ghraib Correctional Facility"

27. In mid-October 2003, the ICRC visited persons deprived of their liberty undergoing interrogation by military intelligence officers in Unit 1A, the "isolation section" of "Abu Ghraib" Correctional Facility. Most of these persons deprived of their liberty had been arrested in early October. During the visit, ICRC delegates directly witnessed and documented a variety of methods used to secure the cooperation of the persons deprived of their liberty with their interrogators. In particular they witnessed the practice of keeping persons deprived of their liberty completely naked in totally empty concrete cells and in total darkness, allegedly for several consecutive days. Upon witnessing such cases, the ICRC interrupted its visits and requested an explanation from the authorities. The military intelligence officer in charge of the interrogation explained that this practice was "part of the process." The process appeared to be a give-and-take policy whereby persons deprived of their liberty were "drip-fed" with new items (clothing, bedding, hygiene articles, lit cell, etc.) in exchange for their "cooperation." The ICRC also visited other persons deprived of their liberty held in total darkness, others in dimly lit cells who had been allowed to dress following periods during which they had been held naked. Several had been given women's underwear to wear under their jumpsuit (men's underwear was not distributed), which they felt to be humiliating.

The ICRC documented other forms of ill-treatment, usually combined with those described above, including threats, insults, verbal violence, sleep deprivation caused by the playing of loud music or constant light in cells devoid of windows, tight hand-cuffing with flexi-cuffs causing lesions and wounds around the wrists. Punishment included being made to walk in the corridors handcuffed and naked, or with women's underwear on the head, or being handcuffed either dressed or naked to the bed bars or the cell door. Some persons deprived of their liberty presented physical marks and psychological symptoms, which were compatible with these allegations. The ICRC medical delegate examined persons deprived of their liberty presenting signs of con-centration difficulties, memory problems, verbal expression difficulties, incoherent speech, acute anxiety reactions, abnormal behaviour and suicidal tendencies. These symptoms appeared to have been caused by the methods and duration of interroga-tion. One person held in isolation that the ICRC examined, was unresponsive to verbal and painful stimuli. His heart rate was 120 beats per minute and his respiratory rate 18 per minute. He was diagnosed as suffering from somatoform (mental) disorder, specifically a conversion disorder, most likely due to the ill-treatment he was subjected to during interrogation.

According to the allegations collected by the ICRC, detaining authorities also con-tinued to keep persons deprived of their liberty during the period of interrogation, uninformed of the reason for their arrest. They were often questioned without know-ing what they were accused of. They were not allowed to ask questions and were not provided with an opportunity to seek clarification about the reason for their arrest. Their treatment tended to vary according to their degree of cooperation with their interrogators: those who cooperated were afforded preferential treatment such as being allowed contacts with other persons deprived of their liberty, being allowed to phone their families, being given clothes, bedding equipment, food, water or ciga-rettes, being allowed access to showers, being held in a lit cell, etc.

3.3. Umm Qasr (JFIT) and Camp Bucca (JIF/ICE)

28. Since the establishment of Umm Qasr camp and its successor, Camp Bucca, persons deprived of their liberty undergoing interrogation, whether they had been arrested by British, Danish, Dutch or Italian armed forces were segregated from other internees in a separate section of the camp designed for investigation. This section was initially operated by the British Armed Forces who called it Joint Field Intelligence Team (JFIT). On 7 April, its administration was handed over to the US Armed Forces, which renamed it Joint Interrogation Facility/Interrogation Control Element (JIF/ ICE). On 25 September 2003, its administration was handed back to the British Armed Forces.

29. CF intelligence personnel interrogated persons deprived of their liberty of concern to them in this section. They were either accused of attacks against the CF or deemed to have an "intelligence value." They could be held there from a few days to several weeks, until their interrogation was completed. During a visit in September 2003, the ICRC interviewed in that section several persons deprived of their liberty that had been held there for periods from three to four weeks.

30. Initially, inmates were routinely treated by their guards with general contempt, with petty violence such as having orders screamed at them and being cursed, kicked, struck with rifle butts, roughed up or pushed around. They were reportedly hand-cuffed in the back and hooded for the duration of the interrogation and were prohib-ited from talking to each other or to the guards. Hooding appeared to be motivated by security concerns as well as to be part of standard intimidation techniques used by mil-itary intelligence personnel to frighten inmates into cooperating. This was combined with deliberately maintaining uncertainty about what would happen to the inmates, and a generally hostile attitude on the part of the guards. Conditions of internment improved according to the degree of cooperation of the persons deprived of his liberty. Interrogated persons deprived of their liberty were held in two separate sections. Those under initial investigation were reportedly not allowed to talk to each other (purportedly to avoid exchange of information and "versions of events" between them). They were not allowed to stand up or walk out of the tent but they had access to water with which to wash themselves. Once they had cooperated with their inter-rogators, they were transferred to the "privileged" tent where the above-mentioned restrictions were lifted.

31. Persons deprived of their liberty undergoing interrogation by the CF were allegedly subjected to frequent cursing, insults and threats, both physical and verbal, such as having rifles aimed at them in a general way or directly against the temple, the back of the head, or the stomach, and threatened with transfer to Guantánamo, death or indef-inite internment. Besides mentioning the general climate of intimidation maintained as one of the methods used to pressure persons deprived of their liberty to cooperate with their interrogators, none of those interviewed by the ICRC in Umm Qasr and Camp Bucca spoke of physical ill-treatment during interrogation. All allegations of ill-treatment referred to the phase of arrest, initial internment (at collecting points, hold-ing areas) and "tactical questioning" by military intelligence officers attached to battle group units, prior to transfer to Camp Bucca.

3.4. Previous actions taken by the ICRC in 2003 on the issue of treatment

32. On 1 April, the ICRC informed orally the political advisor of the commander of British Armed Forces at the CF Central Command in Doha about methods of ill-treatment used by military intelligence personnel to interrogate persons deprived of their liberty in the internment camp of Umm Qasr. This intervention had the immedi-ate effect to stop the systematic use of hoods and flexi-cuffs in the interrogation section of Umm Qasr. Brutal treatment of persons deprived of their liberty also allegedly ceased when the 800th MP Brigade took over the guarding of that section in Umm Qasr. UK Forces handed over Umm Qasr holding area to the 800th MP Brigade on 09.04.03. The 800th MP Brigade then built Camp Bucca two kilometers away.

33. In May 2003, the ICRC sent to the CF a memorandum based on over 200

allegations of ill-treatment of prisoners of war during capture and interrogation at collecting points, battle group stations and temporary holding areas. The allegations were consistent with marks on bodies observed by the medical delegate. The memorandum was handed over to [name blacked out] of the US Central Command in Doha, State of Qatar. Subsequently, one improvement consisted in the removal of wristbands with the remark "terrorist" given to foreign detainees.

34. In early July the ICRC sent the CF a working paper detailing approximately 50 allegations of ill-treatment in the military intelligence section of Camp Cropper, at Baghdad International Airport. They included a combination of petty and deliberate acts of violence aimed at securing the cooperation of the persons deprived of their liberty with their interrogators: threats (to intern individuals indefinitely, to arrest other family members, to transfer individuals to Guantánamo) against persons deprived of their liberty or against members of their families (in particular wives and daughters); hooding; tight handcuffing; use of stress positions (kneeling, squatting, standing with arms raised over the head) for three or four hours; taking aim at individuals with rifles, striking them with rifle butts, slaps, punches, prolonged exposure to the sun, and isolation in dark cells. ICRC delegates witnessed marks on the bodies of several persons deprived of their liberty consistent with their allegations. In one illustrative case, a person deprived of his liberty arrested at home by the CF on suspicion of involvement in an attack against the CF, was allegedly beaten during interrogation in a location in the vicinity of Camp Cropper. He alleged that he had been hooded and cuffed with flexi-cuffs, threatened to be tortured and killed, urinated on, kicked in the head, lower back and groin, force-fed a baseball which was tied into the mouth using a scarf and deprived of sleep for four consecutive days. Interrogators would allegedly take turns ill-treating him. When he said he would complain to the ICRC he was allegedly beaten more. An ICRC medical examination revealed haematoma in the lower back, blood in urine, sensory loss in the right hand due to tight handcuffing with flexi-cuffs, and a broken rib.

Shortly after that intervention was sent, the military intelligence internment section was closed and persons deprived of their liberty were transferred to what became the "High Value Detainees" section of the airport, a regular internment facility under the command of the 115th Military Police Battalion. From this time onwards, the ICRC observed that the ill-treatment of this category of persons deprived of their liberty by military intelligence declined significantly and even stopped, while their interrogation continued through to the end of the year 2003.

3.5. Allegations of ill-treatment by Iraqi police

35. The ICRC has also collected a growing body of allegations relating to widespread abuse of power and ill-treatment of persons in the custody of Iraqi police. This included the extensive practice of threatening to hand over these persons to the CF for internment, or claiming to act under the CF instructions, in order to abuse their power

and extort money from persons taken in custody. Allegations collected by the ICRC indicated that numerous people had been handed over to the CF on the basis of unfounded accusations (of hostility against the CF, or belonging to opposition forces) because they were unable or unwilling, to pay bribes to the police. Alleged ill-treatment during arrest and transportation included hooding, tight handcuffing, verbal abuse, beating with fists and rifle butts, and kicking. During interrogation, the detaining authorities allegedly whipped persons deprived of their liberty with cables on the back, kicked them in the lower parts of the body, including in the testicles, handcuffed and left them hanging from the iron bars of the cell windows or doors in painful positions for several hours at a time, and burned them with cigarettes (signs on bodies witnessed by ICRC delegates). Several persons deprived of their liberty alleged that they had been made to sign a statement that they had not been allowed to read. These allegations concerned several police stations in Baghdad including Al-Qana, Al-Jiran, Al-Kubra in Al-Amariyya, Al-Hurriyyeh in Al-Doura, Al-Salhiyye in Salhiyye, and Al-Baiah. Many persons deprived of their liberty drew parallels between police practices under the occupation with those of the former regime.

36. In early June 2003, for instance, a group of persons deprived of their liberty was taken to the former police academy after they had been arrested. There, they were allegedly hooded and cuffed and made to stand against a wall while a policeman placed his pistol against their heads and pulled the trigger in a mock execution (the pistol was in fact unloaded); they were also allegedly forced to sit on chairs where they were hit on the legs, the soles of their feet and on their sides with sticks. They also allegedly had water poured on their legs and had electrical shocks administered to them with stripped tips of electric wires. The mother of one of the persons deprived of liberty was reportedly brought in and the policemen threatened to mistreat her. Another person deprived of his liberty was threatened with having his wife brought in and raped. They were made to fingerprint their alleged confessions of guilt, which resulted in their transfer to the CF to be interned pending trial.

37. The ICRC reminds the authorities of the CF that prisoners of war and other protected persons in the custody of occupying forces must be humanely treated at all times; they must not be subjected to cruel or degrading treatment; and must be protected against all acts of violence (Art. 13, 14, Third Geneva Convention; Art. 27, Fourth Geneva Convention). Torture and other forms of physical and psychological coercion against prisoners of war and other interned persons for the purpose of extracting confession or information is prohibited in all cases and under all circumstances without exception (Art. 17 and 87, Third Geneva Convention; Art. 5, 31 and 32, Fourth Geneva Convention). Confessions extracted under coercion or torture can never be used as evidence of guilt (Art. 99, Third Geneva Convention; Art. 31, Fourth Geneva Convention). Such violations of International Humanitarian Law should be thoroughly investigated in order to determine responsibilities and prosecute those found responsible (Art. 129, Third Geneva Convention and Art. 146, Fourth Geneva Convention).

4. TREATMENT IN REGULAR INTERNMENT FACILITIES

4.1. General conditions of treatment

38. The ICRC assessed the treatment of persons deprived of their liberty in regular internment facilities by CF personnel as respectful, with a few individual exceptions due to individual personalities or occasional loss of control on the part of the guards. Abusive behavior by guards, when reported to their officers, was usually quickly reprimanded and disciplined by superiors.

39. The ICRC often noted a serious communication gap between detention personnel and persons deprived of their liberty, primarily due to the language barrier, which resulted in frequent misunderstandings. This was compounded by a widespread attitude of contempt on the part of guards, in reaction to which persons deprived of their liberty, which often complained of being treated like inferiors, adopted a similar attitude.

40. The ICRC occasionally observed persons deprived of their liberty being slapped, roughed up, pushed around or pushed to the ground either because of poor communication (a failure to understand or a misunderstanding of orders given in English was construed by guards as resistance or disobedience), a disrespectful attitude on the part of guards, a reluctance by persons deprived of their liberty to comply with orders, or a loss of temper by guards.

41. Disciplinary measures included being taken out of the compound, handcuffed and made to stand, sit, squat or lie down in the sand under the sun for up to three or four hours, depending on the breach of discipline (disrespectful behavior towards guards, communication between persons deprived of their liberty transferring from one compound to another, disobeying orders); temporary suspension of cigarette distribution, and temporary segregation in disciplinary confinement sections of the detention facilities.

42. Despite the fact that reductions in the availability of water or food rations or, more commonly, cigarettes were occasionally observed, the prohibition on collective punishment provided for under International Humanitarian Law (Art. 26.6, 87.3, Third Geneva Convention and Art. 33, Fourth Geneva Convention) appeared to be generally respected by detaining authorities.

4.2. "High Value Detainees" section, Baghdad International Airport

43. Since June 2003, over a hundred "high value detainees" have been held for nearly 23 hours a day in strict solitary confinement in small concrete cells devoid of daylight. This regime of complete isolation strictly prohibited any contact with other persons

deprived of their liberty, guards, family members (except through Red Cross Messages) and the rest of the outside world. Even spouses and members of the same family were subject to this regime. Persons deprived of their liberty whose "investigation" was nearing completion were reportedly allowed to exercise together outside their cells for twenty minutes twice a day or go to the showers or toilets together. The other persons deprived of their liberty still under interrogation reportedly continued to be interned in total "segregation" (i.e. they were allowed to exercise outside their cells for twenty minutes twice a day and to go to the showers or toilets but always alone and without any contact with others). Most had been subjected to this regime for the past five months. Attempts to contact other persons deprived of their liberty or simply to exchange glances or greetings were reportedly sanctioned by reprimand or temporary deprivation of time outside their cells. Since August 2003, the detainees have been provided with the Koran. They have been allowed to receive books of a non-political nature, but no newspapers or magazines on current affairs. The internment regime appeared to be motivated by a combination of security concerns (isolation of the persons deprived of their liberty from the outside world) and the collection of intelligence. All had been undergoing interrogation since their internment, in spite of the fact that none had been charged with criminal offence.

On 30 October 2003, the ICRC wrote to the Detaining Authorities recommending that this policy be discontinued and replaced by a regime of internment consistent with the CF's obligations under the Geneva Conventions.

44. *The internment of persons in solitary confinement for months at a time in cells devoid of daylight for nearly 23 hours a day is more severe than the forms of internment provided for in the Third and Fourth Geneva Conventions (investigation of criminal offences or disciplinary punishment). It cannot be used as a regular, ordinary mode of holding of prisoners of war or civilian internees. The ICRC reminds the authorities of the Coalition Forces in Iraq that internment of this kind contravenes Articles 21, 25, 89, 90, 95, 103 of the Third Geneva Convention and Articles 27, 41, 42, 78, 82, 118, 125 of the Fourth Geneva Convention. The ICRC recommends to the authorities of the CF that they set up an internment regime which ensures respect for the psychological integrity and human dignity of the persons deprived of their liberty and that they make sure that all persons deprived of their liberty are allowed sufficient time every day outside in the sunlight and the opportunity to move about and exercise in the outside yard.*

5. EXCESSIVE AND DISPROPORTIONATE USE OF FORCE AGAINST PERSONS DEPRIVED OF THEIR LIBERTY BY THE DETAINING AUTHORITIES

45. Since March 2003, the ICRC recorded, and in some cases, witnessed, a number of incidents in which guards shot at persons deprived of their liberty with live ammunition, in the context either of unrest relating to internment conditions or of escape attempts by individuals:

Camp Cropper, 24 May 2003: In the context of a hunger strike, unrest broke out in the camp prior to ICRC visit. One person deprived of his liberty suffered a gunshot wound.

Camp Cropper, 9 June 2003: Six persons deprived of their liberty were injured by live ammunition after a guard opened fire on the group in an attempt to quell a demonstration.

Camp Cropper, 12 June 2003: Two, or possibly three, persons deprived of their liberty were shot at when they attempted to escape through the barbed wire fence. One of them, Akheel Abd Al-Hussein from Baghdad, was wounded and later died after being taken to the hospital. The other person deprived of his liberty was recaptured and received treatment for gunshot wounds.

Abu Ghraib, 13 June 2003: When unrest flared up, guards from three watchtowers opened fire at the demonstrators, injuring seven persons deprived of their liberty and killing another, Alaa Jasim Hassan. The authorities investigated the matter and concluded that the "shooting was justified as the three tower [guards] determined that the lives of the interior guards were threatened."

Abu Ghraib, late June 2003: During unrest, one person deprived of his liberty was injured by live ammunition when a guard opened fire.

Abu Ghraib, 24 November 2003: During a riot four detainees were killed by US MP guards. The killing took place after unrest erupted in one of the compounds (no. 4). The detainees claimed to be unhappy with the situation of detention. Specifically, lack of food, clothing, but more importantly the lack of judicial guarantees and, especially important during the time of Eid al-Fitr, lack of family visits or lack of contacts all together. The detainees alleged to have gathered near the gate whereupon the guards panicked and started shooting. Initially, non-lethal ammunition was used which was subsequently replaced by live ammunition.

The report handed over by the CF to the ICRC states that detainees were trying to force open the gate. It further states that several verbal warnings were given and non-lethal ammunition fired at the crowd. After 25 minutes deadly force was applied resulting in the death of four detainees.

[names blacked out]

The narrative report furnished by the CF does not address the reason for the riot in any way and does not give any recommendations as to how a similar incident could be avoided. It does not question the use of lethal force during such an incident.

Camp Bucca, 16–22 April 2003: ICRC delegates witnessed a shooting incident, which caused the death of one person deprived of his liberty and injury of another. A first shot was fired on the ground by a soldier located outside the compound in a bid to rescue one of the guards, allegedly being threatened by a prisoner of war armed with a stick; the second shot injured a prisoner of war in the left forearm, and the third shot killed another prisoner of war.

Camp Bucca, 22 September 2003: Following unrest in a section of the camp, one person deprived of his liberty, allegedly throwing stones, was fired upon by a guard in a watchtower. He suffered a gunshot wound to the upper part of the chest, the bullet passed through the chest and exited from the back. The investigation undertaken by the CF concluded that "the compound guards correctly utilized the rules of engagement and that numerous non-lethal rounds were dispersed to no avail." The person deprived of his liberty "was the victim of a justifiable shooting." An ICRC delegate and an interpreter witnessed most of the events. At no point did the persons deprived of their liberty, and the victim shot at, appear to pose a serious threat to the life or security of the guards who could have responded to the situation with less brutal measures. The shooting showed a clear disregard for human life and security of the persons deprived of their liberty.

46. These incidents were investigated summarily by the CF. They concluded in all cases that a legitimate use of firearms had been made against persons deprived of their liberty, who, except perhaps in Abu Ghraib on 13 June 2003, were unarmed and did not appear to pose any serious threat to anyone's life justifying the use of firearms. In all cases, less extreme measures could have been used to quell the demonstrations or neutralize persons deprived of their liberty trying to escape.

47. In connection with the 22 September 2003 incident, the ICRC wrote on 23 October to the Commander of the 800th MP Brigade and recommended the adoption of crowd control measures consistent with the rules and principles of the Third and Fourth Geneva Conventions and other applicable international norms relating to the use of force or firearms by law-enforcement personnel.

48. Since May 2003, the ICRC repeatedly recommended to the CF to use non-lethal methods to deal with demonstrations, riots or escape attempts. In Camp Cropper, its recommendations were heeded. After initial deplorable incidents no further shooting of persons deprived of their liberty has occurred since November 2003. In mid-July, the ICRC witnessed a demonstration in that camp: in spite of some violence by the persons deprived of their liberty, the problem was efficiently dealt with by the camp commander without any excessive use of force. He called in anti-riot military policemen, refrained from any act that might have provoked further anger from the persons deprived of their liberty, waited patiently for the emotions to calm down and then sought to establish dialogue with the persons deprived of their liberty through their section representatives. The unrest was quieted down without any violence.

49. *The ICRC reminds the authorities of the CF that the use of firearms against persons deprived of their liberty, especially against those who are escaping or attempting to escape is an extreme measure which should not be disproportionate to the legitimate objective to be achieved (to apprehend the individual) and shall always be preceded by warning appropriate to the circumstances (Art. 42, Third Geneva Convention).*

The CF detaining personnel should be provided with adequate training to deal with incidents in their internment facilities. Firearms should not be used except when a suspected offender offers armed resistance or otherwise jeopardizes the lives of others and only when less extreme measures are not sufficient to restrain or apprehend him (Article 3 of the Code of Conduct for Law Enforcement Officials and Article 9 of the Basic Principles on the Use of Force and Firearms by Law Enforcement Officials).

In every instance in which a firearm is discharged, a report should be made promptly to the competent authorities. All deaths or serious injuries of a person deprived of his liberty caused or suspected to have been caused by a sentry should be immediately followed by a proper inquiry by the Detaining Power which should ensure the prosecution of any person(s) found responsible (Art. 121, Third Geneva Convention; Art. 131, Fourth Geneva Convention).

6. SEIZURE AND CONFISCATION OF PRIVATE BELONGINGS OF PERSONS DEPRIVED OF THEIR LIBERTY

50. The ICRC collected numerous allegations of seizure and confiscation of private property (money, cars and other valuables) by the CF in the context of arrests. In only a few cases were receipts issued to the arrested person or his family, detailing the items confiscated. This was perceived by persons deprived of their liberty as outright theft or pillage. The following examples will serve to illustrate the allegations:

- [name blacked out] alleged that the CF took US$22,000 in cash and his personal luggage during his arrest;
- [name blacked out] claimed that large amounts of money and personal effects were confiscated by the CF when he was arrested at his home on 27–28 May 2003. The items confiscated allegedly included 71,450,000 Iraqi dinars, 14,000 US dollars, two wedding rings, a video camera, a watch, real-estate property documents, his wife's residential documents, his father's will, his private diaries, as well as most of the family private documents and personal identity and other papers;
- [name blacked out] claimed that his car was confiscated when he was arrested by the CF in Basrah on 16 July 2003;
- [name blacked out] claimed that CF confiscated two million Iraqi dinars when arrested at his home on 21 August 2003;
- [name blacked out] claimed that his money and two cars were confiscated when he was arrested by the CF on 11 August 2003.

51. In Camp Cropper, Camp Bucca and Abu Ghraib, a system was gradually put in place whereby personal belongings in the possession of persons deprived of their liberty at the time of their arrival in these facilities which they could not keep with them (money, other valuables, spare clothing, identity papers) were registered and kept until their release. In these cases, a receipt was usually issued to the person deprived of his liberty and his belongings were returned when he was released. However, this system took no account of the property seized during arrest.

52. In response to property loss or damage caused to property by the CF during raids

and also to complaints regarding pension or salaries, the CF established a compensation system open to everyone, including internees and the general public. Complaints could be filed at General Information Centers (GIC), set up under the responsibility of the Humanitarian Assistance Coordination Centers (HACC).

Supporting evidence, which is problematic given that arresting authorities rarely issue receipts, should back claims. The ICRC is not yet able to assess the efficiency of this compensation system although it has had the possibility to visit one of the GICs. There are nine GICs in the city of Baghdad and one in the city of Mosul, there are however none in the other parts of the country therefore depriving a large number of persons of the possibility to file complaints.

53. *In accordance with international legal provisions, the ICRC reminds the authorities of the CF that pillage is prohibited by International Humanitarian Law (Art. 33, Fourth Geneva Convention), that private property may not be confiscated (Art. 46.2, 1807 Hague Convention No. IV), and that an army of occupation can only take possession of cash, funds, and realizable securities which are strictly the property of the State (Art. 53, 1907 Hague Convention No. IV).*

In addition, persons deprived of their liberty shall be permitted to retain articles of personal use. Valuables may not be taken from them except in accordance with an established procedure and receipts must be issued (Art. 18, 68.2, Third Geneva Convention and Art. 97, Fourth Geneva Convention).

7. EXPOSURE OF INTERNEES/DETAINEES TO DANGEROUS TASKS

54. On 3 September 2003 in Camp Bucca, three persons deprived of their liberty were severely injured by the explosion of what apparently was a cluster bomb:

[name blacked out] (bilateral below-knee amputation)
[name blacked out] (bilateral above-knee amputation)
[name blacked out] (left above-knee amputation)

They were part of a group of 10 persons deprived of their liberty involved in voluntary work to clear rubbish along the barbed-wire fence of the camp. They were transferred to the British Field Military Hospital where they received appropriate medical treatment. Their injuries required limb amputations.

55. On 23 October 2003, the ICRC wrote to the officer commanding the 800th MP Brigade to request an investigation into the incident. The ICRC encouraged the CF not to engage persons deprived of their liberty in dangerous labour.

56. *The ICRC recommends to the authorities of the CF that all three victims be properly compensated as provided for by both Third and Fourth Geneva Conventions (Art. 68, Third Geneva Convention and Art. 95, Fourth Geneva Convention).*

8. PROTECTION OF PERSONS DEPRIVED OF THEIR LIBERTY AGAINST SHELLING

57. Since its reopening by the CF, Abu Ghraib prison has been the target of frequent night shelling by mortars and other weapons, which resulted, on several occasions, in persons deprived of their liberty being killed or injured. During the month of July, the Commander of the facility reported at least 25 such attacks. On 16 August, three mortar rounds landed in the prison compound, killing at least five and injuring 67 persons deprived of their liberty. Subsequent attacks caused further deaths and injuries. An ICRC team visited Abu Ghraib on 17 August and noticed the lack of protective measures: while the CF personnel were living in concrete buildings, all persons deprived of their liberty were sheltered under tents in compounds which had no bunkers or any other protection, rendering them totally vulnerable to shelling.

Persons deprived of their liberty alleged that they had not been advised on what to do to protect themselves in the event of shelling. They were dismayed and felt that the authorities "did not care." After these attacks, security was improved around the prison compound to reduce the risk of further attacks. However, steps taken to ensure the protection of persons deprived of their liberty remained insufficient. The inmates were allowed to fill and place sandbags around the perimeter of each tent. By late October, sandbags had not been placed around all tents and those sandbags that were in place did not offer adequate protection from shelling or projectile explosions.

58. *In accordance with International Humanitarian Law provisions, the* ICRC *reminds the authorities of the* CF *that the detaining power must not set up places of internment in areas particularly exposed to the dangers of war (Art. 23.1, Third Geneva Convention and Art. 83, Fourth Geneva Convention). In all places of internment exposed to air raids and other hazards of war, shelters adequate in number and structure to ensure the necessary protection must be made available. In the event of an alarm, the internees must be free to enter such shelters as quickly as possible (Art. 23.2, Third Geneva Convention and Art. 88, Fourth Geneva Convention). When a place of internment is found to be unsafe, persons deprived of their liberty should be transferred to other places of interment, offering adequate security and living conditions in accordance with the Third and Fourth Geneva Conventions.*

CONCLUSION

59. This ICRC report documents serious violations of International Humanitarian Law relating to the conditions of treatment of the persons deprived of their liberty held by the CF in Iraq. In particular, it establishes that persons deprived of their liberty face the risk of being subjected to a process of physical and psychological coercion, in some cases tantamount to torture, in the early stages of the internment process.

60. Once the interrogation process is over, the conditions of treatment for the persons deprived of their liberty generally improve, except in the "High Value Detainee" section at Baghdad International Airport where persons deprived of their liberty have been held for nearly 23 hours a day in strict solitary confinement in small concrete cells devoid of daylight, an internment regime which does not comply with provisions of the Third and Fourth Geneva Conventions.

61. During internment, persons deprived of their liberty also risk being victims of disproportionate and excessive use of force on the part of detaining authorities attempting to restore order in the event of unrest or to prevent escapes.

62. Another serious violation of International Humanitarian Law described in the report is the CF's inability or lack of will to set up a system of notifications of arrests for the families of persons deprived of liberty in Iraq. This violation of provisions of International Humanitarian Law causes immense distress among persons deprived of their liberty and their families, the latter fearing that their relatives unaccounted for are dead. The uncaring behaviour of the CF and their inability to quickly provide accurate information on persons deprived of their liberty for the families concerned also seriously affects the image of the Occupying Powers amongst the Iraqi population.

63. In addition to recommendations highlighted in the report relating to conditions of internment, information given to persons deprived of their liberty upon arrest, and the need to investigate violations of International Humanitarian Law and to prosecute those found responsible, the ICRC wishes particularly to remind the CF of their duty:

- to respect at all times the human dignity, physical integrity and cultural sensitivity of persons deprived of their liberty held under their control;
- to set up a system of notifications of arrests to ensure that the families persons deprived of their liberty are quickly and accurately informed;
- to prevent all forms of ill-treatment and moral or physical coercion of persons deprived of their liberty in connection with interrogations;
- to instruct the arresting and detaining authorities that causing serious bodily injury or serious harm to the health of protected persons is prohibited under the Third and Fourth Geneva Conventions;
- to set up an internment regime that ensures respect for the psychological integrity and human dignity of the persons deprived of their liberty;
- to ensure that battle group units arresting individuals and staff in charge of internment facilities receive adequate training enabling them to operate in a proper manner and fulfill their responsibilities without resorting to ill-treatment or using excessive force.

The practices described in this report are prohibited under International Humanitarian Law. They warrant serious attention by the CF. In particular, the CF should review their policies and practices, take corrective action and improve the treatment of prisoners of war and other protected persons under their authority. This report is part of the bilateral and confidential dialogue undertaken by the ICRC with the CF. In the future, the ICRC will continue its bilateral and confidential dialogue with the CF in accordance with provisions of International Humanitarian Law, on the basis of its monitoring of the conditions of arrest, interrogation and internment of persons deprived of their liberty held by the CF.

APPENDIX III

Investigation

WORKING TOWARD TRUTH

TO UNDERSTAND THE series of investigations into the events at Abu Ghraib, one might imagine a chain leading from the military police and military intelligence soldiers in the prison, up through their immediate superiors, through the senior commanders in Iraq, the Middle East, and finally Washington, up through the civilian leadership of the government by way of the secretary of defense to, finally, the President. As I write, each of the investigations that has been conducted—five major ones thus far, the reports of three of which are reprinted here—has examined a set of links. None has begun to look at the entire chain.

The first investigation began on January 13, 2004, four and a half months before the photographs were broadcast, after Specialist Joseph M. Darby handed over CDs containing hundreds of images of abuse to the Army's Criminal Investigation Command (CID) and officers of that command began interviewing Iraqis and Americans. Two weeks later, on January 31, Major General Antonio M. Taguba was appointed to conduct an investigation into the activities of the 800th Military Police Brigade. Major General Taguba submitted the findings of his investigation to his superior officers in early March. On May 1 Seymour M. Hersh, in an article in *The New Yorker*, reported on and quoted from Taguba's investigation.

On April 15—after producers at CBS News had acquired the photographs, but before they broadcast them, having delayed doing so at the request of the Chairman of the Joint Chiefs of Staff—Major General George R. Fay was appointed to conduct an investigation into the activities of military intelligence at Abu Ghraib. In June, Lieutenant General Anthony R. Jones was appointed over Major General Fay, allowing, among other things, interviews to be conducted with officers outranking Fay, notably with Lieutenant General Ricardo Sanchez, the commander in Iraq.

On May 12, Secretary of Defense Donald Rumsfeld appointed one of his predecessors, former secretary of defense James R. Schlesinger, to head an "Independent Panel... to review Department of Defense investigations on detention operations whether completed or ongoing"—in effect, an investigation of the investigations. Schlesinger's panel included another former secretary of defense, Harold Brown, a former Republican congresswoman from Florida, Tillie K. Fowler, and a retired Air Force officer, General Charles A. Horner.

Included here in full are the Taguba, Jones/Fay, and Schlesinger reports, investigating, respectively, the activities of the military police, the activities of military intelligence, and, in effect, the state of the investigations into detention operations. (Note that the Fay report includes sections not released to the public, and published here for the first time; they are printed in italic type.) As I write, at least four more investigations are ongoing. Reading these reports, one gathers a great deal of information about the particular links in the chain of decisions and responsibility that led to Abu Ghraib. One has only intimations of the entire chain.

—MD

Appendix III: Investigation—Working Toward Truth

ARTICLE 15-6 INVESTIGATION OF THE 800TH MILITARY POLICE BRIGADE (THE TAGUBA REPORT)

TABLE OF CONTENTS

References

1. Geneva Convention Relative to the Treatment of Prisoners of War, 12 August 1949
2. Geneva Convention for the Amelioration of the Condition of the Wounded and Sick in the Armed Forces in the Field, 12 August 1949
3. Geneva Convention for the Amelioration of the Condition of the Wounded, Sick and Shipwrecked Members of Armed Forces at Sea, 12 August 1949
4. Geneva Convention Protocol Relative to the Status of Refugees, 1967
5. Geneva Convention Relative to the Status of Refugees, 1951
6. Geneva Convention for the Protection of War Victims, 12 August 1949
7. Geneva Convention Relative to the Protection of Civilian Persons in Time of War, 12 August 1949
8. DOD Directive 5100.69, "DOD Program for Prisoners of War and other Detainees," 27 December 1972
9. DOD Directive 5100.77 "DOD Law of War Program," 10 July 1979
10. STANAG No. 2044, Procedures for Dealing with Prisoners of War (PW) (Edition 5), 28 June 1994
11. STANAG No. 2033, Interrogation of Prisoners of War (PW) (Edition 6), 6 December 1994
12. AR 190-8, Enemy Prisoners of War, Retained Personnel, Civilian Internees, and Other Detainees, 1 October 1997
13. AR 190-47, The Army Corrections System, 15 August 1996
14. AR 190-14, Carrying of Firearms and Use of Force for Law Enforcement and Security Duties, 12 March 1993
15. AR 195-5, Evidence Procedures, 28 August 1992
16. AR 190-11, Physical Security of Arms, Ammunition and Explosives, 12 February 1998
17. AR 190-12, Military Police Working Dogs, 30 September 1993
18. AR 190-13, The Army Physical Security Program, 30 September 1993
19. AR 380-67, Personnel Security Program, 9 September 1988
20. AR 380-5, Department of the Army Information Security, 31 September 2000
21. AR 670-1, Wear and Appearance of Army Uniforms and Insignia, 5 September 2003
22. AR 190-40, Serious Incident Report, 30 November 1993
23. AR 15-6, Procedures for Investigating Officers and Boards of Officers, 11 May 1988
24. AR 27-10, Military Justice, 6 September 2002
25. AR 635-200, Enlisted Personnel, 1 November 2000
26. AR 600-8-24, Officer Transfers and Discharges, 29 June 2002
27. AR 500-5, Army Mobilization, 6 July 1996
28. AR 600-20, Army Command Policy, 13 May 2002

29. AR 623-105, Officer Evaluation Reports, 1 April 1998

30. AR 175-9, Contractors Accompanying the Force, 29 October 1999

31. FM 3-19.40, Military Police Internment/Resettlement Operations, 1 August 2001

32. FM 3-19.1, Military Police Operations, 22 March 2001

33. FM 3-19.4, Military Police Leaders' Handbook, 4 March 2002

34. FM 3-05.30, Psychological Operations, 19 June 2000

35. FM 33-1-1, Psychological Operations Techniques and Procedures, 5 May 1994

36. FM 34-52, Intelligence Interrogation, 28 September 1992

37. FM 19-15, Civil Disturbances, 25 November 1985

38. FM 3-0, Operations, 14 June 2001

39. FM 101-5, Staff Organizations and Functions, 23 May 1984

40. FM 3-19.30, Physical Security, 8 January 2001

41. FM 3-21.5, Drill and Ceremonies, 7 July 2003

42. ARTEP 19-546-30 MTP, Mission Training Plan for Military Police Battalion (IR)

43. ARTEP 19-667-30 MTP, Mission Training Plan for Military Police Guard Company

44. ARTEP 19-647-30 MTP, Mission Training Plan for Military Police Escort Guard Company

45. STP 19-95B1-SM, Soldier's Manual, MOS 95B, Military Police, Skill Level 1, 6 August 2002

46. STP 19-95C14-SM-TG, Soldier's Manual and Trainer's Guide for MOS 95C Internment/Resettlement Specialist, Skill Levels 1/2/3/4, 26 March 1999

47. STP 19-95C1-SM MOS 95C, Corrections Specialist, Skill Level 1, Soldier's Manual, 30 September 2003

48. STP 19-95C24-SM-TG MOS 95C, Corrections Specialist, Skill Levels 2/3/4, Soldier's Manual and Trainer's Guide, 30 September 2003

49. Assessment of DOD Counter-Terrorism Interrogation and Detention Operations in Iraq, (MG Geoffrey D. Miller, Commander JTF-GTMO, Guantanamo Bay, Cuba), 9 September 2003

50. Assessment of Detention and Corrections Operations in Iraq, (MG Donald J. Ryder, Provost Marshal General), 6 November 2003

51. CJTF-7 FRAGO #1108, Subject: *includes*- para 3.C.8 & 3.C.8.A.1, Assignment of 205 MI BDE CDR Responsibilities for the Baghdad Central Confinement Facility (BCCF), 19 November 2003

52. CJTF-7 FRAGO #749, Subject: Intelligence and Evidence-Led Detention Operations Relating to Detainees, 24 August 2003

53. 800th MP BDE FRAGO # 89, Subject: Rules of Engagement, 26 December 2003

54. CG CJTF-7 Memo: CJTF-7 Interrogation and Counter-Resistance Policy, 12 October 2003

55. CG CJTF-7 Memo: Dignity and Respect While Conducting Operations, 13 December 2003

56. Uniform Code of Military Justice and Manual for Courts Martial, 2002 Edition

ARTICLE 15-6 INVESTIGATION OF
THE 800th MILITARY POLICE BRIGADE

BACKGROUND

1. (U) On 19 January 2004, Lieutenant General (LTG) Ricardo S. Sanchez, Commander, Combined Joint Task Force Seven (CJTF-7) requested that the Commander, US Central Command, appoint an Investigating Officer (IO) in the grade of Major General (MG) or above to investigate the conduct of operations within the 800th Military Police (MP) Brigade. LTG Sanchez requested an investigation of detention and internment operations by the Brigade from 1 November 2003 to present. LTG Sanchez cited recent reports of detainee abuse, escapes from confinement facilities, and accountability lapses, which indicated systemic problems within the brigade and suggested a lack of clear standards, proficiency, and leadership. LTG Sanchez requested a comprehensive and all-encompassing inquiry to make findings and recommendations concerning the fitness and performance of the 800th MP Brigade. (ANNEX 2)

2. (U) On 24 January 2003, the Chief of Staff of US Central Command (CENTCOM), MG R. Steven Whitcomb, on behalf of the CENTCOM Commander, directed that the Commander, Coalition Forces Land Component Command (CFLCC), LTG David D. McKiernan, conduct an investigation into the 800th MP Brigade's detention and internment operations from 1 November 2003 to present. CENTCOM directed that the investigation should inquire into all facts and circumstances surrounding recent reports of suspected detainee abuse in Iraq. It also directed that the investigation inquire into detainee escapes and accountability lapses as reported by CJTF-7, and to gain a more comprehensive and all-encompassing inquiry into the fitness and performance of the 800th MP Brigade. (ANNEX 3)

3. (U) On 31 January 2004, the Commander, CFLCC, appointed MG Antonio M. Taguba, Deputy Commanding General Support, CFLCC, to conduct this investigation. MG Taguba was directed to conduct an informal investigation under AR 15-6 into the 800th MP Brigade's detention and internment operations. Specifically, MG Taguba was tasked to:

   a. (U) Inquire into all the facts and circumstances surrounding recent allegations of detainee abuse, specifically allegations of maltreatment at the Abu Ghraib Prison (Baghdad Central Confinement Facility (BCCF));

   b. (U) Inquire into detainee escapes and accountability lapses as reported by CJTF-7, specifically allegations concerning these events at the Abu Ghraib Prison;

c. (U) Investigate the training, standards, employment, command policies, internal procedures, and command climate in the 800th MP Brigade, as appropriate;

d. (U) Make specific findings of fact concerning all aspects of the investigation, and make any recommendations for corrective action, as appropriate. (ANNEX 4)

4. (U) LTG Sanchez's request to investigate the 800th MP Brigade followed the initiation of a criminal investigation by the US Army Criminal Investigation Command (USACIDC) into specific allegations of detainee abuse committed by members of the 372nd MP Company, 320th MP Battalion in Iraq. These units are part of the 800th MP Brigade. The Brigade is an Iraq Theater asset, TACON to CJTF-7, but OPCON to CFLCC at the time this investigation was initiated. In addition, CJTF-7 had several reports of detainee escapes from US/Coalition Confinement Facilities in Iraq over the past several months. These include Camp Bucca, Camp Ashraf, Abu Ghraib, and the High Value Detainee (HVD) Complex/Camp Cropper. The 800th MP Brigade operated these facilities. In addition, four Soldiers from the 320th MP Battalion had been formally charged under the Uniform Code of Military Justice (UCMJ) with detainee abuse in May 2003 at the Theater Internment Facility (TIF) at Camp Bucca, Iraq. (ANNEXES 5–18, 34 and 35)

5. (U) I began assembling my investigation team prior to the actual appointment by the CFLCC Commander. I assembled subject matter experts from the CFLCC Provost Marshal (PM) and the CFLCC Staff Judge Advocate (SJA). I selected COL Kinard J. La Fate, CFLCC Provost Marshal to be my Deputy for this investigation. I also contacted the Provost Marshal General of the Army, MG Donald J. Ryder, to enlist the support of MP subject matter experts in the areas of detention and internment operations. (ANNEXES 4 and 19)

6. (U) The Investigating Team also reviewed the Assessment of DoD Counter-Terrorism Interrogation and Detention Operations in Iraq conducted by MG Geoffrey D. Miller, Commander, Joint Task Force Guantanamo (JTF-GTMO). From 31 August to 9 September 2003, MG Miller led a team of personnel experienced in strategic interrogation to HQ, CJTF-7 and the Iraqi Survey Group (ISG) to review current Iraqi Theater ability to rapidly exploit internees for actionable intelligence. MG Miller's team focused on three areas: intelligence integration, synchronization, and fusion; interrogation operations; and detention operations. MG Miller's team used JTF-GTMO procedures and interrogation authorities as baselines. (ANNEX 20)

7. (U) The Investigating Team began its inquiry with an in-depth analysis of the Report on Detention and Corrections in Iraq, dated 5 November 2003, conducted

by MG Ryder and a team of military police, legal, medical, and automation experts. The CJTF-7 Commander, LTG Sanchez, had previously requested a team of subject matter experts to assess, and make specific recommendations concerning detention and corrections operations. From 13 October to 6 November 2003, MG Ryder personally led this assessment/assistance team in Iraq. (ANNEX 19)

ASSESSMENT OF DoD COUNTER-TERRORISM INTERROGATION AND DETENTION OPERATIONS IN IRAQ (MG MILLER'S ASSESSMENT)

1. (S/NF) The principal focus of MG Miller's team was on the strategic interrogation of detainees/internees in Iraq. Among its conclusions in its Executive Summary were that CJTF-7 did not have authorities and procedures in place to affect a unified strategy to detain, interrogate, and report information from detainees/internees in Iraq. The Executive Summary also stated that detention operations must act as an enabler for interrogation. (ANNEX 20)

2. (S/NF) With respect to interrogation, MG Miller's Team recommended that CJTF-7 dedicate and train a detention guard force subordinate to the Joint Interrogation Debriefing Center (JIDC) Commander that "sets the conditions for the successful interrogation and exploitation of internees/detainees." Regarding Detention Operations, MG Miller's team stated that the function of Detention Operations is to provide a safe, secure, and humane environment that supports the expeditious collection of intelligence. However, it also stated "it is essential that the guard force be actively engaged in setting the conditions for successful exploitation of the internees." (ANNEX 20)

3. (S/NF) MG Miller's team also concluded that Joint Strategic Interrogation Operations (within CJTF-7) are hampered by lack of active control of the internees within the detention environment. The Miller Team also stated that establishment of the Theater Joint Interrogation and Detention Center (JIDC) at Abu Ghraib (BCCF) will consolidate both detention and strategic interrogation operations and result in synergy between MP and MI resources and an integrated, synchronized, and focused strategic interrogation effort. (ANNEX 20)

4. (S/NF) MG Miller's team also observed that the application of emerging strategic interrogation strategies and techniques contain new approaches and operational art. The Miller Team also concluded that a legal review and recommendations on internee interrogation operations by a dedicated Command Judge Advocate is required to maximize interrogation effectiveness. (ANNEX 20)

IO COMMENTS ON MG MILLER'S ASSESSMENT

1. (S/NF) MG Miller's team recognized that they were using JTF-GTMO operational procedures and interrogation authorities as baselines for its observations and recommendations. There is a strong argument that the intelligence value of detainees held at JTF-Guantanamo (GTMO) is different than that of the detainees/internees held at Abu Ghraib (BCCF) and other detention facilities in Iraq. Currently, there are a large number of Iraqi criminals held at Abu Ghraib (BCCF). These are not believed to be international terrorists or members of Al Qaida, Anser Al Islam, Taliban, and other international terrorist organizations. (ANNEX 20)

2. (S/NF) The recommendations of MG Miller's team that the "guard force" be actively engaged in setting the conditions for successful exploitation of the internees would appear to be in conflict with the recommendations of MG Ryder's Team and AR 190-8 that military police "do not participate in military intelligence supervised interrogation sessions." The Ryder Report concluded that the OEF template whereby military police actively set the favorable conditions for subsequent interviews runs counter to the smooth operation of a detention facility. (ANNEX 20)

REPORT ON DETENTION AND CORRECTIONS
IN IRAQ (MG RYDER'S REPORT)

1. (U) MG Ryder and his assessment team conducted a comprehensive review of the entire detainee and corrections system in Iraq and provided recommendations addressing each of the following areas as requested by the Commander CJTF-7:

   a. (U) Detainee and corrections system management
   b. (U) Detainee management, including detainee movement, segregation, and accountability
   c. (U) Means of command and control of the detention and corrections system
   d. (U) Integration of military detention and corrections with the Coalition Provisional Authority (CPA) and adequacy of plans for transition to an Iraqi-run corrections system
   e. (U) Detainee medical care and health management
   f. (U) Detention facilities that meet required health, hygiene, and sanitation standards
   g. (U) Court integration and docket management for criminal detainees
   h. (U) Detainee legal processing
   i. (U) Detainee databases and records, including integration with law enforcement and court databases (ANNEX 19)

2. (U) Many of the findings and recommendations of MG Ryder's team are beyond the scope of this investigation. However, several important findings are clearly relevant to this inquiry and are summarized below (emphasis is added in certain areas):

A. (U) *Detainee Management (including movement, segregation, and accountability)*

1. (U) There is a wide variance in standards and approaches at the various detention facilities. Several Division/Brigade collection points and US monitored Iraqi prisons had flawed or insufficiently detailed use of force and other standing operating procedures or policies (e.g. weapons in the facility, improper restraint techniques, detainee management, etc.) *Though, there were no military police units purposely applying inappropriate confinement practices.* (ANNEX 19)

2. (U) Currently, due to lack of adequate Iraqi facilities, Iraqi criminals (generally Iraqi-on-Iraqi crimes) are detained with security internees (generally Iraqi-on-Coalition offenses) and EPWs in the same facilities, though segregated in different cells/compounds. (ANNEX 19)

3. (U) The management of multiple disparate groups of detained people in a single location by members of the same unit invites confusion about handling, processing, and treatment, and typically facilitates the transfer of information between different categories of detainees. (ANNEX 19)

4. (U) The 800th MP (I/R) units did not receive Internment/Resettlement (I/R) and corrections specific training during their mobilization period. Corrections training is only on the METL of two MP (I/R) Confinement Battalions throughout the Army, one currently serving in Afghanistan, and elements of the other are at Camp Arifjan, Kuwait. MP units supporting JTF-GTMO received ten days of training in detention facility operations, to include two days of unarmed self-defense, training in interpersonal communication skills, forced cell moves, and correctional officer safety. (ANNEX 19)

B. (U) *Means of Command and Control of the Detention and Corrections System*

1. (U) The 800th MP Brigade was originally task organized with eight MP(I/R) Battalions consisting of both MP Guard and Combat Support companies. Due to force rotation plans, the 800th redeployed two Battalion HHCs in December 2003, the 115th MP Battalion and the 324th MP Battalion. In December 2003, the 400th MP Battalion was relieved of its mission and redeployed in January 2004. The 724th MP Battalion redeployed on 11 February 2004 and the remainder is scheduled to redeploy in March and April 2004. They are the

310th MP Battalion, 320th MP Battalion, 530th MP Battalion, and 744th MP Battalion. The units that remain are generally understrength, as Reserve Component units do not have an individual personnel replacement system to mitigate medical losses or the departure of individual Soldiers that have reached 24 months of Federal active duty in a five-year period. (ANNEX 19)

2. (U) The 800th MP Brigade (I/R) is currently a CFLCC asset, TACON to CJTF-7 to conduct Internment/Resettlement (I/R) operations in Iraq. All detention operations are conducted in the CJTF-7 AO; Camps Ganci, Vigilant, Bucca, TSP Whitford, and a separate High Value Detention (HVD) site. (ANNEX 19)

3. (U) The 800th MP Brigade has experienced challenges adapting its task organizational structure, training, and equipment resources from a unit designed to conduct standard EPW operations in the COMMZ (Kuwait). Further, the doctrinally trained MP Soldier-to-detainee population ratio and facility layout templates are predicated on a compliant, self-disciplining EPW population, and not criminals or high-risk security internees. (ANNEX 19)

4. (U) EPWs and Civilian Internees should receive the full protections of the Geneva Conventions, unless the denial of these protections is due to specifically articulated military necessity (e.g., no visitation to preclude the direction of insurgency operations). (ANNEXES 19 and 24)

5. (U) AR 190-8, *Enemy Prisoners of War, Retained Personnel, Civilian Internees, and other Detainees*, FM 3-19.40, *Military Police Internment and Resettlement Operations*, and FM 34-52, *Intelligence Interrogations*, require military police to provide an area for intelligence collection efforts within EPW facilities. Military Police, though adept at passive collection of intelligence within a facility, do not participate in Military Intelligence supervised interrogation sessions. Recent intelligence collection in support of Operation Enduring Freedom posited a template whereby military police actively set favorable conditions for subsequent interviews. Such actions generally run counter to the smooth operation of a detention facility, attempting to maintain its population in a compliant and docile state. *The 800th MP Brigade has not been directed to change its facility procedures to set the conditions for MI interrogations, nor participate in those interrogations.* (ANNEXES 19 and 21-23)

6. MG Ryder's Report also made the following, inter alia, near-term and mid-term recommendations regarding the command and control of detainees:

    a. (U) Align the release process for security internees with DoD Policy. The process of screening security internees should include intelligence findings, interrogation results, and current threat assessment.

b. (U) Determine the scope of intelligence collection that will occur at Camp Vigilant. Refurbish the Northeast Compound to separate the screening operation from the Iraqi run Baghdad Central Correctional Facility. *Establish procedures that define the role of military police Soldiers securing the compound, clearly separating the actions of the guards from those of the military intelligence personnel.*

c. (U) Consolidate all Security Internee Operations, except the MEK security mission, under a single Military Police Brigade Headquarters for OIF 2.

d. (U) *Insist that all units identified to rotate into the Iraqi Theater of Operations (ITO) to conduct internment and confinement operations in support of OIF 2 be organic to CJTF-7.* (ANNEX 19)

IO COMMENTS REGARDING MG RYDER'S REPORT

1. (U) The objective of MG Ryder's Team was to observe detention and prison operations, identify potential systemic and human rights issues, and provide near-term, mid-term, and long-term recommendations to improve CJTF-7 operations and transition of the Iraqi prison system from US military control/oversight to the Coalition Provisional Authority and eventually to the Iraqi Government. The Findings and Recommendations of MG Ryder's Team are thorough and precise and should be implemented immediately. (ANNEX 19)

2. (U) Unfortunately, many of the systemic problems that surfaced during MG Ryder's Team's assessment are the very same issues that are the subject of this investigation. In fact, many of the abuses suffered by detainees occurred during, or near to, the time of that assessment. As will be pointed out in detail in subsequent portions of this report, I disagree with the conclusion of MG Ryder's Team in one critical aspect, that being its conclusion that the 800th MP Brigade had not been asked to change its facility procedures to set the conditions for MI interviews. While clearly the 800th MP Brigade and its commanders were not tasked to set conditions for detainees for subsequent MI interrogations, it is obvious from a review of comprehensive CID interviews of suspects and witnesses that this was done at lower levels. (ANNEX 19)

3. (U) I concur fully with MG Ryder's conclusion regarding the effect of AR 190-8. Military Police, though adept at passive collection of intelligence within a facility, should not participate in Military Intelligence supervised interrogation sessions. Moreover, Military Police should not be involved with setting "favorable conditions" for subsequent interviews. These actions, as will be outlined in this investigation, clearly run counter to the smooth operation of a detention facility. (ANNEX 19)

PRELIMINARY INVESTIGATIVE ACTIONS

1. (U) Following our review of MG Ryder's Report and MG Miller's Report, my investigation team immediately began an in-depth review of all available documents regarding the 800th MP Brigade. We reviewed in detail the voluminous CID investigation regarding alleged detainee abuses at detention facilities in Iraq, particularly the Abu Ghraib (BCCF) Detention Facility. We analyzed approximately fifty witness statements from military police and military intelligence personnel, potential suspects, and detainees. We reviewed numerous photos and videos of actual detainee abuse taken by detention facility personnel, which are now in the custody and control of the US Army Criminal Investigation Command and the CJTF-7 prosecution team. The photos and videos are not contained in this investigation. We obtained copies of the 800th MP Brigade roster, rating chain, and assorted internal investigations and disciplinary actions involving that command for the past several months. (All ANNEXES Reviewed by Investigation Team)

2. (U) In addition to military police and legal officers from the CFLCC PMO and SJA Offices we also obtained the services of two individuals who are experts in military police detention practices and training. These were LTC Timothy Weathersbee, Commander, 705th MP Battalion, United States Disciplinary Barracks, Fort Leavenworth, and SFC Edward Baldwin, Senior Corrections Advisor, US Army Military Police School, Fort Leonard Wood. I also requested and received the services of Col (Dr) Henry Nelson, a trained US Air Force psychiatrist assigned to assist my investigation team. (ANNEX 4)

3. (U) In addition to MG Ryder's and MG Miller's Reports, the team reviewed numerous reference materials including the 12 October 2003 CJTF-7 Interrogation and Counter-Resistance Policy, the AR 15-6 Investigation on Riot and Shootings at Abu Ghraib on 24 November 2003, the 205th MI Brigade's Interrogation Rules of Engagement (IROE), facility staff logs/journals and numerous records of AR 15-6 investigations and Serious Incident Reports (SIRs) on detainee escapes/shootings and disciplinary matters from the 800th MP Brigade. (ANNEXES 5–20, 37, 93, and 94)

4. (U) On 2 February 2004, I took my team to Baghdad for a one-day inspection of the Abu Ghraib Prison (BCCF) and the High Value Detainee (HVD) Complex in order to become familiar with those facilities. We also met with COL Jerry Mocello, Commander, 3rd MP Criminal Investigation Group (CID), COL Dave Quantock, Commander, 16th MP Brigade, COL Dave Phillips, Commander, 89th MP Brigade, and COL Ed Sannwaldt, CJTF-7 Provost Marshal. On 7 February 2004, the team visited the Camp Bucca Detention Facility to familiarize itself with the facility and operating structure. In addition, on 6 and 7 February 2004, at Camp Doha, Kuwait, we conducted extensive training sessions on approved detention

practices. We continued our preparation by reviewing the ongoing CID investigation and were briefed by the Special Agent in Charge, CW2 Paul Arthur. We refreshed ourselves on the applicable reference materials within each team member's area of expertise, and practiced investigative techniques. I met with the team on numerous occasions to finalize appropriate witness lists, review existing witness statements, arrange logistics, and collect potential evidence. We also coordinated with CJTF-7 to arrange witness attendance, force protection measures, and general logistics for the team's move to Baghdad on 8 February 2004. (ANNEXES 4 and 25)

5. (U) At the same time, due to the Transfer of Authority on 1 February 2004 between III Corps and V Corps, and the upcoming demobilization of the 800th MP Brigade Command, I directed that several critical witnesses who were preparing to leave the theater remain at Camp Arifjan, Kuwait until they could be interviewed (ANNEX 29). My team deployed to Baghdad on 8 February 2004 and conducted a series of interviews with a variety of witnesses (ANNEX 30). We returned to Camp Doha, Kuwait on 13 February 2004. On 14 and 15 February we interviewed a number of witnesses from the 800th MP Brigade. On 17 February we returned to Camp Bucca, Iraq to complete interviews of witnesses at that location. From 18 February thru 28 February we collected documents, compiled references, did follow-up interviews, and completed a detailed analysis of the volumes of materials accumulated throughout our investigation. On 29 February we finalized our executive summary and out-briefing slides. On 9 March we submitted the AR 15-6 written report with findings and recommendations to the CFLCC Deputy SJA, LTC Mark Johnson, for a legal sufficiency review. The out-brief to the appointing authority, LTG McKiernan, took place on 3 March 2004. (ANNEXES 26 and 45–91)

FINDINGS AND RECOMMENDATIONS

(PART ONE)

(U) The investigation should inquire into all of the facts and circumstances surrounding recent allegations of detainee abuse, specifically, allegations of maltreatment at the Abu Ghraib Prison (Baghdad Central Confinement Facility).

1. (U) The US Army Criminal Investigation Command (CID), led by COL Jerry Mocello, and a team of highly trained professional agents have done a superb job of investigating several complex and extremely disturbing incidents of detainee abuse at the Abu Ghraib Prison. They conducted over 50 interviews of witnesses, potential criminal suspects, and detainees. They also uncovered numerous photos and videos portraying in graphic detail detainee abuse by Military Police personnel on numerous occasions from October to December 2003. Several potential suspects rendered full and complete confessions regarding their personal involvement and

the involvement of fellow Soldiers in this abuse. Several potential suspects invoked their rights under Article 31 of the Uniform Code of Military Justice (UCMJ) and the 5th Amendment of the U.S. Constitution. (ANNEX 25)

2. (U) In addition to a comprehensive and exhaustive review of all of these statements and documentary evidence, we also interviewed numerous officers, NCOs, and junior enlisted Soldiers in the 800th MP Brigade, as well as members of the 205th Military Intelligence Brigade working at the prison. We did not believe it was necessary to re-interview all the numerous witnesses who had previously provided comprehensive statements to CID, and I have adopted those statements for the purposes of this investigation. (ANNEXES 26, 34, 35, and 45–91)

REGARDING PART ONE OF THE INVESTIGATION, I MAKE THE FOLLOWING SPECIFIC FINDINGS OF FACT:

1. (U) That Forward Operating Base (FOB) Abu Ghraib (BCCF) provides security of both criminal and security detainees at the Baghdad Central Correctional Facility, facilitates the conducting of interrogations for CJTF-7, supports other CPA operations at the prison, and enhances the force protection/quality of life of Soldiers assigned in order to ensure the success of ongoing operations to secure a free Iraq. (ANNEX 31)

2. (U) That the Commander, 205th Military Intelligence Brigade, was designated by CJTF-7 as the Commander of FOB Abu Ghraib (BCCF) effective 19 November 2003. That the 205th MI Brigade conducts operational and strategic interrogations for CJTF-7. That from 19 November 2003 until Transfer of Authority (TOA) on 6 February 2004, COL Thomas M. Pappas was the Commander of the 205th MI Brigade and the Commander of FOB Abu Ghraib (BCCF). (ANNEX 31)

3. (U) That the 320th Military Police Battalion of the 800th MP Brigade is responsible for the Guard Force at Camp Ganci, Camp Vigilant, & Cellblock 1 of FOB Abu Ghraib (BCCF). That from February 2003 to until he was suspended from his duties on 17 January 2004, LTC Jerry Phillabaum served as the Battalion Commander of the 320th MP Battalion. That from December 2002 until he was suspended from his duties, on 17 January 2004, CPT Donald Reese served as the Company Commander of the 372nd MP Company, which was in charge of guarding detainees at FOB Abu Ghraib. I further find that both the 320th MP Battalion and the 372nd MP Company were located within the confines of FOB Abu Ghraib. (ANNEXES 32 and 45)

4. (U) That from July of 2003 to the present, BG Janis L. Karpinski was the Commander of the 800th MP Brigade. (ANNEX 45)

5. (S) That between October and December 2003, at the Abu Ghraib Confinement Facility (BCCF), numerous incidents of sadistic, blatant, and wanton criminal abuses were inflicted on several detainees. This systemic and illegal abuse of detainees was intentionally perpetrated by several members of the military police guard force (372nd Military Police Company, 320th Military Police Battalion, 800th MP Brigade), in Tier (section) 1-A of the Abu Ghraib Prison (BCCF). The allegations of abuse were substantiated by detailed witness statements (ANNEX 26) and the discovery of extremely graphic photographic evidence. Due to the extremely sensitive nature of these photographs and videos, the ongoing CID investigation, and the potential for the criminal prosecution of several suspects, the photographic evidence is not included in the body of my investigation. The pictures and videos are available from the Criminal Investigative Command and the CTJF-7 prosecution team. In addition to the aforementioned crimes, there were also abuses committed by members of the 325th MI Battalion, 205th MI Brigade, and Joint Interrogation and Debriefing Center (JIDC). Specifically, on 24 November 2003, SPC Luciana Spencer, 205th MI Brigade, sought to degrade a detainee by having him strip and returned to cell naked. (ANNEXES 26 and 53)

6. (S) I find that the intentional abuse of detainees by military police personnel included the following acts:

   a. (S) Punching, slapping, and kicking detainees; jumping on their naked feet;
   b. (S) Videotaping and photographing naked male and female detainees;
   c. (S) Forcibly arranging detainees in various sexually explicit positions for photographing;
   d. (S) Forcing detainees to remove their clothing and keeping them naked for several days at a time;
   e. (S) Forcing naked male detainees to wear women's underwear;
   f. (S) Forcing groups of male detainees to masturbate themselves while being photographed and videotaped;
   g. (S) Arranging naked male detainees in a pile and then jumping on them;
   h. (S) Positioning a naked detainee on a MRE Box, with a sandbag on his head, and attaching wires to his fingers, toes, and penis to simulate electric torture;
   i. (S) Writing "I am a Rapest" (sic) on the leg of a detainee alleged to have forcibly raped a 15-year old fellow detainee, and then photographing him naked;
   j. (S) Placing a dog chain or strap around a naked detainee's neck and having a female Soldier pose for a picture;
   k. (S) A male MP guard having sex with a female detainee;
   l. (S) Using military working dogs (without muzzles) to intimidate and frighten detainees, and in at least one case biting and severely injuring a detainee;
   m. (S) Taking photographs of dead Iraqi detainees. (ANNEXES 25 and 26)

7. (U) These findings are amply supported by written confessions provided by several

of the suspects, written statements provided by detainees, and witness statements. In reaching my findings, I have carefully considered the pre-existing statements of the following witnesses and suspects (ANNEX 26):

a. (U) SPC Jeremy Sivits, 372nd MP Company - Suspect
b. (U) SPC Sabrina Harman, 372nd MP Company – Suspect
c. (U) SGT Javal S. Davis, 372nd MP Company - Suspect
c. (U) PFC Lynndie R. England, 372nd MP Company - Suspect
d. (U) Adel Nakhla, Civilian Translator, Titan Corp., Assigned to the 205th MI Brigade - Suspect
e. (U) SPC Joseph M. Darby, 372nd MP Company
f. (U) SGT Neil A. Wallin, 109th Area Support Medical Battalion
g. (U) SGT Samuel Jefferson Provance, 302nd MI Battalion
h. (U) Torin S. Nelson, Contractor, Titan Corp., Assigned to the 205th MI Brigade
j. (U) CPL Matthew Scott Bolanger, 372nd MP Company
k. (U) SPC Mathew C. Wisdom, 372nd MP Company
l. (U) SSG Reuben R. Layton, Medic, 109th Medical Detachment
m. (U) SPC John V. Polak, 229th MP Company

8. (U) In addition, several detainees also described the following acts of abuse, which under the circumstances, I find credible based on the clarity of their statements and supporting evidence provided by other witnesses (ANNEX 26):

a. (U) Breaking chemical lights and pouring the phosphoric liquid on detainees;
b. (U) Threatening detainees with a charged 9mm pistol;
c. (U) Pouring cold water on naked detainees;
d. (U) Beating detainees with a broom handle and a chair;
e. (U) Threatening male detainees with rape;
f. (U) Allowing a military police guard to stitch the wound of a detainee who was injured after being slammed against the wall in his cell;
g. (U) Sodomizing a detainee with a chemical light and perhaps a broom stick.
h. (U) Using military working dogs to frighten and intimidate detainees with threats of attack, and in one instance actually biting a detainee.

9. (U) I have carefully considered the statements provided by the following detainees, which under the circumstances I find credible based on the clarity of their statements and supporting evidence provided by other witnesses:

a. (U) Amjed Isail Waleed, Detainee # 151365
b. (U) Hiadar Saber Abed Miktub-Aboodi, Detainee # 13077
c. (U) Huessin Mohssein Al-Zayiadi, Detainee # 19446
d. (U) Kasim Mehaddi Hilas, Detainee # 151108

  e. (U) Mohanded Juma Juma (sic), Detainee # 152307

  f. (U) Mustafa Jassim Mustafa, Detainee # 150542

  g. (U) Shalan Said Alsharoni, Detainee, # 150422

  h. (U) Abd Alwhab Youss, Detainee # 150425

  i. (U) Asad Hamza Hanfosh, Detainee # 152529

  j. (U) Nori Samir Gunbar Al-Yasseri, Detainee # 7787

  k. (U) Thaar Salman Dawod, Detainee # 150427

  l. (U) Ameen Sa'eed Al-Sheikh, Detainee # 151362

  m. (U) Abdou Hussain Saad Faleh, Detainee # 18470 (ANNEX 26)

10. (U) I find that contrary to the provision of AR 190-8, and the findings found in MG Ryder's Report, Military Intelligence (MI) interrogators and Other US Government Agency's (OGA) interrogators actively requested that MP guards set physical and mental conditions for favorable interrogation of witnesses. Contrary to the findings of MG Ryder's Report, I find that personnel assigned to the 372nd MP Company, 800th MP Brigade were directed to change facility procedures to "set the conditions" for MI interrogations. I find no direct evidence that MP personnel actually participated in those MI interrogations. (ANNEXES 19, 21, 25, and 26).

11. (U) I reach this finding based on the actual proven abuse that I find was inflicted on detainees and by the following witness statements. (ANNEXES 25 and 26):

  a. (U) *SPC Sabrina Harman, 372nd MP Company*, stated in her sworn statement regarding the incident where a detainee was placed on a box with wires attached to his fingers, toes, and penis, "that her job was to keep detainees awake." She stated that MI was talking to CPL Grainer. She stated: "MI wanted to get them to talk. It is Grainer and Frederick's job to do things for MI and OGA to get these people to talk."

  b. (U) *SGT Javal S. Davis, 372nd MP Company*, stated in his sworn statement as follows: "I witnessed prisoners in the MI hold section, wing 1A being made to do various things that I would question morally. In Wing 1A we were told that they had different rules and different SOP for treatment. I never saw a set of rules or SOP for that section just word of mouth. The Soldier in charge of 1A was Corporal Granier. He stated that the Agents and MI Soldiers would ask him to do things, but nothing was ever in writing he would complain (sic)." When asked why the rules in 1A/1B were different than the rest of the wings, SGT Davis stated: "The rest of the wings are regular prisoners and 1A/B are Military Intelligence (MI) holds." When asked why he did not inform his chain of command about this abuse, SGT Davis stated: "Because I assumed that if they were doing things out of the ordinary or outside the guidelines, someone would have said something. Also the wing belongs to MI and it appeared MI personnel approved of the abuse." SGT Davis also stated that he had heard MI insinuate to the guards to abuse the inmates. When asked what MI said he stated: "Loosen this guy up for us." Make sure he has a bad night." "Make sure he gets the treatment." He claimed these comments were made to CPL Granier and SSG Frederick. Finally, SGT Davis stated that (sic): "the MI staffs to my understanding have been giving Granier compliments on the way he has been handling the MI holds. Example being statements like, "Good job, they're breaking down real fast. They answer every question. They're giving out good information, Finally, and Keep up the good work. Stuff like that."

c. (U) *SPC Jason Kennel, 372nd MP Company*, was asked if he were present when any detainees were abused. He stated: "I saw them nude, but MI would tell us to take away their mattresses, sheets, and clothes." He could not recall who in MI had instructed him to do this, but commented that, "if they wanted me to do that they needed to give me paperwork." He was later informed that "we could not do anything to embarrass the prisoners."

d. (U) *Mr. Adel L. Nakhla*, a US civilian contract translator was questioned about several detainees accused of rape. He observed (sic): "They (detainees) were all naked, a bunch of people from MI, the MP were there that night and the inmates were ordered by SGT Granier and SGT Frederick ordered the guys while questioning them to admit what they did. They made them do strange exercises by sliding on their stomach, jump up and down, throw water on them and made them some wet, called them all kinds of names such as "gays" do they like to make love to guys, then they handcuffed their hands together and their legs with shackles and started to stack them on top of each other by insuring that the bottom guys penis will touch the guy on tops butt."

e. (U) *SPC Neil A Wallin, 109th Area Support Medical Battalion*, a medic testified that: "Cell 1A was used to house high priority detainees and cell 1B was used to house the high risk or trouble making detainees. During my tour at the prison I observed that when the male detainees were first brought to the facility, some of them were made to wear female underwear, which I think was to somehow break them down."

12. (U) I find that prior to its deployment to Iraq for Operation Iraqi Freedom, the 320th MP Battalion and the 372nd MP Company had received no training in detention/internee operations. I also find that very little instruction or training was provided to MP personnel on the applicable rules of the Geneva Convention Relative to the Treatment of Prisoners of War, FM 27-10, AR 190-8, or FM 3-19.40. Moreover, I find that few, if any, copies of the Geneva Conventions were ever made available to MP personnel or detainees. (ANNEXES 21–24, 33, and multiple witness statements)

13. (U) Another obvious example of the Brigade Leadership not communicating with its Soldiers or ensuring their tactical proficiency concerns the incident of detainee abuse that occurred at Camp Bucca, Iraq, on May 12, 2003. Soldiers from the 223rd MP Company reported to the 800th MP Brigade Command at Camp Bucca, that four Military Police Soldiers from the 320th MP Battalion had abused a number of detainees during inprocessing at Camp Bucca. An extensive CID investigation determined that four soldiers from the 320th MP Battalion had kicked and beaten these detainees following a transport mission from Talil Air Base. (ANNEXES 34 and 35)

14. (U) Formal charges under the UCMJ were preferred against these Soldiers and an Article-32 Investigation conducted by LTC Gentry. He recommended a general court martial for the four accused, which BG Karpinski supported. Despite this documented abuse, there is no evidence that BG Karpinski ever attempted to remind 800th MP Soldiers of the requirements of the Geneva Conventions regarding detainee treatment or took any steps to ensure that such abuse was not repeated. Nor is there any evidence that LTC(P) Phillabaum, the commander of the Soldiers involved in the Camp Bucca abuse incident, took any initiative to ensure his Soldiers were properly trained regarding detainee treatment. (ANNEXES 35 and 62)

RECOMMENDATIONS AS TO PART ONE OF THE INVESTIGATION:

1. (U) Immediately deploy to the Iraq Theater an integrated multi-discipline Mobile Training Team (MTT) comprised of subject matter experts in internment/resettlement operations, international and operational law, information technology, facility management, interrogation and intelligence gathering techniques, chaplains, Arab cultural awareness, and medical practices as it pertains to I/R activities. This team needs to oversee and conduct comprehensive training in all aspects of detainee and confinement operations.

2. (U) That all military police and military intelligence personnel involved in any aspect of detainee operations or interrogation operations in CJTF-7, and subordinate units, be immediately provided with training by an international/operational law attorney on the specific provisions of The Law of Land Warfare FM 27-10, specifically the Geneva Convention Relative to the Treatment of Prisoners of War, Enemy Prisoners of War, Retained Personnel, Civilian Internees, and Other Detainees, and AR 190-8.

3. (U) That a single commander in CJTF-7 be responsible for overall detainee operations throughout the Iraq Theater of Operations. I also recommend that the Provost Marshal General of the Army assign a minimum of two (2) subject matter

experts, one officer and one NCO, to assist CJTF-7 in coordinating detainee operations.

4. (U) That detention facility commanders and interrogation facility commanders ensure that appropriate copies of the Geneva Convention Relative to the Treatment of Prisoners of War and notice of protections be made available in both English and the detainees' language and be prominently displayed in all detention facilities. Detainees with questions regarding their treatment should be given the full opportunity to read the Convention.

5. (U) That each detention facility commander and interrogation facility commander publish a complete and comprehensive set of Standing Operating Procedures (SOPs) regarding treatment of detainees, and that all personnel be required to read the SOPs and sign a document indicating that they have read and understand the SOPs.

6. (U) That in accordance with the recommendations of MG Ryder's Assessment Report, and my findings and recommendations in this investigation, all units in the Iraq Theater of Operations conducting internment/confinement/detainment operations in support of Operation Iraqi Freedom be OPCON for all purposes, to include action under the UCMJ, to CJTF-7.

7. (U) Appoint the C3, CJTF as the staff proponent for detainee operations in the Iraq Joint Operations Area (JOA). (MG Tom Miller, C3, CJTF-7, has been appointed by COMCJTF-7).

8. (U) That an inquiry UP AR 381-10, Procedure 15 be conducted to determine the extent of culpability of Military Intelligence personnel, assigned to the 205th MI Brigade and the Joint Interrogation and Debriefing Center (JIDC) regarding abuse of detainees at Abu Ghraib (BCCF).

9. (U) That it is critical that the proponent for detainee operations is assigned a dedicated Senior Judge Advocate, with specialized training and knowledge of international and operational law, to assist and advise on matters of detainee operations.

FINDINGS AND RECOMMENDATIONS

(PART TWO)

(U) The Investigation inquire into detainee escapes and accountability lapses as reported by CJTF-7, specifically allegations concerning these events at the Abu Ghraib Prison:

REGARDING PART TWO OF THE INVESTIGATION,
I MAKE THE FOLLOWING SPECIFIC FINDINGS OF FACT:

1. The 800th MP Brigade was responsible for theater-wide Internment and Resettlement (I/R) operations. (ANNEXES 45 and 95)

2. (U) The 320th MP Battalion, 800th MP Brigade was tasked with detainee operations at the Abu Ghraib Prison Complex during the time period covered in this investigation. (ANNEXES 41, 45, and 59)

3. (U) The 310th MP Battalion, 800th MP Brigade was tasked with detainee operations and Forward Operating Base (FOB) Operations at the Camp Bucca Detention Facility until TOA on 26 February 2004. (ANNEXES 41 and 52)

4. (U) The 744th MP Battalion, 800th MP Brigade was tasked with detainee operations and FOB Operations at the HVD Detention Facility until TOA on 4 March 2004. (ANNEXES 41 and 55)

5. (U) The 530th MP Battalion, 800th MP Brigade was tasked with detainee operations and FOB Operations at the MEK holding facility until TOA on 15 March 2004. (ANNEXES 41 and 97)

6. (U) Detainee operations include accountability, care, and well being of Enemy Prisoners of War, Retained Person, Civilian Detainees, and Other Detainees, as well as Iraqi criminal prisoners. (ANNEX 22)

7. (U) The accountability for detainees is doctrinally an MP task IAW FM 3-19.40. (ANNEX 22)

8. (U) There is a general lack of knowledge, implementation, and emphasis of basic legal, regulatory, doctrinal, and command requirements within the 800th MP Brigade and its subordinate units. (Multiple witness statements in ANNEXES 45–91).

9. (U) The handling of detainees and criminal prisoners after in-processing was inconsistent from detention facility to detention facility, compound to compound, encampment to encampment, and even shift to shift throughout the 800th MP Brigade AOR. (ANNEX 37)

10. (U) Camp Bucca, operated by the 310th MP Battalion, had a "Criminal Detainee In-Processing SOP" and a "Training Outline" for transferring and releasing detainees, which appears to have been followed. (ANNEXES 38 and 52)

11. (U) Incoming and outgoing detainees are being documented in the National Detainee Reporting System (NDRS) and Biometric Automated Toolset System (BATS) as required by regulation at all detention facilities. However, it is under-utilized and often does not give a "real time" accurate picture of the detainee population due to untimely updating. (ANNEX 56)

12. (U) There was a severe lapse in the accountability of detainees at the Abu Ghraib Prison Complex. The 320th MP Battalion used a self-created "change sheet" to document the transfer of a detainee from one location to another. For proper accountability, it is imperative that these change sheets be processed and the detainee manifest be updated within 24 hours of movement. At Abu Ghraib, this process would often take as long as 4 days to complete. This lag-time resulted in inaccurate detainee Internment Serial Number (ISN) counts, gross differences in the detainee manifest and the actual occupants of an individual compound, and significant confusion of the MP Soldiers. The 320th MP Battalion S-1, CPT Theresa Delbalso, and the S-3, MAJ David DiNenna, explained that this break-down was due to the lack of manpower to process change sheets in a timely man-ner. (ANNEXES 39 and 98)

13. (U) The 320th Battalion TACSOP requires detainee accountability at least 4 times daily at Abu Ghraib. However, a detailed review of their operational jour-nals revealed that these accounts were often not done or not documented by the unit. Additionally, there is no indication that accounting errors or the loss of a detainee in the accounting process triggered any immediate corrective action by the Battalion TOC. (ANNEX 44)

14. (U) There is a lack of standardization in the way the 320th MP Battalion con-ducted physical counts of their detainees. Each compound within a given encampment did their headcounts differently. Some compounds had detainees line up in lines of 10, some had them sit in rows, and some moved all the detainees to one end of the compound and counted them as they passed to the other end of the compound. (ANNEX 98)

15. (U) FM 3-19.40 outlines the need for 2 roll calls (100% ISN band checks) per day. The 320th MP Battalion did this check only 2 times per week. Due to the lack of real-time updates to the system, these checks were regularly inaccurate. (ANNEXES 22 and 98)

16. (U) The 800th MP Brigade and subordinate units adopted non-doctrinal terms such as "band checks," "roll-ups," and "call-ups," which contributed to the lapses in accountability and confusion at the soldier level. (Annexes 63, 88, and 98)

17. (U) Operational journals at the various compounds and the 320th Battalion TOC

contained numerous unprofessional entries and flippant comments, which high-lighted the lack of discipline within the unit. There was no indication that the journals were ever reviewed by anyone in their chain of command. (Annex 37)

18. (U) Accountability SOPs were not fully developed and standing TACSOPs were widely ignored. Any SOPs that did exist were not trained on, and were never dis-tributed to the lowest level. Most procedures were shelved at the unit TOC, rather than at the subordinate units and guards mount sites. (Annexes 44, 67, 71, and 85)

19. (U) Accountability and facility operations SOPs lacked specificity, implementa-tion measures, and a system of checks and balances to ensure compliance. (Annex ES 76 and 82)

20. (U) Basic Army Doctrine was not widely referenced or utilized to develop the accountability practices throughout the 800th MP Brigade's subordinate units. Daily processing, accountability, and detainee care appears to have been made up as the operations developed with reliance on, and guidance from, junior mem-bers of the unit who had civilian corrections experience. (Annex 21)

21. (U) Soldiers were poorly prepared and untrained to conduct I/R operations prior to deployment, at the mobilization site, upon arrival in theater, and throughout their mission. (ANNEXES 62, 63, and 69)

22. (U) The documentation provided to this investigation identified 27 escapes or attempted escapes from the detention facilities throughout the 800th MP Brigade's AOR. Based on my assessment and detailed analysis of the substandard accountability process maintained by the 800th MP Brigade, it is highly likely that there were several more unreported cases of escape that were probably "written off" as administrative errors or otherwise undocumented. 1LT Lewis Raeder, Platoon Leader, 372nd MP Company, reported knowing about at least two additional escapes (one from a work detail and one from a window) from Abu Ghraib (BCCF) that were not documented. LTC Dennis McGlone, Com-mander, 744th MP Battalion, detailed the escape of one detainee at the High Value Detainee Facility who went to the latrine and then outran the guards and escaped. Lastly, BG Janis Karpinski, Commander, 800th MP Brigade, stated that there were more than 32 escapes from her holding facilities, which does not match the number derived from the investigation materials. (ANNEXES 5–10, 45, 55, and 71)

23. (U) The Abu Ghraib and Camp Bucca detention facilities are significantly over their intended maximum capacity while the guard force is undermanned and under resourced. This imbalance has contributed to the poor living conditions,

escapes, and accountability lapses at the various facilities. The overcrowding of the facilities also limits the ability to identify and segregate leaders in the detainee population who may be organizing escapes and riots within the facility. (ANNEXES 6, 22, and 92)

24. (U) The screening, processing, and release of detainees who should not be in custody takes too long and contributes to the overcrowding and unrest in the detention facilities. There are currently three separate release mechanisms in the theater-wide internment operations. First, the apprehending unit can release a detainee if there is a determination that their continued detention is not warranted. Secondly, a criminal detainee can be released after it has been determined that the detainee has no intelligence value, and that their release would not be detrimental to society. BG Karpinski had signature authority to release detainees in this second category. Lastly, detainees accused of committing "Crimes Against the Coalition," who are held throughout the separate facilities in the CJTF-7 AOR, can be released upon a determination that they are of no intelligence value and no longer pose a significant threat to Coalition Forces. The release process for this category of detainee is a screening by the local US Forces Magistrate Cell and a review by a Detainee Release Board consisting of BG Karpinski, COL Marc Warren, SJA, CJTF-7, and MG Barbara Fast, C-2, CJTF-7. MG Fast is the "Detainee Release Authority" for detainees being held for committing crimes against the coalition. According to BG Karpinski, this category of detainee makes up more than 60% of the total detainee population, and is the fastest growing category. However, MG Fast, according to BG Karpinski, routinely denied the board's recommendations to release detainees in this category who were no longer deemed a threat and clearly met the requirements for release. According to BG Karpinski, the extremely slow and ineffective release process has significantly contributed to the overcrowding of the facilities. (ANNEXES 40, 45, and 46)

25. (U) After Action Reviews (AARs) are not routinely being conducted after an escape or other serious incident. No lessons learned seem to have been disseminated to subordinate units to enable corrective action at the lowest level. The Investigation Team requested copies of AARs, and none were provided. (Multiple Witness Statements)

26. (U) Lessons learned (i.e. Findings and Recommendations from various 15-6 Investigations concerning escapes and accountability lapses) were rubber stamped as approved and ordered implemented by BG Karpinski. There is no evidence that the majority of her orders directing the implementation of substantive changes were ever acted upon. Additionally, there was no follow-up by the command to verify the corrective actions were taken. Had the findings and recommendations contained within their own investigations been analyzed and

actually implemented by BG Karpinski, many of the subsequent escapes, accountability lapses, and cases of abuse may have been prevented. (ANNEXES 5–10)

27. (U) The perimeter lighting around Abu Ghraib and the detention facility at Camp Bucca is inadequate and needs to be improved to illuminate dark areas that have routinely become avenues of escape. (ANNEX 6)

28. (U) Neither the camp rules nor the provisions of the Geneva Conventions are posted in English or in the language of the detainees at any of the detention facilities in the 800th MP Brigade's AOR, even after several investigations had annotated the lack of this critical requirement. (Multiple Witness Statements and the Personal Observations of the Investigation Team)

29. (U) The Iraqi guards at Abu Ghraib (BCCF) demonstrate questionable work ethics and loyalties, and are a potentially dangerous contingent within the Hard-Site. These guards have furnished the Iraqi criminal inmates with contraband, weapons, and information. Additionally, they have facilitated the escape of at least one detainee. (ANNEX 8 and 26-SPC Polak's Statement)

30. (U) In general, US civilian contract personnel (Titan Corporation, CACI, etc...), third country nationals, and local contractors do not appear to be properly supervised within the detention facility at Abu Ghraib. During our on-site inspection, they wandered about with too much unsupervised free access in the detainee area. Having civilians in various outfits (civilian and DCUs) in and about the detainee area causes confusion and may have contributed to the difficulties in the accountability process and with detecting escapes. (ANNEX 51, Multiple Witness Statements, and the Personal Observations of the Investigation Team)

31. (U) SGM Marc Emerson, Operations SGM, 320th MP Battalion, contended that the Detainee Rules of Engagement (DROE) and the general principles of the Geneva Convention were briefed at every guard mount and shift change on Abu Ghraib. However, none of our witnesses, nor our personal observations, support his contention. I find that SGM Emerson was not a credible witness. (ANNEXES 45, 80, and the Personal Observations of the Investigation Team)

32. (U) Several interviewees insisted that the MP and MI Soldiers at Abu Ghraib (BCCF) received regular training on the basics of detainee operations; however, they have been unable to produce any verifying documentation, sign-in rosters, or soldiers who can recall the content of this training. (Annexes 59, 80, and the Absence of any Training Records)

33. (S/NF) The various detention facilities operated by the 800th MP Brigade have

routinely held persons brought to them by Other Government Agencies (OGAs) without accounting for them, knowing their identities, or even the reason for their detention. The Joint Interrogation and Debriefing Center (JIDC) at Abu Ghraib called these detainees "ghost detainees." On at least one occasion, the 320th MP Battalion at Abu Ghraib held a handful of "ghost detainees" (6-8) for OGAs that they moved around within the facility to hide them from a visiting International Committee of the Red Cross (ICRC) survey team. This maneuver was deceptive, contrary to Army Doctrine, and in violation of international law. (Annex 53)

34. (U) The following riots, escapes, and shootings have been documented and reported to this Investigation Team. Although there is no data from other missions of similar size and duration to compare the number of escapes with, the most significant factors derived from these reports are twofold. First, investigations and SIRs lacked critical data needed to evaluate the details of each incident. Second, each investigation seems to have pointed to the same types of deficiencies; however, little to nothing was done to correct the problems and to implement the recommendations as was ordered by BG Karpinski, nor was there any command emphasis to ensure these deficiencies were corrected:

    a. (U) 4 June 03—This escape was mentioned in the 15-6 Investigation covering the 13 June 03 escape, recapture, and shootings of detainees at Camp Vigilant (320th MP Battalion). However, no investigation or additional information was provided as requested by this investigation team. (ANNEX 7)

    b. (U) 9 June 03—Riot and shootings of five detainees at Camp Cropper. (115th MP Battalion) Several detainees allegedly rioted after a detainee was subdued by MPs of the 115th MP Battalion after striking a guard in compound B of Camp Cropper. A 15-6 investigation by 1LT Magowan (115th MP Battalion, Platoon Leader) concluded that a detainee had acted up and hit an MP. After being subdued, one of the MPs took off his DCU top and flexed his muscles to the detainees, which further escalated the riot. The MPs were overwhelmed and the guards fired lethal rounds to protect the life of the compound MPs, whereby 5 detainees were wounded. Contributing factors were poor communications, no clear chain of command, facility-obstructed views of posted guards, the QRF did not have non-lethal equipment, and the SOP was inadequate and outdated. (ANNEX 5)

    c. (U) 12 June 03—Escape and recapture of detainee #8399, escape and shooting of detainee # 7166, and attempted escape of an unidentified detainee from Camp Cropper Holding Area (115th MP Battalion). Several detainees allegedly made their escape in the nighttime hours prior to 0300.

A 15-6 investigation by CPT Wendlandt (115th MP Battalion, S-2) concluded that the detainees allegedly escaped by crawling under the wire at a
location with inadequate lighting. One detainee was stopped prior to
escape. An MP of the 115th MP Battalion search team recaptured detainee
8399, and detainee # 7166 was shot and killed by a Soldier during the
recapture process. Contributing factors were overcrowding, poor lighting,
and the nature of the hardened criminal detainees at that location. It is of
particular note that the command was informed at least 24 hours in
advance of the upcoming escape attempt and started doing amplified
announcements in Arabic stating the camp rules. The investigation
pointed out that rules and guidelines were not posted in the camps in the
detainees' native languages. (ANNEX 6)

d. (U) 13 June 03—Escape and recapture of detainee # 8968 and the shooting of eight detainees at Abu Ghraib (BCCF) (320th MP Battalion). Several detainees allegedly attempted to escape at about 1400 hours from the
Camp Vigilant Compound, Abu Ghraib (BCCF). A 15-6 investigation by
CPT Wyks (400th MP Battalion, S-1) concluded that the detainee
allegedly escaped by sliding under the wire while the tower guard was
turned in the other direction. This detainee was subsequently apprehended
by the QRF. At about 1600 the same day, 30-40 detainees rioted and
pelted three interior MP guards with rocks. One guard was injured and
the tower guards fired lethal rounds at the rioters injuring 7 and killing 1
detainee. (ANNEX 7)

e. (U) 05 November 03—Escape of detainees # 9877 and # 10739 from Abu
Ghraib (320th MP Battalion). Several detainees allegedly escaped at 0345
from the Hard-Site, Abu Ghraib (BCCF). An SIR was initiated by SPC
Warner (320th MP Battalion, S-3 RTO). The SIR indicated that 2 criminal
prisoners escaped through their cell window in tier 3A of the Hard-Site.
No information on findings, contributing factors, or corrective action has
been provided to this investigation team. (ANNEX 11)

f. (U) 07 November 03—Escape of detainee # 14239 from Abu Ghraib
(320th MP Battalion). A detainee allegedly escaped at 1330 from Compound 2 of the Ganci Encampment, Abu Ghraib (BCCF). An SIR was initiated by SSG Hydro (320th MP Battalion, S-3 Asst. NCOIC). The SIR
indicated that a detainee escaped from the North end of the compound
and was discovered missing during distribution of the noon meal, but
there is no method of escape listed in the SIR. No information on findings,
contributing factors, or corrective action has been provided to this investigation team. (ANNEX 12)

g. (U) 08 November 03 — Escape of detainees #115089, #151623, #151624, # 116734, #116735, and #116738 from Abu Ghraib (320th MP Battalion). Several detainees allegedly escaped at 2022 from Compound 8 of the Ganci encampment, Abu Ghraib. An SIR was initiated by MAJ DiNenna (320th MP Battalion, S-3). The SIR indicated that 5-6 prisoners escaped from the North end of the compound, but there is no method of escape listed in the SIR. No information on findings, contributing factors, or corrective action has been provided to this investigation team. (ANNEX 13)

h. (U) 24 November 03 — Riot and shooting of 12 detainees #150216, #150894, #153096, 153165, #153169, #116361, #153399, #20257, #150348, #152616, #116146, and #152156 at Abu Ghraib (320th MP Battalion). Several detainees allegedly began to riot at about 1300 in all of the compounds at the Ganci encampment. This resulted in the shooting deaths of 3 detainees, 9 wounded detainees, and 9 injured US Soldiers. A 15-6 investigation by COL Bruce Falcone (220th MP Brigade, Deputy Commander) concluded that the detainees rioted in protest of their living conditions, that the riot turned violent, the use of non-lethal force was ineffective, and, after the 320th MP Battalion CDR executed "Golden Spike," the emergency containment plan, the use of deadly force was authorized. Contributing factors were lack of comprehensive training of guards, poor or non-existent SOPs, no formal guard-mount conducted prior to shift, no rehearsals or ongoing training, the mix of less than lethal rounds with lethal rounds in weapons, no AARs being conducted after incidents, ROE not posted and not understood, overcrowding, uniforms not standardized, and poor communication between the command and Soldiers. (ANNEX 8)

i. (U) 24 November 03 — Shooting of detainee at Abu Ghraib (320th MP Battalion). A detainee allegedly had a pistol in his cell and around 1830 an extraction team shot him with less than lethal and lethal rounds in the process of recovering the weapon. A 15-6 investigation by COL Bruce Falcone (220th Brigade, Deputy Commander) concluded that one of the detainees in tier 1A of the Hard Site had gotten a pistol and a couple of knives from an Iraqi Guard working in the encampment. Immediately upon receipt of this information, an ad-hoc extraction team consisting of MP and MI personnel conducted what they called a routine cell search, which resulted in the shooting of an MP and the detainee. Contributing factors were a corrupt Iraqi Guard, inadequate SOPs, the Detention ROE in place at the time was ineffective due to the numerous levels of authorization needed for use of lethal force, poorly trained MPs, unclear lanes of responsibility, and ambiguous relationship between the MI and MP assets. (ANNEX 8)

j. (U) 13 December 03—Shooting by non-lethal means into crowd at Abu Ghraib (320th MP Battalion). Several detainees allegedly got into a detainee-on-detainee fight around 1030 in Compound 8 of the Ganci encampment, Abu Ghraib. An SIR was initiated by SSG Matash (320th MP Battalion, S-3 Section). The SIR indicated that there was a fight in the compound and the MPs used a non-lethal crowd-dispersing round to break up the fight, which was successful. No information on findings, contributing factors, or corrective action has been provided to this investigation team. (ANNEX 14)

k. (U) 13 December 03—Shooting by non-lethal means into crowd at Abu Ghraib (320th MP Battalion). Several detainees allegedly got into a detainee-on-detainee fight around 1120 in Compound 2 of the Ganci encampment, Abu Ghraib. An SIR was initiated by SSG Matash (320th MP Battalion, S-3 Section). The SIR indicated that there was a fight in the compound and the MPs used two non-lethal shots to disperse the crowd, which was successful. No information on findings, contributing factors, or corrective action has been provided to this investigation team. (ANNEX 15)

l. (U) 13 December 03—Shooting by non-lethal means into crowd at Abu Ghraib (320th MP Battalion). Approximately 30-40 detainees allegedly got into a detainee-on-detainee fight around 1642 in Compound 3 of the Ganci encampment, Abu Ghraib (BCCF). An SIR was initiated by SSG Matash (320th MP Battalion, S-3 Section). The SIR indicates that there was a fight in the compound and the MPs used a non-lethal crowd-dispersing round to break up the fight, which was successful. No information on findings, contributing factors, or corrective action has been provided to this investigation team. (ANNEX 16)

m. (U) 17 December 03—Shooting by non-lethal means of detainee from Abu Ghraib (320th MP Battalion). Several detainees allegedly assaulted an MP at 1459 inside the Ganci Encampment, Abu Ghraib (BCCF). An SIR was initiated by SSG Matash (320th MP BRIGADE, S-3 Section). The SIR indicated that three detainees assaulted an MP, which resulted in the use of a non-lethal shot that calmed the situation. No information on findings, contributing factors, or corrective action has been provided to this investigation team. (ANNEX 17)

n. (U) 07 January 04—Escape of detainee #115032 from Camp Bucca (310th MP Battalion). A detainee allegedly escaped between the hours of 0445 and 0640 from Compound 12, of Camp Bucca. Investigation by CPT Kaires (310th MP Battalion S-3) and CPT Holsombeck (724th MP

Battalion S-3) concluded that the detainee escaped through an undetected weakness in the wire. Contributing factors were inexperienced guards, lapses in accountability, complacency, lack of leadership presence, poor visibility, and lack of clear and concise communication between the guards and the leadership. (ANNEX 9)

o. (U) 12 January 04—Escape of Detainees #115314 and #109950 as well as the escape and recapture of 5 unknown detainees at the Camp Bucca Detention Facility (310th MP Battalion). Several detainees allegedly escaped around 0300 from Compound 12, of Camp Bucca. An AR 15-6 Investigation by LTC Leigh Coulter (800th MP Brigade, OIC Camp Arif-jan Detachment) concluded that three of the detainees escaped through the front holding cell during conditions of limited visibility due to fog. One of the detainees was noticed, shot with a non-lethal round, and returned to his holding compound. That same night, 4 detainees exited through the wire on the South side of the camp and were seen and apprehended by the QRF. Contributing factors were the lack of a coordinated effort for emplacement of MPs during implementation of the fog plan, overcrowd-ing, and poor communications. (ANNEX 10)

p. (U) 14 January 04—Escape of detainee #12436 and missing Iraqi guard from Hard-Site, Abu Ghraib (320th MP Battalion). A detainee allegedly escaped at 1335 from the Hard Site at Abu Ghraib (BCCF). An SIR was initiated by SSG Hydro (320th MP Battalion, S-3 Asst. NCOIC). The SIR indicates that an Iraqi guard assisted a detainee to escape by signing him out on a work detail and disappearing with him. At the time of the second SIR, neither missing person had been located. No information on findings, contributing factors, or corrective action has been provided to this investi-gation team. (ANNEX 99)

q. (U) 26 January 04—Escape of detainees #s 115236, 116272, and 151933 from Camp Bucca (310th MP Battalion). Several Detainees allegedly escaped between the hours of 0440 and 0700 during a period of intense fog. Investigation by CPT Kaires (310th MP Battalion S-3) concluded that the detainees crawled under a fence when visibility was only 10-15 meters due to fog. Contributing factors were the limited visibility (darkness under foggy conditions), lack of proper accountability reporting, inadequate number of guards, commencement of detainee feeding during low visibil-ity operations, and poorly rested MPs. (ANNEX 18)

36. (U) As I have previously indicated, this investigation determined that there was virtually a complete lack of detailed SOPs at any of the detention facilities. More-over, despite the fact that there were numerous reported escapes at detention

facilities throughout Iraq (in excess of 35), AR 15-6 Investigations following these escapes were simply forgotten or ignored by the Brigade Commander with no dissemination to other facilities. After-Action Reports and Lessons Learned, if done at all, remained at individual facilities and were not shared among other commanders or soldiers throughout the Brigade. The Command never issued standard TTPs for handling escape incidents. (ANNEXES 5–10, Multiple Witness Statements, and the Personal Observations of the Investigation Team)

RECOMMENDATIONS REGARDING PART TWO OF THE INVESTIGATION:

1. (U) ANNEX 100 of this investigation contains a detailed and referenced series of recommendations for improving the detainee accountability practices throughout the OIF area of operations.

2. (U) Accountability practices throughout any particular detention facility must be standardized and in accordance with applicable regulations and international law.

3. (U) The NDRS and BATS accounting systems must be expanded and used to their fullest extent to facilitate real time updating when detainees are moved and or transferred from one location to another.

4. (U) "Change sheets," or their doctrinal equivalent must be immediately processed and updated into the system to ensure accurate accountability. The detainee roll call or ISN counts must match the manifest provided to the compound guards to ensure proper accountability of detainees.

5. (U) Develop, staff, and implement comprehensive and detailed SOPs utilizing the lessons learned from this investigation as well as any previous findings, recommendations, and reports.

6. (U) SOPs must be written, disseminated, trained on, and understood at the lowest level.

7. (U) Iraqi criminal prisoners must be held in separate facilities from any other category of detainee.

8. (U) All of the compounds should be wired into the master manifest whereby MP Soldiers can account for their detainees in real time and without waiting for their change sheets to be processed. This would also have the change sheet serve as a way to check up on the accuracy of the manifest as updated by each compound. The BATS and NDRS system can be utilized for this function.

9. (U) Accountability lapses, escapes, and disturbances within the detainment facilities must be immediately reported through both the operational and administrative Chain of Command via a Serious Incident Report (SIR). The SIRs must then be tracked and followed by daily SITREPs until the situation is resolved.

10. (U) Detention Rules of Engagement (DROE), Interrogation Rules of Engagement (IROE), and the principles of the Geneva Conventions need to be briefed at every shift change and guard mount.

11. (U) AARs must be conducted after serious incidents at any given facility. The observations and corrective actions that develop from the AARs must be analyzed by the respective MP Battalion S-3 section, developed into a plan of action, shared with the other facilities, and implemented as a matter of policy.

12. (U) There must be significant structural improvements at each of the detention facilities. The needed changes include significant enhancement of perimeter lighting, additional chain link fencing, staking down of all concertina wire, hard site development, and expansion of Abu Ghraib (BCCF).

13. (U) The Geneva Conventions and the facility rules must be prominently displayed in English and the language of the detainees at each compound and encampment at every detention facility IAW AR 190-8.

14. (U) Further restrict US civilians and other contractors' access throughout the facility. Contractors and civilians must be in an authorized and easily identifiable uniform to be more easily distinguished from the masses of detainees in civilian clothes.

15. (U) Facilities must have a stop movement/transfer period of at least 1 hour prior to every 100% detainee roll call and ISN counts to ensure accurate accountability.

16. (U) The method for doing head counts of detainees within a given compound must be standardized.

17. (U) Those military units conducting I/R operations must know of, train on, and constantly reference the applicable Army Doctrine and CJTF command policies. The references provided in this report cover nearly every deficiency I have enumerated. Although they do not, and cannot, make up for leadership shortfalls, all soldiers, at all levels, can use them to maintain standardized operating procedures and efficient accountability practices.

FINDINGS AND RECOMMENDATIONS

(PART THREE)

(U) Investigate the training, standards, employment, command policies, internal procedures, and command climate in the 800th MP Brigade, as appropriate:

Pursuant to Part Three of the Investigation, select members of the Investigation team
(Primarily COL La Fate and I) personally interviewed the following witnesses:

1. (U) BG Janis Karpinski, Commander, 800th MP Brigade
2. (U) COL Thomas Pappas, Commander, 205th MI Brigade
3. (U) COL Ralph Sabatino, CFLCC Judge Advocate, CPA Ministry of Justice
   (Interviewed by COL Richard Gordon, CFLCC SJA)
4. (U) LTC Gary W. Maddocks, S-5 and Executive Officer, 800th MP Brigade
5. (U) LTC James O'Hare, Command Judge Advocate, 800th MP Brigade
6. (U) LTC Robert P. Walters Jr., Commander, 165th MI Battalion (Tactical
   Exploitation)
7. (U) LTC James D. Edwards, Commander, 202nd MI Battalion
8. (U) LTC Vincent Montera, Commander, 310th MP Battalion
9. (U) LTC Steve Jordan, former Director, Joint Interrogation and Debriefing
   Center/LNO to the 205th MI Brigade
10. (U) LTC Leigh A. Coulter, Commander, 724th MP Battalion and OIC Arifjan
    Detachment, 800th MP Brigade
11. (U) LTC Dennis McGlone, Commander, 744th MP Battalion
12. (U) MAJ David Hinzman, S-1, 800th MP Brigade
13. (U) MAJ William D. Proietto, Deputy CJA, 800th MP Brigade
14. (U) MAJ Stacy L. Garrity, S-1 (FWD), 800th MP Brigade
15. (U) MAJ David W. DiNenna, S-3, 320th MP Battalion
16. (U) MAJ Michael Sheridan, XO, 320th MP Battalion
17. (U) MAJ Anthony Cavallaro, S-3, 800th MP Brigade
18. (U) CPT Marc C. Hale, Commander, 670th MP Company
19. (U) CPT Donald Reese, Commander, 372nd MP Company
20. (U) CPT Darren Hampton, Assistant S-3, 320th MP Battalion
21. (U) CPT John Kaires, S-3, 310th MP Battalion
22. (U) CPT Ed Diamantis, S-2, 800th MP Brigade
23. (U) CPT Marc C. Hale, Commander, 670th MP Company
24. (U) CPT Donald Reese, Commander, 372nd MP Company
25. (U) CPT James G. Jones, Commander, 229th MP Company
26. (U) CPT Michael Anthony Mastrangelo, Jr., Commander, 310th MP Company
27. (U) CPT Lawrence Bush, IG, 800th MP Brigade
28. (U) 1LT Lewis C. Raeder, Platoon Leader, 372nd MP Company
29. (U) 1LT Elvis Mabry, Aide-de-camp to Brigade Commander, 800th MP Brigade

30. (U) 1LT Warren E. Ford, II, Commander, HHC 320th MP Battalion
31. (U) 2LT David O. Sutton, Platoon Leader, 229th MP Company
32. (U) CW2 Edward J. Rivas, 205th MI Brigade
33. (U) CSM Joseph P. Arrington, Command Sergeant Major, 320th MP Battalion
34. (U) SGM Pascual Cartagena, Acting Command Sergeant Major, 800th MP Brigade
35. (U) CSM Timothy L. Woodcock, Command Sergeant Major, 310th MP Battalion
36. (U) 1SG Dawn J. Rippelmeyer, First Sergeant, 977th MP Company
37. (U) SGM Mark Emerson, Operations SGM, 320th MP Battalion
38. (U) MSG Brian G. Lipinski, First Sergeant, 372nd MP Company
39. (U) MSG Andrew J. Lombardo, Operations Sergeant, 310th MP Battalion
40. (U) SFC Daryl J. Plude, Platoon Sergeant, 229th MP Company
41. (U) SFC Shannon K. Snider, Platoon SGT, 372nd MP Company
42. (U) SFC Keith A. Comer, 372nd MP Company
43. (U) SSG Robert Elliot, Squad Leader, 372nd MP Company
44. (U) SSG Santos A. Cardona, Army Dog Handler, 42nd MP Detachment, 16th MP Brigade
45. (U) SGT Michael Smith, Army Dog Handler, 523rd MP Detachment, 937th Engineer Group
46. (U) MA1 William J. Kimbro, USN Dog Handler, NAS Signal and Canine Unit
47. (U) Mr. Steve Stephanowicz, US civilian Contract Interrogator, CACI, 205th MI Brigade
48. (U) Mr. John Israel, US civilian Contract Interpreter, Titan Corporation, 205th MI Brigade

(ANNEXES 45–91)

REGARDING PART THREE OF THE INVESTIGATION, I MAKE THE FOLLOWING SPECIFIC FINDINGS OF FACT:

1. (U) I find that BG Janis Karpinski took command of the 800th MP Brigade on 30 June 2003 from BG Paul Hill. BG Karpinski has remained in command since that date. The 800th MP Brigade is comprised of eight MP battalions in the Iraqi TOR: 115th MP Battalion, 310th MP Battalion, 320th MP Battalion, 324th MP Battalion, 400th MP Battalion, 530th MP Battalion, 724th MP Battalion, and 744th MP Battalion. (ANNEXES 41 and 45)

2. (U) Prior to BG Karpinski taking command, members of the 800th MP Brigade believed they would be allowed to go home when all the detainees were released from the Camp Bucca Theater Internment Facility following the cessation of major ground combat on 1 May 2003. At one point, approximately 7,000 to 8,000 detainees were held at Camp Bucca. Through Article-5 Tribunals and a screening process, several thousand detainees were released. Many in the command

believed they would go home when the detainees were released. In late May–early June 2003 the 800th MP Brigade was given a new mission to manage the Iraqi penal system and several detention centers. This new mission meant Soldiers would not redeploy to CONUS when anticipated. Morale suffered, and over the next few months there did not appear to have been any attempt by the Command to mitigate this morale problem. (ANNEXES 45 and 96)

3. (U) There is abundant evidence in the statements of numerous witnesses that soldiers throughout the 800th MP Brigade were not proficient in their basic MOS skills, particularly regarding internment/resettlement operations. Moreover, there is no evidence that the command, although aware of these deficiencies, attempted to correct them in any systemic manner other than ad hoc training by individuals with civilian corrections experience. (Multiple Witness Statements and the Personal Observations of the Investigation Team)

4. (U) I find that the 800th MP Brigade was not adequately trained for a mission that included operating a prison or penal institution at Abu Ghraib Prison Complex. As the Ryder Assessment found, I also concur that units of the 800th MP Brigade did not receive corrections-specific training during their mobilization period. MP units did not receive pinpoint assignments prior to mobilization and during the post mobilization training, and thus could not train for specific missions. The training that was accomplished at the mobilization sites were developed and implemented at the company level with little or no direction or supervision at the Battalion and Brigade levels, and consisted primarily of common tasks and law enforcement training. However, I found no evidence that the Command, although aware of this deficiency, ever requested specific corrections training from the Commandant of the Military Police School, the US Army Confinement Facility at Mannheim, Germany, the Provost Marshal General of the Army, or the US Army Disciplinary Barracks at Fort Leavenworth, Kansas. (ANNEXES 19 and 76)

5. (U) I find that without adequate training for a civilian internee detention mission, Brigade personnel relied heavily on individuals within the Brigade who had civilian corrections experience, including many who worked as prison guards or corrections officials in their civilian jobs. Almost every witness we interviewed had no familiarity with the provisions of AR 190-8 or FM 3-19.40. It does not appear that a Mission Essential Task List (METL) based on in-theater missions was ever developed nor was a training plan implemented throughout the Brigade. (ANNEXES 21, 22, 67, and 81)

6. (U) I also find, as did MG Ryder's Team, that the 800th MP Brigade as a whole, was understrength for the mission for which it was tasked. Army Doctrine dictates that an I/R Brigade can be organized with between 7 and 21 battalions, and

that the average battalion size element should be able to handle approximately 4000 detainees at a time. This investigation indicates that BG Karpinski and her staff did a poor job allocating resources throughout the Iraq JOA. Abu Ghraib (BCCF) normally housed between 6000 and 7000 detainees, yet it was operated by only one battalion. In contrast, the HVD Facility maintains only about 100 detainees, and is also run by an entire battalion. (ANNEXES 19, 22, and 96)

7. (U) Reserve Component units do not have an individual replacement system to mitigate medical or other losses. Over time, the 800th MP Brigade clearly suffered from personnel shortages through release from active duty (REFRAD) actions, medical evacuation, and demobilization. In addition to being severely under-manned, the quality of life for Soldiers assigned to Abu Ghraib (BCCF) was extremely poor. There was no DFAC, PX, barbershop, or MWR facilities. There were numerous mortar attacks, random rifle and RPG attacks, and a serious threat to Soldiers and detainees in the facility. The prison complex was also severely over-crowded and the Brigade lacked adequate resources and personnel to resolve serious logistical problems. Finally, because of past associations and familiarity of Soldiers within the Brigade, it appears that friendship often took precedence over appropriate leader and subordinate relationships. (ANNEX 101, Multiple Witness Statements, and the Personal Observations of the Investigation Team)

8. (U) With respect to the 800th MP Brigade mission at Abu Ghraib (BCCF), I find that there was clear friction and lack of effective communication between the Commander, 205th MI Brigade, who controlled FOB Abu Ghraib (BCCF) after 19 November 2003, and the Commander, 800th MP Brigade, who controlled detainee operations inside the FOB. There was no clear delineation of responsibility between commands, little coordination at the command level, and no integration of the two functions. Coordination occurred at the lowest possible levels with little oversight by commanders. (ANNEXES 31, 45, and 46)

9. (U) I find that this ambiguous command relationship was exacerbated by a CJTF-7 Fragmentary Order (FRAGO) 1108 issued on 19 November 2003. Paragraph 3.C.8, Assignment of 205th MI Brigade Commander's Responsibilities for the Baghdad Central Confinement Facility, states as follows:

3.C.8. A. (U) 205 MI BRIGADE.

3.C.8. A. 1. (U) EFFECTIVE IMMEDIATELY COMMANDER 205 MI BRIGADE ASSUMES RESPONSIBILITY FOR THE BAGH-DAD CONFINEMENT FACILITY (BCCF) AND IS APPOINTED THE FOB COMMANDER. UNITS CURRENTLY AT ABU GHRAIB (BCCF) ARE TACON TO 205 MI BRIGADE FOR *"SECURITY OF DETAINEES AND FOB PROTECTION."*

Although not supported by BG Karpinski, FRAGO 1108 made all of the MP units at Abu Ghraib TACON to the Commander, 205th MI Brigade. This effectively made an MI Officer, rather than an MP Officer, responsible for the MP units conducting detainee operations at that facility. This is not doctrinally sound due to the different missions and agendas assigned to each of these respective specialties. (ANNEX 31)

10. (U) Joint Publication 0-2, Unified Action Armed Forces (UNAAF), 10 July 2001 defines Tactical Control (TACON) as the detailed direction and control of movements or maneuvers within the operational area necessary to accomplish assigned missions or tasks. (ANNEX 42)

> "TACON is the command authority over assigned or attached forces or commands or military capability made available for tasking that is limited to the detailed direction and control of movements or maneuvers within the operational area necessary to accomplish assigned missions or tasks. TACON is inherent in OPCON and may be delegated to and exercised by commanders at any echelon at or below the level of combatant commander."

11. (U) Based on all the facts and circumstances in this investigation, I find that there was little, if any, recognition of this TACON Order by the 800th MP Brigade or the 205th MI Brigade. Further, there was no evidence if the Commander, 205th MI Brigade clearly informed the Commander, 800th MP Brigade, and specifically the Commander, 320th MP Battalion assigned at Abu Ghraib (BCCF), on the specific requirements of this TACON relationship. (ANNEXES 45 and 46)

12. (U) It is clear from a comprehensive review of witness statements and personal interviews that the 320th MP Battalion and 800th MP Brigade continued to function as if they were responsible for the security, health and welfare, and overall security of detainees within Abu Ghraib (BCCF) prison. Both BG Karpinski and COL Pappas clearly behaved as if this were still the case. (ANNEXES 45 and 46)

13. (U) With respect to the 320th MP Battalion, I find that the Battalion Commander, LTC (P) Jerry Phillabaum, was an extremely ineffective commander and leader. Numerous witnesses confirm that the Battalion S-3, MAJ David W. DiNenna, basically ran the battalion on a day-to-day basis. At one point, BG Karpinski sent LTC (P) Phillabaum to Camp Arifjan, Kuwait for approximately two weeks, apparently to give him some relief from the pressure he was experiencing as the 320th Battalion Commander. This movement to Camp Arifjan immediately followed a briefing provided by LTC (P) Phillabaum to the CJTF-7 Commander, LTG Sanchez, near the end of October 2003. BG Karpinski placed LTC Ronald Chew, Commander of the 115th MP Battalion, in charge of the

320th MP Battalion for a period of approximately two weeks. LTC Chew was also in command of the 115th MP Battalion assigned to Camp Cropper, BIAP, Iraq. I could find no orders, either suspending or relieving LTC (P) Phillabaum from command, nor any orders placing LTC Chew in command of the 320th. In addition, there was no indication this removal and search for a replacement was communicated to the Commander CJTF-7, the Commander 377th TSC, or to Soldiers in the 320th MP Battalion. Temporarily removing one commander and replacing him with another serving Battalion Commander without an order and without notifying superior or subordinate commands is without precedent in my military career. LTC (P) Phillabaum was also reprimanded for lapses in accountability that resulted in several escapes. The 320th MP Battalion was stigmatized as a unit due to previous detainee abuse which occurred in May 2003 at the Bucca Theater Internment Facility (TIF), while under the command of LTC (P) Phillabaum. Despite his proven deficiencies as both a commander and leader, BG Karpinski allowed LTC (P) Phillabaum to remain in command of her most troubled battalion guarding, by far, the largest number of detainees in the 800th MP Brigade. LTC (P) Phillabaum was suspended from his duties by LTG Sanchez, CJTF-7 Commander on 17 January 2004. (ANNEXES 43, 45, and 61)

14. (U) During the course of this investigation I conducted a lengthy interview with BG Karpinski that lasted over four hours, and is included verbatim in the investigation Annexes. BG Karpinski was extremely emotional during much of her testimony. What I found particularly disturbing in her testimony was her complete unwillingness to either understand or accept that many of the problems inherent in the 800th MP Brigade were caused or exacerbated by poor leadership and the refusal of her command to both establish and enforce basic standards and principles among its soldiers. (ANNEX 45 and the Personal Observations of the Interview Team)

15. (U) BG Karpinski alleged that she received no help from the Civil Affairs Command, specifically, no assistance from either BG John Kern or COL Tim Regan. She blames much of the abuse that occurred in Abu Ghraib (BCCF) on MI personnel and stated that MI personnel had given the MPs "ideas" that led to detainee abuse. In addition, she blamed the 372nd Company Platoon Sergeant, SFC Snider, the Company Commander, CPT Reese, and the First Sergeant, MSG Lipinski, for the abuse. She argued that problems in Abu Ghraib were the fault of COL Pappas and LTC Jordan because COL Pappas was in charge of FOB Abu Ghraib. (ANNEX 45)

16. (U) BG Karpinski also implied during her testimony that the criminal abuses that occurred at Abu Ghraib (BCCF) might have been caused by the ultimate disposition of the detainee abuse cases that originally occurred at Camp Bucca in May 2003. She stated that "about the same time those incidents were taking place out

of Baghdad Central, the decisions were made to give the guilty people at Bucca plea bargains. So, the system communicated to the soldiers, the worst that's gonna happen is, you're gonna go home." I think it important to point out that almost every witness testified that the serious criminal abuse of detainees at Abu Ghraib (BCCF) occurred in late October and early November 2003. The photographs and statements clearly support that the abuses occurred during this time period. The Bucca cases were set for trial in January 2004 and were not finally disposed of until 29 December 2003. There is entirely no evidence that the decision of numerous MP personnel to intentionally abuse detainees at Abu Ghrabid (BCCF) was influenced in any respect by the Camp Bucca cases. (ANNEXES 25, 26, and 45)

17. (U) Numerous witnesses stated that the 800th MP Brigade S-1, MAJ Hinzman and S-4, MAJ Green, were essentially dysfunctional, but that despite numerous complaints, these officers were not replaced. This had a detrimental effect on the Brigade Staff's effectiveness and morale. Moreover, the Brigade Command Judge Advocate, LTC James O'Hare, appears to lack initiative and was unwilling to accept responsibility for any of his actions. LTC Gary Maddocks, the Brigade XO did not properly supervise the Brigade staff by failing to lay out staff priorities, take overt corrective action when needed, and supervise their daily functions. (ANNEXES 45, 47, 48, 62, and 67)

18. (U) In addition to poor morale and staff inefficiencies, I find that the 800th MP Brigade did not articulate or enforce clear and basic Soldier and Army standards. I specifically found these examples of unenforced standards:

a. There was no clear uniform standard for any MP Soldiers assigned detention duties. Despite the fact that hundreds of former Iraqi soldiers and officers were detainees, MP personnel were allowed to wear civilian clothes in the FOB after duty hours while carrying weapons. (ANNEXES 51 and 74)

b. Some Soldiers wrote poems and other sayings on their helmets and soft caps. (ANNEXES 51 and 74)

c. In addition, numerous officers and senior NCOs have been reprimanded/disciplined for misconduct during this period. Those disciplined include: (ANNEXES 43 and 102)

1). (U) BG Janis Karpinski, Commander, 800th MP Brigade
• Memorandum of Admonishment by LTG Sanchez, Commander, CJTF-7, on 17 January 2004.

2). (U) LTC (P) Jerry Phillabaum, Commander, 320th MP Battalion

- GOMOR from BG Karpinski, Commander 800th MP Brigade, on 10 November 2003, for lack of leadership and for failing to take corrective security measures as ordered by the Brigade Commander; filed locally
- Suspended by BG Karpinski, Commander 800th MP Brigade, 17 January 2004; Pending Relief for Cause, for dereliction of duty

3). (U) LTC Dale Burtyk, Commander, 400th MP Battalion
  - GOMOR from BG Karpinski, Commander 800th MP Brigade, on 20 August 2003, for failure to properly train his Soldiers. (Soldier had negligent discharge of M-16 while exiting his vehicle, round went into fuel tank); filed locally.

4). (U) MAJ David DiNenna, S-3, 320th MP Battalion
  - GOMOR from LTG McKiernan, Commander CFLCC, on 25 May 2003, for dereliction of duty for failing to report a violation of CENTCOM General Order #1 by a subordinate Field Grade Officer and Senior Noncommissioned Officer, which he personally observed; returned to soldier unfiled.
  - GOMOR from BG Karpinski, Commander 800th MP Brigade, on 10 November 03, for failing to take corrective security measures as ordered by the Brigade Commander; filed locally.

5). (U) MAJ Stacy Garrity, Finance Officer, 800th MP Brigade
  - GOMOR from LTG McKiernan, Commander CFLCC, on 25 May 2003, for violation of CENTCOM General Order #1, consuming alcohol with an NCO; filed locally.

6). (U) CPT Leo Merck, Commander, 870th MP Company
  - Court-Martial Charges Preferred, for Conduct Unbecoming an Officer and Unauthorized Use of Government Computer in that he was alleged to have taken nude pictures of his female Soldiers without their knowledge; Trial date to be announced.

7). (U) CPT Damaris Morales, Commander, 770th MP Company
  - GOMOR from BG Karpinski, Commander 800th MP Brigade, on 20 August 2003, for failing to properly train his Soldiers (Soldier had negligent discharge of M-16 while exiting his vehicle, round went into fuel tank); filed locally.

8). (U) CSM Roy Clement, Command Sergeant Major, 800th MP Brigade

- GOMOR and Relief for Cause from BG Janis Karpinski, Commander 800th MP Brigade, for fraternization and dereliction of duty for fraternizing with junior enlisted soldiers within his unit; GOMOR officially filed and he was removed from the CSM list.

9). (U) CSM Edward Stotts, Command Sergeant Major, 400th MP Battalion
- GOMOR from BG Karpinski, Commander 800th MP Brigade, on 20 August 2003, for failing to properly train his Soldiers (Soldier had negligent discharge of M-16 while exiting his vehicle, round went into fuel tank); filed locally.

10). (U) 1SG Carlos Villanueva, First Sergeant, 770th MP Company
- GOMOR from BG Karpinski, Commander 800th MP Brigade, on 20 August 2003, for failing to properly train his Soldiers (Soldier had negligent discharge of M-16 while exiting his vehicle, round went into fuel tank); filed locally.

11). (U) MSG David Maffett, NBC NCO, 800th MP Brigade,
- GOMOR from LTG McKiernan, Commander CFLCC, on 25 May 2003, for violation of CENTCOM General Order #1, consuming alcohol; filed locally.

12). (U) SGM Marc Emerson, Operations SGM, 320th MP Battalion,
- Two GO Letters of Concern and a verbal reprimand from BG Karpinski, Commander 800th MP Brigade, for failing to adhere to the guidance/directives given to him by BG Karpinski; filed locally.

d. (U) Saluting of officers was sporadic and not enforced. LTC Robert P. Walters, Jr., Commander of the 165th Military Intelligence Battalion (Tactical Exploitation), testified that the saluting policy was enforced by COL Pappas for all MI personnel, and that BG Karpinski approached COL Pappas to reverse the saluting policy back to a no-saluting policy as previously existed. (ANNEX 53)

19. (U) I find that individual Soldiers within the 800th MP Brigade and the 320th Battalion stationed throughout Iraq had very little contact during their tour of duty with either LTC (P) Phillabaum or BG Karpinski. BG Karpinski claimed, during her testimony, that she paid regular visits to the various detention facilities where her Soldiers were stationed. However, the detailed calendar provided by her Aide-de-Camp, 1LT Mabry, does not support her contention. Moreover,

numerous witnesses stated that they rarely saw BG Karpinski or LTC (P) Phill-abaum. (Multiple Witness Statements)

20. (U) In addition I find that psychological factors, such as the difference in culture, the Soldiers' quality of life, the real presence of mortal danger over an extended time period, and the failure of commanders to recognize these pressures contributed to the perversive atmosphere that existed at Abu Ghraib (BCCF) Detention Facility and throughout the 800th MP Brigade. (ANNEX 1).

21. As I have documented in other parts of this investigation, I find that there was no clear emphasis by BG Karpinski to ensure that the 800th MP Brigade Staff, Commanders, and Soldiers were trained to standard in detainee operations and proficiency or that serious accountability lapses that occurred over a significant period of time, particularly at Abu Ghraib (BCCF), were corrected. AR 15-6 Investigations regarding detainee escapes were not acted upon, followed up with corrective action, or disseminated to subordinate commanders or Soldiers. Brigade and unit SOPs for dealing with detainees if they existed at all, were not read or understood by MP Soldiers assigned the difficult mission of detainee operations. Following the abuse of several detainees at Camp Bucca in May 2003, I could find no evidence that BG Karpinski ever directed corrective training for her soldiers or ensured that MP Soldiers throughout Iraq clearly understood the requirements of the Geneva Conventions relating to the treatment of detainees. (Multiple Witness Statements and the Personal Observations of the Investigation Team)

22. On 17 January 2004 BG Karpinski was formally admonished in writing by LTG Sanchez regarding the serious deficiencies in her Brigade. LTG Sanchez found that the performance of the 800th MP Brigade had not met the standards set by the Army or by CJTF-7. He found that incidents in the preceding six months had occurred that reflected a lack of clear standards, proficiency and leadership within the Brigade. LTG Sanchez also cited the recent detainee abuse at Abu Ghraib (BCCF) as the most recent example of a poor leadership climate that "permeates the Brigade." I totally concur with LTG Sanchez' opinion regarding the performance of BG Karpinski and the 800th MP Brigade. (ANNEX 102 and the Personal Observations of the Investigating Officer)

RECOMMENDATIONS AS TO PART THREE OF THE INVESTIGATION:

1. (U) That BG Janis L. Karpinski, Commander, 800th MP Brigade be Relieved from Command and given a General Officer Memorandum of Reprimand for the following acts which have been previously referred to in the aforementioned findings:
   • Failing to ensure that MP Soldiers at theater-level detention facilities throughout Iraq had appropriate SOPs for dealing with detainees and that

Commanders and Soldiers had read, understood, and would adhere to these SOPs.

- Failing to ensure that MP Soldiers in the 800th MP Brigade knew, understood, and adhered to the protections afforded to detainees in the Geneva Convention Relative to the Treatment of Prisoners of War.
- Making material misrepresentations to the Investigation Team as to the frequency of her visits to her subordinate commands.
- Failing to obey an order from the CFLCC Commander, LTG McKiernan, regarding the withholding of disciplinary authority for Officer and Senior Noncommissioned Officer misconduct.
- Failing to take appropriate action regarding the ineffectiveness of a subordinate Commander, LTC (P) Jerry Phillabaum.
- Failing to take appropriate action regarding the ineffectiveness of numerous members of her Brigade Staff including her XO, S-1, S-3, and S-4.
- Failing to properly ensure the results and recommendations of the AARs and numerous 15-6 Investigation reports on escapes and shootings (over a period of several months) were properly disseminated to, and understood by, subordinate commanders.
- Failing to ensure and enforce basic Soldier standards throughout her command.
- Failing to establish a Brigade METL.
- Failing to establish basic proficiency in assigned tasks for Soldiers throughout the 800th MP Brigade.
- Failing to ensure that numerous and reported accountability lapses at detention facilities throughout Iraq were corrected.

2. (U) That COL Thomas M. Pappas, Commander, 205th MI Brigade, be given a General Officer Memorandum of Reprimand and Investigated UP Procedure 15, AR 381-10, US Army Intelligence Activities for the following acts which have been previously referred to in the aforementioned findings:
- Failing to ensure that Soldiers under his direct command were properly trained in and followed the IROE.
- Failing to ensure that Soldiers under his direct command knew, understood, and followed the protections afforded to detainees in the Geneva Convention Relative to the Treatment of Prisoners of War.
- Failing to properly supervise his soldiers working and "visiting" Tier 1 of the Hard-Site at Abu Ghraib (BCCF).

3. (U) That LTC (P) Jerry L. Phillabaum, Commander, 320th MP Battalion, be Relieved from Command, be given a General Officer Memorandum of Reprimand, and be removed from the Colonel/O-6 Promotion List for the following acts which have been previously referred to in the aforementioned findings:
- Failing to properly ensure the results, recommendations, and AARs from numerous reports on escapes and shootings over a period of several months

were properly disseminated to, and understood by, subordinates.

- Failing to implement the appropriate recommendations from various 15-6 Investigations as specifically directed by BG Karpinski.
- Failing to ensure that Soldiers under his direct command were properly trained in Internment and Resettlement Operations.
- Failing to ensure that Soldiers under his direct command knew and understood the protections afforded to detainees in the Geneva Convention Relative to the Treatment of Prisoners of War.
- Failing to properly supervise his soldiers working and "visiting" Tier 1 of the Hard-Site at Abu Ghraib (BCCF).
- Failing to properly establish and enforce basic soldier standards, proficiency, and accountability.
- Failure to conduct an appropriate Mission Analysis and to task organize to accomplish his mission.

4. (U) That LTC Steven L. Jordan, Former Director, Joint Interrogation and Debriefing Center and Liaison Officer to 205th Military Intelligence Brigade, be relieved from duty and be given a General Officer Memorandum of Reprimand for the following acts which have been previously referred to in the aforementioned findings:

- Making material misrepresentations to the Investigating Team, including his leadership roll at Abu Ghraib (BCCF).
- Failing to ensure that Soldiers under his direct control were properly trained in and followed the IROE.
- Failing to ensure that Soldiers under his direct control knew, understood, and followed the protections afforded to detainees in the Geneva Convention Relative to the Treatment of Prisoners of War.
- Failing to properly supervise soldiers under his direct authority working and "visiting" Tier 1 of the Hard-Site at Abu Ghraib (BCCF).

5. (U) That MAJ David W. DiNenna, Sr., S-3, 320th MP Battalion, be Relieved from his position as the Battalion S-3 and be given a General Officer Memorandum of Reprimand for the following acts which have been previously referred to in the aforementioned findings:

- Received a GOMOR from LTG McKiernan, Commander CFLCC, on 25 May 2003, for dereliction of duty for failing to report a violation of CENTCOM General Order #1 by a subordinate Field Grade Officer and Senior Noncommissioned Officer, which he personally observed; GOMOR was returned to Soldier and not filed.
- Failing to take corrective action and implement recommendations from various 15-6 investigations even after receiving a GOMOR from BG Karpinski, Commander 800th MP Brigade, on 10 November 03, for failing to take corrective security measures as ordered; GOMOR was filed locally.

- Failing to take appropriate action and report an incident of detainee abuse, whereby he personally witnessed a Soldier throw a detainee from the back of a truck.

6. (U) That CPT Donald J. Reese, Commander, 372nd MP Company, be Relieved from Command and be given a General Officer Memorandum of Reprimand for the following acts which have been previously referred to in the aforementioned findings:

    - Failing to ensure that Soldiers under his direct command knew and understood the protections afforded to detainees in the Geneva Convention Relative to the Treatment of Prisoners of War.
    - Failing to properly supervise his Soldiers working and "visiting" Tier 1 of the Hard-Site at Abu Ghraib (BCCF).
    - Failing to properly establish and enforce basic soldier standards, proficiency, and accountability.
    - Failing to ensure that Soldiers under his direct command were properly trained in Internment and Resettlement Operations.

7. (U) That 1LT Lewis C. Raeder, Platoon Leader, 372nd MP Company, be Relieved from his duties as Platoon Leader and be given a General Officer Memorandum of Reprimand for the following acts which have been previously referred to in the aforementioned findings:

    - Failing to ensure that Soldiers under his direct command knew and understood the protections afforded to detainees in the Geneva Convention Relative to the Treatment of Prisoners of War.
    - Failing to properly supervise his soldiers working and "visiting" Tier 1 of the Hard-Site at Abu Ghraib (BCCF).
    - Failing to properly establish and enforce basic Soldier standards, proficiency, and accountability.
    - Failing to ensure that Soldiers under his direct command were properly trained in Internment and Resettlement Operations.

8. (U) That SGM Marc Emerson, Operations SGM, 320th MP Battalion, be Relieved from his duties and given a General Officer Memorandum of Reprimand for the following acts which have been previously referred to in the aforementioned findings:

    - Making a material misrepresentation to the Investigation Team stating that he had "never" been admonished or reprimanded by BG Karpinski, when in fact he had been admonished for failing to obey an order from BG Karpinski to "stay out of the towers" at the holding facility.
    - Making a material misrepresentation to the Investigation Team stating that he had attended every shift change/guard-mount conducted at the 320th MP Battalion, and that he personally briefed his Soldiers on the proper treatment

of detainees, when in fact numerous statements contradict this assertion.

- Failing to ensure that Soldiers in the 320th MP Battalion knew and understood the protections afforded to detainees in the Geneva Convention Relative to the Treatment of Prisoners of War.
- Failing to properly supervise his soldiers working and "visiting" Tier 1 of the Hard-Site at Abu Ghraib (BCCF).
- Failing to properly establish and enforce basic soldier standards, proficiency,
- Failing to ensure that his Soldiers were properly trained in Internment and Resettlement Operations.

9. (U) That 1SG Brian G. Lipinski, First Sergeant, 372nd MP Company, be Relieved from his duties as First Sergeant of the 372nd MP Company and given a General Officer Memorandum of Reprimand for the following acts which have been previously referred to in the aforementioned findings:

- Failing to ensure that Soldiers in the 372nd MP Company knew and understood the protections afforded to detainees in the Geneva Convention Relative to the Treatment of Prisoners of War.
- Failing to properly supervise his soldiers working and "visiting" Tier 1 of the Hard-Site at Abu Ghraib (BCCF).
- Failing to properly establish and enforce basic soldier standards, proficiency, and accountability.
- Failing to ensure that his Soldiers were properly trained in Internment and Resettlement Operations.

10. (U) That SFC Shannon K. Snider, Platoon Sergeant, 372nd MP Company, be Relieved from his duties, receive a General Officer Memorandum of Reprimand, and receive action under the Uniform Code of Military Justice for the following acts which have been previously referred to in the aforementioned findings:

- Failing to ensure that Soldiers in his platoon knew and understood the protections afforded to detainees in the Geneva Convention Relative to the Treatment of Prisoners of War.
- Failing to properly supervise his soldiers working and "visiting" Tier 1 of the Hard-Site at Abu Ghraib (BCCF).
- Failing to properly establish and enforce basic soldier standards, proficiency, and accountability.
- Failing to ensure that his Soldiers were properly trained in Internment and Resettlement Operations.
- Failing to report a Soldier, who under his direct control, abused detainees by stomping on their bare hands and feet in his presence.

11. (U) That Mr. Steven Stephanowicz, Contract US Civilian Interrogator, CACI, 205th Military Intelligence Brigade, be given an Official Reprimand to be placed in his employment file, termination of employment, and generation of a derogatory

report to revoke his security clearance for the following acts which have been previously referred to in the aforementioned findings:
- Made a false statement to the investigation team regarding the locations of his interrogations, the activities during his interrogations, and his knowledge of abuses.
- Allowed and/or instructed MPs, who were not trained in interrogation techniques, to facilitate interrogations by "setting conditions" which were neither authorized and in accordance with applicable regulations/policy. He clearly knew his instructions equated to physical abuse.

12. (U) That Mr. John Israel, Contract US Civilian Interpreter, CACI, 205th Military Intelligence Brigade, be given an Official Reprimand to be placed in his employment file and have his security clearance reviewed by competent authority for the following acts or concerns which have been previously referred to in the aforementioned findings:
- Denied ever having seen interrogation processes in violation of the IROE, which is contrary to several witness statements.
- Did not have a security clearance.

13. (U) I find that there is sufficient credible information to warrant an Inquiry UP Procedure 15, AR 381-10, US Army Intelligence Activities, be conducted to determine the extent of culpability of MI personnel, assigned to the 205th MI Brigade and the Joint Interrogation and Debriefing Center (JIDC) at Abu Ghraib (BCCF). Specifically, I suspect that COL Thomas M. Pappas, LTC Steve L. Jordan, Mr. Steven Stephanowicz, and Mr. John Israel were either directly or indirectly responsible for the abuses at Abu Ghraib (BCCF) and strongly recommend immediate disciplinary action as described in the preceding paragraphs as well as the initiation of a Procedure 15 Inquiry to determine the full extent of their culpability. (Annex 36)

OTHER FINDINGS/OBSERVATIONS

1. (U) Due to the nature and scope of this investigation, I acquired the assistance of Col (Dr.) Henry Nelson, a USAF Psychiatrist, to analyze the investigation materials from a psychological perspective. He determined that there was evidence that the horrific abuses suffered by the detainees at Abu Ghraib (BCCF) were wanton acts of select soldiers in an unsupervised and dangerous setting. There was a complex interplay of many psychological factors and command insufficiencies. A more detailed analysis is contained in ANNEX 1 of this investigation.

2. (U) During the course of this investigation I conducted a lengthy interview with BG Karpinski that lasted over four hours, and is included verbatim in the investi-

gation Annexes. BG Karpinski was extremely emotional during much of her testimony. What I found particularly disturbing in her testimony was her complete unwillingness to either understand or accept that many of the problems inherent in the 800th MP Brigade were caused or exacerbated by poor leadership and the refusal of her command to both establish and enforce basic standards and principles among its Soldiers. (ANNEX 45)

3. (U) Throughout the investigation, we observed many individual Soldiers and some subordinate units under the 800th MP Brigade that overcame significant obstacles, persevered in extremely poor conditions, and upheld the Army Values. We discovered numerous examples of Soldiers and Sailors taking the initiative in the absence of leadership and accomplishing their assigned tasks.

  a. (U) The 744th MP Battalion, commanded by LTC Dennis McGlone, efficiently operated the HVD Detention Facility at Camp Cropper and met mission requirements with little to no guidance from the 800th MP Brigade. The unit was disciplined, proficient, and appeared to understand their basic tasks.

  b. (U) The 530th MP Battalion, commanded by LTC Stephen J. Novotny, effectively maintained the MEK Detention Facility at Camp Ashraf. His Soldiers were proficient in their individual tasks and adapted well to this highly unique and non-doctrinal operation.

  c. (U) The 165th MI Battalion excelled in providing perimeter security and force protection at Abu Ghraib (BCCF). LTC Robert P. Walters, Jr., demanded standards be enforced and worked endlessly to improve discipline throughout the FOB.

4. (U) The individual Soldiers and Sailors that we observed and believe should be favorably noted include:

  a. (U) Master-at-Arms First Class William J. Kimbro, US Navy Dog Handler, knew his duties and refused to participate in improper interrogations despite significant pressure from the MI personnel at Abu Ghraib.

  b. (U) SPC Joseph M. Darby, 372nd MP Company discovered evidence of abuse and turned it over to military law enforcement.

  c. (U) 1LT David O. Sutton, 229th MP Company, took immediate action and stopped an abuse, then reported the incident to the chain of command.

CONCLUSION

1. (U) Several US Army Soldiers have committed egregious acts and grave breaches of international law at Abu Ghraib/BCCF and Camp Bucca, Iraq. Furthermore, key senior leaders in both the 800th MP Brigade and the 205th MI Brigade failed to comply with established regulations, policies, and command directives in preventing detainee abuses at Abu Ghraib (BCCF) and at Camp Bucca during the period August 2003 to February 2004.

2. (U) Approval and implementation of the recommendations of this AR 15-6 Investigation and those highlighted in previous assessments are essential to establish the conditions with the resources and personnel required to prevent future occurrences of detainee abuse.

Annexes

1. Psychological Assessment
2. Request for investigation from CJTF-7 to CENTCOM
3. Directive to CFLCC from CENTCOM directing investigation
4. Appointment Memo from CFLCC CDR to MG Taguba
5. 15-6 Investigation 9 June 2003
6. 15-6 Investigation 12 June 2003
7. 15-6 Investigation 13 June 2003
8. 15-6 Investigation 24 November 2003
9. 15-6 Investigation 7 January 2004
10. 15-6 Investigation 12 January 2004
11. SIR 5 November 2003
12. SIR 7 November 2003
13. SIR 8 November 2003
14. SIR 13 December 2003
15. SIR 13 December 2003
16. SIR 13 December 2003
17. SIR 17 December 2003
18. Commander's Inquiry 26 January 2004
19. MG Ryder's Report, 6 November 2003
20. MG Miller's Report, 9 September 2003
21. AR 190-8, Enemy Prisoners of War, Retained Personnel, Civilian Internees, and Other Detainees, 1 October 1997
22. FM 3-19.40, Military Police Internment/Resettlement Operations, 1 August 2001
23. FM 34-52, Intelligence Interrogation, 28 September 1992
24. Fourth Geneva Convention, 12 August 1949
25. CID Report on criminal abuses at Abu Ghraib, 28 January 2004
26. CID Interviews, 10–25 January 2004

27. 800th MP Brigade Roster, 29 January 2004
28. 205th MI Brigade's IROE, Undated
29. TOA Order (800th MP Brigade) and letter holding witnesses
30. Investigation Team's witness list
31. FRAGO #1108
32. Letters suspending several key leaders in the 800th MP Brigade and Rating Chain with suspensions annotated
33. FM 27-10, Military Justice, 6 September 2002
34. CID Report on abuse of detainees at Camp Bucca, 8 June 2003
35. Article 32 Findings on abuse of detainees at Camp Bucca, 26 August 2003
36. AR 381-10, 1 July 1984
37. Excerpts from log books, 320th MP Battalion
38. 310th MP Battalion's Inprocessing SOP
39. 320th MP Battalion's "Change Sheet"
40. Joint Interrogation and Debriefing Center's (JIDC) Slides, Undated
41. Order of Battle Slides, 12 January 2004
42. Joint Publication 0-2, Unified Actions Armed Forces, 10 July 2001
43. General Officer Memorandums of Reprimand
44. 800th MP Battalion's TACSOP
45. BG Janis Karpinski, Commander, 800th MP Brigade
46. COL Thomas Pappas, Commander, 205th MI Brigade
47. COL Ralph Sabatino, CFLCC Judge Advocate, CPA Ministry of Justice
48. LTC Gary W. Maddocks, S-5 and Executive Officer, 800th MP Brigade
49. LTC James O'Hare, Command Judge Advocate, 800th MP Brigade
50. LTC Robert P. Walters Jr., Commander, 165th MI Battalion (Tactical exploitation)
51. LTC James D. Edwards, Commander, 202nd MI Battalion
52. LTC Vincent Montera, Commander 310th MP Battalion
53. LTC Steve Jordan, former Director, Joint Interrogation and Debriefing Center/LNO to the 205th MI Brigade
54. LTC Leigh A. Coulter, Commander 724th MP Battalion and OIC Arifjan Detachment, 800th MP Brigade
55. LTC Dennis McGlone, Commander, 744th MP Battalion
56. MAJ David Hinzman, S-1, 800th MP Brigade
57. MAJ William D. Proietto, Deputy CJA, 800th MP Brigade
58. MAJ Stacy L. Garrity, S-1 (FWD), 800th MP Brigade
59. MAJ David W. DiNenna, S-3, 320th MP Battalion
60. MAJ Michael Sheridan, XO, 320th MP Battalion
61. MAJ Anthony Cavallaro, S-3, 800th MP Brigade
62. CPT Marc C. Hale, Commander, 670th MP Company
63. CPT Donald Reese, Commander, 372nd MP Company
64. CPT Darren Hampton, Assistant S-3, 320th MP Battalion
65. CPT John Kaires, S-3, 310th MP Battalion
66. CPT Ed Diamantis, S-2, 800th MP Brigade

67. LTC Jerry L. Phillabaum, Commander, 320th MP Battalion
68. CPT James G. Jones, Commander, 229th MP Company
69. CPT Michael A. Mastrangelo, Jr., Commander, 310th MP Company
70. CPT Lawrence Bush, IG, 800th MP Brigade
71. 1LT Lewis C. Raeder, Platoon Leader, 372nd MP Company
72. 1LT Elvis Mabry, Aide-de-Camp to Brigade Commander, 800th MP Brigade
73. 1LT Warren E. Ford, II, Commander, HHC 320th MP Battalion
74. 2LT David O. Sutton, Platoon Leader, 229th MP Company
75. CW2 Edward J. Rivas, 205th MI Brigade
76. CSM Joseph P. Arrison, Command Sergeant Major, 320th MP Battalion
77. SGM Pascual Cartagena, Command Sergeant Major, 800th MP Brigade
78. CSM Timothy L. Woodcock, Command Sergeant Major, 310th MP Battalion
79. 1SG Dawn J. Rippelmeyer, First Sergeant, 977th MP Company
80. SGM Mark Emerson, Operations SGM, 320th MP Battalion
81. MSG Brian G. Lipinski, First Sergeant, 372nd MP Company
82. MSG Andrew J. Lombardo, Operations Sergeant, 310th MP Battalion
83. SFC Daryl J. Plude, Platoon Sergeant, 229th MP Company
84. SFC Shannon K. Snider, Platoon SGT, 372nd MP Company
85. SFC Keith A. Comer, 372nd MP Company
86. SSG Robert Elliot, Squad Leader, 372nd MP Company
87. SSG Santos A. Cardona, Army Dog Handler
88. SGT Michael Smith, Army Dog Handler
89. MA1 William J. Kimbro, USN Dog Handler
90. Mr. Steve Stephanowicz, US civilian contract Interrogator, CACI, 205th MI Brigade
91. Mr. John Israel, US civilian contract Interpreter, Titan Corporation, 205th MI Brigade
92. FM 3-19.1, Military Police Operations, 22 March 2001
93. CJTF-7 IROE and DROE, Undated
94. CJTF-7 Interrogation and Counter Resistance Policy, 12 October 2003
95. 800th MP Brigade Mobilization Orders
96. Sample Detainee Status Report, 13 March 2004
97. 530th MP Battalion Mission Brief, 11 February 2004
98. Memorandum for Record, CPT Ed Ray, Chief of Military Justice, CFLCC, 9 March 2004
99. SIR 14 January 2004
100. Accountability Plan Recommendations, 9 March 2004
101. 2LT Michael R. Osterhout, S-2, 320th MP Battalion
102. Memorandum of Admonishment from LTG Sanchez to BG Karpinski, 17 January 2004
103. Various SIRs from the 800th MP Brigade/320th MP Battalion
104. 205th MI Brigade SITREP to MG Miller, 12 December 2003
105. SGT William A. Cathcart, 372nd MP Company
106. 1LT Michael A. Drayton, Commander, 870th MP Company

FINAL REPORT OF THE INDEPENDENT PANEL TO REVIEW DoD DETENTION OPERATIONS (THE SCHLESINGER REPORT)

August 2004

INDEPENDENT PANEL TO REVIEW DoD DETENTION OPERATIONS

Chairman
The Honorable James R. Schlesinger

Panel Members
The Honorable Harold Brown
The Honorable Tillie K. Fowler
General Charles A. Homer (USAF-RET)

Executive Director
Dr. James A. Blackwell, Jr.

August 24, 2004

To U.S. Secretary of Defense Donald Rumsfeld

We, the appointed members of the Independent Panel to Review DoD Detention Operations, pursuant to our charter do hereby submit the results of our findings and offer our best recommendations.

Sincerely,

[signed]
The Honorable James R. Schlesinger
Chairman

[signed]
The Honorable Harold Brown
Panel Member

[signed]
The Honorable Tillie K. Fowler
Panel Member

[signed]
General Charles A. Horner
(USAF - Ret.)
Panel Member

THE INDEPENDENT PANEL TO REVIEW DEPARTMENT OF DEFENSE
DETENTION OPERATIONS

August 2004

Table of Contents

Table of Appendices

EXECUTIVE SUMMARY

OVERVIEW

The events of October through December 2003 on the night shift of Tier 1 at Abu Ghraib prison were acts of brutality and purposeless sadism. We now know these abuses occurred at the hands of both military police and military intelligence personnel. The pictured abuses, unacceptable even in wartime, were not part of authorized interrogations nor were they even directed at intelligence targets. They represent deviant behavior and a failure of military leadership and discipline. However, we do know that some of the egregious abuses at Abu Ghraib which were not photographed did occur during interrogation sessions and that abuses during interrogation sessions occurred elsewhere.

In light of what happened at Abu Ghraib, a series of comprehensive investigations has been conducted by various components of the Department of Defense. Since the beginning of hostilities in Afghanistan and Iraq, U.S. military and security operations have apprehended about 50,000 individuals. From this number, about 300 allegations of abuse in Afghanistan, Iraq or Guantánamo have arisen. As of mid-August 2004, 155 investigations into the allegations have been completed, resulting in 66 substantiated cases. Approximately one-third of these cases occurred at the point of capture or tactical collection point, frequently under uncertain, dangerous and violent circumstances.

Abuses of varying severity occurred at differing locations under differing circumstances and context. They were widespread and, though inflicted on only a small percentage of those detained, they were serious both in number and in effect. No approved procedures called for or allowed the kinds of abuse that in fact occurred. There is no evidence of a policy of abuse promulgated by senior officials or military authorities. Still, the abuses were not just the failure of some individuals to follow known standards, and they are more than the failure of a few leaders to enforce proper discipline. There is both institutional and personal responsibility at higher levels.

Secretary of Defense Donald Rumsfeld appointed the members of the Independent Panel to provide independent professional advice on detainee abuses, what caused them and what actions should be taken to preclude their repetition. The Panel reviewed various criminal investigations and a number of command and other major investigations. The Panel also conducted interviews of relevant persons, including the Secretary and Deputy Secretary of Defense, other senior Department of Defense officials, the military chain-of-command and their staffs and other officials directly and indirectly involved with Abu Ghraib and other detention operations. However, the Panel did not have full access to information involving the role of the Central Intelligence Agency in detention operations; this is an area the Panel believes needs further investigation and review. It should be noted that information provided to the Panel was that available as of mid-August 2004. If additional information becomes available, the Panel's judgments might be revised.

POLICY

With the events of September 11, 2001, the President, the Congress and the American people recognized we were at war with a different kind of enemy. The terrorists who flew airliners into the World Trade Center and the Pentagon were unlike enemy combatants the U.S. has fought in previous conflicts. Their objectives, in fact, are to kill large numbers of civilians and to strike at the heart of America's political cohesion and its economic and military might. In the days and weeks after the attack, the President and his closest advisers developed policies and strategies in response. On September 18, 2001, by a virtually unanimous vote, Congress passed an Authorization for Use of Military Force. Shortly thereafter, the U.S. initiated hostilities in Afghanistan and the first detainees were held at Mazar-e-Sharrif in November 2001.

On February 7, 2002, the President issued a memorandum stating that he determined the Geneva Conventions did not apply to the conflict with al Qaeda, and although they did apply in the conflict with Afghanistan, the Taliban were unlawful combatants and therefore did not qualify for prisoner of war status (see Appendix C). Nonetheless, the Secretary of State, Secretary of Defense, and the Chairman of the Joint Chiefs of Staff were all in agreement that treatment of detainees should be consistent with the Geneva Conventions. The President ordered accordingly that detainees were to be treated "... humanely and, to the extent appropriate and consistent with military necessity, in a manner consistent with the principles of Geneva." Earlier, the Department of State had argued the Geneva Conventions in their traditional application provided a sufficiently robust legal construct under which the Global War on Terror could effectively be waged. The Legal Advisor to the Chairman, Joint Chiefs of Staff, and many of the military service attorneys agreed with this position.

In the summer of 2002, the Counsel to the President queried the Department of Justice Office of Legal Counsel (OLC) for an opinion on the standards of conduct for interrogation operations conducted by U.S. personnel outside of the U.S. and the applicability of the Convention Against Torture. The OLC responded in an August 1, 2002 opinion in which it held that in order to constitute torture, an act must be specifically intended to inflict severe physical or mental pain and suffering that is difficult to endure.

Army Field Manual 34-52 (FM 34-52), with its list of 17 authorized interrogation methods, has long been the standard source for interrogation doctrine within the Department of Defense (see Appendix D). In October 2002, authorities at Guantánamo requested approval of stronger interrogation techniques to counter tenacious resistance by some detainees. The Secretary of Defense responded with a December 2, 2002 decision authorizing the use of 16 additional techniques at Guantánamo (see Appendix E). As a result of concerns raised by the Navy General Counsel on January 15, 2003, Secretary Rumsfeld rescinded the majority of the approved measures in the

December 2, 2002 authorization. Moreover, he directed the remaining more aggressive techniques could be used only with his approval (see Appendix D).

At the same time, he directed the Department of Defense (DoD) General Counsel to establish a working group to study interrogation techniques. The Working Group was headed by Air Force General Counsel Mary Walker and included wide membership from across the military legal and intelligence communities. The Working Group also relied heavily on the OLC. The Working Group reviewed 35 techniques and after a very extensive debate ultimately recommended 24 to the Secretary of Defense. The study led to the Secretary of Defense's promulgation on April 16, 2003 of a list of approved techniques strictly limited for use at Guantánamo. This policy remains in force at Guantánamo (see Appendix E).

In the initial development of these Secretary of Defense policies, the legal resources of the Services' Judge Advocates General and General Counsels were not utilized to their full potential. Had the Secretary of Defense had a wider range of legal opinions and a more robust debate regarding detainee policies and operations, his policy of April 16, 2003 might well have been developed and issued in early December 2002. This would have avoided the policy changes which characterized the Dec 02, 2002 to April 16, 2003 period.

It is clear that pressures for additional intelligence and the more aggressive methods sanctioned by the Secretary of Defense memorandum, resulted in stronger interrogation techniques that were believed to be needed and appropriate in the treatment of detainees defined as "unlawful combatants." At Guantánamo, the interrogators used those additional techniques with only two detainees, gaining important and time-urgent information in the process.

In Afghanistan, from the war's inception through the end of 2002, all forces used FM 34-52 as a baseline for interrogation techniques. Nonetheless, more aggressive interrogation of detainees appears to have been on-going. On January 24, 2003, in response to a data call from the Joint Staff to facilitate the Working Group efforts, the Commander Joint Task Force-180 forwarded a list of techniques being used in Afghanistan, including some not explicitly set out in FM 34-52. These techniques were included in a Special Operation Forces (SOF) Standard Operating Procedures document published in February 2003. The 519th Military Intelligence Battalion, a company of which was later sent to Iraq, assisted in interrogations in support of SOF and was fully aware of their interrogation techniques.

Interrogators and lists of techniques circulated from Guantánamo and Afghanistan to Iraq. During July and August 2003, the 519th Military Intelligence Company was sent to the Abu Ghraib detention facility to conduct interrogation operations. Absent any explicit policy or guidance, other than FM 34-52, the officer in charge prepared draft interrogation guidelines that were a near copy of the Standard Operating Procedure created by SOF. It is important to note that techniques effective under carefully controlled conditions at Guantánamo became far more problematic when they migrated and were not adequately safeguarded.

Following a CJTF-7 request, Joint Staff tasked SOUTHCOM to send an assistance team to provide advice on facilities and operations, specifically related to screening, interrogations, HUMINT collection, and inter-agency integration in the short and long term. In August 2003, MG Geoffrey Miller arrived to conduct an assessment of DoD counter-terrorism interrogation and detention operations in Iraq. He was to discuss current theater ability to exploit internees rapidly for actionable intelligence. He brought the Secretary of Defense's April 16, 2003 policy guidelines for Guantánamo with him and gave this policy to CJTF-7 as a possible model for the command-wide policy that he recommended be established. MG Miller noted that it applied to unlawful combatants at Guantánamo and was not directly applicable to Iraq where the Geneva Conventions applied. In part as a result of MG Miller's call for strong, command-wide interrogation policies and in part as a result of a request for guidance coming up from the 519th at Abu Ghraib, on September 14, 2003 LTG Sanchez signed a memorandum authorizing a dozen interrogation techniques beyond Field Manual 34-52—five beyond those approved for Guantánamo (see Appendix D).

MG Miller had indicated his model was approved only for Guantánamo. However, CJTF-7, using reasoning from the President's Memorandum of February 7, 2002 which addressed "unlawful combatants," believed additional, tougher measures were warranted because there were "unlawful combatants" mixed in with Enemy Prisoners of War and civilian and criminal detainees. The CJTF-7 Commander, on the advice of his Staff Judge Advocate, believed he had the inherent authority of the Commander in a Theater of War to promulgate such a policy and make determinations as to the categorization of detainees under the Geneva Conventions. CENTCOM viewed the CJTF-7 policy as unacceptably aggressive and on October 12, 2003 Commander CJTF-7 rescinded his September directive and disseminated methods only slightly stronger than those in Field Manual 34–52 (see Appendix D). The policy memos promulgated at the CJTF-7 level allowed for interpretation in several areas and did not adequately set forth the limits of interrogation techniques. The existence of confusing and inconsistent interrogation technique policies contributed to the belief that additional interrogation techniques were condoned.

DETENTION AND INTERROGATION OPERATIONS

From his experience in Guantánamo, MG Miller called for the military police and military intelligence soldiers to work cooperatively, with the military police "setting the conditions" for interrogations. This MP role included passive collection on detainees as well as supporting incentives recommended by the military interrogators. These collaborative procedures worked effectively in Guantánamo, particularly in light of the high ratio of approximately 1 to 1 of military police to mostly compliant detainees. However, in Iraq and particularly in Abu Ghraib the ratio of military police to repeatedly unruly detainees was significantly smaller, at one point 1 to about 75 at Abu Ghraib, making it difficult even to keep track of prisoners. Moreover, because Abu Ghraib was located in a combat zone, the military police were engaged in force protection of the complex as well as escorting convoys of supplies to and from the prison. Compounding these problems was the inadequacy of leadership, oversight and support needed in the face of such difficulties.

At various times, the U.S. conducted detention operations at approximately 17 sites in Iraq and 25 sites in Afghanistan, in addition to the strategic operation at Guantánamo. A cumulative total of 50,000 detainees have been in the custody of U.S. forces since November 2001, with a peak population of 11,000 in the month of March 2004.

In Iraq, there was not only a failure to plan for a major insurgency, but also to quickly and adequately adapt to the insurgency that followed after major combat operations. The October 2002 CENTCOM War Plan presupposed that relatively benign stability and security operations would precede a handover to Iraq's authorities. The contingencies contemplated in that plan included sabotage of oil production facilities and large numbers of refugees generated by communal strife.

Major combat operations were accomplished more swiftly than anticipated. Then began a period of occupation and an active and growing insurgency. Although the removal of Saddam Hussein was initially welcomed by the bulk of the population, the occupation became increasingly resented. Detention facilities soon held Iraqi and foreign terrorists as well as a mix of Enemy Prisoners of War, other security detainees, criminals and undoubtedly some accused as a result of factional rivalries. Of the 17 detention facilities in Iraq, the largest, Abu Ghraib, housed up to 7,000 detainees in October 2003, with a guard force of only about 90 personnel from the 800th Military Police Brigade. Abu Ghraib was seriously overcrowded, under-resourced, and under continual attack. Five U.S. soldiers died as a result of mortar attacks on Abu Ghraib. In July 2003, Abu Ghraib was mortared 25 times; on August 16, 2003, five detainees were killed and 67 wounded in a mortar attack. A mortar attack on April 20, 2004 killed 22 detainees.

Problems at Abu Ghraib are traceable in part to the nature and recent history of the military police and military intelligence units at Abu Ghraib. The 800th Military Police Brigade had one year of notice to plan for detention operations in Iraq. Original projections called for approximately 12 detention facilities in non-hostile, rear areas with a projection of 30,000 to 100,000 Enemy Prisoners of War. Though the 800th had planned a detention operations exercise for the summer of 2002, it was cancelled because of the disruption in soldier and unit availability resulting from the mobilization of Military Police Reserves following 9/11. Although its readiness was certified by U.S. Army Forces Command, actual deployment of the 800th Brigade to Iraq was chaotic. The "Time Phased Force Deployment List," which was the planned flow of forces to the theater of operations, was scrapped in favor of piecemeal unit deployment orders based on actual unit readiness and personnel strength. Equipment and troops regularly arrived out of planned sequence and rarely together. Improvisation was the order of the day. While some units overcame these difficulties, the 800th was among the lowest in priority and did not have the capability to overcome the shortfalls it confronted.

The 205th MI Brigade, deployed to support Combined Joint Task Force-7 (CJTF-7), normally provides the intelligence capability for a Corps Headquarters. However, it was insufficient to provide the kind of support needed by CJTF-7, especially with regard to interrogators and interpreters. Some additional units were mobilized to fill in the gaps, but while these MI units were more prepared than their military police counterparts, there were insufficient numbers of units available. Moreover, unit cohesion was lacking because elements of as many as six different units were assigned to the interrogation mission at Abu Ghraib. These problems were heightened by friction between military intelligence and military police personnel, including the brigade commanders themselves.

ABUSES

As of the date of this report, there were about 300 incidents of alleged detainee abuse across the Joint Operations Areas. Of the 155 completed investigations, 66 have resulted in a determination that detainees under the control of U.S. forces were abused. Dozens of non-judicial punishments have already been awarded. Others are in various stages of the military justice process.

Of the 66 already substantiated cases of abuse, eight occurred at Guantánamo, three in Afghanistan and 55 in Iraq. Only about one-third were related to interrogation, and two-thirds to other causes. There were five cases of detainee deaths as a result of abuse by U.S. personnel during interrogations. Many more died from natural causes and enemy mortar attacks. There are 23 cases of detainee deaths still under investigation; three in Afghanistan and 20 in Iraq. Twenty-eight of the abuse cases are alleged to include Special Operations Forces (SOF) and, of the 15 SOF cases that have been closed, ten were determined to be unsubstantiated and five resulted in disciplinary action. The Jacoby review of SOF detention operations found a range of abuses and causes similar in scope and magnitude to those found among conventional forces.

The aberrant behavior on the night shift in Cell Block 1 at Abu Ghraib would have been avoided with proper training, leadership and oversight. Though acts of abuse occurred at a number of locations, those in Cell Block 1 have a unique nature fostered by the predilections of the noncommissioned officers in charge. Had these noncommissioned officers behaved more like those on the day shift, these acts, which one participant described as "just for the fun of it," would not have taken place.

Concerning the abuses at Abu Ghraib, the impact was magnified by the fact the shocking photographs were aired throughout the world in April 2004. Although CENTCOM had publicly addressed the abuses in a press release in January 2004, the photographs remained within the official criminal investigative process. Consequently, the highest levels of command and leadership in the Department of Defense were not adequately informed nor prepared to respond to the Congress and the American public when copies were released by the press.

POLICY AND COMMAND RESPONSIBILITIES

Interrogation policies with respect to Iraq, where the majority of the abuses occurred, were inadequate or deficient in some respects at three levels: Department of Defense, CENTCOM/CJTF-7, and Abu Ghraib Prison. Policies to guide the demands for actionable intelligence lagged behind battlefield needs. As already noted, the changes in DoD interrogation policies between December 2, 2002 and April 16, 2003 were an element contributing to uncertainties in the field as to which techniques were authorized. Although specifically limited by the Secretary of Defense to Guantánamo, and requiring his personal approval (given in only two cases), the augmented techniques for Guantánamo migrated to Afghanistan and Iraq where they were neither limited nor safeguarded.

At the operational level, in the absence of specific guidance from CENTCOM, interrogators in Iraq relied on Field Manual 34-52 and on unauthorized techniques that had migrated from Afghanistan. On September 14, 2003 CJTF-7 signed the theater's first policy on interrogation, which contained elements of the approved Guantánamo policy and elements of the SOF policy (see Appendix D). Policies approved for use on al Qaeda and Taliban detainees, who were not afforded the protection of the Geneva Conventions, now applied to detainees who did fall under the Geneva Convention protections.

CENTCOM disapproved the September 14, 2003 policy, resulting in another policy signed on October 12, 2003 which essentially mirrored the outdated 1987 version of the FM 34-52 (see Appendix D). The 1987 version, however, authorized interrogators to control all aspects of the interrogation, "to include lighting and heating, as well as food, clothing, and shelter given to detainees." This was specifically left out of the current 1992 version. This clearly led to confusion on what practices were acceptable. We cannot be sure how much the number and severity of abuses would have been curtailed had there been early and consistent guidance from higher levels. Nonetheless, such guidance was needed and likely would have had a limiting effect.

At the tactical level we concur with the Jones/Fay investigation's conclusion that military intelligence personnel share responsibility for the abuses at Abu Ghraib with the military police soldiers cited in the Taguba investigation. The Jones/Fay Investigation found 44 alleged instances of abuse, some which were also considered by the Taguba report. A number of these cases involved MI personnel directing the actions of MP personnel. Yet it should be noted that of the 66 closed cases of detainee abuse in Guantánamo, Afghanistan and Iraq cited by the Naval Inspector General, only one-third were interrogation related.

The Panel concurs with the findings of the Taguba and Jones investigations that serious leadership problems in the 800th MP Brigade and 205th MI Brigade, to include the 320th MP Battalion Commander and the Director of the Joint Debriefing and Interrogation Center (JDIC), allowed the abuses at Abu Ghraib. The Panel endorses the disciplinary actions taken as a result of the Taguba Investigation. The

Panel anticipates that the Chain of Command will take additional disciplinary action as a result of the referrals of the Jones/Fay investigation.

We believe LTG Sanchez should have taken stronger action in November when he realized the extent of the leadership problems at Abu Ghraib. His attempt to mentor BG Karpinski, though well-intended, was insufficient in a combat zone in the midst of a serious and growing insurgency. Although LTG Sanchez had more urgent tasks than dealing personally with command and resource deficiencies at Abu Ghraib, MG Wojdakowski and the staff should have seen that urgent demands were placed to higher headquarters for additional assets. We concur with the Jones findings that LTG Sanchez and MG Wojdakowski failed to ensure proper staff oversight of detention and interrogation operations.

We note, however, in terms of its responsibilities, CJTF-7 was never fully resourced to meet the size and complexity of its mission. The Joint Staff, CJTF-7 and CENTCOM took too long to finalize the Joint Manning Document (JMD). It was not finally approved until December 2003, six months into the insurgency. At one point, CJTF-7 had only 495 of the 1,400 personnel authorized. The command was burdened with additional complexities associated with its mission to support the Coalition Provisional Authority.

Once it became clear in the summer of 2003 that there was a major insurgency growing in Iraq, with the potential for capturing a large number of enemy combatants, senior leaders should have moved to meet the need for additional military police forces. Certainly by October and November when the fighting reached a new peak, commanders and staff from CJTF-7 all the way to CENTCOM to the Joint Chiefs of Staff should have known about and reacted to the serious limitations of the battalion of the 800th Military Police Brigade at Abu Ghraib. CENTCOM and the JCS should have at least considered adding forces to the detention/interrogation operation mission. It is the judgment of this panel that in the future, considering the sensitivity of this kind of mission, the OSD should assure itself that serious limitations in detention/interrogation missions do not occur.

Several options were available to Commander CENTCOM and above, including reallocation of U.S. Army assets already in the theater, Operational Control (OPCON) of other Service Military Police units in theater, and mobilization and deployment of additional forces from the continental United States. There is no evidence that any of the responsible senior officers considered any of these options. What could and should have been done more promptly is evidenced by the fact that the detention/interrogation operation in Iraq is now directed by a Major General reporting directly to the Commander, Multi-National Forces Iraq (MNFI). Increased units of Military Police, fully manned and more appropriately equipped, are performing the mission once assigned to a single under-strength, poorly trained, inadequately equipped and weakly-led brigade.

In addition to the already cited leadership problems in the 800th MP Brigade, there were a series of tangled command relationships. These ranged from an unclear military intelligence chain of command, to the Tactical Control (TACON) relationship of the 800th with CJTF-7 which the Brigade Commander apparently did not adequately understand, and the confusing and unusual assignment of MI and MP responsibilities at Abu Ghraib. The failure to react appropriately to the October 2003 ICRC report, following its two visits to Abu Ghraib, is indicative of the weakness of the leadership at Abu Ghraib. These unsatisfactory relationships were present neither at Guantánamo nor in Afghanistan.

RECOMMENDATIONS

Department of Defense reform efforts are underway and the Panel commends these efforts. They are discussed in more detail in the body of this report. The Office of the Secretary of Defense, the Joint Chiefs of Staff and the Military Services are conducting comprehensive reviews on how military operations have changed since the end of the Cold War. The Military Services now recognize the problems and are studying force compositions, training, doctrine, responsibilities and active duty/reserve and guard/contractor mixes which must be adjusted to ensure we are better prepared to succeed in the war on terrorism. As an example, the Army is currently planning and developing 27 additional MP companies.

The specific recommendations of the Independent Panel are contained in the Recommendations section.

CONCLUSION

The vast majority of detainees in Guantánamo, Afghanistan and Iraq were treated appropriately, and the great bulk of detention operations were conducted in compliance with U.S. policy and directives. They yielded significant amounts of actionable intelligence for dealing with the insurgency in Iraq and strategic intelligence of value in the Global War on Terror. For example, much of the information in the recently released 9/11 Commission's report, on the planning and execution of the attacks on the World Trade Center and Pentagon, came from interrogation of detainees at Guantánamo and elsewhere.

Justice Sandra Day O'Connor, writing for the majority of the Supreme Court of the United States in *Hamdi v. Rumsfeld* on June 28, 2004, pointed out that "The purpose of detention is to prevent captured individuals from returning to the field of battle and taking up arms once again." But detention operations also serve the key purpose of intelligence gathering. These are not competing interests but appropriate objectives which the United States may lawfully pursue.

We should emphasize that tens of thousands of men and women in uniform strive every day under austere and dangerous conditions to secure our freedom and the freedom of others. By historical standards, they rate as some of the best trained, disciplined and professional service men and women in our nation's history.

While any abuse is too much, we see signs that the Department of Defense is now on the path to dealing with the personal and professional failures and remedying the underlying causes of these abuses. We expect any potential future incidents of abuse will similarly be discovered and reported out of the same sense of personal honor and duty that characterized many of those who went out of their way to do so in most of these cases. The damage these incidents have done to U.S. policy, to the image of the U.S. among populations whose support we need in the Global War on Terror and to the morale of our armed forces, must not be repeated.

INTRODUCTION—CHARTER AND METHODOLOGY

The Secretary of Defense chartered the Independent Panel on May 12, 2004, to review Department of Defense (DoD) Detention Operations (see Appendix A). In his memorandum, the Secretary tasked the Independent Panel to review Department of Defense investigations on detention operations whether completed or ongoing, as well as other materials and information the Panel deemed relevant to its review. The Secretary asked for the Panel's independent advice in highlighting the issues considered most important for his attention. He asked for the Panel's views on the causes and contributing factors to problems in detainee operations and what corrective measures would be required.

Completed investigations reviewed by the Panel include the following:
- Joint Staff External Review of Intelligence Operations at Guantánamo Bay, Cuba, September 28, 2002 (Custer Report)
- Joint Task Force Guantánamo assistance visit to Iraq to assess intelligence operations, September 5, 2003 (Miller Report)
- Army Provost Marshal General assessment of detention and corrections operations in Iraq, November 6, 2003 (Ryder Report)
- Administrative investigation under Army Regulation 15–6 (AR 15–6) regarding Abu Ghraib, June 8, 2004 (Taguba Report)
- Army Inspector General assessment of doctrine and training for detention operations, July 23, 2004 (Mikolashek Report)
- The Fay investigation of activities of military personnel at Abu Ghraib and related LTG Jones investigation under the direction of GEN Kern, August 16, 2004
- Naval Inspector General's review of detention procedures at Guantánamo Bay, Cuba and the Naval Consolidated Brig, Charleston, South Carolina (A briefing was presented to the Secretary of Defense on May 8, 2004.)
- Naval Inspector General's review of DoD worldwide interrogation operations, due for release on September 9, 2004
- Special Inspection of Detainee Operations and Facilities in the Combined Forces Command-Afghanistan AOR (CFC-A), June 26, 2004 (Jacoby Report).

- Administrative Investigation of Alleged Detainee Abuse by the Combined Joint Special Operations Task Force—Arabian Peninsula (Formica Report) Due for release in August, 2004. Assessment not yet completed and not reviewed by the Independent Panel
- Army Reserve Command Inspector General Assessment of Military Intelligence and Military Police Training (due for release in December 2004)

Panel interviews of selected individuals either in person or via video-teleconference:

June 14, 2004:

- MG Keith Dayton, Director, Iraq Survey Group (ISG), Baghdad, Iraq
- MG Geoffrey Miller, Director, Detainee Operations, CJTF-7, Baghdad, Iraq
- Hon Donald Rumsfeld, Secretary of Defense
- Hon Steve Cambone, Under Secretary of Defense for Intelligence
- MG Walter Wojdakowski, Deputy Commanding General, V Corps, USAREUR and 7th Army
- MG Donald Ryder, Provost Marshal, U.S. Army/Commanding General, U.S. Army Criminal Investigation Command, Washington, D.C.
- COL Thomas Pappas, Commander, 205th Military Intelligence Brigade, V Corps, USAREUR and 7th Army

June 24, 2004:

- LTG David McKiernan, Commanding General, Third U.S. Army, U.S. Army Forces Central Command, Coalition Forces Land Component Command
- MG Barbara Fast, CJTF-7 C-2, Director for Intelligence, Baghdad, Iraq
- MG Geoffrey Miller, Director, Detainee Operations, CJTF-7, Baghdad, Iraq
- LTG Ricardo Sanchez, Commanding General, CJTF-7, Commanding General, V Corps, USAREUR and 7th Army in Iraq
- Mr. Daniel Dell'Orto, Principal Deputy General Counsel, DoD
- LTG Keith Alexander, G-2, U.S. Army, Washington, D.C.
- LTG William Boykin, Deputy Undersecretary of Defense for Intelligence, Intelligence and Warfighting Support, Office of the Under Secretary of Defense for Intelligence
- Hon Douglas Feith, Under Secretary of Defense for Policy

July 8, 2004:

- COL Marc Warren, Senior Legal Advisor to LTG Sanchez, Iraq
- BG Janis Karpinski, Commander (TPU), 800th Military Police Brigade, Uniondale, NY
- Hon Paul Wolfowitz, Deputy Secretary of Defense
- Hon William Haynes, General Counsel DoD
- Mr. John Rizzo, CIA Senior Deputy General Counsel
- GEN John Abizaid, Commander, U.S. Central Command

- MG George Fay, Deputy to the Army G2, Washington, D.C.
- VADM Albert Church III, Naval Inspector General

July 22, 2004:
- Hon Donald Rumsfeld, Secretary of Defense

The Panel did not conduct a case-by-case review of individual abuse cases. This task has been accomplished by those professionals conducting criminal and commander-directed investigations. Many of these investigations are still on-going. The Panel did review the various completed and on-going reports covering the causes for the abuse. Each of these inquiries or inspections defined abuse, categorized the abuses, and analyzed the abuses in conformity with the appointing authorities' guidance, but the methodologies do not parallel each other in all respects. The Panel concludes, based on our review of other reports to date and our own efforts that causes for abuse have been adequately examined.

The Panel met on July 22nd and again on August 16th to discuss progress of the report. Panel members also reviewed sections and versions of the report through July and mid-August.

An effective, timely response to our requests for other documents and support was invariably forthcoming, due largely to the efforts of the DoD Detainee Task Force. We conducted reviews of multiple classified and unclassified documents generated by DoD and other sources.

Our staff has met and communicated with representatives of the International Committee of the Red Cross and with the Human Rights Executive Directors' Coordinating Group.

It should be noted that information provided to the Panel was that available as of mid-August 2004. If additional information becomes available, the Panel's judgments might be revised.

THE CHANGING THREAT

The date September 11, 2001, marked an historic juncture in America's collective sense of security. On that day our presumption of invulnerability was irretrievably shattered. Over the last decade, the military has been called upon to establish and maintain the peace in Bosnia and Kosovo, eject the Taliban from Afghanistan, defeat the Iraqi Army, and fight ongoing insurgencies in Iraq and Afghanistan. Elsewhere it has been called upon to confront geographically dispersed terrorists who would threaten America's right to political sovereignty and our right to live free of fear.

In waging the Global War on Terror, the military confronts a far wider range of threats. In Iraq and Afghanistan, U.S. forces are fighting diverse enemies with varying ideologies, goals and capabilities. American soldiers and their coalition partners have defeated the armored divisions of the Republican Guard, but are still under attack by forces using automatic rifles, rocket-propelled grenades, roadside bombs and surface-to-air missiles. We are not simply fighting the remnants of dying regimes or opponents of the local governments and coalition forces assisting those governments, but multiple enemies including indigenous and international terrorists. This complex operational environment requires soldiers capable of conducting traditional stability operations associated with peacekeeping tasks one moment and fighting force-on-force engagements normally associated with war-fighting the next moment.

Warfare under the conditions described inevitably generates detainees—enemy combatants, opportunists, trouble-makers, saboteurs, common criminals, former regime officials and some innocents as well. These people must be carefully but humanely processed to sort out those who remain dangerous or possess militarily-valuable intelligence. Such processing presents extraordinarily formidable logistical, administrative, security and legal problems completely apart from the technical obstacles posed by communicating with prisoners in another language and extracting actionable intelligence from them in timely fashion. These activities, called detention operations, are a vital part of an expeditionary army's responsibility, but they depend upon training, skills, and attributes not normally associated with soldiers in combat units.

Military interrogators and military police, assisted by front-line tactical units, found themselves engaged in detention operations with detention procedures still steeped in the methods of World War II and the Cold War, when those we expected to capture on the battlefield were generally a homogenous group of enemy soldiers. Yet this is a new form of war, not at all like Desert Storm nor even analogous to Vietnam or Korea.

General Abizaid himself best articulated the current nature of combat in testimony before the U.S. Senate Armed Services Committee on May 19, 2004:

> Our enemies are in a unique position, and they are a unique brand of ideological extremists whose vision of the world is best summed up by how the Taliban ran Afghanistan. If they can outlast us in Afghanistan and undermine the legitimate government there, they'll once again fill up the seats at the soccer stadium and force people to watch executions. If, in Iraq, the culture of intimidation practiced by our enemies is allowed to win, the mass graves will fill again. Our enemies kill without remorse, they challenge our will through the careful manipulation of propaganda and information, they seek safe havens in order to develop weapons of mass destruction that they will use against us when they are ready. Their targets are not Kabul and Baghdad, but places like Madrid and London and New York. While we can't be defeated militarily, we're not going to win this thing militarily alone.... As we fight this most unconventional war of this new century, we must be patient and courageous.

In Iraq the U.S. commanders were slow to recognize and adapt to the insurgency that erupted in the summer and fall of 2003. Military police and interrogators who had previous experience in the Balkans, Guantánamo and Afghanistan found themselves, along with increasing numbers of less-experienced troops, in the midst of detention operations in Iraq the likes of which the Department of Defense had not foreseen. As Combined Joint Task Force-7 (CJTF-7) began detaining thousands of Iraqis suspected of involvement in or having knowledge of the insurgency, the problem quickly surpassed the capacity of the staff to deal with and the wherewithal to contain it.

Line units conducting raids found themselves seizing specifically targeted persons, so designated by military intelligence; but, lacking interrogators and interpreters to make precise distinctions in an alien culture and hostile neighborhoods, they reverted to rounding up any and all suspicious-looking persons—all too often including women and children. The flood of incoming detainees contrasted sharply with the trickle of released individuals. Processing was overwhelmed. Some detainees at Abu Ghraib had been held 90 days before being interrogated for the first time.

Many interrogators, already in short supply from major reductions during the post-Cold War drawdown, by this time, were on their second or third combat tour. Unit cohesion and morale were largely absent as under-strength companies and battalions from across the United States and Germany were deployed piecemeal and stitched together in a losing race to keep up with the rapid influx of vast numbers of detainees.

As the insurgency reached an initial peak in the fall of 2003, many military policemen from the Reserves who had been activated shortly after September 11, 2001 had reached the mandatory two-year limit on their mobilization time. Consequently, the ranks of soldiers having custody of detainees in Iraq fell to about half strength as MPs were ordered home by higher headquarters.

Some individuals seized the opportunity provided by this environment to give vent to latent sadistic urges. Moreover, many well-intentioned professionals, attempting to resolve the inherent moral conflict between using harsh techniques to gain information to save lives and treating detainees humanely, found themselves in uncharted ethical ground, with frequently changing guidance from above. Some stepped over the line of humane treatment accidentally; some did so knowingly. Some of the abusers believed other governmental agencies were conducting interrogations using harsher techniques than allowed by the Army Field Manual 34-52, a perception leading to the belief that such methods were condoned. In nearly 10 percent of the cases of alleged abuse, the chain of command ignored reports of those allegations. More than once a commander was complicit.

The requirements for successful detainee operations following major combat operations were known by U.S. forces in Iraq. After Operations Enduring Freedom and earlier phases of Iraqi Freedom, several lessons learned were captured in official reviews and were available on-line to any authorized military user. These lessons included the need for doctrine tailored to enable police and interrogators to work together effectively; the need for keeping MP and MI units manned at levels sufficient to the task; and the need for MP and MI units to belong to the same tactical command.

However, there is no evidence that those responsible for planning and executing detainee operations, in the phase of the Iraq campaign following the major combat operations, availed themselves of these "lessons learned" in a timely fashion.

Judged in a broader context, U.S. detention operations were both traditional and new. They were traditional in that detainee operations were a part of all past conflicts. They were new in that the Global War on Terror and the insurgency we are facing in Iraq present a much more complicated detainee population.

Many of America's enemies, including those in Iraq and Afghanistan, have the ability to conduct this new kind of warfare, often referred to as "asymmetric" warfare. Asymmetric warfare can be viewed as attempts to circumvent or undermine a superior, conventional strength, while exploiting its weaknesses using methods the superior force neither can defeat nor resort to itself. Small unconventional forces can violate a state's security without any state support or affiliation whatsoever. For this reason, many terms in the orthodox lexicon of war—e.g., state sovereignty, national borders, uniformed combatants, declarations of war, and even war itself, are not terms terrorists acknowledge.

Today, the power to wage war can rest in the hands of a few dozen highly motivated people with cell phones and access to the Internet. Going beyond simply terrorizing individual civilians, certain insurgent and terrorist organizations represent a higher level of threat, characterized by an ability and willingness to violate the political sovereignty and territorial integrity of sovereign nations.

Essential to defeating terrorist and insurgent threats is the ability to locate cells, kill or detain key leaders, and interdict operational and financial networks. However, the smallness and wide dispersal of these enemy assets make it problematic to focus on signal and imagery intelligence as we did in the Cold War, Desert Storm, and the first phase of Operation Iraqi Freedom. The ability of terrorists and insurgents to blend into the civilian population further decreases their vulnerability to signal and imagery intelligence. Thus, information gained from human sources, whether by spying or interrogation, is essential in narrowing the field upon which other intelligence gathering resources may be applied. In sum, human intelligence is absolutely necessary, not just to fill these gaps in information derived from other sources, but also to provide clues and leads for the other sources to exploit.

Military police functions must also adapt to this new kind of warfare. In addition to organizing more units capable of handling theater-level detention operations, we must also organize those units, so they are able to deal with the heightened threat environment. In this new form of warfare, the distinction between front and rear becomes more fluid. All forces must continuously prepare for combat operations.

THE POLICY PROMULGATION PROCESS

Although there were a number of contributing causes for detainee abuses, policy processes were inadequate or deficient in certain respects at various levels:

345

Department of Defense (DoD), CENTCOM, Coalition Forces Land Component Command (CFLCC), CJTF-7, and the individual holding facility or prison. In pursuing the question of the extent to which policy processes at the DoD or national level contributed to abuses, it is important to begin with policy development as individuals in Afghanistan were first being detained in November 2001. The first detainees arrived at Guantánamo in January 2002.

In early 2002, a debate was ongoing in Washington on the application of treaties and laws to al Qaeda and Taliban. The Department of Justice, Office of Legal Counsel (OLC) advised DoD General Counsel and the Counsel to the President that, among other things:

- Neither the Federal War Crimes Act nor the Geneva Conventions would apply to the detention conditions of al Qaeda prisoners,
- The President had the authority to suspend the United States treaty obligations applying to Afghanistan for the duration of the conflict should he determine Afghanistan to be a failed state,
- The President could find that the Taliban did not qualify for Enemy Prisoner of War (EPW) status under Geneva Convention III.

The Attorney General and the Counsel to the President, in part relying on the opinions of OLC, advised the President to determine the Geneva Conventions did not apply to the conflict with al Qaeda and the Taliban. The Panel understands DoD General Counsel's position was consistent with the Attorney General's and the Counsel to the President's position. Earlier, the Department of State had argued that the Geneva Conventions in their traditional application provided a sufficiently robust legal construct under which the Global War on Terror could effectively be waged.

The Legal Advisor to the Chairman, Joint Chiefs of Staff and many service lawyers agreed with the State Department's initial position. They were concerned that to conclude otherwise would be inconsistent with past practice and policy, jeopardize the United States armed forces personnel, and undermine the United States military culture which is based on a strict adherence to the law of war. At the February 4, 2002 National Security Council meeting to decide this issue, the Department of State, the Department of Defense, and the Chairman of the Joint Chiefs of Staff were in agreement that all detainees would get the treatment they are (or would be) entitled to under the Geneva Conventions.

On February 7, 2002, the President issued his decision memorandum (see Appendix B). The memorandum stated the Geneva Conventions did not apply to al Qaeda and therefore they were not entitled to prisoner of war status. It also stated the Geneva Conventions did apply to the Taliban but the Taliban combatants were not entitled to prisoner of war status as a result of their failure to conduct themselves in accordance with the provisions of the Geneva Conventions. The President's memorandum also stated: "As a matter of policy, United States Armed Forces shall continue to treat detainees humanely and, to the extent appropriate and consistent with military necessity, in a manner consistent with the principles of Geneva."

Regarding the applicability of the Convention Against Torture and Other Cruel

Inhumane or Degrading Treatment, the OLC opined on August 1, 2002 that interrogation methods that comply with the relevant domestic law do not violate the Convention. It held that only the most extreme acts, that were specifically intended to inflict severe pain and torture, would be in violation; lesser acts might be "cruel, inhumane, or degrading" but would not violate the Convention Against Torture or domestic statutes. The OLC memorandum went on to say, as Commander in Chief exercising his wartime powers, the President could even authorize torture, if he so decided.

Reacting to tenacious resistance by some detainees to existing interrogation methods, which were essentially limited to those in Army Field Manual 34-52 (see Appendix E), Guantánamo authorities in October 2002 requested approval of strengthened counter-interrogation techniques to increase the intelligence yield from interrogations. This request was accompanied by a recommended tiered list of techniques, with the proviso that the harsher Category III methods (see Appendix E) could be used only on "exceptionally resistant detainees" and with approval by higher headquarters.

This Guantánamo initiative resulted in a December 2, 2002 decision by the Secretary of Defense authorizing, "as a matter of policy," the use of Categories I and II and only one technique in Category III: mild, non-injurious physical contact (see Appendix E). As a result of concern by the Navy General Counsel, the Secretary of Defense rescinded his December approval of all Category II techniques plus the one from Category III on January 15, 2003. This essentially returned interrogation techniques to FM 34-52 guidance. He also stated if any of the methods from Categories II and III were deemed warranted, permission for their use should be requested from him (see Appendix E).

The Secretary of Defense directed the DoD General Counsel to establish a working group to study interrogation techniques. The working group was headed by Air Force General Counsel Mary Walker and included wide membership from across the military, legal and intelligence communities. The working group also relied heavily on the OLC. The working group reviewed 35 techniques, and after a very expansive debate, ultimately recommended 24 to the Secretary of Defense. The study led to the Secretary's promulgation on April 16, 2003 of the list of approved techniques. His memorandum emphasized appropriate safeguards should be in place and, further, "*Use of these techniques is limited to interrogations of unlawful combatants held at Guantánamo Bay, Cuba.*" He also stipulated that four of the techniques should be used only in case of military necessity and that he should be so notified in advance. If additional techniques were deemed essential, they should be requested in writing, with "recommended safeguards and rationale for applying with an identified detainee."

In the initial development of these Secretary of Defense policies, the legal resources of the Services' Judge Advocates and General Counsels were not utilized to their fullest potential. Had the Secretary of Defense had the benefit of a wider range of legal opinions and a more robust debate regarding detainee policies and operations, his policy of April 16, 2003 might well have been developed and issued in early

December 2002. This could have avoided the policy changes which characterized the December 2, 2002 to April 16, 2003 period.

It is clear that pressure for additional intelligence and the more aggressive methods sanctioned by the Secretary of Defense memorandum resulted in stronger interrogation techniques. They did contribute to a belief that stronger interrogation methods were needed and appropriate in their treatment of detainees. At Guantánamo, the interrogators used those additional techniques with only two detainees, gaining important and time-urgent information in the process.

In Afghanistan, from the war's inception through the end of 2002, all forces used FM 34–52 as a baseline for interrogation techniques. Nonetheless, more aggressive interrogation of detainees appears to have been ongoing. On January 24, 2003, in response to a data call from the Joint Staff to facilitate the Secretary of Defense-directed Working Group efforts, the Commander Joint Task Force-180 forwarded a list of techniques being used in Afghanistan, including some not explicitly set out in FM 34–52. These techniques were included in a Special Operations Forces (SOF) Standard Operating Procedures document published in February 2003. The 519th Military Intelligence Battalion, a Company of which was later sent to Iraq, assisted in interrogations in support of SOF and was fully aware of their interrogation techniques.

In Iraq, the operational order from CENTCOM provided the standard FM 34-52 interrogation procedures would be used. Given the greatly different situations in Afghanistan and Iraq, it is not surprising there were differing CENTCOM policies for the two countries. In light of ongoing hostilities that monopolized commanders' attention in Iraq, it is also not unexpected the detainee issues were not given a higher priority.

Interrogators and lists of techniques circulated from Guantánamo and Afghanistan to Iraq. During July and August 2003, a Company of the 519th MI Battalion was sent to the Abu Ghraib detention facility to conduct interrogation operations. Absent guidance other than FM 34-52, the officer in charge prepared draft interrogation guidelines that were a near copy of the Standard Operating Procedure created by SOF. It is important to note that techniques effective under carefully controlled conditions at Guantánamo became far more problematic when they migrated and were not adequately safeguarded.

In August 2003, MG Geoffrey Miller arrived to conduct an assessment of DoD counterterrorism interrogation and detention operations in Iraq. He was to discuss current theater ability to exploit internees rapidly for actionable intelligence. He brought to Iraq the Secretary of Defense's April 16, 2003 policy guidelines for Guantánamo—which he reportedly gave to CJTF-7 as a potential model—recommending a command-wide policy be established. He noted, however, the Geneva Conventions did apply to Iraq. In addition to these various printed sources, there was also a store of common lore and practice within the interrogator community circulating through Guantánamo, Afghanistan and elsewhere.

At the operational level, in the absence of more specific guidance from CENT-COM, interrogators in Iraq relied on FM 34-52 and on unauthorized techniques that had migrated from Afghanistan. On September 14, 2003, Commander CJTF-7 signed the theater's first policy on interrogation which contained elements of the approved Guantánamo policy and elements of the SOF policy. Policies approved for use on al Qaeda and Taliban detainees who were not afforded the protection of EPW status under the Geneva Conventions now applied to detainees who did fall under the Geneva Convention protections. CENTCOM disapproved the September 14, 2003 policy resulting in another policy signed on October 12, 2003 which essentially mirrored the outdated 1987 version of the FM 34-52. The 1987 version, however, authorized interrogators to control all aspects of the interrogation, "to include lighting and heating, as well as food, clothing, and shelter given to detainees." This was specifically left out of the 1992 version, which is currently in use. This clearly led to confusion on what practices were acceptable. We cannot be sure how much the number and severity of abuses would have been curtailed had there been early and consistent guidance from higher levels. Nonetheless, such guidance was needed and likely would have had a limiting effect.

At Abu Ghraib, the Jones/Fay investigation concluded that MI professionals at the prison level shared a "major part of the culpability" for the abuses. Some of the abuses occurred during interrogation. As these interrogation techniques exceeded parameters of FM 34-52, no training had been developed. Absent training, the interrogators used their own initiative to implement the new techniques. To what extent the same situation existed at other prisons is unclear, but the widespread nature of abuses warrants an assumption that at least the understanding of interrogations policies was inadequate. A host of other possible contributing factors, such as training, leadership, and the generally chaotic situation in the prisons, are addressed elsewhere in this report.

PUBLIC RELEASE OF ABUSE PHOTOS

In any large bureaucracy, good news travels up the chain of command quickly; bad news generally does not. In the case of the abuse photos from Abu Ghraib, concerns about command influence on an ongoing investigation may have impeded notification to senior officials.

Chronology of Events

On January 13, 2004, SPC Darby gave Army criminal investigators a copy of a CD containing abuse photos he had taken from SPC Graner's computer. CJTF-7, CENTCOM, the Chairman of the Joint Chiefs of Staff and the Secretary of Defense were all informed of the issue. LTG Sanchez promptly asked for an outside investigation, and MG Taguba was appointed as the investigating officer. The officials who saw the photos on January 14, 2004, not realizing their likely significance, did not recommend the photos be shown to more senior officials. A CENTCOM press release in Baghdad on January 16, 2004 announced there was an ongoing investigation into reported incidents of detainee abuse at a Coalition Forces detention facility.

An interim report of the investigation was provided to CJTF-7 and CENTCOM commanders in mid-March 2004. It is unclear whether they saw the Abu Ghraib photos, but their impact was not appreciated by either of these officers or their staff officers who may have seen the photographs, as indicated by the failure to transmit them in a timely fashion to more senior officials. When LTG Sanchez received the Taguba report, he immediately requested an investigation into the possible involvement of military intelligence personnel. He told the panel that he did not request the photos be disseminated beyond the criminal investigative process because commanders are prohibited from interfering with, or influencing, active investigations. In mid-April, LTG McKiernan, the appointing official, reported the investigative results through his chain of command to the Department of the Army, the Army Judge Advocate General, and the U.S. Army Reserve Command. LTG McKiernan advised the panel that he did not send a copy of the report to the Secretary of Defense, but forwarded it through his chain of command. Again the reluctance to move bad news farther up the chain of command probably was a factor impeding notification of the Secretary of Defense.

Given this situation, GEN Richard Myers, the Chairman of the Joint Chiefs of Staff, was unprepared in April 2004 when he learned the photos of detainee abuse were to be aired in a CBS broadcast. The planned release coincided with particularly intense fighting by Coalition forces in Fallujah and Najaf. After a discussion with GEN Abizaid, GEN Myers asked CBS to delay the broadcast out of concern the lives of the Coalition soldiers and the hostages in Iraq would be further endangered. The story of the abuse itself was already public. Nonetheless, both GEN Abizaid and GEN Myers understood the pictures would have an especially explosive impact around the world.

Informing Senior Officials

Given the magnitude of this problem, the Secretary of Defense and other senior DoD officials need a more effective information pipeline to inform them of high-profile incidents which may have a significant adverse impact on DoD operations. Had such a pipeline existed, it could have provided an accessible and efficient tool for field commanders to apprise higher headquarters, the Joint Chiefs of Staff, and the Office of the Secretary of Defense, of actual or developing situations which might hinder, impede, or undermine U.S. operations and initiatives. Such a system could have equipped senior spokesmen with the known facts of the situation from all DoD elements involved. Finally, it would have allowed for senior official preparation and Congressional notification.

Such a procedure would make it possible for a field-level command or staff agency to alert others of the situation and forward the information to senior officials. This would not have been an unprecedented occurrence. For example, in December 2002, concerned Naval Criminal Investigative Service agents drew attention to the potential for abuse at Guantánamo. Those individuals had direct access to the highest levels of leadership and were able to get that information to senior levels without encumbrance. While a corresponding flow of information might not have prevented the abuses from occurring, the Office of the Secretary of Defense would have been alerted to a festering issue, allowing for an early and appropriate response.

Another example is the Air Force Executive Issues Team. This office has fulfilled the special information pipeline function for the Air Force since February 1998. The team chief and team members are highly trained and experienced field grade officers drawn from a variety of duty assignments. The team members have access to information flow across all levels of command and staff and are continually engaging and building contacts to facilitate the information flow. The information flow to the team runs parallel and complementary to standard reporting channels in order to avoid bypassing the chain of command but yet ensures a rapid and direct flow of relevant information to Air Force Headquarters.

A proper, transparent posture in getting the facts and fixing the problem would have better enabled the DoD to deal with the damage to the mission of the U.S. in the region and to the reputation of the U.S. military.

COMMAND RESPONSIBILITIES

Although the most egregious instances of detainee abuse were caused by the aberrant behavior of a limited number of soldiers and the predilections of the non-commissioned officers on the night shift of Tier 1 at Abu Ghraib, the Independent Panel finds that commanding officers and their staffs at various levels failed in their duties and that such failures contributed directly or indirectly to detainee abuse. Commanders are responsible for all their units do or fail to do, and should be held accountable for their action or inaction. Command failures were compounded by poor advice provided by staff officers with responsibility for overseeing battlefield functions related to detention and interrogation operations. Military and civilian leaders at the Department of Defense share this burden of responsibility.

Commanders

The Panel finds that the weak and ineffectual leadership of the Commanding General of the 800th MP Brigade and the Commanding Officer of the 205th MI Brigade allowed the abuses at Abu Ghraib. There were serious lapses of leadership in both units from junior non-commissioned officers to battalion and brigade levels. The commanders of both brigades either knew, or should have known, abuses were taking place and taken measures to prevent them. The Panel finds no evidence that organizations above the 800th MP Brigade- or the 205th MI Brigade-level were directly involved in the incidents at Abu Ghraib. Accordingly, the Panel concurs in the judgment and recommendations of MG Taguba, MG Fay, LTG Jones, LTG Sanchez, LTG McKiernan, General Abizaid and General Kern regarding the commanders of these two units. The Panel expects disciplinary action may be forthcoming.

The Independent Panel concurs with the findings of MG Taguba regarding the Director of the Joint Interrogation and Debriefing Center (JIDC) at Abu Ghraib. Specifically, the Panel notes that MG Taguba concluded that the Director, JIDC made material misrepresentations to MG Taguba's investigating team. The panel finds that he failed to properly train and control his soldiers and failed to ensure prisoners were afforded the protections under the relevant Geneva Conventions. The Panel concurs with MG Taguba's recommendation that he be relieved for cause and given a letter of reprimand and notes that disciplinary action may be pending against this officer.

The Independent Panel concurs with the findings of MG Taguba regarding the Commander of the 320th MP Battalion at Abu Ghraib. Specifically, the Panel finds that he failed to ensure that his subordinates were properly trained and supervised and that he failed to establish and enforce basic soldier standards, proficiency and accountability. He was not able to organize tasks to accomplish his mission in an appropriate manner. By not communicating standards, policies and plans to soldiers, he conveyed a sense of tacit approval of abusive behavior towards prisoners and a lax and dysfunctional command climate took hold. The Panel concurs with MG Taguba's recommendation that he be relieved from command, be given a General Officer Memorandum of reprimand, and be removed from the Colonel/O-6 promotion list.

The Independent Panel finds that BG Karpinski's leadership failures helped set the conditions at the prison which led to the abuses, including her failure to establish appropriate standard operating procedures (SOPs) and to ensure the relevant Geneva Conventions protections were afforded prisoners, as well as her failure to take appropriate actions regarding ineffective commanders and staff officers. The Panel notes the conclusion of MG Taguba that she made material misrepresentations to his investigating team regarding the frequency of her visits to Abu Ghraib. The Panel concurs with MG Taguba's recommendation that BG Karpinski be relieved of command and given a General Officer Letter of Reprimand.

Although LTG Sanchez had tasks more urgent than dealing personally with command and resource deficiencies and allegations of abuse at Abu Ghraib, he should have ensured his staff dealt with the command and resource problems. He should have assured that urgent demands were placed for appropriate support and resources through Coalition Forces Land Component Command (CFLCC) and CENTCOM to the Joint Chiefs of Staff. He was responsible for establishing the confused command relationship at the Abu Ghraib prison. There was no clear delineation of command responsibilities between the 320th MP Battalion and the 205th MI Brigade. The situation was exacerbated by CJTF-7 Fragmentary Order (FRAGO) 1108 issued on

November 19, 2003 that appointed the commander of the 205th MI Brigade as the base commander for Abu Ghraib, including responsibility for the support of all MPs assigned to the prison. In addition to being contrary to existing doctrine, there is no evidence the details of this command relationship were effectively coordinated or implemented by the leaders at Abu Ghraib. The unclear chain of command established by CJTF-7, combined with the poor leadership and lack of supervision, contributed to the atmosphere at Abu Ghraib that allowed the abuses to take place.

The unclear command structure at Abu Ghraib was further exacerbated by the confused command relationship up the chain. The 800th MP Brigade was initially assigned to the Central Command's Combined Forces Land Component Commander (CFLCC) during the major combat phase of Operation Iraqi Freedom. When CFLCC left the theater and returned to Fort McPherson Georgia, CENTCOM established Combined Joint Task Force-Seven (CJTF-7). While the 800th MP Brigade remained assigned to CFLCC, it essentially worked for CJTF-7. LTG Sanchez delegated responsibility for detention operations to his Deputy, MG Wojdakowski. At the same time, intelligence personnel at Abu Ghraib reported through the CJTF-7 C-2, Director for Intelligence. These arrangements had the damaging result that no single individual was responsible for overseeing operations at the prison.

The Panel endorses the disciplinary actions already taken, although we believe LTG Sanchez should have taken more forceful action in November when he fully comprehended the depth of the leadership problems at Abu Ghraib. His apparent attempt to mentor BG Karpinski, though well-intended, was insufficient in a combat zone in the midst of a serious and growing insurgency.

The creation of the Joint Interrogation and Debriefing Center (JIDC) at Abu Ghraib was not an unusual organizational approach. The problem is, as the Army Inspector General assessment revealed, joint doctrine for the conduct of interrogation operations contains inconsistent guidance, particularly with regard to addressing the issue of the appropriate command relationships governing the operation of such organizations as a JIDC. Based on the findings of the Fay, Jones and Church investigations, SOUTHCOM and CENTCOM were able to develop effective command relationships for such centers at Guantánamo and in Afghanistan, but CENTCOM and CJTF-7 failed to do so for the JIDC at Abu Ghraib.

Staff Officers

While staff officers have no command responsibilities, they are responsible for providing oversight, advice and counsel to their commanders. Staff oversight of detention and interrogation operations for CJTF-7 was dispersed among the principal and special staff. The lack of one person on the staff to oversee detention operations and facilities complicated effective and efficient coordination among the staff.

The Panel finds the following:

- The CJTF-7 Deputy Commander failed to initiate action to request additional military police for detention operations after it became clear that there were insufficient assets in Iraq.

- The CJTF-7 C-2, Director for Intelligence failed to advise the commander properly on directives and policies needed for the operation of the JIDC, for interrogation techniques and for appropriately monitoring the activities of Other Government Agencies (OGAs) within the Joint Area of Operations.
- The CJTF-7 Staff Judge Advocate failed to initiate an appropriate response to the November 2003 ICRC report on the conditions at Abu Ghraib.

Failure of the Combatant Command to Adjust the Plan

Once it became clear in July 2003 there was a major insurgency growing in Iraq and the relatively benign environment projected for Iraq was not materializing, senior leaders should have adjusted the plan from what had been assumed to be a stability operation and a benign handoff of detention operations to the Iraqis. If commanders and staffs at the operational level had been more adaptive in the face of changing conditions, a different approach to detention operations could have been developed by October 2003, as difficulties with the basic plan were readily apparent by that time. Responsible leaders who could have set in motion the development of a more effective alternative course of action extend up the command chain (and staff), to include the Director for Operations, Combined Joint Task Force 7 (CJTF-7); Deputy Commanding General, CJTF-7; Commander CJTF-7; Deputy Commander for Support, CFLCC; Commander, CFLCC; Director for Operations, Central Command (CENTCOM); Commander, CENTCOM; Director for Operations, Joint Staff; the Chairman of the Joint Chiefs of Staff; and the Office of the Secretary of Defense. In most cases these were errors of omission, but they were errors that should not go unnoted.

There was ample evidence in both Joint and Army lessons learned that planning for detention operations for Iraq required alternatives to standard doctrinal approaches. Reports from experiences in Operation Enduring Freedom and at Guantánamo had already recognized the inadequacy of current doctrine for the detention mission and the need for augmentation of both MP and MI units with experienced confinement officers and interrogators. Previous experience also supported the likelihood that detainee population numbers would grow beyond planning estimates. The relationship between MP and MI personnel in the conduct of interrogations also demanded close, continuous coordination rather than remaining compartmentalized. "Lessons learned" also reported the value of establishing a clear chain of command subordinating MP and MI to a Joint Task Force or Brigade Commander. This commander would be in charge of all aspects of both detention and interrogations just as tactical combat forces are subordinated to a single commander. The planners had only to search the lessons learned databases (available on-line in military networks) to find these planning insights. Nevertheless, CENTCOM's October 2002 planning annex for detention operations reflected a traditional doctrinal methodology.

The change in the character of the struggle signaled by the sudden spike in U.S. casualties in June, July and August 2003 should have prompted consideration of the need for additional MP assets. GEN Abizaid himself signaled a change in operations when he publicly declared in July that CENTCOM was now dealing with a growing "insurgency," a term government officials had previously avoided in characterizing the war. Certainly by October and November when the fighting reached a new peak, commanders and staffs from CJTF-7 all the way to CENTCOM and the Joint Chiefs of Staff knew by then the serious deficiencies of the 800th MP Brigade and should have at least considered reinforcing the troops for detention operations. Reservists, some of whom had been first mobilized shortly after September 11, 2001, began reaching a two-year mobilization commitment, which, by law, mandated their redeployment and deactivation.

There was not much the 800th MP Brigade (an Army Reserve unit), could do to delay the loss of those soldiers, and there was no individual replacement system or a unit replacement plan. The MP Brigade was totally dependent on higher headquarters to initiate action to alleviate the personnel crisis. The brigade was duly reporting readiness shortfalls through appropriate channels. However, its commanding general was emphasizing these shortfalls in personal communications with CJTF-7 commanders and staff as opposed to CFLCC. Since the brigade was assigned to CFLCC, but under the Tactical Control (TACON) of CJTF-7, her communications should been with CFLCC. The response from CJTF-7's Commander and Deputy Commander was that the 800th MP Brigade had sufficient personnel to accomplish its mission and that it needed to reallocate its available soldiers among the dozen or more detention facilities it was operating in Iraq. However, the Panel found the further deterioration in the readiness condition of the brigade should have been recognized by CFLCC and CENTCOM by late summer 2003. This led the Panel to conclude that CJTF-7, CFLCC and CENTCOM failure to request additional forces was an avoidable error.

The Joint Staff recognized intelligence collection from detainees in Iraq needed improvement. This was their rationale for sending MG Miller from Guantánamo to assist CJTF-7 with interrogation operations. However, the Joint Staff was not paying sufficient attention to evidence of broader readiness issues associated with both MP and MI resources.

We note that CJTF-7 Headquarters was never fully resourced to meet the size and complexity of its mission. The Joint Staff, CJTF-7 and CENTCOM took too long to finalize the Joint Manning Document (JMD) which was not finally approved until December 2003—six months into the insurgency. At one point, CJTF-7 Headquarters had only 495 of the 1,400 personnel authorized. The command was burdened with additional complexities associated with its mission to support the Coalition Provisional Authority.

Finally, the Joint Staff failed to recognize the implications of the deteriorating manning levels in the 800th MP Brigade; the absence of combat equipment among detention elements of MP units operating in a combat zone; and the indications of deteriorating mission performance among military intelligence interrogators owing to the stress of repeated combat deployments.

When CJTF-7 did realize the magnitude of the detention problem, it requested an assistance visit by the Provost Marshal General of the Army, MG Ryder. There seemed to be some misunderstanding of the CJTF-7 intent, however, since MG Ryder viewed his visit primarily as an assessment of how to transfer the detention program to the Iraqi prison system.

In retrospect, several options for addressing the detention operations challenge were available. CJTF-7 could have requested a change in command relationships to place the 800th MP Brigade under Operational Control of CJTF-7 rather than Tactical Control. This would have permitted the Commander of CJTF-7 to reallocate tactical assets under his control to the detention mission. While other Military Police units in Iraq were already fully committed to higher-priority combat and combat support missions, such as convoy escort, there were non-MP units that could have been reassigned to help in the conduct of detention operations. For example, an artillery brigade was tasked to operate the CJTF-7 Joint Visitors Center in Baghdad. A similar tasking could have provided additional troop strength to assist the 800th MP Brigade at Abu Ghraib. Such a shift would have supplied valuable experienced sergeants, captains and lieutenant colonels sorely lacking in both the MI and MP units at Abu Ghraib. A similar effect could have been achieved by CENTCOM assigning USMC, Navy and Air Force MP and security units to operational control of CJTF-7 for the detention operations mission.

Mobilization and deployment of additional forces from CONUS was also a feasible option. A system is in place for commands such as CJTF-7, CFLCC, and CENTCOM to submit a formal Request for Forces (RFF). Earlier, CJTF-7 had submitted a RFF for an additional Judge Advocate organization, but CENTCOM would not forward it to the Joint Chiefs of Staff. Perhaps this experience made CJTF-7 reluctant to submit a RFF for MP units, but there is no evidence that any of the responsible officers considered any option other than the response given to BG Karpinski to "wear her stars" and reallocate personnel among her already over-stretched units.

While it is the responsibility of the JCS and services to provide adequate numbers of appropriately trained personnel for missions such as the detention operations in Iraq, it is the responsibility of the combatant commander to organize those forces in a manner to achieve mission success. The U.S. experience in the conduct of post-conflict stability operations has been limited, but the impact of our failure to conduct proper detainee operations in this case has been significant. Combatant commanders and their subordinates must organize in a manner that affords unity of command, ensuring commanders work for commanders and not staff.

The fact that the detention operation mission for all of Iraq is now commanded by a 2-star general who reports directly to the operational commander, and that 1,900 MPs, more appropriately equipped for combat, now perform the mission once assigned to a single under-strength, poorly trained, inadequately equipped, and weakly-led brigade, indicate more robust options should have been considered sooner.

Finally, the panel notes the failure to report the abuses up the chain of command in a timely manner with adequate urgency. The abuses at Abu Ghraib were known and under investigation as early as January 2004. However, the gravity of the abuses was not conveyed up the chain of command to the Secretary of Defense. The Taguba report, including the photographs, was completed in March 2004. This report was transmitted to LTG Sanchez and GEN Abizaid; however, it is unclear whether they ever saw the Abu Ghraib photos. GEN Myers has stated he knew of the existence of the photos as early as January 2004. Although the knowledge of the investigation into Abu Ghraib was widely known, as we noted in the previous section, the impact of the photos was not appreciated by any of these officers as indicated by the failure to transmit them in a timely fashion to officials at the Department of Defense. (See Appendix A for the names of persons associated with the positions cited in this section.)

MILITARY POLICE AND DETENTION OPERATIONS

In Operation Enduring Freedom in Afghanistan and Operation Iraqi Freedom, commanders should have paid greater attention to the relationship between detainees and military operations. The current doctrine and procedures for detaining personnel are inadequate to meet the requirements of these conflicts. Due to the vastly different circumstances in these conflicts, it should not be surprising there were deficiencies in the projected needs for military police forces. All the investigations the Panel reviewed highlight the urgency to augment the prior way of conducting detention operations. In particular, the military police were not trained, organized, or equipped to meet the new challenges.

The Army IG found morale was high and command climate was good throughout forces deployed in Iraq and Afghanistan with one noticeable exception. Soldiers conducting detainee operations in remote or dangerous locations complained of very poor morale and command climate due to the lack of higher command involvement and support and the perception that their leaders did not care. At Abu Ghraib, in particular, there were many serious problems, which could have been avoided, if proper guidance, oversight and leadership had been provided.

Mobilization and Training

Mobilization and training inadequacies for the MP units occurred during the various phases of employment, beginning with peacetime training, activation, arrival at the mobilization site, deployment, arrival in theater and follow-on operations.

Mobilization and Deployment

Problems generally began for the MP units upon arrival at the mobilization sites. As one commander stated, "Anything that could go wrong went wrong." Preparation was not consistently applied to all deploying units, wasting time and duplicating efforts already accomplished. Troops were separated from their equipment for excessive periods of time. The flow of equipment and personnel was not coordinated. The Commanding General of the 800th MP Brigade indicated the biggest problem was getting MPs and their equipment deployed together. The unit could neither train at its stateside mobilization site without its equipment nor upon arrival overseas, as two or three weeks could go by before joining with its equipment. This resulted in assigning equipment and troops in an ad hoc manner with no regard to original unit. It also resulted in assigning certain companies that had not trained together in peacetime to battalion headquarters. The flow of forces into theater was originally planned and assigned on the basis of the Time Phased Force Deployment List (TPFDL). The TPFDL was soon scrapped, however, in favor of individual unit deployment orders assigned by U.S. Army Forces Command based on unit readiness and personnel strength. MP Brigade commanders did not know who would be deployed next. This method resulted in a condition wherein a recently arrived battalion headquarters would be assigned the next arriving MP companies, regardless of their capabilities or any other prior command and training relationships.

Original projections called for approximately 12 detention facilities with a projection of 30,000 to 100,000 enemy prisoners of war. These large projections did not materialize. In fact, the initial commanding general of the 800th MP brigade, BG Hill, stated he had more than enough MPs designated for the Internment/Resettlement (I/R—hereafter called detention) mission at the end of the combat phase in Iraq. This assessment radically changed following the major combat phase, when the 800th moved to Baghdad beginning in the summer of 2003 to assume the detention mission. The brigade was given additional tasks assisting the Coalition Provisional Authority (CPA) in reconstructing the Iraqi corrections system, a mission they had neither planned for nor anticipated.

Inadequate Training for the Military Police Mission

Though some elements performed better than others, generally training was inadequate. The MP detention units did not receive detention-specific training during their mobilization period, which was a critical deficiency. Detention training was conducted for only two MP detention battalions, one in Afghanistan and elements of the other at Camp Arifjan, Kuwait. The 800th MP Brigade, prior to deployment, had planned for a major detention exercise during the summer of 2002; however, this was cancelled due to the activation of many individuals and units for Operation Noble Eagle following the September 11, 2001 attack. The Deputy Commander of one MP brigade stated "training at the mobilization site was wholly inadequate." In addition, there was no theater-specific training.

The Army Inspector General's investigators also found that training at the mobilization sites failed to prepare units for conducting detention operations. Leaders of inspected reserve units stated in interviews that they did not receive a clear mission statement prior to mobilization and were not notified of their mission until after deploying. Personnel interviewed described being placed immediately in stressful situations in a detention facility with thousands of non-compliant detainees and not being trained to handle them. Units arriving in theater were given just a few days to conduct a handover from the outgoing units. Once deployed, these newly arrived units had difficulty gaining access to the necessary documentation on tactics, techniques, and procedures to train their personnel on the MP essential tasks of their new mission. A prime example is that relevant Army manuals and publications were available only on-line, but personnel did not have access to computers or the Internet.

Force Structure Organization

The current military police organizational structure does not address the detention mission on the nonlinear battlefield characteristic of the Global War on Terror.

Current Military Police Structure

The present U.S. Army Reserve and Army National Guard system worked well for the 1991 Gulf War for which large numbers of reserve forces were mobilized, were deployed, fought, and were quickly returned to the United States. These forces, however, were not designed to maintain large numbers of troops at a high operational tempo for a long period of deployment as has been the case in Afghanistan and Iraq.

Comments from commanders and the various inspection reports indicated the current force structure for the MPs is neither flexible enough to support the developing mission, nor can it provide for the sustained detainee operations envisioned for the future. The primary reason is that the present structure lacks sufficient numbers of detention specialists. Currently, the Army active component detention specialists are assigned in support of the Disciplinary Barracks and Regional Correctional Facilities in the United States, all of which are non-deployable.

New Force Structure Initiatives

Significant efforts are currently being made to shift more of the MP detention requirements into the active force structure. The Army's force design for the future will standardize detention forces between active and reserve components and provide the capability for the active component to immediately deploy detention companies. The Panel notes that the Mikolashek inspection found significant shortfalls in training and force structure for field sanitation, preventive medicine and medical treatment requirements for detainees.

Doctrine and Planning

Initial planning envisaged a conflict mirroring operation Desert Storm; approximately 100,000 enemy prisoners of war were forecast for the first five days of the conflict. This expectation did not materialize in the first phase of Operation Iraqi Freedom. As a result, there were too many MP detention companies. The reverse occurred in the second phase of Iraqi Freedom, where the plan envisaged a reduced number of detention MPs on the assumption the initial large numbers of enemy prisoners of war would already have been processed out of the detention facilities. The result was that combat MPs were ultimately reassigned to an unplanned detention mission.

The doctrine of yesterday's battlefield does not satisfy the requirements of today's conflicts. Current doctrine assumes a linear battlefield and is very clear for the handling of detainees from the point of capture to the holding areas and eventually to the detention facilities in the rear. However, Operations Enduring Freedom and Iraqi Freedom, both occurring where there is no distinction between front and rear areas, forced organizations to adapt tactics and procedures to address the resulting voids. Organizations initially used standard operating procedures for collection points and detention facilities. These procedures do not fit the new environment, generally because there are no safe areas behind "friendly lines"—there *are* no friendly lines. The inapplicability of current doctrine had a negative effect on accountability, security, safeguarding of detainees, and intelligence exploitation. Instead of capturing and rapidly moving detainees to secure collection points as prescribed by doctrine, units tended to retain the detainees and attempted to exploit their tactical intelligence value without the required training or infrastructure.

Current doctrine specifies that line combat units hold detainees no longer than 12–24 hours to extract immediately useful intelligence. Nonetheless, the Army IG inspection found detainees were routinely held up to 72 hours. For corps collection points, doctrine specifies detainees be held no longer than three days; the Army IG found detainees were held from 30 to 45 days.

Equipment Shortfalls

The current force structure for MP detention organizations does not provide sufficient assets to meet the inherent force protection requirement on battlefields likely to be characteristic of the future. Detention facilities in the theater may have to be located in a hostile combat zone, instead of the benign secure environment current doctrine presumes.

MP detention units will need to be equipped for combat. Lack of crew-served weapons, e.g., machine guns and mortars, to counter external attacks resulted in casualties to the detainee population as well as to the friendly forces. Moreover, Army-issued radios were frequently inoperable and too few in number. In frustration, individual soldiers purchased commercial radios from civilian sources. This improvisation created an unsecured communications environment that could be monitored by any hostile force outside the detention facility.

Detention Operations and Accountability

Traditionally, military police support the Joint Task Force (JTF) by undertaking administrative processing of detention operations, thereby relieving the war-fighters of concern over prisoners and civilian detainees. The handling of detainees is a tactical and operational consideration the JTF addresses during planning to prevent combat forces from being diverted to handle large numbers of detainees. Military police are structured, therefore, to facilitate the tempo of combat operations by providing for the quick movement of prisoners from the battle area to temporary holding areas and thence to detention facilities.

However, the lack of relevant doctrine meant the design and operation of division, battalion, and company collection points were improvised on an ad hoc basis, depending on such immediate local factors as mission, troops available, weather, time, etc. At these collection points, the SOPs the units had prior to deployment were outdated or ill-suited for the operating environment of Afghanistan and Iraq. Tactical units found themselves taking on roles in detainee operations never anticipated in their prior training. Such lack of proper skills had a negative effect on the intelligence exploitation, security, and safeguarding of detainees.

The initial point of capture may be at any time or place in a military operation. This is the place where soldiers have the least control of the environment and where most contact with the detainees occurs. It is also the place where, in or immediately after battle, abuse may be most likely. And it is the place where the detainee, shocked by capture, may be most likely to give information. As noted earlier, instead of capturing and rapidly transporting detainees to collection points, battalions and companies were holding detainees for excessive periods, even though they lacked the training, materiel, or infrastructure for productive interrogation. The Naval IG found that approximately one-third of the alleged incidents of abuse occurred at the point of capture.

Detention

The decision to use Abu Ghraib as the primary operational level detention facility happened by default. Abu Ghraib was selected by Ambassador Bremer who envisioned it as a temporary facility to be used for criminal detainees until the new Iraqi government could be established and an Iraqi prison established at another site. However, CJTF-7 saw an opportunity to use it as an interim site for the detainees it expected to round up as part of Operation Victory Bounty in July 2003. CJTF-7 had considered Camp Bucca but rejected it, as it was 150 miles away from Baghdad where the operation was to take place.

Abu Ghraib was also a questionable facility from a standpoint of conducting interrogations. Its location, next to an urban area, and its large size in relation to the small MP unit tasked to provide a law enforcement presence, made it impossible to achieve the necessary degree of security. The detainee population of approximately 7,000 outmanned the 92 MPs by approximately a 75:1 ratio. The choice of Abu Ghraib as the facility for detention operations placed a strictly detention mission-driven unit—one designed to operate in a rear area—smack in the middle of a combat environment.

Detainee Accountability and Classification

Adequate procedures for accountability were lacking during the movement of detainees from the collection points to the detainee facilities. During the movement, it was not unusual for detainees to exchange their identification tags with those of other detainees. The diversity of the detainee population also made identification and classification difficult. Classification determined the detainee assignment to particular cells/blocks, but individuals brought to the facility were often a mix of criminals and security detainees. The security detainees were either held for their intelligence value or presented a continuing threat to Coalition Forces. Some innocents were also included in the detainee population. The issue of unregistered or "ghost" detainees presented a limited, though significant, problem of accountability at Abu Ghraib.

Detainee Reporting

Detainee reporting lacked accountability, reliability and standardization. There was no central agency to collect and manage detainee information. The combatant commanders and the JTF commanders have overall responsibility for the detainee programs to ensure compliance with the international law of armed conflict, domestic law and applicable national policy and directives. The reporting system is supposed to process all inquiries concerning detainees and provide accountability information to the International Committee of the Red Cross. The poor reporting system did not meet this obligation.

Release Procedures

Multiple reviews were required to make release recommendations prior to approval by the release authority. Nonconcurrence by area commanders, intelligence organizations, or law enforcement agencies resulted in retention of ever larger numbers of detainees. The Army Inspector General estimated that up to 80 percent of detainees being held for security and intelligence reasons might be eligible for release upon proper review of their cases with the other 20 percent either requiring continued detention on security grounds or uncompleted intelligence requirements. Interviews indicated area commanders were reluctant to concur with release decisions out of concern that potential combatants would be reintroduced into their areas of operation or that the detainees had continuing intelligence value.

INTERROGATION OPERATIONS

Any discussion of interrogation techniques must begin with the simple reality that their purpose is to gain intelligence that will help protect the United States, its forces and interests abroad. The severity of the post-September 11, 2001 terrorist threat and the escalating insurgency in Iraq make information gleaned from interrogations especially important. When lives are at stake, all legal and moral means of eliciting information must be considered. Nonetheless, interrogations are inherently unpleasant, and many people find them objectionable by their very nature.

The relationship between interrogators and detainees is frequently adversarial. The interrogator's goal of extracting useful information likely is in direct opposition to the detainee's goal of resisting or dissembling. Although interrogators are trained to stay within the bounds of acceptable conduct, the imperative of eliciting timely and useful information can sometimes conflict with proscriptions against inhumane or degrading treatment. For interrogators in Iraq and Afghanistan, this tension is magnified by the highly stressful combat environment. The conditions of war and the dynamics of detainee operations carry inherent risks for human mistreatment and must be approached with caution and careful planning and training.

A number of interrelated factors both limited the intelligence derived from interrogations and contributed to detainee abuse in Operations Enduring Freedom and Iraqi Freedom. A shortfall of properly trained human intelligence personnel to do tactical interrogation of detainees existed at all levels. At the larger detention centers, qualified and experienced interrogators and interpreters were in short supply. No doctrine existed to cover segregation of detainees whose status differed or was unclear, nor was there guidance on timely release of detainees no longer deemed of intelligence interest. The failure to adapt rapidly to the new intelligence requirements of the Global War on Terror resulted in inadequate resourcing, inexperienced and untrained personnel, and a backlog of detainees destined for interrogation. These conditions created a climate not conducive to sound intelligence-gathering efforts.

The Threat Environment

The Global War on Terror requires a fundamental reexamination of how we approach collecting intelligence. Terrorists present new challenges because of the way they organize, communicate, and operate. Many of the terrorists and insurgents are geographically dispersed non-state actors who move across national boundaries and operate in small cells that are difficult to surveil and penetrate.

Human Intelligence from Interrogations

The need for human intelligence has dramatically increased in the new threat environment of asymmetric warfare. Massed forces and equipment characteristic of the Cold War era, Desert Storm and even Phase I of Operation Iraqi Freedom relied largely on signals and imagery intelligence. The intelligence problem then was primarily one of monitoring known military sites, troop locations and equipment concentrations. The problem today, however, is discovering new information on widely dispersed terrorist and insurgent networks. Human intelligence often provides the clues to understand these networks, enabling the collection of intelligence from other sources. Information derived from interrogations is an important component of this human intelligence, especially in the Global War on Terror.

The interrogation of al Qaeda members held at Guantánamo has yielded valuable information used to disrupt and preempt terrorist planning and activities. Much of the 9/11 Commission's report on the planning and execution of the attacks on the World Trade Center and Pentagon came from interrogation of detainees. In the case of al Qaeda, interrogations provided insights on organization, key personnel, target selection, planning cycles, cooperation among various groups, and logistical support. This information expanded our knowledge of the selection, motivation, and training of these groups. According to Congressional testimony by the Under Secretary of Defense for Intelligence, we have gleaned information on a wide range of al Qaeda activities, including efforts to obtain weapons of mass destruction, sources of finance, training in use of explosives and suicide bombings, and potential travel routes to the United States.

Interrogations provide commanders with information about enemy networks, leadership, and tactics. Such information is critical in planning operations. Tactically, detainee interrogation is a fundamental tool for gaining insight into enemy positions, strength, weapons, and intentions. Thus, it is fundamental to the protection of our forces in combat. Notably, Saddam Hussein's capture was facilitated by interrogation-derived information. Interrogations often provide fragmentary pieces of the broader intelligence picture. These pieces become useful when combined with other human intelligence or intelligence from other sources.

Pressure on Interrogators to Produce Actionable Intelligence

With the active insurgency in Iraq, pressure was placed on the interrogators to produce "actionable" intelligence. In the months before Saddam Hussein's capture, inability to determine his whereabouts created widespread frustration within the intelligence community. With lives at stake, senior leaders expressed, forcibly at times, their needs for better intelligence. A number of visits by high-level officials to Abu Ghraib undoubtedly contributed to this perceived pressure. Both the CJTF-7 commander and his intelligence officer, CJTF-7 C2, visited the prison on several occasions. MG Miller's visit in August/September, 2003 stressed the need to move from simply collecting tactical information to collecting information of operational and strategic value. In November 2003, a senior member of the National Security Council Staff visited Abu Ghraib, leading some personnel at the facility to conclude, perhaps incorrectly, that even the White House was interested in the intelligence gleaned from their interrogation reports. Despite the number of visits and the intensity of interest in actionable intelligence, however, the Panel found no undue pressure exerted by senior officials. Nevertheless, their eagerness for intelligence may have been perceived by interrogators as pressure.

Interrogation Operations Issues

A number of factors contributed to the problems experienced in interrogation operations. They ranged from resource and leadership shortfalls to doctrinal deficiencies and poor training.

Inadequate Resources

As part of the peace dividend following the Cold War much of the human intelligence capability, particularly in the Army, was reduced. As hostilities began in Afghanistan and Iraq, Army human intelligence personnel, particularly interrogators and interpreters, were ill-equipped to deal with requirements at both the tactical level and at the larger detention centers. At the tactical level, questioning of detainees has been used in all major conflicts. Knowledge of the enemy's positions, strength, equipment and tactics is critical in order to achieve operational success while minimizing casualties. Such tactical questioning to gain immediate battlefield intelligence is generally done at or near the point of capture. In Iraq, although their numbers were insufficient, some of the more seasoned MIs from the MI units supporting Abu Ghraib were assigned to support the Army Tactical HUMINT teams in the field.

In both Afghanistan and Iraq, tactical commanders kept detainees longer than specified by doctrine in order to exploit their unique local knowledge such as religious and tribal affiliation and regional politics. Remaining with the tactical units, the detainees could be available for follow-up questioning and clarification of details. The field commanders were concerned that information from interrogations, obtained in the more permanent facilities, would not be returned to the capturing unit. Tactical units, however, were not properly resourced to implement this altered operating arrangement. The potential for abuse also increases when interrogations are conducted in an emotionally charged field environment by personnel unfamiliar with approved techniques.

At the fixed detention centers such as Abu Ghraib, lack of resources and shortage of more experienced senior interrogators impeded the production of actionable intelligence. Inexperienced and untrained personnel often yielded poor intelligence. Interpreters, particularly, were in short supply, contributing to the backlog of detainees to be interrogated. As noted previously, at Abu Ghraib for instance, there were detainees who had been in custody for as long as 90 days before being interrogated for the first time.

Leadership and Organization Shortfalls at Abu Ghraib

Neither the leadership nor the organization of Military Intelligence at Abu Ghraib was up to the mission. The 205th MI Brigade had no organic interrogation elements; they had been eliminated by the downsizing in the 1990s. Soldiers from Army Reserve units filled the ranks, with the consequence that the Brigade Commander had to rely on disparate elements of units and individuals, including civilians, which had never trained together. The creation of the Joint Interrogation and Debriefing Center (JIDC) introduced another layer of complexity into an already stressed interrogations environment. The JIDC was an ad hoc organization made up of six different units lacking the normal command and control structure, particularly at the senior noncommissioned officer level. Leadership was also lacking, from the Commander of the 800th MP Brigade in charge of Abu Ghraib, who failed to ensure that soldiers had appropriate SOPs for dealing with detainees, to the Commander of the 205th MI Brigade, who failed to ensure that soldiers under his command were properly trained and followed the interrogation rules of engagement. Moreover, the Director of the JIDC was a weak leader who did not have experience in interrogation operations and who ceded the core of his responsibilities to subordinates. He failed to provide appropriate training and supervision of personnel assigned to the Center. None of these leaders established the basic standards and accountability that might have served to prevent the abusive behaviors that occurred.

Interrogation Techniques

Interrogation techniques intended only for Guantánamo came to be used in Afghanistan and Iraq. Techniques employed at Guantánamo included the use of stress positions, isolation for up to 30 days and removal of clothing. In Afghanistan techniques included removal of clothing, isolating people for long periods of time, use of stress positions, exploiting fear of dogs, and sleep and light deprivation. Interrogators in Iraq, already familiar with some of these ideas, implemented them even prior to any policy guidance from CJTF-7. Moreover, interrogators at Abu Ghraib were relying on a 1987 version of FM 34-52, which authorized interrogators to control all aspects of the interrogation to include light, heating, food, clothing and shelter given to detainees.

A range of opinion among interrogators, staff judge advocates and commanders existed regarding what techniques were permissible. Some incidents of abuse were clearly cases of individual criminal misconduct. Other incidents resulted from misinterpretations of law or policy or confusion about what interrogation techniques were permitted by law or local SOPs. The incidents stemming from misinterpretation or confusion occurred for several reasons: the proliferation of guidance and information from other theaters of operation; the interrogators' experiences in other theaters; and the failure to distinguish between permitted interrogation techniques in other theater environments and Iraq. Some soldiers or contractors who committed abuse may honestly have believed the techniques were condoned.

Use of Contractors as Interrogators

As a consequence of the shortage of interrogators and interpreters, contractors were used to augment the workforce. Contractors were a particular problem at Abu Ghraib. The Army Inspector General found that 35 percent of the contractors employed did not receive formal training in military interrogation techniques, policy, or doctrine. The Naval Inspector General, however, found some of the older contractors had backgrounds as former military interrogators and were generally considered more effective than some of the junior enlisted military personnel. Oversight of contractor personnel and activities was not sufficient to ensure intelligence operations fell within the law and the authorized chain of command. Continued use of contractors will be required, but contracts must clearly specify the technical requirements and personnel qualifications, experience, and training needed. They should also be developed and administered in such as way as to provide the necessary oversight and management.

Doctrinal Deficiencies

At the tactical level, detaining individuals primarily for intelligence collection or because they constitute a potential security threat, though necessary, presents units with situations not addressed by current doctrine. Many units adapted their operating procedures for conducting detainee operations to fit an environment not contemplated in the existing doctrinal manuals. The capturing units had no relevant procedures for information and evidence collection, which were critical for the proper disposition of detainees.

Additionally, there is inconsistent doctrine on interrogation facility operations for the fixed detention locations. Commanders had to improvise the organization and command relationships within these elements to meet the particular requirements of their operating environments in Afghanistan and Iraq. Doctrine is lacking to address the screening and interrogation of large numbers of detainees whose status (combatants, criminals, or innocents) is not easily ascertainable. Nor does policy specifically address administrative responsibilities related to the timely release of detainees captured and detained primarily for intelligence exploitation or for the security threat they may pose.

Role of CIA

CIA personnel conducted interrogations in DoD detention facilities. In some facilities these interrogations were conducted in conjunction with military personnel, but at Abu Ghraib the CIA was allowed to conduct its interrogations separately. No memorandum of understanding existed on interrogations operations between the CIA and CJTF-7, and the CIA was allowed to operate under different rules. According to the Fay investigation, the CIA's detention and interrogation practices contributed to a loss of accountability at Abu Ghraib. We are aware of the issue of unregistered detainees, but the Panel did not have sufficient access to CIA information to make any determinations in this regard.

THE ROLE OF MILITARY POLICE AND MILITARY INTELLIGENCE IN DETENTION OPERATIONS

Existing doctrine does not clearly address the relationship between the Military Police (MP) operating detention facilities and Military Intelligence (MI) personnel conducting intelligence exploitation at those facilities. The Army Inspector General report states neither MP nor MI doctrine specifically defines the distinct, but interdependent, roles and responsibilities of the two elements in detainee operations.

In the Global War on Terror, we are dealing with new conditions and new threats. Doctrine must be adjusted accordingly. MP doctrine currently states intelligence personnel may collaborate with MPs at detention sites to conduct interrogations, with coordination between the two groups to establish operating procedures. MP doctrine does not; however, address the subject of approved and prohibited MI procedures in an MP-operated facility. Conversely, MI doctrine does not clearly explain MP detention procedures or the role of MI personnel within a detention setting.

GUANTÁNAMO

The first detainees arrived at Guantánamo in January 2002. The SOUTHCOM Commander established two joint task forces at Guantánamo to execute the detention operations (JTF-160) and the interrogation operations (JTF-170). In August of that year, based on difficulties with the command relationships, the two JTFs were organized into a single command designated as Joint Task Force Guantánamo. This reorganization was conceived to enhance unity of command and direct all activities in support of interrogation and detention operations.

On November 4, 2002, MG Miller was appointed Commander of Joint Task Force Guantánamo. As the joint commander, he called upon the MP and MI soldiers to work together cooperatively. Military police were to collect passive intelligence on detainees. They became key players, serving as the eyes and ears of the cellblocks for military intelligence personnel. This collaboration helped set conditions for successful interrogation by providing the interrogator more information about the detainee—his mood, his communications with other detainees, his receptivity to particular incentives, etc. Under the single command, the relationship between MPs and MIs became an effective operating model.

AFGHANISTAN

The MP and MI commands at the Bagram Detention Facility maintained separate chains of command and remained focused on their independent missions. The Combined Joint Task Force-76 Provost Marshal was responsible for detainee operations. He designated a principal assistant to run the Bagram facility. In parallel fashion, the CJTF-76 Intelligence Officer was responsible for MI operations in the facility, working through an Officer-in-Charge to oversee interrogation operations. The two deputies worked together to coordinate execution of their respective missions. A dedicated judge advocate was assigned full time to the facility, while the CJTF-76 Inspector General provided independent oversight. Based on information from the Naval Inspector General investigation, this arrangement in Afghanistan worked reasonably well.

ABU GHRAIB, IRAQ

The Central Confinement Facility is located near the population center of Baghdad. Abu Ghraib was selected by Ambassador Bremer who envisioned it as a temporary facility to be used for criminal detainees until the new Iraqi government could be established and an Iraqi prison established at another site. Following operations during the summer of 2003, Abu Ghraib also was designated by CJTF-7 as the detention center for security detainees. It was selected because it was difficult to transport prisoners, due to improvised explosives devices (IEDs) and other insurgent tactics, to the more remote and secure Camp Bucca, some 150 miles away.

Request for Assistance

Commander CJTF-7 recognized serious deficiencies at the prison and requested assistance. In response to this request, MG Miller and a team from Guantánamo were sent to Iraq to provide advice on facilities and operations specific to screening, interrogations, HUMINT collection and interagency integration in the short- and long- term. The team arrived in Baghdad on August 31, 2003. MG Miller brought a number of recommendations derived from his experience at Guantánamo to include his model for MP and MI personnel to work together. These collaborative procedures had worked well at Guantánamo, in part because of the high ratio of approximately one-to-one of military police to mostly compliant detainees. However, the guard-to-detainee ratio at Abu Ghraib was approximately 1 to 75, and the Military Intelligence and the Military Police had separate chains of command.

MG Ryder, the Army Provost Marshal, also made an assistance visit in mid-October 2003. He conducted a review of detainee operations in Iraq. He found flawed operating procedures, a lack of training, an inadequate prisoner classification system, under-strength units and a ratio of guard to prisoners designed for "compliant" prisoners of war and not for criminals or high-risk security detainees. However, he failed to detect the warning signs of potential and actual abuse that was ongoing during his visit. The assessment team members did not identify any MP units purposely applying inappropriate confinement practices. The Ryder report continues that "Military Police, though adept at passive collection of intelligence within a facility, do not participate in Military Intelligence-supervised interrogation sessions. The 800th MP Brigade has not been asked to change its facility procedures to set the conditions for MI interviews, nor participate in those interviews."

Prevailing Conditions

Conditions at Abu Ghraib reflected an exception to those prevailing at other theater detainee facilities. U.S. forces were operating Tiers 1A and 1B, while Tiers 2 through 7 were under the complete control of Iraqi prison guards. Iraqis who had committed crimes against other Iraqis were intended to be housed in the tiers under Iraqi control. The facility was under frequent hostile fire from mortars and rocket-propelled grenades. Detainee escape attempts were numerous and there were several riots. Both MI and MP units were seriously under-resourced and lacked unit cohesion and mid-level leadership. The reserve MP units had lost senior noncommissioned officers and other personnel through rotations back to the U.S. as well as reassignments to other missions in the theater.

in a detention facility. The meaning of guidance, such as MPs "setting the conditions" for interrogation, needs to be defined with precision. MG Taguba argued that all detainee operations be consolidated under the responsibility of a single commander reporting directly to Commander CJTF-7. This change has now been accomplished and seems to be working effectively. Other than lack of leadership, training deficiencies in both MP and MI units have been cited most often as the needed measures to prevent detainee abuse. We support the recommendations on training articulated by the reports published by the various other reviews.

3. The nation needs more specialists for detention/interrogation operations, including linguists, interrogators, human intelligence, counter-intelligence, corrections police and behavioral scientists. Accompanying professional development and career field management systems must be put in place concurrently. The Panel agrees that some use of contractors in detention operations must continue into the foreseeable future. This is especially the case with the need for qualified interpreters and interrogators and will require rigorous oversight.

4. Joint Forces Command should chair a Joint Service Integrated Process Team to develop a new Operational Concept for Detention Operations in the new era of warfare, covering the Global War on Terror. The team should place special and early emphasis on detention operations during Counter-Insurgency campaigns and Stability Operations in which familiar concepts of front and rear areas may not apply. Attention should also be given to preparing for conditions in which normal law enforcement has broken down in an occupied or failed state. The Panel recommends that the idea of a deployable detention facility should be studied and implemented as appropriate.

5. Clearly, force structure in both MP and MI is inadequate to support the armed forces in this new form of warfare. Every investigation we reviewed refers to force structure deficiencies in some measure. There should be an active and reserve component mix of units for both military intelligence and military police. Other forces besides the Army are also in need of force structure improvements. Those forces have not been addressed adequately in the reports reviewed by the Panel, and we recommend that the Secretaries of the Navy and Air Force undertake force structure reviews of their own to improve the performance of their Services in detention operations.

6. Well-documented policy and procedures on approved interrogation techniques are imperative to counteract the current chilling effect the reaction to the abuses have had on the collection of valuable intelligence through interrogations. Given the critical role of intelligence in the Global War on Terror, the aggressiveness of interrogation techniques employed must be measured against the value of intelligence sought, to include its importance, urgency and relevance. A policy for interrogation operations should be promulgated early on and acceptable interrogation techniques for each operation must be clearly understood by all interrogation personnel.

7. All personnel who may be engaged in detention operations, from point of capture to final disposition, should participate in a professional ethics program that would equip them with a sharp moral compass for guidance in situations often riven

with conflicting moral obligations. The development of such a values-oriented ethics program should be the responsibility of the individual services with assistance provided by the Joint Chiefs of Staff.

8. Clearer guidelines for the interaction of CIA with the Department of Defense in detention and interrogation operations must be defined.

9. The United States needs to redefine its approach to customary and treaty international humanitarian law, which must be adapted to the realities of the nature of conflict in the 21st Century. In doing so, the United States should emphasize the standard of reciprocity, in spite of the low probability that such will be extended to United States Forces by some adversaries, and the preservation of United States societal values and international image that flows from an adherence to recognized humanitarian standards.

10. The Department of Defense should continue to foster its operational relationship with the International Committee of the Red Cross. The Panel believes the International Committee of the Red Cross, no less than the Defense Department, needs to adapt itself to the new realities of conflict which are far different from the Western European environment from which the ICRC's interpretation of Geneva Conventions was drawn.

11. The assignment of a focal point within the office of the Under Secretary for Policy would be a useful organizational step. The new focal point for Detainee Affairs should be charged with all aspects of detention policy and also be responsible for oversight of DoD relations with the International Committee of the Red Cross.

12. The Secretary of Defense should ensure the effective functioning of rapid reporting channels for communicating bad news to senior Department of Defense leadership without prejudice to any criminal or disciplinary actions already underway. The Panel recommends consideration of a joint adaptation of procedures such as the Air Force special notification process.

13. The Panel notes that the Fay investigation cited some medical personnel for failure to report detainee abuse. As noted in that investigation, training should include the obligation to report any detainee abuse. The Panel also notes that the Army IG found significant shortfalls in training and force structure for field sanitation, preventive medicine and medical treatment requirements for detainees. As the DoD improves detention operations force structure and training, it should pay attention to the need for medical personnel to screen and monitor the health of detention personnel and detainees.

14. The integration of the recommendations in this report and all the other efforts underway on detention operations will require further study. Analysis of the dynamics of program and resource implications, with a view to assessing the trade-offs and opportunity costs involved, must be addressed.

APPENDICES

GLOSSARY

Army Regulation 15-6	AR 15-6	Army regulation which specifies procedures for command investigations. The common name for both formal and informal command investigations.
Active Component	AC	Active military component of the Army, Navy, Air Force or Marines.
Abuse Cases		An incident or allegation of abuse, including, but not limited to death, assault, sexual assault, and theft, that triggers a CID investigation, which may involve multiple individuals.
Behavioral Science Coordination Team	BSCT	Team comprised of medical and other specialized personnel that provides support to special operations forces.
Civilian Internees	CI	Designation of civilians encountered and detained in the theater of war.
Criminal Investigation Command	CID	Investigative agency of the U. S. Army responsible for conducting criminal investigations to which the Army is or may be a party.
Collection Points	CP	Forward locations where prisoners are collected, processed and prepared for movement to the detention center.
Coalition Provisional Authority	CPA	Interim government of Iraq, in place from May 2003 through June 2004.
Convention Against Torture and Other Cruel, Inhumane or Degrading Treatment		An international treaty brought into force in 1987 which seeks to define torture and other cruel, inhuman or degrading punishment and provides a mechanism for punishing those who would inflict such treatment on others.
Enemy Prisoner of War	EPW	International Committee of the Red Cross term for prisoners of war; this status bestows certain

		rights to the individual in the Geneva Conventions.
Force Design Update	FDU	The Army process to review and restructure forces.
Fragmentary Order	FRAGO	An abbreviated form of an operation order (verbal, written or digital) usually issued on a day-to-day basis that eliminates the need for restarting information contained in a basic operation order.
Army Field Manual 34-52 "Intelligence Interrogation"	FM 34-52	Current manual for operations and training in interrogation techniques. The edition dated 1987 was updated in 1992.
Geneva Conventions	GC	The international treaties brought into force in August 1949. These conventions extend protections to, among others, prisoners of war and civilians in time of war.
Global War on Terror	GWOT	Worldwide operation to eradicate individuals and groups that participate in and sponsor terrorism.
Internment/ Resettlement	I/R	Internment/resettlement mission assigned to specific US Army Military Police units who are responsible for the detention of Enemy Prisoners of War during armed conflict.
International Committee of the Red Cross	ICRC	Nongovernmental organization that seeks to help victims of war and internal violence.
In Lieu Of	ILO	When used in reference to manning, indicates that forces were used in a manner other than originally specified.
Initial Point of Capture	IPOC	Location where an enemy prisoner or internee is captured.
Iraq Survey Group	ISG	Organization located in Iraq with the mission to find weapons of mass destruction.

Joint Manning Document	JMD	Master document covering personnel requirements for the joint theater.
Navy Criminal Investigative Service	NCIS	Investigative service for the US Navy and Marine Corps.
National Detainee Reporting Center	NDRC	Agency charged with accounting for and reporting all EPW, retained personnel, civilian internees and other detainees during armed conflict.
Operation Enduring Afghanistan	OEF	Military operation in Afghanistan
Other Government Agencies	OGA	Refers to non-Department of Defense agencies operating in theaters of war.
Operation Iraqi Freedom	OIF	Military operation in Iraq.
Office of Legal Counsel	OLC	Refers to the Department of Justice Office of Legal Counsel.
Operation Noble Eagle	ONE	Operation to activate and deploy forces for homeland defense and civil support in response to the attacks of September 11, 2001.
Operation Victory Bounty	OVB	CJTF-7 operation to sweep Baghdad area for remaining elements of the Saddam Fedayeen in 2003.
Operational Control	OPCON	Command authority over all aspects of military operations.
Republican Guard	RG	Elite Iraqi military forces under the regime of Saddam Hussein.
Reserve Component	RC	Army, Navy, Air Force and Marine Reserves and Army and Air National Guard
Request for Forces	RFF	Commanders request for additional forces to support the mission.

Standing Operating Procedure	SOP	A set of instructions covering those features of operations which lend themselves to a definite or standardized procedures without loss of effectiveness. The procedure is applicable unless ordered otherwise.
Tactical Control	TACON	Command authority to control and task forces for maneuvers within an area of operations.
Tactical Human Intelligence Team	THT	Forward deployed intelligence element providing human intelligence support to maneuver units.
Time Phased Deployment List	TPFDL	Identifies the units needed to support an operational plan and specifies their order and method of deployment.

GLOSSARY (cont'd.)

GUANTÁNAMO			COMMANDER
United States Southern Command	USSOUTHCOM	One of nine Unified Combatant Commands with operational control of U.S. military forces. Area of responsibility includes Guantánamo Bay, Cuba.	GEN James Hill
Joint Task Force 160	JTF-160	Initially responsible for detention operations at Guantánamo, merged in JTF-G 11/4/02.	
Joint Task Force 170	JTF-170	Initially responsible for interrogation operations at Guantánamo, merged in JTF-G 11/4/02.	
Joint Task Force Guantánamo	JTF-G	Joint task force for all operations at Guantánamo, formed 11/4/02.	

AFGHANISTAN			
United States Central Command	USCENTCOM	One of nine Unified Commands with operational control of U.S. military forces. Area of responsibility includes Afghanistan and Iraq.	GEN John Abizaid
Coalition Forces Land Component Command	CFLCC	Senior headquarters element for multi-national land forces in both Iraq and Afghanistan.	LTG David McKiernan
Combined Joint Task Force 180	CJTF-180	Forward deployed headquarters for Afghanistan.	

IRAQ			
United States Central Command	USCENTCOM	One of nine Unified Commands with operational control of U.S. military forces. Area of responsibility includes Afghanistan and Iraq.	GEN John Abizaid
Coalition Forces Land Component Command	CFLCC	Senior headquarters element for multi-national land forces in both Iraq and Afghanistan.	LTG David McKiernan

IRAQ (cont'd.)

Combined Joint Task Force 7	CJTF-7	Forward deployed headquarters for Operation Iraqi Freedom. Replaced in May 04 by Multi National Force–Iraq and Multi National Corps–Iraq	LTG Ricardo Sanchez
Combined Joint Task Force 7 Intelligence Staff	CJTF-7 C2	Intelligence staff support to CJTF-7	MG Barbara Fast
800th Military Police Brigade	800th MP BDE	U.S. Army Reserve Military Police responsible for all internment facilities in Iraq, and assistance to CPA Minister of Justice.	BG Janis Karpinski
Joint Interrogation and Detention Center	JDIC	Element of CJTF-7 for interrogation mission at Abu Ghraib.	LTC Steven Jordan
320th Military Police Battalion	320th MP BN	Element of 800th Bde; assigned to Abu Ghraib	LTC Jerry Phillabaum
372nd Military Police Company	372nd MP CO	Element of 320th Bn; assigned to Abu Ghraib	CPT Donald Reese
72nd Military Police Company	72nd MP CO	Nevada National Guard MP Company, assigned to Abu Ghraib prior to 372nd MP Co.	
205th Military Intelligence Brigade	205th MI BDE	Military Intelligence Brigade responsible for multiple Army intelligence missions throughout Iraq.	COL Thomas Pappas
519th Military Intelligence Battalion	519th MI BN	Tactical exploitation element of Company A was located at Abu Ghraib.	MAJ Michnewicz

OTHER

United States Army Forces Command	FORSCOM	U.S. Army major command responsible for training, readiness and deployment.

SECRETARY OF DEFENSE
1000 DEFENSE PENTAGON
WASHINGTON, DC 20301-1000

MAY 12 2004

MEMORANDUM FOR THE HONORABLE JAMES R. SCHLESINGER,
CHAIRMAN
THE HONORABLE HAROLD BROWN
THE HONORABLE TILLIE K. FOWLER
GENERAL CHARLES A. HORNER, USAF (RET.)

SUBJECT: Independent Panel to Review DoD Detention Operations

Various organizations of the Department of Defense have investigated, or will investigate, various aspects of allegations of abuse at DoD Detention Facilities and other matters related to detention operations. Thus far these inquiries include the following:

—Criminal investigations into individual allegations
—Army Provost Marshal General assessment of detention and corrections operations in Iraq
—Joint Task Force Guantánamo assistance visit to Iraq to assess intelligence operations
—Administrative Investigation under AR 15–6 regarding Abu Ghraib operations
—Army Inspector General assessment of doctrine and training for detention operations
—Commander, Joint Task Force-7 review of activities of military intelligence personnel at Abu Ghraib
—Army Reserve Command Inspector General assessment of training of Reserve units regarding military intelligence and military police
—Naval Inspector General review of detention procedures at Guantánamo Bay, Cuba, and the Naval Consolidated Brig, Charleston, South Carolina

I have been or will be briefed on the results of these inquiries and the corrective actions taken by responsible officials within the Department.

It would be helpful to me to have your independent, professional advice on the issues that you consider most pertinent related to the various allegations, based on your review of completed and pending investigative reports and other materials and information. I am especially interested in your views on the cause of the problems and what should be done to fix them. Issues such as force structure, training of regular and reserve personnel, use of contractors, organization, detention policy and procedures, interrogation policy and procedures, the relationship between detention and interrogation, compliance with the Geneva Conventions, relationship with the International Committee of the Red Cross, command relationships, and operational practices may be contributing factors you might wish to review. Issues of personal accountability will be resolved through established military justice and administrative procedures, although any information you may develop will be welcome.

I would like your independent advice orally and in writing, preferably within 45 days after you begin your review. DoD personnel will collect information for your review and assist you as you deem appropriate. You are to have access to all relevant DoD investigations and other DoD information unless prohibited by law. Reviewing all written materials relevant to these issues may be sufficient to allow you to provide your advice. Should you believe it necessary to travel or conduct interviews, the Director of Administration and Management will make appropriate arrangements.

I intend to provide your report to the Committees on Armed Services, the Secretaries of the Military Departments, the Chairman of the Joint Chiefs of Staff, the Commanders of the Combatant Commands, the Directors of the Defense Agencies, and others as appropriate. If your report contains classified information, please also provide an unclassified version suitable for public release.

By copy of this memorandum, I request the Director of Administration and Management to secure the necessary technical, administrative and legal support for your review from the Department of Defense Components. I appoint you as full-time employees of this Department without pay under 10 U.S.C. §1583. I request all Department of Defense personnel to cooperate fully with your review and to make available all relevant documents and information at your request.

[signed Donald Rumsfeld]

cc: SECRETARIES OF THE MILITARY DEPARTMENTS
CHAIRMAN OF THE JOINT CHIEFS OF STAFF
UNDER SECRETARIES OF DEFENSE
DIRECTOR, DEFENSE RESEARCH AND ENGINEERING
ASSISTANT SECRETARIES OF DEFENSE
GENERAL COUNSEL OF THE DEPARTMENT OF DEFENSE
INSPECTOR GENERAL OF THE DEPARTMENT OF DEFENSE
DIRECTOR, OPERATIONAL TEST AND EVALUATION

ASSISTANTS TO THE SECRETARY OF DEFENSE
DIRECTOR, ADMINISTRATION AND MANAGEMENT
DIRECTOR, FORCE TRANSFORMATION
DIRECTOR, NET ASSESSMENT
DIRECTOR, PROGRAM ANALYSIS AND EVALUATION
DIRECTORS OF THE DEFENSE AGENCIES
DIRECTORS OF THE DOD FIELD ACTIVITIES

THE WHITE HOUSE
WASHINGTON

February 7, 2002

MEMORANDUM FOR THE VICE PRESIDENT
THE SECRETARY OF STATE
THE SECRETARY OF DEFENSE
THE ATTORNEY GENERAL
CHIEF OF STAFF TO THE PRESIDENT
DIRECTOR OF CENTRAL INTELLIGENCE
ASSISTANT TO THE PRESIDENT FOR NATIONAL
SECURITY AFFAIRS
CHAIRMAN OF THE JOINT CHIEFS OF STAFF

SUBJECT: Humane Treatment of al Qaeda and Taliban Detainees

1. Our recent extensive discussions regarding the status of al Qaeda and Taliban
   detainees confirm that the application of the Geneva Convention Relative to the
   Treatment of Prisoners of War of August 12, 1949 (Geneva) to the conflict with
   al Qaeda and the Taliban involves complex legal questions. By its terms, Geneva
   applies to conflicts involving "High Contracting Parties," which can only be
   states. Moreover, it assumes the existence of "regular" armed forces fighting on
   behalf of states. However, the war against terrorism ushers in a new paradigm,
   one in which groups with broad, international reach commit horrific acts against
   innocent civilians, sometimes with the direct support of states. Our Nation recognizes that this new paradigm—ushered in not by us, but by terrorists—
   requires new thinking in the law of war, but thinking that should nevertheless be
   consistent with the principles of Geneva.

2. Pursuant to my authority as Commander in Chief and Chief Executive of the
   United States, and relying on the opinion of the Department of Justice dated
   January 22, 2002, and on the legal opinion rendered by the Attorney General in
   his letter of February 1, 2002, I hereby determine as follows:

   a. I accept the legal conclusion of the Department of Justice and determine that
      none of the provisions of Geneva apply to our conflict with al Qaeda in
      Afghanistan or elsewhere throughout the world because, among other rea-
      sons, al Qaeda is not a High Contracting Party to Geneva.

   b. I accept the legal conclusion of the Attorney General and the Department of

Justice that I have the authority under the Constitution to suspend Geneva as between the United States and Afghanistan, but I decline to exercise that authority at this time. Accordingly, I determine that the provisions of Geneva will apply to our present conflict with the Taliban. I reserve the right to exercise this authority in this or future conflicts.

c. I also accept the legal conclusion of the Department of Justice and determine that common Article 3 of Geneva does not apply to either al Qaeda or Taliban detainees, because, among other reasons, the relevant conflicts are international in scope and common Article 3 applies only to "armed conflict not of an international character."

d. Based on the facts supplied by the Department of Defense and the recommendation of the Department of Justice, I determine that the Taliban detainees are unlawful combatants and, therefore, do not qualify as prisoners of war under Article 4 of Geneva. I note that, because Geneva does not apply to our conflict with al Qaeda, al Qaeda detainees also do not qualify as prisoners of war.

3. Of course, our values as a Nation, values that we share with many nations in the world, call for us to treat detainees humanely, including those who are not legally entitled to such treatment. Our Nation has been and will continue to be a strong supporter of Geneva and its principles. As a matter of policy, the United States Armed Forces shall continue to treat detainees humanely and, to the extent appropriate and consistent with military necessity, in a manner consistent with the principles of Geneva.

4. The United States will hold states, organizations, and individuals who gain control of United States personnel responsible for treating such personnel humanely and consistent with applicable law.

5. I hereby reaffirm the order previously issued by the Secretary of Defense to the United States Armed Forces requiring that the detainees be treated humanely and, to the extent appropriate and consistent with military necessity, in a manner consistent with the principles of Geneva.

6. I hereby direct the Secretary of State to communicate my determinations in an appropriate manner to our allies, and other countries and international organizations cooperating in the war against terrorism of global reach.

[signed]

George Bush

Appendix D

Interrogation Policies in Guantanamo, Afghanistan and Iraq

	GTMO				Afghanistan				Iraq			
Number of Authorized Techniques	Policy	Date	Notes	Number of Authorized Techniques	Policy	Date	Notes	Number of Authorized Techniques	Policy	Date	Notes
17	FM 34-52 (1992)	Jan 02 - 01 Dec 02		17	FM 34-52 (1992)	27 Oct 01 - 24 Jan 03		17	FM 34-52 (1992)		
33	Secretary of Defense Approved Tiered System	02 Dec 02 - 15 Jan 03	1	33	CJTF 180 Response to Director, Joint Staff	24-Jan-03	1,3,6	29	CJTF-7 Signed Policy	14-Sep-03	1
20	FM 34-52 (1992) with 3 Cat I Techniques	16 Jan 03 - 15 Apr 03		32	CJTF 180 Detainee SOP	27-Mar-04	1	19	CJTF-7 Signed Policy	12-Oct-03	4
24	Secretary of Defense Memo	16 Apr 03 - Present	1.2	19	CJTF-A Rev 2 Guidance	Jun-04	4	19	CJTF-7 Signed Policy	13-May-04	4

1 Some techniques specifically delineated in this memo are inherent to techniques contained in FM 34-52, e.g. Yelling as a component of Fear Up
2 Five Approved Techniques require SOUTHCOM approval and SECDEF notification.
3 Figure includes techniques that were not in current use but requested for future use.
4 Figure includes one technique which requires CG approval.
5 Memorandum cited for Afghanistan and Iraq are classified.
6 Figure includes the 17 techniques of FM-34-52, although they are not specified in the Memo.

Appendix D
Source: Naval IG Investigation

Appendix E
Evolution of Interrogation Techniques - GTMO

Interrogation Techniques	FM 34-52 (1992) Jan 02 - 01 Dec 02	Secretary of Defense Approved Tier System 02 Dec 02 - 15 Jan 03	FM 34-52 (1992) with some Cat I 16 Jan 03 - 15 Apr 03	Secretary of Defense Memo 16 Apr 03 - Present
Direct Questioning	X	X	X	X
Incentive/removal of incentive	X	X	X	X
Emotional love	X	X	X	X
Emotional hate	X	X	X	X
Fear up harsh	X	X	X	X
Fear up mild	X	X	X	X
Reduced fear	X	X	X	X
Pride and ego up	X	X	X	X
Pride and ego down	X	X	X	X
Futility	X	X	X	X
We know all	X	X	X	X
Establish your identity	X	X	X	X
Repetition approach	X	X	X	X
File and dossier	X	X	X	X*
Mutt and Jeff		X	X	X
Rapid Fire	X	X	X	X
Silence	X	X	X	X
Change of Scene	X	X	X	X
Yelling		X (Cat I)		
Deception		X (Cat I)		X*
Multiple interrogators		X (Cat I)	X	
Interrogator identity		X (Cat I)	X	
Stress positions, like standing		X (Cat II)		
False documents/reports		X (Cat II)		
Isolation for up to 30 days		X (Cat II)		
Deprivation of light/auditory stimuli		X (Cat II)		
Hooding (transportation & questioning)		X (Cat II)		
20-hour interrogations		X (Cat II)		
Removal of ALL comfort items, including religious items		X (Cat II)		X*
MRE-only diet		X (Cat II)		
Removal of clothing		X (Cat II)		
Forced grooming		X (Cat II)		
Exploiting individual phobias, e.g. dogs		X (Cat II)		
Mild, non-injurious physical contact, e.g. grabbing, poking or light pushing		X (Cat III)		
Environmental manipulation				X
Sleep adjustment				X
False flag				X

Source: Naval IG Investigation
Appendix E

* Techniques require SOUTHCOM approval and SECDEF notification

APPENDIX G

PSYCHOLOGICAL STRESSES

The potential for abusive treatment of detainees during the Global War on Terrorism was entirely predictable based on a fundamental understanding of the principle of social psychology principles coupled with an awareness of numerous known environmental risk factors. Most leaders were unacquainted with these known risk factors, and therefore failed to take steps to mitigate the likelihood that abuses of some type would occur during detainee operations. While certain conditions heightened the possibility of abusive treatment, such conditions neither excuse nor absolve the individuals who engaged in deliberate immoral or illegal behaviors.

The abuse the detainees endured at various places and times raises a number of questions about the likely psychological aspects of inflicting such abuses. Findings from the field of social psychology suggest that the conditions of war and the dynamics of detainee operations carry inherent risks for human mistreatment, and therefore must be approached with great caution and careful planning and training.

The Stanford Prison Experiment

In 1973, Haney, Banks and Zimbardo[1] published their landmark Stanford study, "Interpersonal Dynamics in a Simulated Prison." Their study provides a cautionary tale for all military detention operations. The Stanford Experiment used a set of tested, psychologically sound college students in a benign environment. In contrast, in military detention operations, soldiers work under stressful combat conditions that are far from benign.

The Stanford Prison Experiment (SPE) attempted to "create a prison-like situation" and then observe the behavior of those involved. The researchers randomly assigned 24 young men to either the "prisoner" or "guard" group. Psychological testing was used to eliminate participants with overt psychopathology, and extensive efforts were made to simulate actual prison conditions. The experiment, scheduled to last two weeks, was cancelled after only six days due to the ethical concerns raised by the behaviors of the participants. The study notes that while guards and prisoners were free to engage in any form of interpersonal interactions, the "characteristic nature of their encounters tended to be negative, hostile, affrontive and dehumanizing."

The researchers found that both prisoners and guards exhibited "pathological reactions" during the course of the experiment. Guards fell into three categories: (1) those who were "tough but fair," (2) those who were passive and reluctant to use coercive control and, of special interests, (3) those who "went far beyond their roles to engage in creative cruelty and harassment." With each passing day, guards "were observed to generally escalate their harassment of the prisoners." The researchers reported: "We witnessed a sample of normal, healthy American college students fractionate into a group of prison guards who seemed to derive pleasure from insulting, threatening, humiliating, and dehumanizing their peers."

Because of the random assignment of subjects, the study concluded the observed behaviors were the result of situational rather than personality factors:

> The negative, anti-social reactions observed were not the product of an environment created by combining a collection of deviant personalities, but rather, the result of an intrinsically pathological situation which could distort and rechannel the behaviour of essentially normal individuals. The abnormality here resided in the psychological nature of the situation and not in those who passed through it.

The authors discussed how prisoner-guard interactions shaped the evolution of power use by the guards:

> The use of power was self-aggrandizing and self-perpetuating. The guard power, derived initially from an arbitrary label, was intensified whenever there was any perceived threat by the prisoners and this new level subsequently became the baseline from which further hostility and harassment would begin. The most hostile guards on each shift moved spontaneously into the leadership roles of giving orders and deciding on punishments. They became role models whose behaviour was emulated by other members of the shift. Despite minimal contact between the three separate guard shifts and nearly 16 hours a day spent away from the prison, the absolute level of aggression as well as the more subtle and "creative" forms of aggression manifested, increased in a spiraling function. Not to be tough and arrogant was to be seen as a sign of weakness by the guards and even those "good" guards who did not get as drawn into the power syndrome as the others respected the implicit norm of never contradicting or even interfering with an action of a more hostile guard on their shift.

In an article published 25 years after the Stanford Prison Experiment, Haney and Zimbardo noted their initial study "underscored the degree to which institutional settings can develop a life of their own, independent of the wishes, intentions, and purposes of those who run them." They highlighted the need for those outside the culture to offer external perspectives on process and procedures.[2]

Social Psychology:
Causes of Aggression and Inhumane Treatment

The field of social psychology examines the nature of human interactions. Researchers in the field have long been searching to understand why humans sometimes mistreat fellow humans. The discussions below examine the factors behind human aggression and inhumane treatment, striving to impart a better understanding of why detainee abuses occur.

Human Aggression

Research has identified a number of factors that can assist in predicting human aggression. These factors include:

- **Personality traits.** Certain traits among the totality of an individual's behavioral and emotional make-up predispose to be more aggressive than other individuals.
- **Beliefs.** Research reveals those who believe they can carry out aggressive acts, and that such acts will result in a desired outcome, are more likely to be aggressive than those who do not hold these beliefs.
- **Attitudes.** Those who hold more positive attitudes towards violence are more likely to commit violent acts.
- **Values.** The values individuals hold vary regarding the appropriateness of using violence to resolve interpersonal conduct.
- **Situational Factors.** Aggressive cues (the presence of weapons), provocation (threats, insults, aggressive behaviors), frustration, pain and discomfort (hot temperatures, loud noises, unpleasant odors), and incentives can all call forth aggressive behaviors.
- **Emotional factors.** Anger, fear, and emotional arousal can heighten the tendency to act out aggressively.

The personality traits, belief systems, attitudes, and values of those who perpetrated detainee abuses can only be speculated upon. However, it is reasonable to assume, in any given population, these characteristics will be distributed along a bell curve, which will predispose some more than others within a group to manifest aggressive behaviors. These existing traits can be affected by environmental conditions, which are discussed later.

Abusive Treatment

Psychologists have attempted to understand how and why individuals and groups who usually act humanely can sometimes act otherwise in certain circumstances. A number of psychological concepts explain why abusive behavior occurs. These concepts include:

- **Deindividuation.** Deindividuation is a process whereby the anonymity, suggestibility, and contagion provided in a crowd allows individuals to participate

in behavior marked by the temporary suspension of customary rules and inhibitions. Individuals within a group may experience reduced self-awareness which can also result in disinhibited behavior.

- **Groupthink.** Individuals often make very uncharacteristic decisions when part of a group. Symptoms of groupthink include: (1) Illusion of invulnerability—group members believe the group is special and morally superior; therefore its decisions are sound; (2) Illusion of unanimity in which members assume all are in concurrence, and (3) Pressure is brought to bear on those who might dissent.
- **Dehumanization.** Dehumanization is the process whereby individuals or groups are viewed as somehow less than fully human. Existing cultural and moral standards are often not applied to those who have been dehumanized.
- **Enemy Image.** Enemy image describes the phenomenon wherein both sides participating in a conflict tend to view themselves as good and peace-loving peoples, while the enemy is seen as evil and aggressive.
- **Moral Exclusion.** Moral exclusion is a process whereby one group views another as fundamentally different, and therefore prevailing moral rules and practices apply to one group but not the other.

Abuse and Inhumane Treatment in War

Socialization to Evil and Doubling. Dr. Robert Jay Lifton has extensively examined the nature of inhumane treatment during war. Dr. Lifton suggested that ordinary people can experience "socialization to evil," especially in a war environment. Such people often experience a "doubling." They are socialized to evil in one environment and act accordingly within that environment, but they think and behave otherwise when removed from that environment. For example, doctors committed unspeakable acts while working in Auschwitz, but would go home on weekends and behave as "normal" husbands and fathers.

Moral Disengagement. Moral disengagement occurs when normal self-regulatory mechanisms are altered in a way that allows for abusive treatment and similar immoral behaviors. Certain conditions, identified by Bandura and his colleagues,[3] can lead to moral disengagement, such as:

- **Moral Justification.** Misconduct can be justified if it is believed to serve a social good.
- **Euphemistic Language.** Language affects attitudes and beliefs, and the use of euphemistic language such as "softening up" (and even "humane treatment") can lead to moral disengagement.
- **Advantageous Comparison.** "Injurious conduct can be rendered benign" when compared to more violent behaviors. This factor is likely to occur during war. Essentially, abusive behaviors may appear less significant and somehow justifiable when compared to death and destruction.

- **Displacement of Responsibility.** "People view their actions as springing from the social pressures or dictates of others rather than as something for which they are socially responsible." This is consistent with statements from those under investigation for abuses.
- **Diffusion of Responsibility.** Group decisions and behaviors can obscure responsibility: "When everyone is responsible, no one really feels responsible."
- **Disregarding or Distorting the Consequences of Actions.** Harmful acts can be minimized or ignored when the harm is inflicted for personal gain or because of social inducements.
- **Attribution of Blame.** "Victims get blamed for bringing suffering on themselves."

Detainee and interrogation operations consist of a special subset of human interactions, characterized by one group which has significant power and control over another group which must be managed, often against the will of its members. Without proper oversight and monitoring, such interactions carry a higher risk of moral disengagement on the part of those in power and, in turn, are likely to lead to abusive behaviors.

Environmental Factors

The risk of abusive behaviors is best understood by examining both psychological and environmental risk factors. A cursory examination of situational variables present at Abu Ghraib indicates the risk for abusive treatment was considerable. Many of the problematic conditions at Abu Ghraib are discussed elsewhere in this report, to include such factors as poor training, under nearly daily attack, insufficient staffing, inadequate oversight, confused lines of authority, evolving and unclear policy, and a generally poor quality of life. The stresses of these conditions were certainly exacerbated by delayed troop rotations and by basic issues of safety and security. Personnel needed to contend with both internal threats from volatile and potentially dangerous prisoners and external threats from frequent mortar fire and attacks on the prison facilities.

The widespread practice of stripping detainees, another environmental factor, deserves special mention. The removal of clothing interrogation technique evolved into something much broader, resulting in the practice of groups of detainees being kept naked for extended periods at Abu Ghraib. Interviews with personnel at Abu Ghraib indicated that naked detainees were a common sight within the prison, and this was understood to be a general part of interrogation operations.

While the removal of clothing may have been intended to make detainees feel more vulnerable and therefore more compliant with interrogations, this practice is likely to have had a psychological impact on guards and interrogators as well. The wearing of clothes is an inherently social practice, and therefore the stripping away of clothing may have had the unintended consequence of dehumanizing detainees in the eyes of those who interacted with them. As discussed earlier, the process of dehumanization lowers the moral and cultural barriers that usually preclude the abusive treatment of others.

NOTES

1. C. Haney, C. Banks, and P. Zimbardo, "Interpersonal Dynamics in a Simulated Prison," *International Journal of Criminology and Penology*, Vol. 1 (1973), pp. 69–97.

2. C. Haney and P. Zimbardo, "The Past and Future of U.S. Prison Policy, Twenty-Five Years after the Stanford Prison Experiment," *American Psychologist*, July 1998, pp. 709–727.

3. A. Bandura, C. Barbaranelli, G. Caprara, and C. Pastorelli, "Mechanisms of Moral Disengagement in the Exercise of Moral Agency," *Journal of Personality and Social Psychology*, Vol. 71, No. 2 (August 1996), pp. 364–374.

Appendix H

ETHICAL ISSUES

Introduction

For the United States and other nations with similar value systems, detention and interrogation are themselves ethically challenging activities. Effective interrogators must deceive, seduce, incite, and coerce in ways not normally acceptable for members of the general public. As a result, the U.S. places restrictions on who may be detained and the methods interrogators may employ. Exigencies in the Global War on Terror have stressed the normal American boundaries associated with detention and interrogation. In the ensuing moral uncertainty, arguments of military necessity make the ethical foundation of our soldiers especially important.

Ethical Foundations of Detention and Interrogation

Within our values system, consent is a central moral criterion on evaluating our behavior toward others. Consent is the manifestation of the freedom and dignity of the person and, as such, plays a critical role in moral reasoning. Consent restrains, as well as enables, humans in their treatment of others. Criminals, by not respecting the rights of others, may be said to have consented—in principle—to arrest and possible imprisonment. In this construct—and due to the threat they represent—insurgents and terrorists "consent" to the possibility of being captured, detained, interrogated, or possibly killed.

Permissions and Limits on Detentions

This guideline of implied consent for the U.S. first limits who may be detained. Individuals suspected of insurgent or terrorist activity may be detained to prevent them from conducting further attacks and to gather intelligence to prevent other insurgents and terrorists from conducting attacks. This suggests two categories of persons who may be detained and interrogated: (1) persons who have engaged in or assisted those who engage in terrorist or insurgent activities; and (2) persons who have come by information regarding insurgent and terrorist activity.

By engaging in such activities, persons in the first category may be detained as criminals or enemy combatants, depending on the context. Persons in the second category may be detained and questioned for specific information, but if they do not represent a continuing threat, they may be detained only long enough to obtain the information.

Permissions and Limits on Interrogation Techniques

For the U.S., most cases for permitting harsh treatment of detainees on moral grounds begin with variants of the "ticking time bomb" scenario. The ingredients of such scenarios usually include an impending loss of life, a suspect who knows how to prevent it—and in most versions is responsible for it—and a third party who has no humane alternative to obtain the information in order to save lives. Such cases raise a perplexing moral problem: Is it permissible to employ inhumane treatment when it is believed to be the only way to prevent loss of lives? In periods of emergency, and especially in combat, there will always be a temptation to override legal and moral norms for morally good ends. Many in Operations Enduring Freedom and Iraqi Freedom were not well prepared by their experience, education, and training to resolve such ethical problems.

A morally consistent approach to the problem would be to recognize there are occasions when violating norms is understandable but not necessarily correct—that is, we can recognize that a good person might, in good faith, violate standards. In principle, someone who, facing such a dilemma, committed abuse should be required to offer his actions up for review and judgment by a competent authority. An excellent example is the case of a 4th Infantry Division battalion commander who permitted his men to beat a detainee whom he had good reason to believe had information about future attacks against his unit. When the beating failed to produce the desired results, the commander fired his weapon near the detainee's head. The technique was successful and the lives of U.S. servicemen were likely saved. However, his actions clearly violated the Geneva Conventions and he reported his actions knowing he would be prosecuted by the Army. He was punished in moderation and allowed to retire.

In such circumstances interrogators must apply a "minimum harm" rule by not inflicting more pressure than is necessary to get the desired information. Further, any treatment that causes permanent harm would not be permitted, as this surely constitutes torture. Moreover, any pain inflicted to teach a lesson or after the interrogator has determined he cannot extract information is morally wrong.

National security is an obligation of the state, and therefore the work of interrogators carries a moral justification. But the methods employed should reflect this nation's commitment to our own values. Of course the tension between military necessity and our values will remain. Because of this, military professionals must accept the reality that during crises they may find themselves in circumstances where lives will be at stake and the morally appropriate methods to preserve those lives may not be obvious. This should not preclude action, but these professionals must be prepared to accept the consequences.

Ethics Education

The instances of detainee abuse in Iraq and Afghanistan do indicate a review of military ethics education programs is needed. This is not to suggest that more adequate ethics education will necessarily prevent abuses. Major service programs such as the Army's "core values," however, fail to adequately prepare soldiers working in detention operations.

While there are numerous ethics education programs throughout the services, almost all refer to certain "core values" as their foundation. Core-values programs are grounded in organizational efficacy rather than the moral good. They do not address humane treatment of the enemy and noncombatants, leaving military leaders and educators an incomplete tool box with which to deal with "real-world" ethical problems. A professional ethics program addressing these situations would help equip them with a sharper moral compass for guidance in situations often riven with conflicting moral obligations.

Executive Summary
Investigation of Intelligence Activities At Abu Ghraib
pages 1-5.

AR 15-6 Investigation of the Abu Ghraib Prison and
205th Military Intelligence Brigade
LTG Anthony R. Jones
pages 6-33

AR 15-6 Investigation of the Abu Ghraib Detention
Facility and 205th Military Intelligence Brigade
MG George R. Fay
pages 34-176

Note: Sections of the Fay report not released to the public, marked "S//NF"
("Secret//No foreign distribution") and published here for the first time, appear
in italic type on pages 457–465.

EXECUTIVE SUMMARY

Investigation of Intelligence Activities
At
Abu Ghraib

Background

     This investigation was ordered initially by LTG Ricardo S. Sanchez, Commander, Combined Joint Task Force Seven (CJTF-7). LTG Sanchez appointed MG George R. Fay as investigating officer under the provisions of Army Regulation 381-10, Procedure 15. MG Fay was appointed to investigate allegations that members of the 205th Military Intelligence Brigade (205 MI BDE) were involved in detainee abuse at the Abu Ghraib Detention Facility. Specifically, MG Fay was to determine whether 205 MI BDE personnel requested, encouraged, condoned, or solicited Military Police (MP) personnel to abuse detainees and whether MI personnel comported with established interrogation procedures and applicable laws and regulations.

     On 16 June 2004, Acting Secretary of the Army R. L. Brownlee appointed General Paul J. Kern, Commander, US Army Materiel Command (AMC), as the new Procedure 15 appointing authority. On 25 June 2004, GEN Kern appointed LTG Anthony R. Jones, Deputy Commanding General, US Army Training and Doctrine Command, as an additional Procedure 15 investigating officer. MG Fay was retained as an investigating officer.

     Without reinvestigating areas reviewed by MG Fay, LTG Jones was specifically directed to focus on whether organizations or personnel higher than the 205th MI BDE chain of command, or events and circumstances outside of the 205th MI Brigade, were involved, directly or indirectly, in the questionable activities regarding alleged detainee abuse at Abu Ghraib prison.

     The investigative teams conducted a comprehensive review of all available background documents and statements pertaining to Abu Ghraib from a wide variety of sources. These sources included the reports written by MG Geoffrey Miller, MG Donald Ryder, MG Antonio Taguba and the Department of Army Inspector General. LTG Jones interviewed LTG Sanchez and MG Barbara Fast, the CJTF-7 Senior Intelligence Staff Officer. MG Fay's team conducted over 170 interviews concerning the interviewees' knowledge of interrogation and detention operations at Abu Ghraib and/or their knowledge of and involvement in detainee abuse. MG Fay's interviews included interviews with MG Fast, MG Walter Wojdakowski, MG Geoffrey Miller, MG Thomas Miller, and BG Janis Karpinski.

Operational Environment

The events at Abu Ghraib cannot be understood in a vacuum. Three interrelated aspects of the operational environment played important roles in the abuses that occurred at Abu Ghraib. First, from the time V Corps transitioned to become CJTF-7, and throughout the period under investigation, it was not resourced adequately to accomplish the missions of the CJTF: stability and support operations (SASO) and support to the Coalition Provisional Authority (CPA). The CJTF-7 headquarters lacked adequate personnel and equipment. In addition, the military police and military intelligence units at Abu Ghraib were severely under-resourced. Second, providing support to the Coalition Provisional Authority (CPA) required greater resources than envisioned in operational plans. Third, operational plans envisioned that CJTF-7 would execute SASO and provide support to the CPA in a relatively non-hostile environment. In fact, opposition was robust and hostilities continued throughout the period under investigation. Therefore, CJTF-7 had to conduct tactical counter-insurgency operations, while also executing its planned missions.

These three circumstances delayed establishment of an intelligence architecture and degraded the ability of the CJTF-7 staff to execute its assigned tasks, including oversight of interrogation and detention operations at Abu Ghraib.

When hostilities were declared over, US forces had control of only 600 Enemy Prisoners of War (EPW) and Iraqi criminals. In the fall of 2003, the number of detainees rose exponentially due to tactical operations to capture counter-insurgents dangerous to U.S. forces and Iraqi civilians. At that time, the CJTF-7 commander believed he had no choice but to use Abu Ghraib as the central detention facility.

Command and staff actions and inaction must be understood in the context of the operational environment discussed above. In light of the operational environment, and CJTF-7 staff and subordinate unit's under-resourcing and increased missions, the CJTF-7 Commander had to prioritize efforts. CJTF-7 devoted its resources to fighting the counter-insurgency and supporting the CPA, thereby saving Coalition and civilian Iraqi lives and assisting in the transition to Iraqi self-rule. In the over-all scheme of OIF, the CJTF-7 Commander and staff performed above expectations.

Abuse

Clearly abuses occurred at the prison at Abu Ghraib. There is no single, simple explanation for why this abuse at Abu Ghraib happened. The primary causes are misconduct (ranging from inhumane to sadistic) by a small group of morally corrupt soldiers and civilians, a lack of discipline on the part of the leaders and Soldiers of the 205th MI BDE and a failure or lack of leadership by multiple echelons within CJTF-7. Contributing factors can be traced to issues affecting Command and Control, Doctrine, Training, and the experience of the Soldiers we asked to perform this vital mission.

For purposes of this report, abuse is defined as treatment of detainees that violated U.S. criminal law or international law or treatment that was inhumane or coercive without lawful justification. Whether the Soldier or contractor knew, at the time of the acts, that the conduct violated any law or standard, is not an element of the definition.

The abuses at Abu Ghraib primarily fall into two categories: a) intentional violent or sexual abuse and, b) abusive actions taken based on misinterpretations or confusion regarding law or policy.

LTG Jones found that while senior level officers did not commit the abuse at Abu Ghraib they did bear responsibility for lack of oversight of the facility, failing to respond in a timely manner to the reports from the International Committee of the Red Cross and for issuing policy memos that failed to provide clear, consistent guidance for execution at the tactical level.

MG Fay has found that from 25 July 2003 to 6 February 2004, twenty-seven 205 MI BDE Personnel allegedly requested, encouraged, condoned or solicited Military Police (MP) personnel to abuse detainees and/or participated in detainee abuse and/or violated established interrogation procedures and applicable laws and regulations during interrogation operations at Abu Ghraib.

Most, though not all, of the violent or sexual abuses occurred separately from scheduled interrogations and did not focus on persons held for intelligence purposes. No policy, directive or doctrine directly or indirectly caused violent or sexual abuse. In these cases, Soldiers knew they were violating the approved techniques and procedures.

Confusion about what interrogation techniques were authorized resulted from the proliferation of guidance and information from other theaters of operation; individual interrogator experiences in other theaters; and, the failure to distinguish between interrogation operations in other theaters and Iraq. This confusion contributed to the occurrence of some of the non-violent and non-sexual abuses.

MG Taguba and MG Fay reviewed the same photographs as supplied by the US Army Criminal Investigation Command (CID). MG Fay identified one additional photograph depicting abuse by MI personnel that had not been previously identified by MG Taguba. MG Fay also identified other abuse that had not been photographed.

Alleged incidents of abuse by military personnel have been referred to the CID for criminal investigation and the chain of command for disciplinary action. Alleged incidents of abuse by civilian contractors have been referred through the Department of Defense to the Department of Justice.

Discipline and Leadership

Military Intelligence and Military Police units had missions throughout the Iraqi Theater of Operations (ITO), however, 205th MI Brigade and 800th Military Police Brigade leaders at Abu Ghraib failed to execute their assigned responsibilities. The leaders from units located at Abu Ghraib or with supervision over Soldiers and units at Abu Ghraib, failed to supervise subordinates or provide direct oversight of this important mission. These leaders failed to properly discipline their Soldiers. These leaders failed to learn from prior mistakes and failed to provide continued mission-specific training. The 205th MI Brigade Commander did not assign a specific subordinate unit to be responsible for interrogations at Abu Ghraib and did not ensure that a Military Intelligence chain of command at Abu Ghraib was established. The absence of effective leadership was a factor in not sooner discovering and taking actions to prevent both the violent/sexual abuse incidents and the misinterpretation/confusion incidents.

Neither Department of Defense nor Army doctrine caused any abuses. Abuses would not have occurred had doctrine been followed and mission training conducted. Nonetheless, certain facets of interrogation and detention operations doctrine need to be updated, refined or expanded, including, the concept, organization, and operations of a Joint Interrogation and Debriefing Center (JIDC); guidance for interrogation techniques at both tactical and strategic levels; the roles, responsibilities and relationships between Military Police and Military Intelligence personnel at detention facilities; and, the establishment and organization of a Joint Task Force structure and, in particular, its intelligence architecture.

Other Contributing Factors

Demands on the Human Intelligence (HUMINT) capabilities in a counter-insurgency and in the future joint operational environment will continue to tax tactical and strategic assets. The Army needs trained and experienced tactical HUMINT personnel.

Working alongside non-DOD organizations/agencies in detention facilities proved complex and demanding. The perception that non-DOD agencies had different rules regarding interrogation and detention operations was evident. Interrogation and detention policies and limits of authority should apply equally to all agencies in the Iraqi Theater of Operations.

"Ghost Detainees"

The appointing authority and investigating officers made a specific finding regarding the issue of "ghost detainees" within Abu Ghraib. It is clear that the interrogation practices of other government agencies led to a loss of accountability at Abu Ghraib. DoD must document and enforce adherence by other government agencies with established DoD practices and procedures while conducting detainee interrogation operations at DoD facilities. This matter requires further investigation and, in accordance with the provisions of AR 381-10, Part 15, is being referred to the DoD Inspector General, as the DoD liaison with other government agencies for appropriate investigation and evaluation. Soldiers/Sailors/Airmen/Marines should never be put in a position that potentially puts them at risk for non-compliance with the Geneva Convention or Laws of Land Warfare.

Conclusion

Leaders and Soldiers throughout Operation Iraqi Freedom were confronted with a complex and dangerous operational environment. Although a clear breakdown in discipline and leadership, the events at Abu Ghraib should not blind us from the noble conduct of the vast
majority of our Soldiers. We are a values based profession in which the clear majority of our Soldiers and leaders take great pride.

A clear vote of confidence should be extended by the senior leadership to the leaders and Soldiers who continue to perform extraordinarily in supporting our Nation's wartime mission. Many of our Soldiers have paid the ultimate sacrifice to preserve the freedoms and liberties that America and our Army represent throughout the world.

23 August 2004

AR 15-6 Investigation
of the Abu Ghraib Prison
and 205th Military Intelligence Brigade

LTG Anthony R. Jones

AR 15-6 Investigation of the Abu Ghraib Detention Facility and 205th MI Brigade

LTG Anthony R. Jones

(U) Table of Contents

(U) AR 15-6 Investigation of the
Abu Ghraib Detention Facility
and 205th MI Brigade

1.   (U) Executive Summary

a. (U) Appointment, Charter and Investigative Activity

(1) (U) On 24 June 2004, Acting Secretary of the Army R. L. Brownlee notified me that I was selected to serve as the Senior Investigating Officer in the investigation of the 205th Military Intelligence Brigade. GEN Paul Kern was the appointing authority and in a memorandum, dated 25 June 2004, formally designated me Senior Investigating Officer. MG George Fay, who had been investigating the 205th MI BDE since his appointment by LTG Ricardo Sanchez on 31 March 2004, would continue as an investigating officer. Without reinvestigating areas reviewed by MG Fay, I was specifically directed to focus on whether organizations or personnel higher than the 205th Military Intelligence (MI) Brigade chain of command, or events and circumstances outside of the 205th MI Brigade, were involved, directly or indirectly, in the questionable activities regarding alleged detainee abuse at Abu Ghraib prison.

(2) (U) During the course of my investigation, I interviewed LTG Ricardo Sanchez, the Commander of Combined Joint Task Force-7 (CJTF-7)[1] during the period under investigation, and the senior intelligence officer on his staff, MG Barbara Fast (the "C2"). In addition, I reviewed witness statements that MG Fay' s investigation team had collected; assessment and investigation reports written by MG Geoffrey Miller, MG Donald Ryder, MG Antonio Taguba and the Department of the Army Inspector General (DAIG); and other written materials including relevant law, doctrine, organizational documents, policy, directives, and U.S. Central Command (CENTCOM) and CJTF-7 operational orders (OPORDS) and fragmentary orders (FRAGOs).

b. (U) Background and Operational Environment

(1) (U) The events at Abu Ghraib cannot be understood in a vacuum. Three interrelated aspects of the operational environment played important roles in the abuses that occurred at Abu Ghraib. First, from the time V Corps transitioned to become CJTF-7, and throughout the period under investigation, it was not resourced adequately to accomplish the missions of the CJTF: stability and support operations (SASO) and support to the Coalition Provisional Authority (CPA). The CJTF-7 headquarters lacked adequate personnel and equipment. In addition, the military police and military intelligence units at Abu Ghraib were severely under-resourced. Second, providing support to the Coalition Provisional Authority (CPA) required greater resources than envisioned in operational plans. Third, operational plans envisioned that CJTF-7 would execute SASO and provide support to the CPA in a relatively non-hostile environment. In fact, opposition was robust and hostilities continued throughout the period under investigation. Therefore, CJTF-7 had to conduct tactical counter-insurgency operations, while also executing its planned missions.

1 CJTF-7 was the higher headquarters to which the 205th MI Brigade reported.

(2) (U) These three circumstances delayed establishment of an intelligence architecture and degraded the ability of the CJTF-7 staff to execute its assigned tasks, including oversight of interrogation and detention operations at Abu Ghraib.

(3) (U) When hostilities were declared over, U.S. forces had control of only 600 Enemy Prisoners of War (EPWs) and Iraqi criminals. In the fall of 2003, the number of detainees rose exponentially due to tactical operations to capture counter-insurgents dangerous to U.S. forces and Iraqi civilians. At this time, the CJTF-7 commander believed he had no choice but to use Abu Ghraib as the central detention facility.

c. (U) Abuse at Abu Ghraib

(1) (U) Clearly abuses occurred at the prison at Abu Ghraib. For purposes of this report, I defined abuse as treatment of detainees that violated U.S. criminal law or international law or treatment that was inhumane or coercive without lawful justification. Whether the Soldier or contractor knew, at the time of the acts, that the conduct violated any law or standard, is not an element of the definition. MG Fay's portion of this report describes the particular abuses in detail.

(2) (U) I found that no single, or simple, explanation exists for why some of the Abu Ghraib abuses occurred. For clarity of analysis, my assessment divides abuses at Abu Ghraib into two different types of improper conduct: First, intentional violent or sexual abuses and, second, actions taken based on misinterpretations of or confusion about law or policy.

(3) (U) Intentional violent or sexual abuses include acts causing bodily harm using unlawful force as well as sexual offenses including, but not limited to rape, sodomy and indecent assault. No Soldier or contractor believed that these abuses were permitted by any policy or guidance. If proven, these actions would be criminal acts. The primary causes of the violent and sexual abuses were relatively straight-forward _ individual criminal misconduct, clearly in violation of law, policy, and doctrine and contrary to Army values.

(4) (U) Incidents in the second category resulted from misinterpretations of law or policy or resulted from confusion about what interrogation techniques were permitted. These latter abuses include some cases of clothing removal (without any touching) and some uses of dogs in interrogations (uses without physical contact or extreme fear). Some of these incidents may have violated international law. At the time the Soldiers or contractors committed the acts, however, some of them may have honestly believed the techniques were condoned.

d. (U) Major Findings

(1) (U) The chain of command directly above the 205th MI Brigade was not directly involved in the abuses at Abu Ghraib. However, policy memoranda promulgated by the CJTF-7 Commander led indirectly to some of the non-violent and non-sexual abuses. In addition, the CJTF-7 Commander and Deputy Commander failed to ensure proper staff oversight of detention and interrogation operations. Finally, CJTF-7 staff elements reacted inadequately to earlier indications and warnings that problems existed at Abu Ghraib.

Command and staff actions and inaction must be understood in the context of the operational environment discussed above. In light of the operational environment, and CJTF-7 staff and subordinate unit's under-resourcing and increased missions, the CJTF-7 Commander had to prioritize efforts. CJTF-7 devoted its resources to fighting the counter-insurgency and supporting the CPA, thereby saving Coalition and civilian Iraqi lives and assisting in the transition to Iraqi self-rule. I find that the CJTF-7 Commander and staff performed above expectations, in the over-all scheme of OIF.

(2) (U) Most, though not all, of the violent or sexual abuses occurred separately from scheduled interrogations and did not focus on persons held for intelligence purposes. No policy, directive or doctrine directly or indirectly caused violent or sexual abuse. Soldiers knew they were violating the approved techniques and procedures.

(3) (U) Confusion about what interrogation techniques were authorized resulted from the proliferation of guidance and information from other theaters of operation; individual interrogator experiences in other theaters; and, the failure to distinguish between interrogation operations in other theaters and Iraq. This confusion contributed to the occurrence of some of the non-violent and non-sexual abuses.

(4) (U) Military Intelligence and Military Police units also had missions throughout the Iraqi Theater of Operations (ITO), however, 205th MI Brigade and 800th Military Police Brigade leaders at Abu Ghraib failed to execute their assigned responsibilities. The leaders from these units located at Abu Ghraib or with supervision over Soldiers and units at Abu Ghraib, failed to supervise subordinates or provide direct oversight of this important mission. These leaders failed to properly discipline their Soldiers. These leaders failed to learn from prior mistakes and failed to provide continued mission-specific training. The 205th MI Brigade Commander did not assign a specific subordinate unit to be responsible for interrogations at Abu Ghraib and did not ensure that a Military Intelligence chain of command at Abu Ghraib was established. The absence of effective leadership was a factor in not sooner discovering and taking actions to prevent both the violent/sexual abuse incidents and the misinterpretation/confusion incidents.

(5) (U) Neither Defense nor Army doctrine caused any abuses. Abuses would not have occurred had doctrine been followed and mission training conducted. Nonetheless, certain facets of interrogation and detention operations doctrine need to be updated, refined or expanded, including, the concept, organization, and operations of a Joint Interrogation and Debriefing Center (JIDC); guidance for interrogation techniques at both tactical and strategic levels; the roles, responsibilities and relationships between Military Police and Military Intelligence personnel at detention facilities; and, the establishment and organization of a Joint Task Force structure and in particular, its intelligence architecture.

(6) (U) No single or simple theory can explain why some of the abuses at Abu Ghraib occurred. In addition to individual criminal propensities, leadership failures and, multiple policies, many other factors contributed to the abuses occurring at Abu Ghraib, including:

• Safety and security conditions at Abu Ghraib;

UNCLASSIFIED

- Multiple agencies/organizations involvement in interrogation operations at Abu Ghraib;

- Failure to effectively screen, certify, and then integrate contractor interrogators/analysts/linguists;

- Lack of a clear understanding of MP and MI roles and responsibilities in interrogation operations.

- Dysfunctional command relationships at brigade and higher echelons, including the tactical control (TACON) relationship between the 800th MP Brigade and CJTF-7.

(7) (U) Demands on the Human Intelligence (HUMINT) capabilities in a counter-insurgency and in the future joint operational environment will continue to tax tactical and strategic assets. The Army needs trained and experienced tactical HUMINT personnel.

(8) (U) Working alongside non-DOD organizations/agencies in detention facilities proved complex and demanding. The perception that non-DOD agencies had different rules regarding interrogation and detention operations was evident, Interrogation and detention policies and limits of authority should apply equally to all agencies in the Iraqi Theater of Operations.

(9) (U) Leaders and Soldiers throughout Operation Iraqi Freedom were confronted with a complex and dangerous operational environment. Although a clear breakdown in discipline and leadership, the events at Abu Ghraib should not blind us from the noble conduct of the vast majority of our Soldiers. We are a values based profession in which the clear majority of our Soldiers and leaders take great pride.

(10) (U) A clear vote of confidence should be extended by the senior leadership to the leaders and Soldiers who continue to perform extraordinarily in supporting our Nation's wartime mission. Many of our Soldiers have paid the ultimate sacrifice to preserve the freedoms and liberties that America and our Army represent throughout the world.

UNCLASSIFIED

2. (U) Charter and Investigative Activity

a. (U) On 24 June 2004, Acting Secretary of the Army, R. L. Brownlee, notified me that I was selected to serve as the Senior Investigating Officer in the investigation of the 205th Military Intelligence Brigade. GEN Paul Kern was the appointing authority and in a memorandum dated 25 June 2004, formally designated me Senior Investigating Officer. MG George Fay, who had been investigating the 205th MI BDE since his appointment by LTG Ricardo Sanchez on 31 March 2004, would continue as an investigating officer.

b. (U) My specific duties were to focus on whether organizations or personnel higher than the 205th Military Intelligence (MI) Brigade chain of command, or events and circumstances outside of the 205th MI Brigade, were involved, directly or indirectly, in the questionable activities regarding alleged detainee abuse at Abu Ghraib prison.

c. (U) In accordance with guidance from the Appointing Authority, I would interview LTG Ricardo Sanchez and other Combined Joint Task Force-7 (CJTF-7) staff, as required, to obtain information to make findings and recommendations to GEN Kern on the culpability of senior leaders who had responsibility for interrogation and detainee operations in Iraq. My directions were to not reinvestigate the areas that MG Fay had already reviewed. Rather, I was to look at operational and strategic level events that occurred prior to and during the period under investigation and determine their relationship, if any, to the abuses that occurred while the 205th MI Brigade was involved in interrogations and intelligence analysis at Abu Ghraib.

d. (U) During the course of my investigation, I interviewed LTG Ricardo Sanchez, the Commander of Combined Joint Task Force-7 (CJTF-7) during the period under investigation, and the senior intelligence officer on his staff, MG Barbara Fast (the "C2"). In addition, I reviewed witness statements that MG Fay's investigation team had collected; reviewed the assessment and investigation reports written by MG Geoffrey Miller, MG Donald Ryder, MG Antonio Taguba, and the Department of the Army Inspector General; and reviewed other written materials including relevant law, doctrine, organizational documents, policy, directives, and U.S. Central Command (CENTCOM) and CJTF-7 Operational Orders (OPORDS) and Fragmentary Orders (FRAGOs).

3. (U) Background: Operation Iraqi Freedom During this Period

UNCLASSIFIED

4.   (U) Operational Environment

a.   (U) Before deciding to centralize detainees at Abu Ghraib, major organizational changes were ongoing in the structure of U.S. Forces fighting the Iraqi campaign. Following major ground operations and declaration of the end of hostilities, the U.S. Army V Corps transitioned to become the CJTF-7. Also during this period, then-MG Sanchez was promoted to Lieutenant General and assumed command of V Corps, replacing LTG Wallace who led Phase III, Decisive Operations, in Iraq. LTG Sanchez transitioned from commanding a division, consisting of approximately 15,000 Soldiers, to commanding V Corps. The U.S. Third Army, or ARCENT, was designated the Combined Forces Land Component Command under the U.S. Central Command during the initial phases of OW. When V Corps transitioned to the CJTF-7, the new command assumed responsibility for the Combined Forces Land Component Command (CFLCC) missions and operations in the Iraqi Theater of Operations (IT 0). The Forces under the command of LTG Sanchez grew to approximately 180,000 U.S. and Coalition forces. In addition, the new CJTF-7 was directed to transition to Phase IV of the Iraqi campaign. Phase IV operations were envisioned as stability and support operations (SASO) and direct support to the CPA. CJTF-7 assistance to the CPA was essential to help the CPA succeed in recreating essential government departments under the control of Iraqi leaders. CJTF-7 would also help the CPA transition control of critical government organizations, strategic communications, reconstruction contracts, and lines of operation necessary to enable Iraqi self-rule.

b.   (U) In actuality, LTG Sanchez and his V Corps staff rapidly realized that the war had not ended. They were in a counter-insurgency operation with a complex, adaptive enemy that opposed the rule of law and ignored the Geneva Conventions. This enemy opposed the transition of the new Iraqi governing councils that would enable self-rule, and opposed any occupation by U.S. or coalition forces. The hostilities continued. Operations were planned and executed to counter the insurgency.

c.   (U) In June 2003, when the CJTF-7 organization was established, a vast increase in responsibilities began. A Joint Manning Document (JMD) was developed to delineate the specific skill sets of personnel needed to perform the increased roles and functions of this new headquarters. After multiple reviews, the JMD for the CJTF-7 HQ5 was formally approved for 1400 personnel in December 2003. That JMD included personnel needed to support the Coalition Provisional Authority (CPA), staff the functional elements needed to focus at joint operational and strategic levels, and specifically augment areas such as intelligence, operations, and logistics. Building a coherent, focused team was essential to the success of Phase IV operations.

d.   (U) CJTF-7 remained in the direct chain of command of the U.S. Central Command, but also was charged with a direct support role to the CPA. Command relationships of subordinate tactical commands previously under V Corps remained as previously outlined in Operational Orders. Therefore, the divisions' and Corps' separate brigades, which included the 205th MI Brigade, remained under the CJTF-7. The level of authority and responsibilities of a command of this magnitude is normally vested in a four-star level Army Service Component Command under a Regional Combatant Commander, Of the 1400 personnel required on the JMD, the V Corps staff transitioned to only *495*, or roughly a third, of the manning requirements. The new JMD also required that key staff positions be manned by general officers rather than the normal

UNCLASSIFIED
o

colonel level positions on a Corps staff Although the JMD was properly staffed and approved, personnel and equipment shortages impacted on CJTF-7's ability to execute the mission and remained a critical issue throughout the period in question. The JMD had 169 positions earmarked for support of operations at Abu Ghraib.

(1) (S/NF)

(2) (U) The 800th MP Brigade remained TACON to the CJTF-7 throughout this period. With the essential task and responsibility for all EPW and confinement operations transferring from CFLCC to CJTF-7, this unit would have been more appropriately designated as OPCON instead of TACON to the CJTF. Tactical Control (TACON) allows commanders the detailed and usually local direction and control of movements and maneuver necessary to accomplish missions and tasks. Whereas, Operational Control (OPCON) provides full authority to organize commands and forces and employ them as the commander considers necessary to accomplish assigned missions. The 800th MP Brigade's parent unit in the area of operations remained the 377th Theater Support Command, located in Kuwait. In accordance with the CENTCOM OPLAN, CFLCC (ARCENT) had to provide operational logistic support to Army Forces employed from Kuwait. The TACON relationship of the 800th MP Brigade with CJTF-7 resulted in disparate support from the CJTF-7 staff, lower priority in meeting resource needs for detention facilities, and the lack of intrusive, aggressive oversight of the unit by CJTF-7 leadership. No attempt was made by the CJTF-7 or ARCENT Staff to coordinate a change in this command relationship.

e. (U) Following the period of major ground hostilities in Phase III operations, the infrastructure of the country remained in desperate need of reconstruction. In addition to battle damage, looting, pillaging, and criminal actions had decimated the government buildings and infrastructure necessary to detain enemy prisoners of war or criminals.

f. (U) The logistics system, including local contracted support, to support units in Iraq was slowly catching up to the priority requirements that needed to be executed. Improving living conditions and basic support for Soldiers, as well as ensuring the safety and security of all forces, remained priorities, especially with the advent of the counter-insurgency. Quality of life for Soldiers did not improve in many locations until December of 2003.

g. (U) Prior to the beginning of hostilities, planners estimated 30-100 thousand enemy prisoners of war would need to be secured, segregated, detained, and interrogated. The 800th MP Brigade was given the mission to establish as many as twelve detention centers, to be run by subordinate battalion units. As of May 2003, BG Hill reported that only an estimated 600 detainees were being held _a combination of enemy prisoners and criminals. As a result, additional military police units previously identified for deployment were demobilized in CONUS. The original plan also envisioned that only the prisoners remaining from the initial major combat operations would require detention facilities, and they would eventually be released or turned over to the Iraqi authorities once justice departments and criminal detention facilities were re-established,

h. (U) As major counter-insurgency operations began in the July 2003 timeframe, the demands on the CJTF-7 commander and staff, the CPA, the subordinate units, the Iraqi interim government, and Soldiers at all levels increased dramatically. Decisions were made to keep some units in-country to fight the insurgency. Pressure increased to obtain operational intelligence on the enemy's identity, support systems, locations, leadership, intelligence sources, weapons and ammunition caches, and centers of gravity. In addition, the location of Saddam Hussein and information on WMD remained intelligence priorities. The complexity of missions being conducted by CJTF-7 and subordinate units increased and placed a high demand on leadership at all levels. Leaders had to adapt to the new environment and prosecute hostilities, while at the same time exercising appropriate compassion for non-combatants and protecting the people who were trying to do what was right for their country. Operations were planned to pursue the various factions of the counter-insurgency based on intelligence developed with the Iraqi people and Coalition Forces. A rapid increase in the number of detainees (due to the apprehension of counter-insurgents who posed a security risk to our Soldiers and to the Iraqi people, members of criminal factions, and personnel of intelligence value) demanded a decision on a detention facility and a need to rapidly expand interrogation operations.

i. (U) Throughout the Iraqi Theater of Operations (ITO), synchronization of force protection and security operations between operational forces and forward operating bases, such as Abu Ghraib, demanded more focus by brigade-level leadership. Supported-to-supporting relationships were blurred due to the large geographical areas given to tactical units. At Abu Ghraib, outside-the-wire responsibilities during the period in question were the responsibility of the 3d Armored Cavalry Regiment and then the 82d Airborne Division. Force Protection and security for the Abu Ghraib forward operating base was an implied task for the 320th MP Battalion initially, and then, after the 19 November FRAGO, a specified task for the 205th MI Brigade Commander. The defense and security of the Abu Ghraib forward operating base, to include engaging the communities outside of the base for information, was a key concern of LTG Sanchez during his visits and led to the decision to place the 205th MI Brigade commander in charge of forces at Abu Ghraib for force protection and defense of the base in November 2003.

j. (U) Interrogating detainees was a massive undertaking. In accordance with doctrine, unit level personnel would gather initial battlefield intelligence at the point of apprehension. Tactical interrogations would continue at designated collection points (CP) at Brigade and Division levels. Then a more detailed interrogation to get operational and strategic intelligence was to be conducted at a designated central detention facility. The location and facility for this detention and interrogation was Abu Ghraib. Abu Ghraib was selected by Ambassador Bremer after consultation with his staff and LTG Sanchez. Abu Ghraib was envisioned as a temporary facility to be used for criminal detainees until the new Iraqi government could be established and an Iraqi prison established at another site. Following operations during the summer of 2003, Abu Ghraib also was designated by CJTF-7 as the detention center for security detainees. The population of criminals, security detainees, and detainees with potential intelligence value grew to an estimated 4000-5000 personnel in the fall of 2003.

k. (U) The 800th MP Brigade was designated the responsible unit for the Abu Ghraib detention facility and for securing and safeguarding the detainees. The 205th MI Brigade was given responsibility for screening and interrogating detainees at Abu Ghraib. The 320th MP battalion was the unit specifically charged with operating the Abu Ghraib detainee facility by the 800th MP Brigade. Initially, the 205th MI Brigade commander did not specify an MI unit or organization for interrogation operations at Abu Ghraib. Interrogators, analysts, and linguists arrived at Abu Ghraib from multiple units and locations within the 205th MI Brigade.

10

Contractor personnel were also later used to augment interrogation, analyst, and linguist personnel at Abu Ghraib.

5. (U) Assessments and Visits to Improve Intelligence, Detention and Interrogation Operations

a. (U) As commanders at all levels sought operational intelligence, it became apparent that the intelligence structure was undermanned, under-equipped, and inappropriately organized for counter-insurgency operations. Upon arrival in July 2003, MG Barbara Fast was tasked to do an initial assessment of the intelligence architecture needed to execute the CJTF-7 mission in Iraq. Technical intelligence collection means alone were insufficient in providing the requisite information on an enemy that had adapted to the environment and to a high-tech opponent. Only through an aggressive structure of human intelligence (HUMINT) collection and analysis could the requisite information be obtained. Communications equipment, computers, and access to sufficient bandwidth to allow reachback capabilities to national databases were needed to assist in the fusion and collaboration of tactical through strategic intelligence data. Disparate cells of different agencies had to be co-located to allow access to respective data bases to assist in the fusion and collaboration effort. Interrogation reports had to be standardized and rapidly reviewed to allow dissemination to subordinate tactical units, coalition allies, Iraqis, and other personnel at the unclassified level.

b. (U) Following MG Fast's initial assessment and report to CENTCOM headquarters, changes began to take place to put the right architecture in place. An Intelligence Fusion Cell was established, as were a Joint Inter-Agency Task Force and an expanded JC2X HUMINT Management Cell, at CJTF-7 headquarters. The CPA staff was augmented with military personnel from the CJTF-7 intelligence staff With the assistance of the Department of the Army Staff, CJTF-7 obtained needed communications equipment, computers, and reachback access to the Information Dominance Center (IDC) to collaborate intelligence information. The focus of the previous V Corps staff, which formed the nucleus of the initial CJTF-7 staff, rapidly changed from a tactical focus to a joint operational and strategic level focus. The subsequent successes of this new intelligence architecture created by MG Fast and her team exponentially improved the intelligence process and saved the lives of Coalition Forces and Iraqi civilians. HUMINT operations and the fusion of intelligence led to the capture of key members of the former regime, and ultimately, to the capture of Saddam Hussein himself. During the time period of the Abu Ghraib abuses, the intelligence focus was on Saddam Hussein's capture and exploitation of documents related to Saddam Hussein, preparation for Ramadan, and large scale enemy activity at Fallujah and Najaf. The effort to expand the intelligence organization, obtain operational intelligence about the counter-insurgency, and support the CPA consumed the efforts of the CJTF-7 staff. Responsibilities for oversight of tactical interrogation procedures, Intel analysis, and reporting at Abu Ghraib as throughout the ITO, were entrusted to the commanders in the field.

c. (U) Due to the expanded scope of the mission for this new organization, the need to gain operational intelligence about the counter-insurgency, and the rapid and unexpected number of detainees, assistance was requested to help inform the leadership on proper procedures, techniques, and changes needed for success. The assessment visit by MG Ryder greatly assisted the review and improvement of detention operations. Ryder's recommendations to automate the in-processing and accountability of detainees using the Biometrics Automated Tool Set (BATS), to discipline the audit trail of detainees from point of capture to the central detention facility, and to properly segregate different groups, were implemented.

d.   (S/NF)

e.   (U) MG Fast's initial assessment and report on the intelligence organization and the needed systems architecture to support the mission was invaluable to establishing a roadmap for needed intelligence resources. LTG Alexander, the DA G2, was instrumental in providing needed equipment and guidance to improve the intelligence collection and fusion capabilities in Iraq. LTG Alexander was specifically helpful in getting the equipment necessary to support the intelligence architecture from the tactical to the strategic fusion levels.

6.   (U) Indications and Warnings

a.   (U) In retrospect, indications and warnings had surfaced at the CJTF-7 level that additional oversight and corrective actions were needed in the handling of detainees from point of capture through the central collection facilities, to include Abu Ghraib. Examples of these indications and warnings include: the investigation of an incident at Camp Cropper, the International Committee of the Red Cross (ICRC) reports on handling of detainees in subordinate units, ICRC reports on Abu Ghraib detainee conditions and treatment, CID investigations and disciplinary actions being taken by commanders, the death of an OGA detainee at Abu Ghraib, the lack of an adequate system for identification and accountability of detainees, and division commanders' continual concerns that intelligence information was not returning to the tactical level once detainees were evacuated to the central holding facility. The Commander, CJTF-7, recognized the need to place emphasis on proper handling of detainees and proper treatment of the Iraqi people in close proximity to operations. In October and December 2003, CDR, CJTF-7 published two policy memos entitled "Proper treatment of the Iraqi people during combat operations" and "Dignity and respect while conducting operations." Reports from the assessments of MG Miller and MG Ryder clearly confirmed the CJTF-7 Commander's instincts that action was needed to improve procedures and set the conditions for success in intelligence and detention operations. The report from the CID in January 2004 and subsequent investigation by MG Taguba confirmed that abuses occurred at Abu Ghraib during the period under investigation.

b.   (U) I would be remiss if I did not reemphasize that the 180,000 U.S. and coalition forces, under all echelons of command within the CJTF-7, were prosecuting this complex counter-insurgency operation in a tremendously horrid environment, and were performing above all expectations. Leaders and Soldiers confronted a faceless enemy whose hatred of the United States knew no limits. The actions of a few undisciplined Soldiers at Abu Ghraib have overshadowed the selfless service demonstrated every day, twenty-four hours a day, by the vast majority of our Soldiers and civilians on the battlefield. We, as a Nation, owe a debt of gratitude to our service members who have answered our Nation's call and are in harm's way, every day. This fact became perfectly clear to me as I conducted my investigation.

13

7.   (U) Doctrine, Organizational Structure and Policy Challenges in the Iraqi Theater of Operations

a.   (U) Doctrine and Organizational Structures

(1) (U) Doctrine could not provide quick solutions for all the situations that confronted CJTF-7. In many cases, the situation, mission, and environment dictated the decisions and the actions taken by the CJTF leadership. This situation is not uncommon. Rarely does war follow the pre-planned strategy. As the V Corps staff morphed to form the nucleus of the CJTF-7 staff, doctrine was not available to prescribe a detailed sequence to efficiently and effectively execute the transition. The new JMD focused on supplementing the V Corps headquarters structure to perform the expected mission in the Iraqi environment - stability and support operations and support of the CPA.

(2) (U) <u>Joint Interrogation and Debriefing Center</u>. In accordance with JP 2.01, the use of a JIDC by a JTF is situation-dependent. No defined organization exists for implementing the JIDC concept. At Abu Ghraib, a JIDC was established based on the recommendation of MG Miller during his assessment. At the time, Abu Ghraib had only a few hundred detainees. LTC Jordan was sent to Abu Ghraib to oversee the establishment of the JIDC. On 19 November 2003, when COL Thomas Pappas assumed the role of commander of the forward operating base, he directed activities of the JIDC and LTC Jordan became the deputy director of the JIDC. There are conflicting statements regarding who had the responsibilities to implement and oversee the JIDC at Abu Ghraib. In accordance with doctrine, the CJTF-7 C2, MG Fast, through her JC2-X staff, provided priority intelligence requirements for the interrogators and analysts in the JIIDC. A portion of the approved CJTF-7 JMD earmarked 169 personnel for the interrogation operations and analysis cells in the JIDC. Many of these positions were later filled with contractor personnel. Although a senior officer was directed to be the Chief, JIDC, the establishment and efficient operation of the JIDC was further complicated by the lack of an organizational MI unit and chain of command at Abu Ghraib solely responsible for MI personnel and intelligence operations.

(3) (U) <u>MI & MP Responsibilities at Abu Ghraib</u> The delineation of responsibilities for interrogations between the military intelligence and military police may not have been understood by some Soldiers and some leaders. The doctrinal implications of this issue are discussed later in this report. At Abu Ghraib, the lack of an MI commander and chain of command precluded the coordination needed for effective operations. At the same time, LTC Jordan failed to execute his responsibilities as Chief, JIDC. Tactical doctrine states that interrogators should specify to the guards what types of behavior on their part will facilitate screening of detainees. Normally, interrogation facilities are collocated with detention facilities, requiring close coordination between the MPs who are responsible for detention operations, and the MI personnel who are responsible for screening and interrogations. Both doctrinal manuals, for military police and military intelligence operations, clearly provide that Soldiers and units must obey rules of land warfare and, specifically, the Geneva Conventions when handling detainees. At Abu Ghraib, the delineation of responsibilities seems to have been blurred when military police Soldiers, untrained in interrogation operations, were used to enable interrogations. Problems arose in the following areas: use of dogs in interrogations, sleep deprivation as an interrogation technique and use of isolation as an interrogation technique.

UNCLASSIFIED

(4) (U) <u>CJTF-7 Staff Responsibility</u>. CJTF-7 responsibility for staff oversight of detention operations, facilities, intelligence analysis and fusion, and limits of authority of interrogation techniques was dispersed among the principal and special staff Overall responsibility for detention operations was vested in the C3, MG Tom Miller, with further delegation to the Provost Marshal. Support of facilities was a C4 responsibility, with priorities of work established by the DCG, MG Walter Wojdakowski. MG Wojdakowski also had direct responsibility and oversight of the separate brigades assigned or TACON to CJTF-7. Priorities for intelligence collection, analysis and fusion were the responsibility of the C2, MG Fast. Lastly, LTG Sanchez used his Staff Judge Advocate, Colonel Marc Warren, to advise him on the

limits of authority for interrogation and compliance with the Geneva Conventions for the memos published. The lack of one person on the staff to oversee detention operations and facilities, and the responsibilities of all units at a detention facility complicated effective and efficient coordination among the staff Subordinate brigade commanders and their staffs also had to coordinate different actions for support with the various staff sections responsible for the support requested.

b. (U) Policy

(1) (U) <u>Policy Guidance</u>. DOD-wide, formal written policies for interrogation techniques have been prescribed by various levels of command and authority. In most cases, the doctrinal reference is FM 34-52, Intelligence Interrogation, dated September 1992. As stated, this manual is currently under revision by the proponent. During the period under investigation, there was confusing and sometimes conflicting guidance resulting from the number of policy memos and the specific areas of operation the various policies were intended to cover. Each theater's techniques for interrogation and counter-resistance were reviewed by appropriate legal authorities and subjected to external assessments before commanders were advised of their acceptability. In the wartime settings of each theater, commanders were satisfied that appropriate oversight had been conducted for procedures being used for interrogations. However, when reviewing the various reports on the number of abuses in the ITO, it became clear there is no agreed upon definition of abuse among all legal, investigating and oversight agencies.

(2) (U) Interrogation techniques, including Counter-Resistance Techniques, were developed and approved for the detainees in Guantanamo and Afghanistan who were determined not to be EPWs or protected persons under the Geneva Conventions of 1949. The OSD memo promulgated in December 2002, approving techniques and safeguards for interrogation of unlawful combatants in GTMO, included the use of dogs to induce stress and the removal of clothing as Counter-Resistance Techniques. This memo was rescinded in January 2003. A General Counsel Interrogation Working Group was subsequently formed and published a revised memo in April 2003 under the signature of the SECDEF on Counter-Resistance Techniques. This memo produced by the Working Group and the techniques outlined in FM 34-52 were referenced by Colonel Warren and his staff to develop the limits of authority memo for LTG Sanchez. The provisions of Geneva Convention IV, Relative to Protection of Civilian Persons in Time of War, did apply to detainees in Iraq.

(3) (U) Initially, no theater-specific guidance on approved interrogation techniques was published by CJTF-7 for the ITO. Thus, LTG Sanchez reemphasized the limits of authority for

UNCLASSIFIED
14

interrogations in his memos dated 14 September 2003 and 12 October 2003. The first was rescinded, and the second addressed only security detainees and, inadvertently, left certain issues for interpretation: namely, the responsibility for clothing detainees, the use of dogs in interrogation, and applicability of techniques to detainees who were not categorized as "security detainees." Furthermore, some military intelligence personnel executing their interrogation duties at Abu Ghraib had previously served as interrogators in other theaters of operation, primarily Afghanistan and GTMO. These prior interrogation experiences complicated understanding at the interrogator level. The extent of "word of mouth" techniques that were passed to the interrogators in Abu Ghraib by assistance teams from Guantanamo, Fort Huachuca, or amongst themselves due to prior assignments is unclear and likely impossible to definitively determine. The clear thread in the CJTF-7 policy memos and published doctrine is the humane treatment of detainees and the applicability of the Geneva Conventions. Experienced interrogators will confirm that interrogation is an art, not a science, and knowing the limits of authority is crucial. Therefore, the existence of confusing and inconsistent interrogation technique policies contributed to the belief that additional interrogation techniques were condoned in order to gain intelligence.

8. (U) Specific Comments on Abuse at Abu Ghraib

a. (U) This report, so far, has discussed the OPLAN background, operational environment, and policy, doctrine and structural decisions that created conditions which allowed the abuses at Abu Ghraib to occur. The earlier investigations aptly described what happened at Abu Ghraib. MG Taguba found that "numerous incidents of sadistic, blatant, and wanton criminal abuses were inflicted on detainees." MG Fay identified forty-four incidents of detainee abuse and his report describes the particular abuses in detail. In this section, I rely on the statements and other investigative activity from MG Fay. The conclusions, however, are my own. Clearly, shameful events occurred at the detention facility of Abu Ghraib and the culpable MI and MP Soldiers and leaders should be held responsible. In this section, I set forth an analytical framework for categorizing the abuses propose causes for the incidents of abuse, and also discuss the culpability of organizations and personnel higher than the 205th MI Brigade Commander.

b. (U) For purposes of this report, I defined abuse as treatment of detainees that violated U.S. criminal law (including the Uniform Code of Military Justice (UCMJ)) or international law, or treatment that was inhumane or coercive without lawful justification. Whether the Soldier or contractor knew, at the time of the acts, that the conduct violated any law or standard, is not an element of the definition. In other words, conduct that met the definition would be "abuse" independent of the actor's knowledge that the conduct violated any law or standard.

c. (U) For clarity of analysis, my assessment divides abuses at Abu Ghraib into two different types of improper conduct: first, intentional violent or sexual abuses and, second, actions taken based on misinterpretation of or confusion about law or policy.

(1) (U) Intentional violent or sexual abuses, for purposes of this report, include acts causing bodily harm using unlawful force as well as sexual offenses including, but not limited to rape, sodomy and indecent assault.[2] These incidents of physical or sexual abuse are serious

---

2. As those offenses are defined in the Uniform Code of Military Justice.

UNCLASSIFIED

enough that no Soldier or contractor believed the conduct was based on official policy or guidance. If proven, these actions would be criminal acts. I found that no policy, directive, or doctrine caused the violent or sexual abuse incidents. Soldiers knew they were violating the approved techniques and procedures. The primary causes of these actions were relatively straight-forward _individual criminal misconduct, clearly in violation of law, policy, and doctrine and contrary to Army values.

(2) (U) The second category of abuse consists of <u>incidents that resulted from misinterpretations of law or policy</u> or resulted from confusion about what interrogation techniques were permitted by law or local SOPs. I found that misinterpretation as to accepted practices or confusion occurred due to the proliferation of guidance and information from other theaters of operation; individual interrogator experiences in other theaters; and, the failure to distinguish between permitted interrogation techniques in other theater environments and Iraq. These abuses include some cases of clothing removal (without any touching), some use of dogs in interrogations (uses without physical contact or extreme fear) and some instances of improper imposition of isolation. Some of these incidents involve conduct which, in retrospect, violated international law. However, at the time some of the Soldiers or contractors committed the acts, they may have honestly believed the techniques were condoned. Some of these incidents either took place during interrogations or were related to interrogation. Often, these incidents consisted of MP Soldiers, rather than MI personnel, implementing interrogation techniques.

d. (U) Some abuses may in fact fall in between these two categories or have elements of both. For instance, some Soldiers under the guise of confusion or misinterpretation may actually have intentionally violated approved interrogation techniques. For example, a Soldier may know that clothing removal is prohibited, but still removed some of a detainee's clothing to try to enhance interrogation techniques. This Soldier can later claim to have believed the actions were condoned. Soldier culpability in this area is best left to individual criminal or command investigations. While no analytical scheme can aptly categorize all misconduct, I think using the two categories set forth above helps explain <u>why</u> the entire range of abuses occurred.

e. (U) The appointment memo directed me to determine whether organizations or personnel higher than the 205th MI Brigade chain of command were involved directly or indirectly, in the questionable activities regarding alleged detainee abuse at Abu Ghraib prison.

(1) (U) I find no organization or individual higher in the chain of command of the 205th MI Brigade were directly involved in the questionable activities regarding alleged detainee abuse at Abu Ghraib prison.

(2) (U) CJTF-7 leaders and staff actions, however, contributed indirectly to the questionable activities regarding alleged detainee abuse at Abu Ghraib.

(a) (U) Policy memoranda promulgated by the CJTF-7 Commander led indirectly to some of the non-violent and non-sexual abuses. The policy memos promulgated at the CJTF-7 level allowed for interpretation in several areas, including use of dogs and removal of clothing. Particularly, in light of the wide spectrum of interrogator qualifications, maturity, and experiences (i.e. in GTMO and Afghanistan), the memos did not adequately set forth the limits on interrogation techniques. Misinterpretations of CJTF policy memos led to some of the abuses at Abu Ghraib, but did not contribute to the violent or sexual abuses.

UNCLASSIFIED
16

(b) (U) Inaction at the CJTF-7 staff level may have also contributed to the failure to discover and prevent abuses before January 2004. As discussed above, staff responsibility for detention and interrogation operations was dispersed among the Deputy Commanding General, C2, C3, C4 and SJA. The lack of a single CJTF-7 staff proponent for detention and interrogation operations resulted in no individual staff member focusing on these operations. As discussed in Section V, certain warning signs existed. In addition, there is sufficient evidence to reasonably believe that personnel in the CJTF-7 staff, principally in the OSJA and JC2X had knowledge of potential abuses and misconduct in violation of the Geneva Conventions at Abu Ghraib. This knowledge was not presented to the CJTF-7 leadership. Had the pace of combat operations and support to the CPA not been so overwhelming, the CJTF-7 staff may have provided additional oversight to interrogation operations at Abu Ghraib. The Commander, CJTF-7 had to prioritize efforts and CJTF-7, by necessity, devoted its resources to fighting the counter-insurgency and supporting the CPA, thereby saving U.S. and civilian Iraqi lives and assisting in the transition to Iraqi self-rule. Further, LTG Sanchez and MG Wojdakowski relied upon two senior officer Brigade Commanders (BG Janice Karpinski and COL Pappas) to run detention and interrogation operations at Abu Ghraib. In my professional opinion, in light of all the circumstances, the CJTF-7 staff did everything they could have reasonably been expected to do to successfully complete all their assigned missions.

f. (U) Assessing the materials from MG Fay and from MG Taguba, I agree that leadership failure, at the brigade level and below, clearly was a factor in not sooner discovering and taking actions to prevent both the violent/sexual abuse incidents and the misinterpretation/confusion incidents. At Abu Ghraib, interrogation operations were also plagued by a lack of an organizational chain of command presence and by a lack of proper actions to establish standards and training by the senior leaders present.

(1) (U) The leaders from 205th MI and 800th MP Brigades located at Abu Ghraib or with supervision over Abu Ghraib, failed to supervise subordinates or provide direct oversight of this important mission. The lack of command presence, particularly at night, was clear.

(2) (U) The 205th Brigade Commander did not specifically assign responsibility for interrogation operations to a specific subordinate MI unit at Abu Ghraib and did not ensure that a chain of command for the interrogation operations mission was established at Abu Ghraib. The presence of a clear chain of Military Intelligence command and associated responsibilities would have enhanced effective operations.

(3) (U) The leaders from 205th MI and 800th MP Brigades located at Abu Ghraib or with supervision over Soldiers and units at Abu Ghraib, failed to properly discipline their Soldiers and failed to develop and learn from AARs and lessons learned.

(4) (U) These leaders failed to provide adequate mission-specific training to execute a mission of this magnitude and complexity.

(5) (U) A dysfunctional command relationship existed between the MI Brigade and the MP Brigade, including:

(a) Failure to coordinate and document specific roles and responsibilities;

17

(b) Confusion at the Soldier level concerning the clarity of the MP role in interrogations.

(6) (U) Despite these leadership deficiencies, the primary cause of the most egregious violent and sexual abuses was the individual criminal propensities of the particular perpetrators. These individuals should not avoid personal responsibility, despite the failings of the chain of command.

g. (U) Other Contributing Factors. No single, or simple, cause explains why some of the Abu Ghraib abuses happened. In addition to the leadership failings discussed above, other contributing factors include:

(1) (U) Safety and security conditions at Abu Ghraib. Resources that might otherwise have been put towards detention operations instead had to be dedicated to force protection. In addition, the difficult circumstances for Soldiers, including a poor quality of life and the constant threat of death or serious injury, contributed to Soldiers' frustrations and increased their levels of stress. Facilities at Abu Ghraib were poor. Working and living conditions created a poor climate to conduct interrogation and detention operations to standard.

(2) (U) The lack of clear and consistent guidance, promulgated at the CJTF level on interrogation procedures coupled with the availability of information on Counter-Resistance Techniques used in other theaters.

(3) (U) Soldier knowledge of interrogation techniques permitted in GTMO and Afghanistan and failure to distinguish between those environments and Iraq.

(4) (U) Interaction with OGA and other agency interrogators who did not follow the same rules as U.S. Forces. There was at least the perception, and perhaps the reality, that non-DOD agencies had different rules regarding interrogation and detention operations. Such a perception encouraged Soldiers to deviate from prescribed techniques.

(5) (U) Integration of some contractors without training, qualifications, and certification created ineffective interrogation teams and the potential for non-compliance with doctrine and applicable laws.

(6) (U) Under-resourcing of personnel in both the 800th MP BDE (including the inability to replace personnel leaving theater) and in the 205th MI Brigade, specifically in the interrogator, analyst, and linguist fields. (Under-resourcing at the CJTF-7 level also contributed and was previously discussed.)

(7) (U) Lack of a clear understanding of MP and MI roles and responsibilities by some Soldiers and leaders.

(8) (U) Lack of clear roles and responsibilities for tactical, as opposed to, strategic interrogation.

UNCLASSIFIED

9. (U) Assessments as the Senior Investigating Officer

a. (U) Introduction. Due to the previous assessments and investigations conducted on Abu Ghraib, I was able to develop my own assessments based on interviews I conducted, the findings and conclusions in the earlier reports, as well as the materials in MG Fay's report. The following assessments provide insight on the challenges that CJTF-7 faced, as well as areas that need to be addressed by our military in the near future. The specific investigations and assessments were provided by the reports of MG Miller, MG Ryder, MG Taguba, the DAIG, and MG Fay.

b. (U) Charters. MG Miller's and MG Ryder's assessments were conducted on interrogation and detention operations as a result of the request and/or discussions by the CJTF Commander and the Commander, CENTCOM. MG Taguba and MG Fay were directed to investigate personnel in the MP Brigade and the MI Brigade after the discovery of abuses at Abu Ghraib. The DAIG was specifically tasked to conduct an assessment of Detainee Operations as the Army executes its role as DOD Executive Agent for Enemy Prisoners of War and Detention Program.

c. (U) Summaries of assessment visits. The assistance visits by MG Miller and MG Ryder, discussed briefly above, confirmed the instincts of the Commander, CJTF-7, and provided solid recommendations for improving procedures. MG Miller's assessment set forth what had to be done to synchronize intelligence efforts, and provided different techniques in interrogation and analysis. MG Ryder provided processes for more efficient and effective chain of custody of, and accountability for, detainees. MG Taguba's and MG Fay's investigative reports confirmed that abuses occurred and assigned specific responsibility for the actions. The DAIG report provided insights across doctrine, organizations, training, materiel, leadership, personnel and facilities (DOTMLPF) and on capability and standards shortfalls. I found that the assistance visits by senior leaders with experience in detention and interrogation operations, subject matter experts, and mobile training teams were extremely helpful in validating needed procedures and increasing the effectiveness of interrogation and detention operations. The investigative reports and DAIG findings will be used to fix deficiencies that have been found in current operations.

d. (U) Doctrine.

(1) (U) Doctrine is meant to be a guideline to focus efforts in a specific area. Doctrine is the culmination of years of experience, Doctrine allows leaders at all levels to adapt to the different environments and situations that their units may encounter. When prosecuting hostilities, doctrine does not replace the inherent responsibilities of commanders to execute their missions, care for the safety and security of their Soldiers, train their Soldiers and their organizations to be competent and confident in their assigned duties and responsibilities, or uphold the rule of law and legal authority such as the Geneva Convention. An overarching doctrine allows commanders the latitude to develop tactics, techniques, and procedures, as well as unit standard operating procedures, to focus Soldier and unit operations. Commander policies and directives often supplement or emphasize specific items that the commander wants to ensure are clearly understood within their command.

(2) (U) Basic Army and Joint doctrine for detention and interrogation operations served as a guideline for operations in OIF. Doctrine did not cause the abuses at Abu Ghraib. Had Army

UNCLASSIFIED
10

doctrine and training been followed, the abuses at Abu Ghraib would not have occurred. Several areas, however, need to be updated, refined or expanded: roles, responsibilities and relationships between MP and MI personnel; the concept, structure, and organization of a JIDC; the transition to and organization of a JTF structure and in particular, the intelligence organization within the JTF headquarters.

(a)(U) <u>Roles, responsibilities and relationships between MP and MI personnel</u>. The various investigations indicate that the delineation of responsibilities for interrogations between the military intelligence and military police may not have been understood by some Soldiers and some leaders. At Abu Ghraib, non-violent and non-sexual abuses may have occurred as a result of confusion in three areas of apparent MI/MP overlap: use of dogs during interrogations, nudity, and implementation of sleep deprivation. Doctrinal manuals prescribe responsibilities for military intelligence and military police personnel at detention facilities. These manuals do not address command or support relationships. Subordinate units of the military intelligence brigade of a Corps are normally tasked with running the Corps Interrogation Facility (CIF). Centralized EPW collection and holding areas, as well as detention centers, are the responsibility of the Military Police with staff oversight by the Provost Marshal. FM 34-52, Intelligence Interrogation, does state that in the screening process of EPWs, MPs and MI Soldiers should coordinate roles.

(b)(U) Relationships between MP and MI personnel and leadership responsibilities at a detention facility of this magnitude need to be more prescriptive. Doctrine establishes the need for coordination and designates detention operations as a military police responsibility. Responsibility for interrogation of detainees remains with the military intelligence community. Doctrine for Interrogation operations states that MPs can enable, in coordination with MI personnel, a more successful interrogation. Exact procedures for how MP Soldiers assist with informing interrogators about detainees or assist with enabling interrogations can be left to interpretation. Our doctrinal manuals are clear on humane treatment of detainees and compliance with the Geneva Conventions by MI, MP and all U.S. Forces. The current version of FM 34-52, Intelligence Interrogation, is under revision to incorporate lessons learned in ongoing theaters of operations. Lessons learned have also resulted in changes to programs of instruction by military police and military intelligence proponents. My assessment is that the ongoing revision of Intelligence Interrogation manuals will assist in clarification of roles and responsibilities. At Abu Ghraib, doctrinal issues did not preclude on-site leaders from taking appropriate action to execute their missions.

(c)(U) <u>The Joint Interrogation and Debriefing Center</u>. The JIDC was formed at Abu Ghraib by personnel from a number of organizations, creating an ad hoc relationship. Further, the establishment of the JIDC at Abu Ghraib, coupled with implementing the new Tiger Team approach to interrogations (where an interrogator, analyst, and linguist operate as a team) were new to Abu Ghraib personnel and demanded creation of a detailed standard operating procedure (SOP). A SOP was initially developed and published in October 2003 by MI personnel at the facility. Joint doctrine needs to expand on the operation and organization for a JIDC at centralized detention facilities. A template for a JIDC needs to be developed, to include identifying Joint and other agency resources with strategic interrogation expertise, to provide insight for combatant commanders in specific areas of operation.

20

(d)(U) Joint doctrine and policy should also address the roles of military personnel and other agencies in collocated detention and interrogation facilities. All detainees must be in-processed, medically screened, accounted for, and properly documented when interned in a military facility. This did not happen at Abu Ghraib.

(3) (U) Transition to and Organization of JTF Structure and its Intelligence Architecture. The intelligence architecture for the missions tasked to the CJTF-7 was inadequate due to the expanded mission and continuation of hostilities in theater. Several reports stated that lack of manning provided significant challenges due to the increased mission work load and the environment. Certainly, the V Corps Headquarters was not trained, manned or equipped to assume the role of a CJTF. Although the mission was initially considered to be SASO, in fact hostilities continued. CI/HUMINT capabilities in current force structure, among all services, needs a holistic review. The Army has significantly reduced tactical interrogators since Desert Shield/Desert Storm. Creation of the Defense HUMINT Service and worldwide demands for these skills has depleted the number of experienced interrogators that may be needed in the future joint operational environment. The HUMINT management organization within the Intelligence Staff of a JTF needs to be institutionalized and resourced. Specifically, work needs to be done to institutionalize the personnel and equipment needs for future command and control headquarters to include the JIATF and C2X cells within a JTF intelligence staff.

(4) (U) In addition, the ongoing review by the Army and Joint Forces Command to create JTF capable headquarters and Standing Joint Task Force Headquarters organic to combatant commands should be expedited and resourced. Such efforts may have helped transition V Corps to the CJTF-7 staff more rapidly by assigning a Standing Joint Task Force to the CJTF-7. Similarly, the Army's initiative to develop stand alone command and control headquarters, currently known as Units of Employment, that are JTF-capable would have greatly facilitated the transition of the V Corps staff to the new organization.

e. (U) Policy and Procedures

(1) (U) Detention Operations. At first, at Abu Ghraib and elsewhere in Iraq, the handling of detainees, appropriately documenting their capture, and identifying and accounting for them, were all dysfunctional processes, using little or no automation tools. The assistance visits by MG Miller and MG Ryder revealed the need to adhere to established policies and guidance, discipline the process, properly segregate detainees, and use better automation techniques to account for detainees and to provide timely information.

(2) (U) Interrogation Techniques Policy. A review of different theaters' interrogation technique policies reveals the need for clear guidance for interrogation techniques at both the tactical and strategic levels, especially where multiple agencies are involved in interrogation operations. The basic Field Manuals provide guidance for Soldiers conducting interrogations at the tactical level. Different techniques and different authorities currently exist for other agencies. When Army Soldiers and other agency personnel operate in the same areas, guidelines become blurred. The future joint operational environment presents a potential for a mix of lawful and unlawful combatants and a variety of different categories of detainees. Techniques used during initial battlefield interrogations as opposed to at a central detention facility differ in terms of tactical versus more strategic level information collection. The experience, maturity, and source of interrogators at each of these locations may also dictate a change in techniques. In each

theater, commanders were seeking guidance and information on the applicability of the articles of the Geneva Conventions to specific population sets and on what techniques could be used to improve intelligence production and remain within the limits of lawful authorities.

(a)(U) At Abu Ghraib, the lack of consistent policy and command oversight regarding interrogation techniques, coupled with changing policies, contributed to the confusion concerning which techniques could be used, which required higher level approval, and what limits applied to permitted techniques. Initially, CJTF-7 had no theater-specific guidance other than the basic Field Manuals which govern Intelligence Interrogations and Internment and Resettlement operations. Policies for interrogation techniques including policies for Counter-Resistance Techniques, were provided for different theaters of operation—-namely Guantanamo, Afghanistan, and Iraq. Some interrogators conducting operations at Abu Ghraib had experience in different theaters and used their experiences to develop procedures at Abu Ghraib. An example of this is the SOP for the JIDC created by personnel of the 519th MI Battalion.

(b)(U) When policies, SOPs, or doctrine were available, Soldiers were inconsistently following them. In addition, in some units, training on standard procedures or mission tasks was inadequate. In my assessment, I do not believe that multiple policies resulted in the violent or sexual abuses discovered at Abu Ghraib. However, confusion over policies contributed to some of the non-violent and non-sexual abuses. There is a need, therefore, to further refine interrogation techniques and limits of authority at the tactical versus the strategic level, and between Soldiers and other agency personnel.

(3) (U) Use of Military Detention Centers by Other Agencies. In joint military detention centers, service members should never be put in a position that potentially puts them at risk for non-compliance with the Geneva Conventions or Laws of Land Warfare. At Abu Ghraib, detainees were accepted from other agencies and services without proper in-processing, accountability, and documentation. These detainees were referred to as "ghost detainees." Proper procedures must be followed, including, segregating detainees of military intelligence value and properly accounting and caring for detainees incarcerated at military detention centers. The number of ghost detainees temporarily held at Abu Ghraib, and the audit trail of personnel responsible for capturing, medically screening, safeguarding and properly interrogating the "ghost detainees," cannot be determined.

f. (U) Training. The need for additional training during the mobilization phase or in-country on unit and specific individual tasks was clearly an issue in the reports and assessments. Some military police units found themselves conducting detention operations which was not a normal unit mission essential task, and those units needed additional training to properly accomplish the missions they were given. The collocation and mixture of other agency and civilian personnel conducting detention and interrogation operations became confusing for junior leaders and Soldiers not normally accustomed to working with other organizations. Collective training to standard by MP and MI units in combined scenarios as rigorous as the situations faced in OIF is needed to prepare for the future.

In addition, V Corps personnel, to include commanders and staff, were not trained to execute a JTF mission. The transition from major combat operations to a headquarters focused on SASO and support to the Coalition Provisional Authority was a major transition which the unit did not have time to train or prepare. Most importantly, we must continue to place rigor and values in our training regimen. Our values are non-negotiable for members of our profession. They are what a professional military force represents to the world. As addressed before, leaders need rigorous training to be able to adapt to this level of complexity.

g. (U) Materiel. Priorities for logistical support remained with the operational units who were conducting combat operations and providing force protection and security of U.S. and coalition forces. Creating an intelligence organization to provide tactical through strategic intelligence in a seamless manner and the dramatic increase in detention operations demanded communications, computers, and a network to support operations. The concept of a Joint Logistics Command should be further examined using lessons learned from OIF/OEF. Automation equipment needed to provide seamless connectivity of intelligence information from tactical through strategic levels, and enable an Intelligence Fusion Center in a JTF should be documented and embedded in JTF capable headquarters. Equipment currently undergoing research and development and commercial off—the-shelf solutions which enable CI/HUMINT operations and enable Soldiers to serve as sensors and collectors should be rapidly pursued. The process of accounting for detainees, their equipment, and their personal property, and documenting their intelligence value, should be automated from the tactical level to the centralized detention facilities.

h. (U) Leader Development. The OIF environment demanded adaptive, confident, and competent leadership at all echelons. Leaders must set the example and be at the critical centers of gravity for their respective operations. Leaders set the example in a values-based profession. The risk to Soldiers and the security of all personnel demanded continued leader involvement in operations, planning, after-action reviews, and clear dissemination of lessons learned, to adapt to the dynamics of the counter-insurgency. Successful leaders were involved in their operations and were at the tip of the spear during critical periods. Leadership failure was seen when leaders did not take charge, failed to provide appropriate guidance, and did not conduct continual training. In some cases, leaders failed to accept responsibility or apply good judgment in executing assigned responsibilities. This latter fact is evident in the lack of a coordinated defense at Abu Ghraib, inconsistent training and standards, and lack of discipline by Soldiers. Commanders and leaders at all levels remain responsible for execution of their mission and the welfare of their Soldiers, In Iraq, leaders had to adapt to a new complex operational environment. Some of our leaders adapted faster than others. We must continue to put rigor in our leader and unit training. Leaders must be trained for certainty and educated for uncertainty. The ability to know how to think rather than what to think is critical in the future Joint Operational Environment. Specific leader and Soldier failures in the 800th MP Brigade and the 205th MI Brigade are identified in the investigative reports by MG Taguba and MG Fay. As discussed above, my review of echelons above brigade revealed that CJTF-7 leaders were not directly involved in the abuses at Abu Ghraib. Their actions and inaction did indirectly contribute to the non-sexual and non-violent abuses.

i. (U) Facilities. Facilities and quality of life for Soldiers and detainees were representative of the conditions throughout the AOR initially. Only when the logistics system became responsive to the needs of units and Soldiers, contracting mechanisms were put in place to support operations, and the transportation system matured to move supplies, were improvements seen in facilities and quality of life. The conditions at Abu Ghraib were representative of the conditions found throughout the country during post Phase III, Decisive Operations. The slow process of developing the logistics system and providing secure lines of communication directly impeded Soldier security and quality of life.

10. (U) Concluding Findings and Recommendations

a. (U) SUMMARY AS SENIOR INVESTIGATING OFFICER. I derived these findings and recommendations from the observations and assessments discussed in sections 2-9, from the interviews I conducted, and from the documents I have reviewed. Furthermore, I support the recommendations of the Fay and Taguba Reports concerning individual culpability for actions that violated U.S. criminal law (including the Uniform Code of Military Justice (UCMJ)) or international law, or that was inhumane or coercive without lawful justification. The personnel who committed these acts did not act in accordance with the discipline and values that the U.S. Army represents. Leaders who had direct responsibilities for the actions of these individuals failed to adequately exercise their responsibilities in the execution of this mission.

b. (U) RESPONSIBILITY ABOVE 205th MI BRIGADE

(1) (U)Findings:

(a) (U) I find that the chain of command above the $_{205th}$ MI Brigade was not directly involved in any of the abuses that occurred at Abu Ghraib.

(b) (U) I find that the chain of command above the $_2$OSthMI Brigade promulgated policy memoranda that, inadvertently, left room for interpretation and may have indirectly led to some of the non-violent and non-sexual abuse incidents.

(c) (U) I find that LTG Sanchez, and his DCG, MG Wojdakowski, failed to ensure proper staff oversight of detention and interrogation operations. As previously stated, MG Wojdakowski had direct oversight of two new Brigade Commanders. Further, staff elements of the CJTF-7 reacted inadequately to some of the Indications and Warnings discussed above. However, in light of the operational environment, and CJTF-7's under-resourcing and unplanned missions, and the Commander's consistent need to prioritize efforts, I find that the CJTF-7 Commander and staff performed above expectations, in the over-all scheme of OIF.

(d) (U) I find that the TACON relationship of the 800th MP Brigade to the CJTF-7 created a dysfunctional relationship for proper oversight and effective detention operations in the Iraqi Theater of Operations (ff0). In addition, the relationship between leaders and staff of the 205th MI Brigade and 800th MP Brigade was ineffective as they failed to effect proper coordination of roles and responsibilities for detention and interrogation operations.

(e) (U) I find that a number of causes outside of the control of CJTF-7 also contributed to the abuses at Abu Ghraib. These are discussed in Section 8 and include, individuals' criminal propensity; Soldier knowledge of interrogation techniques permitted in GTMO and Afghanistan and failure to distinguish between those environments and Iraq; interaction with OGA and other agency interrogators who did not follow the same rules as U.S. Forces; integration of some contractors without training, qualifications, and certification; under-resourcing of personnel in both the 800th MP BDE (including the inability to replace personnel leaving theater) and in the 205th MI Brigade, specifically in the interrogator, analyst, and linguist fields.

(2) (U) Recommendations:

(a) (U) That CJTF-7 designate a single staff proponent for Detention and Interrogation Operations. The grade of this officer should be commensurate with the level of responsibilities of the particular operation. Further, that the Army in concert with JFCOM should review the concept and clarify responsibilities for a single staff position for Detention and Interrogation operations as part of a JTF capable organization.

(b) (U) That CJTF-7 in concert with CENTCOM publish clear guidance that applies to all units and agencies on roles and responsibilities for Detention and Interrogation Operations, and publish clear guidance on the limits of interrogation authority for interrogation techniques as pertains to the detainee population in the ITO.

(c) (U) That CENTCOM review command relationship and responsibilities for the 800th MP Brigade with CJTF-7 in the conduct of detention operations in the ITO.

(d) (U) That the CJTF-7 Inspector General be designated the staff proponent to rapidly investigate ICRC allegations. That the CJTF-7 Inspector General periodically conduct unscheduled inspections of detention and interrogation operations providing direct feedback to the commander.

c. (U) DOCTRINE

(1) (U) Finding: Army and Joint doctrine did not directly contribute to the abuses found at Abu Ghraib. Abuses would not have occurred had doctrine been followed. Nonetheless, certain areas need to updated, expanded or refined.

(2) (U) Recommendations:

(a) (U) That JFCOM in concert with the Army update Joint and Army publications to clearly address the concept, organization and operations of a Joint Interrogation and Debriefing Center in a future joint operational environment.

(b) (U) That the Army update interrogation operations doctrine to clarify responsibilities for interrogation techniques at both tactical and strategic levels. The ongoing revision and update of FM 34-52, Intelligence Interrogations, should clarify the roles and responsibilities of MP and MI units at centralized detention facilities.

(c)(U) That DOD assess the impact of current policies on Detention and Interrogation Operations. That DOD review the limits of authority for interrogation techniques and publish guidance that applies to all services and agencies.

d. (U) V CORPS TRANSITION TO CJTF

(1) (U)Findings:

UNCLASSIFIED

(a)(U) V Corps was never adequately resourced as a CJTF. The challenge of transitioning from V Corps HQ5 to CJTF-7 without adequate personnel, equipment, and intelligence architecture, severely degraded the commander and staff during transition. Personnel shortages documented in the JMD continued to preclude operational capabilities.

(b)(U) Command and control headquarters that can perform as a Joint Task Force in a joint operational environment will be the norm for the future. This fact warrants action by supporting commands and services to resource and train JTF capable headquarters for success.

(2) (U) Recommendations:

(a)(U) That the Army expedite the development and transition of Corps-level command and control headquarters into JTF-capable organizations.

(b)(U) That the Army in concert with JFCOM institutionalize and resource the personnel and equipment needs of future JTF-capable headquarters, including the intelligence architecture of such headquarters.

e. (U) INTELLIGENCE ARCHITECTURE and INTELLIGENCE PERSONNEL RESOURCES

(I) (U)Findings:

(a)(U) Demands on the HUMINT capabilities in a counter-insurgency and in the future joint operational environment will continue to tax tactical and strategic assets. An Intelligence Fusion Center, a Joint Inter-agency Task Force and a JC2X are essential to provide seamless tactical through strategic level intelligence in a JTF headquarters.

(b)(U) Future land forces, especially the Army, need trained and experienced tactical HUMINT personnel to operate in the future Joint Operational Environment,

(2) (U) Recommendations:

(a) (U) That the Army conduct a holistic review of the CIIHUMINT intelligence force structure and prioritize needs for the future joint operational environment. The review should consider the personnel, equipment and resources needed to provide a seamless intelligence capability from the tactical to the strategic level to support the combatant commander.

(b) (U) That the Army align and train HUMINT assets geographically to leverage language skills and knowledge of culture.

(c) (U) That land forces, particularly MI and MP personnel, conduct rigorous collective training to replicate the complex environment experienced in OIF and in likely future areas of conflict.

f. (U) FACILITIES

UNCLASSIFIED

(1) (U) finding: Abu Ghraib detention facility was inadequate for safe and secure detention and interrogation operations. CJTF-7 lacked viable alternatives due to the depleted infrastructure in Iraq.

(2) (U) Recommendation: That the Army review the concept of detainee contingency facilities that can be rapidly deployed and established to safeguard and secure detainees, while providing necessary facilities to conduct screening and interrogations (similar to the concept of the Force Provider or Red Horse contingency facilities, where pre-fabricated buildings can be set up quickly). Adopting this recommendation would provide commanders an option for rapidly deploying and establishing detention facilities.

g. (U) OTHER GOVERNMENT AGENCIES

(1) (U) Findings:

(a) (U) Working alongside non-military organizations/agencies to jointly execute missions for our Nation, proved to be complex and demanding on military units at the tactical level. There was at least the perception that non-DOD agencies had different rules regarding interrogation and detention operations. Policies and specific limits of authority need review to ensure applicability to all organizations operating in the designated theater of operations

(b) (U) Seamless sharing of operational intelligence was hindered by lack of a fusion center that received, analyzed, and disseminated all intelligence collected by CJTF-7 units and other agencies/units outside of the CJTF-7 chain of command.

(c) (U) Proliferation of Interrogation and Counter-Resistance Technique memorandums, with specific categorization of unlawful combatants in various theaters of operations, and the inter-mingling of tactical, strategic, and other agency interrogators at the central detention facility of Abu Ghraib, provided a permissive and compromising climate for Soldiers.

(d) (U) Soldiers/Sailors/Airmen/Marines should never be put in a position that potentially puts them at risk for non-compliance with the Geneva Conventions or Laws of Land Warfare

(2) (U) Recommendations:

(a)(U) That DOD review inter-agency policies to ensure that all parties in a specific theater of operations are required to adhere to the same guidance and rules in the use of military Interrogation and Detention Facilities, including limits of authority for interrogation techniques.

(b)(U) That CENTCOM publish guidance for compliance by all agencies/organizations utilizing military detention facilities in the Iraqi theater of operation.

(c)(U) That DOD review the responsibilities for interrogations by other agencies and other agencies responsibilities to the combatant commander to provide intelligence information and support.

(d)(U) That DOD assess the impact of current policies and guidance on unlawful combatants in the conduct of Detention and Interrogation Operations. And, that DOD review the limits of authority for use of interrogation techniques and publish guidance that is applicable to all parties using military facilities.

h. (U) LEADERSHIP and SUCCESSES

(1) (U) Findings:

(a) (U) Leaders throughout Operation Iraqi Freedom were confronted with a complex operational environment. The speed at which leaders at all echelons adapted to this environment varied based on level of training, maturity in command, and ability to see the battlefield. The adaptability of leaders in future operational environments will be critical.

(b) (U) In Operation Iraqi Freedom, as the intelligence architecture matured and became properly equipped and organized, and close working relationships with all intelligence agencies and other OIF forces developed, there were clear successes in obtaining intelligence.

(c) (U) HUMINT management and Intelligence Fusion were essential to enable success in this complex operational environment.

(2) (U) Recommendations.

(a) (U) That rigorous leader training in our institutions, at home stations, and at the Army's Training Centers (Joint Readiness Training Center, National Training Center, Combat Maneuver Training Center, and Battle Command Training Program) continue.

(b) (U) That DOD/CENTCOM and the senior leaders of all services recognize and provide a vote of confidence to our military's leaders and Soldiers executing the OIF mission and supporting the Iraqi people.

AR 15-6 INVESTIGATION OF THE
ABU GHRAIB DETENTION FACILITY AND
205th MILITARY INTELLIGENCE BRIGADE (U)

MG GEORGE R. FAY
INVESTIGATING OFFICER

SUBJECT: (U) AR 15-6 Investigation of the Abu Ghraib Detention Facility and 205th MI Brigade

1. (U) Appointing Officials' Instructions and Investigative Methodology

    a. (U) Appointing Officials' Instruction.

    (1) (U) On 31 March 2004, LTG Ricardo S. Sanchez, Commander, Combined Joint Task Force 7 (CJTF-7), appointed MG George R. Fay as an Army Regulation (AR) 381-10 Procedure 15 Investigating Officer. LTG Sanchez determined, based upon MG Antonio Taguba's out brief of the results of an Article 15-6 investigation of the Abu Ghraib Detention Facility in Iraq, that another investigation was warranted. MG Fay was to investigate allegations that members of the 205th Military Intelligence Brigade were involved in detainee abuse at the Abu Ghraib Detention Facility.

    (a) (U) MG Fay was instructed as follows: Pursuant to AR 381-10, Procedure 15, you are hereby appointed as an investigating officer to conduct an investigation in accordance with (IAW) Army Regulation (AR) 15-6 into all the relevant facts and circumstances surrounding the alleged misconduct on the part of personnel assigned and/or attached to the 205th Military Intelligence (MI) Brigade, to include civilian interrogators and/or interpreters, from 15 August 2003 to 1 February 2004 at the Abu Ghraib (AG) Detention Facility.

    (b) (U) Specifically, you will investigate the following areas:

    [1] (U) Whether 205th MI Brigade personnel requested, encouraged, condoned, or solicited Military Police (MP) personnel to abuse detainees at AG as preparation for interrogation operations.

    [2] (U) Whether 205th MI Brigade personnel comported with established interrogation procedures and applicable laws and regulations when questioning Iraqi security internees at the Joint Interrogation and Debriefing Center.

    (2) (U) The Commander, United States Central Command (CENTCOM) requested a new appointing authority and investigating officer be assigned to the investigation. On 14 June 2004, Secretary of Defense (SECDEF) Donald Rumsfeld requested the Acting Secretary of the Army (SECARMY) R.L.Brownlee assign an "officer senior to LTG Sanchez" to assume his duties as appointing authority, and a new or additional investigating officer should one be required. SECDEF provided the following additional guidance to the Acting SECARMY:

    (U) The new appointing authority shall refer recommendations concerning issues at the Department of the Army level to the Department of the Army and recommendations concerning issues at the Department of Defense (DoD) level to the Department of Defense for appropriate action. The appointing authority shall refer the completed report to the Commander,

4

SUBJECT: (U) AR 15-6 Investigation of the Abu Ghraib Detention Facility and
205th MI Brigade

United States Central Command for further action as appropriate, including forwarding to the
ATSD(IO) [Assistant to the Secretary of Defense for Intelligence Oversight] in accordance with
DoD Directive 5240.1-R and CJCS-I 5901.01. Matters concerning accountability, if any, should
be referred by the appointing authority, without recommendation, to the appropriate level of the
chain of command for disposition.

(3) (U) On 16 June 2004, Acting SECARMY Brownlee designated GEN Paul J. Kern,
Commander of the US Army Materiel Command, as the new Procedure 15 appointing authority.
Acting SECARMY Brownlee's instructions included the following:

(a) (U) I am designating you as the appointing authority. Major General Fay remains
available to perform duties as the investigating officer. If you determine, however, after
reviewing the status of the investigation, that a new or additional investigating officer is
necessary, please present that request to me.

(b) (U) Upon receipt of the investigation, you will refer all recommendations
concerning issues at the Department of the Army level to me and all recommendations
concerning issues at the Department of Defense level to the Secretary of Defense for appropriate
action. You will refer the completed report to the Commander, United States Central Command,
for further action as appropriate, including forwarding to ATSD(IO) IAW DoD Directive
5240.1-R and CJCS-I 5901.01. Finally, you should refer matters concerning accountability, if
any, without recommendation, to the appropriate level of the chain of command for disposition.
If you determine that you need further legal resources to accomplish this mission, you should
contact the Judge Advocate General.

(4) (U) On 25 June 2004, GEN Kern appointed LTG Anthony R. Jones, Deputy
Commanding General, US Army Training and Doctrine Command (TRADOC), as an additional
Procedure 15 investigating officer. GEN Kern's instructions to LTG Jones included the
following:

(a) (U) Pursuant to AR 381-10, Procedure 15, and AR 15-6, you are hereby appointed
as an investigating officer to conduct an investigation of alleged misconduct involving personnel
assigned or attached to the 205th Military Intelligence Brigade at the Abu Ghraib Detention
Facility. Your appointment is as an additional investigating officer. MG Fay and his
investigative team are available to assist you.

(b) (U) Specifically, the purpose of the investigation is to determine the facts and to
determine whether the questionable activity at Abu Ghraib is legal and is consistent with
applicable policy. In LTG Sanchez's 31 March 2004 appointment letter to MG Fay, which I have
adopted, he specified three areas into which the investigation was to look: whether the 205th

5

SUBJECT: (U) AR 15-6 Investigation of the Abu Ghraib Detention Facility and
205th MI Brigade

responsibility or complicity in the abuses that occurred at Abu Ghraib. Twenty-seven (27) were cited in this report for some degree of culpability and seventeen (17) were cited for misunderstanding of policy, regulation or law. Three (3) MI Soldiers, who had previously received punishment under UCMJ, were recommended for additional investigation. Seven (7) MP Soldier identified in the MG Taguba Report and currently under criminal investigation and/or charges are also central figures in this investigation and are included in the above numbers. One (1) person cited in the MG Taguba Report was exonerated.

(4) (U) Looking beyond personal responsibility, leader responsibility and command responsibility, systemic problems and issues also contributed to the volatile environment in which the abuse occurred. These systemic problems included: inadequate interrogation doctrine and training, an acute shortage of MP and MI Soldiers, the lack of clear lines of responsibility between the MP and MI chains of command, the lack of a clear interrogation policy for the Iraq Campaign, and intense pressure felt by the personnel on the ground to produce actionable intelligence from detainees. Twenty-four (24) additional findings and two (2) observations regarding systemic failures are included in the final investigative report. These findings ranged from doctrine and policy concerns, to leadership and command and control issues, to resource and training issues.

b. (U) Problems: Doctrine, Policy, Training, Organization, and Other Government Agencies.

(1) (U) Inadequacy of doctrine for detention operations and interrogation operations was a contributing factor to the situations that occurred at Abu Ghraib. The Army's capstone doctrine for the conduct of interrogation operations is Field Manual (FM) 34-52, Intelligence Interrogation, dated September 1992. Non-doctrinal approaches, techniques, and practices were developed and approved for use in Afghanistan and GTMO as part of the Global War on Terrorism (GWOT). These techniques, approaches, and practices became confused at Abu Ghraib and were implemented without proper authorities or safeguards. Soldiers were not trained on non-doctrinal interrogation techniques such as sleep adjustment, isolation, and the use of dogs. Many interrogators and personnel overseeing interrogation operations at Abu Ghraib had prior exposure to or experience in GTMO or Afghanistan. Concepts for the non-doctrinal, non field-manual approaches and practices came from documents and personnel in GTMO and Afghanistan. By October 2003, interrogation policy in Iraq had changed three times in less than thirty days and it became very confusing as to what techniques could be employed and at what level non-doctrinal approaches had to be approved.

(2) (U) MP personnel and MI personnel operated under different and often incompatible rules for treatment of detainees. The military police referenced DoD-wide regulatory and procedural guidance that clashed with the theater interrogation and counter-resistance policies that the military intelligence interrogators followed. Further, it appeared that neither group knew

SUBJECT: (U) AR 15-6 Investigation of the Abu Ghraib Detention Facility and
205th MI Brigade

or understood the limits imposed by the other's regulatory or procedural guidance concerning the treatment of detainees, resulting in predictable tension and confusion. This confusion contributed to abusive interrogation practices at Abu Ghraib. Safeguards to ensure compliance and to protect against abuse also failed due to confusion about the policies and the leadership's failure to monitor operations adequately.

(3) (U) By December 2003, the JIDC at Abu Ghraib had a total of approximately 160 personnel with 45 interrogators and 18 linguists/translators assigned to conduct interrogation operations. These personnel were from six different MI battalions and groups – the 519 MI BN, 323 MI BN, 325 MI BN, 470 MI GP, the 66th MI GP, the 500 MI GP. To complicate matters, interrogators from a US Army Intelligence Center and School, Mobile Training Team (MTT) consisting of analysts and interrogators, and three interrogation teams consisting of six personnel from GTMO, came to Abu Ghraib to assist in improving interrogation operations. Additionally, contract interrogators from CACI and contract linguists from Titan were hired in an attempt to address shortfalls. The JIDC was created in a very short time period with parts and pieces of various units. It lacked unit integrity, and this lack was a fatal flaw.

(4) (U) The term Other Government Agencies (OGA) most commonly referred to the Central Intelligence Agency (CIA). The CIA conducted unilateral and joint interrogation operations at Abu Ghraib. The CIA's detention and interrogation practices contributed to a loss of accountability and abuse at Abu Ghraib. No memorandum of understanding existed on the subject interrogation operations between the CIA and CJTF-7, and local CIA officers convinced military leaders that they should be allowed to operate outside the established local rules and procedures. CIA detainees in Abu Ghraib, known locally as "Ghost Detainees," were not accounted for in the detention system. With these detainees unidentified or unaccounted for, detention operations at large were impacted because personnel at the operations level were uncertain how to report or classify detainees.

c. (U) Detainee Abuse at Abu Ghraib.

(1) (U) Physical and sexual abuses of detainees at Abu Ghraib were by far the most serious. The abuses spanned from direct physical assault, such as delivering head blows rendering detainees unconscious, to sexual posing and forced participation in group masturbation. At the extremes were the death of a detainee in OGA custody, an alleged rape committed by a US translator and observed by a female Soldier, and the alleged sexual assault of a female detainee. These abuses are, without question, criminal. They were perpetrated or witnessed by individuals or small groups. Such abuse can not be directly tied to a systemic US approach to torture or approved treatment of detainees. The MPs being prosecuted claim their actions came at the direction of MI. Although self-serving, these claims do have some basis in fact. The environment created at Abu Ghraib contributed to the occurrence of such abuse and the fact that

SUBJECT: (U) AR 15-6 Investigation of the Abu Ghraib Detention Facility and
205th MI Brigade

it remained undiscovered by higher authority for a long period of time. What started as nakedness and humiliation, stress and physical training (exercise), carried over into sexual and physical assaults by a small group of morally corrupt and unsupervised Soldiers and civilians.

(2) (U) Abusing detainees with dogs started almost immediately after the dogs arrived at Abu Ghraib on 20 November 2003. By that date, abuses of detainees was already occurring and the addition of dogs was just one more device. Dog Teams were brought to Abu Ghraib as a result of recommendations from MG G. Miller's assessment team from GTMO. MG G. Miller recommended dogs as beneficial for detainee custody and control issues. Interrogations at Abu Ghraib, however, were influenced by several documents that spoke of exploiting the Arab fear of dogs. The use of dogs in interrogations to "fear up" detainees was utilized without proper authorization.

(3) (U) The use of nudity as an interrogation technique or incentive to maintain the cooperation of detainees was not a technique developed at Abu Ghraib, but rather a technique which was imported and can be traced through Afghanistan and GTMO. As interrogation operations in Iraq began to take form, it was often the same personnel who had operated and deployed in other theaters and in support of GWOT, who were called upon to establish and conduct interrogation operations in Abu Ghraib. The lines of authority and the prior legal opinions blurred. They simply carried forward the use of nudity into the Iraqi theater of operations. The use of clothing as an incentive (nudity) is significant in that it likely contributed to an escalating "de-humanization" of the detainees and set the stage for additional and more severe abuses to occur.

(4) (U) There was significant confusion by both MI and MPs between the definitions of "isolation" and "segregation." LTG Sanchez approved the extended use of isolation on several occasions, intending for the detainee to be kept apart, without communication with their fellow detainees. His intent appeared to be the segregation of specific detainees. The technique employed in several instances was not, however, segregation but rather isolation - the complete removal from outside contact other than required care and feeding by MP guards and interrogation by MI. Use of isolation rooms in the Abu Ghraib Hard Site was not closely controlled or monitored. Lacking proper training, clear guidance, or experience in this technique, both MP and MI stretched the bounds into further abuse; sensory deprivation and un-safe or unhealthy living conditions. Detainees were sometimes placed in excessively cold or hot cells with limited or poor ventilation and no light.

3. (U) Background and Environment.

   a. (U) Operational Environment.

10

SUBJECT: (U) AR 15-6 Investigation of the Abu Ghraib Detention Facility and
205th MI Brigade

(1) (U) The Global War on Terrorism began in earnest on 11 September 2001 (9/11). Soon after the 9/11 attacks, American forces entered Afghanistan to destroy the primary operating and training base of Al Qaida. Prisoners collected in these and other global counter-terrorist operations were transferred to Guantanamo Naval Base, Cuba. Two Task Forces were formed at JTF-GTMO to manage intelligence collection operations with the newly captured prisoners. Military and civilian interrogators, counterintelligence agents, analysts, and other intelligence personnel from a variety of services and agencies manned the task forces and exploited the captured personnel for information.

(2) (U) US and coalition partners attacked Iraq on 20 March 2003 and soon after toppled Saddam Hussein's regime. The Iraq conflict transitioned quickly and unexpectedly to an insurgency environment. Coalition forces began capturing and interrogating alleged insurgents. Abu Ghraib prison, opened after the fall of Saddam to house criminals, was soon used for collecting and interrogating insurgents and other persons of intelligence interest. The unit responsible for managing Abu Ghraib interrogations was the 205 MI BDE.

b. (U) Law, Policy, Doctrine and Training.

(1) (U) Applicable Law.

(a) (U) Military Order of November 13th 2001 – Detention, Treatment and Trial of Certain Non-Citizens in the War Against Terrorism (Reference Annex J, Appendix 1).

(b) (U) Geneva Convention (IV) Relative to the Protection of Civilian Persons in Time of War, 12 August 1949 (Reference Annex J, Appendix 5).

(c) (U) AR 190-8 / OPNAVINST 3461.6 / AFJI 31-302/MCO 3461.1, Enemy Prisoners of War, Retained Personnel, Civilian Internees and other Detainees, 1 October 1997 (Reference Annex M, Appendix 2).

(d) (U) FM 34-52, Intelligence Interrogation, 28 September 1992 (Reference Annex M, Appendix 3).

(e) (U) Classification of Detainees. The overwhelming evidence in this investigation shows that most "detainees" at Abu Ghraib were "civilian internees." Therefore, this discussion will focus on "civilian internees."

[1] (U) Detainee. AR 190-8 defines a detainee as any person captured or otherwise detained by an armed force. By this definition, a detainee could be an Enemy Prisoner of War (EPW), a Retained Person, such as a doctor or chaplain, or a Civilian Internee. The term

11

SUBJECT: (U) AR 15-6 Investigation of the Abu Ghraib Detention Facility and
205th MI Brigade

[7] (U) Article 143. Representatives or delegates of the Protecting Powers shall have permission to go to all places where protected persons are, particularly to places of internment, detention and work. They shall have access to all premises occupied by protected persons and shall be able to interview the latter without witnesses, personally or through an interpreter. Such visits may not be prohibited except for reasons of military imperative, and then only as an exceptional and temporary measure. Their duration and frequency shall not be restricted. Such representatives and delegates shall have full liberty to select the places they wish to visit. The Detaining or Occupying Power, the Protecting Power, and when occasion arises the Power of origin of the persons to be visited, may agree that compatriots of the internees shall be permitted to participate in the visits. The delegates of the International Committee of the Red Cross shall also enjoy the above prerogatives. The appointment of such delegates shall be submitted for the approval of the Power governing the territories where they will carry out their duties.

(2) (U) AR 190-8, Enemy Prisoners of War, Retained Personnel, Civilian Internees and other Detainees is a joint publication between all services of the Armed Forces (Reference Annex M, Appendix 2).

(a) (U) US Policy Overview. The regulation (Reference Annex M, Appendix 2, AR 190-8, Paragraph 1-5) sets out US Policy stating that "US policy, relative to the treatment of EPW, Civilian Internees and RP in the custody of the US Armed Forces, is as follows: All persons captured, detained, interned, or otherwise held in US Armed Forces custody during the course of conflict will be given humanitarian care and treatment from the moment they fall into the hands of the US forces until final release and repatriation." The regulation further defines this policy.

(b) (U) Inhumane Treatment. Specifically, inhumane treatment of detainees is prohibited and is considered a serious and punishable offense under international law and the UCMJ. The following acts are prohibited: murder, torture, corporal punishment, mutilation, the taking of hostages, sensory deprivation, collective punishment, execution without trial, and all cruel and degrading treatment. (Reference Annex M, Appendix 2, AR 190-8, Paragraph 1-5(b)).

(c) (U) Protection from Certain Acts. All detainees will be protected against all acts of violence to include rape, forced prostitution, assault and theft, insults, public curiosity, bodily injury, and reprisals of any kind. (Reference Annex M, Appendix 2, AR 190-8, Paragraph 1-5(c)). This is further reinforced in FM 34-52 (Reference Annex M, Appendix 3), which states that the Geneva Conventions and US policy expressly prohibit acts of violence or intimidation, including physical or mental torture, threats, insults, or exposure to inhumane treatment as a means of or aid to interrogation.

14

SUBJECT: (U) AR 15-6 Investigation of the Abu Ghraib Detention Facility and
205th MI Brigade

(d) (U) Photographs. Photographs of detainees are strictly prohibited except for
internal administrative purposes of the confinement facility. (Reference Annex M, Appendix 2,
AR 190-8, Paragraph 1-5(d)).

(e) (U) Physical torture or moral coercion. No form of physical or moral coercion will
be exercised against the Civilian Internee. (Reference Annex M, Appendix 2, AR 190-8,
Paragraph 1-5(a)(1)).

(f) (U) At all times, the Civilian Internee will be humanely treated and protected against
all acts of violence or threats and insults and public curiosity. The Civilian Internee will be
especially protected against all acts of violence, insults, public curiosity, bodily injury, reprisals
of any kind, sexual attacks such as rape, forced prostitution, or any form of indecent assault.
(Reference Annex M, Appendix 2, AR 190-8, Paragraph 1-5(a)(2) & (3)).

(3) (U) Military Intelligence Doctrine and Training.

(a) (U) Doctrine.

[1] (U) The Army's capstone doctrine for the conduct of interrogation operations is
FM 34-52, Intelligence Interrogation, dated September, 1992. This doctrine provides an
adequate basis for the training of interrogators at the Soldier level (e.g., in the art of tactical
interrogation and the Geneva Conventions); however, it is out of date with respect to the
management and conduct of detainee operations. Joint Doctrine on the conduct of detainee
operations is sparse even though the Army has operated JIDCs since 1989 in Operation JUST
CAUSE, and because the Army is normally tasked by the Joint Force Commander to establish
and manage EPW/Detainee operations for the deployed force (Reference Annex M, Appendix 1,
APPENDIX G-3, Joint Publication 2-01, Joint Intelligence Support to Military Operations).
National level doctrine, in the form of a Defense Intelligence Agency Manual (DIAM), also
contains very little doctrinal basis for the conduct and management of joint interrogation
operations. A critical doctrinal gap at the joint and service level is the role of national level
agencies (e.g., other governmental agencies [OGA]) in detainee operations to include appropriate
protocols for sharing valuable intelligence assets. The Center for Army Lessons Learned
(CALL) reported the following in a recent assessment of Operation Iraqi Freedom detainee and
interrogation operations (Reference Annex C, Appendix 5):

> MP and MI doctrine at division and below must be modified for stability
> operations and support operations to reflect the need for long-term
> detention facilities and interrogation of captives at the tactical level.

15

SUBJECT: (U) AR 15-6 Investigation of the Abu Ghraib Detention Facility and 205th MI Brigade

[2] (U) It is possible that some of the unauthorized interrogation techniques employed in Iraq may have been introduced through the use of an outdated training manual (FM 34-52 dated 1987 vice FM 34-52 dated 1992). The superseded version (FM 34-52, dated 1987) has been used at various locations in OIF. In a prior AR 15-6 investigation of Camp Cropper (Reference Annex C, Appendix 2), the 1987 version was again used as the reference (Reference Annex M, Appendix 3). On 9 June 2004, CJTF-7 published an email (Reference Annex L, Appendix 4, email) that indicated the May 1987 version was used as CJTF-7's primary reference. The section encapsulated below from the 1987 version has been removed from the 1992 version of FM 34-52. To the untrained, the reference in the outdated version could appear as a license for the interrogator to go beyond the current doctrine as established in the current FM 34-52. The 1987 version suggests the interrogator controls lighting, heating, and configuration of the interrogation room, as well as the food, shelter, and clothing given to the source. The section from the 1987 version that could be misunderstood is from Chapter 3 and reads as follows:

> FM 34-52 (1987) Chapter 3, Establish and Maintain Control. The interrogator should appear to be the one who controls all aspects of the interrogation to include the lighting, heating, and configuration of the interrogation room, as well as the food, shelter, and clothing given to the source. The interrogator must always be in control, he must act quickly and firmly. However, everything that he says and does must be within the limits of the Geneva and Hague Conventions, as well as the standards of conduct outlined in the UCMJ.

[3] (U) Doctrine provides the foundation for Army operations. A lack of doctrine in the conduct of non-conventional interrogation and detainee operations was a contributing factor to the abuses at Abu Ghraib.

(b) (U) Training

[1] (U) Formal US Army interrogation training is conducted at the Soldier level, primarily as part of a Soldier's Initial Entry Training (IET). There is no formal advanced interrogation training in the US Army. Little, if any, formal training is provided to MI leaders and supervisors (Commissioned Officers, Warrant Officers, and Non-Commissioned Officers) in the management of interrogation and detainee operations. These skills can only be developed in the unit environment through assignments to an interrogation unit, involvement in interrogation training exercises, or on deployments. Unfortunately, unit training and exercises have become increasingly difficult to conduct due to the high pace of deployments of interrogation personnel

SUBJECT: (U) AR 15-6 Investigation of the Abu Ghraib Detention Facility and
205th MI Brigade

and units. With very few exceptions, combined MI and MP training on the conduct of detainee operations is non-existent.

[2] (U) The IET course at the USAIC, Fort Huachuca, AZ, provides a 16.5 week course of instruction. The course consists of 758.2 hours of academic training time that includes collection prioritization, screening, planning and preparation, approaches, questioning, termination of interrogations, and report writing in the classroom and practical exercise environments. The course focuses on the conduct of tactical interrogations in conventional war. Each student receives eight hours of classroom training on AR 381-10, Army Intelligence Activities (Reference Annex M, Appendix 2) and FM 27-10, Law of Land Warfare (Reference Annex M, Appendix 3) and 184 hours of practical exercise. The student's understanding of the Geneva Conventions and Law of Land Warfare is continually evaluated as a critical component. If at any time during an exercise, the student violates the Geneva Conventions, they will fail the exercise. A failure does not eliminate the student from the course. Students are generally given the chance to recycle to the next class; however, egregious violations could result in dismissal from the course.

[3] (U) The reserve components use the same interrogator program of instruction as does the active component. They are exposed to the same classes and levels of instruction. Like the active component, the reserve components' training opportunities prior to deployment in recent years have been minimal, if any. Those slated for deployment to the JTF-GTMO attend the Intelligence Support to Counter Terrorism (ISCT) Course.

[4] (U) Army Regulations require interrogators to undergo refresher training on the Geneva Conventions annually. Units are also expected to conduct follow-up training for Soldiers to maintain and improve their interrogation skills. This becomes difficult given that Soldiers fresh from the basic interrogation course are deployed almost as soon as they arrive to their unit of assignment. This leaves little, if any, time to conduct that follow-on training with their unit to hone the skills they have learned in school. In addition to the unit deployments, the individual interrogators find themselves deployed to a wide variety of global engagements in a temporary duty status–not with their units of assignments. It is not uncommon for an individual to be deployed two or three times in the course of a year (e.g., the Balkans, Cuba [JTF-GTMO], Afghanistan, Iraq, or in support of Special Operations Forces [SOF]).

[5] (U) There is no formal advanced interrogation training in the US Army. The DoD manages a Strategic Debriefing Course for all services. While some of the skills are similar, the Strategic Debriefing Course is not an advanced interrogation course. Further, only interrogators being assigned to strategic debriefing assignments are authorized to attend this course. This prevents the tactical interrogator, the operator at Abu Ghraib, from further developing skills. Junior NCOs receive only limited interrogation-related training during his or

SUBJECT: (U) AR 15-6 Investigation of the Abu Ghraib Detention Facility and
205th MI Brigade

practices developed and approved for use on Al Qaeda and Taliban detainees who were not afforded the protection of the Geneva Conventions, now applied to detainees who did fall under the Geneva Conventions' protections. Furthermore, the Geneva Conventions protect both EPWs and detainees, with somewhat different levels of protections and rights accorded to each. The 14 September 2003 memo established a requirement to obtain LTG Sanchez's approval prior to using certain techniques on EPWs. The policy failed to address what, if any, approval authority had to be obtained for using any of the interrogation techniques on civilian internees, who were the bulk of the detainees at that time. Additionally, there were discrepancies within the memo. One (1) discrepancy was that the cover memo required LTG Sanchez's approval for isolation, whereas Enclosure 1, Paragraph X of the policy, indicates approval authority came from the Commander, 205 MI BDE, for isolation exceeding 30 days. (Reference Annex J, Appendix 3, 030914 CJTF-7 Interrogation and Counter-Resistance Policy)

(8) (S//NF) CENTCOM disapproved of the 14 September 2003 policy, prompting new drafts of proposed interrogation policy for Iraq. On 28 September 2003, CJTF-7 OSJA drafted a new policy memo tending to provide the interrogators broader leeway in creating inter-rogation approaches. On 5 October 2003, another policy memo, substantively identical to the 28 September 2003 draft memo, was staffed through HQ, CJTF-7 (Reference Annex J, Appendix 3, 030928 Interrogation and Counter Resistance Policy; Annex J, Appendix 3, 031005 Interrogation and Counter-Resistance Policy).

(9) (S//NF) On 12 October 2003, LTG Sanchez signed a second CJTF-7 Interrogation and Counter-Resistance Policy for use in Iraq, substantially derived from the 5 October 2003 memo. LTG Sanchez granted approval for all listed approaches, identical to those in the superseded 1987 FM 34-52, and stipulated that he must approve the use of any approach not listed. The 12 October 2003 policy superseded the CJTF-7 ICRP signed 14 September 2003 (Reference Annex J, Appendix 3, 031012 Interrogation and Counter-Resistance Policy).

(10) (U) The 12 October 2003 policy significantly changed the tone and substance of the previous policy. It removed any approach not listed in the 1987 FM 34-52. While acknowledging the applicability of the Geneva Conventions and the duty to treat all detainees humanely, it also cited Articles 5 and 78 noting specifically that those "detainees engaged in activities hostile to security of coalition forces had forfeited their Geneva Convention rights of communication." It also included provisions found in the superseded 1987 FM 34-52 that authorized interrogators to control all aspects of the interrogation, "to include lighting, and heating, as well as food, clothing and shelter given to detainees." This phrase was specifically left out of the 1992 version (See section 3a(2), above). The 12 October 2003 policy also deleted references to EPWs and specified the policy was for use on civilian security internees.

26

SECRET//NOFORN//X1

SUBJECT: (U) AR 15-6 Investigation of the Abu Ghraib Detention Facility and
205th MI Brigade

(11) (S//NF) This 12 October 2003 memorandum, intended by CJTF SJA staff to be clear, succinct, and understandable at all levels, confused doctrine and policy even further. The drafters of the 28 September 2003 and 5 October 2003 policy specifically referred to language in the 1987 field manual. It is unclear how the staff in Iraq came to reference the older version, but this reference clearly led to confusion on what practices were acceptable. Specifically, the earlier manual was quoted in several policy memos: "the interrogator should appear to be the one who controls all aspects of the interrogation to include the lighting, heating, and configuration of the interrogation room, as well as the food, clothing and shelter given" to the security internee. This phrase was used to justify the use of stress positions, the presence of dogs, sleep management, and yelling, loud music and light control in the policies from Afghanistan and Iraq. Over time, interrogators and staff accepted the phrase and its justifications for approaches as doctrinal truth. Given the interrogators' generally poor understanding of the Geneva Conventions, requirements of the new policy further confused an already murky situation. (Reference Annex B, Appendix 1, SANCHEZ; Annex M, Appendix 3; FM 34-52, Interrogation Operations, [1987 and 1992 versions]).

(12) (S//NF) The 12 October 2003 policy removed isolation as an interrogation approach requiring LTG Sanchez's approval. It also muddied the practice of segregation. FM 3-19.40 describes the rationale and basis for segregation. The practice of segregation in EPW/civilian internee operations is done primarily to keep prisoners from exchanging stories prior to interrogation. CPT Fitch and MAJ Kazmier told investigators that the word segregation was substituted for the word isolation so that the practice would be more in keeping with the Geneva Conventions. It appears the policy drafters invoked Article 5, which justifies forfeiture of a security detainee's rights of communication, to justify segregation. The justification was necessary because the word segregation itself does not appear in either Geneva Convention III (EPW) or Geneva Convention IV (Civilians). Nor does the word segregation appear in current interrogation doctrine, the 1992 FM 34-52, although tangential references to the MP duties of segregating EPWs appear in the 1987 FM 34-52. In the Geneva Conventions, the words isolation and separation appear in health and personal safety contexts only. Therefore, the change of wording had no impact on the requirement to comply with the Geneva Conventions. MI personnel continued to direct the MPs to segregate detainees to prevent communication of interrogation tactics or other collaboration between civilian internees as part of the interrogation process.

(13) (S//NF) The 12 October 2003 policy allowed segregating detainees at the interrogator's discretion for up to 30 days without LTG Sanchez's approval. In practice though, segregation often became isolation, because there was no clear distinction between the two at the Abu Ghraib level. While segregation is doctrinally approved to limit communication among prisoners prior to interrogation, isolation is an interrogation technique used to induce fear and punish uncooperative detainees, per the 1987 FM 34-52. Isolation became an abusive practice,

SECRET//NOFORN//X1

27

SUBJECT: (U) AR 15-6 Investigation of the Abu Ghraib Detention Facility and 205th MI Brigade

(i.e., often used as punishment for failure to cooperate), a perversion of the practice of segregation. At Abu Ghraib, isolation conditions sometimes included being kept naked in very hot or very cold, small rooms, and/or completely darkened rooms, clearly in violation of the Geneva Conventions.

(14) (S//NF) Another confusing change involved removing the use of dogs from the list of approaches. The 12 October 2003 policy did not specifically preclude it. In fact, the safeguards section of the policy established the conditions for the use of dogs, should they be present during interrogations: They had to be muzzled and they had to be under the control of a trained handler. Even though it was not listed in the approved techniques section, which meant that it required the LTG Sanchez's approval, its inclusion in the safeguards section is confusing. In fact, the Commander, 205 MI BDE, COL Pappas, believed that he could approve the use of dogs. Dogs as an interrogation tool should have been specifically excluded because the practice was never doctrine. In approving the concept, LTG Sanchez did not adequately consider the distinction between using dogs at the facility to patrol for security and using them as an interrogation tool, and the implications for interrogation policy. Interrogators at Abu Ghraib used both dogs and isolation as interrogation practices. The manner in which they were used on some occasions clearly violated the Geneva Conventions. (Reference Annex B, Appendix 1, SANCHEZ)

(15) (U) On 16 October 2003, the JIDC Interrogation Operations Officer, CPT Carolyn A. Wood, produced an "Interrogation Rules of Engagement" chart as an aid for interrogators, graphically portraying the 12 October 2003 policy. It listed the approved approaches, and identified the approaches which had been removed as authorized interrogation approaches, which nonetheless could be used with LTG Sanchez's approval. The chart was confusing, however. It was not completely accurate and could be subject to various interpretations. For example, the approved approaches list left off two techniques which previously had been included in the list (the Pride and Ego Down approach and the Mutt and Jeff approach). The right side of the chart listed approaches that required LTG Sanchez's prior approval. What was particularly confusing was that nowhere on the chart did it mention a number of techniques that were in use at the time: removal of clothing, forced grooming, hooding, and yelling, loud music and light control. Given the detail otherwise noted on the aid, the failure to list some techniques left a question of whether they were authorized for use without approval. (Reference Annex J, Appendix 4, CJTF-7 IROE training card)

(16) (U) By mid-October, interrogation policy in Iraq had changed three times in less than 30 days. Various versions of each draft and policy were circulated among Abu Ghraib, 205 MI BDE, CJTF-7 C2, and CJTF-7 SJA. Anecdotal evidence suggests that personnel were confused about the approved policy from as early as 14 September 2003. The SJA believed that the 14 September 2003 policy was not to be implemented until CENTCOM approved it. Meanwhile, interrogators in Abu Ghraib began operating under it immediately. It was not always clear to JIDC officers what approaches required LTG Sanchez's approval, nor was the level of

28

SUBJECT: (U) AR 15-6 Investigation of the Abu Ghraib Detention Facility and
205th MI Brigade

approval consistent with requirements in other commands. The JIDC October 2003 SOP, likewise created by CPT Wood, was remarkably similar to the Bagram (Afghanistan) Collection Point SOP. Prior to deployment to Iraq, CPT Wood's unit (A/519 MI BN) allegedly conducted the abusive interrogation practices in Bagram resulting in a Criminal Investigation Command (CID) homicide investigation. The October 2003 JIDC SOP addressed requirements for monitoring interrogations, developing detailed interrogation plans, delegating interrogation plan approval authority to the Interrogation Officer in Charge (OIC), and report writing. It failed to mention details concerning ICRP, approval requirements or procedures. Interrogators, with their section leaders' knowledge, routinely utilized approaches/techniques without obtaining the required authority, indicating confusion at a minimum of two levels of supervision. (Reference Annex J, Appendix 4, JIDC Interrogation SOP; Annex J, Appendix 4, CJTF-180 Bagram Collection Point SOP)

(17) (U) Concepts for the non-doctrinal, non-field manual approaches and practices clearly came from documents and personnel in Afghanistan and Guantanamo. The techniques employed in JTF-GTMO included the use of stress positions, isolation for up to thirty days, removal of clothing, and the use of detainees' phobias (such as the use of dogs) as the 2 December 2002 Counter-Resistance memo, and subsequent statements demonstrate. As the CID investigation mentioned above shows, from December 2002, interrogators in Afghanistan were removing clothing, isolating people for long periods of time, using stress positions, exploiting fear of dogs and implementing sleep and light deprivation. Interrogators in Iraq, already familiar with the practice of some of these new ideas, implemented them even prior to any policy guidance from CJTF-7. These practices were accepted as SOP by newly-arrived interrogators. Some of the CJTF-7 ICRPs neither effectively addressed these practices, nor curtailed their use. (Annex J, Appendix 2, Tab A, Counter-Resistance Techniques; Annex J, Appendix 2, Interrogation Techniques; Annex E, Appendix 4, CID Report)

(18) (S//REL to USA and MCFI) FRAGO 749, paragraph 3.D.7, states that "Coalition Forces will treat all detainees/internees with dignity and respect and will provide at least the standard of humane treatment required under international law. This means that detainees/internees will be treated in a manner accorded EPWs pursuant to the principles outlined in Geneva Convention III. Coalition Forces will protect detainees from physical harm and against insults and public curiosity and will treat detainees/internees without dis-tinction based upon gender, race, nationality, religion or political opinion." (Reference Annex J, Appendix 3)

(6) (U) Other Regulatory Procedural Guidance

(a) (U) On 13 November 2001, the President issued a military order entitled the Detention, Treatment and Trial of Certain Non-Citizens in the War Against Terrorism. The

SUBJECT: (U) AR 15-6 Investigation of the Abu Ghraib Detention Facility and 205th MI Brigade

order authorized US military forces to detain non-US citizens suspected of terrorism, and try them for violations of the law of war and other applicable laws. The order also authorized the SECDEF to detain individuals under such conditions he may prescribe and to issue related orders and regulations as necessary. (Reference Annex J, Appendix 1, Presidential Military Order)

(b) (S//NF)

(c) (U) The MP personnel and the MI personnel operated under different and often incompatible rules for treatment of detainees. The MPs referenced DoD-wide regulatory and procedural guidance that clashed with the theater interrogation and counter-resistance policies that the MI interrogators followed. Further, it appears that neither group knew or understood the limits imposed by the other's regulatory or procedural guidance concerning the treatment of detainees, resulting in predictable tension and confusion.

(d) (U) For instance, a MI order to strip a detainee as an interrogation process conflicted with the AR 190-8 directive to treat detainees with respect for their person and honor (Reference Annex M, Appendix 2, AR 190-8, paragraph 5-1a(2)); or to protect detainees against violence, insults, public curiosity, or any form of indecent assault (Reference Annex M, Appendix 2, AR 190-8, paragraph 5-1a(3)); and FM 3-19.40 (Reference Annex M, Appendix 3) (which specifically directs that internees will retain their clothing). A MI order to place a detainee in isolation violated the AR 190-8 directive to not imprison a detainee in a place without daylight (Reference Annex M, Appendix 2, AR 190-8, paragraph 6-11a(5)); to not confine for more than 30 consecutive days, (Reference Annex M, Appendix 2, AR 190-8, paragraph 6-12d(1)); and FM 3-19.40 which specifically directs that the facility commander must authorize any form of punishment. Finally, when interrogators ordered the use of dogs as an interrogation technique, the order violated the policy and intent of AR 190-12. (Reference Annex M, Appendix 2)

4. (U) Summary of Events at Abu Ghraib.

30

SUBJECT: (U) AR 15-6 Invest
205th MI Briga

(3) (S//NF)

SUBJECT: (U) AR 15-6 Invest
205th MI Briga

personnel were present in the 20
All of these personnel were fron
JIDC) had approximately 160 2(
linguists/translators assigned to (
different MI battalions and grou|
(USAR), the 470th MI Group (4
(500 MI GP). Additional resour
analysts and interrogators, and a
personnel from JTF-GTMO, can
(See paragraph 4.j.(2)). Still sho
CACI International, and contrac
shortfalls (See paragraph 4.g.). :
been deployed to combat operati
of selected personnel home with

b. (U) Establishment of the F

(1) (U) The Coalition Prov
Ghraib Prison as a criminal detei
SANCHEZ). Abu Ghraib began
Holds or security detainees in the
Cropper (located at BIAP) or to
Bucca (Reference Annex F, App

(2) (S//NF)

(4) (S//NF)

(5) (S//NF)

SUBJECT: (U) AR 15-6 Investigation of the Abu Ghraib Detention Facility and
205th MI Brigade

a. (U) Military Intelligence Organization and Resources.

(1) (U) Task Organization.

(a) (U) The 205 MI BDE was organizationally, and geographically, the size of two MI Brigades. It was composed of four Active and three Reserve Battalions. The 205 MI BDE possessed no organic interrogation elements or personnel. All HUMINT assets (units and personnel) assigned to the 205 MI BDE were from other organizations. Major subordinate elements of the 205 MI BDE included three Tactical Exploitation Battalions (HUMINT and Counterintelligence), one Aerial Exploitation Battalion (Signal Intelligence [SIGINT]) and Imagery Intelligence (IMINT), an Operations Battalion (ANALYSIS), a Linguist Battalion (HUMINT Support) and a Corps Support Battalion (HUMINT). Elements of the Brigade were located throughout Iraq supporting a wide variety of combat operations. (Reference Annex H, Appendix 6, Tab C, 205 MI BDE Command Brief).

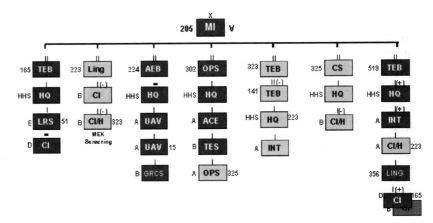

205th MI Brigade Task Organization (August 2003)

(b) (U) The 205 MI BDE Commander, COL Thomas Pappas, had a reputation for being an excellent MI officer with a great background and experience before being selected for command. He took command of the 205 MI BDE on 1 July 2003 while the unit was already deployed in Iraq. His performance as Brigade Commander prior to the Abu Ghraib incidents was "outstanding" according to his rater, MG Wojdakowski, DCG, V Corps/CJTF-7 (Reference Annex B, Appendix 1, WOJDAKOWSKI). LTG Sanchez also believed COL Pappas was an

SUBJECT: (U) AR 15-
205th I

excellent and dedicated
members of COL Pappa
Brigade Operations Offi

(2) (U) Resources.

(a) (U) As host
intelligence priorities. I
SASO with interrogatior
Annex B, Appendix 1, S
operations were growing
The 205 MI BDE had th
elements consisting of ar
maneuver elements to cc
deployed combat forces

(b) (U) As prev
capability. Those assets
of the Army in the 1990'
Command were A/519 N
BN), US Army Reserve
the USAR units were sig
many Soldiers from othe
as "cross-leveling." Alth
inserting Soldiers into ur
The Soldiers did not kno
The Army has always str
efforts on interrogation o
including civilians, that h

(c) (U) Interesti
interrogation operations
interrogators. Roughly tl
BIAP, even though the IS
interest to exploit than di
Unfortunately, these muc
mission needs (Reference

(d) (U) The nun
for a small detainee popu

SUBJECT: (U) AR 15-
205th I

(3) (U) The Hard
occupancy until 25 Aug
the beginning of the seri
based on her experience
of MI value would enha
for use of part of the Ha
from the 205 MI BDE, s
was then granted use of
diagram) to house detair

c. (U) Detention Opc

(1) (S//NF)

(2) (S//NF)

SUBJECT: (U) AR 15-6 Investigation of the Abu Ghraib Detention Facility and
205th MI Brigade

36

SUBJECT: (U) AR 15-6 Investigation of the Abu Ghraib Detention Facility and
205th MI Brigade

(6) (U) The problems cited above contributed significantly to the overcrowding at Abu Ghraib. Overcrowding was even further exacerbated with the transfer of detainees from Camp Bucca to Abu Ghraib. The physical plant was totally inadequate in size and the construction and renovations that were underway were incomplete. Scarcity of resources – both personnel and equipment – to conduct effective confinement or interrogation operations made the situation worse.

(7) (U) There was general consensus (Reference Annex B, Appendix 1, FAST, CIVILIAN-12, LYONS, WOOD, SOLDIER14, SANCHEZ) that as the pace of operations picked up in late November – early December 2003, it became a common practice for maneuver elements to round up large quantities of Iraqi personnel in the general vicinity of a specified target as a cordon and capture technique. Some operations were conducted at night resulting in some detainees being delivered to collection points only wearing night clothes or under clothes. SGT Jose Garcia, assigned to the Abu Ghraib Detainee Assessment Board, estimated that 85% - 90% of the detainees were of no intelligence value based upon board interviews and debriefings of detainees. The Deputy C2X, CJTF-7, CIVILIAN-12, confirmed these numbers. (Reference Annex B, Appendix 1, GARCIA, CIVILIAN-12). Large quantities of detainees with little or no intelligence value swelled Abu Ghraib's population and led to a variety of overcrowding difficulties. Already scarce interrogator and analyst resources were pulled from interrogation operations to identify and screen increasing numbers of personnel whose capture documentation was incomplete or missing. Complicated and unresponsive release procedures ensured that these detainees stayed at Abu Ghraib – even though most had no value.

(8) (U) To make matters worse, Abu Ghraib increasingly became the target of mortar attacks (Reference Annex F, Appendix 3 shows an image of mortar round strikes at Abu Ghraib prior to February 2004 and the times of mortar strikes from January-April 2004) which placed detainees – innocent and guilty alike – in harms way. Force protection was a major issue at Abu Ghraib. The prison is located in a hostile portion of Iraq, adjacent to several roads and highways, and near population centers. BG Karpinski recognized Abu Ghraib's vulnerabilities and raised these concerns frequently to both MG Wojdakowski and LTG Sanchez (Reference Annex B, Appendix 1, KARPINSKI). LTG Sanchez was equally concerned with both the inherent vulnerability of Abu Ghraib and frustrated with the lack of progress in establishing even rudimentary force protection measures and plans (Reference Annex B, Appendix 1, SANCHEZ). LTG Sanchez directed that measures be taken to improve the force protection situation even to the point of having the 82nd Airborne Division Commander meet with Abu Ghraib officers concerning the issue. But, little progress was made and the mortar attacks continued. In an effort to improve force protection at Abu Ghraib, LTG Sanchez directed COL Pappas assume Tactical Control (TACON) of the Abu Ghraib Forward Operating Base (FOB) (Reference Annex H, Appendix 1, FRAGO 1108) on 19 November 2003. COL Pappas devoted considerable energy to improving security, even to the point of bringing a subordinate battalion commander to Abu

37

SUBJECT: (U) AR 15-6 Investigation of the Abu Ghraib Detention Facility and
205th MI Brigade

Ghraib to coordinate force protection plans and operations. In spite of these efforts, the mortar attacks continued and culminated in an attack in April 2004 killing 22 detainees and wounding approximately 80 others, some seriously. This highlights the critical need for adequate force protection for a detainee center.

(9) (U) The Security Internee Review and Appeal Board was established on 15 August 2003. It served as the release authority for security internees and/or those on MI Hold who were deemed to be of no security threat or (further) intelligence value. It consisted of three voting members - the C2, CJTF-7 (MG Fast), the Commander 800 MP BDE (BG Karpinski), and the CJTF-7 SJA (COL Warren), and two non-voting members (a SJA recorder and a MI assistant recorder). When first instituted, it was to meet on an "as required" basis; however, it appeared to be difficult to balance the schedules of three senior officers and the necessary support staff on a recurring, regular basis. Due to poor record keeping, accurate detainee release statistics are not available. We do know that by 2 October 2003, only 220 files had been reviewed by the board (Reference Annex H, Appendix 9, 031002 Oct CJTF7 JA Memo for CG). A preliminary screening board (Appellate Review Panel) at a level of authority below the General Officers on the Security Internee Review and Appeal Board was established to speed up the review of files by the General Officers. In the October – November 2003 timeframe, only approximately 100 detainee files a week were considered for release (Reference Annex B, Appendix 1, SUMMERS). As the detainee population increased, it became necessary to have the meetings on a much more frequent basis – initially twice a week. In the January 2004 timeframe, the board was meeting six times a week (Reference Annex B, Appendix 1, FAST). By February 2004, a standing board was established to deal with the ever increasing backlog. Even with more frequent meetings, the release of detainees from Abu Ghraib did not keep pace with the inflow. BG Karpinski believed that MG Fast was unreasonably denying detainees' release. By 11 January 2004, 57 review boards had been held and 1152 detained personnel had been released out of a total of 2113 considered. From February 2004 on, the release flow increased. (Reference Annex C, Appendix 1, Tab B, Annex 104)

(10) (U) As of late May 2004, over 8500 detainees had been reviewed for release, with 5300 plus being released and 3200 plus being recommended for continued internment. (Reference Annex H, Appendix 9, CJTF-7 C2X email). Even those that were initially deemed of no intelligence value and those that had been drained of intelligence information were not released on a timely basis – not as the result of any specific policy, but simply because the system that supported the release board (screening, interviews, availability of accurate records, and coordination) and the release board itself could not keep up with the flow of detainees into Abu Ghraib. Even with these long release delays (often 6 months and longer), there were concerns between the intelligence and tactical sides of the house. Combat Commanders desired that no security detainee be released for fear that any and all detainees could be threats to coalition forces. On occasion, Division Commanders overturned the recommendations of

SUBJECT: (U) AR 15-6 Investigation of the Abu Ghraib Detention Facility and
205th MI Brigade

Division Staffs to release some detainees at the point of capture (Reference Annex B, Appendix 1, PHILLABAUM). The G2, 4 ID informed MG Fast that the Division Commander did not concur with the release of any detainees for fear that a bad one may be released along with the good ones. MG Fast described the 4ID's response to efforts to coordinate the release of selected detainees, "…we wouldn't have detained them if we wanted them released." (Reference Annex B, Appendix 1, FAST, CIVILIAN-12). MG Fast responded that the board would ultimately release detainees if there was no evidence provided by capturing units to justify keeping them in custody.

(11) (U) The chart below depicts the rise in detainee 'MI Hold' population (those identified by the "system" to be deemed of intelligence interest) (Reference Annex H, Appendix 5). SOLDIER-14, the officer at Abu Ghraib primarily responsible for managing collection requirements and intelligence reporting, estimated that only 10-15% of the detainees on MI Hold were of actual intelligence interest. (Reference Annex B, Appendix 1, SOLDIER-14)

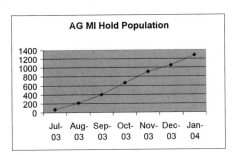

(12) (U) Interrogation operations in Abu Ghraib suffered from the effects of a broken detention operations system. In spite of clear guidance and directives, capturing units failed to perform the proper procedures at the point-of-capture and beyond with respect to handling captured enemy prisoners of war and detainees (screening, tactical interrogation, capture cards, sworn statements, transportation, etc.). Failure of capturing units to follow these procedures contributed to facility overcrowding, an increased drain on scarce interrogator and linguist resources to sort out the valuable detainees from innocents who should have been released soon after capture, and ultimately, to less actionable intelligence.

d. (U) Establishment of MP Presence at Abu Ghraib. The first Army unit to arrive was the 72nd MP Company (72 MP CO), Nevada Army National Guard. When first assigned to Abu Ghraib, the 72 MP CO was a subordinate unit of the 400th MP Battalion (400 MP BN)

SUBJECT: (U) AR 15-6 Investigation of the Abu Ghraib Detention Facility and
205th MI Brigade

headquartered at BIAP. The 320th MP Battalion (320 MP BN) advance party was the next to arrive at Abu Ghraib on 24 July 2003. The rest of the 320 MP BN Headquarters, commanded by LTC Phillabaum arrived on 28 July 2003. With the 320 MP BN came one of its subordinate units, the 447th MP Company (447 MP CO). The 72 MP CO was then reassigned from the 400 MP BN to the 320 MP BN. The next unit to arrive was the 229th MP Company (229 MP CO) on or about 3 August 2003. On 1 October 2003, SSG Frederick, CPL Graner and other MPs who have allegedly abused detainees, arrived as part of the 372 MP CO. The rest of the 320 MP CO arrived in late October 2003, followed by the 870th MP Company (870 MP CO) and 670 MP Company (670 MP CO) on approximately 14 November 2003.

e. (U) Establishment of MI Presence at Abu Ghraib.

(1) (U) The first MI unit to arrive at Abu Ghraib was a detachment from A/519 MI BN on 25 July 2003. The person in charge of that contingent was 1SGT McBride. Soldiers from the 519 MI BN had been sent there to prepare for OVB. CPT Wood arrived at Abu Ghraib on 4 August 2003 to assume the duties of Interrogation Operations OIC. MAJ Thompson arrived on or about 10 September 2003 along with elements of the 325 MI BN. MAJ Thompson was sent by COL Pappas to set up the JIDC at Abu Ghraib. LTC Jordan arrived at Abu Ghraib on 17 September 2003 to become the Director of the JIDC. MAJ Price and elements of the 323 MI BN arrived at the end of September 2003. MAJ Price had been the OIC of the interrogation operation at Camp Bucca. He became the Operations Officer of the JIDC, working closely with MAJ Thompson and CPT Wood. Most of the personnel from the 323 MI BN element that arrived with MAJ Price were used as the Headquarters element and did not directly participate in interrogations.

(2) (U) Civilian CACI contract interrogators began to arrive in late September 2003. There are a number of shortfalls connected to this issue (See paragraph 4.g., below). It was another complicating factor with respect to command and control. CPT Wood relied on the CACI site manager, CIVILIAN-18, to interview contractors as they arrived and to assign them based on his interviews. She knew little of their individual backgrounds or experience and relied on "higher headquarters" to screen them before arrival. Such screening was not occurring.

(3) (U) During October 2003, in addition to the elements of the already mentioned MI units and the Titan and CACI civilians, elements of the 470 MI GP, 500 MI GP, and 66 MI GP appeared. These units were from Texas, Japan, and Germany, and were part of the US Army Intelligence and Security Command (INSCOM), which tasked those subordinate units to send whatever interrogator and analyst support they had available. MAJ Thompson rotated back to the US on 15 November 2003. CPT Wood left on emergency leave on 4 December 2003 and never returned. MAJ Price, then, was the only commissioned officer remaining in the Operations Section.

SUBJECT: (U) AR 15-6 Investigation of the Abu Ghraib Detention Facility and
205th MI Brigade

(4) (U) It is important to understand that the MI units at Abu Ghraib were far from complete units. They were small elements from those units. Most of the elements that came to Abu Ghraib came without their normal command structure. The unit Commanders and Senior NCOs did not go to Abu Ghraib but stayed with the bulk of their respective units. The bringing together of so many parts of so many units, as well as civilians with very wide backgrounds and experience levels in a two month time period, was a huge challenge from a command and control perspective.

f. (U) Establishment, Organization, and Operation of the Joint Interrogation Debriefing Center (JIDC)

(1) (U) The idea for the creation of the JIDC came about after a number of briefings and meetings were held among LTG Sanchez, MG Fast, COL Pappas, and COL Steven Boltz, Assistant C2, CJTF-7. These meetings and briefings occurred about mid-August 2003 through early September 2003. They partially coincided with MG G. Miller's arrival from GTMO. He and his team provided an assessment of detainee operations in Iraq from 31 August to 9 September 2003 (See Paragraph 4.j.(1)). MG G. Miller's discussions with the CJTF personnel and the 205 MI BDE personnel influenced the decision to create a JIDC and how it would be organized, but those discussions were already underway before his arrival. The objective for the establishment of the JIDC was to enhance the interrogation process with a view toward producing better, timelier, actionable intelligence (actionable intelligence provides commanders and Soldiers a high level of situational understanding, delivered with speed, accuracy, and timeliness, in order to conduct successful operations).

(2) (U) On 6 September 2003, COL Pappas briefed LTG Sanchez on a plan to improve interrogation operations resulting from a 31 August 2003 meeting (Reference Annex H, Appendix 10). LTG Sanchez approved the concept and directed COL Pappas to accelerate all aspects of the plan. This decision established the JIDC and modified previous interrogation operations at Abu Ghraib. COL Pappas decided when standing up the JIDC not to make it a battalion operation (Reference Annex B, Appendix 1, WILLIAMS), therefore deciding not to place one of his battalion commanders in charge of the JIDC but instead rely upon staff personnel to manage the entire operation. The current operation would be transitioned to a JIDC by personnel already assigned at Abu Ghraib with additional manning provided by the consolidation of security detainee interrogation operations from other locations (e.g., Camp Cropper). LTC Jordan would become the Director of the JIDC on 17 September 2003. Other key JIDC personnel included CPT Wood (OIC ICE), MAJ Thompson (JIDC Operations Officer), MAJ Price (JIDC Operations Officer), SOLDIER-14 and SOLDIER-23 (Interrogation Technicians). CJTF-7 decided to use the JTF-GTMO Tiger Team concept which uses an interrogator, an intelligence analyst, and an interpreter on each team. A re-organization of the

41

SUBJECT: (U) AR 15-6 Investigation of the Abu Ghraib Detention Facility and
205th MI Brigade

JIDC took place in the late September to October 2003 timeframe which divided Tiger Teams
into functional categories.

(3) (U) The reorganization introduced another layer of complexity into an already stressed
Abu Ghraib interrogation operations environment. The Tiger Team worked well at GTMO.
JTF-GTMO's target population and mission, however, were different from what was faced in
Iraq. The Tiger Team method was designed to develop strategic level information from the
GTMO detainees who were primarily captured in Afghanistan. By the time they reached GTMO
any tactical value they may have had was gone. The same is true for Abu Ghraib relative to Iraq.
The best place to collect tactical intelligence from interrogations is at the tactical level. Tactical
intelligence is the most perishable, and the faster you harvest it the more useful it will be to help
that tactical unit. JIDC personnel at Abu Ghraib believed the thirst for intelligence reporting to
feed the national level systems was driving the train. There was then a focus to fill that
perceived void and feed that system. LTG Sanchez did not believe significant pressure was
coming from outside of CJTF-7, but does confirm that there was great pressure placed upon the
intelligence system to produce actionable intelligence (Reference Annex B, Appendix 1,
SANCHEZ). The Tiger Team concept should have only been used at Abu Ghraib for any high
value targets identified. Those targets should receive careful planning and preparation, and be
interrogated by the most experienced interrogators, analysts, and interpreters. Using a Tiger
Team at Corps (the JIDC) for developing tactical intelligence did not work.

(4) (U) The JIDC is a non-doctrinal organization. Initially, there was no joint manning
document for the JIDC (though one was developed by the 205 MI BDE over time and was
submitted to CJTF-7). There was no approved structure for the JIDC. The manning document
was being created as the JIDC was already operating (Reference Annex B, Appendix 1,
WILLIAMS, Maurice). Because there is no JIDC doctrine (or training), procedures were ad hoc
in nature – adapted from FM 34-52 where possible, though most processes and procedures were
developed on the fly based upon the needs of the situation. The organization of the JIDC
changed often (Reference Annex H, Appendix 6, Tab B) and contributed to the general state of
turmoil at Abu Ghraib. Interrogators were not familiar with the new working arrangements (e.g.,
working with analysts) and were only slightly trained on the conduct of interrogations using
translators. Note that most interrogators are only trained in conducting tactical interrogations in
a conventional war environment (See paragraph 3.b.(3)). In spite of this turmoil, lack of training
and doctrine, and shortages, the JIDC did mature over time and improved intelligence production
derived from interrogations at Abu Ghraib.

(5) (U) Early in the formation of the JIDC, COL Pappas requested COL Boltz provide him
with a Lieutenant Colonel to run the new organization because the responsibilities would require
someone of that rank and commensurate experience. LTC Jordan had just arrived in Iraq four
days earlier. He was originally sent to be COL Boltz's Deputy C2 but then a decision was made

SUBJECT: (U) AR 15-6 Investigation of the Abu Ghraib Detention Facility and
205th MI Brigade

to upgrade the C2 position from a COL to a MG. MG Fast was sent to CJTF-7 to be the C2, COL Boltz became the Deputy C2 and LTC Jordan became excess. Since LTC Jordan was available, COL Boltz assigned him to Abu Ghraib to run the JIDC. COL Boltz expected LTC Jordan to report to COL Pappas because COL Pappas had command responsibility for the JIDC. LTC Jordan was assigned to the JIDC verbally. He states that he never received orders (Reference Annex B, Appendix 1, JORDAN, BOLTZ).

(6) (U) There is a significant difference between what LTC Jordan claims he was told when he was sent to Abu Ghraib and what COL Pappas and COL Boltz say he was told. LTC Jordan says he was sent to be a "liaison" officer between CJTF-7 and the JIDC. COL Pappas and COL Boltz say he was sent there to be in charge of it. Reference to titles is useless as a way to sort through this because there was no actual manning document for reference; people made up their own titles as things went along. Some people thought COL Pappas was the Director; some thought LTC Jordan was the Director. A major shortcoming on the part of COL Pappas and LTC Jordan was the failure to do a formal Officer Evaluation Report (OER) support form, Department of Army (DA) Form 67-8-1, to clearly delineate LTC Jordan's roles and responsibilities. It is clear that both had their own ideas as to roles and responsibilities, and an initial goal-setting session formalized via the support form would have forced both parties to deal in specifics. Such sessions are frequently done after the fact; especially in stress-filled combat situations. The less organized the situation, however, the more such a process is needed in order to sort out the boundaries and lanes in the road. Abu Ghraib was certainly a place and a situation that required both clear boundaries and clear lanes in the road. LTC Jordan did provide a support form that he said he did some weeks after his assignment to Abu Ghraib and which he sent to COL Boltz. COL Boltz claims he never received it. LTC Jordan never received a signed copy back from COL Boltz and never followed up to get one. Even if LTC Jordan had sent the support form a few weeks later as he states, it was by then too late. The confusion/damage had been done. The early stages of the Abu Ghraib operation were the most critical to the disastrous end results (Reference Annex B, Appendix 1 BOLTZ, PAPPAS, JORDAN).

(7) (U) The preponderance of evidence supports the COLs Pappas/Boltz position that LTC Jordan was sent to run the JIDC. (Reference Annex B, Appendix 1, PAPPAS and BOLTZ). MAJ M. Williams, Operations Officer of the 205 MI BDE, and MAJ L. Potter, Deputy Commander of the 205 MI BDE, were adamant that LTC Jordan was sent for that reason. LTC Phillabaum believed LTC Jordan was in charge once he arrived at Abu Ghraib and started dealing directly with him. In all but one important aspect, interrogation operations, LTC Jordan began to act as if he were in charge.

(8) (U) As is now evident, LTC Jordan was a poor choice to run the JIDC. He was a Civil Affairs officer. He was an MI officer early in his career, but transferred to Civil Affairs in 1993. The MI experience he did have had not been in interrogation operations. LTC Jordan left the

43

SUBJECT: (U) AR 15-6 Investigation of the Abu Ghraib Detention Facility and
205th MI Brigade

actual management, organization, and leadership of the core of his responsibilities to MAJ Thompson and CPT Wood. The reality of the situation was that MAJ Thompson and CPT Wood were overwhelmed by the huge demands of trying to organize, staff, equip, and train the JIDC while at the same time answering incessant requests for information from both the 205 MI BDE as well as from CJTF-7. What the JIDC needed in the beginning, more than ever, was a trained, experienced MI LTC. COL Pappas was correct in his assessment of what was required. In the critical early stages of the JIDC, as it was being formed, Abu Ghraib needed a LTC to take total control. The need was for a leader to get the JIDC organized, to set standards, enforce discipline, create checks and balances, establish quality controls, communicate a zero tolerance for abuse of detainees, and enforce that policy by quickly and efficiently punishing offenders so that the rest of the organization clearly understood the message. Well-disciplined units that have active, involved leaders both at the NCO and Officer level are less likely to commit abuses or other such infractions. If such instances do occur, they are seldom repeated because those leaders act aggressively to deal with the violators and reemphasize the standards (Reference Annex B, Appendix 1, BOLTZ, PAPPAS, JORDAN).

(9) (U) LTC Jordan gravitated to what he knew, and what he was comfortable with, rather than filling the void noted above. He was actually a very hard working officer who dedicated himself to improving life for all of the Soldiers at Abu Ghraib. He is physically brave, volunteered for Iraq, and was wounded in action at Abu Ghraib during the mortar attack on 20 September 2003. He addressed shortcomings in the mess situation, lack of exercise equipment, protective gear, living conditions, and communications. He also enforced stricter adherence to the uniform policies and the wearing of protective gear by Soldiers and contractors. Many of the Soldiers that we spoke to, both MPs and MI, considered LTC Jordan the "go to guy" to get the types of things just enumerated done. BG Karpinski even remarked once to LTC Jordan during one of her visits "Do you ever sleep?" (Reference Annex B, Appendix 2, KARPINSKI). Unfortunately, all of the issues he was addressing should have been left to the staffs of the 205 MI BDE and the 320 MP BN. He was not the FOB Commander. LTC Phillabaum was the FOB Commander until the 19 November 2003 FRAGO. (Annex B, Appendix 1, JORDAN).

(10) (U) LTC Jordan became fascinated with the "Other Government Agencies," a term used mostly to mean Central Intelligence Agency (CIA), who were operating at Abu Ghraib. The OGA "Ghost Detainee" issue (housing of detainees not formally accounted for) was well known within both the MI and MP communities and created a mystique about what "they" were doing (See paragraph 4.h.). LTC Jordan allowed OGA to do interrogations without the presence of Army personnel (Reference Annex B, Appendix 1, WOOD, THOMPSON, and PRICE). Prior to that time, JIDC policy was that an Army interrogator had to accompany OGA if they were interrogating one of the detainees MI was also interrogating. As noted above, LTC Jordan was little involved in the interrogation operations, but in this aspect he did become involved and it did not help the situation. The lack of OGA adherence to the practices and procedures

SUBJECT: (U) AR 15-6 Investigation of the Abu Ghraib Detention Facility and
205th MI Brigade

established for accounting for detainees eroded the necessity in the minds of Soldiers and civilians for them to follow Army rules.

(11) (U) LTC Jordan and ten other Soldiers were wounded in the mortar attack that occurred on 20 September 2003. Two Soldiers died in that attack. LTC Jordan was extremely traumatized by that attack, especially by the two deaths and the agony suffered by one of those Soldiers before his death. He was still very emotional about that attack when interviewed for this investigation on 27 May 2004. He said he thinks about the attack and the deaths daily. That attack also had an impact on a number of other Soldiers at Abu Ghraib as did the very frequent mortar attacks that occurred at Abu Ghraib during this entire period The Soldiers' and civilians' morale at Abu Ghraib suffered as the attacks continued. Additionally, there was a general feeling by both MI and MP personnel that Abu Ghraib was the forgotten outpost receiving little support from the Army. (Reference Annex F, Appendix 3, Mortar Attacks). The frequency of these attacks and the perceived lack of aggressive action to prevent them were contributing factors to the overall poor morale that existed at Abu Ghraib.

(12) (U) COL Pappas perceived intense pressure for intelligence from interrogations. This began soon after he took Command in July 2003. In fact, as the time progressed from July 2003 through January 2004, interrogation operations at Abu Ghraib became the central focus of his efforts despite the fact that he was in command of the entire MI Brigade. That pressure for better results was passed from COL Pappas to the rest of the JIDC leadership (including MAJ Thompson, MAJ Price, CPT Wood, SOLDIER-23, and SOLDIER-14) and from them to the interrogators and analysts operating at Abu Ghraib. Pressure consisted in deviation from doctrinal reporting standards (pressure to report rapidly any and all information in non-standard formats such as Interrogator Notes in lieu of standard intelligence reports), directed guidance and prioritization from "higher," outside of doctrinal or standard operating procedures, to pursue specific lines of questioning with specific detainees, and high priority 'VFR Direct' taskings to the lowest levels in the JIDC. This pressure should have been expected in such a critical situation, but was not managed by the leadership and was a contributing factor to the environment that resulted in abuses. (Reference Annex B, Appendix 1, PAPPAS, BOLTZ, LYONS, WOOD, JORDAN,WILLIAMS, Maurice, POTTER, THOMAS, PRICE; and Annex B, Appendix 2, FAST, GEOFFREY MILLER, THOMAS MILLER).

(13) (U) The most critical period of time for Abu Ghraib was when COL Pappas committed a critical error in judgment by failing to remove LTC Jordan as soon as his shortcomings were noted, on approximately 10 October 2003. Very shortly after LTC Jordan's arrival at Abu Ghraib, on or about 17 September 2003, the 205 MI BDE Staff began to note LTC Jordan's involvement in staff issues and his lack of involvement in interrogation operations. The situation as described above would have been a daunting challenge for the most experienced, well trained, MI Officer. COL Pappas knew LTC Jordan was not who was needed to fulfill the JIDC

SUBJECT: (U) AR 15-6 Investigation of the Abu Ghraib Detention Facility and
205th MI Brigade

functions early on, but nevertheless chose to see if LTC Jordan could work out over time. COL Pappas made more frequent visits during this time period both because he was receiving increasing pressure for results but also because he could not rely on LTC Jordan to run the entire operation.

(14) (U) As pointed out clearly in the MG Taguba report, MP units and individuals at Abu Ghraib lacked sufficient training on operating a detainment/interrogation facility. MI units and individuals also lacked sufficient, appropriate, training to cope with the situation encountered at Abu Ghraib (See Paragraph 3.b.(4)). An insurgency is HUMINT intensive. The majority of that HUMINT comes from interrogations and debriefings. Yet at the JIDC, which was set up to be the focal point for interrogation operations, there was only one officer, CPT Wood, with significant interrogation operations experience. There were four MI Warrant Officers but all were used for staff functions rather than directly supervising and observing interrogations. There was a shortage of trained NCOs at the E-7/E-6 level. Each Section Leader had four or five Tiger Teams, too many to closely observe, critique, counsel, consult, and supervise. One Section Leader was an E-5. Several of the interrogators were civilians and about half of those civilians lacked sufficient background and training. Those civilians were allowed to interrogate because there were no more military assets to fill the slots. (Reference Annex B, Appendix 1, PAPPAS). Such a mixture together with constant demands for reports and documentation overwhelmed the Section Leaders. The analysts assigned to Tiger Teams were not all trained 96Bs, but were a mixture of all available intelligence Military Occupational Specialties (MOS). Many of those assigned as analysts had never been trained nor had they ever served as analysts.

(15) (U) Guard and interrogation personnel at Abu Ghraib were not adequately trained or experienced and were certainly not well versed in the cultural understanding of the detainees. MI personnel were totally ignorant of MP lanes in the road or rules of engagement. A common observation was that MI knew what MI could do and what MI couldn't do; but MI did not know what the MPs could or could not do in their activities. The same was true of MP ignorance of MI operational procedures. Having two distinct command channels (MI and MP – see Command and Control) in the same facility with little understanding of each other's doctrinal and regulatory responsibilities caused uncertainty and confusion. There was a perception among both MI and MP personnel that the other group was not doing its fair share in mutually supportive tasks of running the physical plant. CIVILIAN-12 (Assistant CJTF-7 C2X) observed that confusion seemed to be the order of the day at Abu Ghraib. There was hostility between MI and MP personnel over roles and responsibilities (Reference Annex B, Appendix 1, CIVILIAN-12). There was a distinct lack of experience in both camps. Except for some of the Reserve Component MPs who had civilian law enforcement experience, most of the MPs were never trained in prison operations. Because of the shortage of MPs, some MI personnel had to assume detainee escort duties, for which they received only the most rudimentary training.

46

SUBJECT: (U) AR 15-6 Investigation of the Abu Ghraib Detention Facility and
205th MI Brigade

(16) (U) Abu Ghraib rapidly evolved from a tactical interrogation operation in July 2003 to a JIDC beginning in September 2003. Doctrine, SOPs, and other tactics, techniques and procedures (TTP) for a JIDC were initially non-existent. The personnel manning the JIDC came from numerous units, backgrounds, and experiences. Equipment such as computers, software, IT infrastructure (networks, data storage), and connectivity to relevant intelligence data bases was very limited. Even file cabinets were in short supply which resulted in lost documents. One JIDC Soldier stated, "I can believe them (files for requests for exceptions to policy) getting lost because we often lost complete files. Our filing system was not the best. We did not have serviceable file cabinets and teams were given approval to place files in cardboard boxes." (Reference Annex B, Appendix 1, ADAMS) Initially there was only one computer available for every four interrogators. Ad hoc data bases were built, employed, and modified as requirements dictated. Data connectivity between interrogators and analysts was established using "thumb drives." Forms, intelligence products, and database formats came and went based upon their immediate utility – many times dictated by the changing structure of the JIDC itself as directed by leadership. Critical records regarding each detainee were located in several electronic and hardcopy locations – the operations officers maintained some files, others were maintained by section leaders, others by collection management personnel, and others by Detainee Release Board (DRB) personnel. Some interrogation related information was recorded on a whiteboard which was periodically erased. No centralized management system existed to manage interrogation operations. One result was that detainee records critical to the evaluation of prisoners for a variety of reasons (for intelligence value assessment, release, medical evaluation, etc.) were difficult to find or construct. MP records at Abu Ghraib were equally primitive. These documentation shortfalls not only hindered effective interrogation operations and information sharing, but also hindered the ability of the Security Internee Review and Appeal Board (which relied upon records reviews to make decisions to release or retain detainees). As addressed earlier, many detainees arrived at Abu Ghraib with little or no documentation from capturing units. Follow-on records maintained by the MP and MI personnel at Abu Ghraib would be sparse if the detainee had not been thoroughly interrogated. DRBs were reluctant to release a detainee if they knew little about him. MG Fast noted that one detainee file that was reviewed by the release board was completely empty. Even detainee medical records that should have been created and stored (Reference Annex H, Appendix 8) were not maintained appropriately. Medical doctors on site at Abu Ghraib claim that excellent medical records were maintained on detainees (Reference Annex B, Appendix 1, ACKERSON). Only a few detainee medical records could be found, indicating that they are not being maintained IAW AR 40-66 (Medical Records Administration and Healthcare Documentation).

g. (U) Contract Interrogators and Linguists

(1) (U) Contracting-related issues contributed to the problems at Abu Ghraib prison. Several of the alleged perpetrators of the abuse of detainees were employees of government

SUBJECT: (U) AR 15-6 Investigation of the Abu Ghraib Detention Facility and
205th MI Brigade

contractors. Two contractual arrangements were involved: one with CACI, for interrogators and several other intelligence - related occupational categories; and one with BTG, for linguists. Since 28 November 2001, BTG has been part of Titan Corporation. The contract is still in the name of BTG. Most people have referred to it as the Titan Contract. A brief description of these two contractual arrangements follows:

(a) (U) Linguist contract- Titan, Inc. - Contract DASC01-99-D-0001.

[1] (U) The need to supplement the Army's capacity for linguists was first raised to the Vice Chief of Staff of the Army in a 1997 "Foreign Language Lay down." It was proposed to establish a contract with the private sector to provide linguists, as needed, for contingencies and current intelligence operations.

[2] (U) As a result of this perceived need, INSCOM awarded Contract DASC01-99-D-0001 to Titan, in March 1999. The contract called for Titan initially to develop a plan to provide and manage linguists throughout the world, and later, implement the plan as required. The contract called for three levels of linguists- some were required to obtain security clearances and some were not. The linguist candidates were subject to some level of background investigations, based on individual requirements for security clearances. Since the award of the contract, hundreds of linguists have been provided, with generally positive results. It is noted that the contract calls for translation services only, and makes no mention of contractor employees actually conducting interrogations. Since the statement of work is limited to translation services, the linguists apparently were not required to review and sign the IROE at Abu Ghraib. A recent review of the contract indicated that the current contract ceiling is approximately $650 Million. Other agencies can order linguist services under this contract. For the most part, the ordering activity also provides the funds for these delivery orders. The contract contains a clause that allows the Contracting Officer to direct the contractor to remove linguists from the theater in which they are performing. This clause has been invoked on occasion for misconduct.

(b) Interrogator contract-CACI, Inc.

[1] (U) The second contractual arrangement is a series of Delivery Orders awarded to CACI, in August 2003, which call for the provision of numerous intelligence-related services such as "Interrogator Support," "Screening Cell Support," "Open Source Intelligence," "Special Security Office," "HUMINT Augmentee Contractors" (which includes "Interrogation Support," "Junior Interrogators," "Senior and Junior Counter-Intelligence Agents," and "Tactical/Strategic Interrogators").

48

SUBJECT: (U) AR 15-6 Investigation of the Abu Ghraib Detention Facility and 205th MI Brigade

[2] (U) These Delivery Orders were awarded under a Blanket Purchase Agreement (BPA) (NBCHA01-0005) with the National Business Center (NBC), a fee for service activity of the Interior Department. The BPA between CACI and NBC set out the ground rules for ordering from the General Services Administration (GSA) pursuant to GSA Schedule Contract GS-35F-5872H, which is for various Information Technology (IT) Professional Services. Approximately eleven Delivery Orders were related to services in Iraq. While CJTF-7 is the requiring and funding activity for the Delivery Orders in question, it is not clear who, if anyone, in Army contracting or legal channels approved the use of the BPA, or why it was used.

[3] (U) There is another problem with the CACI contract. A CACI employee, Thomas Howard, participated with the COR, LTC Brady, in writing the Statement of Work (SOW) prior to the award of the contract (Reference Annex B, Appendix 1, BOLTZ). This situation may violate the provisions of Federal Acquisition Regulation (FAR) 9. 505-2 (b) (1).

[4] (U) On 13 May 2004, the Deputy General Counsel (Acquisition) of the Army issued an opinion that all Delivery Orders for Interrogator Services should be cancelled immediately as they were beyond the scope of the GSA Schedule contract.

(2) (U) Although intelligence activities and related services, which encompass interrogation services, should be performed by military or government civilian personnel wherever feasible, it is recognized that contracts for such services may be required in urgent or emergency situations. The general policy of not contracting for intelligence functions and services was designed in part to avoid many of the problems that eventually developed at Abu Ghraib, i.e., lack of oversight to insure that intelligence operations continued to fall within the law and the authorized chain of command, as well as the government's ability to oversee contract operations.

(3) (U) Performing the interrogation function in-house with government employees has several tangible benefits for the Army. It enables the Army more readily to manage the function if all personnel are directly and clearly subject to the chain of command, and other administrative and/or criminal sanctions, and it allows the function to be directly accessible by the commander/supervisor without going through a Contracting Officer Representative (COR). In addition, performing the function in-house enables Army Commanders to maintain a consistent approach to training (See Paragraph 3.b.(3)) and a reliable measure of the qualifications of the people performing the function.

(4) (U) If it is necessary to contract for interrogator services, Army requiring activities must carefully develop the applicable SOW to include the technical requirements and requisite personnel qualifications, experience, and training. Any such contracts should, to the greatest extent possible, be awarded and administered by an Army contracting activity in order to provide for the necessary oversight, management, and chain of command. Use of contracting vehicles

SUBJECT: (U) AR 15-6 Investigation of the Abu Ghraib Detention Facility and
205th MI Brigade

such as GSA Federal Supply Schedule (FSS) contracts should be carefully scrutinized given the complexity and sensitivities connected to interrogation operations.

(5) (U) Some of the employees at Abu Ghraib were not DoD contractor employees. Contractor employees under non-DoD contracts may not be subject to the Military Extraterritorial Jurisdiction Act (18 US Code 3261- 3267). The Act allows DoD contractor employees who are "accompanying the Armed Forces outside the United States" to be subject to criminal prosecution if they engage in conduct that would constitute an offense punishable by imprisonment for more than one year if the conduct had occurred within the jurisdiction of the United States.

(6) (U) In the performance of such sensitive functions as interrogation, the Army needs to maintain close control over the entire operation. If a decision is made to contract for these services, the most effective way to do that and maintain a direct chain of command is to award, administer, and manage the contract with Army personnel. As learned in the current situation, it is very difficult, if not impossible, to effectively administer a contract when the COR is not on site.

(7) (U) The Army needs to improve on-site contract monitoring by government employees (using CORs) to insure that the Army's basic interests are protected. The inadequacy of the on-site contract management at Abu Ghraib is best understood by reviewing the statement of CPT Wood (Reference Annex B, Appendix 1, WOOD), the Interrogation OIC, who indicated she never received any parameters or guidance as to how the CACI personnel were to be utilized. She also indicates that her primary point of contact (POC) on matters involving the CACI Delivery Orders was the CACI on-site manager. There is no mention of a COR. Another indication of the inadequacy of the contract management is reflected in the statement of SOLDIER14 (Reference Annex B, Appendix 1, SOLDIER-14), who indicated he was never informed that the Government could reject unsatisfactory CACI employees. It would appear that no effort to familiarize the ultimate user of the contracted services of the contract's terms and procedures was ever made. In order to improve this situation, training is required to ensure that the COR is thoroughly familiar with the contract and gains some level of familiarity with the Geneva Conventions standards. It needs to be made clear that contractor employees are bound by the requirements of the Geneva Conventions.

(8) (U) If it is necessary to contract for interrogator services, more specific training requirements and personnel standards must be incorporated into the solicitation/contract to insure that the contractor hires properly trained and qualified personnel.

(9) (U) Emerging results from a DA Inspector General (DAIG) Investigation indicate that approximately 35% of the contract interrogators lacked formal military training as interrogators.

SUBJECT: (U) AR 15-6 Investigation of the Abu Ghraib Detention Facility and
205th MI Brigade

While there are specific technical requirements in the linguist contract, the technical requirements for the interrogator contract were not adequate. It appears that the only mention of qualifications in the contract stated merely that the contractor employee needs to have met the requirements of one of two MOS, 97E or 351E, or "equivalent". Any solicitation/contract for these services needs to list specific training, if possible, not just point to an MOS. If the training from the MOS is what is required, those requirements should be listed in the solicitation/contract in full, not just referenced. Perhaps the best way of insuring that contractor interrogators receive adequate training would be to utilize existing government training. For example, prospective contractor employees could be sent, at contractor expense, to the Tactical Human Intelligence Course for the 97E MOS, "Human Intelligence Collector." Such a step would likely require some adjustments to the current program of instruction. Prospective contract interrogators could be given the course tests on Interrogation and the Geneva Conventions. If they can pass the examinations, no further training would be required. After a reasonable training period, prospective contractor interrogators who are unable to pass the exam would be rejected. There are, of course other training possibilities. The key point would be agreement on some standardization of the training of contractor interrogators. The necessity for some sort of standard training and/or experience is made evident by the statements of both contractor employees and military personnel. CIVILIAN-21 (CACI) seemingly had little or no interrogator experience prior to coming to Abu Ghraib (Reference Annex B, Appendix 1,CIVILIAN-21, ADAMS), even though he was a Navy Reserve Intelligence Specialist. Likewise, numerous statements indicated that little, if any, training on Geneva Conventions was presented to contractor employees (Reference Annex B, Appendix 1, SOLDIER-25, CIVILIAN-10, CIVILIAN-21 and CIVILIAN-11). Prior to deployment, all contractor linguists or interrogators should receive training in the Geneva Conventions standards for the treatment of detainees/prisoners. This training should include a discussion of the chain of command and the establishment of some sort of "hotline" where suspected abuses can be reported in addition to reporting through the chain of command. If the solicitation/contract allows "equivalent" training and experience, the Contracting Officer, with the assistance of technical personnel, must evaluate and assess the offerors'/contractor's proposal/written rationale as to why it believes that the employee has "equivalent" training. It appears that under the CACI contract, no one was monitoring the contractor's decisions as to what was considered "equivalent."

(10) (U) In addition, if functions such as these are being contracted, MI personnel need to have at least a basic level of contract training so they can protect the Army's interests. Another indication of the apparent inadequacy of on-site contract management and lack of contract training is the apparent lack of understanding of the appropriate relationship between contractor personnel, government civilian employees, and military personnel. Several people indicated in their statements that contractor personnel were "supervising" government personnel or *vice versa*. SGT Adams indicated that CACI employees were in positions of authority, and appeared to be supervising government personnel. She indicated a CACI employee named "First Name"

51

SUBJECT: (U) AR 15-6 Investigation of the Abu Ghraib Detention Facility and
205th MI Brigade

was listed as being in charge of screening. CIVILIAN-08 (CACI) was in charge of "B Section" with military personnel listed as subordinates on the organization chart. SOLDIER-14 also indicated that CIVILIAN-08 was a supervisor for a time. CPT Wood stated that CACI "supervised" military personnel in her statement, but offered no specifics. Finally, a government organization chart (Reference Annex H, Appendix 6, Tab B) showed a CIVILIAN-02 (CACI) as the Head of the DAB. CIVILIAN-02 is a CACI employee. On the other side of the coin, CIVILIAN-21 indicated in his statement that the Non-Commissioned Officer in Charge (NCOIC) was his supervisor. (Reference Annex B, Appendix 1, SOLDIER-14, CIVILIAN-21, ADAMS, WOOD)

(11) (U) Given the sensitive nature of these sorts of functions, it should be required that the contractor perform some sort of background investigation on the prospective employees. A clause that would allow the government to direct the contractor to remove employees from the theater for misconduct would seem advisable. The need for a more extensive pre-performance background investigation is borne out by the allegations of abuse by contractor personnel.

(12) (U) An important step in precluding the recurrence of situations where contractor personnel may engage in abuse of prisoners is to insure that a properly trained COR is on-site. Meaningful contract administration and monitoring will not be possible if a small number of CORs are asked to monitor the performance of one or more contractors who may have 100 or more employees in the theater, and in some cases, perhaps in several locations (which seems to have been the situation at Abu Ghraib). In these cases, the CORs do well to keep up with the paper work, and simply have no time to actively monitor contractor performance. It is apparent that there was no credible exercise of appropriate oversight of contract performance at Abu Ghraib.

(13) (U) Proper oversight did not occur at Abu Ghraib due to a lack of training and inadequate contract management and monitoring. Failure to assign an adequate number of CORs to the area of contract performance puts the Army at risk of being unable to control poor performance or become aware of possible misconduct by contractor personnel. This lack of monitoring was a contributing factor to the problems that were experienced with the performance of the contractors at Abu Ghraib. The Army needs to take a much more aggressive approach to contract administration and management if interrogator services are to be contracted. Some amount of advance planning should be utilized to learn from the mistakes made at Abu Ghraib.

h. (U) Other Government Agencies and Abu Ghraib.

(1) (U) Although the FBI, JTF-121, Criminal Investigative Task Force, ISG and the Central Intelligence Agency (CIA) were all present at Abu Ghraib, the acronym "Other Government Agency" (OGA) referred almost exclusively to the CIA. CIA detention and interrogation

52

SUBJECT: (U) AR 15-6 Investigation of the Abu Ghraib Detention Facility and
205th MI Brigade

practices led to a loss of accountability, abuse, reduced interagency cooperation, and an unhealthy mystique that further poisoned the atmosphere at Abu Ghraib.

(2) (U) CIA detainees in Abu Ghraib, known locally as "Ghost Detainees," were not accounted for in the detention system. When the detainees were unidentified or unaccounted for, detention operations at large were impacted because personnel at the operations level were uncertain how to report them or how to classify them, or how to database them, if at all. Therefore, Abu Ghraib personnel were unable to respond to requests for information about CIA detainees from higher headquarters. This confusion arose because the CIA did not follow the established procedures for detainee in-processing, such as fully identifying detainees by name, biometric data, and Internee Serial Number (ISN) number.

(3) (U) DETAINEE-28, suspected of having been involved in an attack against the ICRC, was captured by Navy SEAL Team 7 during a joint TF-121/CIA mission. He reportedly resisted arrest, so a SEAL Team member butt-stroked DETAINEE-28 on the side of the head to subdue him. CIA representatives brought DETAINEE-28 into Abu Ghraib early in the morning of 4 November 2003, sometime around 0430 to 0530 hours. Under a supposed verbal agreement between the JIDC and the CIA, the CIA did not announce its arrival to JIDC Operations. SPC Stevanus, the MP on duty at the Hard Site at the time, observed the two CIA representatives come in with DETAINEE-28 and place him in a shower room in Tier 1B. About 30 to 45 minutes later, SPC Stevanus was summoned to the shower stall and when he arrived, DETAINEE-28 appeared to be dead. Removing the sandbag covering DETAINEE-28's head, SPC Stevanus checked DETAINEE-28's pulse. Finding none, he called for medical assistance, and notified his chain of command. LTC Jordan arrived on site at approximately 0715 hours, and found several MPs and US medical staff with DETAINEE-28 in the Tier 1B shower stall, face down, handcuffed with his hands behind his back. CIVILIAN-03, an Iraqi prison medical doctor, informed him DETAINEE-28 was dead. "OTHER AGENCY EMPLOYEE01," a CIA representative, un-cuffed DETAINEE-28 and turned his body over. Where DETAINEE-28's head had lain against the floor, LTC Jordan noted a small spot of blood. LTC Jordan notified COL Pappas (205 MI BDE Commander), and "OTHER AGENCY EMPLOYEE01" said he would notify "OTHER AGENCY EMPLOYEE02," his CIA supervisor. Once "OTHER AGENCY EMPLOYEE02" arrived, he requested that the Hard Site hold DETAINEE28's body until the following day. DETAINEE-28's body was placed in a body bag, packed in ice, and stored in the shower area. CID was notified. The next day, DETAINEE-28's body was removed from Abu Ghraib on a litter, to make it appear as if he were only ill, so as not to draw the attention of the Iraqi guards and detainees. The body was transported to the morgue at BIAP for an autopsy, which concluded that DETAINEE-28 died of a blood clot in the head, likely a result of injuries he sustained during apprehension. (Reference Annex B, Appendix 1, JORDAN, PAPPAS, PHILLABAUM, SNIDER, STEVANUS, THOMPSON; Annex I, Appendix 1, photographs C5-21, D5-11, M65-69)

SECRET//NOFORN//X1

SUBJECT: (U) AR 15-6 Investigation of the Abu Ghraib Detention Facility and
205th MI Brigade

(4) (U) The systemic lack of accountability for interrogator actions and detainees plagued detainee operations in Abu Ghraib. It is unclear how and under what authority the CIA could place prisoners like DETAINEE-28 in Abu Ghraib because no memorandums of understanding existed on the subject between the CIA and CJTF-7. Local CIA officers convinced COL Pappas and LTC Jordan that they should be allowed to operate outside the established local rules and procedures. When COL Pappas raised the issue of CIA use of Abu Ghraib with COL Boltz, COL Boltz encouraged COL Pappas to cooperate with the CIA because everyone was all one team. COL Boltz directed LTC Jordan to cooperate. (Reference Annex B, Appendix 1, PAPPAS, BOLTZ)

(5) (U) In many instances, failure to adhere to in-processing procedures caused confusion and acrimony between the Army and OGA, and in at least one instance, acrimony between the US and Saudi Arabian entities. (Reference Annex K, Appendix 3, emails) For example, the CIA interned three Saudi national medical personnel working for the coalition in Iraq. CIA officers placed them in Abu Ghraib under false names. The Saudi General in charge of the men asked US authorities to check the records for them. A search of all databases using their true names came back negative. Ambassador Bremer then requested a search, which produced the same results. The US Embassy in Riyadh also requested a search, which likewise produced no information. Ultimately, the Secretary of State, Colin Powell, requested a search, and as with the other requestors, had to be told that the three men were not known to be in US custody. Shortly after the search for the Secretary of State, a JIDC official recalled that CIA officers once brought three men together into the facility. A quick discussion with the detainees disclosed their true names, which matched the name search requests, and the men were eventually released. (Reference Annex B, Appendix 1, CIVILIAN-12)

(6) (U) Another instance showing lack of accountability to the procedures or rules involved a CIA officer who entered the interrogation room after a break in the interrogation, drew his weapon, chambered a round, and placed the weapon in his holster. This action violated the rule that no weapons be brought into an interrogation room, especially weapons with live rounds. Detainees who have been interrogated by CIA officers have alleged abuse. (Reference Annex B, Appendix 1, CIVILIAN-12)

(7) (U) The death of DETAINEE-28 and incidents such as the loaded weapon in the interrogation room, were widely known within the US community (MI and MP alike) at Abu Ghraib. Speculation and resentment grew over the lack of personal responsibility, of some people being above the laws and regulations. The resentment contributed to the unhealthy environment that existed at Abu Ghraib. The DETAINEE-28 death remains unresolved. CIA officers operating at Abu Ghraib used alias' and never revealed their true names. "OTHER AGENCY EMPLOYEE01" (alias) was the CIA officer with DETAINEE-28 on the morning of

SECRET//NOFORN//X1

54

SUBJECT: (U) AR 15-6 Investigation of the Abu Ghraib Detention Facility and
205th MI Brigade

his death. "OTHER AGENCY EMPLOYEE02" (alias) was not directly involved in
DETAINEE-28's death, but participated in the discussions after his death. Had the CIA followed
established Army procedures and in-processed DETAINEE-28 in accordance with those
procedures, DETAINEE-28 would have been medically screened.

(8) (U) OGA never provided results of their abuse investigations to Commander, CJTF-7.
This resulted in a total lack of visibility over OGA interaction with detainees held in CJTF-7
spaces. Additionally, the CJTF-7 charter provided no oversight or control over the ISG. LTG
Sanchez could neither leverage ISG interrogation assets to assist the detainee operations in Abu
Ghraib, nor could he compel ISG to share substantive intelligence reports with CJTF-7.
(Reference Annex B, Appendix 1, SANCHEZ)

i. (U) The Move of the 205 MI BDE Commander to Abu Ghraib.

(1) (U) In September 2003, COL Pappas began visiting Abu Ghraib two or three times per
week as opposed to once every week or two, his previous routine. He was also beginning to stay
overnight occasionally. His visit schedule coincided with the increased emphasis being placed
on interrogation operations and the newly formed JIDC. (Reference Annex B, Appendix 1,
PAPPAS)

(2) (U) On 16 November 2003, COL Pappas took up full time residence at Abu Ghraib
after once again speaking with LTG Sanchez and MG Fast and deciding that he needed to be
there. He was appointed FOB Commander on 19 November 2003 in FRAGO 1108. The
issuance of FRAGO 1108 has been pointed to and looked upon by many as being a significant
change and one that was a major factor in allowing the abuses to occur. It was not. The abuses
and the environment for them began long before FRAGO 1108 was ever issued. That FRAGO
appointed the Commander, 205 MI BDE, the Commander FOB Abu Ghraib for Force Protection
and Security of Detainees. COL Pappas then had TACON of the 320 MP BN. TACON has
been misinterpreted by some to mean that COL Pappas then took over the running of the prison,
or what has been referred to as Warden functions. COL Pappas never took over those functions,
and LTC Phillabaum agrees that the running of the prison was always his responsibility. LTG
Sanchez has stated that he never intended to do anything except improve the Force Protection
posture of the FOB. That improved force protection posture would have thus improved the
security of detainees as well. COL Pappas' rater, MG Wojdakowski, also stated that COL
Pappas was never given responsibility for running the prison, but that the MPs retained that
responsibility. It would appear from MG Taguba's investigation and the interview for this
investigation that BG Karpinski was the only person among the Army leadership involved at the
time who interpreted that FRAGO differently. (Reference Annex B, Appendix 1, KARPINSKI
and Annex B, Appendix 2, KARPINSKI)

55

SUBJECT: (U) AR 15-6 Investigation of the Abu Ghraib Detention Facility and
205th MI Brigade

(3) (U) Upon being appointed FOB Commander, COL Pappas brought in one of his subordinate units, the 165th MI Battalion (165 MI BN) to enhance base security and to augment forces providing perimeter security as well as to conduct reconnaissance and surveillance outside the perimeter. That unit had reconnaissance and surveillance elements similar to line combat units that the MP Battalions did not possess. COL Pappas, on 8 December 2003, requested additional forces to support his force protection mission (Reference Annex H, Appendix 6, TAB – Request for Forces (RFF)). Requested forces included personnel for additional guards and a rapid reaction force.

(4) (U) The fact that COL Pappas did not have control of the MP force after the 19 November 2003 FRAGO regarding prison operations is further supported by the fact that at some point near the end of November 2003, the MPs stopped escorting detainees from the camps to the interrogation sites due to personnel shortages. This required MI to take over this function despite their protests that they were neither trained nor manned to do it. COL Pappas would have ordered the MPs to continue the escorts if he had had such authority (See paragraph 4.c.)

(5) (U) A milestone event at Abu Ghraib was the shooting incident that occurred in Tier 1A on 24 November 2003 (See paragraph 5.e.). COL Pappas was by then in residence at Abu Ghraib. LTC Jordan displayed personal bravery by his direct involvement in the shoot-out, but also extremely poor judgment. Instead of ordering the MPs present to halt their actions and isolate the tier until the 320 MP BN Commander and COL Pappas could be notified, he became directly involved. As the senior officer present, LTC Jordan became responsible for what happened. Eventually, COL Pappas was notified, and he did visit the scene. By then the shooting was over, and the MPs were searching the cells. COL Pappas did not remain long but admits to being told by SOLDIER-23 that the Iraqi Police were being interrogated by MI personnel. COL Pappas left LTC Jordan in charge of the situation after the shooting which came to be known as the IP Roundup. The IP Roundup was, by all accounts chaotic. The Iraqi Police, hence the name "IP," became detainees and were subjected to strip searching by the MPs in the hallway, with female Soldiers and at least one female interpreter present. The IP were kept in various stages of dress, including nakedness, for prolonged periods as they were interrogated. This constitutes humiliation, which is detainee abuse. Military working dogs were being used not only to search the cells, but also to intimidate the IPs during interrogation without authorization. There was a general understanding among the MI personnel present that LTG Sanchez had authorized suspending existing ICRP (known by the Abu Ghraib personnel locally as the IROE) because of the shooting (Reference Annex C, Appendix 1, Tab B, Annex 8, AR 15-6 Investigation, 24 November 2003). Nobody is sure where that information came from, but LTG Sanchez never gave such authorization (Reference Annex B, Appendix 1, SANCHEZ). LTC Jordan and the Soldiers should have known the Interrogation Rules would not and could not have been suspended. LTC Jordan should have controlled the situation and should have taken steps to reinforce proper standards at a time when emotions were likely high given the

SUBJECT: (U) AR 15-6 Investigation of the Abu Ghraib Detention Facility and
205th MI Brigade

circumstances. LTC Jordan is responsible for allowing the chaotic situation, the unauthorized nakedness and resultant humiliation, and the military working dog abuses that occurred that night. LTC Jordan should have obtained any authorizations to suspend ICRP in writing, via email, if by no other means. The tone and the environment that occurred that night, with the tacit approval of LTC Jordan, can be pointed to as the causative factor that set the stage for the abuses that followed for days afterward related to the shooting and the IP Roundup. COL Pappas is also responsible and showed poor judgment by leaving the scene before normalcy returned, as well as for leaving LTC Jordan in charge.

(6) (U) The small quantity of MI personnel had a difficult time managing the large number of MI holds which moved from the hundreds to over a thousand by December 2003 (See paragraph 4.c.(12)). In December 2003, COL Pappas, in his role as FOB Commander, requested additional forces be allocated to support the difficult and growing force protection mission. Prior to his designation as FOB Commander, COL Pappas had requested additional forces to support the JIDC mission. One of the reasons he cited in the December request was that the mixing of MI and MP functions was worsening the already difficult personnel resource situation.

j. (U) Advisory and Training Team Deployments

(1) (U) MG Geoffrey Miller Visit

(a) (U) MG G. Miller's visit was in response to a J3, JCS, request to SOUTHCOM for a team to assist CENTCOM and ISG in theater (Reference Annex L, Appendix 1, Electrical Message, DTG: 181854Z Aug 03, FM JOINT STAFF WASHINGTON DC // J3). The team was directed to assist with advice on facilities and operations specific to screening, interrogations, HUMINT collection, and interagency integration in the short and long term. MG G. Miller was tasked as the result of a May 2003 meeting he had with MG Ronald Burgess, J2, JCS. MG Burgess indicated there were some challenges in CJTF-7 with the transition from major combat operations to SASO in the areas of intelligence, interrogation, and detention (Reference Annex B, Appendix 1, MILLER). COL Boltz believed LTG Sanchez had requested the support (Reference Annex B, Appendix 1, BOLTZ).

(b) (U) From 31 August to 9 September 2003, MG G. Miller led a team to Iraq to conduct an "Assessment of DoD Counterterrorism Interrogation and Detention Operations in Iraq." Specifically, MG G. Miller's team was to conduct assistance visits to CJTF-7, TF-20, and the ISG to discuss current theater ability to exploit internees rapidly for actionable intelligence. MG G. Miller and his team of 17 experts assessed three major areas of concern: intelligence integration, synchronization, and fusion; interrogation operations; and detention operations. The team's assessment (Reference Annex L, Appendix 1, MG Miller's Report, Assessment of DoD Counterterrorism Interrogation and Detention Operations in Iraq, undated, and MG Miller's

SUBJECT: (U) AR 15-6 Investigation of the Abu Ghraib Detention Facility and
205th MI Brigade

Briefing of his findings, dated 6 September 2003) identified several areas in need of attention: the interrogators didn't have the authorities and procedures in place to effect a unified strategy to detain, interrogate, and report information from detainees in Iraq; the information needs required an in-theater analysis capability integrated in the interrogation operations to allow for access/leverage of the worldwide intelligence databases; and the detention operations function must support the interrogation process.

(c) (U) MG G. Miller's visit also introduced written GTMO documentation into the CJTF-7 environment. LTG Sanchez recalled MG G. Miller left behind a whole series of SOPs that could be used as a start point for CJTF-7 interrogation operations. It was clear that these SOPs had to be adapted to the conditions in Iraq and that they could not be implemented blindly. LTG Sanchez was confident the entire CJTF-7 staff understood that the conditions in GTMO were different than in Iraq, because the Geneva Conventions applied in the Iraqi theater.

(d) (U) The assessment team essentially conducted a systems analysis of the intelligence mission in Iraq and did not concentrate on specific interrogation techniques. While no "harsh techniques" were briefed, COL Pappas recalled a conversation with MG G. Miller regarding the use of military working dogs to support interrogations (See paragraph 5.f.). According to COL Pappas, MG G. Miller said they, GTMO, used military working dogs, and that they were effective in setting the atmosphere for interrogations (Reference Annex B, Appendix 2, PAPPAS). MG G. Miller contradicted COL Pappas in his statement (Reference Annex B, Appendix 1, MILLER), saying he only discussed using military working dogs to help the MPs with detainee custody and control issues. According to MG G. Miller, the dogs help provide a controlled atmosphere (not interrogations as recalled by COL Pappas) that helps reduce risk of detainee demonstrations or acts of violence. According to MG G. Miller, his team recommended a strategy to work the operational schedule of the dog teams so the dogs were present when the detainees were awake, not when they are sleeping.

(e) (U) Several things occurred subsequent to MG G. Miller's visit to Abu Ghraib. The JIDC was established. The use of Tiger Teams was implemented based on the JTF-GTMO model, which teamed an interrogator and an analyst together, giving each team an organic analytical capability. There was also a moderate increase in the number of interrogators reassigned to the Abu Ghraib operation. This increase was probably not connected to MG G. Miller's visit as much as to the arrival of elements of the 325 MI BN which began to arrive 10 September 2003--the same day MG G. Miller departed Iraq. Prior to their arrival, the interrogation assets consisted of one OIC (captain), one technician (chief warrant officer), 12 HUMINT collectors (MOS 97E/97B), an analyst, and a communications team. While the number of interrogators increased, the JIDC requirements for a staff and leadership also increased. Those positions were filled from within the assigned units. It is indeterminate what impact the MG G. Miller Team's concepts had on operations at Abu Ghraib. There was an

SUBJECT: (U) AR 15-6 Investigation of the Abu Ghraib Detention Facility and
205th MI Brigade

increase in intelligence reports after the visit but that appears more likely due to the assignment
of trained interrogators and an increased number of MI Hold detainees to interrogate.

(2) JTF-GTMO Training Team.

(a) (U) Subsequent to MG G. Miller's visit, a team of subject matter experts was
dispatched from JTF-GTMO to Abu Ghraib (approximately 4 October to 2 December 2003) to
assist in the implementation of the recommendations identified by MG G. Miller. The JTF-
GTMO Team included three interrogators and three analysts, organized into three teams, with
one interrogator and one analyst on each, which is the GTMO "Tiger Team" concept. The JTF
GTMO Team included SOLDIER28 (351E Team Chief), SOLDIER27, CIVILIAN-14 (97E),
SOLDIER-03 (97E), SSG Miller (96B), and SOLDIER-11 (96B). The Team Chief understood
his task was to assist CJTF-7 for a period not to exceed 90 days with the mission of building a
robust and effective JIDC, and identifying solutions and providing recommendations for the
JIDC (Reference Annex B, Appendix 1, SOLDIER-28). Upon arrival at Abu Ghraib,
SOLDIER-28 and SOLDIER-27, both of whom had been on the original MG G. Miller
assessment visit, concentrated on establishing the various JIDC elements. Particular emphasis
was given to formalizing the JIDC staff and the collection, management and dissemination
(CM&D) function at Abu Ghraib, to alleviate many of the information distribution issues
surfaced during MG G. Miller's visit. Some interrogation policies were already in place.
Consistent with its charter to assist in establishment of a GTMO-like operation, the team
provided copies of the current JTF-GTMO policies, SOPs (Reference, Annex L, Appendix 2,
SOP for JTF-GTMO, Joint Intelligence Group [JIG], Interrogation Control Element [ICE],
Guantanamo Bay, CU, dated 21 January 2003, revised 12 June 2003), and the SECDEF Letter
(Reference, Annex J, Appendix 2, MEMORANDUM FOR COMMANDER, US SOUTHERN
COMMAND, Subject: Counter-Resistance Techniques in the War on Terrorism (S), dated 16
April 2003) outlining the techniques authorized for use with the GTMO detainees. The four
other JTF-GTMO team members were split up and integrated into interrogation operations as
members/leaders of the newly formed Tiger Teams under the ICE. SOLDIER-28 and
SOLDIER-27 did not directly participate in any interrogation operations and reported that they
never observed, or heard about, any detainee abuse or mistreatment. SOLDIER-28's assertion as
regards knowledge of abuses is contradicted by one of his Soldiers (Reference Annex B,
Appendix 1, SOLDIER-03) (See paragraphs 4.j.(2)(c) and 4.j.(2)(d), below).

(b) (U) While the JTF-GTMO team's mission was to support operations and assist in
establishment of the JIDC, there was a great deal of animosity on the part of the Abu Ghraib
personnel, especially some A/519 MI BN Personnel. This included an intentional disregard for
the concepts and techniques the GTMO Team attempted to instill, as well as contempt for some
of the team's work ethic, professional judgment, and ideas. Because of this, the GTMO Team's
ability to effect change at Abu Ghraib may have been severely limited. This information was

SUBJECT: (U) AR 15-6 Investigation of the Abu Ghraib Detention Facility and
205th MI Brigade

obtained during a review of email exchanged between SOLDIER-14, CW2 Grace, CW3
Sammons, SFC McBride, with info copies to CPT Wood and SOLDIER-23. It should be noted
that senior managers at Abu Ghraib thought highly of the JTF-GTMO team and believed they
positively impacted the operations.

(c) (U) SOLDIER-11, a JTF-GTMO analyst assigned to the "Former Regime Loyalists"
Tiger Team, stated that he witnessed and reported two incidents of abuse (Reference Annex B,
Appendix 1, SOLDIER-11). In his first report, SOLDIER-11 reported that he was observing an
interrogation being conducted by SOLDIER19 A/519 MI BN. As SOLDIER-11 observed from
behind a glass, SOLDIER-19 directed a detainee to roll his jumpsuit down to his waist and
insinuated that the detainee would be stripped further if he did not cooperate. The interrogation
ended abruptly when the translator objected to the tactic and refused to continue. SOLDIER-11
reported the incident to both SOLDIER-16, his Tiger Team Leader, and to SOLDIER-28, his
JTF GTMO Team Chief. SOLDIER-16 invoked her rights under UCMJ and chose not to make
any statement regarding this or any other matters (Reference Annex B, Appendix
1SOLDIER16). When asked, SOLDIER-28 stated that he could not recall what SOLDIER11
reported to him regarding the rolling down of the detainee's jumpsuit, but does recall a
conversation about a translator walking out of an interrogation due to a "cultural difference"
(Reference Annex B, Appendix 1, SOLDIER-28). SOLDIER-11 is adamant that he reported the
incident in detail (Reference Annex B, Appendix 1, SOLDIER-11) and that he never used the
phrase "cultural difference."

(d) (U) In another report to SOLDIER-28, SOLDIER-11 reported a second incident.
SOLDIER-11 and SOLDIER--19 were conducting an interrogation around mid-October 2003.
The detainee was uncooperative and was not answering questions. SOLDIER19 became
frustrated and suggested to SOLDIER11 that the detainee be placed in solitary. SOLDIER-11
did not agree with the recommendation and suggested it would be counterproductive. About 15
minutes later (two hours into the interrogation), SOLDIER-19 exercised his authority as the lead
interrogator and had the detainee placed in solitary confinement. About a half an hour later,
SOLDIER-11 and SOLDIER-19 went to the Hard Site to see the detainee, and found him lying
on the floor, completely naked except for a hood that covered his head from his upper lip,
whimpering. SOLDIER-11 andSOLDIER-19 had the MPs redress the detainee before escorting
him back to the general population. SOLDIER-11 was disturbed by what he had seen and
considered reporting it to several different people. Ultimately, SOLDIER-11 reported this
incident to SOLDIER-28 (Reference Annex B, Appendix 1, SOLDIER-11). SOLDIER-11
added that SOLDIER-28 accepted the report and indicated he would surface the issue to COL
Pappas (not due to return to Abu Ghraib for 2 - 3 days). Also according to SOLDIER-11,
SOLDIER-28 was very ill and placed on 30 days quarters shortly after SOLDIER-11 made his
report. When asked, SOLDIER-28 could not recall such a report being made to him (Reference
Annex B, Appendix 1, SOLDIER-28).

60

SUBJECT: (U) AR 15-6 Investigation of the Abu Ghraib Detention Facility and
205th MI Brigade

(e) (U) SSG Miller does not recall the JTF-GTMO team ever discussing specific interrogation techniques employed, abuse, or unauthorized interrogation methods. He observed only approved interrogation techniques in line with FM 34-52, and never saw any detainee abuse, mistreatment, or nakedness (Reference Annex B, Appendix 1, MILLER).

(f) (U) CIVILIAN-14 never observed any activity or training event that was not in compliance with basic human rights and the Geneva Conventions. CIVILIAN-14 did, however, notice "a lot of detainee nakedness at Abu Ghraib," possibly, he speculated, attributable to the lack of available clothing. There was nothing he observed or heard that he considered detainee abuse. Relating to his JTF-GTMO experience/training, CIVILIAN-14 believed the removal of clothing for interrogation purposes was an option available with the appropriate approvals; however, it was rarely used at JTF-GTMO. This misunderstanding of the rules and regulations was evident in his reaction to the detainee nakedness at Abu Ghraib. Clearly CIVILIAN-14 was not aware of the fact the SECDEF had withdrawn that authority. (Reference Annex B, Appendix 1, CIVILIAN-14)

(g) (U) In reviewing his activities while at Abu Ghraib, SOLDIER-03 recalled his team submitted two requests to use techniques requiring approvals beyond the team level. In cases requiring such approvals, the request went to the Operations Officer (either MAJ Thompson or MAJ Price) (Operations Officer) and they would approve or disapprove the technique. Those requests requiring a CJTF-7 approval level went to CPT Wood who would forward them for approval. SOLDIER-03 recalled submitting the requests several days in advance of the interrogation to ensure it was approved or disapproved before the interrogation began. His first request (detainee sitting against a wall) was initiated by SOLDIER-21 (analyst) and SOLDIER-30 (interrogator). SOLDIER-03 reviewed the request and forwarded it for approval (SOLDIER-03 could not recall to whom he submitted the request or who had approved it). The request was approved and was implemented. After "observing for a couple of minutes," SOLDIER-03 ended the interrogation. In preparation for another interrogation, the same two females (SOLDIER-21 and SOLDIER-30) submitted a request to interrogate a detainee naked. The request was reviewed by SOLDIER-03 and forwarded to MAJ Price. MAJ Price denies ever approving a naked interrogation. SOLDIER-03 recalled that the technique had been approved, but could not recall by whom. As with the above interrogation, SOLDIER-03 observed the interrogation. After about 15 minutes, he determined the nudity was not a productive technique and terminated the session. SOLDIER-03 never discussed this incident with SOLDIER-28. In his opinion, he had obtained the appropriate authorities and approvals for an "acceptable technique." When asked, SOLDIER-03 recalled hearing about nakedness at GTMO, but never employed the technique. (Reference Annex B, Appendix 1, SOLDIER-03, PRICE).

(h) (U) The JTF-GTMO Team viewed itself as having the mission of setting up and organizing an effective and efficient JIDC staff, and assisting in establishing the Tiger Team

SECRET//NOFORN//X1

SUBJECT: (U) AR 15-6 Investigation of the Abu Ghraib Detention Facility and
205th MI Brigade

concept based on the GTMO model and experience. They did not view their mission as being for training specific interrogation techniques. This is contrary to MG G. Miller's understanding of the mission. There is no evidence that the JTF-GTMO team intentionally introduced any new/prohibited interrogation techniques. Clearly, however, they were operating without a full understanding of the current JTF-GTMO ICRP.

(i) (U) According to SOLDIER-28, no After Action Report (AAR) was prepared for this mobile training team's effort. He provided a post-mission briefing to MG G. Miller upon his return to GTMO. The team's mission was not clearly defined until they arrived at Abu Ghraib. According to MAJ Price (Reference Annex B, Appendix 1, PRICE), the JTF-GTMO Team arrived without a defined charter; however, in his opinion, the team's suggestions were very good and exactly what the Abu Ghraib operation needed. MAJ Price felt that the real changes began to show after COL Pappas arrived on or about 16 November 2003.

(3) (U) Fort Huachuca Mobile Training Team

(a) (U) From 7 to 21 October 2003, a five person ISCT MTT from the USAIC, Fort Huachuca, AZ, was dispatched to conduct an overall assessment of interrogation operations, present training, and provide advice and assistance at the Abu Ghraib JIDC. This course was developed in response to requirements surfaced during interrogation operations at JTF-GTMO, specifically to prepare reserve interrogators and order of battle analysts for deployment to JTF-GTMO. The course consists of a refresher in interrogation procedures and an introduction to strategic debriefing procedures (Reference Annex L, Appendix 4, ISCT POI; ISCT MTT AAR). The MTT consisted of a team chief, CW3 Norris (351B), three 97E interrogators, MSG Filhanessian, SFC Fierro and SFC Walters, and one analyst (96B) SOLDIER-56. The MTT spent the first few days at Abu Ghraib observing ongoing JIDC interrogation operations and establishing a training schedule based on their observations. The training phase lasted approximately five days and focused on interrogation skills and elicitation techniques, cultural awareness, collection management, and use of interpreters. The team discussed the use of Tiger Teams, but did not conduct any training in their use. The Tiger Team concept of teaming an Interrogator and an Analyst together had been previously recommended by the GTMO Assessment Team and was already being employed at Abu Ghraib when the ISCT MTT arrived. Following the training, at least two ISCT MTT Interrogators participated in approximately 19 interrogations and observed several others. The MTT prepared an After Action Report (Reference Annex L, Appendix 4, ISCT MTT AAT, Joint Detainee Interrogation Center, CJTF-7, Abu Ghurayb (sic), Iraq, dated 3 November 2003), which noted eleven issues and provided recommendations for each. The issues mainly concerned screening procedures, interrogation planning and preparation, approaches, questioning, interpreter control, deception detection, and administrative and reporting issues. SFC Filhanessian did recall they had access to the 16 April 2003 SECDEF Memorandum and devoted some time to discussing approach strategies outside

SECRET//NOFORN//X1

62

SUBJECT: (U) AR 15-6 Investigation of the Abu Ghraib Detention Facility and
205th MI Brigade

the ones mentioned in FM 34-52, Intelligence Interrogations, 28 September 1992, like the issue of military working dogs, sleep deprivation, etc., (Reference Annex B, Appendix 1, FILHANESSIAN). According to SOLDIER-25 (Reference Annex B, Appendix 1,SOLDIER25), "A team from Fort Huachuca ... gave us 3 days of classes, including rules of engagement and the use of sleep deprivation and sleep management." The ISCT MTT AAR did not note any incidents of detainee abuse or mistreatment. Three interviewed ISCT MTT members stated that they did not witness, or hear of any incidents of detainee abuse or mistreatment. Neither did they observe or know of any incidents where MI instructed or insinuated that the MP should abuse detainees. Further, MTT members stated that the 519 MI BN interrogators at Abu Ghraib demonstrated experience, "did things by the book," and used techniques that were within the limitations established by FM 34-52 (Interrogation Operations). Some team members, however, expressed some concerns about what appeared to them to be a lack of experience with some of the civilian contracted CACI Interrogators, and the fact that the MTT did not have the opportunity to train and work with some newly arriving contractors (Reference Annex B, Appendix 1, WALTERS; CIVILIAN-07; and FIERRO).

(b) (U) On 21 June 2004, SFC Walters contacted the investigative team via email and indicated he wanted to make additions to his statement (Reference Annex B, Appendix 1, WALTERS 20040621, email). SFC Walters was concerned that as a member of the ISCT MTT, he may have contributed to the abuse at Abu Ghraib. When questioned by CACI employee CIVILIAN-21 for ideas to use to get these prisoners to talk, SFC Walters related several stories about the use of dogs as an inducement, suggesting he (CIVILIAN-21) talk to the MPs about the possibilities. SFC Walters further explained that detainees are most susceptible during the first few hours after capture. "The prisoners are captured by Soldiers, taken from their familiar surroundings, blindfolded and put into a truck and brought to this place (Abu Ghraib); and then they are pushed down a hall with guards barking orders and thrown into a cell, naked; and that not knowing what was going to happen or what the guards might do caused them extreme fear." SFC Walters also suggested CIVILIAN-21 could take some pictures of what seemed to be guards being rough with prisoners...so he could use them to scare the prisoners. Lastly, SFC Walters also shared what he described as a formal, professional prisoner in-processing as he observed it in Bagram (a reference to the detainee operations that had taken place Afghanistan).

(c) (U) On 26 June 2004, during a follow-on interview (Reference Annex B, Appendix 1, WALTERS); SFC Walters confirmed the information he provided in his email. He clarified that his conversation with CIVILIAN-21 occurred before the training was conducted and that he was certain CIVILIAN-21 clearly understood the rules with regard to interrogations. SFC Walters was adamant he had stressed the need to obtain the appropriate authorities before using any of the techniques discussed. SFC Walters knew of no other "off line" conversations between the MTT members and assigned interrogators. SFC Walters said he had related stories he had heard, but did not personally observe. In addressing the ISCT MTT training objectives, SFC

63

SUBJECT: (U) AR 15-6 Investigation of the Abu Ghraib Detention Facility and
205th MI Brigade

Walters noted they (ISCT MTT) did not agree with the JTF-GTMO modus operandi. The (ISCT MTT) felt the use of Tiger Teams wasted limited analytical support. Analysts should support interrogation teams and not be part of the interrogation. This mirrors the opinions of the Abu Ghraib team (Reference Annex B, Appendix 1, WOOD).

(d) (U) Throughout OIF I, USAIC assisted in sending MTTs to all divisional locations within Iraq in order to provide instruction on THT operations, G2X staff functions, and tactical questioning for non-military intelligence Soldiers. Prior to this training, a separate team traveled to Afghanistan and Iraq to provide similar training at Bagram Airfield and Abu Ghraib Detention Facility. This training was the same training provided to OIF units in Iraq that also incorporated lessons learned during that MTT.

k. (U) International Committee of the Red Cross (ICRC)

(1) (U) The ICRC visits to Abu Ghraib have been the source of great concern since the abuses at Abu Ghraib became public knowledge. The ICRC are independent observers who identified abuses to the leadership of Abu Ghraib as well as to CJTF-7. Their allegations were not believed, nor were they adequately investigated.

(2) (U) During the 9-12 and 21-23 October 2003 visits to Abu Ghraib, the ICRC noted that the ill treatment of detainees during interrogation was not systemic, except with regard to persons arrested in connection with suspected security offenses or deemed to have an "intelligence value." These individuals were probably the MI holds. "In these cases, persons deprived of their liberty [and] under supervision of the Military Intelligence were at high risk of being subjected to a variety of harsh treatments. These ranged from insults, threat and humiliations, to both physical and psychological coercion (which in some cases was tantamount to torture) in order to force cooperation with their interrogators (Reference Annex G, Appendix 1, Executive Summary)." The ICRC noted that some detainees in Tier 1A were held naked in their cells, with meals ready to eat (MRE) packing being used to cover their nudity. The ICRC immediately informed the authorities, and the detainees received clothes for the remainder of the ICRC visit. Additionally, the ICRC complained about MI-imposed restrictions on visiting certain security detainees in Camp Vigilant and in Tier 1A. Red Cross delegates were informed they could visit those areas the following day and then only on the basis of a list of detainees and tasks agreed on with Abu Ghraib officials. (Reference Annex G, Appendix 1, TAB B)

(3) (U) The ICRC found a high level of depression, feelings of helplessness, stress, and frustration, especially by those detainees in isolation. Detainees made the following allegations during interviews with the ICRC: threats during interrogation; insults and verbal insults during transfer in Tier 1A; sleep deprivation; walking in the corridors handcuffed and naked, except for female underwear over the head; handcuffing either to the upper bed bars or doors of the cell for

64

SUBJECT: (U) AR 15-6 Investigation of the Abu Ghraib Detention Facility and
205th MI Brigade

3-4 hours. Some detainees presented physical marks and psychological symptoms which were compatible with these allegations. Also noted were brutality upon capture, physical or psychological coercion during interrogation, prolonged isolation, and excessive and disproportionate use of force. (Reference Annex G, Appendix 1, TAB B)

(4) (U) The ICRC made a number of recommendations after the October 2003 visits, including: grant ICRC full and unimpeded access to all detainees; improve the security related to the accommodation structure; clarify and improve conditions of detention and treatment; distribute hygiene items, spare clothes, blankets, etc.; inform detainees of the reason for their detention; implement regular family visits for detainees; and increase recreational and educational activities. (Reference Annex G, Appendix 1, Tab B, ICRC Working Paper, dated 6 November 2003).

(5) (U) LTC Phillabaum, regarding the 9 – 12 October 2003 visit, stated he was told of naked detainees by the ICRC and immediately contacted LTC Jordan. The two went to see the situation first hand. LTC Phillabaum claimed that LTC Jordan acknowledged that it was common practice for some of the detainees to be kept naked in their cells. In November 2003, after having received the written ICRC report, CJTF-7 sent an Australian Judge Advocate officer, MAJ George O'Kane, to Abu Ghraib to meet with LTC Jordan and other officers to craft a response to the ICRC memo. (Reference Annex B, Appendices 1 and 2, PHILLABAUM)

(6) (U) Stemming from those October 2003 visits, the ICRC also made the following request of the Coalition Forces: respect at all times the human dignity, physical integrity, and cultural sensitivity of detainees; set up a system of notification of arrest to the families of detainees; prevent all forms of ill-treatment; respect and protect the dignity of detainees; allow sufficient time for outside activity and exercise; define and apply regulations compatible with international Humanitarian Law; thoroughly investigate violation of international Humanitarian Law; ensure that capturing forces and interment facility personnel are trained to function in a proper manner without resorting to ill-treatment of detainees. (Reference ANNEX G, Appendix 1, Tab A, ICRC Report February 2004)

(7) (U) COL Warren, the CJTF-7 SJA, stated that neither he nor anyone else from CJTF-7 Headquarters was present at Abu Ghraib during the ICRC visit in October 2003. Throughout 2003, all ICRC reports were addressed to the commander or subordinate commanders of the 800 MP BDE. The OSJA received a copy of the reports. Letters on specific topics addressed to LTG Sanchez were given to COL Warren and he would prepare the response for LTG Sanchez. MAJ O'Kane prepared an analysis of the report on 25 November 2003 and the draft was sent to CJTF-7 C2 and the 800 MP BDE for review. On 4 December 2003, a meeting was held at Abu Ghraib, attended by MP, MI, and legal personnel, in order to discuss the report. In mid-December, the draft response was sent by OSJA to the 800 MP BDE for review and coordination. BG

SUBJECT: (U) AR 15-6 Investigation of the Abu Ghraib Detention Facility and 205th MI Brigade

Karpinski signed the response, dated 24 December 2003. (Reference Annex G, Appendix 3, KARPINSKI Letter)

(8) (U) During the 4-8 January 2004 visit, the ICRC expressed special concern over being informed by COL Pappas and COL Warren that they were invoking Article 143 of Geneva Convention IV, thereby denying the ICRC access to eight of the detainees in the interrogation section. Of particular interest was the status of detainee DETAINEE-14, a Syrian national and self-proclaimed Jihadist, who was in Iraq to kill coalition troops. DETAINEE-14 was detained in a totally darkened cell measuring about 2 meters long and less than a meter across, devoid of any window, latrine or water tap, or bedding. On the door the ICRC delegates noticed the inscription "the Gollum," and a picture of the said character from the film trilogy "Lord of the Rings." During the 14-18 March 2004 visit, the ICRC was once again denied access to nine detainees, including DETAINEE-14. They noted that DETAINEE-14 was no longer in the same cell as he was previously, but was still in one of the more "difficult" cells. (Reference Annex G, Appendix 1, ICRC Working Paper, dated 6 November 2003; Appendix 2, ICRC Letter dated February 2004; Appendix 2, Tab B, ICRC Letter dated 25 March 2004)

(9) (U) Article 143, Fourth Geneva Convention, reads in part "Such visits may be prohibited except for reasons of imperative military necessity, and then only for an exceptional and temporary measure." COL Warren and COL Pappas both acknowledge denying access to specified detainees by the ICRC on each of two occasions (in January and March 2004), invoking the above cited provision. The ICRC, in their memorandum of 25 March 2004, acknowledged the right of COL Warren and COL Pappas to invoke the "imperative military necessity clause." It questioned the "exceptional and temporary" nature of the denial of access to DETAINEE-14 on both occasions, however, given that DETAINEE-14 (by the time of the second visit) had been under interrogation for some four months. This was the same DETAINEE-14 that was viewed a "special project" and who was abused by the use of dogs. (See paragraph 5.f.) (Reference Annex B, Appendix 1, PAPPAS, WARREN)

(10) (U) COL Pappas acknowledges in his statement that the ICRC visited Abu Ghraib twice (January and March 2004). He received a copy of the results and noted there were allegations of maltreatment and detainees wearing women's underwear on their heads. He did not believe it. He recalled he might have related to the staff that "this stuff couldn't have been happening." He added that when the ICRC came by the second time (March 2004), he invoked Article 143, preventing the eight detainees in Tier 1A from talking to the ICRC while undergoing active interrogation. COL Pappas states: "COL Warren informed me that I had the authority to do this." (Reference Annex B, Appendices 1 and 2, PAPPAS)

(11) (U) COL Warren also stated that when he saw the ICRC report on naked detainees and detainees wearing women's underwear, he couldn't believe it. He saw the report when he

66

SUBJECT: (U) AR 15-6 Investigation of the Abu Ghraib Detention Facility and
205th MI Brigade

returned to CJTF-7 from leave on 30 November 2003. His office probably had received the report on 16 November 2003. He regrets not having taken the report earlier to LTG Sanchez or MG Wojdakowski. While this would not have prevented the abuse they subsequently discovered (because it had taken place in November 2003), it may have resulted in CID beginning an investigation a month earlier than they did. During the ICRC's next visit to Abu Ghraib, during the period 4-8 January 2004, COL Warren states they invoked Article 143 of the Fourth Geneva Conventions and did not allow the ICRC to have private interviews with eight detainees who were undergoing active interrogations. He did allow the ICRC delegate to see the detainees, observe the conditions of their detention, and obtain their names and Internee Serial Numbers." (Reference Annex B, Appendix 1, WARREN)

(12) (U) LTC Chew, Commander of the 115th MP Battalion (115 MP BN), has stated that although he attended the ICRC out-brief, after the 21-23 October 2003 visits, he never saw or heard of any detainees being stripped or held naked, nor did he ever see a written report from the ICRC. He stated that a doctor with the ICRC team provided information concerning a few detainees having psychological problems and stating that they should be evaluated. ICRC also related charges of handcuffing, nakedness, wearing of female underwear, and sleep deprivation. The ICRC also complained about lack of access to certain detainees, and he discussed the matter with LTC Jordan. He also discussed the allegations made by the ICRC with MAJ Potter, BG Karpinski, and MAJ Cavallero. BG Karpinski does not recall hearing about the report until early December 2003 when it was discussed at CJTF-7 Headquarters with COL Warren. (Reference Annex B, Appendix 1, CHEW, KARPINSKI)

(13) (U) LTC Jordan has stated that after the ICRC visited Abu Ghraib, COL Pappas and BG Karpinski received the final report, but that he did not see the report. When asked by COL Pappas if he had ever seen or heard any rumors of abuse, LTC Jordan told COL Pappas that he (LTC Jordan) had not. He was not aware of COL Pappas ever doing anything concerning the ICRC allegations (Reference Annex B, Appendix 1, JORDAN and Annex B, Appendix 2, JORDAN).

(14) (U) The only response to the ICRC was a letter signed by BG Karpinski, dated 24 December 2003. According to LTC Phillabaum and COL Warren (as quoted above) an Australian Judge Advocate officer, MAJ O'Kane, was the principal drafter of the letter. Attempts to interview MAJ O'Kane were unsuccessful. The Australian Government agreed to have MAJ O'Kane respond to written questions, but as of the time of this report, no response has been received. The section of the BG Karpinski letter pertaining to Abu Ghraib primarily addresses the denial of access to certain detainees by the ICRC. It tends to gloss over, close to the point of denying the inhumane treatment, humiliation, and abuse identified by the ICRC. The letter merely says: Improvement can be made for the provision of clothing, water, and personal hygiene items. (Reference Annex G, Appendix 3, KARPINSKI Letter)

SECRET//NOFORN//X1

SUBJECT: (U) AR 15-6 Investigation of the Abu Ghraib Detention Facility and 205th MI Brigade

5. Summary of Abuses at Abu Ghraib

a. (U) Several types of detainee abuse were identified in this investigation: physical and sexual abuse; improper use of military working dogs; humiliating and degrading treatments; and improper use of isolation.

(1) (U) Physical Abuse. Several Soldiers reported that they witnessed physical abuse of detainees. Some examples include slapping, kicking, twisting the hands of a detainee who was hand-cuffed to cause pain, throwing balls at restrained internees, placing gloved hand over the nose and mouth of an internee to restrict breathing, "poking" at an internee's injured leg, and forcing an internee to stand while handcuffed in such a way as to dislocate his shoulder. These actions are clearly in violation of applicable laws and regulations.

(2) (U) Use of Dogs. The use of military working dogs in a confinement facility can be effective and permissible under AR 190-12 as a means of controlling the internee population. When dogs are used to threaten and terrify detainees, there is a clear violation of applicable laws and regulations. One such impermissible practice was an alleged contest between the two Army dog handlers to see who could make the internees urinate or defecate in the presence of the dogs. An incident of clearly abusive use of the dogs occurred when a dog was allowed in the cell of two male juveniles and allowed to go "nuts." Both juveniles were screaming and crying with the youngest and smallest trying to hide behind the other juvenile. (Reference Annex B, Appendix 1, SOLDIER-17)

(3) (U) Humiliating and Degrading Treatments. Actions that are intended to degrade or humiliate a detainee are prohibited by GC IV, Army policy and the UCMJ. The following are examples of such behavior that occurred at Abu Ghraib, which violate applicable laws and regulations.

(4) (U) Nakedness. Numerous statements, as well as the ICRC report, discuss the seemingly common practice of keeping detainees in a state of undress. A number of statements indicate that clothing was taken away as a punishment for either not cooperating with interrogators or with MPs. In addition, male internees were naked in the presence of female Soldiers. Many of the Soldiers who witnessed the nakedness were told that this was an accepted practice. Under the circumstances, however, the nakedness was clearly degrading and humiliating.

(5) (U) Photographs. A multitude of photographs show detainees in various states of undress, often in degrading positions.

SECRET//NOFORN//X1

68

SUBJECT: (U) AR 15-6 Investigation of the Abu Ghraib Detention Facility and
205th MI Brigade

(6) (U) Simulated Sexual Positions. A number of Soldiers describe incidents where detainees were placed in simulated sexual positions with other internees. Many of these incidents were also photographed.

(7) (U) Improper Use of Isolation. There are some legitimate purposes for the segregation (or isolation) of detainees, specifically to prevent them from sharing interrogation tactics with other detainees or other sensitive information. Article 5 of Geneva Convention IV supports this position by stating that certain individuals can lose their rights of communication, but only when absolute military security requires. The use of isolation at Abu Ghraib was often done as punishment, either for a disciplinary infraction or for failure to cooperate with an interrogation. These are improper uses of isolation and depending on the circumstances amounted to violation of applicable laws and regulations. Isolation could properly be a sanction for a disciplinary infraction if applied through the proper process set out in AR 190-8 and the Geneva Conventions.

(8) (U) Failure to Safeguard Detainees. The Geneva Conventions and Army Regulations require that detainees be "protected against all acts of violence and threats thereof and against insults and public curiosity." Geneva Convention IV, Article 27 and AR 190-8, paragraph 5-1(a)(2). The duty to protect imposes an obligation on an individual who witnesses an abusive act to intervene and stop the abuse. Failure to do so may be a violation of applicable laws and regulations.

(9) (U) Failure to Report Detainee Abuse. The duty to report detainee abuse is closely tied to the duty to protect. The failure to report an abusive incident could result in additional abuse. Soldiers who witness these offenses have an obligation to report the violations under the provision of Article 92, UCMJ. Soldiers who are informed of such abuses also have a duty to report violations. Depending on their position and their assigned duties, the failure to report detainee abuse could support a charge of dereliction of duty, a violation of the UCMJ. Civilian contractors employed as interrogators and translators would also have a duty to report such offenses as they are also bound by the Geneva Conventions and are charged with protecting the internees.

(10) (U) Other traditional prison guard issues were far less clear. MPs are responsible for the clothing of detainees; however, MI interrogators started directing nakedness at Abu Ghraib as early as 16 September 2003 to humiliate and break down detainees. MPs would also sometimes discipline detainees by taking away clothing and putting detainees in cells naked. A severe shortage of clothing during the September, October, November 2003, time frame was frequently mentioned as the reason why people were naked. Removal of clothing and nakedness were being used to humiliate detainees at the same time there was a general level of confusion as to what was allowable in terms of MP disciplinary measures and MI interrogation rules, and what

69

SUBJECT: (U) AR 15-6 Investigation of the Abu Ghraib Detention Facility and
205th MI Brigade

clothing was available. This contributed to an environment that would appear to condone
depravity and degradation rather than the humane treatment of detainees.

b. (U) The original intent by MI leadership (205 MI BDE) was for Tier 1A to be reserved for
MI Holds only. In fact, CPT Wood states in an email dated 7 September 2003, during a visit
from MG Miller and BG Karpinski, that BG Karpinski confirmed "we (MI) have all the iso
(Isolation) cells in the wing we have been working. We only had 10 cells to begin with but that
has grown to the entire wing." LTC Phillabaum also thought that MI had exclusive authority to
house MI holds in Tier 1A. The fact is, however, that a number of those cells were often used by
the MPs to house disciplinary problems. That fact is supported by the testimony of a large
number of people who were there and further supported by the pictures and the detainee records.
In fact, 11 of a total of 25 detainees identified by the CID as victims of abuse were not MI holds
and were not being interrogated by MI. The MPs put the problem detainees (detainees who
required separation from the general population for disciplinary reasons) in Tier 1A because
there was no other place available to isolate them. Neither CPT Wood nor MAJ Williams
appreciated the mixing because it did not allow for a pure MI environment, but the issue never
made its way up to either LTC Phillabaum or to BG Karpinski.

c. (U) The "sleep adjustment" technique was used by MI as soon as the Tier 1A block
opened. This was another source of confusion and misunderstanding between MPs and MI
which contributed to an environment that allowed detainee abuse, as well as its perpetuation for
as long as it continued. Sleep adjustment was brought with the 519 MI BN from Afghanistan. It
is also a method used at GTMO. (See paragraph 3.b.(5)). At Abu Ghraib, however, the MPs
were not trained, nor informed as to how they actually should do the sleep adjustment. The MPs
were just told to keep a detainee awake for a time specified by the interrogator. The MPs used
their own judgment as to how to keep them awake. Those techniques included taking the
detainees out of their cells, stripping them and giving them cold showers. CPT Wood stated she
did not know this was going on and thought the detainees were being kept awake by the MPs
banging on the cell doors, yelling, and playing loud music. When one MI Soldier inquired about
water being thrown on a naked detainee he was told that it was an MP discipline technique.
Again, who was allowed to do what and how exactly they were to do it was totally unclear.
Neither of the communities (MI and MP) knew what the other could and could not do.
(Reference Annex B, Appendix 1, WOOD, JOYNER)

d. (U) This investigation found no evidence of confusion regarding actual physical abuse,
such as hitting, kicking, slapping, punching, and foot stomping. Everyone we spoke to knew it
was prohibited conduct except for one Soldier. (Reference Annex B, Appendix 1, SOLDIER-
29). Physical discomfort from exposure to cold and heat or denial of food and water is not as
clear-cut and can become physical or moral coercion at the extreme. Such abuse did occur at
Abu Ghraib, such as detainees being left naked in their cells during severe cold weather without

SUBJECT: (U) AR 15-6 Investigation of the Abu Ghraib Detention Facility and
205th MI Brigade

blankets. In Tier 1A some of the excesses regarding physical discomfort were being done as directed by MI and some were being done by MPs for reasons not related to interrogation. (See paragraph 5.e.-h.)

e. (U) The physical and sexual abuses of detainees at Abu Ghraib are by far the most serious. The abuses spanned from direct physical assault, such as delivering head blows rendering detainees unconscious, to sexual posing and forced participation in group masturbation. At the extremes were the death of a detainee in OGA custody, an alleged rape committed by a US translator and observed by a female Soldier, and the alleged sexual assault of an unknown female. They were perpetrated or witnessed by individuals or small groups. Such abuse can not be directly tied to a systemic US approach to torture or approved treatment of detainees. The MPs being investigated claim their actions came at the direction of MI. Although self- serving, these claims do have some basis in fact. The climate created at Abu Ghraib provided the opportunity for such abuse to occur and to continue undiscovered by higher authority for a long period of time. What started as undressing and humiliation, stress and physical training (PT), carried over into sexual and physical assaults by a small group of morally corrupt and unsupervised Soldiers and civilians. Twenty-four (24) serious incidents of physical and sexual abuse occurred from 20 September through 13 December 2003. The incidents identified in this investigation include some of the same abuses identified in the MG Taguba investigation; however, this investigation adds several previously unreported events. A direct comparison cannot be made of the abuses cited in the MG Taguba report and this one.

(1) (U) **Incident #1.** On 20 September 2003, two MI Soldiers beat and kicked a passive, cuffed detainee, suspected of involvement in the 20 September 2003 mortar attack on Abu Ghraib that killed two Soldiers. Two Iraqis (male and female) were detained and brought to Abu Ghraib immediately following the attack. MI and the MP Internal Reaction Force (IRF) were notified of the apprehension and dispatched teams to the entry control point to receive the detainees. Upon arrival, the IRF observed two MI Soldiers striking and yelling at the male detainee whom they subsequently "threw" into the back of a High- Mobility Multipurpose Wheeled Vehicle (HMMWV). 1LT Sutton, 320th MP BN IRF intervened to stop the abuse and was told by the MI Soldiers "we are the professionals; we know what we are doing." They refused 1LT Sutton's lawful order to identify themselves. 1LT Sutton and his IRF team (SGT Spiker, SFC Plude) immediately reported this incident, providing sworn statements to MAJ Dinenna, 320 MP BN S3 and LTC Phillabaum, 320 MP BN Commander. 1SG McBride, A/205 MI BN interviewed and took statements from SGT Lawson, identified as striking the detainee, and each MI person present: SSG Hannifan, SSG Cole, SGT Claus, SGT Presnell. While the MP statements all describe abuse at the hands of an unidentified MI person (SGT Lawson), the MI statements all deny any abuse occurred. LTC Phillabaum subsequently reported the incident to the CID who determined the allegation lacked sufficient basis for prosecution. The detainee was interrogated and released that day (involvement in the mortar attack was unlikely); therefore, no

SUBJECT: (U) AR 15-6 Investigation of the Abu Ghraib Detention Facility and 205th MI Brigade

detainee is available to confirm either the MP or MI recollection of events. This incident was not further pursued based on limited data and the absence of additional investigative leads. (Reference Annex B, Appendix 1, DINENNA, LAWSON, MCBRIDE, PHILLABAUM, PLUDE, SPIKER, SUTTON; Annex B, Appendix 2, DINENNA, PHILLABAUM, PLUDE; Annex B, Appendix 3, PLUDE, SPIKER)

(2) (U) **Incident #2.** On 7 October 2003, three MI personnel allegedly sexually assaulted female DETAINEE-29. CIVILIAN-06 (Titan) was the assigned interpreter, but there is no indication he was present or involved. DETAINEE-29 alleges as follows: First, the group took her out of her cell and escorted her down the cellblock to an empty cell. One unidentified Soldier stayed outside the cell (SOLDIER33, A/519 MI BN); while another held her hands behind her back, and the other forcibly kissed her (SOLDIER32, A/519 MI BN). She was escorted downstairs to another cell where she was shown a naked male detainee and told the same would happen to her if she did not cooperate. She was then taken back to her cell, forced to kneel and raise her arms while one of the Soldiers (SOLDIER31, A/519 MI BN) removed her shirt. She began to cry, and her shirt was given back as the Soldier cursed at her and said they would be back each night. CID conducted an investigation and SOLDIER33, SOLDIER32, and SOLDIER31 invoked their rights and refused to provide any statements. DETAINEE-29 identified the three Soldiers as SOLDIER33, SOLDIER32, and SOLDIER31 as the Soldiers who kissed her and removed her shirt. Checks with the 519 MI BN confirmed no interrogations were scheduled for that evening. No record exists of MI ever conducting an authorized interrogation of her. The CID investigation was closed. SOLDIER33, SOLDIER32, and SOLDIER31 each received non-judicial punishment, Field Grade Article 15's, from the Commander, 205 MI BDE, for failing to get authorization to interrogate DETAINEE-29. Additionally, COL Pappas removed them from interrogation operations. (Reference Annex B, Appendix 1, PAPPAS; Annex B, Appendix 2, PAPPAS; Annex B, Appendix 3, DETAINEE-29).

(3) **Incident #3.** On 25 October 2003 detainees DETAINEE-31, DETAINEE-30, and DETAINEE-27 were stripped of their clothing, handcuffed together nude, placed on the ground, and forced to lie on each other and simulate sex while photographs were taken. Six photographs depict this abuse. Results of the CID investigation indicate on several occasions over several days, detainees were assaulted, abused and forced to strip off their clothing and perform indecent acts on each other. DETAINEE-27 provided a sworn statement outlining these abuses. Those present and/or participating in the abuse were CPL Graner, 372 MP CO, SSG Frederick, 372 MP CO, SPC England, 372 MP CO, SPC Harman, 372 MP CO, SOLDIER34, 372 MP CO, CIVILIAN-17, Titan Corp., SOLDIER-24, B/325 MI BN, SOLDIER19, 325 MI BN, and SOLDIER10, 325 MI BN. SOLDIER-24 claimed he accompanied SOLDIER10 to the Hard Site the evening of 25 October 2003 to see what was being done to the three detainees suspected of raping a young male detainee. SOLDIER-10 appeared to have foreknowledge of the abuse, possibly from his friendship with SPC Harman, a 372 MP CO MP. SOLDIER-24 did not believe

72

SUBJECT: (U) AR 15-6 Investigation of the Abu Ghraib Detention Facility and
205th MI Brigade

the abuse was directed by MI and these individuals were not interrogation subjects. PFC
England, however, claimed "MI Soldiers instructed them (MPs) to rough them up." When
SOLDIER-24 arrived the detainees were naked, being yelled at by an MP through a megaphone.
The detainees were forced to crawl on their stomachs and were handcuffed together. SOLDIER-
24 observed SOLDIER-10 join in the abuse with CPL Graner and SSG Frederick. All three
made the detainees act as though they were having sex. He observed SOLDIER-19 dump water
on the detainees from a cup and throw a foam football at them. SOLDIER-24 described what he
saw to SOLDIER-25, B/321 MI BN, who reported the incident to SGT Joyner, 372 MP CO.
SGT Joyner advised SOLDIER-25 he would notify his NCOIC and later told SOLDIER-25 "he
had taken care of it." SOLDIER-25 stated that a few days later both she and SOLDIER24 told
SOLDIER-22 of the incident. SOLDIER-22 subsequently failed to report what he was told.
SOLDIER-25 did not report the abuse through MI channels because she felt it was an MP matter
and would be handled by them.

(U) This is a clear incident of direct MI personnel involvement in detainee abuse;
however, it does not appear to be based on MI orders. The three detainees were incarcerated for
criminal acts and were not of intelligence interest. This incident was most likely orchestrated by
MP personnel (CPL Graner, SSG Frederick, SOLDIER34, SPC Harman, PFC England), with the
MI personnel (SOLDIER-19, SOLDIER-10, and SOLDIER-24, CIVILIAN-17, and another
unidentified interpreter) joining in and/or observing the abuse. (Reference Annex B, Appendix
1, JOYNER, SOLDIER-19, CIVILIAN-17, SOLDIER-25; Annex B, Appendix 3, SOLDIER34,
ENGLAND, HARMAN, DETAINEE-31, DETAINEE-30, DETAINEE-27; Annex I, Appendix
1, Photographs M36-41).

(4) (U) **Incident #4.** DETAINEE-08, arrived at Abu Ghraib on 27 October 2003 and was
subsequently sent to the Hard Site. DETAINEE-08 claims when he was sent to the Hard Site, he
was stripped of his clothing for six days. He was then given a blanket and remained with only
the blanket for three more days. DETAINEE-08 stated the next evening he was transported by
CPL Graner, 372 MP CO MP, to the shower room, which was commonly used for interrogations.
When the interrogation ended, his female interrogator left, and DETAINEE-08 claims CPL
Graner and another MP, who meets the description of SSG Fredrick, then threw pepper in
DETAINEE-08's face and beat him for half an hour. DETAINEE-08 recalled being beaten with
a chair until it broke, hit in the chest, kicked, and choked until he lost consciousness. On other
occasions DETAINEE-08 recalled that CPL Graner would throw his food into the toilet and say
"go take it and eat it." DETAINEE-08's claims of abuse do not involve his interrogator(s) and
appear to have been committed by CPL Graner and SSG Frederick, both MPs. Reviewing the
interrogation reports; however, suggests a correlation between this abuse and his interrogations.
DETAINEE-08's interrogator for his first four interrogations was SOLDIER-29, a female, and
almost certainly the interrogator he spoke of. Her Analyst was SOLDIER-10. In the first
interrogation report they concluded he was lying and recommended a "fear up" approach if he
continued to lie. Following his second interrogation it was recommended DETAINEE-08 be

SUBJECT: (U) AR 15-6 Investigation of the Abu Ghraib Detention Facility and
205th MI Brigade

moved to isolation (the Hard Site) as he continued "to be untruthful." Ten days later, a period roughly correlating with DETAINEE-08's claim of being without clothes and/or a blanket for nine days before his beating, was interrogated for a third time. The interrogation report references his placement in "the hole," a small lightless isolation closet, and the "Mutt and Jeff" interrogation technique being employed. Both techniques as they were used here were abusive and unauthorized. According to the report, the interrogators "let the MPs yell at him" and upon their return, "used a fear down," but "he was still holding back." The following day he was interrogated again and the report annotates "use a direct approach with a reminder of the unpleasantness that occurred the last time he lied." Comparing the interrogation reports with DETAINEE-08's recollections, it is likely the abuse he describes occurred between his third and forth interrogations and that his interrogators were aware of the abuse, the "unpleasantness." SGT Adams stated that SOLDIER-29 and SSG Frederick had a close personal relationship and it is plausible she had CPL Graner and SSG Frederick "soften up this detainee" as they have claimed "MI" told them to do on several, unspecified, occasions (Reference Annex B, Appendix 1, ADAMS, SOLDIER-29; Annex B, Appendix 3, DETAINEE-08; Annex I, Appendix 4, DETAINEE-08).

(5) (U) **Incident #5.** In October 2003, DETAINEE-07, reported alleged multiple incidents of physical abuse while in Abu Ghraib. DETAINEE-07 was an MI Hold and considered of potentially high value. He was interrogated on 8, 21, and 29 October; 4 and 23 November and 5 December 2003. DETAINEE-07's claims of physical abuse (hitting) started on his first day of arrival. He was left naked in his cell for extended periods, cuffed in his cell in stressful positions ("High cuffed"), left with a bag over his head for extended periods, and denied bedding or blankets. DETAINEE-07 described being made to "bark like a dog, being forced to crawl on his stomach while MPs spit and urinated on him, and being struck causing unconsciousness." On another occasion DETAINEE-07 was tied to a window in his cell and forced to wear women's underwear on his head. On yet another occasion, DETAINEE-07 was forced to lie down while MPs jumped onto his back and legs. He was beaten with a broom and a chemical light was broken and poured over his body. DETAINEE-04 witnessed the abuse with the chem-light. During this abuse a police stick was used to sodomize DETAINEE-07 and two female MPs were hitting him, throwing a ball at his penis, and taking photographs. This investigation surfaced no photographic evidence of the chemical light abuse or sodomy. DETAINEE-07 also alleged that CIVILIAN-17, MP Interpreter, Titan Corp., hit DETAINEE-07 once, cutting his ear to an extent that required stitches. He told SOLDIER-25, analyst, B/321 MI BN, about this hitting incident during an interrogation. SOLDIER-25 asked the MPs what had happened to the detainee's ear and was told he had fallen in his cell. SOLDIER-25 did not report the detainee's abuse. SOLDIER-25 claimed the detainee's allegation was made in the presence of CIVILIAN-21, Analyst/Interrogator, CACI, which CIVILIAN-21 denied hearing this report. Two photos taken at 2200 hours, 1 November 2003 depict a detainee with stitches in his ear; however, we could not confirm the photo was DETAINEE-07. Based on the details provided by the detainee and the

74

SUBJECT: (U) AR 15-6 Investigation of the Abu Ghraib Detention Facility and
205th MI Brigade

close correlation to other known MP abuses, it is highly probable DETAINEE-07's allegations are true. SOLDIER-25 failed to report the detainee's allegation of abuse. His statements and available photographs do not point to direct MI involvement. However, MI interest in this detainee, his placement in Tier 1A of the Hard Site, and initiation of the abuse once he arrived there, combine to create a circumstantial connection to MI (knowledge of or implicit tasking of the MPs to "set conditions") which are difficult to ignore. MI should have been aware of what was being done to this detainee based on the frequency of interrogations and high interest in his intelligence value. (Reference Annex B, Appendix 1, SOLDIER-25, CIVILIAN-21; Annex B, Appendix 3, DETAINEE-04, DETAINEE-07; Annex I, Appendix 1, Photographs M54-55).

(6) (U) **Incident #6**. DETAINEE-10 and DETAINEE-12 claimed that they and "four Iraqi Generals, were abused upon their arrival at the Hard Site. DETAINEE-10 was documented in MP records as receiving a 1.5 inch laceration on his chin, the result of his resisting an MP transfer. His injuries are likely those captured in several photographs of an unidentified detainee with a lacerated chin and bloody clothing which were taken on 14 November, a date coinciding with his transfer. DETAINEE-12 claimed he was slammed to the ground, punched, and forced to crawl naked to his cell with a sandbag over his head. These two detainees as well as the other four (DETAINEE-20, DETAINEE-19, DETAINEE-22, DETAINEE-21) were all high value Iraqi General Officers or senior members of the Iraqi Intelligence Service. MP logs from the Hard Site indicate they attempted to incite a riot in Camp Vigilant while being transferred to the Hard Site. There is no documentation of what occurred at Camp Vigilant or of detainees receiving injuries. When DETAINEE-10 was in-processed into the Hard Site, he was resisting and was pushed against the wall. At that point the MPs noticed blood coming from under his hood and they discovered the laceration on his chin. A medical corpsman was immediately called to suture the detainee's chin. These events are all documented, indicating the injury occurred before the detainee's arrival at the Hard Site and that he received prompt medical attention. When, where, and by whom this detainee suffered his injuries could not be determined nor could an evaluation be made of whether it constituted "reasonable force" in conjunction with a riot. Our interest in this incident stems from MP logs concerning DETAINEE-10 indicating MI provided direction about his treatment. CPL Graner wrote an entry indicating he was told by SFC Joyner, who was in turn told by LTC Jordan, to "Strip them out and PT them." Whether "strip out" meant to remove clothing or to isolate we couldn't determine. Whether "PT them" meant physical stress or abuse can't be determined. The vagueness of this order could, however, have led to any subsequent abuse. The alleged abuse, injury, and harsh treatment correlating with the detainees' transfer to MI hold also suggest MI could have provided direction or MP could have been given the perception they should abuse or "soften up detainees," however, there is no clear proof. (Reference Annex B, Appendix 1, JORDAN, JOYNER; Annex C).

(7) (U) **Incident #7**. On 4 November 2003, a CIA detainee, DETAINEE-28 died in custody in Tier 1B. Allegedly, a Navy SEAL Team had captured him during a joint TF-121/CIA

75

SUBJECT: (U) AR 15-6 Investigation of the Abu Ghraib Detention Facility and
205th MI Brigade

mission. DETAINEE-28 was suspected of having been involved in an attack against the ICRC and had numerous weapons with him at the time of his apprehension. He was reportedly resisting arrest, and a SEAL Team member butt-stroked him on the side of the head to suppress the threat he posed. CIA representatives brought DETAINEE-28 into Abu Ghraib sometime around 0430 to 0530 without notifying JIDC Operations, in accordance with a supposed verbal agreement with the CIA. While all the details of DETAINEE-28's death are still not known (CIA, DOJ, and CID have yet to complete and release the results of their investigations), SPC Stevanus, an MP on duty at the Hard Site at the time DETAINEE-28 was brought in, stated that two CIA representatives came in with DETAINEE-28 and he was placed in a shower room (in Tier 1B). About 30 to 45 minutes later, SPC Stevanus was summoned to the shower stall, and when he arrived, DETAINEE-28 appeared to be dead. SPC Stevanus removed the sandbag which was over DETAINEE-28's head and checked for the detainee's pulse. He found none. He un-cuffed DETAINEE-28 called for medical assistance, and notified his chain of command. LTC Jordan stated that he was informed of the death shortly thereafter, at approximately 0715 hours. LTC Jordan arrived at the Hard Site and talked to CIVILIAN03, an Iraqi prison medical doctor, who informed him DETAINEE-28 was dead. LTC Jordan stated that DETAINEE-28 was in the Tier 1B shower stall, face down, handcuffed with his hands behind his back. LTC Jordan's version of the handcuffs conflicts with SPC Stevanus' account that he un-cuffed DETAINEE-28. This incident remains under CID and CIA investigation.

(U) A CIA representative identified only as "OTHER AGENCY EMPLOYEE-01" was present, along with several MPs and US medical staff. LTC Jordan recalled that it was "OTHER AGENCY EMPLOYEE-01" who uncuffed DETAINEE-28 and the body was turned over. LTC Jordan stated that he did not see any blood anywhere, except for a small spot where DETAINEE-28's head was touching the floor. LTC Jordan notified COL Pappas (205 MI BDE Commander), and "OTHER AGENCY EMPLOYEE-01" said he would notify "OTHER AGENCY EMPLOYEE-02," his CIA supervisor. Once "OTHER AGENCY EMPLOYEE-02" arrived, he stated he would call Washington, and also requested that DETAINEE-28's body be held in the Hard Site until the following day. The body was placed in a body bag, packed in ice, and stored in the shower area. CID was notified and the body was removed from Abu Ghraib the next day on a litter to make it appear as if DETAINEE-28 was only ill, thereby not drawing the attention of the Iraqi guards and detainees. The body was transported to the morgue at BIAP for an autopsy, which concluded that DETAINEE-28 died of a blood clot in the head, a likely result of injuries he sustained while resisting apprehension. There is no indication or accusations that MI personnel were involved in this incident except for the removal of the body. (Reference Annex B, Appendix 1, JORDAN, PAPPAS, PHILLABAUM, SNIDER, STEVANUS, THOMPSON; Annex I, Appendix 1, Photographs C5-21, D5-11, M65-69).

(8) (U) **Incident #8**. On 20 October 2003, DETAINEE-03, was allegedly stripped and physically abused for sharpening a toothbrush to make a shank (knife-like weapon).

76

SUBJECT: (U) AR 15-6 Investigation of the Abu Ghraib Detention Facility and
205th MI Brigade

DETAINEE-03 claimed the toothbrush was not his. An MP log book entry by SSG Frederick, 372 MPs, directed DETAINEE-03 to be stripped in his cell for six days. DETAINEE-03 claimed he was told his clothing and mattress would be taken away as punishment. The next day he claims he was cuffed to his cell door for several hours. He claims he was taken to a closed room where he had cold water poured on him and his face was forced into someone's urine. DETAINEE-03 claimed he was then beaten with a broom and spat upon, and a female Soldier stood on his legs and pressed a broom against his anus. He described getting his clothes during the day from SGT Joyner and having them taken away each night by CPL Graner for the next three days. DETAINEE-03 was an MI Hold but was not interrogated between 16 September and 2 November 2003. It is plausible his interrogators would be unaware of the alleged abuse and DETAINEE-03 made no claim he informed them (Reference Annex B, Appendix 3, DETAINEE-03).

(9) (U) **Incident #9**. Three photographs taken on 25 October 2003 depicted PFC England, 372 MP CO, holding a leash which was wrapped around an unidentified detainee's neck. Present in the photograph is SPC Ambuhl who was standing to the side watching. PFC England claimed in her initial statement to CID that CPL Graner had placed the tie-down strap around the detainee's neck and then asked her to pose for the photograph. There is no indication of MI involvement or knowledge of this incident (Reference Annex E, CID Report and Reference Annex I, Appendix 1, Photographs M33-35).

(10) (U) **Incident #10**. Six Photographs of DETAINEE-15, depict him standing on a box with simulated electrical wires attached to his fingers and a hood over his head. These photographs were taken between 2145 and 2315 on 4 November 2003. DETAINEE-15 described a female making him stand on the box, telling him if he fell off he would be electrocuted, and a "tall black man" as putting the wires on his fingers and penis. From the CID investigation into abuse at Abu Ghraib it was determined SGT J. Davis, SPC Harman, CPL Graner, and SSG Frederick, 372 MP CO, were present during this abuse. DETAINEE-15 was not an MI Hold and it is unlikely MI had knowledge of this abuse (Reference Annex B, Appendix 3, DETAINEE-15; Annex I, Appendix 1, Photographs C1-2, D19-21, M64).

(11) (U) **Incident #11**. Twenty-nine photos taken between 2315 and 0024, on 7 and 8 November 2003 depict seven detainees (DETAINEE-17, DETAINEE-16, DETAINEE-24, DETAINEE-23, DETAINEE-26, DETAINEE-01, DETAINEE-18) who were physically abused, placed in a pile and forced to masturbate. Present in some of these photographs are CPL Graner and SPC Harman. The CID investigation into these abuses identified SSG Frederick, CPL Graner, SGT J. Davis, SPC Ambuhl, SPC Harman, SPC Sivits, and PFC England; all MPs, as involved in the abuses which occurred. There is no evidence to support MI personnel involvement in this incident. CID statements from PFC England, SGT J. Davis, SPC Sivits, SPC Wisdom, SPC Harman, DETAINEE-17, DETAINEE-01, and DETAINEE-16 detail that the

SUBJECT: (U) AR 15-6 Investigation of the Abu Ghraib Detention Facility and
205th MI Brigade

detainees were stripped, pushed into a pile, and jumped on by SGT J. Davis, CPL Graner, and SSG Frederick. They were photographed at different times by SPC Harman, SPC Sivits, and SSG Frederick. The detainees were subsequently posed sexually, forced to masturbate, and "ridden like animals." CPL Graner knocked at least one detainee unconscious and SSG Frederick punched one so hard in the chest that he couldn't breath and a medic was summoned. SSG Frederick initiated the masturbation and forced the detainees to hit each other. PFC England stated she observed SSG Frederick strike a detainee in the chest during these abuses. The detainee had difficulty breathing and a medic, SOLDIER-01, was summoned. SOLDIER-01 treated the detainee and while in the Hard Site observed the "human pyramid" of naked detainees with bags over their heads. SOLDIER-01 failed to report this abuse. These detainees were not MI Holds and MI involvement in this abuse has not been alleged nor is it likely. SOLDIER-29 reported seeing a screen saver for a computer in the Hard Site that depicted several naked detainees stacked in a "pyramid." She also once observed, unrelated to this incident, CPL Graner slap a detainee. She stated that she didn't report the picture of naked detainees to MI because she did not see it again and also did not report the slap because she didn't consider it abuse (Reference Annex B, Appendix 1, SOLDIER-29; Annex B, Appendix 3, DETAINEE-01, DETAINEE-17, DETAINEE-16, ENGLAND, DAVIS, HARMAN,SIVITS, WISDOM; Annex B, Appendix 3, TAB A, SOLDIER-01, and Annex I, Appendix 1, Photographs C24-42, D22-25, M73-77, M87).

(12) (U) **Incident #12**. A photograph taken circa 27 December 2003, depicts a naked DETAINEE-14, apparently shot with a shotgun in his buttocks. This photograph could not be tied to a specific incident, detainee, or allegation and MI involvement is indeterminate (Reference Annex I, Appendix 1, Photographs D37-38, H2, M111).

(13) (U) **Incident #13**. Three photographs taken on 29 November 2003, depict an unidentified detainee dressed only in his underwear, standing with each foot on a separate box, and bent over at the waist. This photograph could not be tied to a specific incident, detainee, or allegation and MI involvement is indeterminate. (Reference Annex I, Appendix1, Photographs D37-38, M111)

(14) (U) **Incident #14**. An 18 November 2003 photograph depicts a detainee dressed in a shirt or blanket lying on the floor with a banana inserted into his anus. This as well as several others show the same detainee covered in feces, with his hands encased in sandbags, or tied in foam and between two stretchers. These are all identified as DETAINEE-25 and were determined by CID investigation to be self-inflicted incidents. Even so, these incidents constitute abuse; a detainee with a known mental condition should not have been provided the banana or photographed. The detainee has a severe mental problem and the restraints depicted in these photographs were allegedly used to prevent the detainee from sodomizing himself and assaulting himself and others with his bodily fluids. He was known for inserting various objects

78

SUBJECT: (U) AR 15-6 Investigation of the Abu Ghraib Detention Facility and
205th MI Brigade

into his rectum and for consuming and throwing his urine and feces. MI had no association with this detainee (Reference Annex C; Annex E; Annex I, Appendix 1, Photographs, C22-23, D28-36, D39, M97-99, M105-110, M131-133).

(15) (U) **Incident #15.** On 26 or 27 November 2003, SOLDIER-15, 66 MI GP, observed CIVILIAN-11, a CACI contractor, interrogating an Iraqi policeman. During the interrogation, SSG Frederick, 372 MP CO, alternated between coming into the cell and standing next to the detainee and standing outside the cell. CIVILIAN-11 would ask the policeman a question stating that if he did not answer, he would bring SSG Frederick back into the cell. At one point, SSG Frederick put his hand over the policeman's nose, not allowing him to breathe for a few seconds. At another point SSG Frederick used a collapsible nightstick to push and possibly twist the policeman's arm, causing pain. When SSG Frederick walked out of the cell, he told SOLDIER-15 he knew ways to do this without leaving marks. SOLDIER-15 did not report the incident. The interpreter utilized for this interrogation was CIVILIAN-16. (Reference Annex B, Appendix 1, SOLDIER-15)

(16) (U) **Incident #16.** On an unknown date, SGT Hernandez, an analyst, observed CIVILIAN-05, a CACI contractor, grab a detainee from the back of a High-Mobility, Multipurpose, Wheeled Vehicle (HMMWV) and drop him on the ground. CIVILIAN-05 then dragged the detainee into an interrogation booth. The detainee was handcuffed the entire time. When the detainee tried to get up to his knees, CIVILIAN-05 would force him to fall. SGT Hernandez reported the incident to CID but did not report it in MI channels. (Reference Annex B, Appendix 1, HERNANDEZ)

(17) (U) **Incident #17.** A 30 November 2003, MP Log entry described an unidentified detainee found in a cell covered in blood. This detainee had assaulted CPL Graner, 372 MP CO, while they moved him to an isolation cell in Tier 1A. CPL Graner and CPL Kamauf, subdued the detainee, placed restraints on him and put him in an isolation cell. At approximately 0320 hours, 30 November 2003, after hearing banging on the isolation cell door, the cell was checked and the detainee was found in the cell standing by the door covered in blood. This detainee was not an MI Hold and there is no record of MI association with this incident or detainee. (Reference Annex I, Appendix 1, Photographs M115-129, M134).

(18) (U) **Incident #18.** On approximately 12 or 13 December 2003, DETAINEE-06 claimed numerous abuse incidents against US Soldiers. DETAINEE-06 was a Syrian foreign fighter and self-proclaimed Jihadist who came to Iraq to kill Coalition troops. DETAINEE-06 stated the Soldiers supposedly retaliated against him when he returned to the Hard Site after being released from the hospital following a shooting incident in which he attempted to kill US Soldiers. DETAINEE-06 had a pistol smuggled into him by an Iraqi Policeman and used that pistol to try to kill US personnel working in the Hard Site on 24 November 2003. An MP

SUBJECT: (U) AR 15-6 Investigation of the Abu Ghraib Detention Facility and
205th MI Brigade

returned fire and wounded DETAINEE-06. Once DETAINEE-06 ran out of ammunition, he surrendered and was transported to the hospital. DETAINEE-06 claimed CIVILIAN-21 visited him in the hospital and threatened him with terrible torture upon his return. DETAINEE-06 claimed that upon his return to the Hard Site, he was subjected to various threats and abuses which included Soldiers threatening to torture and kill him, being forced to eat pork and having liquor put in his mouth, having a "very hot" substance put in his nose and on his forehead, having the guards hit his "broken" leg several times with a solid plastic stick, being forced to "curse" his religion, being urinated on, being hung by handcuffs from the cell door for hours, being "smacked" on the back of the head, and "allowing dogs to try to bite" him. This claim was substantiated by a medic, SOLDIER-20, who was called to treat a detainee (DETAINEE-06) who had been complaining of pain. When SOLDIER-20 arrived DETAINEE-06 was cuffed to the upper bunk so that he could not sit down and CPL Graner was poking at his wounded legs with an asp with DETAINEE-06 crying out in pain. SOLDIER-20 provided pain medication and departed. He returned the following day to find DETAINEE-06 again cuffed to the upper bunk and a few days later returned to find him cuffed to the cell door with a dislocated shoulder. SOLDIER-20 failed to either stop or report this abuse. DETAINEE-06 also claimed that prior to the shooting incident, which he described as when "I got shot with several bullets" without mentioning that he ever fired a shot, he was threatened "every one or two hours... with torture and punishment", was subjected to sleep deprivation by standing up "for hours and hours", and had a "black man" tell him he would rape DETAINEE-06 on two occasions. Although DETAINEE-06 stated that CPL Graner led "a number of Soldiers" into his cell, he also stated that he had never seen CPL Graner beat a prisoner. These claims are from a detainee who attempted to kill US service members. While it is likely some Soldiers treated DETAINEE-06 harshly upon his return to the Hard Site, DETAINEE-06's accusations are potentially the exaggerations of a man who hated Americans. (Reference Annex B, Appendix 3, DETAINEE-06, SOLDIER-20).

(19) (U) **Incident #19**. SGT Adams, 470 MI GP, stated that sometime between 4 and 13 December 2003, several weeks after the shooting of "a detainee who had a pistol" (DETAINEE-06), she heard he was back from the hospital, and she went to check on him because he was one of the MI Holds she interrogated. She found DETAINEE-06 without clothes or blanket, his wounds were bleeding and he had a catheter on without a bag. The MPs told her they had no clothes for the detainee. SGT Adams ordered the MPs to get the detainee some clothes and went to the medical site to get the doctor on duty. The doctor (Colonel) asked what SGT Adams wanted and was asked if he was aware the detainee still had a catheter on. The Colonel said he was, the Combat Army Surgical Hospital (CASH) had made a mistake, and he couldn't remove it because the CASH was responsible for it. SGT Adams told him this was unacceptable, he again refused to remove it and stated the detainee was due to go back to the CASH the following day. SGT Adams asked if he had ever heard of the Geneva Conventions, and the Colonel responded "fine Sergeant, you do what you have to do, I am going back to bed."

80

SUBJECT: (U) AR 15-6 Investigation of the Abu Ghraib Detention Facility and
205th MI Brigade

(U) It is apparent from this incident that DETAINEE06 did not receive proper medical treatment, clothing or bedding. The "Colonel" has not been identified in this investigation, but efforts continue. LTC Akerson was chief of the medical team for "security holds" at Abu Ghraib from early October to late December 2003. He treated DETAINEE06 following his shooting and upon his return from the hospital. He did not recall such an incident or DETAINEE06 having a catheter. It is possible SGT Adams was taken to a different doctor that evening. She asked and was told the doctor was a Colonel, not a Lieutenant Colonel and is confident she can identify the Colonel from a photograph. LTC Akerson characterized the medical records as being exceptional at Abu Ghraib, however, the records found by this investigation were poor and in most cases non-existent. (Reference Annex B, Appendix 1, ADAMS, AKERSON; Annex B, Appendix 3, DETAINEE-06).

(20) (U) **Incident #20**. During the fall of 2003, a detainee stated that another detainee, named DETAINEE-09, was stripped, forced to stand on two boxes, had water poured on him and had his genitals hit with a glove. Additionally, the detainee was handcuffed to his cell door for a half day without food or water. The detainee making the statement did not recall the exact date or participants. Later, "Assad" was identified as DETAINEE-09, who stated that on 5 November 2003 he was stripped naked, beaten, and forced to crawl on the floor. He was forced to stand on a box and was hit in his genitals. The participants in this abuse could not be determined. MI involvement is indeterminate. (Reference Annex B, Appendix 3, DETAINEE-09; Annex I, Appendix 1, Photographs D37-38, M111)

(21) (U) **Incident #21**. Circa October 2003, CIVILIAN-17, an interpreter of the Titan Corporation, observed the following incident: CPL Graner, 372 MP CO, pushed a detainee, identified as one of the "three stooges" or "three wise men", into a wall, lacerating the detainee's chin. CIVILIAN-17 specifically stated the detainee was pushed into a wall and "busted his chin." A medic, SGT Wallin, stated he was summoned to stitch the detainee and treated a 2.5 inch laceration on the detainee's chin requiring 13 stitches. SGT Wallin did not know how the detainee was injured. Later that evening, CPL Graner took photos of the detainee. CPL Graner was identified in another incident where he stitched an injured detainee in the presence of medics. There is no indication of MI involvement, knowledge, or direction of this abuse. (Reference Annex B, Appendix 1,CIVILIAN-17; Annex B, Appendix 3,CIVILIAN-17, WALLIN, DETAINEE-02; Annex I, Appendix 1, Photographs M88-96).

(22) (U) **Incident #22**. On an unknown date, an interpreter named "CIVILIAN-01" allegedly raped a 15-18 year old male detainee according to DETAINEE-05. DETAINEE-05 heard screaming and climbed to the top of his cell door to see over a sheet covering the door of the cell where the abuse was occurring. DETAINEE-05 observed CIVILIAN-01, who was wearing a military uniform, raping the detainee. A female Soldier was taking pictures.

SUBJECT: (U) AR 15-6 Investigation of the Abu Ghraib Detention Facility and
205th MI Brigade

DETAINEE-05 described CIVILIAN-01 as possibly Egyptian, "not skinny or short," and effeminate. The date and participants of this alleged rape could not be confirmed. No other reporting supports DETAINEE-05's allegation, nor have photographs of the rape surfaced. A review of all available records could not identify a translator by the name of CIVILIAN-01. DETAINEE05's description of the interpreter partially matches CIVILIAN-17, Interpreter, Titan Corp. CIVILIAN-17 is a large man, believed by several witnesses to be homosexual, and of Egyptian extraction. CIVILIAN-17 functioned as an interpreter for a Tactical HUMINT Team at Abu Ghraib, but routinely provided translation for both MI and MP. CID has an open investigation into this allegation. (Reference Annex B, Appendix 3, DETAINEE-05)

(23) (U) **Incident #23**. On 24 November 2003, a US Army officer, CPT Brinson, MP, allegedly beat and kicked a detainee. This is one of three identified abuses associated with the 24 November shooting. A detainee obtained a pistol from Iraqi police guards, shot an MP and was subsequently shot and wounded. During a subsequent search of the Hard Site and interrogation of detainees, SGT Spiker, 229 MP CO, a member of the Abu Ghraib Internal Reaction Force (IRF), observed an Army Captain dragging an unidentified detainee in a choke hold, throwing him against a wall, and kicking him in the mid-section. SPC Polak, 229 MP CO, IRF was also present in the Hard Site and observed the same abuse involving two Soldiers and a detainee. The detainee was lying on his stomach with his hands cuffed behind his back and a bag over his head. One Soldier stood next to him with the barrel of a rifle pressed against the detainee's head. The other Soldier was kneeling next to the detainee punching him in the back with a closed fist. The Soldier then stood up and kicked the detainee several times. The Soldier inflicting the beating was described as a white male with close cropped blond hair. SPC Polak saw this Soldier a few days later in full uniform, identifying him as a Captain, but could not see his name. Both SPC Polak and SGT Spiker reported this abuse to their supervisors, SFC Plude and 1LT Sutton, 372 MP CO. Photos of company grade officers at Abu Ghraib during this time were obtained and shown to SPC Polak and SGT Spiker, who positively identified the "Captain" as CPT Brinson. This incident was investigated by CID and the assault was determined to be unfounded; a staged event to protect the fact the detainee was a cooperative MP Source. (Reference Annex B, Appendix 1, PLUDE, POLAK, SPIKER, SUTTON; Annex B, Appendix 3, PLUDE, SUTTON; Annex E, Appendix 5, CID Report of Investigation 0005-04-CID149-83131)

(24) (U) **Incident #24**. A photograph created circa early December 2003 depicts an unidentified detainee being interrogated by CIVILIAN-11, CACI, Interrogator, and CIVILIAN-16, Titan, linguist. The detainee is squatting on a chair which is an unauthorized stress position. Having the detainee on a chair which is a potentially unsafe situation, and photographing the detainee are violations of the ICRP. (Reference Annex I, Appendix 2, Photograph "Stress Position").

82

SUBJECT: (U) AR 15-6 Investigation of the Abu Ghraib Detention Facility and
205th MI Brigade

f. (U) Incidents of Detainee Abuse Using Dogs. (U) Abusing detainees with dogs started almost immediately after the dogs arrived at Abu Ghraib on 20 November 2003. By that date, abuses of detainees was already occurring and the addition of dogs was just one more abuse device. Dog Teams were brought to Abu Ghraib as a result of recommendations from MG G. Miller's assessment team from JTF-GTMO. MG G. Miller recommended dogs as beneficial for detainee custody and control issues, especially in instances where there were large numbers of detainees and few guards to help reduce the risk of detainee demonstrations or acts of violence, as at Abu Ghraib. MG G. Miller never recommended, nor were dogs used for interrogations at GTMO. The dog teams were requested by COL Pappas, Commander, 205 MI BDE. COL Pappas never understood the intent as described by MG G. Miller. Interrogations at Abu Ghraib were also influenced by several documents that spoke of exploiting the Arab fear of dogs: a 24 January 2003 "CJTF 180 Interrogation Techniques," an 11 October 2002 JTF 170 "Counter-Resistance Strategies," and a 14 September 2003 CJTF-7 ICRP. Once the dogs arrived, there was controversy over who "owned" the dogs. It was ultimately decided that the dogs would be attached to the Internal Reaction Force (IRF). The use of dogs in interrogations to "fear up" detainees was generally unquestioned and stems in part from the interrogation techniques and counter-resistance policy distributed from CJTF 180, JTF 170 and CJTF-7. It is likely the confusion about using dogs partially stems from the initial request for dog teams by MI, not MPs, and their presence being associated with MG G. Miller's visit. Most military intelligence personnel believed that the use of dogs in interrogations was a "non-standard" technique which required approval, and most also believed that approval rested with COL Pappas. COL Pappas also believed, incorrectly, that he had such authority delegated to him from LTG Sanchez. COL Pappas's belief likely stemmed in part from the changing ICRP. The initial policy was published on 14 September 2003 and allowed the use of dogs subject to approval by LTG Sanchez. On 12 October 2003, these were amended to eliminate several techniques due to CENTCOM objections. After the 12 October 2003 amendment, the ICRP safeguards allowed that dogs present at interrogations were to be muzzled and under the control of a handler. COL Pappas did not recall how he got the authority to employ dogs; just that he had it. (Reference Annex B, Appendix 1, G. MILLER and PAPPAS, and Annex J, Appendix 3)

(U) SFC Plude stated the two Army dog teams never joined the Navy teams as part of the IRF and remained separate and under the direct control of MAJ Dinenna, S3, 320 MP BN. These teams were involved in all documented detainee abuse involving dogs; both MP and MI directed. The Navy dog teams were properly employed because of good training, excellent leadership, personal moral character, and professionalism exhibited by the Navy Dog Handlers, MA1 Kimbro, MA1 Clark, and MA2 Pankratz, and IRF personnel. The Army teams apparently agreed to be used in abusive situations by both MPs and MI in contravention to their doctrine, training, and values. In an atmosphere of permissiveness and absence of oversight or leadership the Army dog teams became involved in several incidents of abuse over the following weeks

83

SUBJECT: (U) AR 15-6 Investigation of the Abu Ghraib Detention Facility and
205th MI Brigade

(Reference Annex B, Appendix 1, KIMBRO, PLUDE; Annex B, Appendix 2, PLUDE; Annex B, Appendix 3, PLUDE).

(1) (U) **Incident #25**. The first documented incident of abuse with dogs occurred on 24 November 2003, just four days after the dogs teams arrived. An Iraqi detainee was smuggled a pistol by an Iraqi Police Guard. While attempting to confiscate the weapon, an MP was shot and the detainee was subsequently shot and wounded. Following the shooting, LTC Jordan ordered several interrogators to the Hard Site to screen eleven Iraqi Police who were detained following the shooting. The situation at the Hard Site was described by many as "chaos," and no one really appeared to be in charge. The perception was that LTG Sanchez had removed all restrictions that night because of the situation; however, that was not true. No one is able to pin down how that perception was created. A Navy Dog Team entered the Hard Site and was instructed to search for additional weapons and explosives. The dogs searched the cells, no explosives were detected and the Navy Dog Team eventually completed their mission and left. Shortly thereafter, MA1 Kimbro, USN, was recalled when someone "needed" a dog. MA1 Kimbro went to the top floor of Tier 1B, rather than the MI Hold area of Tier 1A. As he and his dog approached a cell door, he heard yelling and screaming and his dog became agitated. Inside the cell were CIVILIAN-11 (CACI contract interrogator), a second unidentified male in civilian clothes who appeared to be an interrogator and CIVILIAN16 (female contract interpreter), all of whom were yelling at a detainee squatting in the back right corner. MA1 Kimbro's dog was barking a lot with all the yelling and commotion. The dog lunged and MA1 Kimbro struggled to regain control of it. At that point, one of the men said words to the effect "You see that dog there, if you don't tell me what I want to know, I'm gonna get that dog on you!" The three began to step out of the cell leaving the detainee inside and MA1 Kimbro backed-up to allow them to exit, but there was not much room on the tier. After they exited, the dog lunged and pulled MA1 Kimbro just inside the cell. He quickly regained control of his dog, and exited the cell. As CIVILIAN-11, CIVILIAN-16, and the other interrogator re-entered the cell, MA1 Kimbro's dog grabbed CIVILIAN-16's forearm in its mouth. It apparently did not bite through her clothes or skin and CIVILIAN-16 stated the dog did not bite her. Realizing he had not been called for an explosives search, MA1 Kimbro departed the area with his dog and as he got to the bottom of the tier stairs, he heard someone calling for the dog again, but he did not return. No record of this interrogation exists, as was the case for the interrogations of Iraqi Police in the hours and days following the shooting incident. The use of dogs in the manner directed by CIVILIAN-11 was clearly abusive and unauthorized (Reference Annex B, Appendix 1, SOLDIER-11, KIMBRO, PAPPAS, CIVILIAN-11; Annex B, Appendix 2, PAPPAS).

(U) Even with all the apparent confusion over roles, responsibilities and authorities, there were early indications that MP and MI personnel knew the use of dog teams in interrogations was abusive. Following this 24 November 2003, incident the three Navy dog teams concluded that some interrogators might attempt to misuse Navy Dogs to support their

84

SUBJECT: (U) AR 15-6 Investigation of the Abu Ghraib Detention Facility and
205th MI Brigade

interrogations. For all subsequent requests they inquired what the specific purpose of the dog
was and when told "for interrogation" they explained that Navy dogs were not intended for
interrogations and the request would not be fulfilled. Over the next few weeks, the Navy dog
teams received about eight similar calls, none of which were fulfilled. In the later part of
December 2003, COL Pappas summoned MA1 Kimbro and wanted to know what the Navy
dogs' capabilities were. MA1 Kimbro explained Navy dog capabilities and provided the Navy
Dog Use SOP. COL Pappas never asked if they could be used in interrogations and following
that meeting the Navy Dog teams received no additional requests to support interrogations.

(2) (U) **Incident #26**. On or about 8 January 2004, SOLDIER-17 was conducting an
interrogation of a Baath Party General Officer in the shower area of Tier 1B of the Hard Site.
Tier 1B was the area of the Hard Site dedicated to female and juvenile detainees. Although Tier
1B was not the normal location for interrogations, due to a space shortage in Tier 1A, SOLDIER-
17 was using this area. SOLDIER-17 witnessed an MP guard and an MP Dog Handler, whom
SOLDIER-17 later identified from photographs as SOLDIER27, enter Tier 1B with SOLDIER-
27's black dog. The dog was on a leash, but was not muzzled. The MP guard and MP Dog
Handler opened a cell in which two juveniles, one known as "Casper," were housed. SOLDIER-
27 allowed the dog to enter the cell and "go nuts on the kids," barking at and scaring them. The
juveniles were screaming and the smaller one tried to hide behind "Casper." SOLDIER-27
allowed the dog to get within about one foot of the juveniles. Afterward, SOLDIER-17
overheard SOLDIER-27 say that he had a competition with another handler (likely SOLDIER-
08, the only other Army dog handler) to see if they could scare detainees to the point that they
would defecate. He mentioned that they had already made some detainees urinate, so they
appeared to be raising the competition. This incident has no direct MI involvement; however,
SOLDIER-17 failed to properly report what he observed. He stated that he went to bed and
forgot the incident until asked about misuse of dogs during this investigation (Reference Annex
B, Appendix 1, SOLDIER-17).

(3) (U) **Incident #27**. On 12 December 2003, an MI Hold detainee named DETAINEE-11,
was recommended by MI (SOLDIER-17) for an extended stay in the Hard Site because he
appeared to be mentally unstable. He was bitten by a dog in the Hard Site, but at the time he was
not undergoing an interrogation and no MI personnel were present. DETAINEE-11 told
SOLDIER-17 that a dog had bitten him and SOLDIER-17 saw dog bite marks on
DETAINEE11's thigh. SOLDIER-08, who was the dog handler of the dog that bit DETAINEE-
11, stated that in December 2003 his dog bit a detainee and he believed that MPs were the only
personnel around when the incident occurred, but he declined to make further statements
regarding this incident to either the MG Taguba inquiry or to this inquiry. SOLDIER-27,
another Army dog handler, also stated that SOLDIER-08's dog had bitten someone, but did not
provide further information. This incident was captured on digital photograph 0178/CG LAPS
and appears to be the result of MP harassment and amusement, no MI involvement is suspected

85

SUBJECT: (U) AR 15-6 Investigation of the Abu Ghraib Detention Facility and
205th MI Brigade

(Reference Annex B, Appendix 1,SOLDIER-17; Annex B, Appendix 2, SOLDIER-08, SMITH;
Annex I, Appendix 1, Photographs, D45-54, M146-171).

    (4) (U) **Incident #28.** In an apparent MI directed use of dogs in detainee abuse, circa 18
December 2003, a photograph depicts a Syrian detainee (DETAINEE-14) kneeling on the floor
with his hands bound behind his back. DETAINEE-14 was a "high value" detainee who had
arrived at Abu Ghraib in December 2003, from a Navy ship. DETAINEE-14 was suspected to
be involved with Al-Qaeda. Military Working Dog Handler SOLDIER-27 is standing in front of
DETAINEE-14 with his black dog a few feet from DETAINEE-14's face. The dog is leashed,
but not muzzled. SGT Eckroth was DETAINEE-14's interrogator from 18 to 21 December
2003, and CIVILIAN-21, CACI contract interrogator, assumed the lead after SGT Eckroth
departed Abu Ghraib on 22 December 2003. SGT Eckroth identified DETAINEE14 as his
detainee when shown a photo of the incident. CIVILIAN-21 claimed to know nothing about this
incident; however, in December 2003 he related to SSG Eckroth he was told by MPs that
DETAINEE-14's bedding had been ripped apart by dogs. CIVILIAN-21 was characterized by
SOLDIER25 as having a close relationship with the MPs, and she was told by SGT Frederick
about dogs being used when CIVILIAN-21 was there. It is highly plausible that CIVILIAN-21
used dogs without authorization and directed the abuse in this incident as well as others related to
this detainee (Reference Annex B, Appendix 1, ECKROTH, SOLDIER25, CIVILIAN-21;
Annex I, Appendix 1, Photographs Z1-6).

    (5) (U) **Incident #29.** On or about 14 - 15 December 2003, dogs were used in an
interrogation. SPC Aston, who was the Section Chief of the Special Projects team, stated that on
14 December, one of his interrogation teams requested the use of dogs for a detainee captured in
conjunction with the capture of Saddam Hussein on 13 December 2003. SPC Aston verbally
requested the use of dogs from COL Pappas, and COL Pappas stated that he would call higher to
request permission. This is contrary to COL Pappas's statement that he was given authority to
use dogs as long as they were muzzled. About one hour later, SPC Aston received approval.
SPC Aston stated that he was standing to the side of the dog handler the entire time the dog was
used in the interrogation. The dog never hurt anyone and was always muzzled, about five feet
away from the detainee (Reference Annex B, Appendix 1, ASTON, PAPPAS).

    (6) (U) **Incident #30.** On another occasion, SOLDIER-26, an MI Soldier assigned to the
S2, 320 MP BN, was present during an interrogation of a detainee and was told the detainee was
suspected to have Al Qaeda affiliations. Dogs were requested and approved about three days
later. SOLDIER-26 didn't know if the dog had to be muzzled or not, likely telling the dog
handler to un-muzzle the dog, in contravention to CJTF-7 policy. The interrogators were
CIVILIAN-20, CACI, and CIVILIAN-21 (CACI), SOLDIER-14, Operations Officer, ICE stated
that CIVILIAN-21, used a dog during one of his interrogations and this is likely that occasion.
According to SOLDIER-14, CIVILIAN-21 had the dog handler maintain control of the dog and

SUBJECT: (U) AR 15-6 Investigation of the Abu Ghraib Detention Facility and
205th MI Brigade

did not make any threatening reference to the dog, but apparently "felt just the presence of the dog would be unsettling to the detainee." SOLDIER-14 did not know who approved the procedure, but was verbally notified by SOLDIER-23, who supposedly received the approval from COL Pappas. CIVILIAN-21 claimed he once requested to use dogs, but it was never approved. Based on the evidence, CIVILIAN-21 was deceitful in his statement (Reference Annex B, Appendix 1, SOLDIER-14, SOLDIER-26, CIVILIAN-21).

(7) (U) **Incident #31**. In a 14/15 December 2003 interrogation, military working dogs were used but were deemed ineffective because the detainee had little to no response to them. CIVILIAN-11, SOLDIER-05 and SOLDIER-12, all who participated in the interrogation, believed they had authority to use the dogs from COL Pappas or from LTG Sanchez; however, no documentation was found showing CJTF7 approval to use dogs in interrogations. It is probable that approval was granted by COL Pappas without such authority. LTG Sanchez stated he never approved use of dogs. (Reference Annex B, Appendix 1, CIVILIAN-11, SOLDIER-12, SOLDIER-14, PAPPAS, SOLDIER-23, CIVILIAN-21, SANCHEZ).

(8) (U) **Incident #32**. In yet another instance, SOLDIER-25, an interrogator, stated that when she and SOLDIER15 were interrogating a female detainee in the Hard Site, they heard a dog barking. The female detainee was frightened by dogs, and SOLDIER-25 and SOLDIER-15 returned her to her cell. SOLDIER-25 went to see what was happening with the dog barking and saw a detainee in his underwear on a mattress on the floor of Tier 1A with a dog standing over him. CIVILIAN-21 was upstairs giving directions to SSG Fredrick (372 MP Co), telling him to "take him back home." SOLDIER-25 opined it was "common knowledge that CIVILIAN-21 used dogs while he was on special projects, working directly for COL Pappas after the capture of Saddam on 13 December 2003." SOLDIER25 could not identify anyone else specifically who knew of this "common knowledge." It appeared CIVILIAN-21 was encouraging and even directing the MP abuse with dogs; likely a "softening up" technique for future interrogations. The detainee was one of CIVILIAN-21's. SOLDIER-25 did not see an interpreter in the area, so it is unlikely that CIVILIAN-21 was actually doing an interrogation.

(9) (U) SOLDIER-25 stated that SSG Frederick would come into her office every other day or so and tell her about dogs being used while CIVILIAN-21 was present. SSG Fredrick and other MPs used to refer to "doggy dance" sessions. SOLDIER-25 did not specify what "doggy dance" was (Reference Annex B, Appendix 1, SOLDIER-25), but the obvious implication is that it referred to an unauthorized use of dogs to intimidate detainees.

g. (U) Incidents of Detainee Abuse Using Humiliation. Removal of clothing was not a technique developed at Abu Ghraib, but rather a technique which was imported and can be traced through Afghanistan and GTMO. The 1987 version of FM 34-52, Interrogation, talked about "controlling all aspects of the interrogation to include... clothing given to the source," while the

SUBJECT: (U) AR 15-6 Investigation of the Abu Ghraib Detention Facility and
205th MI Brigade

current 1992 version does not. The 1987 version was, however, cited as the primary reference for CJTF-7 in Iraq, even as late as 9 June 2004. The removal of clothing for both MI and MP objectives was authorized, approved, and employed in Afghanistan and GTMO. At GTMO, the JTF 170 "Counter-Resistance Strategy," documented on 11 October 2002, permitted the removal of clothing, approved by the interrogation officer-in-charge, as an incentive in detention operations and interrogations. The SECDEF granted this authority on 2 December 2002, but it was rescinded six weeks later in January 2003. This technique also surfaced in Afghanistan. The CJTF-180 "Interrogation Techniques," documented on 24 January 2003, highlighted that deprivation of clothing had not historically been included in battlefield interrogations. However, it went on to recommend clothing removal as an effective technique that could potentially raise objections as being degrading or inhumane, but for which no specific written legal prohibition existed. As interrogation operations in Iraq began to take form, it was often the same personnel who had operated and deployed in other theaters and in support of GWOT, who were called upon to establish and conduct interrogation operations in Abu Ghraib. The lines of authority and the prior legal opinions blurred. Soldiers simply carried forward the use of nudity into the Iraqi theater of operations.

(U) Removal of clothing is not a doctrinal or authorized interrogation technique but appears to have been directed and employed at various levels within MI as an "ego down" technique. It was also employed by MPs as a "control" mechanism. Individual observation and/or understanding of the use and approval of clothing removal varied in each interview conducted by this investigation. LTC Jordan was knowledgeable of naked detainees and removal of their clothing. He denied ordering it and blamed it on the MPs. CPT Wood and SOLDIER14 claimed not to have observed nudity or approved clothing removal. Multiple MPs, interrogators, analysts, and interpreters observed nudity and/or employed clothing removal as an incentive, while an equal number didn't. It is apparent from this investigation that removal of clothing was employed routinely and with the belief it was not abuse. SOLDIER-03, GTMO Tiger Team believed that clothing as an "ego down" technique could be employed. He thought, mistakenly, that GTMO still had that authority. Nudity of detainees throughout the Hard Site was common enough that even during an ICRC visit they noted several detainees without clothing, and CPT Reese, 372 MP CO, stated upon his initial arrival at Abu Ghraib, "There's a lot of nude people here." Some of the nudity was attributed to a lack of clothing and uniforms for the detainees; however, even in these cases we could not determine what happened to the detainee's original clothing. It was routine practice to strip search detainees before their movement to the Hard Site. The use of clothing as an incentive (nudity) is significant in that it likely contributed to an escalating "de-humanization" of the detainees and set the stage for additional and more severe abuses to occur (Reference Annex I, Appendix 1, Photographs D42-43, M5-7, M17-18, M21, M137-141).

SUBJECT: (U) AR 15-6 Investigation of the Abu Ghraib Detention Facility and
205th MI Brigade

(1) (U) **Incident #33**. There is also ample evidence of detainees being forced to wear women's underwear, sometimes on their heads. These cases appear to be a form of humiliation, either for MP control or MI "ego down." DETAINEE-07 and DETAINEE-05 both claimed they were stripped of their clothing and forced to wear women's underwear on their heads. CIVILIAN-15 (CACI) and CIVILIAN-19 (CACI), a CJTF-7 analyst, alleged CIVILIAN-21 bragged and laughed about shaving a detainee and forcing him to wear red women's underwear. Several photographs include unidentified detainees with underwear on their heads. Such photos show abuse and constitute sexual humiliation of detainees (Reference Annex B, Appendix 1, SOLDIER-03, SOLDIER-14, JORDAN, REESE, CIVILIAN-21, WOOD; Annex B, Appendix 3, DETAINEE-05,CIVILIAN-15, CIVILIAN-19, DETAINEE-07; Annex C; Annex G; Annex I, Appendix 1, photographs D12, D14, M11-16).

(2) (U) **Incident #34**. On 16 September 2003, MI directed the removal of a detainee's clothing. This is the earliest incident we identified at Abu Ghraib. An MP log indicated a detainee "was stripped down per MI and he is neked (sic) and standing tall in his cell." The following day his interrogators, SPC Webster and SSG Clinscales, arrived at the detainee's cell, and he was unclothed. They were both surprised. An MP asked SSG Clinscales, a female, to stand to the side while the detainee dressed and the detainee appeared to have his clothing in his cell. SSG Clinscales was told by the MP the detainee had voluntarily removed his clothing as a protest and, in the subsequent interrogation, the detainee did not claim any abuse or the forcible removal of his clothing. It does not appear the detainee was stripped at the interrogator's direction, but someone in MI most likely directed it. SPC Webster and SOLDIER-25 provided statements where they opined SPC Claus, in charge of in-processing MI Holds, may have directed removal of detainee clothing on this and other occasions. SPC Claus denies ever giving such orders (Reference Annex B, Appendix 1, CLAUS, CLINSCALES, SOLDIER-25, WEBSTER).

(3) (U) **Incident #35**. On 19 September 2003, an interrogation "Tiger Team" consisting of SOLDIER-16, SOLDIER-07, and a civilian contract interpreter identified only as "Maher" (female), conducted a late night/early morning interrogation of a 17 year old Syrian foreign fighter. SOLDIER-16 was the lead interrogator. SOLDIER-07 was told by SOLDIER-16 that the detainee they were about to interrogate was naked. SOLDIER-07 was unsure if SOLDIER-16 was simply passing along that fact or had directed the MPs to strip the detainee. The detainee had fashioned an empty "Meals-Ready-to-Eat" (MRE) bag to cover his genital area. SOLDIER-07 couldn't recall who ordered the detainee to raise his hands to his sides, but when he did, the bag fell to the floor exposing him to SOLDIER-07 and the two female interrogation team members. SOLDIER-16 used a direct interrogation approach with the incentive of getting back clothing, and the use of stress positions.

SUBJECT: (U) AR 15-6 Investigation of the Abu Ghraib Detention Facility and
205th MI Brigade

(U) There is no record of an Interrogation Plan or any approval documents which
would authorize these techniques. The fact these techniques were documented in the
Interrogation Report suggests, however, that the interrogators believed they had the authority to
use clothing as an incentive, as well as stress positions, and were not attempting to hide their use.
Stress positions were permissible with Commander, CJTF-7 approval at that time. It is probable
that use of nudity was sanctioned at some level within the chain-of-command. If not, lack of
leadership and oversight permitted the nudity to occur. Having a detainee raise his hands to
expose himself in front of two females is humiliation and therefore violates the Geneva
Conventions (Reference Annex B, Appendix 1, SOLDIER-07, SOLDIER-14, SOLDIER-16,
SOLDIER-24, WOOD).

(4) (U) **Incident #36.** In early October 2003, SOLDIER-19 was conducting an
interrogation and ordered a detainee to roll his orange jumpsuit down to his waist, insinuating to
the detainee that he would be further stripped if he did not cooperate. SOLDIER-19's interpreter
put up his hand, looked away, said that he was not comfortable with the situation, and exited the
interrogation booth. SOLDIER-19 was then forced to stop the interrogation due to lack of
language support. SOLDIER-11, an analyst from a visiting JTF GTMO Tiger Team, witnessed
this incident through the booth's observation window and brought it to the attention of
SOLDIER-16, who was SOLDIER-19's Team Chief and first line supervisor. SOLDIER-16
responded that SOLDIER-19 knew what he was doing and did not take any action regarding the
matter. SOLDIER-11 reported the same information to SOLDIER-28, his JTF GTMO Tiger
Team Chief, who, according to SOLDIER-11, said he would "take care of it." SOLDIER-28
recalled a conversation with SOLDIER-11 concerning an interpreter walking out of an
interrogation due to a "cultural difference," but could not remember the incident. This incident
has four abuse components: the actual unauthorized stripping of a detainee by SOLDIER-19, the
failure of SOLDIER-10 to report the incident he witnessed, the failure of SOLDIER-16 to take
corrective action, reporting the incident up the chain of command, and the failure of SOLDIER-
28 to report. (Reference Annex B, Appendix 1, SOLDIER-11, SOLDIER-16, SOLDIER-19,
SOLDIER-28)

(5) (U) **Incident #37.** A photograph taken on 17 October 2003 depicts a naked detainee
chained to his cell door with a hood on his head. Several other photographs taken on 18 October
2003 depict a hooded detainee cuffed to his cell door. Additional photographs on 19 October
2003 depict a detainee cuffed to his bed with underwear on his head. A review of available
documents could not tie these photos to a specific incident, detainee or allegation, but these
photos reinforce the reality that humiliation and nudity were being employed routinely enough
that photo opportunities occurred on three successive days. MI involvement in these apparent
abuses cannot be confirmed. (Reference Annex I, Appendix 1, Photographs D12, D14, D42-44,
M5-7, M17-18, M21, M11-16, M137-141)

90

SUBJECT: (U) AR 15-6 Investigation of the Abu Ghraib Detention Facility and
205th MI Brigade

(6) (U) **Incident #38**. Eleven photographs of two female detainees arrested for suspected prostitution were obtained. Identified in these photographs are SPC Harman and CPL Graner, both MPs. In some of these photos, a criminal detainee housed in the Hard Site was shown lifting her shirt with both her breasts exposed. There is no evidence to confirm if these acts were consensual or coerced; however in either case sexual exploitation of a person in US custody constitutes abuse. There does not appear to be any direct MI involvement in either of the two incidents above. (Reference Annex I, Appendix 1, Photographs M42-52)

(7) (U) **Incident #39**. On 16 November 2003, SOLDIER-29 decided to strip a detainee in response to what she believed was uncooperative and physically recalcitrant behavior. She had submitted an Interrogation Plan in which she planned to use the "Pride and Ego Down," technique but did not specify that she would strip the detainee as part of that approach. SOLDIER-29 felt the detainee was "arrogant," and when she and her analyst, SOLDIER-10, "placed him against the wall" the detainee pushed SOLDIER-10. SOLDIER-29 warned if he touched SOLDIER-10 again, she would have him remove his shoes. A bizarre tit-for-tat scenario then ensued where SOLDIER-29 would warn the detainee about touching SOLDIER-10, the detainee would "touch" SOLDIER-10, and then had his shirt, blanket, and finally his pants removed. At this point, SOLDIER-29 concluded that the detainee was "completely uncooperative" and terminated the interrogation. While nudity seemed to be acceptable, SOLDIER-29 went further than most when she walked the semi-naked detainee across the camp. SGT Adams, SOLDIER-29's supervisor, commented that walking a semi-naked detainee across the camp could have caused a riot. CIVILIAN-21, a CACI contract interrogator, witnessed SOLDIER-29 and SOLDIER-10 escorting the scantily clad detainee from the Hard Site back to Camp Vigilant, wearing only his underwear and carrying his blanket. CIVILIAN-21 notified SGT Adams, who was SOLDIER-29's section chief, who in turn notified CPT Wood, the ICE OIC. SGT Adams immediately called SOLDIER-29 and SOLDIER-10 into her office, counseled them, and removed them from interrogation duties.

(U) The incident was relatively well known among JIDC personnel and appeared in several statements as second hand information when interviewees were asked if they knew of detainee abuse. LTC Jordan temporarily removed SOLDIER-29 and SOLDIER-10 from interrogation duties. COL Pappas left the issue for LTC Jordan to handle. COL Pappas should have taken sterner action such as an Article 15, UCMJ. His failure to do so did not send a strong enough message to the rest of the JIDC that abuse would not be tolerated. CPT Wood had recommended to LTC Jordan that SOLDIER-29 receive an Article 15 and SFC Johnson, the interrogation NCOIC, recommended she be turned over to her parent unit for the non-compliance. (Reference Annex B, Appendix 1, ADAMS, CIVILIAN-04, JORDAN, PAPPAS, SOLDIER-29, CIVILIAN-21, WOOD; Annex B, Appendix 2, JORDAN).

SUBJECT: (U) AR 15-6 Investigation of the Abu Ghraib Detention Facility and 205th MI Brigade

(8) (U) **Incident #40**. On 24 November 2003, there was a shooting of a detainee at Abu Ghraib in Tier 1A. DETAINEE-06, had obtained a pistol. While the MPs attempted to confiscate the weapon, an MP and DETAINEE-06 were shot. It was alleged that an Iraqi Police Guard had smuggled the pistol to DETAINEE-06 and in the aftermath of the shooting forty-three Iraqi Police were screened and eleven subsequently detained and interrogated. All but three were released following intense questioning. A fourth did not report for work the next day and is still at large. The Iraqi guard detainees admitted smuggling the weapons into the facility hiding them in an inner tube of a tire and several of the Iraqi guards were identified as Fedayeen trainers and members. During the interrogations of the Iraqi Police, harsh and unauthorized techniques were employed to include the use of dogs, discussed earlier in this report, and removal of clothing (See paragraph 5.e(18), above). Once detained, the police were strip-searched, which was a reasonable precaution considering the threat of contraband or weapons. Following such search, however, the police were not returned their clothes before being interrogated. This is an act of humiliation and was unauthorized. It was the general understanding that evening that LTG Sanchez and COL Pappas had authorized all measures to identify those involved, however, that should not have been construed to include abuse. LTC Jordan was the senior officer present at the interrogations and is responsible for the harsh and humiliating treatment of the police (Reference Annex B, Appendix 1, JORDAN, PAPPAS; Annex B, Appendix 2, JORDAN, PAPPAS, Annex B, Appendix 1, DETAINEE-06).

(9) (U) **Incident #41**. On 4 December 2003, documentation in the MP Logs indicated that MI leadership was aware of clothing removal. An entry indicated "Spoke with LTC Jordan (205 MI BDE) about MI holds in Tier 1A/B. He stated he would clear up with MI and let MPs run Tiers 1A/B as far as what inmate gets (clothes)." Additionally, in his statement, LTC Phillabaum claims he asked LTC Jordan what the situation was with naked detainees, and LTC Jordan responded with, "It was an interrogation technique." Whether this supports allegations of MI involvement in the clothing and stripping of detainees is uncertain, but it does show that MI at least knew of the practice and was willing to defer decisions to the MPs. Such vague guidance, if later combined with an implied tasking from MI, or perceived tasking by MP, potentially contributed to the subsequent abuse (Reference Annex B, Appendix 2, PHILLABAUM).

h. (U) Incidents of Detainee Abuse Using Isolation. Isolation is a valid interrogation technique which required approval by the CJTF-7 Commander. We identified documentation of four instances where isolation was approved by LTG Sanchez. LTG Sanchez stated he had approved 25 instances of isolation. This investigation, however, found numerous incidents of chronic confusion by both MI and MPs at all levels of command, up through CJTF-7, between the definitions of "isolation" and "segregation." Since these terms were commonly interchanged, we conclude Segregation was used far more often than Isolation. Segregation is a valid procedure to limit collaboration between detainees. This is what was employed most often in Tier 1A (putting a detainee in a cell by himself vice in a communal cell as was common outside

SUBJECT: (U) AR 15-6 Investigation of the Abu Ghraib Detention Facility and
205th MI Brigade

the Hard Site) and was sometimes incorrectly referred to as "isolation." Tier 1A did have
isolation cells with solid doors which could be closed as well as a small room (closet) which was
referred to as the isolation "Hole." Use of these rooms should have been closely controlled and
monitored by MI and MP leaders. They were not, however, which subjected the detainees to
excessive cold in the winter and heat in the summer. There was obviously poor air quality, no
monitoring of time limits, no frequent checks on the physical condition of the detainee, and no
medical screening, all of which added up to detainee abuse. A review of interrogation reports
identified ten references to "putting people in the Hole," "taking them out of the Hole," or
consideration of isolation. These occurred between 15 September 2003 and 3 January 2004.
(Reference Annex B, Appendix 1, SANCHEZ)

(1) (U) **Incident #42**. On 15 September 2003, at 2150 hours, unidentified MI personnel,
using the initials CKD, directed the use of isolation on a unidentified detainee. The detainee in
cell #9 was directed to leave his outer cell door open for ventilation and was directed to be taken
off the light schedule. The identification of CKD, the MI personnel, or the detainee could not be
determined. This information originated from the prison log entry and confirms the use of
isolation and sensory deprivation as interrogation techniques. (Reference MP Hard Site log book
entry, 15 September 2003).

(2) (U) **Incident #43**. In early October 2003, SOLDIER-11 was interrogating an
unidentified detainee with SOLDIER-19, an interrogator, and an unidentified contract
interpreter. About an hour and 45 minutes into the interrogation, SOLDIER-19 turned to
SOLDIER-11 and asked if he thought they should place the detainee in solitary confinement for
a few hours, apparently because the detainee was not cooperating or answering questions.
SOLDIER-11 expressed his misgivings about the tactic, but deferred to SOLDIER-19 as the
interrogator. About 15 minutes later, SOLDIER-19 stopped the interrogation, departed the
booth, and returned about five minutes later with an MP, SSG Frederick. SSG Frederick jammed
a bag over the detainee's head, grabbed the handcuffs restraining him and said something like
"come with me piggy", as he led the detainee to solitary confinement in the Hard Site, Tier 1A of
Abu Ghraib.

(U) About half an hour later, SOLDIER-19 and SOLDIER-11 went to the Hard Site
without their interpreter, although he was available if needed. When they arrived at the
detainee's cell, they found him lying on the floor, completely naked except for a hood that
covered his head from his upper lip, whimpering, but there were no bruises or marks on him.
SSG Frederick then met SOLDIER-19 and SOLDIER-11 at the cell door. He started yelling at
the detainee, "You've been moving little piggy, you know you shouldn't move", or words to that
effect, and yanked the hood back down over the detainee's head. SOLDIER-19 and SOLDIER-
11 instructed other MPs to clothe the detainee, which they did. SOLDIER-11 then asked
SOLDIER-19 if he knew the MPs were going to strip the detainee, and SOLDIER-19 said that he

SUBJECT: (U) AR 15-6 Investigation of the Abu Ghraib Detention Facility and
205th MI Brigade

did not. After the detainee was clothed, both SOLDIER-19 and SOLDIER-11 escorted him to
the general population and released him without interrogating him again. SSG Frederick made
the statement "I want to thank you guys, because up until a week or two ago, I was a good
Christian." SOLDIER-11 is uncertain under what context SSG Frederick made this statement.
SOLDIER-11 noted that neither the isolation technique, nor the "striping incident" in the cell,
was in any "interrogator notes" or "interrogation plan."

(U) More than likely, SOLDIER-19 knew what SSG Frederick was going to do. Given
that the order for isolation appeared to be a spontaneous reaction to the detainee's recalcitrance
and not part of an orchestrated Interrogation Plan; that the "isolation" lasted only approximately
half an hour; that SOLDIER-19 chose to re-contact the detainee without an interpreter present;
and that SOLDIER-19 was present with SSG Frederick at another incident of detainee abuse; it
is possible that SOLDIER-19 had a prearranged agreement with SSG Frederick to "soften up"
uncooperative detainees and directed SSG Frederick to strip the detainee in isolation as
punishment for being uncooperative, thus providing the detainee an incentive to cooperate during
the next interrogation. We believe at a minimum, SOLDIER-19 knew or at least suspected this
type of treatment would take place even without specific instructions (Reference Annex B,
Appendix 1,SOLDIER-11, SOLDIER-19, PAPPAS, SOLDIER-28).

(3) (U) **Incident(s) #44**. On 13 November 2003, SOLDIER-29 and SOLDIER-10, MI
interrogators, noted that a detainee was unhappy with his stay in isolation and visits to the hole.

(U) On 11, 13, and 14 November 2003, MI interrogators SOLDIER-04, SOLDIER-09,
SOLDIER-02, and SOLDIER-23 noted that a detainee was "walked and put in the Hole," "pulled
out of extreme segregation," "did not seem to be bothered to return to the Hole," "Kept in the
Hole for a long time unless he started to talk," and "was in good spirits even after three days in
the Hole." (Reference Annex I, Appendix 3, Photo of "the Hole").

(U) A 5 November 2003 interrogation report indicates in the recommendations/future
approaches paragraph: "Detainee has been recommended for the hole in ISO. Detainee should
be treated harshly because friendly treatment has not been productive and because COL Pappas
wants fast resolution, or he will turn the detainee over to someone other than the 205th [MI]."

(U) On 12 November 2003, MI interrogators SOLDIER-18 and SOLDIER13 noted that
a detainee "feared the isolation Hole, and it made him upset, but not enough to break."

(U) On 29 November 2003, MI interrogators SOLDIER-18 and SOLDIER-06 told a
detainee that "he would go into the Hole if he didn't start cooperating."

94

SUBJECT: (U) AR 15-6 Investigation of the Abu Ghraib Detention Facility and
205th MI Brigade

(U) On 8 December 2003, unidentified interrogators told a detainee that he was
"recommended for movement to ISO and the Hole - he was told his sun [sunlight] would be
taken away, so he better enjoy it now."

(U) These incidents all indicate the routine and repetitive use of total isolation and light
deprivation. Documentation of this technique in the interrogation reports implies those
employing it thought it was authorized. The manner it was applied is a violation of the Geneva
Conventions, CJTF-7 policy, and Army policy (Reference Annex M, Appendix 2, AR 190-8).
Isolation was being employed without proper approval and with little oversight, resulting in
abuse (Reference Annex I, Appendix 4, DETAINEE-08).

i. (U) Several alleged abuses were investigated and found to be unsubstantiated. Others
turned out to be no more than general rumor or fabrication. This investigation established a
threshold below which information on alleged or potential abuse was not included in this report.
Fragmentary or difficult to understand allegations or information at times defied our ability to
investigate further. One such example is contained in a statement from an alleged abuse victim,
DETAINEE-13, who claimed he was always treated well at Abu Ghraib but was abused earlier
by his captors. He potentially contradicts that claim by stating his head was hit into a wall. The
detainee appears confused concerning the times and locations at which he was abused. Several
incidents involved numerous victims and/or occurred during a single "event," such as the Iraqi
Police Interrogations on 24 November 2003. One example receiving some visibility was a report
by SOLDIER-22 who overheard a conversation in the "chow hall" between SPC Mitchell and his
unidentified "friends." SPC Mitchell was alleged to have said: "MPs were using detainees as
practice dummies. They would hit the detainees as practice shots. They would apply strikes to
their necks and knock them out. One detainee was so scared; the MPs held his head and told him
everything would be alright, and then they would strike him. The detainees would plead for
mercy and the MPs thought it was all funny." SPC Mitchell was interviewed and denied having
knowledge of any abuse. He admitted that he and his friends would joke about noises they heard
in the Hard Site and say things such as "the MPs are doing their thing." SPC Mitchell never
thought anyone would take him seriously. Several associates of SPC Mitchell were interviewed
(SPC Griffin, SOLDIER-12, PVT Heidenreich). All claimed their discussions with SPC
Mitchell were just rumor, and they didn't think anyone would take him seriously or construe he
had personal knowledge of abuse. SPC Mitchell's duties also make it unlikely he would have
witnessed any abuse. He arrived at Abu Ghraib as an analyst, working the day shift, in late
November 2003. Shortly after his arrival, the 24 November "shooting incident" occurred and the
following day, he was moved to Camp Victory for three weeks. Upon his return, he was
transferred to guard duty at Camp Wood and Camp Steel and never returned to the Hard Site.
This alleged abuse is likely an individual's boastful exaggeration of a rumor which was rampant
throughout Abu Ghraib, nothing more (Reference Annex B, Appendix 1, SOLDIER-12,
GRIFFIN, HEIDENREICH, MITCHELL, SOLDIER-22).

95

SECRET//NOFORN//X1

SUBJECT: (U) AR 15-6 Investigation of the Abu Ghraib Detention Facility and 205th MI Brigade

Allegations of Abuse Incidents, the Nature of Reported Abuse, and Associated Personnel

Note: The chart lists all allegations considered. The specific abuse claimed and entities involved are not confirmed in all cases. The category of abuse are underlined. (See paragraph 5e-h, above)

Date/ Time	Incident	Nature of Alleged Abuse						Comments
		Nudity/ Humiliation	Assault	Sexual Assault	Use of Dogs	The "Hole"	Other	
15 SEP 03/ 2150	Use of Isolation. Incident **#42**.					MI/MP		MP log entry confirms MI use of isolation and sensory deprivation as an interrogation technique.
16 SEP 03/ 1315-1445	MI Directs Removal of Clothing. Incident **#34**.	MI/MP						MPs respond to MI tasking. Detainee apparently stripped upon arrival to Hard Site at MI direction.
19-20 SEP 03	Naked Detainee During Interrogation. Incident **#35**.	MI/MP						
20 SEP 03	Two MI Soldiers Beat and Kicked a Cuffed Detainee. Incident **#1**.		MI					CID investigated and referred the case back to the command.

SECRET//NOFORN//X1

SUBJECT: (U) AR 15-6 Investigation of the Abu Ghraib Detention Facility and 205th MI Brigade

Allegations of Abuse Incidents, the Nature of Reported Abuse, and Associated Personnel
Note: The chart lists all allegations considered. The specific abuse claimed and entities involved are not confirmed in all cases. The category of abuse are underlined. (See paragraph 5e-h, above)

Date/ Time	Incident	Nature of Alleged Abuse						Comments
		Nudity/ Humiliation	Assault	Sexual Assault	Use of Dogs	The "Hole"	Other	
7 OCT 03	Unauthorized Interrogation and Alleged Assault of a Female Detainee. Incident #2.	MI		<u>MI</u>				Unauthorized interrogation. MI personnel received Field Grade Article 15s.
Early OCT 03	Interrogator Directs Partial Removal of Clothing/Failure to Report. Incident #36.	<u>MI</u>						
Early OCT 03	Interrogator Directs Unauthorized Solitary Confinement/Milita ry Police Stripping of Detainee/Failure to Report. Incident #43.	MP	MP			<u>MI/MP</u>		MI directed the MP place the detainee in solitary confinement (apparently the "Hole") for a few hours. The MPs carried out the request, stripped and hooded the detainee.

SECRET//NOFORN//X4

SUBJECT: (U) AR 15-6 Investigation of the Abu Ghraib Detention Facility and 205th MI Brigade

Allegations of Abuse Incidents, the Nature of Reported Abuse, and Associated Personnel

Note: The chart lists all allegations considered. The specific abuse claimed and entities involved are not confirmed in all cases. The category of abuse are underlined. (See paragraph 5e-h, above)

Date/ Time	Incident	Nature of Alleged Abuse						Comments
		Nudity/ Humiliation	Assault	Sexual Assault	Use of Dogs	The "Hole"	Other	
17 OCT 03 - 19 Oct 03	Photos Depicting a Naked Hooded Detainee Cuffed to His Cell Door. Detainee Cuffed to His Bed with Underwear on his Head. Incident #37.	UNK						Nudity, hooding, and restraint. No indication of association with MI.
20 OCT 03	Detainee Was Stripped and Abused for Making a Shank from a Toothbrush. Incident #8.	MP	MP	MP				No indication of association with MI.
25 OCT 03/2015 (est)	Photos of a Naked Detainee on a Dog Leash. Incident #9.	MP		MP				Humiliation and degradation. No indication of association with MI.

SECRET//NOFORN//X1

SUBJECT: (U) AR 15-6 Investigation of the Abu Ghraib Detention Facility and 205th MI Brigade

Allegations of Abuse Incidents, the Nature of Reported Abuse, and Associated Personnel
Note: The chart lists all allegations considered. The specific abuse claimed and entities involved are not confirmed in all cases. The category of abuse are underlined. (See paragraph 5e-h, above)

Date/ Time	Incident	Nature of Alleged Abuse						Comments
		Nudity/ Humiliation	Assault	Sexual Assault	Use of Dogs	The "Hole"	Other	
25 OCT 03/ 2300 – 2317 (est)	Three Naked Detainees Handcuffed Together and Forced to Simulate Sex While Photographed and Abused. Incident #3	MI/MP	MI/MP	MI/MP				Incident not associated with interrogation operations. MI personnel observed and participated as individuals.
28 OCT 03	Photographs of Female Detainees. Incident #38.	MP		MP				MPs took many photos of two female detainees. One detainee photographed exposing her breasts.
OCT 03	Abuse and Sodomy of a Detainee (Chem Light Incident). Incident #5.	MP	MP	MP				Detainee on MI Hold. No other indication of association with MI.

SECRET//NOFORN//X1

SUBJECT: (U) AR 15-6 Investigation of the Abu Ghraib Detention Facility and 205th MI Brigade

Allegations of Abuse Incidents, the Nature of Reported Abuse, and Associated Personnel

Note: The chart lists all allegations considered. The specific abuse claimed and entities involved are not confirmed in all cases. The category of abuse are underlined. (See paragraph 5e-h, above)

Date/ Time	Incident	Nature of Alleged Abuse						Comments
		Nudity/ Humiliation	Assault	Sexual Assault	Use of Dogs	The "Hole"	Other	
OCT 03	Detainee's Chin Lacerated. Incident #21.		MP					No indication of association with MI. Assailant unknown.
4 NOV 03/ 2140 - 2315	Detainee Forced to Stand on a Box With Simulated Electrical Wires Attached to his Fingers and Penis. Incident #10.	MP		MP				No indication of association with MI. Attached wire to penis. Threatened detainee with electrocution
4 NOV 03	CIA Detainee Dies in Custody. Incident #7.		CIA					SEAL Team involved in apprehending detainee. MPs photographed body. Tampered with evidence
5 NOV 03	Detainee Forced to Stand on Boxes, Water is Poured on Him, His Genitals are Hit. Incident #20.	MP	MP	MP				Detainee on MI Hold. No other indication of association with MI.

SECRET//NOFORN//X1

SUBJECT: (U) AR 15-6 Investigation of the Abu Ghraib Detention Facility and 205th MI Brigade

Allegations of Abuse Incidents, the Nature of Reported Abuse, and Associated Personnel
Note: The chart lists all allegations considered. The specific abuse claimed and entities involved are not confirmed in all cases. The category of abuse are underlined. (See paragraph 5e-h, above)

Date/ Time	Incident	Nature of Alleged Abuse						Comments
		Nudity/ Humiliation	Assault	Sexual Assault	Use of Dogs	The "Hole"	Other	
7-8 NOV 03/ 2315 – 0024 (est)	Naked "Dog pile and Forced Masturbation of Detainees Following the 6 NOV 03 Riot at Camp Vigilant. Incident #11.	MP	MP	MP				
13 NOV 03	Detainee Claim of MP Abuse Corresponds with Interrogations. Incident #4.	MP	MP					Interrogation reports suggest MI directed abuse. Withholding of bedding
14 NOV 03	MP Log-Detainees Were Ordered "PT'd" By MI. Incident #6.	MP	MP					MPs performed unauthorized medical procedures – stitching detainee wounds

SECRET//NOFORN//X1

SUBJECT: (U) AR 15-6 Investigation of the Abu Ghraib Detention Facility and 205th MI Brigade

Allegations of Abuse Incidents, the Nature of Reported Abuse, and Associated Personnel
Note: The chart lists all allegations considered. The specific abuse claimed and entities involved are not confirmed in all cases. The category of abuse are underlined. (See paragraph 5e-h, above)

Date/ Time	Incident	Nature of Alleged Abuse						Comments
		Nudity/ Humiliation	Assault	Sexual Assault	Use of Dogs	The "Hole"	Other	
16 NOV 03	Stripping of Detainee During Interrogation. Incident #39.	MI						MI interrogator counseled and removed as lead interrogator.
18 NOV 03	Photo Depicting Detainee on the Floor with a Banana Inserted into his Anus. Incident #14.		MP					Detainee had an apparent mental disorder. Photos were taken of him on other dates included showing him naked, praying upside down or covered in feces; blood on a door from an apparently self-inflicted wound; and efforts to restrain him. Appropriate psychiatric care and facilities apparently were not available.
24 NOV 03	MP CPT Beat and Kicked a Detainee. Incident #23.			MP				Subsequent investigation determined to be a staged event and not an abusive incident.

SECRET//NOFORN//X1

SUBJECT: (U) AR 15-6 Investigation of the Abu Ghraib Detention Facility and 205th MI Brigade

Allegations of Abuse Incidents, the Nature of Reported Abuse, and Associated Personnel
Note: The chart lists all allegations considered. The specific abuse claimed and entities involved are not confirmed in all cases. The category of abuse are underlined. (See paragraph 5e-h, above)

Date/ Time	Incident	Nature of Alleged Abuse						Comments
		Nudity/ Humiliation	Assault	Sexual Assault	Use of Dogs	The "Hole"	Other	
24 NOV 03	Interrogator Threatens Use of Military Working Dog. Incident #25.				MP/MI			
24 NOV 03	The use of dogs and humiliation (clothing removal) was approved by MI. Incident #40.	MI/MP			MI/MP			COL Pappas authorized, and LTC Jordan supervised, the harsh treatment of Iraqi Police during interrogations, to include humiliation (clothing removal) and the use of dogs.
26 or 27 Nov 03	MI/MP Abuse During an Interrogation of Iraqi Policeman. Incident #15.		MI/MP					MP cutoff air supply by covering nose and mouth of detainee and twisted his arm at direction of contract interrogator during interrogation of Iraqi policeman.
29 NOV 04	Photo Depicting a detainee in his underwear standing on a box. Incident #13.	UNK	UNK					Photo could not be tied to any specific incident, detainee, or allegation and MI involvement is indeterminate.

SECRET//NOFORN//X1

SUBJECT: (U) AR 15-6 Investigation of the Abu Ghraib Detention Facility and 205th MI Brigade

Allegations of Abuse Incidents, the Nature of Reported Abuse, and Associated Personnel
Note: The chart lists all allegations considered. The specific abuse claimed and entities involved are not confirmed in all cases. The category of abuse are underlined. (See paragraph 5e-h, above)

Date/ Time	Incident	Nature of Alleged Abuse						Comments
		Nudity/ Humiliation	Assault	Sexual Assault	Use of Dogs	The "Hole"	Other	
30 NOV 03	MP Log Entry- Detainee Was Found in Cell Covered in Blood. Incident #17.		UNK					Wounds apparently self-inflicted. No indication of association with MI.
Circa Dec 03	Photo Depicting detainee in stress position on chair. Incident #24.		MI					Photo shows detainee kneeling on a chair with Interrogators watching. No associated interrogation summaries to ID detainee
4 DEC 03	MP Log- Determination of Inmate Clothing by MI. Incident #41.	MI/MP						Suggests MI direction to remove selected detainee's clothing, with MP collaboration.

SUBJECT: (U) AR 15-6 Investigation of the Abu Ghraib Detention Facility and 205th MI Brigade

Allegations of Abuse Incidents, the Nature of Reported Abuse, and Associated Personnel
Note: The chart lists all allegations considered. The specific abuse claimed and entities involved are not confirmed in all cases. The category of abuse are underlined. (See paragraph 5e-h, above)

Date/Time	Incident	Nature of Alleged Abuse						Comments
		Nudity/ Humiliation	Assault	Sexual Assault	Use of Dogs	The "Hole"	Other	
12-13 DEC 03 (est)	Detainee Involved in Attempted Murder of MPs Claims Retaliatory Acts Upon Return to the Hard Site. Incident #18.		MP		MP			Detainee allegations may have been exaggerated. MP – Forced him to eat pork and forced alcohol in his mouth. MPs may have retaliated in response to the detainee shooting an MP on 24 NOV 03.
4-13 DEC 03 (est)	Withholding of Clothing, Bedding, and Medical Care. Incident #19.	MP	UNK					MI Soldier discovered and attempted to rectify the situation. A U/I COL or LTC medical officer refused to remove a catheter when notified by MI.
12 DEC 03	Dog Bites Iranian Detainee. Incident #27.	MP	MP		MP			Detainee on MI Hold. No other indication of association with MI.
14/15 DEC 03	MI Uses Dog in Interrogation. Incident #29.				MI/MP			Used allegedly in response to COL Pappas's blanket approval for use of harsher techniques against Saddam associates.

SECRET//NOFORN//X1

SUBJECT: (U) AR 15-6 Investigation of the Abu Ghraib Detention Facility and 205th MI Brigade

Allegations of Abuse Incidents, the Nature of Reported Abuse, and Associated Personnel

Note: The chart lists all allegations considered. The specific abuse claimed and entities involved are not confirmed in all cases. The category of abuse are underlined. (See paragraph 5e-h, above)

Date/ Time	Incident	Nature of Alleged Abuse						Comments
		Nudity/ Humiliation	Assault	Sexual Assault	Use of Dogs	"The Hole"	Other	
14/15 DEC 03	MI Uses Dog in Interrogation. Incident #31.				MI/MP			Interrogation report indicates dogs used with little effect during an interrogation.
Late DEC 03	Contract Interrogator Possibly Involved in Dog Use on Detainee. Incident #32.				MI/MP			
18 DEC 03 or later	Dog Handler Uses Dog on Detainee. Incident #28.						MP	Photos of incident show only MP personnel; however, it is possible MI directed the dogs to prepare the detainee for interrogation.
27 DEC 03 (est)	Photo Depicting Apparent Shotgun Wounds on Detainee's Buttocks. Incident #12.	UNK	UNK					Detainee apparently shot by MP personnel with shotgun using less-than-lethal rounds. Nudity may have been required to have medics observe and treat wounds. No indication of association with MI.

SUBJECT: (U) AR 15-6 Investigation of the Abu Ghraib Detention Facility and
205th MI Brigade

Allegations of Abuse Incidents, the Nature of Reported Abuse, and Associated Personnel
Note: The chart lists all allegations considered. The specific abuse claimed and entities involved are not confirmed in all cases. The category of abuse are underlined. (See paragraph 5e-h, above)

Date/ Time	Incident	Nature of Alleged Abuse						Comments
		Nudity/ Humiliation	Assault	Sexual Assault	Use of Dogs	The "Hole"	Other	
8 JAN 04 (Estimated)	Dog Used to Scare Juvenile Inmates. Incident #26.				MP			MI Soldier observed the event while in the area during an interrogation. MP motivation unknown. MI Soldier failed to report it.
Unspecified	Un-muzzled dog used during an interrogation. Incident #30.				MI/MP			MI approved the use of dogs during an interrogation. The dog was un-muzzled without such approval.
Unspecified	Possible Rape of a Detainee by a US Translator. Incident #22.			MI				

SECRET//NOFORN//X1

SUBJECT: (U) AR 15-6 Investigation of the Abu Ghraib Detention Facility and 205th MI Brigade

Allegations of Abuse Incidents, the Nature of Reported Abuse, and Associated Personnel

Note: The chart lists all allegations considered. The specific abuse claimed and entities involved are not confirmed in all cases. The category of abuse are underlined. (See paragraph 5e-h, above)

Date/ Time	Incident	Nature of Alleged Abuse						Comments
		Nudity/ Humiliation	Assault	Sexual Assault	Use of Dogs	The "Hole"	Other	
Unspeci fied	Civilian Interrogator Forcibly Pulls Detainee from Truck and Drags Him Across Ground. Incident #16.		MI					The incident was reported by MI, but CID apparently did not pursue the case.
Various Dates	MI Use of Isolation as an Interrogation Technique. Incident #44.					MI/MP		Seven detainees are associated with this line item.
Various Dates	MI Forces Detainee to Wear Women's Underwear on his Head. Incident #33.	MI/MP						MPs may have performed two of the incidents identified in photos, and may have no MI association.

SUBJECT: (U) AR 15-6 Investigation of the Abu Ghraib Detention Facility and
205th MI Brigade

6. (U) Findings and Recommendations.

a. (U) **Major Finding**: From 25 July 2003 to 6 February 2004, twenty-seven (27) 205 MI
BDE personnel allegedly:

- Requested, encouraged, condoned, or solicited MP personnel to abuse detainees or;

- Participated in detainee abuse or;

- Violated established interrogation procedures and applicable laws and regulations as
preparation for interrogation operations at Abu Ghraib.

(U) **Explanation**: Some MI personnel encouraged, condoned, participated in, or ignored
abuse. In a few instances, MI personnel acted alone in abusing detainees. MI abuse and MI
solicitation of MP abuse included the use of isolation with sensory deprivation ("the Hole"),
removal of clothing and humiliation, the use of dogs to "fear up" detainees, and on one occasion,
the condoned twisting of a detainee's cuffed wrists and the smothering of this detainee with a
cupped hand in MI's presence. Some MI personnel violated established interrogation practices,
regulations, and conventions which resulted in the abuse of detainees. While Interrogation and
Counter-Resistance Policies (ICRP) were poorly defined and changed several times, in most
cases of detainee abuse the MI personnel involved knew or should have known what they were
doing was outside the bounds of their authority. Ineffective leadership at the JIDC failed to
detect violations and discipline those responsible. Likewise, leaders failed to provide adequate
training to ensure Soldiers understood the rules and complied.

(U) **Recommendation**: The Army needs to re-emphasize Soldier and leader
responsibilities in interrogation and detention operations and retrain them to perform in
accordance with law, regulations, and Army values and to live up to the responsibilities of their
rank and position. Leaders must also provide adequate training to ensure Soldiers understand
their authorities. The Army must ensure that future interrogation policies are simple, direct and
include safeguards against abuse. Organizations such as the JIDC must possess a functioning
chain of command capable of directing interrogation operations.

b. (U) Other Findings and Recommendations.

(1) (U) **Finding**: There was a lack of clear Command and Control of Detainee Operations
at the CJTF-7 level.

(U) **Explanation**: COL Pappas was rated by MG Wojdakowski, DCG, V Corps/CJTF-
7. MG Wojdakowski, however, was not directly involved with interrogation operations. Most of
COL Pappas' direction was coming from LTG Sanchez directly as well as from MG Fast, the C2.

SUBJECT: (U) AR 15-6 Investigation of the Abu Ghraib Detention Facility and 205th MI Brigade

BG Karpinski was rated by BG Diamond, Commander, 377th Theater Support Command (377 TSC). However, she testified that she believed her rater was MG Wojdakowski and in fact it was he she received her direction from the entire time she was in Iraq (Reference Annex B, Appendix 1, KARPINSKI). The 800 MP BDE was TACON to CJTF-7. Overall responsibility for detainee operations never came together under one person short of LTG Sanchez himself until the assignment of MG G. Miller in April 2004.

(U) **Recommendation**: There should be a single authority designated for command and control for detention and interrogation operations. (DoD/DA)

(2) (U) **Finding**: FRAGO 1108 appointing COL Pappas as FOB Commander at Abu Ghraib was unclear. This issue did not impact detainee abuse.

(U) **Explanation**: Although FRAGO 1108 appointing COL Pappas as FOB Commander on 19 November 2003 changed the command relationship, it had no specific effect on detainee abuses at Abu Ghraib. The FRAGO giving him TACON of the 320 MP BN did not contain any specified or implied tasks. The TACON did not include responsibility for conducting prison or "Warden" functions. Those functions remained the responsibility of the 320 MP BN. This FRAGO has been cited as a significant contributing factor that allowed the abuses to happen, but the abuses were already underway for two months before CJTF-7 issued this FRAGO. COL Pappas and the Commander of the 320 MP BN interpreted that FRAGO strictly for COL Pappas to exercise the external Force Protection and Security of Detainees. COL Pappas had a Long Range Reconnaissance Company in the 165 MI BN that would augment the external protection of Abu Ghraib. The internal protection of detainees, however, still remained the responsibility of the 320 MP BN. The confusion and disorganization between MI and MPs already existed by the time CJTF-7 published the FRAGO. Had there been no change of FOB Command, it is likely abuse would have continued anyway.

(U) **Recommendation**: Joint Task Forces such as CJTF-7 should clearly specify relationships in FRAGOs so as to preclude confusion. Terms such as Tactical Control (TACON) should be clearly defined to identify specific command relationships and preclude confusion. (DoD/CJTF-7)

(3) (U) **Finding**: The JIDC was manned with personnel from numerous organizations and consequently lacked unit cohesion. There was an absence of an established, effective MI chain of command at the JIDC.

(U) **Explanation**: A decision was made not to run the JIDC as a unit mission. The JIDC was manned, led and managed by staff officers from multiple organizations as opposed to a unit with its functioning chain of command. Responsibilities for balancing the demands of

110

SUBJECT: (U) AR 15-6 Investigation of the Abu Ghraib Detention Facility and
205th MI Brigade

managing interrogation operations and establishing good order and discipline in this environment
were unclear and lead to lapses in accountability.

(U) **Recommendation**: JIDCs need to be structured, manned, trained and equipped as
standard military organizations. These organizations should be certified by TRADOC and/or
JFCOM. Appropriate Army and Joint doctrine should be developed defining JIDCs' missions
and functions as separate commands. (DoD/DA/CJTF-7)

(4) (U) **Finding**: Selecting Abu Ghraib as a detention facility placed soldiers and detainees
at an unnecessary force protection risk.

(U) **Explanation**: Failure adequately to protect and house detainees is a violation of
the Third and Fourth Geneva Conventions and AR 190-8. Therefore, the selection of Abu
Ghraib as a detention facility was inappropriate because of its inherent indefensibility and poor
condition. The selection of Abu Ghraib as a detention center was dictated by the Coalition
Provisional Authority officials despite concerns that the Iraqi people would look negatively on
Americans interning detainees in a facility associated with torture. Abu Ghraib was in poor
physical condition with buildings and sections of the perimeter wall having been destroyed,
resulting in completely inadequate living conditions. Force protection must be a major
consideration in selecting any facility as a detention facility. Abu Ghraib was located in the
middle of the Sunni Triangle, an area known to be very hostile to coalition forces. Further, being
surrounded by civilian housing and open fields and encircled by a network of roads and
highways, its defense presented formidable force protection challenges. Even though the force
protection posture at Abu Ghraib was compromised from the start due to its location and poor
condition, coalition personnel still had a duty and responsibility to undertake appropriate
defensive measures. However, the poor security posture at Abu Ghraib resulted in the deaths
and wounding of both coalition forces and detainees.

(U) **Recommendations**:

- Detention centers must be established in accordance with AR 190-8 to ensure
safety and compliance with the Geneva Conventions. (DoD/DA/CJTF-7).
- As a matter of policy, force protection concerns must be applicable to any
detention facility and all detention operations. (DoD/DA/CJTF-7)
- Protect detainees in accordance with Geneva Convention IV by providing
adequate force protection. (DoD/DA/CJTF-7)

(5) (U) **Finding**: Leaders failed to take steps to effectively manage pressure placed upon
JIDC personnel.

(U) **Explanation**: During our interviews, leaders within the MI community
commented upon the intense pressure they felt from higher headquarters, to include CENTCOM,

SECRET//NOFORN//X1

SUBJECT: (U) AR 15-6 Investigation of the Abu Ghraib Detention Facility and
205th MI Brigade

the Pentagon, and DIA for timelier, actionable intelligence (Reference Annex B, Appendix 1, WOOD, PAPPAS, and PRICE). These leaders have stated that this pressure adversely affected their decision making. Requests for information were being sent to Abu Ghraib from a number of headquarters without any prioritization. Based on the statements from the interrogators and analysts, the pressure was allowed to be passed down to the lowest levels.

(U) **Recommendation**: Leaders must balance mission requirements with unit capabilities, soldier morale and effectiveness. Protecting Soldiers from unnecessary pressure to enhance mission effectiveness is a leader's job. Rigorous and challenging training can help prepare units and soldiers for the stress they face in combat. (DoD/DA/CENTCOM/CJTF-7)

(6) (U) **Finding**: Some capturing units failed to follow procedures, training, and directives in the capture, screening, and exploitation of detainees.

(U) **Explanation**: The role of the capturing unit was to conduct preliminary screening of captured detainees to determine if they posed a security risk or possessed information of intelligence value. Detainees who did not pose a security risk and possessed no intelligence value should have been released. Those that posed a security risk and possessed no intelligence value should have been transferred to Abu Ghraib as a security hold. Those that possessed intelligence information should have been interrogated within 72 hours at the tactical level to gather perishable information of value to the capturing unit. After 72 hours, these personnel should have been transferred to Abu Ghraib for further intelligence exploitation as an MI hold. Since most detainees were not properly screened, large numbers of detainees were transferred to Abu Ghraib, who in some cases should not have been sent there at all, and in almost all cases, were not properly identified or documented in accordance with doctrine and directives. This failure led to the arrival of a significant number of detainees at Abu Ghraib. Without proper detainee capture documentation, JIDC interrogators were diverted from interrogation and intelligence production to screening operations in order to assess the value of the incoming detainees (no value, security hold, or MI Hold). The overall result was that less intelligence was produced at the JIDC than could have been if capturing forces had followed proper procedures.

(U) **Recommendation**: Screening, interrogation and release procedures at the tactical level need to be properly executed. Those detainees who pose no threat and are of no intelligence value should be released by capturing units within 72 hours. Those detainees thought to be a threat but of no further intelligence value should be sent to a long term confinement facility. Those detainees thought to possess further intelligence value should be sent to a Corps/Theater Interrogation Center. (DA/CENTCOM/CJTF-7)

(7) (U) **Finding**: DoD's development of multiple policies on interrogation operations for use in different theaters or operations confused Army and civilian Interrogators at Abu Ghraib.

SECRET//NOFORN//X1

112

SUBJECT: (U) AR 15-6 Investigation of the Abu Ghraib Detention Facility and
205th MI Brigade

(U) **Explanation**: National policy and DoD directives were not completely consistent with Army doctrine concerning detainee treatment or interrogation tactics, resulting in CJTF-7 interrogation and counter-resistance policies and practices that lacked basis in Army interrogation doctrine. As a result, interrogators at Abu Ghraib employed non-doctrinal approaches that conflicted with other DoD and Army regulatory, doctrinal and procedural guidance.

(U) **Recommendation**: Adopt one DoD policy for interrogation, within the framework of existing doctrine, adhering to the standards found in doctrine, and enforce that standard policy across DoD. Interrogation policy must be simple and direct, with reference to existing doctrine, and possess effective safeguards against abuse. It must be totally understandable by the interrogator using it. (DoD/DA/CJTF-7)

(8) (U) **Finding**: There are an inadequate number of MI units to satisfy current and future HUMINT missions. The Army does not possess enough interrogators and linguists to support interrogation operations.

(U) **Explanation**: The demand for interrogators and linguists to support tactical screening operations at the point-of-capture of detainees, tactical HUMINT teams, and personnel to support interrogation operations at organizations like the JIDC cannot be supported with the current force structure. As a result, each of these operations in Iraq was undermanned and suffered accordingly.

(U) **Recommendation**: The Army must increase the number of HUMINT units to overcome downsizing of HUMINT forces over the last 10 years and to address current and future HUMINT requirements.

(9) (U) **Finding**: The JIDC was not provided with adequate personnel resources to effectively operate as an interrogation center.

(U) **Explanation**: The JIDC was established in an ad hoc manner without proper planning, personnel, and logistical support for the missions it was intended to perform. Interrogation and analyst personnel were quickly kluged together from a half dozen units in an effort to meet personnel requirements. Even at its peak strength, interrogation and analyst manpower at the JIDC was too shorthanded to deal with the large number of detainees at hand. Logistical support was also inadequate.

(U) **Recommendation**: The Army and DoD should plan on operating JIDC organizations in future operational environments, establish appropriate manning and equipment authorizations for the same. (DoD/DA)

113

SUBJECT: (U) AR 15-6 Investigation of the Abu Ghraib Detention Facility and
205th MI Brigade

(10) (U) **Finding**: There was/is a severe shortage of CAT II and CAT III Arab linguists available in Iraq.

(U) **Explanation**: This shortage negatively affected every level of detainee operations from point-of-capture through detention facility. Tactical units were unable to properly screen detainees at their levels not only because of the lack of interrogators but even more so because of the lack of interpreters. The linguist problem also existed at Abu Ghraib. There were only 20 linguists assigned to Abu Ghraib at the height of operations. Linguists were a critical node and limited the maximum number of interrogations that could be conducted at any time to the number of linguists available.

(U) **Recommendation**: Army and DoD need to address the issue of inadequate linguist resources to conduct detention operations. (DA/DoD)

(11) (U) **Finding**: The cross leveling of a large number of Reserve Component (RC) Soldiers during the Mobilization process contributed to training challenges and lack of unit cohesion of the RC units at Abu Ghraib.

(U) **Recommendation**: If cross leveling of personnel is necessary in order to bring RC units up to required strength levels, then post mobilization training time should be extended. Post mobilization training should include unit level training in addition to Soldier training to ensure cross leveled Soldiers are made part of the team. (DA)

(12) (U) **Finding**: Interrogator training in the Laws of Land Warfare and the Geneva Conventions is ineffective.

(U) **Explanation**: The US Army Intelligence Center and follow on unit training provided interrogators with what appears to be adequate curriculum, practical exercises and man-hours in Law of Land Warfare and Geneva Conventions training. Soldiers at Abu Ghraib, however, remained uncertain about what interrogation procedures were authorized and what proper reporting procedures were required. This indicates that Initial Entry Training for interrogators was not sufficient or was not reinforced properly by additional unit training or leadership.

(U) **Recommendation**: More training emphasis needs to be placed on Soldier and leader responsibilities concerning the identification and reporting of detainee abuse incidents or concerns up through the chain of command, or to other offices such as CID, IG or SJA. This training should not just address the rules, but address case studies from recent and past detainee and interrogation operations to address likely issues interrogators and their supervisors will encounter. Soldiers and leaders need to be taught to integrate Army values and ethical decision-

SUBJECT: (U) AR 15-6 Investigation of the Abu Ghraib Detention Facility and
205th MI Brigade

making to deal with interrogation issues that are not clearly prohibited or allowed. Furthermore, it should be stressed that methods employed by US Army interrogators will represent US values.

(13) (U) **Finding**: MI, MP, and Medical Corps personnel observed and failed to report instances of Abuse at Abu Ghraib. Likewise, several reports indicated that capturing units did not always treat detainees IAW the Geneva Convention.

(U) **Recommendation**: DoD should improve training provided to all personnel in Geneva Conventions, detainee operations, and the responsibilities of reporting detainee abuse. (DoD)

(14) (U) **Finding**: Combined MI/MP training in the conduct of detainee/interrogation operations is inadequate.

(U) **Explanation**: MI and MP personnel at Abu Ghraib had little knowledge of each other's missions, roles and responsibilities in the conduct of detainee/interrogation operations. As a result, some "lanes in the road" were worked out "on the fly." Other relationships were never fully defined and contributed to the confused operational environment.

(U) **Recommendation**: TRADOC should initiate an effort to develop a cross branch training program in detainee and interrogation operations training. FORSCOM should reinstitute combined MI/MP unit training such as the Gold Sword/Silver Sword Exercises that were conducted annually. (DA)

(15) (U) **Finding**: MI leaders do not receive adequate training in the conduct and management of interrogation operations.

(U) **Explanation**: MI Leaders at the JIDC were unfamiliar with and untrained in interrogation operations (with the exception of CPT Wood) as well as the mission and purposes of a JIDC. Absent any knowledge from training and experience in interrogation operations, JIDC leaders had to rely upon instinct to operate the JIDC. MTTs and Tiger Teams were deployed to the JIDC as a solution to help train interrogators and leaders in the management of HUMINT and detainee/interrogator operations.

(U) **Recommendation**: MI Officer, NCO and Warrant Officer training needs to include interrogation operations to include management procedures, automation support, collection management and JIDC operations. Officer and senior NCO training should also emphasize the potential for abuse involved in detention and interrogation operations. (DA)

115

SUBJECT: (U) AR 15-6 Investigation of the Abu Ghraib Detention Facility and
205th MI Brigade

(16) (U) **Finding**: Army doctrine exists for both MI interrogation and MP detainee operations, but it was not comprehensive enough to cover the situation that existed at Abu Ghraib.

(U) **Explanation**: The lines of authority and accountability between MI and MP were unclear and undefined. For example, when MI would order sleep adjustment, MPs would use their judgment on how to apply that technique. The result was MP taking detainees from their cells stripping them and giving them cold showers or throwing cold water on them to keep them awake.

(U) **Recommendation**: DA should conduct a review to determine future Army doctrine for interrogation operations and detention operations. (DA)

(17) (U) **Finding**: Because of a lack of doctrine concerning detainee and interrogation operations, critical records on detainees were not created or maintained properly thereby hampering effective operations.

(U) **Explanation**: This lack of record keeping included the complete life cycle of detainee records to include detainee capture information and documentation, prison records, medical records, interrogation plans and records, and release board records. Lack of record keeping significantly hampered the ability of this investigation to discover critical information concerning detainee abuse.

(U) **Recommendation:** As TRADOC reviews and enhances detainee and interrogation operations doctrine, it should ensure that record keeping and information sharing requirements are addressed. (DA)

(18) (U) **Finding**: Four (4) contract interrogators allegedly abused detainees at Abu Ghraib.

(U) **Explanation**: The contracting system failed to ensure that properly trained and vetted linguist and interrogator personnel were hired to support operations at Abu Ghraib. The system also failed to provide useful contract management functions in support of the facility. Soldiers and leaders at the prison were unprepared for the arrival, employment, and oversight of contract interrogators.

(U) **Recommendations**: The Army should review the use contract interrogators. In the event contract interrogators must be used, the Army must ensure that they are properly qualified from a training and performance perspective, and properly vetted. The Army should establish standards for contract requirements and personnel. Additionally, the Army must

116

SUBJECT: (U) AR 15-6 Investigation of the Abu Ghraib Detention Facility and
205th MI Brigade

provide sufficient contract management resources to monitor contracts and contractor
performance at the point of performance.

(19) (U) **Observation**: MG Miller's visit did not introduce "harsh techniques" into the
Abu Ghraib interrogation operation.

(U) **Explanation**: While there was an increase in intelligence reports after the visit, it
appears more likely it was due to the assignment of trained interrogators and an increased
number of MI Hold detainees to interrogate. This increase in production does not equate to an
increase in quality of the collected intelligence. MG G. Miller's visit did not introduce "harsh
techniques" into the Abu Ghraib interrogation operation.

(20) (U) **Finding**: The JTF-GTMO training team had positive impact on the operational
management of the JIDC; however, the JTF-GTMO training team inadvertently validated
restricted interrogation techniques.

(U) **Explanation**: The JTF-GTMO team stressed the conduct of operations with a
strategic objective, while the Abu Ghraib team remained focused on tactical operations. Instead
of providing guidance and assistance, the team's impact was limited to one-on-one interaction
during interrogations. Clearly a significant problem was the JTF-GTMO's lack of understanding
of the approved interrogation techniques, either for GTMO or CJTF-7 or Abu Ghraib. When the
training team composed of the experts from a national level operation failed to recognize, object
to, or report detainee abuse, such as the use of nudity as an interrogation tactic, they failed as a
training team and further validated the use of unacceptable interrogation techniques.

(U) **Recommendation**: TRADOC should initiate an Army-wide effort to ensure all
personnel involved in detention and interrogation operations are properly trained with respect to
approved doctrine. There should be a MTT to assist ongoing detention operations. This MTT
must be of the highest quality and understand the mission they have been sent to support. They
must have clearly defined and unmistakable objectives. Team members with varied experience
must be careful to avoid providing any training or guidance that contradicts local or national
policy. (DA/DoD)

(21) (U) **Finding**: The Fort Huachuca MTT failed to adapt the ISCT training (which was
focused upon improving the JTF-GTMO operational environment) to the mission needs of CJTF-
7 and JIDC; however, actions of one team member resulted in the inadvertent validation of
restricted interrogation techniques.

(U) **Explanation**: Although the Fort Huachuca Team (ISCT) team was successful in
arranging a few classes and providing some formal training, to include classes on the Geneva
Conventions, both the JIDC leadership and the ISCT team failed to include/require the contract

117

SUBJECT: (U) AR 15-6 Investigation of the Abu Ghraib Detention Facility and
205th MI Brigade

personnel to attend the training. Furthermore, the training that was given was ineffective and certainly did nothing to prevent the abuses occurring at Abu Ghraib, e.g., the "Hole," nakedness, withholding of bedding, and the use of dogs to threaten detainees. The ISCT MTT members were assigned to the various Tiger Teams/sections to conduct interrogations. The ISCT team's lack of understanding of approved doctrine was a significant failure. This lack of understanding was evident in SFC Walters' "unofficial" conversation with one of the Abu Ghraib interrogators (CIVILIAN21). SFC Walters related several stories about the use of dogs as an inducement, suggesting the interrogator talk to the MPs about the possibilities. SFC Walters noted that detainees are most susceptible during the first few hours after capture. "The prisoners are captured by Soldiers, taken from their familiar surroundings, blindfolded and put into a truck and brought to this place (Abu Ghraib); and then they are pushed down a hall with guards barking orders and thrown into a cell, naked; and that not knowing what was going to happen or what the guards might do caused them extreme fear." It was also suggested that an interrogator could take some pictures of what seemed to be guards being rough with prisoners so he could use them to scare the prisoners. This conversation certainly contributed to the abusive environment at Abu Ghraib. The team validated the use of unacceptable interrogation techniques. The ISCT team's Geneva Conventions training was not effective in helping to halt abusive techniques, as it failed to train Soldiers on their responsibilities for identifying and reporting those techniques.

(U) **Recommendation**: TRADOC should initiate an Army-wide effort to ensure all personnel involved in detention and interrogation operations are properly trained with respect to approved doctrine. There should be a MTT to assist ongoing detention operations. This MTT must be of the highest quality and understand the mission they have been sent to support. They must have clearly defined and unmistakable objectives. Team members with varied experience must be careful to avoid providing any training or guidance that contradicts local or national policy. (DA/DoD)

(22) (U) **Finding**: Other Government Agency (OGA) interrogation practices led to a loss of accountability at Abu Ghraib.

(U) **Explanation**: While the FBI, JTF-121, Criminal Investigative Task Force, Iraq Survey Group, and the CIA were all present at Abu Ghraib, the acronym "Other Government Agency" referred almost exclusively to the CIA. Lack of military control over OGA interrogator actions or lack of systemic accountability for detainees plagued detainee operations in Abu Ghraib almost from the start. Army allowed CIA to house "Ghost Detainees" who were unidentified and unaccounted for in Abu Ghraib. This procedure created confusion and uncertainty concerning their classification and subsequent DoD reporting requirements under the Geneva Conventions. Additionally, the treatment and interrogation of OGA detainees occurred under different practices and procedures which were absent any DoD visibility, control, or oversight. This separate grouping of OGA detainees added to the confusion over proper treatment of detainees and created a perception that OGA techniques and practices were suitable

118

SUBJECT: (U) AR 15-6 Investigation of the Abu Ghraib Detention Facility and
205th MI Brigade

and authorized for DoD operations. No memorandum of understanding on detainee
accountability or interrogation practices between the CIA and CJTF-7 was created.

(U) **Recommendation**: DoD must enforce adherence by OGA with established DoD
practices and procedures while conducting detainee interrogation operations at DoD facilities.

(23) (U) **Finding**: There was neither a defined procedure nor specific responsibility within
CJTF-7 for dealing with ICRC visits. ICRC recommendations were ignored by MI, MP and
CJTF-7 personnel.

(U) **Explanation**: Within this investigation's timeframe, 16 September 2003 through
31 January 2004, the ICRC visited Abu Ghraib three times, notifying CJTF-7 twice of their visit
results, describing serious violations of international Humanitarian Law and of the Geneva
Conventions. In spite of the ICRC's role as independent observers, there seemed to be a
consensus among personnel at Abu Ghraib that the allegations were not true. Neither the
leadership, nor CJTF-7 made any attempt to verify the allegations.

(U) **Recommendation**: DoD should review current policy concerning ICRC visits and
establish procedures whereby findings and recommendations made by the ICRC are investigated.
Investigation should not be done by the units responsible for the facility in question. Specific
procedures and responsibilities should be developed for ICRC visits, reports, and responses.
There also needs to be specific inquiries made into ICRC allegations of abuse or maltreatment by
an independent entity to ensure that an unbiased review has occurred. (DoD/CJTF-7)

(24) (U) **Finding**: Two soldiers that the 519 MI BN had reason to suspect were involved in
the questionable death of a detainee in Afghanistan were allowed to deploy and continue
conducting interrogations in Iraq. While in Iraq, those same soldiers were alleged to have
abused detainees.

(U) **Recommendation**: Once soldiers in a unit have been identified as possible
participants in abuse related to the performance of their duties, they should be suspended from
such duties or flagged.

(25) (U) **Observation**: While some MI Soldiers acted outside the scope of applicable laws
and regulations, most Soldiers performed their duties in accordance with the Geneva
Conventions and Army Regulations.

(U) **Explanation**: MI Soldiers operating the JIDC at Abu Ghraib screened thousands
of Iraqi detainees, conducted over 2500 interrogations, and produced several thousand valuable
intelligence products supporting the war fighter and the global war on terrorism. This great effort

SUBJECT: (U) AR 15-6 Investigation of the Abu Ghraib Detention Facility and
205th MI Brigade

was executed in difficult and dangerous conditions with inadequate physical and personnel resources.

c. (U) Individual Responsibility for Detainee Abuse at Abu Ghraib.

(1) (U) **Finding**: **COL Thomas M. Pappas, Commander, 205 MI BDE.** A preponderance of evidence supports that COL Pappas did, or failed to do, the following:

- Failed to insure that the JIDC performed its mission to its full capabilities, within the applicable rules, regulations and appropriate procedures.
- Failed to properly organize the JIDC.
- Failed to put the necessary checks and balances in place to prevent and detect abuses.
- Failed to ensure that his Soldiers and civilians were properly trained for the mission.
- Showed poor judgment by leaving LTC Jordan in charge of the JIDC during the critical early stages of the JIDC.
- Showed poor judgment by leaving LTC Jordan in charge during the aftermath of a shooting incident known as the Iraqi Police Roundup (IP Roundup).
- Improperly authorized the use of dogs during interrogations. Failed to properly supervise the use of dogs to make sure they were muzzled after he improperly permitted their use.
- Failed to take appropriate action regarding the ICRC reports of abuse.
- Failed to take aggressive action against Soldiers who violated the ICRP, the CJTF-7 interrogation and Counter-Resistance Policy and the Geneva Conventions.
- Failed to properly communicate to Higher Headquarters when his Brigade would be unable to accomplish its mission due to lack of manpower and/or resources. Allowed his Soldiers and civilians at the JIDC to be subjected to inordinate pressure from Higher Headquarters.
- Failed to establish appropriate MI and MP coordination at the brigade level which would have alleviated much of the confusion that contributed to the abusive environment at Abu Ghraib.
- The significant number of systemic failures documented in this report does not relieve COL Pappas of his responsibility as the Commander, 205th MI BDE for the abuses that occurred and went undetected for a considerable length of time.

(U) **Recommendation**: This information should be forwarded to COL Pappas' chain of command for appropriate action.

SUBJECT: (U) AR 15-6 Investigation of the Abu Ghraib Detention Facility and
205th MI Brigade

(2) (U) **Finding**: **LTC Stephen L. Jordan, Director, Joint Interrogation Debriefing Center.** A preponderance of evidence supports that LTC Jordan did, or failed to do, the following:

- Failed to properly train Soldiers and civilians on the ICRP.
- Failed to take full responsibility for his role as the Director, JIDC.
- Failed to establish the necessary checks and balances to prevent and detect abuses.
- Was derelict in his duties by failing to establish order and enforce proper use of ICRP during the night of 24 November 2003 (IP Roundup) which contributed to a chaotic situation in which detainees were abused.
- Failed to prevent the unauthorized use of dogs and the humiliation of detainees who were kept naked for no acceptable purpose while he was the senior officer-in-charge in the Hard Site.
- Failed to accurately and timely relay critical information to COL Pappas, such as:
  - The incident where a detainee had obtained a weapon.
  - ICRC issues.
- Was deceitful during this, as well as the MG Taguba, investigations. His recollection of facts, statements, and incidents were always recounted to avoid blame or responsibility. His version of events frequently diverged from most others.
- Failed to obey a lawful order to refrain from contacting anyone except his attorney regarding this investigation. He conducted an e-mail campaign soliciting support from others involved in the investigation.

(U) **Recommendation**: This information should be forwarded to LTC Jordan's chain of command for appropriate action.

SUBJECT: (U) AR 15-6 Investigation of the Abu Ghraib Detention Facility and
205th MI Brigade

(3) (U) **Finding**: **MAJ David M. Price, Operations Officer, Joint Interrogation and Debriefing Center, 141st MI Battalion.** A preponderance of evidence indicates that MAJ Price did, or failed to do, the following:

- Failed to properly train Soldiers and civilians on the ICRP.
- Failed to understand the breadth of his responsibilities as the JIDC Operations Officer. Failed to effectively assess, plan, and seek command guidance and assistance regarding JIDC operations.
- Failed to intervene when the Interrogation Control Element (ICE) received pressure from Higher Headquarters.
- Failed to plan and implement the necessary checks and balances to prevent and detect abuses.
- Failed to properly review interrogation plans which clearly specified the improper use of nudity and isolation as punishment.

(U) **Recommendation**: This information should be forwarded to MAJ Price's chain of command for appropriate action.

(4) (U) **Finding**: **MAJ Michael D. Thompson, Deputy Operations Officer, Joint Interrogation and Debriefing Center, 325 MI BN.** A preponderance of evidence supports that MAJ Thompson failed to do the following:

- Failed to properly train Soldiers and civilians on the ICRP.
- Failed to understand the breadth of his responsibilities as the JIDC Deputy Operations Officer. Failed to effectively assess, plan, and seek command guidance and assistance regarding JIDC operations.
- Failed to intervene when the ICE received pressure from Higher Headquarters.
- Failed to plan and implement the necessary checks and balances to prevent and detect abuses.
- Failed to properly review interrogation plans which clearly specified the improper use of nudity and isolation as punishment.

(U) **Recommendation**: This information should be forwarded to MAJ Thompson's chain of command for appropriate action.

SUBJECT: (U) AR 15-6 Investigation of the Abu Ghraib Detention Facility and
205th MI Brigade

(5) (U) **Finding**: **CPT Carolyn A. Wood, Officer in Charge, Interrogation Control
Element (ICE), Joint Interrogation and Debriefing Center, 519 MI BDE.** A preponderance
of evidence supports that CPT Wood failed to do the following:

- Failed to implement the necessary checks and balances to detect and prevent detainee
abuse. Given her knowledge of prior abuse in Afghanistan, as well as the reported sexual
assault of a female detainee by three 519 MI BN Soldiers working in the ICE, CPT Wood
should have been aware of the potential for detainee abuse at Abu Ghraib. As the
Officer-in-Charge (OIC) she was in a position to take steps to prevent further abuse. Her
failure to do so allowed the abuse by Soldiers and civilians to go undetected and
unchecked.
- Failed to assist in gaining control of a chaotic situation during the IP Roundup, even after
SGT Eckroth approached her for help.
- Failed to provide proper supervision. Should have been more alert due to the following
incidents:
    o An ongoing investigation on the 519 MI BN in Afghanistan.
    o Prior reports of 519 MI BN interrogators conducting unauthorized interrogations.
    o SOLDIER29's reported use of nudity and humiliation techniques.
    o Quick Reaction Force (QRF) allegations of detainee abuse by 519th MI Soldiers.
- Failed to properly review interrogation plans which clearly specified the improper use of
nudity and isolation in interrogations and as punishment.
- Failed to ensure that Soldiers were properly trained on interrogation techniques and
operations.
- Failed to adequately train Soldiers and civilians on the ICRP.

(U) **Recommendation**: This information should be forwarded to CPT Wood's chain of
command for appropriate action.

(6) (U) **Finding**: **SOLDIER-28, Guantanamo Base Team Chief, 260th MI Battalion.**
A preponderance of evidence supports that SOLDIER28 did, or failed to do, the following:

- Failed to report detainee abuse when he was notified by SOLDIER-11 that a detainee was
observed in a cell naked, hooded, and whimpering, and when SOLDIER-11 reported an
interrogator made a detainee pull his jumpsuit down to his waist.

(U) **Recommendation**: This information should be forwarded to SOLDIER-28's chain of
command for appropriate action.

(7) (U) **Finding**: **SOLDIER-23, Operations Section, ICE, JIDC, 325 MI BN.** A
preponderance of evidence supports that SOLDIER23 did, or failed to do, the following:

123

SUBJECT: (U) AR 15-6 Investigation of the Abu Ghraib Detention Facility and 205th MI Brigade

- Failed to prevent detainee abuse and permitted the unauthorized use of dogs and unauthorized interrogations during the IP Roundup. As the second senior MI officer during the IP Roundup, his lack of leadership contributed to detainee abuse and the chaotic situation during the IP Roundup.
- Failed to properly supervise and ensure Soldiers and civilians followed the ICRP.
- Failed to properly review interrogation plans which clearly specified the improper use of nudity and isolation as interrogation techniques and punishment.

(U) **Recommendation**: This information should be forwarded to SOLDIER23' chain of command for appropriate action.

(8) (U) **Finding**: **SOLDIER-14, Night Shift OIC, ICE, JIDC, 519 MI BN.** A preponderance of evidence supports that SOLDIER-14 did, or failed to do, the following:

- Failed to properly supervise and ensure Soldiers and civilians followed the ICRP.
- Failed to provide proper supervision. SOLDIER-14 should have been aware of the potential for detainee abuse at Abu Ghraib: The following incidents should have increased his diligence in overseeing operations:
  - An ongoing investigation of the 519 MI BN in Afghanistan.
  - Allegations by a female detainee that 519 MI BN interrogators sexually assaulted her. The Soldiers received non-judicial punishment for conducting unauthorized interrogations.
  - SOLDIER-29's reported use of nudity and humiliation techniques.
  - Quick Reaction Force (QRF) allegations of detainee abuse by 519 MI BN Soldiers.
- Failed to properly review interrogation plans which clearly specified the improper use of nudity and isolation as punishment.

(U) **Recommendation**: This information should be forwarded to SOLDIER-14's chain of command for appropriate action.

124

SUBJECT: (U) AR 15-6 Investigation of the Abu Ghraib Detention Facility and
205th MI Brigade

(9) (U) **Finding**: **SOLDIER-15, Interrogator, 66 MI GP.** A preponderance of evidence
supports that SOLDIER15 did, or failed to do, the following:

• Failed to report detainee abuse. He witnessed SSG Frederick twisting the handcuffs of a
detainee causing pain and covering the detainee's nose and mouth to restrict him from
breathing.
  o Witnessed during that same incident, CIVILIAN-11 threaten a detainee by
  suggesting he would be turned over to SSG Frederick for further abuse if he did
  not cooperate.

(U) **Recommendation**: This information should be forwarded to SOLDIER-15's chain of
command for appropriate action.

(10) (U) **Finding**: **SOLDIER-22, 302d MI Battalion.** A preponderance of evidence
supports that SOLDIER22 did, or failed to do, the following:

• Failed to report detainee abuse.
  o He was made aware by SOLDIER-25 of an incident where three detainees were
  abused by MPs (Reference Annex I, Appendix 1, Photographs M36-37, M39-41).
  o He was made aware by SOLDIER-25 of the use of dogs to scare detainees.
  o He overheard Soldiers stating that MPs were using detainees as "practice
  dummies;" striking their necks and knocking them unconscious.
  o He was made aware of MPs conducting "PT" (Physical Training) sessions with
  detainees and MI personnel participating:

• Failed to obey a direct order. He interfered with this investigation by talking about the
investigation, giving interviews to the media, and passing the questions being asked by
investigators to others via a website.

(U) **Recommendation**: This information should be forwarded to SOLDIER-22's chain of
command for appropriate action.

125

SUBJECT: (U) AR 15-6 Investigation of the Abu Ghraib Detention Facility and
205th MI Brigade

(11) (U) **Finding**: **SOLDIER-10, Analyst, 325 MI BN (currently attached to HHC, 504 MI BDE).** A preponderance of evidence supports that SOLDIER10 did, or failed to do, the following:

- Actively participated in abuse when he threw water on three detainees who were hand-cuffed together and made to lie on the floor of the detention facility (Reference Annex I, Appendix 1, Photographs M36-37).
- Failed to stop detainee abuse in the above incident and in the incident when SOLDIER-29 stripped a detainee of his clothes and walked the detainee naked from an interrogation booth to Camp Vigilant during a cold winter day.
- Failed to report detainee abuse.

(U) **Recommendation**: This information should be forwarded to SOLDIER-10's chain of command for appropriate action.

(12) (U) **Finding**: **SOLDIER-17, Interrogator, 2d MI Battalion.** A preponderance of evidence supports that SOLDIER17 did, or failed to do, the following:

- Failed to report the improper use of dogs. He saw an un-muzzled black dog go into a cell and scare two juvenile detainees. The dog handler allowed the dogs to "go nuts" on the juveniles (Reference Annex I, Appendix 1, Photograph D-48).
- Failed to report inappropriate actions of dog handlers. He overheard Dog Handlers state they had a competition to scare detainees to the point they would defecate. They claimed to have already made several detainees urinate when threatened by their dogs.

(U) **Recommendation**: This information should be forwarded to SOLDIER-17's chain of command for appropriate action.

126

SUBJECT: (U) AR 15-6 Investigation of the Abu Ghraib Detention Facility and
205th MI Brigade

(13) (U) **Finding**: **SOLDIER-19, Interrogator, 325 MI BN.** A preponderance of
evidence supports that SOLDIER-19 did, or failed to do, the following:

- Abused detainees:
    - o Actively participated in the abuse of three detainees depicted in photographs
      (Reference Annex I, Appendix 1, Photographs M36-37, M39-41). He threw a
      Foam-ball at their genitals and poured water on the detainees while they were
      bound, nude, and abused by others.
    - o Turned over a detainee to the MPs with apparent instructions for his abuse. He
      returned to find the detainee naked and hooded on the floor whimpering.
    - o Used improper interrogation techniques. He made a detainee roll down his
      jumpsuit and threatened the detainee with complete nudity if he did not cooperate.
- Failed to stop detainee abuse in the above incidents.
- Failed to report detainee abuse for above incidents.

(U) **Recommendation**: This information should be forwarded to SOLDIER-19's chain of
command for appropriate action.

(14) (U) **Findings**: **SOLDIER-24, Analyst, 325 MI BN (currently attached to HHC,
504 MI BDE).** A preponderance of evidence supports that SOLDIER24 did, or failed to do, the
following:

- Failed to report detainee abuse. He was present during the abuse of detainees depicted in
  photographs (Reference Annex I, Appendix 1, Photographs M36-37, M39, M41).
- Failed to stop detainee abuse.

(U) **Recommendation**: This information should be forwarded to SOLDIER-24's chain of
command for appropriate action.

127

SECRET//NOFORN//X1

SUBJECT: (U) AR 15-6 Investigation of the Abu Ghraib Detention Facility and
205th MI Brigade

(15) (U) **Findings**: **SOLDIER-25, Interrogator, 321st MI BN.** A preponderance of
evidence supports that SOLDIER25 did, or failed to do, the following:

- Failed to report detainee abuse.
    - o She saw Dog Handlers use dogs to scare detainees. She "thought it was funny" as
      the detainees would run into their cells from the dogs.
    - o She was told by SOLDIER-24 that the detainees who allegedly had raped another
      detainee were handcuffed together, naked, in contorted positions, making it look
      like they were having sex with each other.
    - o She was told that MPs made the detainees wear women's underwear.
- Failed to stop detainee abuse.

(U) **Recommendation**: This information should be forwarded to SOLDIER-25's chain of
command for appropriate action.

(16) (U) **Finding**: **SOLDIER-29, Interrogator, 66 MI GP.** A preponderance of evidence
supports that SOLDIER29 did, or failed to do, the following:

- Failed to report detainee abuse.
    - o She saw CPL Graner slap a detainee.
    - o She saw a computer screen saver depicting naked detainees in a "human
      pyramid."
    - o She was aware MPs were taking photos of detainees.
    - o She knew MPs had given a detainee a cold shower, made him roll in the dirt, and
      stand outside in the cold until he was dry. The detainee was then given another
      cold shower.
- Detainee abuse (Humiliation). She violated interrogation rules of engagement by stripping
  a detainee of his clothes and walking him naked from an interrogation booth to Camp
  Vigilant on a cold winter night.
- Gave MPs instruction to mistreat/abuse detainees.
    - o SOLDIER2-9's telling MPs (SSG Frederick) when detainees had not cooperated
      in an interrogation appeared to result in subsequent abuse.
    - o One of the detainees she interrogated was placed in isolation for several days and
      allegedly abused by the MPs. She annotated in an interrogation report (IN-
      AG00992-DETAINEE-08-04) that a "direct approach" was used with "the
      reminder of the unpleasantness that occurred the last time he lied to us."

(U) **Recommendation**: This information should be forwarded to SOLDIER-29's chain of
command for appropriate action.

SECRET//NOFORN//X1

128

SUBJECT: (U) AR 15-6 Investigation of the Abu Ghraib Detention Facility and
205th MI Brigade

(17) (U) **Findings: SOLDIER-08, Dog Handler, Abu Ghraib, 42 MP Detachment, 16 MP BDE (ABN).** A preponderance of evidence supports that SOLDIER08 did, or failed to do, the following:

- Inappropriate use of dogs. Photographs (Reference Annex I, Appendix 1, D46, D52, M149-151) depict SOLDIER-08 inappropriately using his dog to terrorize detainees.
- Abused detainees. SOLDIER-08 had an on-going contest with SOLDIER-27, another dog handler, to scare detainees with their dogs in order to see who could make the detainees urinate and defecate first.

(U) **Recommendation**: This information should be forwarded to SOLDIER-08's chain of command for appropriate action.

(18) (U) **Findings: SOLDIER34, 372 MP CO.** A preponderance of evidence supports that SOLDIER34 did, or failed to do, the following:

- Failed to report detainee abuse. He was present during the abuse of detainees depicted in photographs (Reference Annex I, Appendix 1, Photographs M36-37, M39-41).
- Failed to stop detainee abuse.

(U) **Recommendation**: This information should be forwarded to SOLDIER34's chain of command for appropriate action.

(19) (U) **Findings: SOLDIER-27, 372 MP CO.** A preponderance of evidence supports that SOLDIER27 did, or failed to do, the following:

- Actively participated in detainee abuse.
  - o During the medical treatment (stitching) of a detainee, he stepped on the chest of the detainee (Reference Annex I, Appendix 1, Photograph M163).
  - o He participated in the abuse of naked detainees depicted in photographs (Reference Annex I, Appendix 1, Photographs M36-37, M39-41).
- Failed to stop detainee abuse.

(U) **Recommendation**: This information should be forwarded to SOLDIER27's chain of command for appropriate action.

129

SUBJECT: (U) AR 15-6 Investigation of the Abu Ghraib Detention Facility and
205th MI Brigade

(20) (U) **Findings**: **SOLDIER-27, Dog Handler, Abu Ghraib, 523 MP Detachment.** A
preponderance of evidence supports that SOLDIER27 did, or failed to do, the following:

- Inappropriate use of dogs. Photographs (Reference Annex I, Appendix 1, Photographs
  D46, D48, M148, M150, M151, M153, Z1, Z3-6) depict SOLDIER-27 inappropriately
  using his dog terrorizing detainees.
- Detainee abuse. SOLDIER-27 had an on-going contest with SOLDIER-08, another dog
  handler, to scare detainees with their dogs and cause the detainees to urinate and defecate.
- Led his dog into a cell with two juvenile detainees and let his dog go "nuts." The two
  juveniles were yelling and screaming with the youngest one hiding behind the oldest.

(U) **Recommendation**: This information should be forwarded to SOLDIER-27's chain of
command for appropriate action.

(21) (U) **Finding**: **SOLDIER-20, Medic, 372 MP CO.** A preponderance of evidence
supports that SOLDIER20 did, or failed to do, the following:

- Failed to report detainee abuse.
  - When called to assist a detainee who had been shot in the leg, he witnessed CPL
    Graner hit the detainee in his injured leg with a stick.
  - He saw the same detainee handcuffed to a bed over several days, causing great
    pain to the detainee as he was forced to stand.
  - He saw the same detainee handcuffed to a bed which resulted in a dislocated
    shoulder.
  - He saw pictures of detainees being abused (stacked naked in a "human pyramid").

(U) **Recommendation**: This information should be forwarded to SOLDIER-20's chain of
command for appropriate action.

(22) (U) **Finding**: **SOLDIER-01, Medic, Abu Ghraib.** A preponderance of evidence
supports that SOLDIER01 did, or failed to do, the following:

- Failed to report detainee abuse. She saw a 'human pyramid" of naked Iraqi prisoners, all
  with sandbags on their heads when called to the Hard Site to provide medical treatment.

(U) **Recommendation**: This information should be forwarded to SOLDIER-01's chain of
command for appropriate action.

(23) (U) **Finding**: **CIVILIAN-05, CACI employee.** A preponderance of evidence
supports that CIVILIAN-05 did, or failed to do, the following:

SUBJECT: (U) AR 15-6 Investigation of the Abu Ghraib Detention Facility and
205th MI Brigade

- He grabbed a detainee (who was handcuffed) off a vehicle and dropped him to the ground. He then dragged him into an interrogation booth and as the detainee tried to get up, CIVILIAN-05 would yank the detainee very hard and make him fall again.
- Disobeyed General Order Number One; drinking alcohol while at Abu Ghraib.
- Refused to take instructions from a Tiger Team leader and refused to take instructions from military trainers.
  - o When confronted by SSG Neal, his Tiger Team leader, about his inadequate interrogation techniques, he replied, "I have been doing this for 20 years and I do not need a 20 year old telling me how to do my job."
  - o When placed in a remedial report writing class because of his poor writing, he did not pay attention to the trainer and sat in the back of the room facing away from the trainer.

(U) **Recommendation**: This information should be forwarded to the Army General Counsel for determination of whether CIVILIAN-05 should be referred to the Department of Justice for prosecution. This information should be forwarded to the Contracting Officer (KO) for appropriate contractual action.

(24) (U) **Finding**: **CIVILIAN-10, Translator, Titan employee.** After a thorough investigation, we found no direct involvement in detainee abuse by CIVILIAN-10. Our investigation revealed CIVILIAN-10 had a valid security clearance until it was suspended.

(U) **Recommendation**: This information should be forwarded to Titan via the KO. CIVILIAN-10 is cleared of any wrong doing and should retain his security clearance.

SUBJECT: (U) AR 15-6 Investigation of the Abu Ghraib Detention Facility and
205th MI Brigade

(25) (U) **Finding**: <u>**CIVILIAN-11, Interrogator, CACI employee.**</u> A preponderance of
evidence supports that CIVILIAN11 did, or failed to do, the following:

- Detainee abuse.
    - o He encouraged SSG Frederick to abuse Iraqi Police detained following a shooting
      incident (IP Roundup). SSG Frederick twisted the handcuffs of a detainee being
      interrogated; causing pain.
    - o He failed to prevent SSG Frederick from covering the detainee's mouth and nose
      restricting the detainee from breathing:
- Threatened the Iraqi Police "with SSG Frederick." He told the Iraqi Police to answer his
  questions or he would bring SSG Frederick back into the cell.
- Used dogs during the IP Roundup in an unauthorized manner. He told a detainee, "You see
  that dog there, if you do not tell me what I want to know, I'm going to get that dog on
  you."
- Placed a detainee in an unauthorized stress position (Reference Annex I, Appendix 2,
  Photograph "Stress Positions"). CIVILIAN-11 is photographed facing a detainee who is
  in a stress position on a chair with his back exposed. The detainee is in a dangerous
  position where he might fall back and injure himself.
- Failed to prevent a detainee from being photographed.

(U) **Recommendation**: This information should be forwarded to the Army General Counsel for
determination of whether CIVILIAN-11 should be referred to the Department of Justice for
prosecution. This information should be forwarded to the KO for appropriate contractual action.

132

SUBJECT: (U) AR 15-6 Investigation of the Abu Ghraib Detention Facility and
205th MI Brigade

(26) (U) **Finding**: **CIVILIAN-16, Translator, Titan employee.** A preponderance of
evidence supports that CIVILIAN-16 did, or failed to do, the following:

- Failed to report detainee abuse.
  - o She participated in an interrogation during the IP Roundup, where a dog was
    brought into a cell in violation of approved ICRP.
  - o She participated in the interrogation of an Iraqi Policeman who was placed in a
    stress position; squatting backwards on a plastic lawn chair. Any sudden
    movement by the IP could have resulted in injury (Reference Annex I, Appendix
    2, Photograph "Stress Positions").
  - o She was present during an interrogation when SSG Frederick twisted the
    handcuffs of a detainee, causing the detainee pain.
  - o She was present when SSG Frederick covered an IP's mouth and nose, restricting
    the detainee from breathing.
- Failed to report threats against detainees.
  - o She was present when CIVILIAN-11 told a detainee, "You see that dog there, if
    you do not tell me what I want to know, I'm going to get that dog on you."
  - o She was present when CIVILIAN-11 threatened a detainee "with SSG Frederick."

(U) **Recommendation**: This information should be forwarded to the Army General Counsel for
determination of whether CIVILIAN-16 should be referred to the Department of Justice for
prosecution. This information should be forwarded to the KO for appropriate contractual action.

(27) (U) **Finding**: **CIVILIAN-17, Interpreter, Titan employee.** A preponderance of
evidence supports that CIVILIAN-17 did, or failed to do, the following:

- Actively participated in detainee abuse.
  - o He was present during the abuse of detainees depicted in photographs (Reference
    Annex I, Appendix 1, Photographs M36-37, M39, M41).
  - o A detainee claimed that CIVILIAN-17 (sic), an interpreter, hit him and cut his ear
    which required stitches.
  - o Another detainee claimed that someone fitting CIVILIAN-17's description raped
    a young detainee.
- Failure to report detainee abuse.
- Failure to stop detainee abuse.

(U) **Recommendation**: This information should be forwarded to the Army General Counsel for
determination of whether CIVILIAN-17 should be referred to the Department of Justice for
prosecution. This information should be forwarded to the KO for appropriate contractual action.

133

SUBJECT: (U) AR 15-6 Investigation of the Abu Ghraib Detention Facility and
205th MI Brigade

(28) (U) Finding: **CIVILIAN-21, Interrogator, CACI employee.** A preponderance of
evidence supports that CIVILIAN-21 did, or failed to do, the following:

- Inappropriate use of dogs. SOLDIER-26 stated that CIVILIAN-21 used a dog during an
  interrogation and the dog was unmuzzled. SOLDIER-25 stated she once saw
  CIVILIAN21 standing on the second floor of the Hard Site, looking down to where a dog
  was being used against a detainee, and yelling to the MPs "Take him home." The dog
  had torn the detainee's mattress. He also used a dog during an interrogation with SSG
  Aston but stated he never used dogs.
- Detainee abuse. CPT Reese stated he saw "NAME" (his description of "NAME"' matched
  CIVILIAN-21) push (kick) a detainee into a cell with his foot.
- Making false statements. During questioning about the use of dogs in interrogations,
  CIVILIAN21 stated he never used them.
- Failed to report detainee abuse. During an interrogation, a detainee told SOLDIER-25 and
  CIVILIAN-21 that CIVILIAN-17, an interpreter, hit him and cut his ear which required
  stitches. SOLDIER-25 stated she told CIVILIAN-21 to annotate this on the interrogation
  report. He did not report it to appropriate authorities.
- Detainee Humiliation.
  - CIVILIAN-15 stated he heard CIVILIAN-21 tell several people that he had
    shaved the hair and beard of a detainee and put him in red women's underwear.
    CIVILIAN-21 was allegedly bragging about it.
  - CIVILIAN-19 stated he heard OTHER AGENCY EMPLOYEE02 laughing about
    red panties on detainees.

(U) **Recommendation**: This information should be forwarded to the Army General Counsel for
determination of whether CIVILIAN-21 should be referred to the Department of Justice for
prosecution. This information should be forwarded to the KO for appropriate contractual action.

SUBJECT: (U) AR 15-6 Investigation of the Abu Ghraib Detention Facility and
205th MI Brigade

(29) (U) **Finding**: There were several personnel who used clothing removal, improper isolation, or dogs as techniques for interrogations in violation of the Geneva Conventions. Several interrogators documented these techniques in their interrogation plans and stated they received approval from the JIDC, Interrogation Control Element. The investigative team found several entries in interrogation reports which clearly specified clothing removal; however, all personnel having the authority to approve interrogation plans claim they never approved or were aware of clothing removal being used in interrogations. Also found were interrogation reports specifying use of isolation, "the Hole." While the Commander, CJTF-7 approved "segregation" on 25 occasions, this use of isolation sometimes trended toward abuse based on sensory deprivation and inhumane conditions. Dogs were never approved, however on several occasions personnel thought they were. Personnel who committed abuse based on confusion regarding approvals or policies are in need of additional training.

(U) **Recommendation**: This information should be forwarded to the Soldiers' chain of command for appropriate action.

CIVILIAN-14 (formally with 368 Military Intelligence Battalion)
SOLDIER-04, 500 Military Intelligence Group
SOLDIER-05, 500 Military Intelligence Group
SOLDIER-03, GTMO Team, 184 Military Intelligence Company
SOLDIER-13, 66 Military Intelligence Group
SOLDIER-18, 66 Military Intelligence Group
SOLDIER-02, 66 Military Intelligence Group
SOLDIER-11 6 Battalion 98 Division (IT)
SOLDIER-16, 325 Military Intelligence Battalion
SOLDIER-30, 325 Military Intelligence Battalion
SOLDIER-26, 320 Military Police Battalion
SOLDIER-06, 302 Military Intelligence Battalion
SOLDIER-07, 325 Military Intelligence Battalion
SOLDIER-21, 325 Military Intelligence Battalion
SOLDIER-09, 302 Military Intelligence Battalion
SOLDIER-12, 302 Military Intelligence Battalion
CIVILIAN-20, CACI Employee

SUBJECT: (U) AR 15-6 Investigation of the Abu Ghraib Detention Facility and
205th MI Brigade

(30) (U) **Finding**: In addition to SOLDIER-20 and SOLDIER01, medical personnel may have been aware of detainee abuse at Abu Ghraib and failed to report it. The scope of this investigation was MI personnel involvement. SOLDIER-20 and SOLDIER-01 were cited because sufficient evidence existed within the scope of this investigation to establish that they were aware of detainee abuse and failed to report it. Medical records were requested, but not obtained, by this investigation. The location of the records at the time this request was made was unknown.

(U) **Recommendation**: An inquiry should be conducted into 1) whether appropriate medical records were maintained, and if so, were they properly stored and collected and 2) whether medical personnel were aware of detainee abuse and failed to properly document and report the abuse.

(31) (U) **Finding**: A preponderance of the evidence supports that SOLDIER-31, SOLDIER-32, and SOLDIER-33 participated in the alleged sexual assault of a female detainee by forcibly kissing her and removing her shirt (Reference CID Case–0216-03-CID259-6121). The individuals received non-judicial punishment for conducting an unauthorized interrogation, but were not punished for the alleged sexual assault.

(U) **Recommendation**: CID should review case # 0216-03-CID259-61211 to determine if further investigation is appropriate. The case should then be forwarded to the Soldiers' chain of command for appropriate action.

(32) (U) **Finding**: An unidentified person, believed to be a contractor interpreter, was depicted in six photographs taken on 25 October 2003 showing the abuse of three detainees. The detainees were nude and handcuffed together on the floor. This investigation could not confirm the identity of this person; however, potential leads have been passed to and are currently being pursued by CID.

(U) **Recommendation**: CID should continue to aggressively pursue all available leads to identify this person and determine the degree of his involvement in detainee abuse.

136

SUBJECT: (U) AR 15-6 Investigation of the Abu Ghraib Detention Facility and
205th MI Brigade

7. (U) Personnel Listing. Deleted in accordance with the Privacy Act and 10 USC §130b

137

SUBJECT: (U) AR 15-6 Investigation of the Abu Ghraib Detention Facility and 205th MI Brigade

8. (U) Task Force Members.

LTG Anthony R. CIVILIAN08 Command	Investigating Officer	HQs, Training and Doctrine
MG George R. Fay	Investigating Officer	HQs, Dept of the Army, G2
Mr. Thomas A. Gandy	Deputy	HQs, Dept of the Army, G2
LTC Phillip H. Bender	Chief Investigator	HQs, Dept of the Army, G2
LTC Michael Benjamin	Legal Advisor	TJAG
MAJ(P) Maricela Alvarado	Executive Officer	HQs, Dept of the Army, G2
CPT Roseanne M. Bleam	Staff Judge Advocate, CJTF-7	CJTF-7 (MNF-I) SJA
CW5 Donald Marquis	SME – Training & Doctrine	HQs, US Army Intelligence Center
CW3 Brent Pack	CID Liaison	US Army CID Command
CW2 Mark Engan	Investigator – Baghdad Team	HQs, 308th MI Bn, 902nd MI Group
SGT Patrick D. Devine	All Source Analyst	ACIC, 310th MI Bn, 902nd MI Group
CPL Ryan Hausterman	Investigator – Baghdad Team	HQs, 310th MI Bn, 902nd MI Group
Mr. Maurice J. Sheley	Investigator	HQs, US Army INSCOM
Mr. Michael P. Scanland	Investigator	HQs, 902nd MI Group
Mr. Claude B. Benner	Investigative Review	ACIC, 902nd MI Group
Mr. Michael Wright	Investigator	HQs, 308th MI Bn, 902nd MI Group
Mr. Scott Robertson	Investigator	HQs, Dept of the Army, G2
Mr. Paul Stark	Chief of Analysis	ACIC, 310th MI Bn, 902nd MI Group
Mr. Kevin Brucie	Investigator – Baghdad Team	Det 13, FCA, 902nd MI Group
Ms. Linda Flanigan	Analyst	ACIC, 310th MI Bn, 902nd MI Group
Mr. Albert Scott	Cyber-Forensic Analyst	HQs, 310th MI Bn, 902nd MI Group
Ms. Saoirse Spain	Analyst	ACIC, 310th MI Bn, 902nd MI group
Mr. Albert J. McCarn Jr.	Chief of Logistics	HQs, Dept of the Army, G2
Ms. Cheryl Clowser	Administrator	HQs, Dept of the Army, G2
Mr. Alfred Moreau	SME – Contract Law	HQs, Dept of the Army, OTJAG
Mr. Rudolph Garcia	Senior Editor	HQs, Dept of the Army, G2

Contract Services provided by Object Sciences Corp. and SYTEX

138

SUBJECT: (U) AR 15-6 Investigation of the Abu Ghraib Detention Facility and
205th MI Brigade

9. (U) Acronyms.

2 MI BN	2d Military Intelligence Battalion
B/321 MI BN	B Company, 321st Military Intelligence Battalion
B/325 MI BN	B Company, 325th Military Intelligence Battalion
A/205 MI BN	A Company, 205th Military Intelligence Battalion
115 MP BN	115th Military Police Battalion
165 MI BN	165th Military Intelligence Battalion
205 MI BDE	205th Military Intelligence Brigade
229 MP CO	229th Military Police Battalion
320 MP BN	320th Military Police Battalion
320 MP CO	320th Military Police Company
323 MI BN	323d Military Intelligence Battalion
325 MI BN	325th Military Intelligence Battalion
372 MP CO	372d Military Police Company
377 TSC	377th Theater Support Command
400 MP BN	400th Military Police Battalion
470 MI GP	470th Military Intelligence Group
447 MP CO	447th Military Police Company
500 MI GP	500th Military Intelligence Group
504 MI BDE	504th Military Intelligence Battalion
519 MI BN	519th Military Intelligence Battalion
66 MI GP	66th Military Intelligence Group
670 MP CO	670th Military Police Company
72 MP CO	72d Military Police Company
800 MP BDE	800th Military Police Brigade
870 MP CO	870th Military Police Company
1SG	First Sergeant
A/519 MI BN	A Company, 519th Military Intelligence Battalion
AAR	After Action Report
AFJI	Air Force Joint Instructor
AG	Abu Ghraib
ANCOC	Advanced Non-Commission Officer's Course
AR	Army Regulation
ATSD (IO)	Assistant to the Secretary of Defense for Intelligence Oversight
BDE	Brigade
BG	Brigadier General
BIAP	Baghdad International Airport
BN	Battalion
BNCOC	Basic Non-Commission Officer's Course
BPA	Blanket Purchase Agreement
C2X	Command and Control Exercise

SECRET//NOFORN//X1

SUBJECT: (U) AR 15-6 Investigation of the Abu Ghraib Detention Facility and 205th MI Brigade

CALL	Center for Army Lessons Learned
CENTCOM	US Central Command
CG	Commanding General
CHA	Corps Holding Area
CIA	Central Intelligence Agency
CID	Criminal Investigation Command
CJCS-I	Chairman, Joint Chief of Staff Instruction
CJTF-7	Combined Joint Task Force 7
CM&D	Collection Management and Dissemination
COL	Colonel
COR	Contracting Officers Representative
CP	Collection Point
CPA	Coalition Provisional Authority
CPL	Corporal
CPT	Captain
CSH	Combat Support Hospital
DA	Department of the Army
DAIG	Department of the Army Inspector General
DCI	Director of Central Intelligence
DCG	Deputy Commanding General
DIAM	Defense Intelligence Agency Manual
DoD	Department of Defense
1LT	First Lieutenant
CASH	Combat Army Surgical Hospital
DIA	Defense Intelligence Agency
KO	Contracting Officer
DOJ	Department of Justice
DRA	Detention Review Authority
DRB	Detainee Release Branch
EPW	Enemy Prisoner of War
FM	Field Manual
FOB	Forward Operating Base
FRAGO	Fragmentary Order
G-3	Army Training Division
GCIV	Geneva Conventions IV
GP	Group
GSA	General Services Administration
GTMO	Guantanamo Naval Base, Cuba
GWOT	Global War On Terrorism
HQ	Headquarters
HUMINT	Human Intelligence
IAW	In Accordance With
ICE	Interrogation and Control Element
ICRC	International Committee of the Red Cross

SECRET//NOFORN//X1

140

SUBJECT: (U) AR 15-6 Investigation of the Abu Ghraib Detention Facility and
205th MI Brigade

ICRP	Interrogation and Counter-Resistance Policies
IET	Initial Entry Training
ID	Infantry Division
IG	Inspector General
IMINT	Imagery Intelligence
INSCOM	Intelligence and Security Command
IP	Iraqi Police
IR	Interment/Resettlement
IROE	Interrogation Rules Of Engagement
ISCT	Interrogation Support to Counterterrorism
ISG	Iraqi Survey Group
JA	Judge Advocate
JCS	Joint Chiefs of Staff
JIDC	Joint Interrogation and Detention Center
JTF-GTMO	Joint Task Force Guantanamo
MAJ	Major
MCO	Marine Corps Order
LTC	Lieutenant Colonel
LTG	Lieutenant General
MFR	Memorandum For Record
MG	Major General
MI	Military Intelligence
MIT	Mobile Interrogation Team
MOS	Military Occupational Specialty
MOU	Memorandum of Understanding
MP	Military Police
MRE	Meals Ready to Eat
MSC	Major Subordinate Command
MSG	Master Sergeant
MTT	Mobile Training Team
NCO	Non-Commissioned Officer
NCOIC	Non-Commissioned Officer In Charge
OER	Officer Evaluation Report
OGA	Other Government Agency
OGC	Office Of General Counsel
OIC	Officer In Charge
OIF	Operation Iraqi Freedom
OPORD	Operations Order
OPNAVINST	Office of the Chief of Naval Operations Instructions
OSJA	Office Of the Staff Judge Advocate
OVB	Operation Victory Bounty
RP	Retained Personnel
SASO	Stability And Support Operations
SECARMY	Secretary of the Army

141

SUBJECT: (U) AR 15-6 Investigation of the Abu Ghraib Detention Facility and
205th MI Brigade

SECDEF	Secretary of Defense
SFC	Sergeant First Class
SGT	Sergeant
SIGINT	Signals Intelligence
SITREP	Situation Report
HMMWV	High-Mobility, Multipurpose Wheeled Vehicle
PFC	Private First Class
MA1	Master at Arms 1
MA2	Master at Arms 2
PVT	Private
QRF	Quick Reaction Force
SJA	Staff Judge Advocate
SOF	Special Operations Forces
SOP	Standard Operating Procedure
SOUTHCOM	US Southern Command
SOW	Statement of Work
SSG	Staff Sergeant
TACON	Tactical Control
THT	Tactical HUMINT Team
TRADOC	Training and Doctrine Command
TTP	Tactics, Techniques, and Procedures
UCMJ	Uniform Code Of Military Justice
USAIC	US Army Intelligence Center
USAR	US Army Reserve
VFR	Visual Flight Rules
E-6	Enlisted Grade 6 (Staff Sergeant)
E-7	Enlisted Grade 7 (Sergeant First Class)
E-5	Enlisted Grade 5 (Sergeant)
96B	Intelligence Analyst
NBC	National Business Center
FSS	Federal Supply Schedule
POC	Point of Contact
DAIG	Department of the Army Inspector General
97E	Human Intelligence Collector
351E	Interrogation Warrant Officer
FBI	Federal Bureau of Investigation
ISN	Internee Serial Number
JTF-21	Joint Task Force – 21
TF-121	Task Force – 121
SEAL	Sea, Air, Land
SPC	Specialist
RFF	Request for Forces
TF-20	Task Force – 20
97B	Counterintelligence Agent

142

SUBJECT: (U) AR 15-6 Investigation of the Abu Ghraib Detention Facility and 205th MI Brigade

CM&D	Collection, Management and Dissemination
JIG	Joint Intelligence Group
351B	Counterintelligence Warrant Officer
PT	Physical Training
IRF	Internal Reaction Force

About the Author

MARK DANNER has been reporting on and writing about foreign affairs for twenty years. A longtime staff writer at *The New Yorker* and a regular contributor to *The New York Review of Books*, Danner has covered Central America, Haiti, the Balkans, and Iraq, among other stories. He is the author of *The Massacre at El Mozote: A Parable of the Cold War* and *The Road to Illegitimacy: One Reporter's Travels Through the 2000 Florida Recount*. His work has been honored with a National Magazine Award, two Overseas Press Awards, and an Emmy. In 1999, Danner was named a MacArthur Fellow. He is Professor of Journalism at the University of California at Berkeley and Henry R. Luce Professor of Human Rights and Journalism at Bard College. Danner divides his time between New York and San Francisco.